Taking Sides: Clashing Views
in Educational Psychology, 8/e

Esther S. Chang

http://create.mheducation.com

ISBN-10: 1259675262    ISBN-13: 9781259675263

# Contents

i. Detailed Table of Contents by Chang   1
ii. Preface by Chang   5
iii. Introduction by Chang   7

## Unit 1   13

1. Basic Theories of Learning and Education by Chang   14
   1.1. Can Psychological Science Improve the Quality of Education? by Chang   15
   1.2. Should Students Be Free? by Chang   25
   1.3. Are Constructivist Teaching Methods Superior to Traditional Methods of Teaching? by Chang   37
   1.4. Should Schools Aim for Students' "Happiness"? by Chang   58

## Unit 2   69

2. Basic Educational Issues by Chang   70
   2.1. Are International Comparisons Helpful? by Chang   71
   2.2. Do Recent Discoveries About the Brain Have Implications for Classroom Practice? by Chang   84
   2.3. Can Schools Close the Achievement Gap between Students from Different Ethnic and Racial Backgrounds? by Chang   95

## Unit 3   111

3. Best Practices by Chang   112
   3.1. Does Grading Help Students Learn? by Chang   113
   3.2. Is Full Inclusion Always the Best Option for Children with Disabilities? by Chang   127
   3.3. Are Single-Gender Classes Necessary to Create Equal Opportunities for Boys and Girls? by Chang   142
   3.4. Does Homework Improve Student Achievement? by Chang   153
   3.5. Is Parental Involvement in Education Critical for Student Achievement? by Chang   195
   3.6. Should We Be "Tiger" Parents? by Chang   245

## Unit 4   279

4. Educational Interventions by Chang   280
   4.1. Should Schools Use Cash Incentives to Promote Educational Goals? by Chang   281
   4.2. Is There Anything Good about Abstinence-Only Sex Education? by Chang   305
   4.3. Does Reducing Class Size Improve Student Achievement? by Chang   327
   4.4. Are School-Wide Anti-Bullying Programs Effective? by Chang   346
   4.5. Are Charter Schools Advancing Educational Reforms? by Chang   376

# DETAILED TABLE OF CONTENTS

## Unit 1: Basic Theories of Learning and Education

**Issue: Can Psychological Science Improve the Quality of Education?**
**YES: Edward L. Thorndike**, from "The Contribution of Psychology to Education," *Journal of Educational Psychology* (1910)
**NO: John Dewey**, from "Education as Engineering," *New Republic* (1922)

Edward Thorndike argued that psychology forms the basis of educational practice and the knowledge generated by the discipline will promote better practices. Moreover, he argued that the procedures psychologists use to generate knowledge can be used directly to improve progress toward educational goals. John Dewey acknowledged that while psychological science may be good at improving current practices, it is limited in making progress in education. Psychological science does not promote revolutionary changes that support progressive education.

**Issue: Should Students Be Free?**
**YES: Carl Rogers**, from "Difficulties and Opportunities: The Challenge of Present-Day Teaching," Charles Merrill Publishing (1969)
**NO: B. F. Skinner**, from "A Technology of Behavior," "Values," "What Is Man?" in *Beyond Freedom & Dignity*, Hackett Publishing (1971)

Founder of humanistic psychology Carl Rogers argued that students learn best when they are allowed to be autonomous and can exercise choice. He proposed that learning be based on students' own curiosity and inner meaning. Founder of behaviorism B. F. Skinner argued that any notion of personal freedom is an illusion. He offers a critique of "inner freedom" and proposes that all learning and motivation is influenced by external forces.

**Issue: Are Constructivist Teaching Methods Superior to Traditional Methods of Teaching?**
**YES: Sam Hausfather**, from "Content and Process in Constructivist Teacher Education," Kendal Hunt Publishing (2002)
**NO: R. E. Clark, P. A. Kirschner, and J. Sweller**, from "Putting Students on the Path to Learning: The Case for Fully Guided Instruction," *American Educator* (2012)

Sam Hausfather argues that constructivism, which challenges the stability of content knowledge, improves teaching by focusing teaching students not only on content knowledge but also on the processes involved in producing it. Richard Clark and colleagues argues that ideal learning environments differ between experts and novices and that constructivist pedagogy, which fosters individual discovery without full guidance from the teacher, has not proven to be ideal for novice learners.

**Issue: Should Schools Aim for Students' "Happiness"?**
**YES: Nel Noddings**, from "What Does It Mean to Educate the WHOLE CHILD?" *Educational Leadership* (2005)
**NO: Kenneth R. Stunkel**, from "Quality in Liberal Education and Illusions of the Academy," *Liberal Education* (1999)

Nel Noddings argues that schools should be "genuinely happy places" to remind us why we engage in academics and to address children as they are, "whole persons." Kenneth Stunkel observes that the decline of liberal studies in college is fostered by an increasing number of academically unprepared students every year and identifies that a major problem has been in accepting and enforcing academic standards regardless of student background.

## Unit 2: Basic Educational Issues

**Issue: Are International Comparisons Helpful?**
**YES: OECD**, from "Learning from High-Performing Education Systems," OECD Publishing (2011)
**NO: Anna Dall**, from "Is PISA Counter-Productive to Building Successful Educational Systems?" *Social Alternatives* (2011)

The OECD argues that if a country is committed to children and their education, the real test of their commitment is how they prioritize education against other commitments, such as youth sports. International comparisons therefore help illuminate why the United States is outperformed by other countries in math, science, and reading. Anna Dall argues that the PISA model is problematic and is counterproductive to building a successful educational system. She critiques the testing culture and believes that there needs to be a paradigm shift away from test performance.

**Issue: <ins>Do Recent Discoveries About the Brain Have Implications for Classroom Practice?</ins>**
**YES: Judy Willis**, from "Building a Bridge from Neuroscience to the Classroom," *Phi Delta Kappan* (2008)
**NO: Dan Willingham**, from "When and How Neuroscience Applies to Education," *Phi Delta Kappan* (2008)

Judy Willis argues that current research on brain function does inform educational practice and she provides some examples from recent brain science findings. Dan Willingham argues that not every finding about how the brain works can or should lead to an accommodation of educational practice.

**Issue: <ins>Can Schools Close the Achievement Gap between Students from Different Ethnic and Racial Backgrounds?</ins>**
**YES: Carol Corbett Burris and Kevin G. Welner**, from "Closing the Achievement Gap by Detracking," *Phi Delta Kappan* (2005)
**NO: William H. Schmidt, Leland S. Cogan, and Curtis C. McKnight**, from "Equality of Educational Opportunity: Myth or Reality in U.S. Schooling?" *American Educator* (2010–2011)

Carol Burris and Kevin Welner argue that the achievement gap between whites and African American and Latino students can be closed by "detracking" and having similarly high expectations and similar curricular demands on all students. William Schmidt and colleagues argue that minority students are exposed to pervasive and persistent inequalities that make school-based reforms unrealistic.

## Unit 3: Best Practices

**Issue: <ins>Does Grading Help Students Learn?</ins>**
**YES: Kyle Spencer**, from "Standards-Based Grading," *Harvard Education Letter* (2012)
**NO: Alfie Kohn**, from "The Case Against Grades," *Educational Leadership* (2011)

Kyle Spencer argues that grades provide useful information if they are linked to standards, or targeted competences to be acquired. Alfie Kohn argues that grades interfere with learning because they subvert one's enjoyment of learning and lead the student to work for grades instead.

**Issue: <ins>Is Full Inclusion Always the Best Option for Children with Disabilities?</ins>**
**YES: Michael F. Giangreco**, from "Extending Inclusive Opportunities," *Educational Leadership* (2007)
**NO: James M. Kauffman, Kathleen McGee, and Michele Brigham**, from "Enabling or Disabling? Observation on Changes in Special Education," *Phi Delta Kappan* (2004)

Michael F. Giangreco argues that even students with severe disabilities are best served within the "regular" education classroom along with their typically developing peers. James M. Kauffman and colleagues argue that the goal of education for students with disabilities should be to increase their level of competence and independence.

**Issue: <ins>Are Single-Gender Classes Necessary to Create Equal Opportunities for Boys and Girls?</ins>**
**YES: Frances R. Spielhagen**, from "How Tweens View Single-Sex Classes," *Educational Leadership* (2006)
**NO: Kelley King and Michael Gurian**, from "Teaching to the Minds of Boys," *Educational Leadership* (2006)

Frances Spielhagen argues that single-gender classes are viewed as more conducive to learning than are coeducational classes by students, especially younger students. Kelley King and Michael Gurian argue that coeducational classrooms can be made to be more accommodating to the learning profiles of both boys and girls.

**Issue: <ins>Does Homework Improve Student Achievement?</ins>**
**YES: Swantje Dettmers, et al.**, from "Homework Works if Homework Quality Is High: Using Multilevel Modeling to Predict the Development of Achievement in Mathematics," *Journal of Educational Psychology* (2010)
**NO: Harris Cooper, et al.**, from "Relationships Among Attitudes About Homework, Amount of Homework Assigned and Completed, and Student Achievement," *Journal of Educational Psychology* (1998)

On the basis of a one-year, two-time point, longitudinal study of a nationally representative German sample of high school students in Grade 9, Swantje Dettmers and colleagues demonstrated that high homework quality fosters motivation to do homework, which in turn leads to higher achievement over time among high school students. Although advocates of homework in general, Harris Cooper and colleagues conducted a study of parents, teachers, and students at lower and upper grades and found that the amount of homework assigned was associated with negative student attitudes weakly related to student grades.

**Issue:  Is Parental Involvement in Education Critical for Student Achievement?**
**YES: Nancy E. Hill and Diana F. Tyson**, from "Parental Involvement in Middle School: A Meta-Analytic Assessment of the Strategies That Promote Achievement," *Developmental Psychology* (2009)
**NO: Cecilia S. S. Cheung and Eva M. Pomerantz**, from "Value Development Underlies the Benefits of Parents' Involvement in Children's Learning: A Longitudinal Investigation in the United States and China," *Journal of Educational Psychology* (2015)

Nancy Hill and Diana Tyson conducted a meta-analysis and found a positive and significant association for most types of parental involvement even after considering publication biases. Cecilia S. S. Cheung and Eva M. Pomerantz demonstrated that the association between parental involvement and students' academic achievement could be explained by the parent–child transmission of values placed on academics.

**Issue:  Should We Be "Tiger" Parents?**
**YES: Ruth K. Chao and Christine Aque**, from "Interpretations of Parental Control by Asian Immigrant and European American Youth," *Journal of Family Psychology* (2009)
**NO: Su Yeong Kim, et al.**, from "Does 'Tiger Parenting' Exist? Parenting Profiles of Chinese Americans and Adolescent Developmental Outcomes," *Asian American Journal of Psychology* (2013)

Ruth Chao and Christine Aque argue that parental control can be viewed as a virtue, especially in Asian-influenced cultures. They conduct a cross-sectional study that demonstrates that Asian youth report lower levels of anger on average in reaction to parental strictness and limit setting compared to European Americans, and that parental control will be effective as long as it does not make youth angry. Su Yeong Kim and colleagues found that tiger parenting was not common perhaps because it is maladaptive. They conducted a 3-point longitudinal study spanning 8 years to demonstrate that tiger parenting existed among Chinese immigrant families in the United States but did not have beneficial influences over time.

## Unit 4:  Educational Interventions

**Issue:  Should Schools Use Cash Incentives to Promote Educational Goals?**
**YES: W. David Pierce, et al.**, from "Positive Effects of Rewards and Performance Standards on Intrinsic Motivation," *Psychological Record* (2003)
**NO: Roy F. Baumeister**, from "Choking Under Pressure: Self-Consciousness and Paradoxical Effects of Incentives on Skillful Performance," *Journal of Personality and Social Psychology* (1984)

W. D. Pierce and colleagues demonstrated that cash rewards can promote intrinsic motivation, particularly if the rewards are used progressively (i.e., after work is completed, more work is given to individuals after cash is given) compared to when rewards were not used and/or given work constantly. Thus, rewarding individuals with cash followed by giving them more work communicates positive messages that significantly enhance intrinsic motivation. Roy Baumeister conducted a classic series of experiments that underscore how situations that demand performance, including the use of cash incentives, cause the individual to "choke"—or fail—due to increased self-consciousness. The role of cash in this study was to communicate "pressure."

**Issue:  Is There Anything Good about Abstinence-Only Sex Education?**
**YES: Elaine A. Borawski, et al.**, from "Effectiveness of Abstinence-Only Intervention in Middle School Teens," *American Journal of Health Behavior* (2005)
**NO: Kathrin F. Stanger-Hall and David W. Hall**, from "Abstinence-Only Education and Teen Pregnancy Rates: Why We Need Comprehensive Sex Education in the U.S.," *PLoS One* (2011)

Elaine Borawski and colleagues tested an abstinence-only sex education curriculum against a matched control group of middle school students in seven schools. They demonstrated that an abstinence-until-marriage curriculum can positively influence abstinence as well as reduce the frequency of sex among sexually experienced youths. Kathrin Stanger-Hall and David Hall argue that as a matter of policy an abstinence-only curriculum is ineffective in reducing teen sex. They show that the more the states emphasized abstinence in sex education programs, the higher their teen pregnancy and birth rates.

**Issue:  Does Reducing Class Size Improve Student Achievement?**
**YES: Jeremy D. Finn, Susan B. Gerber, and Jayne Boyd-Zaharias**, from "Small Classes in the Early Grades, Academic Achievement, and Graduating from High School," *Journal of Educational Psychology* (2005)
**NO: Eric A. Hanushek**, from "The Tennessee Class Size Experiment (Project STAR)," Economic Policy Institute (2002)

Jeremy Finn and colleagues analyzed longitudinal data based on a subsample of children who were tracked from kindergarten to high school because they participated in Project STAR. They found that 4 years of small classes in K-3 during Project STAR was associated with a significant increase in the likelihood of graduating from high school. Eric Hanushek contends that there is little evidence that supports any beneficial effects of classroom reduction, nor does it indicate what effects could be expected from reductions.

**Issue: Are School-Wide Anti-Bullying Programs Effective?**
**YES: Antti Kärnä, et al.**, from "Going to Scale: A Nonrandomized Nationwide Trial of the KiVa Antibullying Program for Grades 1–9," *Journal of Consulting and Clinical Psychology* (2011)
**NO: Sabina Low and Mark Van Ryzin**, from "The Moderating Effects of School Climate on Bullying Prevention Efforts," *School Psychology Quarterly* (2014)

Antti Kärnä, with support from a team of experts and colleagues, reported upon the positive effects of a nationwide school-based anti-bullying program in Finland. Sabina Low and Mark Van Ryzin propose and provide evidence that a positive psychosocial school climate plays a foundational role in the effective prevention of bullying.

**Issue: Are Charter Schools Advancing Educational Reforms?**
**YES: RAND Education**, from "Are Charter Schools Making a Difference? A Study of Student Outcomes in Eight States (Research Brief)," RAND Corporation (2009)
**NO: Martin Carnoy, et al.**, from "Worth the Price? Weighing the Evidence on Charter School Achievement," *Education Finance and Policy* (2006)

Based on the results from data gathered across eight states, RAND researchers found that charter schools can make a difference with regard to long-term student attainment despite their lack of progress on achievement-related indicators compared to traditional public schools. Martin Carnoy and colleagues question whether any gains observed by charter schools is worth the price of closing down traditional public schools. They point out that charters have not made any progress related to achievement when compared to traditional public schools and recreate many of the same problems associated with public schools rather than take advantage of the autonomy to create educational innovations.

# Preface

The field of educational psychology seems to be constantly enmeshed in controversy. Some of the controversies are ongoing; occasionally, a controversy may die down a bit only to return in full force again, perhaps in a slightly different form. Other controversies are more short-lived; either they are resolved or they are abandoned as intractable. From the outside it may seem that these controversies reflect inefficiency and a lack of progress in the field of educational psychology and even that "educational psychologists just like to argue." But are these controversies really as counterproductive as they appear?

In fact, controversies provide the foundation for deeper understanding of the educational issues involved, thereby leading to progress. This is not merely our personal belief. There is considerable empirical evidence from research in educational psychology and cognitive science to support this claim. It is not too difficult to see why this is the case. When we engage in discussion of a controversy, we are forced to muster evidence to support our position and to fully develop in a systematic fashion all of its implications. This can lead us to see gaps in our evidence and fallacies in our reasoning, or to recognize previously unrealized implications. As a result, we may decide to gather additional evidence, modify our position, or even abandon it entirely. It is this spirit of controversy and argumentation that is the basis of this textbook.

In the second unit, the focus is on basic educational issues, such as the importance of international comparisons, the usefulness of brain research for classroom practice, and whether schools are able to close the persistent achievement gap.

The third unit addresses the question of best practices relating to grading, children with disabilities, gender segregated classrooms, homework, parental involvement, and parental expectations (e.g., tiger parents).

Finally, the fourth unit surveys the effectiveness or usefulness of a variety of educational interventions: cash incentives, sex education, class size, anti-bullying programs, and charter schools.

Each issue is stated as a question and is represented by two previously published articles, the first supporting a "yes" answer to the question and the second arguing a "no" response. Each issue is preceded by learning outcomes and an introduction, which provides background and a context for evaluating the articles. Each issue ends with questions to encourage critical reflection and an "Is There Common Ground?" section, which briefly summarizes the complexities of the controversy and possible routes to resolution. We also include additional resources and Internet resources.

**Esther S. Chang**
*Soka University of America*

## Book Organization

This book addresses current and sometimes enduring controversies in educational psychology with the aim of introducing students of psychology to the real-world complexities of educational contexts and introducing students of Education to the disciplinary concerns of psychological theory, measurement (i.e., definition) and research design (i.e., how psychology develops an argument).

This edition is organized into four units. In the first unit, classic debates relating to basic psychological theories of learning and philosophical perspectives in education are revisited, beginning with the role of psychological science in educational reform, questions relating to how students learn optimally (should they be free?), constructivist teaching approaches, and the purpose of and meaning of education (should schools aim for students to be happy?).

## Editor of This Volume

Esther S. Chang, PhD, is associate professor of psychology at Soka University of America. She is a developmental psychologist with specialization in adolescent development. Her research aims at understanding how life goals are pursued with important social partners (parents, peers, important nonparental adults) in the transition to adulthood. She earned her PhD in psychology and social behavior from the University of California at Irvine in 2007.

## Acknowledgments

I gratefully acknowledge the contributions of the previous editors, Leonard Abbeduto and Frank Symons, who had been involved in developing this particular title for a very long time.

In addition, I would like to acknowledge that this edition would not have been possible without Jill Meloy's help and encouragement from McGraw-Hill; technical support from Carin Rogers-Bronstein and Jianmin Shao; and the boundless understanding of my husband, children, and family dog.

Finally, I am indebted to my parents who sacrificed their lives for my education and dedicate this volume to them as well as in the memory of my late uncle, Kwen Joo Choi.

**Esther S. Chang**

## Academic Advisory Board Members

Members of the Academic Advisory Board are instrumental in the final selection of articles for Taking Sides books. Their review of the articles for content, level, and appropriateness provides critical direction to the editor(s) and staff. We think that you will find their careful consideration reflected in this book.

# Introduction

# What Is Educational Psychology?

Educational psychology has traditionally been defined as the application of psychological theories, methods, and findings to the study of learning and teaching. This has led educational psychologists to study such topics as the development of particular academic skills (e.g., reading); the ways in which children acquire and represent knowledge in particular substantive domains (e.g., mathematics) and how those representations can be supported by classroom instruction; individual differences in intelligence and achievement and their relation to classroom instruction; how student motivation is related to learning and to different pedagogical practices; the relationships among different domains of ability and functioning, including the relationship between the cognitive and social domains; how best to assess ability, achievement, and teaching effectiveness; and how to change the beliefs and practices of teachers.

Such a diverse range of interests have always required an eclectic approach. Thus, educational psychologists have traditionally drawn on the concepts and tools of many of the sub-disciplines of psychology: developmental psychology, psychometrics, cognitive psychology, clinical psychology, learning science, and social psychology, to name but a few. In recent years, moreover, educational psychologists have begun to more fully understand the complexity of the factors and systems at play in teaching and learning. This has led them to cross disciplinary boundaries and draw on theories, methods, and findings from other disciplines, including cultural anthropology, linguistics, philosophy, educational administration, political science, sociology, social work, and neuroscience. In turn, educational psychologists have begun to ask questions and examine variables that have not previously been seen as within their purview, such as the relationship between family functioning and academic performance, the role of cultural identity in student achievement, the relationships between economic conditions and pedagogical practices, the impact of changing societal conceptions of juvenile crime on the educational process, the role of the school in the life of a community, and the interaction between experience and the biological processes underlying brain structure, function, and development. Educational psychologists have also begun to see the need to more fully understand the domains that form the subject matter of schools, which has led them to address questions about the nature of expertise in domains such as mathematics and science. And finally, educational psychologists have come to view themselves as the agents of educational reform.

In short, traditional boundaries between educational psychology and other disciplines concerned with children, families, learning, education, and social change have begun to blur. This expansion of scope and crossing of disciplinary boundaries, however, has meant that educational psychologists have become enmeshed in an increasing number of controversies.

## Controversies in Educational Psychology: Where They Come from and How They Can Be Resolved

In this text, we have framed each of the current controversies in educational psychology as a question, such as *Is full inclusion always the best option for children with disabilities?* This approach is useful because, at its most basic level, educational psychology is the science of providing answers to questions about teaching and learning. Sometimes these questions arise from outside the field of educational psychology or even from outside the field of education, as when business leaders turn to educators with questions about how to prepare children for the technological workplace they will face as adults, or when political leaders ask educational psychologists whether or not the inclusion of students with disabilities within the regular classroom is "working." At other times, the questions come from within the field of educational psychology itself, as in the case of questions about whether a constructivist approach (child-centered and discovery-oriented rather than teacher-controlled and scaffolded) is effective in promoting student mastery of academic content. Whatever the sources of these questions, it often happens that educational psychologists and other stakeholders in the educational process end up holding sharply different views about the answers. What creates these controversies? Why do experts in the field hold contrasting theories and beliefs? Analyzing some of the causes of controversies in educational psychology may allow us to understand the paths that must be taken to resolve them.

## Empirical Data

Many questions become controversial because the empirical data needed to supply the answer are lacking. In some cases, the lack of data simply reflects the fact that the question has been asked only recently and thus, there has not been sufficient time to conduct the necessary research. In other cases, however, the question has become controversial *because* of the data that have been collected. That is, the data generated have been inconsistent across studies or can be interpreted as providing support for conflicting theories. Such ambiguity often occurs when the question has been addressed through a *correlational* approach rather than through an *experimental* approach.

In a correlational study, an investigator examines the relationship that exists naturally between two or more variables. In this approach, the scientist does not control or manipulate nature but rather measures it or at least parts of it. Consider, for example, a hypothetical controversy between the relative effectiveness of two approaches to teaching reading (A and B). One way to address this controversy would be to find schools that adopted the different approaches and ask whether students' reading achievement scores are better for schools adopting approach A or approach B. At first glance, this seems likely a relatively straightforward way to decide the controversy. The interpretive problem for such a study, as for any correlational study, is that there may be other differences between the two types of schools in addition to their approaches to teaching reading, and these unmeasured differences may really be responsible for any differences in student achievement that are observed. These differences between the schools might include differences in family demographics (e.g., socioeconomic status, race, and ethnicity), resources available to the schools, level of parental commitment, and so on.

Such alternative interpretations could be ruled out by adopting an experimental approach. In an experiment, the researcher exerts control over the variables of interest. In a true experiment, participants (e.g., students, classes, or schools) are assigned at random the various *conditions* of interest (e.g., instructional approach A and approach B in our example). The value of such random assignment is that, given a large enough sample of participants, we can be confident that the conditions being compared are similar on all variables except those being studied. So, for example, if we have a large number of schools in our sample and we assign them randomly to approach and approach B, we will end up, on average, with about the same number of affluent and economically disadvantaged schools in each condition, the same number of ethnically diverse and ethnically homogeneous schools in each condition, the same number of initially high-achieving and low-achieving schools in each condition, and so on. Such similarity across conditions makes for unambiguous results. In this example, an experimental approach would entitle us to conclude unambiguously that any differences in student achievement observed between the two types of schools had been caused by the difference in their approaches to teaching reading.

If the experimental approach allows for unambiguous interpretation and the correlational approach does not, it would seem sensible to always opt for the experimental approach and thereby avoid any controversy about what the data say. Unfortunately, it is not that simple. For many questions about teaching and learning, it is not possible to do an experiment. Either the situation does not allow the researcher to control the relevant variables or control can be achieved only by creating such an artificial version of the phenomenon to be studied that the possibility of generalizing from the results of the experiment to the "real world" seems remote. Examining the relative effectiveness of gender-segregated and coeducational classes provides an example of a question that does not easily lend itself to an experimental approach. In particular, it is likely that many students, parents, teachers, and school administrators will feel strongly about whether gender segregation is a good idea or not. This means that it is highly unlikely that they will submit to being randomly assigned to a gender-segregated or coeducational class. And if random assignment is not possible, neither is the experimental approach. In this case, we might need to be content with comparisons among naturally formed classes (i.e., the correlational approach), trying to rule out some of the alternative interpretations by recourse to other statistical or logical means.

In each of the controversies we consider in this volume, we have tried to briefly summarize the empirical data that are available and discussed whether or not these data have helped to fuel the controversy (see the section entitled "Is There Common Ground?"). Much of what we have had to say in this regard hinges on the distinction between the correlational and experimental approaches. We also have made suggestions, when possible, about the studies needed to resolve the controversies, as well as pointing out the difficulties that might be encountered in such studies.

# Theoretical Perspectives

Questions can also become controversial because different theories can lead to different answers. The role of theory in advancing scientific understanding is frequently misunderstood. This misunderstanding most often takes the form of a statement (or an attitude) such as "It's only a theory" (meaning "as opposed to a fact or objective truth"). But it would be impossible for any science, including the science of educational psychology, to advance very far without theories. Theories serve three purposes:

1. Theories specify which observations are relevant and which are irrelevant to understanding the phenomena of interest. By way of illustration, consider the task of understanding children's cognitive development. Think of all the things that a child does in his or her very busy day. Although the child engages in many behaviors, not all will be relevant to understanding how his or her cognitive skills develop. We might easily dismiss behaviors such as sneezing, blinking, coughing, giggling, and a host of other seemingly irrelevant behaviors. But what about cases in which the child talks to himself or herself while trying to figure out how a toy works? Or how about the length of time he or she stares at a math problem before beginning to work on it with pencil and paper? For these and a host of other behaviors, theories tell us whether these behaviors are relevant or irrelevant to understanding cognitive development.

2. Theories help to explain the observations that have been collected about the phenomena of interest. In the theory of Jean Piaget, for example, preschool-age children's self-talk (i.e., talking aloud to the self) is relevant to understanding cognitive development because it reflects the child's egocentrism, or self-centeredness. Egocentrism prevents the child from recognizing flaws in his or her reasoning about other people and about problems in the physical world. In Piaget's theory, self-talk is a behavior to be overcome by development and helps to explain the limitations of the preschooler's thinking and behaving.

3. Theories generate predictions that can then be tested by collecting new observations. If the predictions are supported, then we can have more confidence in the theory. If the predictions are not supported, then we must either revise the theory or abandon it. Consider, for example, the explanation of the infant's formation of an attachment to its parent. Behaviorist theories traditionally proposed that the infant "learns" to become attached to its mother, not because of any quality of the mother or infant, but because the mother typically provides food and thus, comes to have reinforcing properties. One of the predictions of such a theory is that the failure of a mother to provide food should preclude the infant's attachment to her. In fact, this prediction was not supported either by experimental work with nonhuman primates or by correlational studies involving humans. Hence, behaviorist theories have been largely abandoned by researchers seeking to understand attachment.

Although theories serve valuable roles, typically the process of theory testing is a protracted one. Seldom do the results of a single empirical study lead to the rise of one theory and the downfall of another. In part, this is because theories often can be revised to accommodate inconsistent results, although at some point the revisions may become so extensive as to render the theory useless. In addition, different theories often lead their proponents to examine very different sorts of observations (i.e., those depicted as relevant by the theory), which means that direct comparison of the predictions of contrasting theories is sometimes difficult or impossible. Whatever the reasons, the fact is that different theories, each of which attempts to explain the same phenomena (e.g., classroom learning), can coexist and enjoy support, which, of course, ensures controversy. Eventually, however, these controversies will be resolved as evidence accumulates in favor of one theory and against the others.

The role of theory in generating (and resolving) controversy is an important theme throughout this book. In fact, the controversies in Unit 2 of this book are motivated almost entirely by theoretical disputes. The reader will see that often the controversies emerge from the clash of formal theories built within, and explicitly recognized by, a particular academic discipline, such as educational psychology. In some instances, however, the reader will see that the controversy is fueled by informal theories that are held tacitly by the people involved (e.g., teachers, parents, lawmakers) and that are the product of the contexts in which they themselves have lived and grown.

# Contextual Influences on the Stakeholders in the Educational Process

Many of the controversies that arise in educational psychology are not the product of vagaries in empirical data or of the existence of competing theories. Instead, many controversies result from contextual influences on the various stakeholders in the educational process (i.e., students, teachers, administrators, parents, civic leaders, and politicians). The late William Kessen, who was a professor at Yale University, was among the first to draw attention to the influence of context on children and on those who care for and study children. He outlined these influences in the provocatively entitled article "The American Child and Other Cultural Inventions," *American Psychologist* (October 1979). Three of Kessen's points are particularly important for understanding the source (and the potential resolution) of many of the controversies considered in the present volume.

1. *Children's lives and development are shaped by the contexts in which they live.* These contexts are multidimensional and can be defined by, among other things, physical variables (e.g., whether or not children are exposed to lead paint through living in an older home), family variables (e.g., whether they live in a two-parent or single-parent home), economic variables (e.g., whether their families are economically disadvantaged or affluent), social variables (e.g., whether they live in a safe or high-crime neighborhood), institutional variables (e.g., whether they are required to attend school or to hold down a job), cultural variables (e.g., parental beliefs and practices related to disciplining children), and historical variables (e.g., whether they happen to live during a time of war or peace). When we think about children attending schools in the United States today, for example, we need to remember that those children are living in very different contexts than were children living during, for example, the early part of the twentieth century. We should also remember—especially as we compare today's students in the United States to those attending schools in other countries— that the contexts for children in the United States may differ in important respects from those of children in Japan or in South Africa. And finally, we should remember that not all children attending U.S. schools today are growing up in precisely

the same contexts. Unfortunately, far too many children come to school carrying the scars of homelessness, abuse, and racial discrimination— scars that may interfere with their ability to derive maximum benefit from the educational opportunities afforded them. In other words, Kessen argued that the diverse circumstances of children's lives—diversity across historical time, across cultures or nations, and even within a culture or nation—can lead to a diversity of outcomes.

Many of the questions considered in this text have arisen in part because of such contextually determined diversity. Concerns about the diversity within any classroom with regard to student background, preparation, and needs have led to a host of questions about whether and how to accommodate such diversity in the classroom. In fact, it is questions of the latter sort that form Unit 1 of this book. Questions about contextually determined diversity have become controversial in part because of empirical data. They also have become controversial, however, because of two other types of contextual influences identified by Kessen.

2. *The views and behaviors of those who care for children are also shaped by the contexts in which they have lived.* By this, Kessen meant that the parents, teachers, community leaders, politicians, and other adults who directly or indirectly influence children's lives are themselves the product of the contexts in which they have lived. As a result, the attitudes they have about the nature of children (e.g., whether children are born inherently willful or inherently loving), about appropriate child-rearing practices (e.g., whether or not children should be spanked), about the developmental outcomes that are optimal (e.g., whether it is better for children to grow into compliant and conforming adults or into autonomous and critical adults), and, of course , about education will differ depending on the contexts of their own lives. In short, the answers that teachers, administrators, civic leaders, and politicians arrive at when faced with questions about education are sometimes determined more by the contexts of their lives than by any formal theory or the results of any empirical investigations.

Many of the questions considered in this text have become controversial precisely because of this type of contextual influence. Consider, for example, the controversy surrounding the inclusion of students with disabilities in classrooms alongside their peers without disabilities (as opposed to being in separate classrooms). For many advocates of inclusion, the issue is rooted in questions about the civil rights of students with disabilities. In fact, these advocates see the issue as the same as that faced in the 1950s and 1960s when racial segregation was battled on the grounds that "separate" social institutions and systems preclude "equal" opportunities.

3. *The views and behaviors of scholars who study children, development, and education are also shaped by the contexts in which they have lived.* Kessen was among the first to chastise education researchers and theorists for their rather "superior attitude;" that is, the assumption that somehow they were immune from the same influences that affect parents, teachers, and the rest of the public, and the assumption that somehow their scientific objectivity transcended historical time and place. Kessen was not simply arguing that scholars have incomplete knowledge and that somehow, as they learn more, they get closer to the truth and less susceptible to contextual influence. Instead, he argued that scholars are people too and that they can never escape the influence of the contexts in which they have lived. Some of the controversies considered in this text have arisen from these types of contextual influence. We see this, for example, in a tendency of researchers to have an almost blind devotion to a particular investigative approach or method of measurement; one in which they see only the advantages and none of the disadvantages.

# Unit 1

# UNIT

# Basic Theories of Learning and Education

*T*his unit covers the basic psychological theories of learning and of educational philosophy that remain to be enduring and classic debates in educational psychology. In fact, many debates in the other units can be related to one or more of these fundamental questions in educational psychology. It will be interesting to revisit these debates after going through other units in this volume.

The unit begins with the most important debate encountered by psychologists as they begin engaging with people in education. Although students in educational psychology are trained with the assumption that psychological science is the only way in which education can move forward, the reality is that so many in education (including other psychologists) are not convinced that psychological science is helpful. Other debates involve the tension between humanistic psychology and behaviorism, which include primary readings that students are not exposed to anymore, as well as practical questions that attempt to translate Piaget's theory of cognitive development to the classroom. Finally, it is important for students in educational psychology to question how students' happiness can be a concern and whether the pursuit of academic excellence counters our hope that all children are able to have "happy" lives.

Selected, Edited, and with Issue Framing Material by:
**Esther S. Chang,** *Soka University of America*

# ISSUE

# Can Psychological Science Improve the Quality of Education?

**YES: Edward L. Thorndike,** from "The Contribution of Psychology to Education," *Journal of Educational Psychology* (1910)

**NO: John Dewey,** from "Education as Engineering," *New Republic* (1922)

---

## Learning Outcomes

**After reading this issue, you will be able to:**

- Define psychological science.
- Identify and explain the advantages to a psychological approach to problem solving.
- Define educational progress in both authors' viewpoints.
- Identify the limitations of psychological science in education.

---

## ISSUE SUMMARY

**YES:** Edward Thorndike argued that psychology forms the basis of educational practice and the knowledge generated by the discipline will promote better practices. Moreover, he argued that the procedures psychologists use to generate knowledge can be used directly to improve progress toward educational goals.

**NO:** John Dewey acknowledged that while psychological science may be good at improving current practices, it is limited in making progress in education. Psychological science does not promote revolutionary changes that support progressive education.

**P**sychology's influence on educational practices in contemporary school contexts can be seen every day and by nearly all stakeholders in education (e.g., students, parents, teachers, principals, school chancellors, the Secretary of Education, etc.). The most obvious influence can be seen in the widespread and frequent use of educational assessments, particularly in the standardized testing of students as well as in the establishment of different criterion for establishing a "proficient" student within each state. Other practices also hint at psychological research methods, such as President Obama's College Scorecard, which allows users to compare colleges on various dimensions, including college's graduation rates, graduates' earnings after graduation, and information relating to students' ability to pay back their college loans (see collegescorecard.ed.gov).

Indeed, the use of psychological measures and methods does not automatically imply that it is being implemented wisely and, in the most careless cases, can completely ignore that psychology is a science. Thus, it is essential to start with the most basic questions for those who work at the intersection of Education and Psychology. That is, what is the role of psychology in education? Can it be used to make education "good"?

First, it would be a mistake to assume that there would be a consensus among psychologists in the answers to these basic questions. Furthermore, going back in history and referring to the writings of two pioneering and prominent psychologists with divergent opinions not only provides an important lesson in the history of educational psychology but also demonstrates how little the debate has changed despite 100 years of existence and use in education.

Psychologists would agree that the use of psychological science entails the use of unbiased observations of educational settings and conducting theoretically informed studies specifically designed to test theories of teaching and learning. However, educational settings are not perfect laboratories but a real-world setting with many "uncontrollable" factors of influence, and educational practices are not as easily quantifiable despite our persistence. Can psychological science be applied in ways that will inform stakeholders wisely?

In 1910, Edward Thorndike helped to launch the inaugural issue of the *Journal of Educational Psychology*, a publication of the APA that continues to publish rigorous original studies in the field, by outlining the unique contributions of psychology to education. In the first issue, he primarily argued that the aims of education can be easily misguided without psychological methods (Thorndike, 1910). Therefore, in his view, psychology's role in education is paramount to educational progress because through its application, the scientific method can be applied to identify and fix problems in education. Otherwise, how can one *really* identify "good" teaching? The use of the scientific method is important because it reduces human bias in selecting "best" practices. Thorndike reminds the reader that reliance on human intuition and common sense impedes educational progress because our aims remain unclear and our teaching activities lack purpose as a result. For instance, science allows us to test the presumptions of various stakeholders who believe that they have the best interests of students in mind but fundamentally disagree on educational solutions. His argument was consistent with much of his scholarly contributions, which generally aimed to make education more efficient and successful through the use of quantitative measurements and the use of statistics in hypothesis testing.

John Dewey, on the other hand, argued in the *New Republic* that educational progress is more than the precise identification of educational goals and the careful documentation of our progress toward them. To Dewey, educational progress had to be much more exciting than the slow, gradual changes led by science. He hoped that the outcome of educational progress would produce schools that were so radically different from current schools that scientists were incapable of envisioning it, supporting it, and participating in its emergence. In short, scientists lacked the moral virtues required of change, namely, of courage and honesty. He feared that psychological science would simply justify existing problems in the schools and at best, veil problems in a way that was more harmful for both teachers and students in the end. For example, psychologists could effectively convince educators that they are "scientifically up-to-date" even though they are simply re-enacting old practices. He was a proponent of progressive education, which fostered democratic classrooms and student experiences that were consistent with the real world (Dewey, 1938). Even though "psychologist" was a part of his identity, he did not believe that progressive education could be spearheaded by psychological science. The changes Dewey envisioned could only be possible by revolutionary changes in thinking about education, not in capturing the status quo of education as precisely as possible.

With the proliferation of educational assessments and a wider range of school types to select from today compared to 100 years ago, the differences between Thorndike and Dewey appear small compared to the differences seen in the two sides today. Today, for those who believe that psychological science can improve education, there is no doubt. Reference to empirical data is a must on an individual level, i.e., making decisions related to student placement, as well as on a national level. Yet, we often sense that teachers are either completely on board with educational and institutional assessment or completely resistant and avoid them as much as they can. Some parents rely solely on standardized test scores to assess schools, whereas others completely ignore the test performance of a school but are more interested in teachers' teaching philosophy and the quality of the school climate. In many respects, if people are not debating this topic, it is because each side may be entrenched.

# YES

**Edward L. Thorndike**

## The Contribution of Psychology to Education

Psychology is the science of the intellects, characters and behavior of animals including man. Human education is concerned with certain changes in the intellects, characters and behavior of men, its problems being roughly included under these four topics: Aims, materials, means and methods.

Psychology contributes to a better understanding of the aims of education by defining them, making them clearer; by limiting them, showing us what can be done and what cannot; and by suggesting new features that should be made parts of them.

Psychology makes ideas of educational aims clearer. When one says that the aim of education is culture, or discipline, or efficiency, or happiness, or utility, or knowledge, or skill, or the perfection of all one's powers, or development, one's statements, and probably one's thoughts, need definition. Different people, even amongst the clearest-headed of them, do not agree concerning just what culture is, or just what is useful. Psychology helps here by requiring us to put our notions of the aims of education into terms of the exact changes that education is to make, and by describing for us the changes which do actually occur in human beings.

Psychology helps to measure the probability that an aim is attainable. For example, certain writers about education state or imply that the knowledge and skill and habits of behavior which are taught to the children of today are of service not only to this generation and to later generations through the work this generation does, but also to later generations forever through the inheritance of increased capacity for knowledge and skill and morals. But if the mental and moral changes made in one generation are not transmitted by heredity to the next generation, the improvement of the race by direct transfer of acquisitions is a foolish, because futile aim.

Psychology enlarges and refines the aim of education. Certain features of human nature may be and have been thought to be unimportant or even quite valueless because of ignorance of psychology. Thus for hundreds of years in the history of certain races even the most gifted thinkers of the race have considered it beneath the dignity of education to make physical health an important aim. Bodily welfare was even thought of as a barrier to spiritual growth, an undesirable interferer with its proper master. Education aimed to teach it its proper place, to treat it as a stupid and brutish slave. It is partly because psychology has shown the world that the mind is the servant and co-worker as well as the master of the body, that the welfare of our minds and morals is intimately bound up with the welfare of our bodies, particularly of our central nervous systems, that today we can all see the eminence of bodily health as an aim of education.

To an understanding of the material of education, psychology is the chief contributor.

Psychology shares with anatomy, physiology, sociology, anthropology, history and the other sciences that concern changes in man's bodily or mental nature the work of providing thinkers and workers in the field of education with knowledge of the material with which they work. Just as the science and art of agriculture depend upon chemistry and botany, so the art of education depends upon physiology and psychology.

A complete science of psychology would tell every fact about every one's intellect and character and behavior, would tell the cause of every change in human nature, would tell the result which every educational force—every act of every person that changed any other or the agent himself—would have. It would aid us to use human beings for the world's welfare with the same surety of the result that we now have when we use falling bodies or chemical elements. In proportion as we get such a science we shall become masters of our own souls as we now are masters of heat and light. Progress toward such a science is being made.

Psychology contributes to understanding of the means of education, first, because the intellects and characters of

Thorndike, Edward L. "The Contribution of Psychology to Education," *Journal of Educational Psychology*, January 1910. © Copyright 1910 by the American Psychological Association.

any one's parents, teachers and friends are very important means of educating him, and, second, because the influence of any other means, such as books, maps or apparatus, cannot be usefully studied apart from the human nature which they are to act upon.

Psychology contributes to knowledge of methods of teaching in three ways. First, methods may be deduced outright from the laws of human nature. For instance, we may infer from psychology that the difficulty pupils have in learning to divide by a fraction is due in large measure to the habit established by all the thousands of previous divisions which they have done or seen, the habit, that is, of "division—decrease" or "number divided—result smaller than the number." We may then devise or select such a method as will reduce this interference from the old habits to a minimum without weakening the old habits in their proper functioning.

Second, methods may be chosen from actual working experience, regardless of psychology, as a starting point. Thus it is believed that in the elementary school a class of fifteen pupils for one teacher gives better results than either a class of three or a class of thirty. Thus, also, it is believed that family life is better than institutional life in its effects upon character and enterprise. Thus, also, it is believed that in learning a foreign language the reading of simple discussions of simple topics is better than the translation of difficult literary masterpieces that treat subtle and complex topics. Even in such cases psychology may help by explaining *why* one method does succeed better and so leading the way to new insights regarding other questions not yet settled by experience.

Third, in all cases psychology, by its methods of measuring knowledge and skill, may suggest means to test and verify or refute the claims of any method. For instance, there has been a failure on the part of teachers to decide from their classroom experience whether it is better to teach the spelling of a pair of homonyms together or apart in time. But all that is required to decide the question for any given pair is for enough teachers to use both methods with enough different classes, keeping everything else except the method constant, and to measure the errors in spelling the words thereafter in the two cases. Psychology, which teaches us how to measure changes in human nature, teaches us how to decide just what the results of any method of teaching are.

So far I have outlined the contribution of psychology to education from the point of view of the latter's problems. I shall now outline very briefly the work being done by psychologists which is of special significance to the theory and practice of education and which may be expected to result in the largest and most frequent contributions.

It will, of course, be understood that directly or indirectly, soon or late, every advance in the sciences of human nature will contribute to our success in controlling human nature and changing it to the advantage of the common weal. If certain lines of work by psychologists are selected for mention here, it is only because they are the more obvious, more direct and, so far as can now be seen, greater aids to correct thinking about education.

The first line of work concerns the discovery and improvement of means of measurement of intellectual functions. (The study of means of measuring moral functions such as prudence, readiness to sacrifice an immediate for a later good, sympathy, and the like, has only barely begun.) Beginning with easy cases such as the discrimination of sensory differences, psychology has progressed to measuring memory and accuracy of movement, fatigue, improvement with practice, power of observing small details, the quantity, rapidity and usefulness of associations, and even to measuring so complex a function as general intelligence and so subtle a one as suggestibility.

The task of students of physical science in discovering the thermometer, galvanometer and spectroscope, and in defining the volt, calorie erg, and ampère, is being attempted by psychologists in the sphere of human nature and behavior. How important such work is to education should be obvious. At least three-fourths of the problems of educational practice are problems whose solution depends upon the *amount* of some change in boys and girls. Of two methods, which gives the *greater* skill? Is the gain in general ability from a "disciplinary" study so great as to outweigh the loss in specially useful habits? Just how much more does a boy learn when thirty dollars a year is spent for his teaching than when only twenty dollars is spent? Units in which to measure the changes wrought by education are essential to an adequate science of education. And, though the students of education may establish these units by their own investigations, they can use and will need all the experience of psychologists in the search for similar units.

The second line of work concerns race, sex, age and individual differences in all the many elements of intellect and character and behavior.

How do the Igorottes, Ainus, Japanese and Esquimaux differ in their efficiency in learning to operate certain mechanical contrivances? Is the male sex more variable than the female in mental functions? What happens to keenness of sensory discrimination with age? How do individuals of the same race, sex and age differ in efficiency in perceiving small visual details or in accuracy in equaling a given length, or in the rapidity of movement? These are samples of many questions which psychologists have tried to answer by appropriate measurements. Such knowledge of the differences which exist amongst men for whatever reason is of service to the thinker about the particular differences which education aims to produce between a man and his former self.

These studies of individual differences or variability are being supplemented by studies of correlations. How far does superior vividness and fidelity in imagery from one sense go with inferiority in other sorts of imagery? To what extent is motor ability a symptom of intellectual ability? Does the quick learner soon forget? What are the mental types that result from the individual variations in mental functions and their intercorrelations? Psychology has already determined with more or less surety the answers to a number of such questions instructive in their bearing upon both scientific insight into human nature and practical arrangements for controlling it.

The extent to which the intellectual and moral differences found inhuman beings are consequences of their original nature and determined by the ancestry from which they spring, is a matter of fundamental importance for education. So also is the manner in which ancestral influence operates. Whether such qualities as leadership, the artistic temperament, originality, persistence, mathematical ability, or motor skill are represented in the germs each by one or a few unit characters so that they "Mendelize" in inheritance, or whether they are represented each by the cooperation of so many unit characters that the laws of their inheritance are those of "blending" is a question whose answer will decide in great measure the means to be employed for racial improvement. Obviously both the amount and the mode of operation of ancestral influence upon intellect and character are questions which psychology should and does investigate.

The results and methods of action of the many forces which operate in childhood and throughout life to change a man's original nature are subjects for study equally appropriate to the work of a psychologist, a sociologist or a student of education, but the last two will naturally avail themselves of all that the first achieves. Although as yet the studies of such problems are crude, speculative and often misguided, we may hope that the influence of climate, food, city life, the specialization of industry, the various forms of the family and of the state, the different "studies" of the schools, and the like will come to be studied by as careful psychologists and with as much care as is now the case with color-vision or the perception of distance.

The foundation upon which education builds is the equipment of instincts and capacity given by nature apart from training. Just as knowledge of the peculiar inheritance

characteristic of any individual is necessary to efficient treatment of him, so knowledge of the unlearned tendencies of man as a species is necessary to efficient planning for education in general. Partly in conscious response to this demand and partly as a result of growing interest in comparative and genetic psychology, there have been in the last two decades many studies by psychologists of both the general laws of instinct and their particular natures, dates of appearance and disappearance, and conditions of modifiability. The instincts of attitude—of interest and aversion—are of course to be included here, as well as the tendencies to more obviously effective responses.

It is unfortunately true that the unlearned tendencies to respond of ants and chickens have been studied with more care than those of men, and also that the extreme complexity and intimate mixture with habits in the case of human instincts prevent studies of them, even when made with great care, from giving entirely unambiguous and elegant results. But the educational theorist or practitioner who should conclude that his casual observations of children in homes and schools needs no reinforcement from the researches of psychologists would be making the same sort of, thought not so great, an error as the pathologist or physician who should neglect the scientific studies of bacteria and protozoa. Also the psychologist who condemns these studies in toto because they lack the precision and surety of his own studies of sensations and perceptual judgments is equally narrow, though from a better motive.

The modifications of instincts and capacities into habits and powers and the development of the latter are the subjects of researches in dynamic psychology which are replacing the vague verbal and trite maxims of what used to be called "applied psychology" by definite insights into reality far in advance of those which common-sense sagacity alone can make. We are finding out when and why "practice makes perfect" and when and why it does not; wherein the reinforcement of a connection between situation and response by resulting satisfaction is better than the inhibition of alternative connections by discomfort and wherein it is not; what the law of diminishing returns from equal amounts of practice is, what it implies, and how it is itself limited; how far the feelings of achievement, of failure and of fatigue are symptomatic of progress, retardation and unfitness for work. Such a list of topics could be much extended even now and is being increased rapidly as more psychologists and more gifted psychologists come to share in the study of the learning process.

Only twenty years ago a student could do little more than add to his own common-sense deductions from the common facts of life the ordered series of similar deductions by the sagacious Bain. Bain utilized all the psychology of his day as well as the common fund of school-room experience, but today his book is hopelessly outgrown. Although it was the source of the minor books on the topic during the eighties and nineties, no one would now think of presenting the facts of the science of education by a revised edition of Bain.

Other lines of psychological work deserve more than mention. Incidental contributions from studies of sensory and perceptual processes, imagery and memory, attention and distraction, facilitation, inhibition and fatigue, imitation and suggestion, the rate and accuracy of movement and other topics—even from studies made with little or no concern about the practical control of human nature—sum up to a body of facts which do extend and economize that control. The special psychology of babies, children and adolescents is obviously important to education. False infant psychology or false child psychology is harmful, not because it is infant psychology, but because it is false.

I give only mention to these so as to save space in which to call attention to another relation between psychology and education which is not sufficiently known. The science of education can and will itself contribute abundantly to psychology. Not only do the laws derived by psychology from simple, specially arranged experiments help us to interpret and control mental action under the conditions of school-room life. School-room life itself is a vast laboratory in which are made thousands of experiments of the utmost interest to "pure" psychology. Not only does psychology help us to understand the mistakes made by children in arithmetic. These mistakes afford most desirable material for studies of the action of the laws of association, analysis and selective thinking. Experts in education studying the responses to school situations for the sake of practical control will advance knowledge not only of the mind as a learner under school conditions but also of the mind for every point of view.

Indeed I venture to predict that this journal will before many years contain a notable proportion of articles reporting answers to psychological questions got from the facts of educational experience, in addition to its list of papers reporting answers to educational questions got from the experiments of the laboratory.

All that is here written may seem very obvious and needless, and meet the tragic fate of being agreed with by every one who reads it. I hope that it is obvious and needless, and that the relation between psychology and education is not, in the mind of any competent thinker, in any way an exception to the general case that action in the world should be guided by the truth about the world; and that any truth about it will directly or indirectly, soon or late, benefit action.

---

EDWARD L. THORNDIKE (1874–1949) is often referred to as the modern founder of Educational Psychology and is best known for his theory of the Law of Effect and related animal experiments in learning, which provided the essential framework for behavioral psychology to take form. He was the past president of the American Psychological Association (APA) in 1912 and was the very first psychologist to be admitted to the National Academy of the Sciences in 1917.

**John Dewey**

# Education as Engineering

**M**rs. Mary Austin in her illuminating article on The Need for a New Social Concept gives an apt expression of the contrast in contemporary behavior between our power in physical engineering and in basic human' concerns. We can, as she points out, easily construct a new type of bridge; we cannot create a new type of education. It would be a comparatively simple matter if schools were destroyed to restore them out of a denuded social consciousness; it would be very difficult under like circumstances to recover ability to make a modern bridge. "The reason is that we have been thinking about education long enough to form a pattern in our minds but not long enough of the multitudinous processes involved in the building of steel bridges."

The meaning is clear, and there is nothing to be gained by a meticulous critique of words. But for radical renovation. . . . of the school system, a revision, almost a reversal, of wording would seem to be required. Instead of saying that we have thought so long about education—if thinking means anything intellectual—it would be closer to 'the realities of the situation to say we have only just begun to think about it. The school system represents not thinking but the domination of thought by the inertia of immemorial customs. Modern bridge building, on the other hand, is quite inconceivable apart from the use of materials determined by purely intellectual methods. Our steel cantilever bridges represent precisely the kind of thing that custom unmodified by thought could never achieve no matter how far it was carried. Because bridge building is dependent upon thinking it is easy for thinking to change the mode; because education depends upon habits which arose before there was scientific method, thinking with great difficulty makes even a little dent.

Consequently if our school system were destroyed, we should not have to recover our "minds"—our intellectual equipment—to restore our schools. It would be enough if we retained our habits. To restore modern bridges we could dispense with formed habits provided we retained our intellectual technique. There is an ambiguity in referring to a "mental pattern" in connection with schools. The pattern is not mental, if we mean a pattern formed *by* mind. There is doubtless a pattern *in* our minds, but that signifies only a sense of a comfortable scheme of action which has been deposited by wont and use. The pattern is so deep-seated and clearly outlined that the ease of its recognition gives rise to a deceptive sense that there is something intellectual in the pattern itself. In engineering the pattern is mental in quite a different way. It summarizes a distinctively intellectual type of behavior.

A sense of this contrast seems essential to adequate reflection on the question of how educational procedure is to become a form of constructive engineering. William James said that anyone grasps the significance of a generalization only in the degree in which he is familiar with the detail covered by it. Now detail means things in concrete existence. We are familiar only with things which specifically enter into our lives and with which we steadily reckon and deal. All concepts, theories, general ideas are thin, meagre and ineffectual in the degree in which they are not reflective expressions of acts and events already embodied, achieved, in experience. New conceptions in education will not of themselves carry us far in modifying schools, for until the schools are modified the new conceptions will be themselves pale, remote, vague, formal. They will become thick, substantial, only in the degree in which they are not indispensably required. For they will offer precise and definite modes of thinking only when new meanings and values have become embodied in concrete life-experiences and are thus sustained by them. Till that time arrives the importance of new concepts is mainly negative and critical. They enable us to criticize existing modes of practice; they point out to us .the fact that concrete detail of the right sort does *not* exist. Their positive function is to inspire experimental action rather than to give information as to how to execute it.

There was, I take it, no definite art or science of modern bridge building until after bridges of the new sort had been constructed. It was impossible that the new art should precede the new achievement. The formulae for construction, the rules of specific procedure, the specific classification of types of problems and solutions had to wait upon presentation of appropriate concrete material, that is upon successful experimentation. Nevertheless the pioneers had something to go upon and go ahead with, even, if they had no specified art of bridge building to rely upon. They had a certain amount of dependable knowledge in mathematics and physics. The difficulty they suffered from was that no one before them had employed this knowledge in building the kind of bridge that new social conditions called for. When they tried to imagine a new type, the minds of all but a few were surely held in bondage by habituation to what was already familiar.

The essential need was thus human rather than scientific. Some one had to have the imagination to get away from the "thought" of the existing easily recognized pattern. This took daring, the courage to think out of line with convention and custom; it took inventiveness in using existing scientific material in a new way, for new consequences. It took intellectual initiative to conduct experiment against almost universal indifference or reprobation; it took intellectual honesty to learn from failure as well as from success in experimentation. The pioneer succeeded in making his bridge—and ultimately making a new art or scientific technique—because he had the courage of a creative mind. Consider the history of any significant invention or discovery, and you will find a period when there was enough knowledge to make a new mode of action or observation possible but no definite information or instruction as to how to make it actual. Every time it was a courageous imagination, a quality which is personal, human, moral, rather than scientific or technical, which built the bridge—in every sense of the word bridge.

There is at present no art of educational engineering. There will not be any such art until considerable progress has been made in creating new modes of education in the home and school. But there does already exist a considerable body of observations and ideas in biology, psychology and the like which serves to criticize and condemn much of our existing practice, and to suggest to a mind not weighed down by fear the possibility of new leads and openings. Given imagination, courage and the desire to experiment and to learn from its results, there is a push toward, a momentum for creative work. Its concrete consequences if subjected to honest or discriminating reflection will afford material for the elaboration of an art, a fairly definite body of suggestions and instructions for the later intelligent conduct of an educative art. But this technique will be largely ex post facto. It is equally fatal to postpone effort till we have the art and to try to deduce the art in advance from the scientific knowledge in biology, psychology and sociology we actually possess. If earlier mathematicians and physicists had attempted to anticipate the result of inventive experimentation in bridge building by deducing from their sciences the rules of the new art, it is certain that they would have arrived only at improved rules for making the old and familiar type of bridge; they would have retarded the day of the new type; they would have concealed from view the necessity of the indispensable human factor—emancipation from routine and timidity. The case is the same with the creation of new types of schools and the ulterior development of an art of education.

There is no question that would-be pioneers in the educational field need an extensive and severe intellectual equipment. Experimentation is something other than blindly trying one's luck or mussing around in the hope that something nice will be the result. Teachers who are to develop a new type of education need a more exacting and comprehensive training in science, philosophy and history than teachers who follow conventionally safe lines. But they do not at present need a translation of this knowledge into a science and art of education. They do not need it because it cannot be had and the pretence of supplying it makes conditions worse rather than better. When, for example, psychology is employed simply to improve the existing teaching of arithmetic or spelling for pre-existing ends, or to measure the technical results of such teaching, let that fact be clearly acknowledged. Let it not be supposed that there is really any advance in the science of education merely because there is a technical improvement in the tools of managing an educational scheme conspicuous for its formation prior to the rise of science. Such "science" only rationalizes old, customary education while improving it in minor details. Given the required intellectual equipment, the further immediate demand is for human qualities of honesty, courage and invention which will enable one to go ahead without the props of custom or the specious pretensions of custom masquerading in the terminology of science.

At present we are still largely in the "rationalizing" stage. Consequently, as was pointed out in an earlier article on Education as Religion, educational concepts nominally as diverse as culture, discipline, social serviceableness work out in practice to mean only a little more of this or that study. The scope of our rationalizing is seen in the fact that educational theory as taught in our teachers' training schools has been revolutionized in the last generation, largely in a decade. But where is the evidence 'of any corresponding change in practice? The most optimistic soul, if candid, will admit that we are mostly doing the old things with new names attached. The change makes little difference—except for advertising purposes. We used to lay out a course prescribed by authority for the improvement of the minds of the young. Now we initiate them into their cultural heritage. The staples used to be taught in certain ways on the ground that the crude and lawless minds of the young needed to be chastened by discipline in things above and beyond them. Now we appeal to "inner motivation." But we teach much the same topics, only in a more gracious, less repellent way. Strange, though, that the opposed needs of external discipline and of inner purpose should be met by so nearly the same subjects and topics!

I am not insinuating that there is personal insincerity in this state of affairs. In part it is due to the fact that docility has been emphasized in education, plus the fact that in the main the most docile among the young are the ones who become teachers when they are adults. Consequently they still listen docilely to the voice of authority. More fundamentally the outcome is due to the fact that a premature attempt is being made to lay down a procedure, definite proper courses of subjects and methods, by which teachers may guide themselves, the procedure being nominally derived from our new knowledge in biology, psychology, etc. But as we have seen, this cannot be done; no results so definite as this can be reached until after the change in educational practice is well under way. When the attempt is made in advance to answer specific questions which will arise in the course of employing the new knowledge, to supply in advance definite suggestions as to courses of procedure, it is inevitable that the minds of both "authorities" and of students intending to teach should fall back upon just the old practices which they are nominally striving to get away from. For here alone is there material concrete enough to permit the formulation of definite problems, answers and steps to be undertaken.

In short, at present, both students and teachers of education are excessively concerned with trying to evolve a body of definite, usable, educational directions out of the new body of science. The attempt is only too natural. But it is pathetic. The endeavor to forestall experiment and its failures and achievements, the attempt to tell in advance how successfully to do a new kind of thing ends, at most, in a rectification of old ways and results, plus a complacent assurance that the best methods of modern science are employed and sanction what is done. This sense of being scientifically up-to-date does endless harm. It retards the creation of a new type of education, because it obscures the one thing deeply needful: a new personal attitude in which a teacher shall be an inventive pioneer in use of what is known, and shall learn in the process of experience to formulate and deal with those problems which a premature "science" of education row tries to state and solve in advance of experience.

I do not underestimate the value of the guidance which some time in the future individuals may derive from the results of prior collective experience. I only say that the benefit of such an art cannot be had until a sufficient number of individuals have experimented without its beneficial aid in order to provide its materials. And what they need above all else is the creatively courageous disposition. Fear, routine, sloth, identification of success with ease, and approbation of others are the enemies that now stand in the way of educational advance. Too much of what is called educational science and art only perpetuate a regime of wont and use by pretending to give scientific guidance and guarantees in advance. There is in existence knowledge which gives a compass to those who enter on the uncharted seas, but only a stupid insincerity will claim that a compass is a chart. The call is to the creative adventurous mind. Religious faith in education working through this medium of individual courage with the aid of non-educational science will end in achieving education as a science and an art. But as usual we confuse faith with worship, and term science what is only justification of habit.

---

**JOHN DEWEY** (1859–1952) was an educational philosopher and psychologist who was best known for his support for progressive education, which emphasized meaningful activity and classroom democracy. He penned the first textbook in psychology, *Psychology* (1886), was president of the APA in 1899, and was one of the founders of the American Civil Liberties Union. He was also a social commentator who wrote in popular publications such as the *New Republic*.

# EXPLORING THE ISSUE

## Can Psychological Science Improve the Quality of Education?

## Critical Thinking and Reflection

1. Is the role of psychological science limited to what Thorndike enumerates in his article?
2. What aspects of psychological science are ignored by Thorndike?
3. In what ways can social scientists exercise courage? In what ways can they exercise honesty?

## Is There Common Ground?

There can be a great deal of common ground between Dewey and Thorndike because both can be seen to value the goals of Enlightenment (e.g., Kant, 1784). Typical of Enlightenment thinkers, Thorndike adamantly believed that science could solve problems not just within the educational domain but for all of society. Likewise, Dewey's call for courage is consistent with the character virtues necessary to conduct scientific studies and apply them to real world problems without worrying about the political consequences.

In Thorndike (1910), the advantages of understanding the knowledge that psychological studies generate was mentioned but much more emphasis was placed on our ability to develop psychometric measurements and in the experimental testing of different practices. The latter two are unique technical skills that psychologists offer to interdisciplinary fields, such as the study of education. Thus, when several specialists collaborate, it is natural for each to hold on to their unique contributions. However, in doing so, we relegate psychologists to technical positions and refer to them for technical advice. Thus, they are often put in situations that allow them to forget the bigger picture. For example, the educational psychologist who studies intrinsic motivation may not think often about how their research informs different educational reform agendas. Thus, Dewey's critique of social scientists in educational contexts is common even today. To avoid this problem educational psychologists should be trained to think philosophically about education.

## Additional Resources

D. C. Berliner, "Telling the Stories of Educational Psychology," *Educational Psychologist* (vol. 27, 1992). doi: 10.1207/s15326985ep2702_2.

J. Dewey, *Experience and Education* (Macmillan, 1938).

R. Glaser, "Education and Thinking: The Role of Knowledge," *American Psychologist* (vol. 39, 1984). doi: http://dx.doi.org/10.1037/0003-066X.39.2.93.

E. O. Wilson, *Consilience: The Unity of Knowledge* (Random House, 1998).

# Internet References . . .

**The Internet Encyclopedia of Philosophy**

www.iep.utm.edu/dewey

**The John Dewey Society for the Study of Education and Culture**

www.johndeweysociety.org

**The Online Books**

http://onlinebooks.library.upenn.edu/webbin /book/lookupname?key=Thorndike%2C%20 Edward%20L.%20(Edward%20Lee)%2C%201874-1949

**Selected, Edited, and with Issue Framing Material by:**
Esther S. Chang, *Soka University of America*

# ISSUE

## Should Students Be Free?

**YES: Carl Rogers**, from "Difficulties and Opportunities: The Challenge of Present-Day Teaching," Charles Merrill Publishing (1969)

**NO: B. F. Skinner**, from "A Technology of Behavior," "Values," "What Is Man," in *Beyond Freedom & Dignity*, Hackett Publishing (1971)

| Learning Outcomes |
|---|
| **After reading this issue, you will be able to:** |
| • Define humanistic psychology. |
| • Define whole person learning. |
| • Define behaviorism. |
| • Compare and contrast the definition of learning between the two perspectives. |
| • Compare and contrast the definition of freedom between the two perspectives. |

### ISSUE SUMMARY

**YES:** Founder of humanistic psychology Carl Rogers argued that students learn best when they are allowed to be autonomous and can exercise choice. He proposed that learning be based on students' own curiosity and inner meaning.

**NO:** Founder of behaviorism B. F. Skinner argued that any notion of personal freedom is an illusion. He offers a critique of "inner freedom" and proposes that all learning and motivation is influenced by external forces.

Historically, the atmosphere of schooling has often been characterized by harsh discipline, regimentation, and restriction. The prison metaphor often used by critics in describing school conditions rings true all too often. Although calls to make schools pleasant have been sounded frequently, they have seldomly been heeded. Roman rhetorician Marcus Fabius Quintilian (ca. A.D. 35–100) advocated a constructive and enjoyable learning atmosphere. John Amos Comenius in the seventeenth century suggested a gardening metaphor in which learners were given kindly nurturance. Johann Heinrich Pestalozzi established a model school in the nineteenth century that replaced authoritarianism with love and respect.

Yet school as an institution retains the stigma of authoritarian control, attendance is compelled, social and psychological punishment is meted out, and the decision-making freedom of students is limited and often curtailed.

These practices lead to rather obvious conclusions: the prevailing belief is either that young people are naturally evil and wild and therefore must be tamed in a restricting environment or that schooling as such is so unpalatable that people must be forced and cajoled to reap its benefits—or both.

Certainly, philosopher John Dewey (1895–1952) was concerned about this circumstance, citing at one time the superintendent of his native Burlington, Vermont, school district as admitting that the schools were a source of "grief and mortification" and were "unworthy of patronage." Dewey rejected both the need for "taming" and the defeatist attitude that the school environment must remain unappealing. He hoped to create a motivational atmosphere that would engage learners in real problem-solving activities, thereby sustaining curiosity, creativity, and attachment. The rewards were to flow from the sense of accomplishment and freedom, which was to be achieved through the disciplined actions necessary to solve the problem at hand.

More recent treatment of the allied issues of freedom, control, and motivation has come from the two major camps in the field of educational psychology: the behaviorists (rooted in the early-twentieth-century theories of Ivan Pavlov, Edward L. Thorndike, and John B. Watson) and the humanists (emanating from the Gestalt and field theory psychologies developed in Europe and America earlier in the twentieth century).

B. F. Skinner has been the dominant force in translating behaviorism into recommendations for school practices. He and his disciples, often referred to as "neobehaviorists," have contributed to widely used innovations such as behavioral objectives in instruction and testing, competency-based education, mastery learning, assertive discipline, and outcome-based education. The humanistic viewpoint has been championed by Carl R. Rogers, Abraham Maslow, Fritz Perls, Rollo May, and Erich Fromm, most of whom ground their psychological theories in the philosophical assumptions of existentialism and phenomenology.

Skinner believes that "inner" states are merely convenient myths, that motives and behaviors are shaped by environmental factors. These shaping forces, however, need not be negative, nor must they operate in an uncontrolled manner. Our present understanding of human behavior allows us the freedom to shape the environmental forces, which in turn shape us. With this power, Skinner contends, we can replace aversive controls in schooling with positive reinforcements that heighten the students' motivation level and make learning more efficient.

Recent manifestations of the continuing interest in Skinner's behaviorism and the humanistic psychology of Rogers include Virginia Richardson's "From Behaviorism to Constructivism in Teacher Education," *Teacher Education and Special Education* (Summer 1996) and Tobin Hart's "From Category to Contact: Epistemology and the Enlivening and Deadening of Spirit in Education," *Journal of Humanistic Education and Development* (September 1997). In the first selection, Carl Rogers critiques Skinner's behaviorist approach and sets forth his argument supporting the reality of freedom as an inner human state that is the wellspring of responsibility, will, and commitment. Skinner deals with the problem of freedom and control in the selection that follows. (Introduction by James Noll.)

# YES

Carl Rogers

## Difficulties and Opportunities: The Challenge of Present-Day Teaching

### What Is Learning?

If the purpose of teaching is to promote learning, then we need to ask what we mean by learning. Here I become passionate. I want to talk about learning, but not the lifeless, sterile, futile, quickly forgotten stuff that is crammed into the mind of the helpless individual tied into this seat by ironclad bonds of conformity! I am talking about *learning*—insatiable curiosity that drives the adolescent mind to absorb everything he can see or hear or read about a topic that has inner meaning. I am talking about the student who says, "I am discovering, drawing in from the outside, and making what I discover a real part of me." I am talking about any learning in which the experience of the learner progresses this way:

> *"No, no, that's not what I want."*
> *"Wait! This is closer to what I'm interested in, what I need."*
> *"Ah, here it is! Now I'm grasping and comprehending what I need and what I want to know!"*

. . .

### Whole-person Learning

Let me look at this from another angle. Educators have traditionally thought of learning as an orderly type of cognitive, left-brain activity. The left hemisphere of the brain tends to function in ways that are logical and linear. It goes step by step in a straight line, emphasizing the parts, the details that make up the whole. It accepts only what is sure and clear. It deals in ideas and concepts; it is associated with masculine aspects of life. This is the only kind of functioning that has been fully acceptable to our schools and colleges.

But to involve the whole person in learning means to set the right brain free, to use it as well. The right hemisphere functions in quite a different way. It is intuitive.

It grasps the essence before it understands the details. It takes in a whole gestalt, the total configuration. It operates in metaphors. It is aesthetic rather than logical. It makes creative leaps. It is the way of artist, of the creative scientist. It is associated with the feeling qualities of life. Frances Vaughn, in her classic work entitled *Awakening Intuition*, says,

> Intuition is known to everyone by experience, yet frequently remains repressed or underdeveloped. As a psychological function, like sensation, feeling, and thinking, intuition is a way of knowing. When you know something intuitively, it has the ring of truth; yet often we do not know *how* we know what we know. . . . Learning to use intuition is learning to be your own teacher.

Significant learning combines the logical and the intuitive, the intellect and the feelings, the concept and the experience, the idea and the meaning. When we learn in that way, we are whole; we use all our masculine and feminine capacities.

. . .

### The Individual Is Free

I am impressed by the scientific advances illustrated in the examples I have given. I regard them as a great tribute to the ingenuity, insight, and persistence of the individuals making the investigations. They have added enormously to our knowledge. Yet for me they leave something very important unsaid. Let me try to illustrate this, first from my experience in therapy and then from the classroom.

I think of a young man classed as schizophrenic with whom I had been working for a long time in a state hospital. He was a very inarticulate man, and during one hour he made only a few remarks about individuals who had recently left the hospital; then he remained silent for almost forty minutes. When he got up to go, he mumbled almost under his breath, "If some of *them* can do it, maybe I can too." That was all—not a dramatic statement, not uttered with force and vigor, yet a statement of choice by this young man to work toward his own improvement and eventual release from the hospital. It is not too surprising that about eight months after that statement he was out of the hospital. I believe this experience of responsible choice is one of the deepest aspects of psychotherapy and one of the elements that most solidly underlies personality change.

I think of another young person, this time a young female graduate student who was deeply disturbed and on the borderline of a psychotic break. Yet after a number of interviews in which she talked very critically about all of the people who had failed to give her what she needed, she finally concluded: "Well, with that sort of a foundation, it's really up to me. I mean it seems to be really apparent to me that I can't depend on someone else to give me an education." And then she added very softly, "I'll really have to get it myself." She went on to explore this experience of important and responsible choice. She found it a frightening experience, and yet one that gave her a feeling of strength. A force seemed to surge up within her that was big and strong, and yet she also felt very much alone and sort of cut off from support. She added, "I am going to begin to do more things that I know I should do." And she did.

. . .

The need to have choices in the classroom is just as important in the evolution of healthy individuals. If all parts of a child's life are controlled, then control becomes the driving force in decisions about teaching and learning. What is taught and how it will be taught become controlling issues. After the child's learning life is controlled for thirteen years in school, suddenly at age eighteen he or she is free to choose. The newfound freedom comes with little or no prior experience. If experience is the best teacher, then choosing and freedom are alien experiences for too many students in our schools.

A colleague shared an experience about a talk he had with a clinical psychologist who works with students in a public school district. The psychologist was attending one of a series of workshops that was being offered to improve the learning climate of middle-school students. The sixth-grade teachers talked and shared examples about the way they were involving students in classroom decisions and creating avenues for young adolescents to develop outlets for their feelings. They also talked about the importance of choices in the classroom. Teachers discussed how students select from a range of projects to work, and their sharing of the operations of the classroom

with the students. For example, students working in teams prepared mini-lessons based on subject areas they had been studying and presented them to the class using visual aids and demonstrations. The discussion by the teachers about their newfound partners in learning was animated and exciting. At the conclusion of the session, a school psychologist who asked to sit in on the session said that the discussion was important for him because he usually only hears about problems and the lack of choices given to students. He commented, "Usually, they give me a student and say, 'He has a problem; fix it.'" He also realized the potential for teachers working together with students to create healthy learning environments, which could prevent the need for him to see some of the students he is currently counseling. Teachers usually do not receive education in counseling, but a supportive and caring learning environment can go a long way in reducing the numbers of students who need specialized counseling services. This would allow time for psychologists to work with those students with the greatest needs.

Let me spell out a trifle more fully the way such choosings occur in the classroom. A student, Dexter, was retained a second time in sixth grade; he had failed all his subjects due to excessive absences. He was placed in a different sixth-grade classroom with a teacher new to the school. After only a week it became clear that Dexter was very bright and capable but also a disruptive factor in the classroom. After several talks, the student explained that he was ashamed about not being with his peers in the next grade and didn't want to be in sixth grade for another year. The teacher asked Dexter if he would be willing to work independently in the library, in school, and at home to make up the learning he had missed. He said, "I need to move on; I can't stay here any longer." With that statement, the teacher developed a learning contract detailing what Dexter needed to move to seventh grade. The contract was approved by the principal and signed by the teacher and Dexter. Dexter completed his work in seven weeks. He moved to seventh grade where some tutoring was provided. Follow-ups with Dexter and his teachers showed he was doing well and was helping other students with their work. He took responsibility for his actions and was able to turn around a situation that would most likely have led him to drop out physically from a situation he had already mentally distanced himself from in the past.

In previous chapters of this book you read about students who had choice and freedom in school. But many students choose to be free earlier, a choice the educational establishment calls *dropping out*. In many cases it's the only way a young adult can express his or her need to choose. Not all students have Dexter's option.

I am trying to suggest in these examples that I would be at a loss to explain the positive change that can occur in psychotherapy or in education if I had to omit the importance of the sense of free and responsible choice on the part of clients, teachers, and students in schools. I believe that the freedom to choose is one of the deepest elements underlying change.

## The Meaning of Freedom

Considering the scientific advantages that I have mentioned, how can we even speak of freedom? In what sense is a client, teacher, or student free? In what sense are any of us free? What possible definition of freedom can there be in the modern world?

Let me attempt such a definition. In the first place, the freedom that I am talking about is essentially an inner element, something that exists in the living person quite aside from any of the outward choices of alternatives that we so often think of as constituting freedom. I am speaking of the kind of freedom that Viktor Frankl vividly describes in his experience of the concentration camp, when everything—possessions, status, identity—was taken from the victim. But even months and years in such an environment showed only "that everything can be taken from a man but one thing: the last of the human freedoms—to choose one's own attitude in any given set of circumstances, to choose one's own way" (1). It is this inner, subjective, existential freedom that I have observed. It is the realization that "I can live myself, here and now, by my own choice." It is the quality of courage that enables a person to step into the uncertainty of the unknown as she chooses herself. It is the discovery of meaning from within oneself, meaning that comes from listening sensitively and openly to the complexities of what one is experiencing. It is the burden of being responsible for the self one chooses to be. It is a person's recognition that she is an emerging process, not a static end product. The individual who is thus deeply and courageously thinking her own thoughts, becoming her own uniqueness, responsibly choosing herself may be fortunate in having hundreds of objective outer alternatives from which to choose, or she may be unfortunate in having none. But her freedom exists regardless. So we are first of all speaking of something that exists within the individual, something phenomenological rather than external, but nonetheless to be prized.

The second point in defining this experience of freedom is that it exists not as a contradiction of the picture of the psychological universe as a sequence of cause and effect, but as a complement to such a universe. Freedom rightly understood is a fulfillment by the person of the ordered sequence of her life. The free person moves out voluntarily, freely, responsibly to play her significant part in a world whose determined events move through her spontaneous choice and will.

I see this freedom of which I am speaking, then, as existing in a different dimension than the determined sequence of cause and effect. I regard it as a freedom that exists in the subjective person, a freedom that she courageously uses to live her potentialities. . . .

## The Irreconcilable Contradiction

. . . On the one hand, modern psychological science, and many other forces in modern life as well, hold the view that the person is unfree, that she is controlled, that words such as *purpose, choice, commitment* have no significant meaning, that the individual is nothing but an object that we can more fully understand and more fully control. Enormous strides have been and are being made in implementing this perspective. It would seem heretical indeed to question this view.

Yet as Polanyi has pointed out in another of his writings, the dogmas of science can be in error (2). He says:

> In the days when an idea could be silenced by showing that it was contrary to religion, theology was the greatest single source of fallacies. Today, when any human thought can be discredited by branding it as unscientific, the power previously exercised by theology has passed over to science; hence science has become in its turn the greatest single source of error.

So I am emboldened to say that over against this view of the individual as unfree, as an object, is the evidence from therapy, from the schoolhouse, from subjective living, and from objective research as well that personal freedom and responsibility have a crucial significance, that one cannot live a complete life without such personal freedom and responsibility, and that self-understanding and responsible choice make a sharp and measurable difference in the behavior of the individual. In this context, commitment does have meaning. Commitment is the emerging and changing total direction of the individual based on a close and acceptant relationship between the person and all of the trends of his or her life, conscious and unconscious. Unless as individuals and as a society we can make constructive use of this capacity for freedom and commitment, humans are, it seems to me set on a collision course with fate.

. . .

## An Update on the Paradox

[S]cientists have moved a long way in recognizing the deficiencies of a mechanistic world view and the inadequacy of the linear cause-effect science on which behaviorism rests. The universe is far more mysterious than it once seemed, and we find prominent physicists likening this view of the cosmos to that of a fluid puzzle—always in a state of flux. As to the issues I have discussed in this chapter, I will include here some quotations by Fritjof Capra, a theoretical physicist, although the same ideas have been expressed by other scientists and philosophers of science.

I'll mention Capra's discussion of the modern world view, including his ideas on the disappearance of a narrow cause-effect science:

> The universe is thus experienced as a dynamic, inseparable whole which always includes the observer in an essential way. In this experience the traditional concepts of space and time, of isolated objects, and of cause and effect lose their meaning. Such an experience, however, is very similar to that of the Eastern mystics. (3, p. 81)

Capra also considers the question of choice: "A living organism is a self-organizing system, which means that its order in structure and function is not imposed by the environment, but is established by the system itself. . . ." Living systems interact with the environment continually, "but this interaction does not determine their organization." Capra continues:

> The relative autonomy of self-organizing systems sheds new light on the age-old philosophical question of free will. From the systems point of view, both determinism and freedom are relative concepts. To the extent that a system is autonomous from its environment it is free; to the extent that it depends on it through continuous interaction its activity will be shaped by environmental influences. The relative autonomy of organisms usually increases with their complexity, and it reaches its culmination in human beings.
>
> This relative concept of free will seems to be consistent with the view of mystical traditions that exhort their followers to transcend the notion of an isolated self and become aware that we are inseparable parts of the cosmos in which we are embedded. The goal of these traditions is to shed all ego sensations completely and, in mystical experience, merge with the totality of the cosmos. Once such a state is reached, the question

of free will seems to lose its meaning. If I am the universe, there can be no "outside" influences and all my actions will be spontaneous and free. (4, pp. 269–70)

Stephen Hawking, physicist and author of *A Brief History of Time*, says that current theory holds that there are either many universes or that there is one large universe with many shapes. The universe based on the best case evidence is chaotic and irregular rather than smooth. Yet we see our part of the universe as smooth. If only the smooth part of the universe can support life then, "we see the universe the way it is because it exists" (5, p. 124). Perhaps as we see more about ourselves, the paradox of freedom will become less chaotic and more "smooth."

I look back to my statement earlier in this chapter: "The free person moves out voluntarily, freely, responsibly, to play her significant part in a world whose determined events move through her spontaneous choice and will." For me these words acquire an added meaning and a new richness in light of Capra's and Hawking's statements. It is a confirming thing to find that views based primarily on experience in psychotherapy are paralleled by the thinking of theoretical physicists, which is based on experimentation and mathematics. The paradoxical quality of our freedom is still there, but it is a paradox with its roots in the nature of the universe.

## References

1. V. E. Frankl, *From Death Camp to Existentialism* (Boston: Beacon Press, 1959).
2. M. Polanyi, "Scientific Outlook: Its Sickness and Cure," *Science* 125 (1957): 480–84.
3. Fritjof Capra, *The Tao of Physics* (Boulder, Colo.: Shambala Press, 1975).
4. Fritjof Capra, *The Turning Point* (New York: Simon and Schuster, 1982).
5. Stephen Hawking, *A Brief History of Time* (New York: Bantam Books, 1990).

---

**CARL ROGERS** (1902–1987) was a widely cited and popular psychotherapist who founded humanistic psychology. He taught and directed centers that treated abused children, which led him to innovative therapies that were client-centered. He authored many books and was awarded many prestigious medals and honors from the APA and served as APA president in 1947.

**B. F. Skinner**                                              **NO**

# A Technology of Behavior

Twenty-five hundred years ago it might have been said that man understood himself as well as any other part of his world. Today he is the thing he understands least. Physics and biology have come a long way, but there has been no comparable development of anything like a science of human behavior. Greek physics and biology are now of historical interest only (no modern physicist or biologist would turn to Aristotle for help), but the dialogues of Plato are still assigned to students and cited as if they threw light on human behavior. Aristotle could not have understood a page of modern physics or biology, but Socrates and his friends would have little trouble in following most current discussions of human affairs. And as to technology, we have made immense strides in controlling the physical and biological worlds, but our practices in government, education, and much of economics, though adapted to very different conditions, have not greatly improved.

We can scarcely explain this by saying that the Greeks knew all there was to know about human behavior. Certainly they knew more than they knew about the physical world, but it was still not much. Moreover, their way of thinking about human behavior must have had some fatal flaw. Whereas Greek physics and biology, no matter how crude, led eventually to modern science, Greek theories of human behavior led nowhere. If they are with us today, it is not because they possessed some kind of eternal verity, but because they did not contain the seeds of anything better.

It can always be argued that human behavior is a particularly difficult field. It is, and we are especially likely to think so just because we are so inept in dealing with it. But modern physics and biology successfully treat subjects that are certainly no simpler than many aspects of human behavior. The difference is that the instruments and methods they use are of commensurate complexity. The fact that equally powerful instruments and methods are not available in the field of human behavior is not an explanation; it is only part of the puzzle. Was putting a man on the moon actually easier than improving education in our public schools? Or than constructing better kinds of living space for everyone? Or than making it possible for everyone to be gainfully employed and, as a result, to enjoy a higher standard of living? The choice was not a matter of priorities, for no one could have said that it was more important to get to the moon. The exciting thing about getting to the moon was its feasibility. Science and technology had reached the point at which, with one great push, the thing could be done. There is no comparable excitement about the problems posed by human behavior. We are not close to solutions.

. . .

Two features of autonomous man are particularly troublesome. In the traditional view, a person is free. He is autonomous in the sense that his behavior is uncaused. He can therefore be held responsible for what he does and justly punished if he offends. That view, together with its associated practices, must be re-examined when a scientific analysis reveals unsuspected controlling relations between behavior and environment. A certain amount of external control can be tolerated. Theologians have accepted the fact that man must be predestined to do what an omniscient God knows he will do, and the Greek dramatist took inexorable fate as his favorite theme. Soothsayers and astrologers often claim to predict what men will do, and they have always been in demand. Biographers and historians have searched for "influences" in the lives of individuals and peoples. Folk wisdom and the insights of essayists like Montaigne and Bacon imply some kind of predictability in human conduct, and the statistical and actuarial evidences of the social sciences point the same direction.

Autonomous man survives in the face of all this because he is the happy exception. Theologians have reconciled predestination with free will, and the Greek audience, moved by the portrayal of an inescapable destiny, walked out of the theater free men. The course of history has been turned by the death of a leader or a storm at sea, as a life has been changed by a teacher or a love affair, but these things do not happen to everyone, and they do not affect everyone in the same way. Some historians have made a virtue of the unpredictability of history. Actuarial evidence is easily ignored; we read that hundreds of people will be killed in traffic accidents on a holiday weekend and take to the road as if personally exempt. Very little behavioral science raises "the specter of predictable man." On the contrary, many anthropologists, sociologists, and psychologists have used their expert knowledge to prove that man is free, purposeful, and responsible. Freud was a determinist—on faith, if not on the evidence—but many Freudians have no hesitation in assuring their patients that they are free to choose among different courses of action and are in the long run the architects of their own destinies.

This escape route is slowly closed as new evidences of the predictability of human behavior are discovered. Personal exemption from a complete determinism is revoked as a scientific analysis progresses, particularly in accounting for the behavior of the individual. Joseph Wood Krutch has acknowledged the actuarial facts while insisting on personal freedom: "We can predict with a considerable degree of accuracy how many people will go to the seashore on a day when the temperature reaches a certain point, even how many will jump off a bridge . . . although I am not, nor are you, compelled to do either." But he can scarcely mean that those who go to the seashore do not go for good reason, or that circumstances in the life of a suicide do not have some bearing on the fact that he jumps off a bridge. The distinction is tenable only so long as a word like "compel" suggests a particularly conspicuous and forcible mode of control. A scientific analysis naturally moves in the direction of clarifying all kinds of controlling relations.

By questioning the control exercised by autonomous man and demonstrating the control exercised by the environment, a science of behavior also seems to question dignity or worth. A person is responsible for his behavior, not only in the sense that he may be justly blamed or punished when he behaves badly, but also in the sense that he is to be given credit and admired for his achievements. A scientific analysis shifts the credit as well as the blame to the environment, and traditional practices can then no longer be justified. These are sweeping changes, and those who are committed to traditional theories and practices naturally resist them.

. . .

Almost all our major problems involve human behavior, and they cannot be solved by physical and biological technology alone. What is needed is a technology of behavior, but we have been slow to develop the science from which such a technology might be drawn. One difficulty is that almost all of what is called behavioral science continues to trace behavior to states of mind, feelings, traits of character, human nature, and so on. Physics and biology once followed similar practices and advanced only when they discarded them. The behavioral sciences have been slow to change partly because the explanatory entities often seem to be directly observed and partly because other kinds of explanations have been hard to find. The environment is obviously important, but its role has remained obscure. It does not push or pull, it *selects*, and this function is difficult to discover and analyze. The role of natural selection in evolution was formulated only a little more than a hundred years ago, and the selective role of the environment in shaping and maintaining the behavior of the individual is only beginning to be recognized and studied. As the interaction between organism and environment has come to be understood, however, effects once assigned to states of mind, feelings, and traits are beginning to be traced to accessible conditions, and a technology of behavior may therefore become available. It will not solve our problems, however, until it replaces traditional prescientific views, and these are strongly entrenched. Freedom and dignity illustrate the difficulty. They are the possessions of the autonomous man of traditional theory, and they are essential to practices in which a person is held responsible for his conduct and given credit for his achievements. A scientific analysis shifts both the responsibility and the achievement to the environment. It also raises questions concerning "values." Who will use a technology and to what ends? Until these issues are resolved, a technology of behavior will continue to be rejected, and with it possibly the only way to solve our problems.

## Values

In what we may call the prescientific view (and the word is not necessarily pejorative) a person's behavior is at least to some extent his own achievement. He is free to deliberate, decide, and act, possibly in original ways, and he is to be given credit for his successes and blamed for his failures. In the scientific view (and the word is not necessarily honorific) a person's behavior is determined by a genetic endowment traceable to the evolutionary history of the species and by the environmental circumstances to which as an individual he has been exposed. Neither view can be proved, but it is in the nature of scientific inquiry that the evidence should shift in favor of the second. As we learn more about the effects of the environment, we have less reason to attribute any part of human behavior to an autonomous controlling agent. And the second view shows a marked advantage when we begin to do something about behavior. Autonomous man is not easily changed; in fact, to the extent that he is autonomous, he is by definition not changeable at all. But the environment can be changed, and we are learning how to change it. The measures we use are those of physical and biological technology, but we use them in special ways to affect behavior.

Something is missing in this shift from internal to external control. Internal control is presumably exerted not only by but for autonomous man. But for whom is a powerful technology of behavior to be used? Who is to use it? And to what end? We have been implying that the effects of one practice are better than those of another, but on what grounds? What is the good against which something else is called better? Can we define the good life? Or progress toward a good life? Indeed, what is progress? What, in a word, is the meaning of life, for the individual or the species?

Questions of this sort seem to point toward the future, to be concerned not with man's origins but with his destiny. They are said, of course, to involve "value judgments"—to raise questions not about facts but about how men feel about facts, not about what man *can* do but about what he *ought* to do. It is usually implied that the answers are out of reach of science. Physicists and biologists often agree, and with some justification, since their sciences do not, indeed, have the answers. Physics may tell us how to build a nuclear bomb but not whether it should be built. Biology may tell us how to control birth and postpone death but not whether we ought to do so. Decisions about the uses of science seem to demand a kind of wisdom which, for some curious reason, scientists are denied. If they are to make value judgments at all, it is only with the wisdom they share with people in general.

It would be a mistake for the behavioral scientist to agree. How people feel about facts, or what it means to feel anything, is a question for which a science of behavior should have an answer. A fact is no doubt different from what a person feels about it, but the latter is a fact also. What causes trouble, here as elsewhere, is the appeal to what people feel. A more useful form of the question is this: If a scientific analysis can tell us how to change behavior, can it tell us what changes to make? This is a question about the behavior of those who do in fact propose and make changes. People act to improve the world and to progress toward a better way of life for good reasons, and among the reasons are certain consequences of their

behavior, and among these consequences are the things people value and call good.

. . .

The struggle for freedom and dignity has been formulated as a defense of autonomous man rather than as a revision of the contingencies of reinforcement under which people live. A technology of behavior is available which would more successfully reduce the aversive consequences of behavior, proximate or deferred, and maximize the achievements of which the human organism is capable, but the defenders of freedom oppose its use. The opposition may raise certain questions concerning "values." Who is to decide what is good for man? How will a more effective technology be used? By whom and to what end? These are really questions about reinforcers. Some things have become "good" during the evolutionary history of the species, and they may be used to induce people to behave for "the good of others." When used to excess, they may be challenged, and the individual may turn to things good only to him. The challenge may be answered by intensifying the contingencies which generate behavior for the good of others or by pointing to previously neglected individual gains, such as those conceptualized as security, order, health, wealth, or wisdom. Possibly indirectly, other people bring the individual under the control of some remote consequences of his behavior, and the good of others then redounds to the good of the individual. Another kind of good which makes for human progress remains to be analyzed.

## What Is Man?

As a science of behavior adopts the strategy of physics and biology, the autonomous agent to which behavior has traditionally been attributed is replaced by the environment—the environment in which the species evolved and in which the behavior of the individual is shaped and maintained. The vicissitudes of "environmentalism" show how difficult it has been to make this change. That a man's behavior owes something to antecedent events and that the environment is a more promising point of attack than man himself has long been recognized. As Crane Brinton observed, "a program to change things not just to convert people" was a significant part of the English, French, and Russian revolutions. It was Robert Owen, according to Trevelyan, who first "clearly grasped and taught that environment makes character and that environment is under human control" or, as Gilbert Seldes wrote, "that man is a creature of circumstance, that if you changed the environments of thirty little Hottentots and thirty little aristocratic English children, the aristocrats would become Hottentots, for all practical purposes, and the Hottentots little conservatives."

The evidence for a crude environmentalism is clear enough. People are extraordinarily different in different places, and possibly just because of the places. The nomad on horseback in Outer Mongolia and the astronaut in outer space are different people, but, as far as we know, if they had been exchanged at birth, they would have taken each other's place. (The expression "change places" shows how closely we identify a person's behavior with the environment in which it occurs.) But we need to know a great deal more before that fact becomes useful. What is it about the environment that produces a Hottentot? And what would need to be changed to produce an English conservative instead?

Both the enthusiasm of the environmentalist and his usually ignominious failure are illustrated by Owen's utopian experiment at New Harmony. A long history of environmental reform—in education, penology, industry, and family life, not to mention government and religion—has shown the same pattern. Environments are constructed on the model of environments in which good behavior has been observed, but the behavior fails to appear. Two hundred years of this kind of environmentalism has very little to show for itself, and for a simple reason. We must know how the environment works before we can change it to change behavior. A mere shift in emphasis from man to environment means very little.

. . .

An experimental analysis shifts the determination of behavior from autonomous man to the environment—an environment responsible both for the evolution of the species and for the repertoire acquired by each member. Early versions of environmentalism were inadequate because they could not explain how the environment worked, and much seemed to be left for autonomous man to do. But environmental contingencies now take over functions once attributed to autonomous man, and certain questions arise. Is man then "abolished"? Certainly not as a species or as an individual achiever. It is the autonomous inner man who is abolished, and that is a step forward. But does man not then become merely a victim or passive observer of what is happening to him? He is indeed controlled by his environment, but we must remember that it is an environment largely of his own making. The evolution of a culture is a gigantic exercise in self-control. It is often said that a scientific view of man leads to wounded vanity, a sense of hopelessness, and nostalgia. But no theory changes what it is a theory about; man remains what he has always been. And a new theory may change what can be done with its subject matter. A scientific view of man offers exciting possibilities. We have not yet seen what man can make of man.

---

**B. F. SKINNER** (1904–1990) is a pioneer in the field of behaviorism and has been referred to by many as the most influential psychologist in the twentieth century. He articulated the principles of operant conditioning and developed the Skinner box. Skinner was prolific in research and made several contributions to the study of learning. He received several distinguished awards from the APA and the National Medal of Science in 1968.

# EXPLORING THE ISSUE

## Should Students Be Free?

## Critical Thinking and Reflection

1. How can teachers allow each student to exercise choice in their assignments?
2. Under what social conditions (e.g., socioeconomic status, ethnic/cultural, parenting contexts, etc.) can reinforcements work successfully in the schools?
3. Is the concept of "inner freedom" by C. Rogers culturally universal?
4. Does the use of operant conditioning and choice depend upon children's developmental stage?

## Is There Common Ground?

The freedom–determinism or freedom–control argument has raged in philosophical, political, and psychological circles down through the ages. Is freedom of choice and action a central, perhaps *the* central, characteristic of being human? Or is freedom only an illusion, a refusal to acknowledge the external shaping of all human actions?

Moving the debate into the field of education, John Dewey depicted a developmental freedom that is acquired through improving one's ability to cope with problems. A. S. Neill (*Summerhill: A Radical Approach to Child Rearing*,1984), who advanced the ideas of early-twentieth-century progressive educators and the establishment of free schools, sees a more natural inborn freedom in human beings, which must be protected and allowed to flourish. Skinner refuses to recognize this "inner autonomous man" but sees freedom resulting from the scientific reshaping of the environment that influences us.

Just as Skinner has struggled to remove the stigma from the word control, arguing that it is the true gateway to freedom, John Holt, in *Freedom and Beyond* (1972), contends that freedom and free activities are not "unstructured"— indeed, that the structure of an open classroom is vastly more complicated than the structure of a traditional classroom.

If both of these views have validity, then we are in a position, as Dewey counselled, to go beyond either-or polemics on these matters and build a more constructive educational atmosphere. Jerome S. Bruner has consistently suggested ways in which free inquiry and subject matter structure can be effectively blended. Arthur W. Combs, in a report titled *Humanistic Education: Objectives and Assessment* (1978), helped to bridge the ideological gap between humanists and behaviorists by demonstrating that subjective outcomes can be assessed by direct or modified behavioral techniques. (By James Noll.)

## Additional Resources

J. Chen, "Teachers' Conceptions of Approaches to Teaching: A Chinese Perspective," *The Asia-Pacific Education Researcher* (vol. 24, no. 2, 2015).

C. S. DeBell, "B.F. Skinner: Myth and Misperception." *Teaching of Psychology* (vol. 19, 1992).

F. Gatongi, "Person-Centred Approach in Schools: Is It the Answer to Disruptive Behaviour in Our Classrooms?" *Counselling Psychology Quarterly* (vol. 20, 2007). doi:10.1080/09515070701403406.

C. Heim, "Tutorial Facilitation in the Humanities Based on the Tenets of Carl Rogers," *Higher Education* (vol. 63, 2012). doi:10.1007/s10734-011-9441-z.

W. T. O'Donohue and K. E. Ferguson, *The Psychology of B.F. Skinner* (Sage, 2001).

J. Staddon, "Did Skinner Miss the Point about Teaching?" *International Journal of Psychology* (vol. 41, 2006). doi:10.1080/00207590500492708.

# Internet References . . .

**B. F. Skinner Foundation**

www.bfskinner.org/archives/biographical-information

**The Carl R. Rogers Collection**

www.oac.cdlib.org/findaid/ark:/13030/tf2f59n977/

**The Freedom to Learn Project**

www.freedomtolearnproject.com

**Teachnology**

www.teach-nology.com/tutorials/teaching
/operantcond.html

Selected, Edited, and with Issue Framing Material by:
Esther S. Chang, *Soka University of America*

# ISSUE

# Are Constructivist Teaching Methods Superior to Traditional Methods of Teaching?

**YES: Sam Hausfather**, from "Content and Process in Constructivist Teacher Education," Kendall Hunt (2002)

**NO: R. E. Clark, P. A. Kirschner, and J. Sweller**, from "Putting Students on the Path to Learning: The Case for Fully Guided Instruction," *American Educator* (2012)

| Learning Outcomes |
|---|
| After reading this issue, you will be able to: <br><br> • Compare and contrast constructivism with traditional models of teaching/learning. <br> • Identify the different learning needs between a novice and an expert. <br> • Identify examples of partially guided instruction. <br> • Define mental schemas. <br> • Explain the worked-example effect. |

## ISSUE SUMMARY

**YES:** Sam Hausfather argues that constructivism, which challenges the stability of content knowledge, improves teaching by focusing teaching students not only on content knowledge but also on the processes involved in producing it.

**NO:** Richard Clark and colleagues argue that ideal learning environments differ between experts and novices and that constructivist pedagogy, which fosters individual discovery without full guidance from the teacher, has not proven to be ideal for novice learners.

**I**n contemplating what good teaching is, one must also contemplate how students learn, how they remember what they learn, and the usefulness of learning anything a teacher hopes students learn. The debate over the proper role of constructivism as a teaching method brings such questions to the forefront. Those in support of constructivist teaching methods are quick to critique traditional instructional models that rely upon knowledge transmission that flows unidirectionally from the teacher to the student. The main problem for constructivists is that deeper levels of understanding and internalization of knowledge among students is not a main concern in traditional models of teaching.

In traditional models of instruction, students are actively processing information by attending to it and practicing the information in an attempt to transfer it from working memory to long-term memory. Testing students is a way to assess not only whether information made its way into long-term memory, but also whether it could be recalled effectively. Although testing outcomes are often referred to as what students "know"—they are more specifically what students can recall from long-term memory. Good teachers are identified when students in their classes score well on tests, or recall information on tests. The challenge that the question this debate poses is to examine whether or not this is the knowledge that supports the educational aims of producing good thinkers.

The constructivist questions the effectiveness of the traditional method because it treats the child as a recipient who is disconnected from what s/he should know. The constructivist approach, as articulated in detail by Sam Hausfather in the "Yes" selection, is to train teachers to appreciate the importance of the learning process (i.e., knowledge construction) as much as the learning outcome because it is believed that students construct knowledge all the time, even before they walk into schools. Students naturally know things, and they have the capacity to learn before being exposed to schools. However, the extent to which what they know is *true* is highly questionable. In short, constructivist teaching aims to invite the learner to question what they already know and to expose them to new ways of knowing. An understanding of the psychological theories of cognitive development originally articulated by the Swiss philosopher and developmental psychologist, Jean Piaget, and Soviet psychologist, Lev Vygotsky, helps to understand the underlying foundations of constructivist teaching strategies.

Jean Piaget was a biologist and philosopher who was mainly interested in how individuals come to know something, and he was curious about whether what an individual knows is consistent with reality. He articulated a theory of knowledge acquisition that coincided with children's physical and biological timetables of development; and is best known for a series of procedures that demonstrated how children and infants fail to know things about objects and their properties until they reach the final stage of cognitive development, that is, formal operations. Piaget's fundamental contribution to understanding how learners learn was in identifying the biased nature of knowledge acquisition by describing knowledge as if it were like any other biological system.

The metaphor of a biological system is useful because all biological systems seek equilibrium, or a state in which the individual feels satisfied. In interacting with the world, the individual assimilates information using previous modes of understanding until a state of disequilibrium is reached. For example, disequilibrium can occur when first-year students in college use their high school methods of studying (e.g., memorizing key words at the end of a textbook chapter) until they encounter situations in which these modes of studying are no longer effective (e.g., essay examinations). Disequilibrium naturally motivates students to change their ways, or accommodate in order to achieve equilibrium again. In accommodating, knowledge is organized more effectively, which leads the individual to function more efficiently. Thus, seeking knowledge is natural and part of a self-regulating system that needs very little external influence due to our motivation to be in equilibrium.

According to Piaget, cognitive development is driven by physical maturation and its physical interaction with the environment. Until children reach formal operations in adolescence, they are limited in their ability to interact with the environment and therefore limited in their ability to question reality. Thus, they are usually wrong about their views of reality. A major limitation among children is their ego-centration, or their inability to understand the perspective of others. However, once the brain matures during puberty, they become more competent than young children in being able to think hypothetically.

Educators have applied Piaget's theory to educational contexts across several levels of instruction. Many teachers of young children use the concept of "readiness," which indicates that a child is cognitively ready to learn. In Piagetian terms, the child has the mental schemes available to assimilate information at a given level. Still other teachers support individualizing instruction within a classroom, perhaps for accelerated learners in a big class, which recognizes that knowledge is best built when responding to individual needs. Finally, the Montessori schools website acknowledges that "the child, through individual choice, makes use of what the environment offers to develop himself," which underscores the importance of children's active engagement in the production of knowledge among the youngest learners. This debate extends these practices to teaching and instruction. Although educators apply constructivist concepts in many ways, can we also apply it to improve our teaching process?

Lev Vygotsky argued that although individuals are active agents of knowledge construction, they are embedded within sociocultural contexts. Thus, the role of teachers is extremely important for student learning. Vygotsky placed greater emphasis on the social nature of knowledge construction whereas Piaget was concerned primarily with how individuals create knowledge. Knowledge is socially constructed by the child in interaction with his/her social environment (e.g., teachers, parents, siblings, peers, etc.). The basic unit of analysis is the child in social context, which cannot be decontextualized from each other. Therefore, content knowledge (i.e., scientific laws and "facts") cannot be fully understood without understanding the social and cultural processes involved in constructing it. For example, the national political landscape, the cultural backgrounds of textbook writers, and the social status of scientists who determine among themselves what is "true" will be highly relevant in assessing its truthfulness. In understanding the social processes involved in creating knowledge, one can uncover the cultural variables that determine the curriculum. Learning processes are therefore potentially more important than content knowledge because knowledge that exists among people is inherently biased by culture. Indeed, scientific facts can be disputed and the conclusions of scientific studies (i.e., content knowledge) may be different depending upon time in history or culture.

In sum, constructivist theories compel teachers to recognize that knowledge is continually created by the individual (and therefore biased) and that information they are using in the classroom is highly culture-specific (and therefore biased). The extent to which these theories of learning can improve teaching remains a controversy.

In the selections that follow, Sam Hausfather explains the need for constructivist teacher education for the "Yes" side. It is argued that the more teachers can appreciate how learning processes and content knowledge are linked, the more effective they will be as teachers. Richard E. Clark and colleagues want to put an end to the practice of partially guided instruction for a majority of learners by arguing that most learners need complete guidance and worked examples.

**Sam Hausfather**

# Content and Process in Constructivist Teacher Education

Teaching involves the process of leading learners to understand and use content. While content remains the goal of constructivist teachers, the process of learning becomes both method and goal as well. In the process of learning lie the roots of our understanding of content as well as our goal to create independent learners. The dichotomy between content and process disappears as we take a constructivist approach to knowledge and teaching. Content does not exist outside the process of acquiring that content (Tobin & Tippins, 1993). Controversies exist in taking this position. These controversies go to the very heart of our understanding of content and the ability to teach content to students. As teacher educators we take a stand on these controversies in how we approach both the process and content of teacher education programs. Teacher educators face a philosophical dilemma in differentiating content and process and understanding how they are intertwined. We also face a practical dilemma in promoting the collaboration between education faculty and arts and sciences faculty necessary to bride content and process in teacher education. In this chapter I discuss implications of constructivism as a way of thinking about content, approaches to learning content that derive from cognitive research, and pedagogical content knowledge as an aspect of teacher education. Examples that illustrate these elements in the practice of teacher education are then given.

## Perspectives of Constructivism on Content Knowledge

Constructivism challenges the core of our understanding of the nature of content (von Glaserfeld, 1993). The nature of content is our beginning point, the philosophical basis of constructivism. Constructivism as an epistemology or way of knowing is based on a theory of the possibility of knowing objective reality (Staver, 1998). Constructivism confronts the wishes of many disciplines to portray ultimate truths in a content area, postulating we can not know objective reality. Constructivism questions the separation between the observer and the observations, the knower and the known. "A constructivist perspective acknowledges the existence of an external reality but realizes that cognizing beings can never know what that reality is actually like" (Tobin & Tippins, 1993, p. 4). Empirical theories of truth postulate that knowledge corresponds to facts in reality. Constructivism views knowledge as being true in relation to other knowledge in an internally coherent network. This coherence view acknowledges that knowledge "works," without supposing that we can reveal an objective reality outside the individual and social interpretations of reality. Not denying an objective reality, human experience is seen as the only viable connection to the real world (Staver, 1998). Kuhn (1970) showed how understandings of the world progressed through revolutionary paradigm shifts that influenced how we as individuals experience the world. We know the world through our experiences, through the interface of our sensation and our constructed meanings of those sensations. While we would prefer to believe the world corresponds to our experience of it, constructivism posits that humans interpret the world in ways that cohere with reality (von Glaserfeld, 1989). Where a correspondence view implies that reality exists exactly as we perceive it, a coherence view implies we actively build a collective, internally coherent understanding of the world that works to explain phenomena (Staver, 1998). Whether that view actually corresponds with reality is beyond our ability to distinguish since only our collective perceptions inform our understanding of reality.

These views raise the most controversial aspects of constructivist perspectives. If content is a human construction, it can change over time. Although certain content areas are more clearly linked to human experience and interpretation as their source (the humanities, arts, and social sciences), the "hard" sciences including mathematics have the greatest difficulty with constructivist epistemology. The humanities and social sciences derive from human creativity and action and seek to interpret and record human progress, whereas the sciences purport to exactly map objective reality. A constructivist approach to the nature of content knowledge should affect how teacher educators look at content across many disciplines. English, history, and the social sciences can be seen more as process and the result of personal viewpoints. Mathematics is seen as a social construction, and thus open to discourse as a method for understanding. Science is often portrayed less as a social institution than as the pursuit of laws for an independent reality that we can explain, predict, control, and know as true. Constructivism challenges this view, denying our ability to fully know objective reality (Staver, 1998). The nature of science will continue to be debated given the various faces of constructivist thought (Good et al., 1993; Phillips, 1995). If we take a constructivist view of the nature of knowledge then we need to raise questions about the approach teacher educators should take in developing teachers' approaches to knowledge. At the same time, the natural and mathematical sciences provide some of the greatest support for educational practices related to constructivism. In this dichotomy lies a source for continued exploration and discussion between teacher educators and content-area faculty.

## Constructivist Approaches to Learning Content

Constructivism brings important insights that speak to pedagogical approaches to learning content. Research in cognitive science has supported constructivist theory and progressed to the point that clear implications are apparent in educational practice. Gaea Leinhardt (1992) has synthesized the cognitive research on learning that supports constructivism and summarized the implications around three fundamental aspects: multiple forms of knowledge, the role of prior knowledge, and the social nature of knowledge and its acquisition. While each of these aspects has clear implications for school practice, less has been written about how teacher education responds to these understandings about learning.

## Institutional Responses

Research on learning has led to the understanding that there are both different types and amounts of knowledge. Declarative knowledge of content concepts and principles becomes powerful for students when it is connected with procedural knowledge of actions and skills (Best, 1995). Knowledge varies across content areas as we examine the different arrangements of facts, notations, and reasoning in different subjects. Knowledge varies within content areas

as one looks at how documentation, arguments or explanations are structured in different disciplines. In addition, metaknowledge, knowing what and how well you know, is seen as a powerful factor in developing understanding in students (Schoenfeld, 1987). These multiple forms of knowledge highlight the complexity of learning. Knowledge is seen as not just information, but an active process, retained when embedded in some organizing structure (Bereiter, 1985). When students interact with information, using it in solving problems, answering questions, or discussing their interpretations, the information becomes their knowledge, tied to their unique understandings. The implications of the nature of knowledge for pedagogy point toward teaching that integrates knowing content with using content, dissolving the line between content and process (Leinhardt, 1992). Active, problem-solving approaches should be apparent no matter what the content approach taken. Since knowledge also does not exist in isolation, it must be connected to student prior knowledge and larger contexts in order to be incorporated into the deep understanding of students. Interdisciplinary approaches can connect the richness of separate disciplines while acknowledging their interrelationships and modes of inquiry (Martinello & Cook, 2000).

The separation of schools of education from schools of arts and sciences within the university often creates a situation where content courses are disconnected from courses on teaching methods and learning (NCTAF, 1996). While teacher education has sought to provide more integration of content with process within teacher education courses, the content prospective teachers learn in their arts and sciences courses is left separate and inactivated through the teacher education sequence. Teacher education students often take 50% to 85% of their course work in the arts and sciences (Gollnick, 1996). Traditionally, arts and sciences courses seldom challenge students' prior knowledge and often reinforce a transmission view of knowledge. A compilation of broad knowledge is emphasized over in-depth study that would challenge student misconceptions. Teacher education faculty can work closely with arts and sciences faculty to plan and implement courses of study that provide strong disciplinary preparation linked closely with the methods and content of pedagogical studies. Brooklyn College of the City University of New York has developed a teacher education program where students take several three-course sequences made up of a liberal arts course, an education "bridging" course, and a pedagogy course (Grumet, 1992). The arts and sciences faculty and the education faculty teaching these paired courses plan syllabi, readings, and discussions together. Other teacher education programs have closely examined their own curriculum to determine the extent to which they model interdisciplinary integration of content areas and pedagogy. For example, Berry College is in the process of blocking its education methods courses to align courses horizontally across a year of similar disciplinary studies (literacy, inquiry, arts and cultures) and vertically so that college faculty can plan integrated experiences for students across disciplinary areas.

## Pedagogical Responses

Learning involves combining what you know with what was taught, continually connecting prior knowledge with new information (Leinhardt, 1992). This prior knowledge can facilitate, inhibit, or transform learning. In reading, comprehension has been shown to depend on what you already know or want to know (Smith, 1988). Research into the nature of "children's science," the ideas and experiences students bring into class with them (Driver et al., 1985; West & Pines, 1985), shows students hold tenaciously to their prior ideas. These alternative conceptions or misconceptions grow out of students' prior experiences with the world around them, and can interfere considerably with teachers' attempts to foster learning. Research in mathematics education shows students come to class with effective but alternative routes to mathematics processes that are often confounded by teaching (Carpenter et al., 1989). Research on the construction of history reveal students' tendency to see historical events in terms of individuals' personal intentions and interactions and to ignore the role of societal institutions (Barton, 1997).

The acknowledgment of alternative conceptions held by students has led to deeper understandings of the process necessary to deal with student constructions. Teachers need to surface students' prior knowledge, connect to it or challenge it, and allow students to build from and onto their prior knowledge. Often the results of teaching produce unintended learning outcomes, as students combine existing ideas with the new ideas presented by teachers (Osborne & Freyberg, 1985). In order for students to make use of ideas taught by teachers in the ways teachers intend, knowledge must present itself as intelligible, fruitful, and plausible. Beyond these qualities, students may also have to find dissatisfaction with their current knowledge and its use in understanding (Posner et al., 1982). This is a clear move away from a "discovery" approach, where students construct knowledge solely based on their own experience, to knowledge construction where students have the opportunity to test their knowledge within a social context, teachers challenge some conceptions, and students involve themselves in a process of constructing understanding

(Watson & Konicek, 1990). Conceptual change instruction in science has emphasized a lesson format that includes an orientation phase, elicitation of ideas, restructuring of ideas, application of ideas, and reviewing change of ideas (Osborne & Freyberg, 1985). Cognitively Guided Instruction (Carpenter et al., 1989) emphasizes allowing students to surface their explanations of mathematical processes as the teacher leads students to see alternative routes to solving problems. Scardamalia and Bereiter (1985) have developed models for teaching writing that use a combination of modeling, coaching, scaffolding, and fading. The use of narrative has been shown to promote students' historical understanding and challenge students' prior conceptions (Levstik & Pappas, 1992).

Teacher education programs are caught in the bind of informing teacher candidates about the importance of prior experiences and misconceptions while also having to deal with these candidates' own prior experiences and misconceptions about both teaching and content. The "apprenticeship of observation" (Lortie, 1975) through lengthy personal experience with schooling prevents preservice teachers from searching beyond what they already know and from questioning the practices they see (Feiman-Nemser & Buchmann, 1987). Some teacher education programs promote conceptual change in their students toward viewing schools as they could be, not merely as they are. Experiences that challenge student conceptions of schooling include provocative readings and discussion (such as Kozol, 1991, etc.), simulations, and experiences in experimental schools that can give different vision of education. In their content studies, preservice teachers' own misconceptions can also be challenged. Teacher education programs that work with faculty in arts and sciences to understand the preconceptions students bring to their classes can promote approaches that will challenge these preconceptions. Through both having their own conceptions challenged and learning about the prior knowledge of their students, teacher candidates will be better prepared to provide their students content knowledge linked with student prior knowledge.

Finally, the social aspect of knowledge provides clear implications in practice. As outlined above, learning is seen to be an active process of knowledge construction and sense making. Beyond that, knowledge is understood as a cultural artifact of people. It is created and transformed by each individual and by groups of people (Vygotsky, 1978). As a result, learning should involve talk, public reasoning, and shared problem solving. Too often the social environment of schools is counterproductive to learning (Hausfather, 1996). Instead of a focus on individual achievement, learning involves social interaction that supports thinking, surfaces prior knowledge, and allows skills to be used in the context of content knowledge. Participating in communities of discourse allows students to clarify, defend, elaborate, evaluate, and argue over the knowledge constructed (Brown, 1994). Many teachers use cooperative learning as a route to building communities of discourse in their classrooms. Cooperative learning has been shown to be a powerful vehicle to improve learning outcomes for students (Slavin, 1996).

Teacher education has a clear role in clarifying a vision of a social environment supportive to learning. Preservice methods courses can model collaboration between and among the teacher and students. College teaching has traditionally stressed individual processes over social processes in learning. Teacher education needs to provide opportunities where college students learn within social situations. College students can metacognitively experience zones of proximal development (Vygotsky, 1978) within college classrooms by working within cooperative or discourse groups while analyzing their own experiences as a guide to their teaching. Instructional conversations can occur within the classic Socratic seminar, where instructor and students together explore problems as a small community of learners. Pairing students for field experience placements in schools is one way to promote peer collaboration that fosters deeper understandings of classroom situations (Hausfather et al., 1996). Pairing allows more opportunities for students to get feedback on their classroom behaviors, as partners observe each other teaching, provide different perspectives on classroom events, and collaborate in planning. Pairing allows preservice teachers to see the value of collegial reflection in contrast to the usual individuality prevalent in schools.

These implications from cognitive science research help us to understand the difficulty of separating content from process in learning. Research in teaching has identified the linking of content with the process of teaching; such links occur as the teacher continually restructures subject matter knowledge for the purpose of teaching (Cochran et al., 1993). Termed pedagogical content knowledge (PCK), this concept connects research on teaching with research on learning, helping determine constructivist approaches to learning content for teaching.

## Pedagogical Content Knowledge

Lee Shulman (1986) introduced the term pedagogical content knowledge as "the ways of representing and formulating the subject that make it comprehensible to others" (p. 9). This goes beyond knowledge of the content per se to include issues of teaching the content, including typical curricular choices, powerful ideas, common learning difficulties, and student conceptions in the specific subject. Shulman included PCK in the broader knowledge base for teaching, which included content knowledge, PCK, curriculum knowledge, general pedagogy, learners and their characteristics, educational contexts, and educational purposes (Shulman, 1987). PCK involves the transformation of content knowledge by teachers in ways that allow learners to construct knowledge during classroom practice. Teachers derive PCK from their understandings of content, their own teaching practice, and their own schooling experience. As such, PCK is closely intertwined with both content knowledge and pedagogical process knowledge (Van Driel et al., 1998).

Different scholars have included different aspects within their conceptualizations of PCK, although all agree PCK differs considerably from content knowledge and that it is developed through an integrative process during classroom practice (Van Driel et al., 1998). Cochran, et al. (1993) renamed PCK as pedagogical content knowing (PCKg) based on a constructivist view of teaching and teacher education. Their model includes subject matter content and specific pedagogical knowledge but adds teachers' understanding of students and of the environmental context of learning. Understanding students includes student abilities and learning strategies, developmental levels, attitudes, motivations, and prior conceptions. Context includes teachers' understandings of the social, political, cultural and physical environment. Teachers simultaneously experience these four components as they prepare for and progress through their career.

Research in pedagogical content knowledge reinforces the research in cognitive science (Cochran et al., 1993) and many of the implications listed above (Ashton, 1990). Teacher education programs can enhance the development of PCK in teacher candidates by modeling and sharing teaching decisions and strategies with students, both by education and content-area faculty. Faculty should have opportunities to demonstrate and reflect on how they use PCK in their own teaching (Cochran et al., 1993). Contexts that promote active simultaneous learning about the many components of teaching within the content area allow for the development of PCK. These contexts should be similar to classroom environments, which suggest the incorporation of multiple field-based opportunities within the teacher education program. Early, continued, and authentic field experiences include real teaching, much contact with experienced teachers, and reflection and feedback (Hausfather et al., 1996).

Although it is difficult to separate PCK from content knowledge, it appears as though a thorough and coherent understanding of content is necessary for effective PCK (Van Driel et al., 1998). Teacher education programs can assist preservice teachers in constructing a deep understanding of disciplinary content from a teaching perspective so it can be used to help specific students understand specific concepts (Cochran et al., 1993). This involves both working closely with arts and sciences faculty to understand pedagogical perspectives as well as integrating methods courses with or alongside content courses.

A teacher education program which balances attention to the process of learning with the content of what is being learned can ultimately result in helping teachers be better able to understand both their content and the learning of their students. Too often content is taught without any attention to process, or process is taught without a deep understanding of the nature of the content involved. Teacher education programs seek to find the balance. We now turn our attention to examples of program efforts that work to obliterate the lines between content and process.

. . .

## Berry College

There is much in teacher education that is process focused. This makes sense given the process nature of teaching. Generally, there is important content as well, such as the theoretical bases of constructivism in the work of Piaget, Vygotsky, and Dewey. Berry College's undergraduate teacher education program tries to continually mix content with process, so as theories are discussed, applications can be modeled. The program is structured to involve a back and forth between college classroom and field experience, allowing students opportunities to continually test the content of teacher education against the process of teaching in real classrooms. There are aspects of the theoretical content where mastery is expected, both in demonstrations to faculty and on the national certification tests. Assessments are constructed which allow demonstration, both authentic and traditional.

Subject-matter content (math, science, social studies, phonics, etc.) is a clear part of the responsibility of an undergraduate teacher education program. Faculty strive to model the way they want students to teach this content while at the same time teaching them the content. Because they cannot teach all the content teachers should know, the emphasis goes more to big ideas, inquiries, and the attitudes necessary to help our students become lifelong learners. This starts with an understanding of the nature of knowledge and how knowledge changes through time. It is important to give credence to students' preconceptions while at the same time understanding the currently accepted conceptions. Teacher education students must understand how to use the tools given to them to continue to learn. They must understand the content deeply in order to teach it. For teacher educators, paying attention to deep understanding of content means you cannot cover everything you hope to. Teachers and teacher educators should not be afraid of exploring their own understandings and delving on their own to understand further. The tools at our disposal are powerful to do this, with the web, electronic encyclopedias, linked communications, etc. Faculty expect students to do the self-learning necessary to prepare well to teach others, both in college classrooms and in their field experiences. Faculty model for students their own attempts to keep up with the burgeoning knowledge in their fields and their continual revision and updating of courses. One group of faculty began a self-study of their attempts to integrate technology in their teacher-education courses (Strehle et al., in press). They openly shared with college students their challenges and learnings as they attempted to use technology in constructivist ways. And faculty honor student expertise as they learn from student explorations into particular content. Content and process become as inseparable as teacher and learner.

What about the teaching of particular content? College faculty depend on their colleagues in the arts and sciences for the content background of teacher education students. Faculty from across the campus were brought together to design the teacher-education curriculum. Discussion and debate helped all faculty understand the perspectives each brought on the role of content and process in teacher education. At first, arts and sciences faculty questioned the content and rigor of education courses. As they participated in the deconstruction and recreation of the teacher education courses, they participated in and came to understand the links between content and process that exist in education courses. Constructivist teacher education cannot occur in a vacuum. Too often students move from teacher education classes to arts and sciences classes where behavioristic techniques prevail. Teacher education faculty continue to struggle with the role of helping colleagues across campus understand changes in pedagogy. Historically teacher education has held a low status within colleges and universities, viewed as a professional school committed to practice instead of research (Schneider, 1987; Goodlad, 1999). This is beginning to change as calls for reform of both teacher education and general undergraduate education are opening to view the entire higher education experience. In smaller institutions such as Berry College, the commitment to teacher education has allowed for long-term curricular and budgetary investments. We continue to struggle with working with our arts and sciences colleagues to understand the process aspects of their content teaching.

Teacher education faculty also deal with teacher education students as we expect them to deal with their own pupils. This involves surfacing students' alternative conceptions or misconceptions, and then building understanding of the alternative conceptions pupils will bring to the classroom. Content is thus revealed, making it approachable but challenging. In the teacher education classroom, an approach to teaching content is modeled that begins with experiences orienting students to a content issue. Student ideas are then elicited, and a process of restructuring ideas is modeled which challenges student ideas and introduces accepted ideas. Students then have the chance to apply their ideas through experience, and review their change in thinking. This "constructivist teaching model" (Scott, 1987) is taught not as a pattern to be reproduced but as a way of understanding constructivist teaching, allowing for variety based on context. Students then explore the understanding of the pupils they may teach. In science methods for example, students are given the assignment of interviewing a child about conceptions in one area of science. The instructor models surfacing alternative conceptions in several science content areas, providing experiences that challenge student conceptions and then discussing current scientific views. Students then watch and discuss videos of child interviews that reveal specific content misconceptions. Students research a science concept and interview a child. They videotape their interview and write a reflective summary on what they learned about student understandings of science concepts. College students are amazed at how differently children think about everyday phenomena.

Although there is clear need for understanding of disciplinary content, that understanding must become a part of interdisciplinary thinking. Once one steps outside the classroom, there is little in life that narrowly follows disciplines. Berry College is in the process of breaking down course walls, moving all courses to become "blocks" team taught by professors bringing different perspectives together. A literacy block will bring together reading, language arts, and literature. An inquiry block will share math and science. An integrated arts block will allow social studies, art, music, and PE to create integrated units. A foundations block will bring together psychology and education. Curriculum brokers will ensure that technology, child development, special education, and second-language learners are integrated throughout all blocks. Blocks will be integrated vertically through faculty sharing of expertise and the development and modeling of interdisciplinary units, with faculty time and expertise choreographed

to "dance" through disciplinary walls. In this way, content areas will be given meaning within integrated blocks emphasizing active/inquisitory approaches to knowledge.

## Georgia State University

The Collaborative Master's Program (CMP) at Georgia State University is a master's degree program based on constructivist principles and the work of Dewey. The ongoing nature of program allows for the following (Rainer & Guyton, 1999):

- living the process of a constructivist model is part of the content of the program
- contextually bound part of work (classroom teaching) gives meaning to content and process
- integrated content
- deep engagement with content

The process of teaching is the content of the CMP, as teacher education faculty model constructivist approaches to pedagogy. Faculty lead students to negotiate the content of the program. For example, work in math methods is begun by discussing current professional standards in mathematics education (NCTM) and the relationship of these standards to the teachers' practice. As the teachers look at both of these in light of constructivist theory, they begin to ask questions of faculty and faculty ask questions of teachers. Together a very ambitious list of topics is generated that the group would like to explore together. Topics are sorted into relevant categories, for example, topics such as problem solving, critical thinking and technology are grouped together with the NCTM standards on communication and reasoning. After narrowing the list to a manageable set of integrated concepts, the ideas are discussed and assigned, including a time line and designation of individuals responsible for discussions and resources. Faculty members prepare a "proposed" agenda based on these decisions. As each class begins, the agenda is presented for additions and revisions. Faculty contributions include providing reflective questions, current research on the topics, and an activity involving children's literature and physical models. Teacher's contributions involve demonstrating effective practice, reflecting on changes in pedagogy, and sharing resources.

Teachers select one area about which they want to study in some depth, collaboratively in focus groups. Example topics have been teaching math, the teaching of reading, culturally relevant curriculum, assessment and evaluation. These groups design not only the content they will study, but also the process through which to study it. Each group has a faculty advisor for resources, coaching, and guiding. In addition to documenting the knowledge of mathematics and literacy teachers gain through this process, they are asked to document their own learning process. The goal is for them to be metacognitive and articulate about their own learning process. The learning frameworks help teachers design their current and future studies.

When teachers engage in designing the benchmark, rubric, capstone, and grading process, the understanding of assessment and evaluation becomes personal. These are probably the most challenging experiences of the year for teachers in the CMP. What teachers learn about assessment and evaluation of content becomes important to them personally. Rather than learning about assessment and evaluation mostly by reading, they are living the content through the process of designing assessments of their own learning.

## Mansfield University of Pennsylvania

The teacher education program at Mansfield University of Pennsylvania works with inservice teachers in their classrooms to contextualize their content. The program encourages deep engagement with content.

In an emerging literacy course, students are held accountable for content by checking that they have completed a log based on chapters. Five or 10 entries are required depending on the length of the chapter. The entries include one paragraph about an idea expressed in their own words and one paragraph about the reactions. The logs are used in small group discussions and in writing their final philosophy paper. The latter must demonstrate that they have grasped the critical content (the five major topics are specified that the paper must address). The instructor models this process while collaborating with a local third-grade teacher. Students read about emerging literacy, experience it as a learner through simulation and modeling, and then have a third-grade writing partner with whom they experience literacy issues.

Early Childhood Curriculum follows emerging literacy. The course included nine classes where students must work for two hours in second grade classrooms. They are observed on a rotating basis and create lesson plans and reflections after each class. During the rest of the course, content is introduced using parts of several NAEYC texts. Students develop a resource notebook organized around the seven topics and then make a concept map. This helps them link information they have learned in many courses.

## Mills College

Inherent in the concept of constructivism are the notions of content and process. The teacher education program at Mills College strives to help students think about this dichotomy as complementary. One program principle articulates this area as "Teaching for the acquisition and construction of subject matter knowledge." A primary focus of the Mills College graduate-level credential programs is to help candidates think in different ways about the subject matter knowledge they already possess. Opportunities are provided for students to transform their content knowledge into working knowledge often referred to in the literature as pedagogical content knowledge. That is, students analyze and reorganize their subject matter knowledge in ways that will make it possible for them to provide similar opportunities for their students to organize knowledge. In addition, candidates construct and reconstruct their own subject matter knowledge where necessary as a means to obtain and develop more pedagogical content knowledge in the future.

To emphasize the contrast and dichotomy of process and content, students engage with content at an adult level while thinking about the teaching of that content (or process) at the instructional level—whether it be for a child or an adult. For example, all elementary-education students participate in Writers' Workshop during the second semester. The semester ends with a publishing party where a collection of writing with a contribution from each class member is published. By participating in writers' workshop, student teachers think about content and process in several ways. First they think about the nature of learning to write; we might consider this content about learner development. Second they think about different aspects of writing, like genre, writing conventions, the process of writing and rewriting. Here, process is the content. Third they think about writers' workshop as an instructional technique, from the perspective of the learner and the perspective of the teacher. As learners, they connect this aspect with the developmental content, and as teachers they connect this aspect with the process of writing and the pedagogy of writing instruction. This "activity" helps clarify the dichotomy and overlap of content and process.

In both the methodology classes and in child development classes, students examine children's learning of mathematics and literacy and apply that understanding to thinking about how best to teach the content. Thus, throughout the program there is a goal of coordinating the nature of the discipline, children's learning, instructional practice and an overall view of the curriculum.

## Conclusions

Constructivist approaches to teacher education must deal with the issues of content and process, acknowledging the vital link between content and its acquisition. Constructivism challenges some basic understandings of content knowledge. At the same time, research supporting constructivist approaches brings insights to teacher education practice that makes for more powerful teaching and student understanding of content. An understanding of the nature of pedagogical content knowledge leads teacher educators to work more closely with arts and sciences faculty to help students integrate their experiences in content courses with their experiences in teacher education courses. Examples at several teacher education programs reinforce these understandings.

These program examples share an understanding that content and process are inseparable. Programs consciously link methods courses with content, focusing teacher candidates on thinking in different ways about content. Modeling by teacher education faculty engages students with content while they learn strategies to teach that content. Content is negotiated with students, with an emphasis on concepts over facts. Courses are blocked across content areas to model interdisciplinary teaching and learning. Finally, efforts are underway to increase collaboration with arts and sciences faculty toward creating a seamless teacher education program.

Teacher education provides a multiplier effect. As we model approaches that lead our students to understand content deeply and to view content and process as inseparable aspects of knowledge construction, our students gain the perspectives and abilities to move their students to deeper understandings of content. Powerful teacher education should lead to students at all levels of schooling coming to better appreciations of the world around them. A constructivist approach shows us that content and process are not dichotomous. As more teachers come to that understanding, many more students will benefit.

# References

Ashton, P. T. (1990). Editorial: Theme issue on pedagogical content knowledge. *Journal of Teacher Education,* 41(3), 2.

Barton, K. C. (1997). "Bossed around by the queen:" Elementary students' understanding of individuals and institutions in history. *Journal of Curriculum and Supervision,* 12(4), 290–314.

Bereiter, C. (1985). Toward a solution of the learning paradox. Review of Educational Research, 55, 201–226.

Best, J. B. (1995). *Cognitive Psychology.* (4th Ed.). St. Paul, MN: West Publishing Co.

Brown, A. L. (1994). The advancement of learning. *Educational Researcher,* 23(8), 4–12.

Carpenter, T. P., Fennema, E., Peterson, P.L., Chiang, C.P., & Loef, M. (1989). Using knowledge of children's mathematics thinking in classroom teaching: An experimental study. *American Educational Research Journal,* 26(4), 499–531.

Cochran, K. F., DeRuiter, J. A., & King, R. A. (1993). Pedagogical content knowing: An integrative model for teacher preparation. *Journal of Teacher Education,* 44(4), 263–272.

Driver, R., Guesne, E. & Tiberghien, A. (Eds.) (1985). *Children's ideas in science.* Philadelphia, PA: Open University Press.

Feiman-Nemser, S. & Buchmann, M. (1987). When is student teaching teacher education? *Teaching and Teacher Education,* 3(4), 255–273.

Gollnick, D. (1996). Can arts and sciences faculty prepare quality teachers? *American Behavioral Scientist,* 40(3), 233–241.

Good, R.G., Wandersee, J.H., & St. Julien, J. (1993). Cautionary notes on the appeal of the new "ism" (constructivism) in science education. In K. Tobin (Ed.) *The practice of constructivism in science education* (pp. 71–87). Hillsdale, NJ: Erlbaum.

Goodlad, J. I. (1999). Rediscovering teacher education: School renewal and educating educators. *Change,* 31(5), 28–33.

Grumet, M. (1992). The language in the middle: Bridging the liberal arts and teacher education. *Liberal Education,* 78(3), 2–7.

Hausfather, S. J. (1996). Vygotsky and schooling: Creating a social context for learning. Action in *Teacher Education,* 18(2), 1–10.

Hausfather, S. J., Outlaw, M. E., & Strehle, E. L. (1996). Relationships as a foundation: Emerging field experiences within multiple college-school partnerships. In T. Warren (Ed.), *Partnerships in teacher education: Schools and colleges working together* (pp. 27–41). Lanham, MD: University Press of America.

Kozol, J. (1991). *Savage inequalities: Children in America's schools.* New York: Crown Publications.

Kuhn, T. S. (1970). *The structure of scientific revolutions.* (2nd ed.). Chicago: University of Chicago Press.

Leinhardt, G. (1992) What research on learning tells us about teaching. *Educational Leadership* 49(7) 20–25.

Levstik, L. S. & Pappas, C. C. (1992). New directions for studying historical understanding. *Theory and Research in Social Education,* 20(4), 369–385.

Lortie, D. (1975). *Schoolteacher: A sociological study.* Chicago: University of Chicago Press.

Martinello, M. L. & Cook, G. E. (2000). *Interdisciplinary inquiry in teaching and learning* (2nd Edition). Upper Saddle River, NJ: Prentice-Hall, Inc.

NCTAF (1996). *What matters most: Teaching for America's future.* New York: National Commission on Teaching & America's Future.

Osborne, R. & Freyberg, P. (1985). *Learning in science: The implications of children's science.* Portsmouth, NH: Heinemann Publishers.

Phillips, D.C. (1995). The good, the bad, and the ugly: The many faces of constructivism. *Educational Researcher,* 24, 5–12.

Posner, G.J., Strike, K.A., Hewson, P.W., & Gertzog, W.A. (1982). Accommodation of a scientific conception: Toward a theory of conceptional change. *Science Education,* 66, 211–227.

Rainer, J., & Guyton, E. (1999). A constructivist approach to teacher education. A paper presented at the annual meeting of the Association of Teacher Educators, Chicago, February.

Scardamalia, M., & Bereiter, C. (1985). Fostering the development of self-regulation in children's knowledge processing. In S. Chipman, J. Segal, & R. Glaser, (Eds.), *Thinking and learning skills: Research and open questions.* Hillsdale NJ: Erlbaum.

Schneider, B. (1987). Tracing the provenance of teacher education. In T. Popkewitz (Ed.), *Critical studies in teacher education: Its folklore, theory, and practice* (pp. 211–241). New York: Falmer Press.

Schoenfeld, A.H. (1987). What's all the fuss about metacognition? In A. H. Schoenfeld (Ed.), *Cognitive science and mathematics education* (pp. 189–253). New York: W. H. Freeman.

Scott, P. (1987). *Children's learning in science project: A constructivist view of learning and teaching in science.* Leeds, England: University of Leeds, Centre for Studies in Science and Mathematics Education.

Shulman, L.S. (1986). Those who understand: Knowledge growth in teaching. *Educational Researcher,* 15, 4–14.

Shulman, L.S. ( 1987). Knowledge and Teaching: Foundations of the new reform. *Harvard Educational Review,* 57, 1–22.

Slavin, R. E. (1996). Research on cooperative learning and achievement: What we know, what we need to know. *Contemporary Educational Psychology,* 21(1), 43–69.

Smith, F. (1988). *Understanding reading: A psycholinguistic analysis of reading and learning to read.* Hillsdale, NJ: Erlbaum.

Staver, J. R. (1998). Constructivism: Sound theory for explicating the practice of science and science teaching. *Journal of Research in Science Teaching,* 35(5), 501–520.

Strehle, E. L., Whatley, A., Kurz, K. A., & Hausfather, S. J. (in press). Narratives of collaboration: Inquiring into technology integration in teacher education. *The Journal of Technology and Teacher Education.*

Tobin, K., & Tippins, D. (1993). Constructivism as a referent for teaching and learning. In K. Tobin (Ed.) *The practice of constructivism in science education.* Hillsdale, NJ: Erlbaum.

Van Driel, J. H., Verloop, N., & De Vos, W. (1998). Developing science teachers' pedagogical content knowledge. *Journal of Research in Science Teaching,* 35(6), 673–695.

von Glaserfeld, E. (1989). Cognition, construction of knowledge, and teaching. *Synthese,* 80, 121–140.

von Glaserfeld, E. (1993). Questions and answers about radical constructivism. In K. Tobin (Ed.) *The practice of constructivism in science education* (pp. 23–38). Hillsdale, NJ: Erlbaum

Vygotsky, L. S. (1978). *Mind in society: The development of higher psychological processes.* Cambridge, MA: Harvard University Press.

Watson, B. & Konicek, R. (1990). Teaching for conceptual change: Confronting children's experience. *Phi Delta Kappan,* 71(9), 680–685.

West, L.H., & Pines, A. L. (Eds.) (1985). *Cognitive structure and conceptual change.* Orlando, FL: Academic Press.

**SAM HAUSFATHER** is a seasoned educator who has taught K-8, has been involved in teacher education, and has served in educational administration. He received his PhD in teacher education and is currently an educational consultant.

**Richard E. Clark, Paul A. Kirschner, and John Sweller**

# Putting Students on the Path to Learning: The Case for Fully Guided Instruction

**D**isputes about the impact of instructional guidance during teaching have been ongoing for more than a half century.[1] On one side of this argument are those who believe that all people—novices and experts alike—learn best when provided with instruction that contains unguided or partly guided segments. This is generally defined as instruction in which learners, rather than being presented with all essential information and asked to practice using it, must discover or construct some or all of the essential information for themselves.[2] On the other side are those who believe that ideal learning environments for experts and novices differ: while experts often thrive without much guidance, nearly everyone else thrives when provided with full, explicit instructional guidance (and should not be asked to discover any essential content or skills).[3]

Our goal in this article is to put an end to this debate. Decades of research clearly demonstrate that *for novices* (comprising virtually all students), direct, explicit instruction is more effective and more efficient than partial guidance.[4] So, when teaching new content and skills to novices, teachers are more effective when they provide explicit guidance accompanied by practice and feedback, not when they require students to discover many aspects of what they must learn. As we will discuss, this does not mean direct, expository instruction all day every day. Small group and independent problems and projects can be effective—not as vehicles for making discoveries, but as a means of *practicing* recently learned content and skills.

Before we describe this research, let's clarify some terms. Teachers providing explicit instructional guidance *fully explain* the concepts and skills that students are required to learn. Guidance can be provided through a variety of media, such as lectures, modeling, videos, computer-based presentations, and realistic demonstrations. It can also include class discussions and activities—if the teacher ensures that through the discussion or activity, the relevant information is explicitly provided and practiced. In a math class, for example, when teaching students how to solve a new type of problem, the teacher may begin by showing students how to solve the problem and fully explaining the how and why of the mathematics involved. Often, in following problems, step-by-step explanations may gradually be faded or withdrawn until, through practice and feedback, the students can solve the problem themselves. In this way, before trying to solve the problem on their own, students would already have been walked through both the procedure and the concepts behind the procedure.

In contrast, those teachers whose lessons are designed to offer partial or minimal instructional guidance expect students to discover on their own some or all of the concepts and skills they are supposed to learn. The partially guided approach has been given various names, including discovery learning,[5] problem-based learning,[6] inquiry learning,[7] experiential learning,[8] and constructivist learning.[9] Continuing the math example, students receiving partial instructional guidance may be given a new type of problem and asked to brainstorm possible solutions in small groups with or without prompts or hints. Then there may be a class discussion of the various groups' solutions, and it could be quite some time before the teacher indicates which solution is correct. Through the process of trying to solve the problem and discussing different students' solutions, each student is supposed to discover the relevant mathematics. (In some minimal guidance classrooms, teachers use explicit instruction of the solution as a backup method for those students who did not make the necessary discoveries and who were confused during the class discussion.) Additional examples of minimally guided approaches include (1) inquiry-oriented science instruction in which students are expected to discover fundamental principles by mimicking the investigatory activities of professional researchers,[10] and (2) medical students being expected to discover well-established solutions for common patient problems.[11]

Two bodies of research reveal the weakness of partially and minimally guided approaches: research comparing pedagogies, and research on how people learn. The past

Reprinted with permission from the Spring 2012 issue of *American Educator*, the quarterly journal of the American Federation of Teachers, AFL-CIO.

half century of empirical research has provided overwhelming and unambiguous evidence that, for every one but experts, partial guidance during instruction is significantly less effective and efficient than full guidance. And, based on our current knowledge of how people learn, there is no reason to expect that partially guided instruction in K–12 classrooms would be as effective as explicit, full guidance.

## Research Comparing Fully Guided and Partially Guided Instruction

Controlled experiments almost uniformly indicate that when dealing with novel information (i.e., information that is new to learners), students should be explicitly shown what to do and how to do it, and then have an opportunity to practice doing it while receiving corrective feedback.[12] A number of reviews of empirical studies on teaching novel information have established a solid research-based case against the use of instruction with minimal guidance. Although an extensive discussion of those studies is outside the scope of this article, one recent review is worth noting: Richard Mayer (a cognitive scientist at the University of California, Santa Barbara) examined evidence from studies conducted from 1950 to the late 1980s comparing pure discovery learning (defined as unguided, problem-based instruction) with guided forms of instruction.[13] He suggested that in each decade since the mid-1950s, after empirical studies provided solid evidence that the then-popular unguided approach did not work, a similar approach soon popped up under a different name with the cycle repeating itself. Each new set of advocates for unguided approaches seemed unaware of, or uninterested in, previous evidence that unguided approaches had not been validated. This pattern produced discovery learning, which gave way to experiential learning, which gave way to problem-based and inquiry learning, which has recently given way to constructivist instructional techniques. Mayer concluded that the "debate about discovery has been replayed many times in education, but each time, the research evidence has favored a guided approach to learning."[14] . . .

Evidence from well-designed, properly controlled experimental studies from the 1980s to today also supports direct instructional guidance.[15] Some researchers[16] have noted that when students learn science in classrooms with pure-discovery methods or with minimal feedback, they often become lost and frustrated, and their confusion can lead to misconceptions. Others[17] found that because false starts (in which students pursue misguided hypotheses) are common in such learning situations, unguided discovery is most often inefficient. In a very important study, researchers not only tested whether science learners learned more via discovery, compared with explicit instruction, but also, once learning had occurred, whether the quality of learning differed.[18] Specifically, they tested whether those who had learned through discovery were better able to transfer their learning to new contexts (as advocates for minimally guided approaches often claim). The findings were unambiguous. Direct instruction involving considerable guidance, including examples, resulted in vastly more learning than discovery. Those relatively few students who learned via discovery showed no signs of superior quality of learning.

In real classrooms, several problems occur when different kinds of minimally guided instruction are used. First, often only the brightest and most well-prepared students make the discovery. Second, many students, as noted above, simply become frustrated. Some may disengage, others may copy whatever the brightest students are doing—either way, they are not actually discovering anything. Third, some students believe they have discovered the correct information or solution, but they are mistaken and so they learn a misconception that can interfere with later learning and problem solving.[19] Even after being shown the right answer, a student is likely to recall his or her discovery—not the correction. Fourth, even in the unlikely event that a problem or project is devised that all students succeed in completing, minimally guided instruction is much less efficient than explicit guidance. What can be taught directly in a 25-minute demonstration and discussion, followed by 15 minutes of independent practice with corrective feedback by a teacher, may take several class periods to learn via minimally guided projects and/or problem solving.

As if these four problems were not enough cause for concern, there is one more problem that we must highlight: *minimally guided instruction can increase the achievement gap*. A review[20] of approximately 70 studies, which had a range of more- and less-skilled students as well as a range of more- and less-guided instruction, found the following: more-skilled learners tend to learn more with less-guided instruction, but less-skilled learners tend to learn more with more-guided instruction. Worse, a number of experiments found that less-skilled students who chose or were assigned to less-guided instruction received significantly *lower* scores on posttests than on pretest measures. For these relatively weak students, the failure to provide strong instructional support produced a *measurable loss of learning*. The implication of these results is that teachers should provide explicit instruction when introducing a new topic, but gradually fade it out as knowledge and skill increase.

Even more distressing is evidence[21] that when learners are asked to select between a more-guided or less-guided version of the same course, less-skilled learners who choose the less-guided approach tend to like it even though they learn less from it. It appears that guided instruction helps less-skilled learners by providing taskspecific learning strategies. However, these strategies require learners to engage in explicit, attention-driven effort and so tend not to be liked, even though they are helpful to learning.

Similarly, more-skilled learners who choose the more-guided version of a course tend to like it even though they too have selected the environment in which they learn less. The reason more guidance tends to be less effective with these learners is that, in most cases, they have already acquired task-specific learning strategies that are more effective for them than those embedded in the more-guided version of the course. And some evidence suggests that they like more guidance because they believe they will achieve the required learning with minimal effort.

If the evidence against minimally guided approaches is so strong, why is this debate still alive? We cannot say with any certainty, but one major reason seems to be that many educators mistakenly believe partially and minimally guided instructional approaches are based on solid cognitive science. Turning again to Mayer's review of the literature, many educators confuse "constructivism," which is a theory of how one learns and sees the world, with a prescription for how to teach.[22] In the field of cognitive science, constructivism is a widely accepted theory of learning; it claims that learners must construct mental representations of the world by engaging in active cognitive processing. Many educators (especially teacher education professors in colleges of education) have latched on to this notion of students having to "construct" their own knowledge, and have *assumed* that the best way to promote such construction is to have students try to discover new knowledge or solve new problems without explicit guidance from the teacher. Unfortunately, this assumption is both widespread and incorrect. Mayer calls it the "constructivist teaching fallacy." Simply put, cognitive activity can happen with or without behavioral activity, and behavioral activity does not in any way guarantee cognitive activity. In fact, the type of active cognitive processing that students need to engage in to "construct" knowledge can happen through reading a book, listening to a lecture, watching a teacher conduct an experiment while simultaneously describing what he or she is doing, etc. Learning requires the construction of knowledge. Withholding information from students does not facilitate the construction of knowledge.

# The Human Brain: Learning 101

In order to really comprehend why full instructional guidance is more effective and efficient than partial or minimal guidance for novices, we need to know how human brains learn. There are two essential components: long-term memory and working memory (often called short-term memory). Long-term memory is that big mental warehouse of things (be they words, people, grand philosophical ideas, or skateboard tricks) we know. Working memory is a limited mental "space" in which we think. The relations between working and long-term memory, in conjunction with the cognitive processes that support learning, are of critical importance to developing effective instruction.

Our understanding of the role of long-term memory in human cognition has altered dramatically over the last few decades. It is no longer seen as a passive repository of discrete, isolated fragments of information that permit us to repeat what we have learned. Nor is it seen as having only peripheral influence on complex cognitive processes such as critical thinking and problem solving. Rather, long-term memory is now viewed as the central, dominant structure of human cognition. Everything we see, hear, and think about is dependent on and influenced by our long-term memory.

A seminal series of studies[23] on chess players, for example, demonstrated that expert players perform well even in "blitz" games (which are played in five minutes) because they are not actually puzzling through each move. They have tens of thousands of board configurations, and the best move for each configuration, stored in long-term memory. Those configurations are learned by studying previous games for 10 years or more. Expert players can play well at a fast pace because all they are doing is recalling the best move—not figuring it out. Similar studies of how experts function have been conducted in a variety of other areas.[24] Altogether, the results suggest that expert problem solvers derive their skill by drawing on the extensive experience stored in their long-term memory in the form of concepts and procedures, known as mental schemas. They retrieve memories of past procedures and solutions, and then quickly select and apply the best ones for solving problems. We are skillful in an area if our long-term memory contains huge amounts of information or knowledge concerning the area. That information permits us to quickly recognize the characteristics of a situation and indicates to us, often immediately and unconsciously, what to do and when to do it. (For instance, think about how much easier managing student behavior was in your fifth year of teaching than in your first year of teaching.) Without our huge store of information in long-term memory, we would be largely incapable of everything from simple acts such as avoiding traffic while crossing a street (information many other animals are unable to store in their long-term memory), to complex activities such as playing chess, solving mathematical problems, or keeping students' attention. In short, our long-term memory incorporates a massive knowledge base that is central to all of our cognitively based activities.

What are the instructional consequences of long-term memory? First and foremost, long-term memory provides us with the ultimate justification for instruction: the aim of all instruction is to add knowledge and skills to long-term memory. If nothing has been added to long-term memory, nothing has been learned.

Working memory is the cognitive structure in which conscious processing occurs. We are only conscious of the information currently being processed in working memory and are more or less oblivious to the far larger amount of information stored in long-term memory. When processing novel information, working memory is very limited in duration and capacity. We have known at least since the 1950s that almost all information stored in working memory is lost within 30 seconds[25] if it is not rehearsed and that the capacity of working memory is limited to only a very small number of elements.[26] That number is usually estimated at about seven, but may be as low as four, plus or minus one.[27] Furthermore, when processing (rather than merely storing) information, it may be reasonable to conjecture that the number of items that can be processed may only be two or three, depending on the nature of the processing required.

For instruction, the interactions between working memory and long-term memory may be even more important than the processing limitations.[28] The limitations of working memory only apply to new, to-be-learned information (that has not yet been stored in long-term memory). When dealing with previously learned, organized information stored in long-term memory, these limitations disappear. Since information can be brought back from long-term memory to working memory as needed, the 30-second limit of working memory becomes irrelevant. Similarly, there are no known limits to the amount of such information that can be brought into working memory from long-term memory.

These two facts—that working memory is very limited when dealing with novel information, but that it is not limited when dealing with organized information stored in long-term memory—explain why partially or minimally guided instruction typically is ineffective for novices, but can be effective for experts. When given a problem to solve, novices' only resource is their very constrained working memory. But experts have both their working memory and all the relevant knowledge and skill stored in long-term memory.

One of the best examples of an instructional approach that takes into account how our working and long-term memories interact is the "worked-example effect." A worked example is just what it sounds like: a problem that has already been solved (or "worked out") for which every step is fully explained and clearly shown; it constitutes the epitome of direct, explicit instruction. The "worked-example effect" is the name given to the widely replicated finding that novice learners who try to learn by being required to solve problems perform worse on subsequent test problems, including transfer problems different from the ones seen previously, than comparable learners who learn by studying equivalent worked examples.

The worked-example effect was first demonstrated in the 1980s.[29] Researchers found that algebra students learned more by studying worked examples than by solving equivalent problems. Since those early demonstrations of the effect, it has been replicated on numerous occasions using a large variety of learners studying an equally large variety of materials—from mathematics and science to English literature and world history.[30] For novices, studying worked examples seems invariably superior to discovering or constructing a solution to a problem.

Why does the worked-example effect occur? The limitations of working memory and the relations between working memory and long-term memory discussed earlier can explain it. Solving a problem requires searching for a solution, which must occur using our limited working memory. If the learner has no relevant concepts or procedures in long-term memory, the only thing to do is blindly search for possible solution steps that bridge the gap between the problem and its solution. This process places a great burden on working-memory capacity because the problem solver has to continually hold and process the current problem state in working memory (e.g., Where am I right now in the problem solving process? How far have I come toward finding a solution?) along with the goal state (e.g., Where do I have to go? What is the solution?), the relations between the goal state and the problem state (e.g., Is this a good step toward solving the problem? Has what I've done helped me get nearer to where I need to go?), the solution steps that could further reduce the differences between the two states (e.g., What should the next step be? Will that step bring me closer to the solution? Is there another solution strategy I can use that might be better?), and any subgoals along the way. Thus, searching for a solution overburdens limited working memory and diverts working- memory resources away from storing information in long-term memory. As a consequence, novices can engage in problem-solving activities for extended periods and learn almost nothing.[31]

In contrast, studying a worked example reduces the burden on working memory (because the solution only has to be comprehended, not discovered) and directs attention (i.e., directs working-memory resources) toward storing the essential relations between problem-solving moves in long-term memory. Students learn to recognize which moves are required for particular problems, which is the basis for developing knowledge and skill as a problem solver.[32]

It is important to note that this discussion of worked examples applies to novices—not experts. In fact, the worked-example effect first disappears and then *reverses* as the learners' expertise increases. That is, for experts, solving a problem is more effective than studying a worked example. When learners are sufficiently experienced, studying a worked example is a redundant activity that places a greater burden on working memory than retrieving a known solution from long-term memory.[33] This reversal in effectiveness is not limited to worked examples; it's true of many explicit, fully guided instructional approaches and is known as the "expertise reversal effect."[34] In general, the expertise reversal effect states that "instructional techniques that are highly effective with inexperienced learners can lose their effectiveness and even have negative consequences when used with more experienced learners."[35] This is why, from the very beginning of this article, we have emphasized that guidance is best for teaching *novel* information and skills. This shows the wisdom of instructional techniques that begin with lots of guidance and then fade that guidance as students gain mastery. It also shows the wisdom of using minimal guidance techniques to reinforce or practice previously learned material.

Recommending partial or minimal guidance for novices was understandable back in the early 1960s, when the acclaimed psychologist Jerome Bruner[36] proposed discovery learning as an instructional tool. At that time, researchers knew little about working memory, long-term memory, and how they interact. We now are in a quite different environment; we know much more about the structures, functions, and characteristics of working memory and long-term memory, the relations between them, and their consequences for learning, problem solving, and critical thinking. We also have a good deal more experimental evidence as to what constitutes effective instruction: controlled experiments almost uniformly indicate that when dealing with novel information, learners should be explicitly shown all relevant information, including what to do and how to do it. We wonder why many teacher educators who are committed to scholarship and research ignore the evidence and continue to encourage minimal guidance when they train new teachers.

After a half century of advocacy associated with instruction using minimal guidance, it appears that there is no body of sound research that supports using the technique with anyone other than the most expert students. Evidence from controlled, experimental (a.k.a., "gold standard") studies almost uniformly supports full and explicit instructional guidance rather than partial or minimal guidance for novice to intermediate learners. These findings and their associated theories suggest teachers should provide their students with clear, explicit instruction rather than merely assisting students in attempting to discover knowledge themselves.

# References

1. David P. Ausubel, "Some Psychological and Educational Limitations of Learning by Discovery," *The Arithmetic Teacher* 11 (1964): 290–302; Robert C. Craig, "Directed versus Independent Discovery of Established Relations," *Journal of Educational Psychology* 47, no. 4 (1956): 223–234; Richard E. Mayer, "Should There Be a Three-Strikes Rule against Pure Discovery Learning? The Case for Guided Methods of Instruction," *American Psychologist* 59, no. 1 (2004): 14–19; and Lee S. Shulman and Evan R. Keislar, eds., *Learning by Discovery: A Critical Appraisal* (Chicago: Rand McNally, 1966).

2. See, for example, Jerome S. Bruner, "The Art of Discovery," *Harvard Educational Review* 31 (1961). 21–32; Seymour Papert, *Mindstorms: Children, Computers, and Powerful Ideas* (New York: Basic Books, 1980); and Leslie P. Steffe and Jerry Gale, eds., *Constructivism in Education* (Hillsdale, NJ: Lawrence Erlbaum Associates, 1995).

3. See, for example, Lee J. Cronbach and Richard E. Snow, *Aptitudes and Instructional Methods: A Handbook for Research on Interactions* (New York: Irvington, 1977); David Klahr and Milena Nigam, "The Equivalence of Learning Paths in Early Science Instruction: Effects of Direct Instruction and Discovery Learning," *Psychological Science* 15 (2004): 661–667; Mayer, "Three-Strikes Rule"; Shulman and Keislar, *Learning by Discovery*, and John Sweller, "Evolution of Human Cognitive Architecture," in *The Psychology of Learning and Motivation,* ed. Brian Ross, vol. 43 (San Diego: Academic, 2003), 215–266.

4. John Sweller, Paul Ayres, and Slava Kalyuga, *Cognitive Load Theory* (New York: Springer, 2011).

5. W. S. Anthony, "Learning to Discover Rules by Discovery," *Journal of Educational Psychology* 64, no. 3 (1973): 325–328; and Bruner, "The Art of Discovery."

6. Howard S. Barrows and Robyn M. Tamblyn, *Problem- Based Learning: An Approach to Medical Education* (New York: Springer, 1980); and Henk G. Schmidt, "Problem-Based Learning: Rationale and Description," *Medical Education* 17, no. 1 (1983): 11–16.

7. Papert, *Mindstorms*; and F. James Rutherford, "The Rofe of Inquiry in Science Teaching," *Journal of Research in Science Teaching* 2, no. 2 (1964): 80–84.

8. David Boud, Rosemary Keogh, and David Walker, eds., *Reflection: Turning Experience into Learning* (London: Kogan Page, 1985); and David A. Kolb and Ronald E. Fry, "Toward an Applied Theory of Experiential Learning," in *Studies Theories of Group Processes*, ed. Cary L. Cooper (New York: Wiley, 1975), 33–57.

9. David Jonassen, "Objectivism vs. Constructivism," *Educational Technology Research and Development* 39, no. 3 (1991): 5–14; and Leslie P. Steffe and Jerry Gale, eds., *Constructivism in Education* (Hillsdale, NJ: Lawrence Erlbaum Associates, 1995).

10. Wouter R. van Joolingen, Ton de Jong, Ard W. Lazonder, Elwin R. Savelsbergh, and Sarah Manlove, "Co-Lab: Research and Development of an Online Learning Environment for Collaborative Scientific Discovery Learning," *Computers in Human Behavior* 21, no. 4 (2005): 671–688.

11. Henk G. Schmidt, "Problem-Based Learning: Does It Prepare Medical Students to Become Better Doctors?" *Medical Journal of Australia* 168, no. 9 (May 4, 1998): 429–430; and Henk G. Schmidt, "Assumptions Underlying Self-Directed Learning May Be False," *Medical Education* 34, no, 4 (2000): 243–245.

12. Jeroen J. G. van Merriënboer and Paul A. Kirschner, *Ten Steps to Complex Learning* (Mahwah, NJ: Lawrence Erlbaum Associates, 2007).

13. Mayer, "Three-Strikes Rule."

14. Mayer, "Three-Strikes Rule," 18.

15. See, for example, Roxana Moreno, "Decreasing Cognitive Load in Novice Students: Effects of Explanatory versus Corrective Feedback in Discovery-Based Multimedia," *Instructional Science*

32, nos. 1–2 (2004): 99–113; and Juhani E. Tuovinen and John Sweller, "A Comparison of Cognitive Load Associated with Discovery Learning and Worked Examples," *Journal of Educational Psychology* 91, no. 2 (1999): 334–341.

16. Ann L. Brown and Joseph C. Campione, "Guided Discovery in a Community of Learners," in *Classroom Lessons: Integrating Cognitive Theory and Classroom Practice*, ed. Kate McGilly (Cambridge, MA: MIT Press, 1994), 229–270; and Pamela Thibodeau Hardiman, Alexander Pollatsek, and Arnold D. Well, "Learning to Understand the Balance Beam," *Cognition and Instruction* 3, no. 1 (1986): 63–86.

17. See, for example, Richard A. Carlson, David H. Lundy, and Walter Schneider, "Strategy Guidance and Memory Aiding in Learning a Problem-Solving Skill," *Human Factors* 34, no. 2 (1992): 129–145; and Leona Schauble, "Belief Revision in Children: The Role of Prior Knowledge and Strategies for Generating Evidence," *Journal of Experimental Child Psychology* 49, no. 1 (1990): 31–57.

18. Klahr and Nigam, "The Equivalence of Learning Paths."

19. Eve Kikas, "Teachers' Conceptions and Misconceptions Concerning Three Natural Phenomena," *Journal of Research in Science Teaching* 41, no. 5 (2004): 432–448.

20. Richard E. Clark, "When Teaching Kills Learning: Research on Mathemathantics," in *Learning and Instruction: European Research in an International Context*, ed. Heinz Mandl, Neville Bennett, Erik De Corte, and Helmut Friedrich, vol. 2 (London: Pergamon, 1989), 1–22.

21. Richard E. Clark, "Antagonism between Achievement and Enjoyment in ATI Studies," *Educational Psychologist* 17, no. 2 (1982): 92–101.

22. Mayer, "Three-Strikes Rule"; and Richard E. Mayer, "Constructivism as a Theory of Learning versus Constructivism as a Prescription for Instruction," in *Constructivist Instruction: Success or Failure?* ed. Sigmund Tobias and Thomas M. Duffy (New York: Taylor and Francis, 2009), 184–200.

23. See Adriaan D. de Groot, *Thought and Choice in Chess* (The Hague, Netherlands: Mouton Publishers, 1965) (original work published in 1946); followed by William G. Chase and Herbert A. Simon, "Perception in Chess," *Cognitive Psychology* 4, no. 1 (1973): 55–81; and Bruce D. Burns, "The Effects

of Speed on Skilled Chess Performance," *Psychological Science* 15, no. 7 (2004): 442–447.

24. See, for example, Dennis E. Egan and Barry J. Schwartz, "Chunking in Recall of Symbolic Drawings," *Memory and Cognition* 7, no. 2 (1979): 149–158; Robin Jeffries, Althea A. Turner, Peter G. Polson, and Michael E. Atwood, "The Processes Involved in Designing Software," in *Cognitive Skills and Their Acquisition,* ed. John R. Anderson (Hillsdale, NJ: Lawrence Erlbaum Associates, 1981), 255–283; and John Sweller and Graham A. Cooper, "The Use of Worked Examples as a Substitute for Problem Solving in Learning Algebra," *Cognition and Instruction* 2, no. 1 (1985): 59–89.

25. Lloyd Peterson and Margaret Jean Peterson, "Short-Term Retention of Individual Verbal Items," *Journal of Experimental Psychology: General* 58, no. 3 (1959): 193–198.

26. George A. Miller, "The Magical Number Seven, Plus or Minus Two: Some Limits on Our Capacity for Processing Information," *Psychological Review* 63, no. 2 (1956): 81–97.

27. See, for example, Nelson Cowan, "The Magical Number 4 in Short-Term Memory; A Reconsideration of Mental Storage Capacity," *Behavioral and Brain Sciences* 24, no. 1 (2001): 87–114.

28. Sweller, "Evolution of Human Cognitive Architecture"; and John Sweller, "Instructional Design Consequences of an Analogy between Evolution by Natural Selection and Human Cognitive Architecture," *Instructional Science* 32, no. 1–2 (2004): 9–31.

29. Sweller and Cooper, "The Use of Worked Examples"; and Graham Cooper and John Sweller, "Effects of Schema Acquisition and Rule Automation on Mathematical Problem-Solving Transfer," *Journal of Educational Psychology* 79, no. 4 (1987): 347–362.

30. William M. Carroll, "Using Worked Examples as an Instructional Support in the Algebra Classroom," *Journal of Educational Psychology* 86, no. 3 (1994): 360–367; Craig S. Miller, Jill Fain Lehman, and Kenneth R. Koedinger, "Goals and learning in Microworlds," *Cognitive Science* 23, no. 3 (1999): 305–336; Fred Paas, "Training Strategies for Attaining Transfer of Problem-Solving Skill in Statistics: A Cognitive-Load Approach," *Journal of Educational Psychology* 84, no. 4 (1992): 429–434; Fred Paas and Jeroen J. G. van Merriënboer, "Variability of Worked Examples and Transfer of Geometrical Problem-Solving Skills: A Cognitive-Load Approach," *Journal of Educational Psychology* 86, no. 1 (1994): 122–133; Hitendra K. Pillay, "Cognitive Load and Mental Rotation: Structuring Orthographic Projection for Learning and Problem Solving," *Instructional Science* 22, no. 2 (1994): 91–113; Jill L. Quilici and Richard E. Mayer, "Role of Examples in How Students Learn to Categorize Statistics Word Problems," *Journal of Educational Psychology* 88, no. 1 (1996): 144–161; Arianne Rourke and John Sweller, "The Worked-Example Effect Using Ill-Defined Problems: Learning to Recognise Designers' Styles," *Learning and Instruction* 19, no. 2 (2009): 185–199; and J. Gregory Trafton and Brian J. Reiser, "The Contributions of Studying Examples and Solving Problems to Skill Acquisition," in *Proceedings of the Fifteenth Annual Conference of the Cognitive Science Society* (Hillsdale, NJ: Lawrence Erlbaum Associates, 1993), 1017–1022.

31. John Sweller, Robert F. Mawer, and Walter Howe, "Consequences of History-Cued and Means-End Strategies in Problem Solving," *American Journal of Psychology* 95, no. 3 (1982): 455–483.

32. Michelene T. H. Chi, Robert Glaser, and Ernest Rees, "Expertise in Problem Solving," in *Advances in the Psychology of Human Intelligence,* ed. Robert J. Sternberg, vol. 1 (Hillsdale, NJ: Lawrence Erlbaum Associates, 1982), 7–75.

33. Slava Kalyuga, Paul Chandler, Juhani Tuovinen, and John Sweller, "When Problem Solving Is Superior to Studying Worked Examples," *Journal of Educational Psychology* 93, no, 3 (2001): 579–588.

34. Kalyuga et al., "When Problem Solving Is Superior."

35. Slava Kalyuga, Paul Ayres, Paul Chandler, and John Sweller, "Expertise Reversal Effect," *Educational Psychologist* 38, no. 1 (2003): 23.

36. Bruner, "The Art of Discovery."

**RICHARD E. CLARK** is a Research Professor of Education at Rossier School of Education at University of Southern California.

**PAUL A. KIRSCHNER** is a University Distinguished Professor at the Open University of the Netherlands and a Visiting Professor of Education at University of Oulu, Finland.

**JOHN SWELLER** is a fellow of the Academy of the Social Sciences in Australia and is Professor Emeritus at the University of New South Wales.

# EXPLORING THE ISSUE

## Are Constructivist Teaching Methods Superior to Traditional Methods of Teaching?

### Critical Thinking and Reflection

1. Is it possible for a child to be an expert?
2. Can teachers allow for children to discover within a fully guided classroom/lesson?
3. Can a novice teacher paired with an expert learner be successful?

## Is There Common Ground?

During the first week of my son's entry into middle school, he came home very excited by one of his teachers, Ms. Smith (not her real name, obviously). He told me that Ms. Smith "knows everything" and he expected that she would teach him "a lot." During that year of school, he was very inspired by Ms. Smith's knowledge and expertise. He often commented on things by saying: "Ms. Smith thinks . . . ." As a parent, I finally came to a point where I admitted to him that I didn't care at all about Ms. Smith, and much less about what she "thinks." What I really wanted to know is what my son "thinks." When I would ask him directly, "what do *you* think?," he would reply, "Ms. Smith knows everything!" This personal experience taught me a great deal and I try to remember it when report cards come around. Although knowledgeable teachers can be an inspiration to young children and a source of respect, do I send my child to school in order to learn what Ms. Smith knows and thinks?

Constructivist teaching methods, which can take the teacher away from the spotlight of the classroom, may be seen as impractical, difficult for novice teachers, and/or too time consuming for general use. Many deem these methods as impractical. The problem may be that it is easier to give students the "right answer" and move on to the next concept or next topic. In other words, traditional models of teaching appear to be efficient for the teacher and for schools, and at younger grade levels, they help students from "reinventing the wheel" every time they encounter new topics. In seeking common ground, I am reminded of the results of a cross-national study of 8th grade math lessons (NCES, 1999; TIMSS Video Study), which illustrates how constructivist teaching methods can be applied in the classroom successfully.

In an effort to understand why U.S. youth in 8th grade are outperformed on international assessments in math, the United States conducted a detailed study of math lessons. In the United States, it was found that a typical 8th grade math lesson began with the teacher instructing students on a concept or a skill. The teacher also solved problems with the class by working through examples in front of the students after his/her instruction. Students would then practice the concept or skill on their own while the teacher assisted students individually and as needed. In Japan, a typical math lesson began with the teacher posing a complex problem that provoked student curiosity and thinking. Students were given time to work out the problem, giving them the opportunity to individually struggle with the problem. Individual students were then asked to present their ideas or solutions to the class and the teacher eventually ended the lesson by summarizing the different ways the students solved the problem. At the end of the lesson, students were allowed to practice similar problems on their own. In the typical Japanese math lesson I just described, constructivist methods were used to actively engage students to think independently and creatively (e.g., inviting the learner to attend to the problem and engage their mind). The teacher facilitated what they constructed individually by sharing their answers in class (e.g., social construction). In the typical U.S. math lesson, traditional methods of teaching modeled for students what knowledge is via the worked example and students were asked to imitate it. Needless to say, after the researchers identified and agreed upon the criterion for high-quality math lessons, they found the content of lessons in Japan to be far higher than in the United States.

## Additional Resources

M. Al-Weher, "The Effect of a Training Course Based on Constructivism on Student Teachers' Perceptions of the Teaching/Learning Process," *Asia-Pacific Journal of Teacher Education* (vol. 32, 2004).

J. M. Applefield, R. Huber, and M. Moallem, "Constructivism in Theory and Practice: Toward a Better Understanding," *The High School Journal* (vol. 84, 2001).

J. Cronjé, "Paradigms Regained: Toward Integrating Objectivism and Constructivism in Instructional Design and the Learning Sciences. Educational Technology," *Research and Development* (vol. 54, 2006).

D. Elkind, "The Problem with Constructivism," *The Educational Forum* (vol. 68, 2004).

R. Fox, "Constructivism Examined," *Oxford Review of Education* (vol. 27, 2001). doi:10.1080/30549800 20030583

K. C. Powell and C. J. Kalina, "Cognitive and Social Constructivism: Developing Tools for an Effective Classroom," *Education* (vol. 130, 2009).

M. Windschitl, "Framing Constructivism in Practice as the Negotiation of Dilemmas: An Analysis of the Conceptual, Pedagogical, Cultural, and Political Challenges Facing Teachers," *Review of Educational Research* (vol. 72, 2002).

# *Internet References . . .*

**Constructivism**

https://carbon.ucdenver.edu/~mryder/itc
/constructivism.html

**Jean Piaget Society**

www.piaget.org/index.html

**Vygotsky's Social Constructivism**

www.muskingum.edu/~psych/psycweb/history
/vygotsky.htm#Theory

**The Society Pages**

http://thesocietypages.org/socimages/2009/09/15
/piagets-stages-of-cognitive-development
-experiments-with-kids/

**How Experts Differ from Novices**

www.csun.edu/science/ref/reasoning/how
-students-learn/2.html

Selected, Edited, and with Issue Framing Material by:
Esther S. Chang, *Soka University of America*

# ISSUE

# Should Schools Aim for Students' "Happiness"?

**YES: Nel Noddings,** from "What Does It Mean to Educate the Whole Child?" *Educational Leadership* (2005)

**NO: Kenneth R. Stunkel,** from "Quality in Liberal Education and Illusions of the Academy," *Liberal Education* (1999)

---

## Learning Outcomes

**After reading this issue, you will be able to:**

- Define happiness within the context of schooling.
- Articulate the aim of schools from the two viewpoints.
- Define and give examples of character education programs.
- Describe a liberal education and its aims.
- Understand the concept of the whole child.

---

### ISSUE SUMMARY

**YES:** Nel Noddings argues that schools should be "genuinely happy places" to remind us why we engage in academics and to address children as they are "whole persons."

**NO:** Kenneth Stunkel observes that the decline of liberal studies in college is fostered by an increasing number of academically unprepared students every year and identifies that a major problem has been in accepting and enforcing academic standards regardless of student background.

**M**ost students in educational psychology are exposed to traditional theories of learning and motivation but not always exposed to theories of education and the philosophical underpinnings of formal education. Yet, almost all of the issues in this series will challenge you on the question of the real aims and purposes of schools in society. If students in psychology have plans to apply their work to educational contexts, this debate is as important as other debates. Many social institutions in society contribute to developing the child, such as families, schools, churches, neighborhoods, and community centers. The unique role of schools is mainly in their responsibility in ensuring children are intellectually prepared to survive in an advanced industrial society. This debate asks whether the social and emotional needs of children are significant to this end.

Schools are societal institutions with specific functions to prepare the young to assume the full responsibilities and obligations of citizenship in adulthood. Yet, it is curious that the word "school" comes from the Greek word *scholē*, meaning "leisure," which was intended to describe a place where one has the freedom to pursue knowledge (see Nisbett, 2004). Even more perplexing is that today, we have begun to associate school with college preparation, so what role does citizenship, happiness, and liberal arts education have in the discussion of the purposes of schooling?

The lay definition of happiness in the United States is usually limited to feelings of pleasure and joy, which can be experienced in a wide range of activities from having sex to simply watching good television. Unfortunately, pleasure of this variety is relatively short-lived and rarely reported in activities related to school or at work, which make up most of our day. Thus, psychologists like to supplement reports of positive emotions with cognitive evaluations of one's life, such as the extent to which one positively evaluates the conditions of their life (Diener, 1984). Therefore, the amount of happiness a person has will be a sum or average of positive affect levels and positive evaluations of life. Based on research conducted by Carol Dweck and colleagues, it appears that if schools were aimed at increasing students' positive affect and positive evaluations of the conditions of their lives, we would have schools that produce more students who have learned to feel helpless rather than self-confident. For example, educators who seek to have a "happy" class may be tempted to praise a child's ability after s/he succeeds at a task in order to boost the child's self-esteem and enhance the motivation to learn more. However, experimental research has suggested that praise that is person or ability oriented was more likely to make students feel "helpless" compared with process praise or criticism (see Kamins & Dweck, 1999).

The focus on positive affect and positive evaluation of life has led a growing number of psychologists to focus on aspects of happiness that extend beyond hedonic experiences. Happiness, as the cultivation of personal meaning, authenticity, and excellence, is referred to as eudaemonia. Aristotle spoke of eudaemonia, which is translated from Greek into English as happiness, in the *Nicomachean Ethics*. Aristotle proposed that happiness "is an activity of soul in accord with virtue." It is a type of life that "is pleasant without need of more pleasure" and one that is "lasting, without easy reversals." The focus is on activity and the pursuit of moral virtues, or habits that make a person "good." This particular aspect of happiness is most relevant to Nel Noddings' "Yes" piece. She refers to character virtues throughout the writing selection and connects it to a curriculum that educates the whole child rather than just the cognitive skills of a child. She argues that schools can and need to focus on aspects of the child that are beyond the fundamental skills (e.g., reading and math).

On the other hand, when educators are focused on other, non-cognitive aspects of children's development, it can be seen to dilute the aims of schooling, which can otherwise be concrete (e.g., to write an essay without spelling errors). The perspective of college faculty and administration is informative in the debate over the aims of schooling. Their perspective allows one to question the end goal of student learning altogether, and not just college-level learning.

At the time of this writing, it was reported by the U.S. Labor Bureau (2015) that 68 percent of high school graduates enrolled in college. As college attendance becomes more normative, college faculty, who are at the receiving end of the products of secondary education, begin to question the purpose of college learning altogether. Do you, as a student, pursue a college degree in order to increase your employment prospects or do you pursue a college degree in order to learn how to think better and independently (just for the sake of it)? Ideally, you would want both as a consumer of college education. However, for those who stand by the liberal arts tradition, learning how to think critically and independently has very little to do with what you decide to pursue as your occupation after graduation. In other words, a truck driver is as good an outcome as a Wall Street banker (perhaps better?) so long as the individual understands how to reason without the help of others. Thus, the purpose of schooling is to educate each citizen to be able to think for themselves. Consistent with this view, schools are not mere agents of socialization, schools aim to improve us by educating us. An education is about making society "good."

The "No" selection uses the issue of a liberal arts education as a platform to counter arguments that support the idea that schools should aim for student happiness. A liberal arts education generally refers to a broad multidisciplinary curriculum at the college level. It continues to expose students to both the humanities and sciences but at a higher level of critical thinking. Thus, students must be prepared to read Plato's writings independently and be able to understand his sarcasm as well as to be able to follow logical arguments in order to prepare for college-level discussions on Plato.

Kenneth Stunkel (along with many who have taught for several years) reports upon an observed decline in these types of student skills in the "No" selection. He observes that many are unprepared for a liberal college education because they lack college readiness in reading and writing in particular. Interestingly, he cites education's grandiose learning outcomes that obscure the true aims of schools. He generally believes that schools should simply work on students' intellectual abilities and hone them to a point whereby the college instructor is no longer needed.

Unfortunately, the reality is that many students decry their general education classes because they fail to see the relevance of Plato or Marx in what they *really* want to do after college. In the following selections, though based on different periods of the lifespan, will ask you to determine the extent to which you think it is important for schools to be "happy places." For Nel Noddings, it is critical to the development of healthy minds, but for Kenneth Stunkel, it is at the expense of our nation's standards and it clouds the true aim of schooling and education.

# YES ⤹

**Nel Noddings**

# What Does It Mean to Educate the WHOLE CHILD?

*In a democratic society, schools must go beyond teaching fundamental skills.*

Public schools in the United States today are under enormous pressure to show—through improved test scores—that they are providing every student with a thorough and efficient education. The stated intention of No Child Left Behind (NCLB) is to accomplish this goal and reverse years of failure to educate many of our inner-city and minority children. But even if we accept that the motives behind NCLB are benign, the law seems fatally flawed.

Some critics have declared NCLB an unfunded mandate because it makes costly demands without providing the resources to meet them. Others point to its bureaucratic complexity; its unattainable main goal (100 percent of students proficient in reading and math by 2014); its motivationally undesirable methods (threats, punishments, and pernicious comparisons); its overdependence on standardized tests; its demoralizing effects; and its corrupting influences on administrators, teachers, and students.

All these criticisms are important, but NCLB has a more fundamental problem: its failure to address, or even ask, the basic questions raised in this issue of *Educational Leadership*: What are the proper aims of education? How do public schools serve a democratic society? What does it mean to educate the whole child?

## The Aims of Education

Every flourishing society has debated the aims of education. This debate cannot produce final answers, good for all times and all places, because the aims of education are tied to the nature and ideals of a particular society. But the aims promoted by NCLB are clearly far too narrow. Surely, we should demand more from our schools than to educate people to be proficient in reading and mathematics. Too many highly proficient people commit fraud, pursue paths to success marked by greed, and care little about how their actions affect the lives of others.

Surely, we should demand more from our schools than to educate people to be proficient in reading and mathematics.

Some people argue that schools are best organized to accomplish academic goals and that we should charge other institutions with the task of pursuing the physical, moral, social, emotional, spiritual, and aesthetic aims that we associate with the whole child. The schools would do a better job, these people maintain, if they were freed to focus on the job for which they were established.

Those who make this argument have not considered the history of education. Public schools in the United States— as well as schools across different societies and historical eras—were established as much for moral and social reasons as for academic instruction. In his 1818 *Report of the Commissioners for the University of Virginia*, for example, Thomas Jefferson included in the "objects of primary education" such qualities as morals, understanding of duties to neighbors and country, knowledge of rights, and intelligence and faithfulness in social relations.

Periodically since then, education thinkers have described and analyzed the multiple aims of education. For example, the National Education Association listed seven aims in its 1918 report, *Cardinal Principles of Secondary Education*: (1) health; (2) command of the fundamental processes; (3) worthy home membership; (4) vocation; (5) citizenship; (6) worthy use of leisure; and (7) ethical character (Kliebard, 1995, p. 98). Later in the century, educators trying to revive the progressive tradition advocated open education, which aimed to encourage creativity, invention, cooperation, and democratic participation in the classroom and in lifelong learning (Silberman, 1973).

Recently, I have suggested another aim: happiness (Noddings, 2003). Great thinkers have associated happiness with such qualities as a rich intellectual life, rewarding human relationships, love of home and place, sound character, good parenting, spirituality and a job that one loves. We incorporate this aim into education not only by helping our students understand the components of happiness but also by making classrooms genuinely happy places.

Few of these aims can be pursued directly, the way we attack behavioral objectives. Indeed, I dread the day when I will enter a classroom and find *Happiness* posted as an instructional objective. Although I may be able to state exactly what students should be able to do when it comes to adding fractions, I cannot make such specific statements about happiness, worthy home membership, use of leisure, or ethical character. These great aims are meant to guide our instructional decisions. They are meant to broaden our thinking—to remind us to ask *why* we have chosen certain curriculums, pedagogical methods, classroom arrangements, and learning objectives. They remind us, too, that students are whole persons—not mere collections of attributes, some to be addressed in one place and others to be addressed elsewhere.

In insisting that schools and other social institutions share responsibility for nurturing the whole child, I recognize that different institutions will have different emphases. Obviously, schools will take greater responsibility for teaching reading and arithmetic; medical clinics for health checkups and vaccinations; families for housing and clothing; and places of worship for spiritual instruction.

## Aims of Education

*The habits we form from childhood make no small difference, but rather they make all the difference.*
                                                    —*Aristotle*

But needs cannot be rigidly compartmentalized. The massive human problems of society demand holistic treatment. For example, leading medical clinics are now working with lawyers and social workers to improve housing conditions for children and to enhance early childhood learning (Shipler, 2004). We know that healthy families do much more than feed and clothe their children. Similarly, schools must be concerned with the total development of children.

## Democracy and Schools

A productive discussion of education's aims must acknowledge that schools are established to serve both individuals and the larger society. What does the society expect of its schools?

From the current policy debates about public education, one would think that U.S. society simply needs competent workers who will keep the nation competitive in the world market. But both history and common sense tell us that a democratic society expects much more: It wants graduates who exhibit sound character, have a social conscience, think critically, are willing to make commitments, and are aware of global problems (Soder, Goodlad, & McMannon, 2001).

In addition, a democratic society needs an education system that helps to sustain its democracy by developing thoughtful citizens who can make wise civic choices. By its very nature, as Dewey (1916) pointed out, a democratic society is continually changing—sometimes for the better, sometimes for the worse—and it requires citizens who are willing to participate and competent enough to distinguish between the better and the worse.

If we base policy debate about education on a serious consideration of society's needs, we will ask thoughtful questions: What modes of discipline will best contribute to the development of sound character? What kinds of peer interactions might help students develop a social conscience? What topics and issues will foster critical thinking? What projects and extracurricular activities might call forth social and personal commitment? Should we assign the task of developing global awareness to social studies courses, or should we spread the responsibility throughout the entire curriculum (Noddings, 2005b)?

In planning education programs for a democratic society, we must use our understanding of the aims of education to explore these questions and many more. Unfortunately, public policy in the United States today concentrates on just one of the *Cardinal Principles* proposed by NEA in 1918: "command of the fundamental processes." Although reading and math are important, we need to promote competence in these subjects while also promoting our other aims. Students can develop reading, writing, speaking, and mathematical skills as they plan and stage dramatic performances, design classroom murals, compose a school paper, and participate in establishing classroom rules.

If present reports about the effects of NCLB on the education of inner-city and minority children are supported by further evidence, we should be especially concerned about our democratic future. Wealthier students are enjoying a rich and varied curriculum and many opportunities to engage in the arts, whereas many of our less wealthy students spend their school days bent over worksheets in an effort to boost standardized test scores (Meier & Wood, 2004). Such reports call into question the notion that NCLB will improve schooling for our poorest students. Surely all students deserve rich educational experiences—experiences that will enable them to become active citizens in a democratic society.

Life in a healthy democracy requires participation, and students must begin to practice participation in our schools. Working together in small groups can furnish such practice, provided that the emphasis is consistently on working together—not on formal group processes or the final grade for a product. Similarly, students can participate in establishing the rules that will govern classroom conduct. It is not sufficient, and it may actually undermine our democracy, to concentrate on producing people who do well on standardized tests and who define success as getting a well-paid job. Democracy means more than voting and maintaining economic productivity, and life means more than making money and beating others to material goods.

> All students deserve rich educational experiences that will enable them to become active citizens in a democratic society.

## The Whole Child

Most of us want to be treated as persons, not as the "sinus case in treatment room 3" or the "refund request on line 4." But we live under the legacy of bureaucratic thought—the idea that every physical and social function should be assigned to its own institution. In the pursuit of efficiency, we have remade ourselves into a collection of discrete attributes and needs. This legacy is strong in medicine, law, social work, business, and education.

Even when educators recognize that students are whole persons, the temptation arises to describe the whole in terms of collective parts and to make sure that every aspect, part, or attribute is somehow "covered" in the curriculum. Children are moral beings; therefore, we must provide character education programs. Children are artistically inclined; therefore, we must provide art classes. Children's physical fitness is declining; therefore, we must provide physical education and nutrition classes. And then we complain that the curriculum is overloaded!

We should not retreat to a curriculum advisory committee and ask, "Now where should we fit this topic into the already overloaded curriculum?" Although we cannot discard all the fragmented subjects in our present school system and start from scratch, we can and should ask all teachers to stretch their subjects to meet the needs and interests of the whole child. Working within the present subject-centered curriculum, we can ask math and science teachers as well as English and social studies teachers to

address moral, social, emotional, and aesthetic questions with respect and sensitivity when they arise (Simon, 2001). In high school math classes, we can discuss Descartes' proof of God's existence (is it flawed?); the social injustices and spiritual longing in *Flatland*, Edwin Abbott's 1884 novel about geometry; the logic and illogic in *Alice's Adventures in Wonderland*; and the wonders of numbers such as $\phi$ and $\pi$.

For the most part, discussions of moral and social issues should respond to students' expressed needs, but some prior planning can be useful, too. When a math teacher recites a poem or reads a biographical piece or a science fiction story, when she points to the beauty or elegance of a particular result, when she pauses to discuss the social nature of scientific work, students may begin to see connections—to see a whole person at work (Noddings, 2005a). Teachers can also look carefully at the subjects that students are required to learn and ask, "How can I include history, literature, science, mathematics, and the arts in my own lessons?" This inclusion would in itself relieve the awful sense of fragmentation that students experience.

The benefits of a more holistic perspective can also extend beyond the academic curriculum and apply to the school climate and the issue of safety and security. Schools often tackle this problem the way they tackle most problems, piece by piece: more surveillance cameras, more security guards, better metal detectors, more locks, shorter lunch periods, more rules. It seems like a dream to remember that most schools 40 years ago had no security guards, cameras, or metal detectors. And yet schools are not safer now than they were in the 1960s and 1970s. We need to ask why there has been a decline in security and how we should address the problem. Do we need more prison-like measures, or is something fundamentally wrong with the entire school arrangement?

Almost certainly, the sense of community and trust in our schools has declined. Perhaps the most effective way to make our schools safer would be to restore this sense of trust. I am not suggesting that we get rid of all our security paraphernalia overnight, but rather that we ask what social arrangements might reduce the need for such measures. Smaller schools? Multiyear assignment of teachers and students? Class and school meetings to establish rules and discuss problems? Dedication to teaching the whole child in every class? Serious attention to the integration of subject matter? Gentle but persistent invitations to all students to participate? More opportunities to engage in the arts and in social projects? More encouragement to speak out with the assurance of being heard? More opportunities to work together? Less competition? Warmer hospitality for parents? More public forums on school issues? Reduction of test-induced stress? More opportunities for informal conversation? Expanding, not reducing, course offerings? Promoting the idea of fun and humor in learning? Educating teachers more broadly? All of the above?

If we base policy debate about education on a serious consideration of society's needs, we will ask thoughtful questions.

We will not find the solution to problems of violence, alienation, ignorance, and unhappiness in increasing our security apparatus, imposing more tests, punishing schools for their failure to produce 100 percent proficiency, or demanding that teachers be knowledgeable in "the subjects they teach." Instead, we must allow teachers and students to interact as whole persons, and we must develop policies that treat the school as a whole community. The future of both our children and our democracy depend on our moving in this direction.

## References

Dewey, J. (1916). *Democracy and education*. New York: Macmillan.

Jefferson, T. (1818). *Report of the commissioners for the University of Virginia*. Available: www.libertynet.org/edcivic/jefferva.html

Kliebard, H. (1995). *The struggle for the American curriculum*. New York: Routledge.

Meier, D., & Wood, G. (Eds.). (2004). *Many children left behind*. Boston: Beacon Press.

Noddings, N. (2003). *Happiness and education*. Cambridge, MA: Cambridge University Press.

Noddings, N. (2005a). *The challenge to care in schools* (2nd ed.). New York: Teachers College Press.

Noddings, N. (Ed.). (2005b). *Educating citizens for global awareness*. New York: Teachers College Press.

Shipler, D. K. (2004). *The working poor: Invisible in America*. New York: Alfred A. Knopf.

Silberman, C. E. (1973). *The open classroom reader*. New York: Vintage Books.

Simon, K. G. (2001). *Moral questions in the classroom*. New Haven, CT: Yale University Press.

Soder, R., Goodlad, J. I., & McMannon, T. J. (Eds.). (2001). *Developing democratic character in the young*. San Francisco: Jossey-Bass.

NEL NODDINGS is Professor Emerita of Education at Stanford University and became well known in the 1980s since writing about care theory (Noddings, 1984). She has been highly prolific, having authored 20 books and literally hundreds of articles. She has been the president of the National Academy of Education, the John Dewey Society, and the Philosophy of Education Society. She has also received several honors, awards, and honorary doctorates.

Kenneth R. Stunkel  **NO**

# Quality in Liberal Education and Illusions of the Academy

The devaluation of liberal learning in mission and substance has exceeded the power of an earnest manifesto to restore its credibility.

This essay is a response to the Statement on Liberal Learning, published in the Spring issue of *Liberal Education*, Vol. 85, No. 2. We welcome responses to the statement as well as expressions of qualification, reservation, and dissent. The previous issue of *Liberal Education* (Spring 1999) bravely tries to map a course for liberal education in a "Statement on Liberal Learning." The goals enumerated are pleasingly idealistic but largely unreachable in the present state of higher education. The formidable obstacle is lack of consensus about purposes of a liberal education and measures necessary to fulfill them. Back in the 1960s I entered the profession with a hope that teaching, thought, scholarship, and contact with young people eager to learn would justify the pittance earned. It is ironic that the latter has improved somewhat while the former has deteriorated. From the vantage point of faculty (a professor of history for thirty-four years) and administration (a dean of humanities and social sciences for eleven years), I have seen almost two generations of students pass through the system. Strong impressions are unavoidable, and for me they are not cheerfully upbeat. Yes, liberal education still happens. Yes, there are able, serious students from all quarters who can profit from it. Yes, there are professors who understand it and resist all the foolishness that saps its integrity. But the other side of the coin is sufficiently tarnished to fault the currency. The tarnished side is our collective problem. The devaluation of liberal learning in mission and substance has exceeded the power of an earnest manifesto to restore its credibility. I wonder at optimists in the academy who think a New Jerusalem is around the corner. No doubt transformations are in the works, but they are the wrong kind and often self-defeating. Quality is proclaimed as a goal in every college catalogue, yet no idea has been more corrupted by a drift into expedience.

## Lost in Space

The words "quality" and "excellence" have become vacuous slogans cheaply used. They have no meaning in liberal education without clear objectives hitched to standards that permit judgment as to whether or not they have been achieved. There are too many objectives, and standards have been fudged to accommodate all of them. Quality has been compromised and obscured by forces outside the academy, for which professors are not wholly at fault, and by choices within, for which they are fully responsible. While a determined body of academics might effect repairs on a battered tradition of liberal learning, they cannot alone undo all the harm or neutralize all the damaging influences. Society at large has shaped a generation of students unreceptive to liberal study. Poor schooling is not the only blight, although it bears a huge share of blame, which reflects a parallel failure of education departments to produce teachers with firm skills and usable knowledge. Judging from polls and studies, as well as from anecdotes and my own experience, the idea of liberal study is misunderstood by students, parents, employers, faculty, and administrators. It is not highly valued or eagerly pursued despite much supportive rhetoric. At best, some parents, students, or employers believe a liberal education may increase chances of employment. At worst, most believe it results in unemployment and a dead end. That all of them think only of employment is part of the difficulty. They are right that liberal education is impractical. It does not train students for careers. But they have lost touch altogether with its unique advantages. Consumer activities, entertainment, and self-absorption are higher priorities than anything so exotic as learning to respect truth (an ideal the academy has diminished) or to explore the 99 percent of knowledge and experience lying outside a student's parochial upbringing.

Inside the academy, a symptom of disarray is the eclectic industry that hums away to rethink, reconsider, rework, or redesign liberal education. A consequence of this "rethinking" has been an expansion of liberal study to include tasks for which it is not suited. These include redressing past injustices of racism and sexism and reforming other social evils. Liberal education is supposed to foster global consciousness, good citizenship, community service, and diversity training, all presumably on top of broad learning, critical thought, decent writing, and serious reading. Tasks that once were clear and manageable have been diluted or replaced by others that are vague and unwieldy, but without evidence that liberal education under the best conditions can reform society or consummate the world's salvation. Such grandiose aims are at odds with achievable purposes, the chief of which is to expand the topography of individual minds and sensibilities.

By absorbing a plethora of social and political agendas, liberal education has lost shape and direction. Confusion about aims has vindicated public skepticism. It has also bewildered and alienated immature students who feel rightly comfortable with tasks and expectations that are more specific and less global. More than a few academics in the humanities and social sciences have aggravated the situation by turning liberal study into a battleground (the "culture wars") for social ideologues or a playground for scholars who claim they are revolutionizing knowledge by showing it does not exist. In the humanities, pretentious theories and methods like social construction and deconstruction undermine subject matter. History becomes social fiction, literature bare "textuality" at the mercy of analysts or readers who overlay novels and poems with their own "narratives," art whatever people who call themselves artists say it is, and science a myth. The theories and methods then turn inward and collapse on their own premises, leaving a void. Amidst this spectacle of intellectual desolation, no one should be surprised that students prefer a fast track to career success and view liberal education as a waste of time and money.

The decline of liberal studies is powered by an unprecedented influx of academically unprepared students (total enrollment is up from some 3 million in the early 1950s to 15 million now), which has effectively transformed higher education into mass postsecondary training. A nearly universal outcome of this inundation of people ill-prepared for higher study is ongoing remediation as a way of life, which has been duly rationalized and justified as harried teachers have scrambled to "rethink" liberal study and redefine standards. Good evidence for standards on the slide is the prevalence of remedial classes. In 1995, they were provided by 72 percent of four-year institutions. The figure for community colleges was 96 percent. In the CUNY system, the third largest public network in the country, four year schools in 1999 had 72 percent of entering students doing remedial work, while community colleges were at 87 percent. The Ivy League and other selective schools also do remedial work, but with quiet discretion.

In the smoke and dust of educational politics, quality, excellence, and standards have been demeaned as "code words" for exclusion of the disadvantaged by dominant elites. What is lost in this suicidal talk is the basis for competence in any undertaking. For example, what we want, or what many of us say we want, is competence with the written word—just plain competence, not fine writing, much less creative writing. Seldom does it come to pass. Haunting the wish is a stern reality, for competence has no meaning without the guidance of specific, enforceable standards. A competent person can perform a desired or needed task consistently and at will. Competence is recognized because tasks upon which life depends are guided by standards that tell us to what end and how the tasks are to be performed. Standards define an acceptable result in a public realm where it makes a difference.

A true standard for competence applies impartially to everyone. Race, class, gender, and ethnicity are irrelevant to the issue of standards. A surgeon understands the connection between competence and standards when an appendix is removed and the patient recovers; an engineer understands it when a new bridge stands firm under loading; a piano teacher understands it when a student modulates properly from one key to another; a cook understands it when the souffle rises; a business executive understands it when a subsidiary gets correct written instructions about disposing of inventory; a history teacher understands it when a student's unambiguous prose conveys facts and ideas without a tangle of misspellings, grammatical mutilations, and inaccuracies. There is no mystery about standards. The problem is widespread unwillingness to accept and enforce them lest someone be offended or left out. No one has explained how quality can be reconciled with the belief that college is for everyone, or how both can be accommodated without one or the other taking a back seat. The poet Goethe observed rightly that a condition for achievement is knowing how to accept limits. So it is with liberal education and what it is best fitted to do.

## About Liberal Education

The distinctive purpose of liberal study is to cultivate powers of mind and feeling through graded stages of reading, writing, thinking, aesthetic contemplation, and the dialectic of informed give and take. These developed and tuned powers are means for acquiring fresh knowledge and assessing experience over a lifetime. Without powers bequeathed by liberal study, life can go on and provide elementary satisfactions, as it always has, but without sounding deeper possibilities of understanding and fulfillment. Such powers might be directed at social purposes and political action, but a liberally educated man or woman may choose other uses of time and energy, such as writing poetry, learning a new language, enjoying Chinese landscape painting, studying the Mozart string quartets, pursuing amateur astronomy, or any number of things, perhaps just gazing out a window in thought, all without regard to social passions and issues of the moment.

The liberally educated mind can distinguish quality from mediocrity, sense from nonsense, authenticity from phoniness, and is not reticent about separating what is excellent from what is merely adequate or palpably inferior. A liberal education for which these distinctions do not exist is an amorphous phantom. Liberal learning entails a disciplined understanding that all artifacts and voices do not repay invested time and effort at an equal rate. Some provide instruction, wonder, and pleasure indefinitely. Others fray and crumble in a moment. Some are solid and enduring. Others are hollow and ephemeral. A liberally educated person knows the difference.

With powers of study, expression, and thought developed and active, limitations imposed by geographical and historical accident are seen for what they are. A wider perspective on self and the world emerges. Tribal sensibility is blunted and recedes. Of course the individual self (who I am alone) must come to terms with the social self (who I am with others), but the rapprochement unfolds in its own way and time with each liberally educated individual. Otherwise, we have indoctrination rather than education. Entering a wider universe of thought and feeling has much potential for causing offense. Acquiring a proper education is risky business, which includes jolts to self-esteem as knowledge replaces ignorance and untenable beliefs are altered or jettisoned. What can be more troubling in the short run than insight that one knows little, understands even less, and has yet to grow up?

Finally, the aim of liberal education is not to shape students into marketable commodities, convert them to social causes, or make technicians of them in history, literature, or other academic subjects. To these restrictions can be added the arcane, antihumanistic world of "cultural studies," where all texts are equal and meaning is an exclusive creature of race, class, gender, and ethnicity. Liberal study is an opportunity to escape such narrow paths and claustrophobic spaces with the help of literature, history, philosophy, art, music, science, and mathematics. Confinement to one dimension of knowledge or partisan immersion in the lore of one's ethnic group are incompatible with liberal thought and sensibility.

The core and spirit of liberal education were explained succinctly by William James in a talk at a women's college at the turn of this century. He argued that liberal study "should help you to know a good man when you see him" ("man" is a generic term meaning human being and hence woman). The liberally educated person is not merely "an efficient instrument for doing a definite thing." After professional training, "you may remain a crude and smoky kind of petroleum, incapable of spreading light." But even the most narrowly trained person grasps standards built into the job and can judge the skill of others, recognizing "sound work, clean work, finished work; feeble work, slack work, sham work." Liberal study carries one beyond this level to an awareness of many kinds of excellence and into the domain of activities and achievements that "have stood the test of time." With the reach of both mind and feeling extended, there comes "the feeling for a good human job anywhere, the admiration of the really admirable, the disesteem of what is cheap and trashy and impermanent." These powers of discernment and judgment enable one to recognize a good man or woman when they turn up.

What are the prospects of liberal education? I suspect that most institutions, especially those dependent on enrollment and retention for revenue, will continue to buckle under and offer mostly painless satisfaction to their customers. Some professors will defend and practice true liberal study and battle the current, although they are in danger of extinction. Others will adjust easily to the brave new world of mass post-secondary training on the premise that lofty goals of liberal learning are Eurocentric and elitist and continue turning it into something else. Still others will find peace in scholarly esotericism or lose themselves and their students in the postmodern maelstrom. That seems to be the probable latitude and longitude of liberal education as the curtain drops on the twentieth century.

---

**KENNETH R. STUNKEL** is Professor of History at Monmouth University. He has published seven books and several scholarly articles. He has an extensive administrative background, serving as dean of faculty for more than 10 years.

# EXPLORING THE ISSUE

## Should Schools Aim for Students' "Happiness"?

## Critical Thinking and Reflection

1. How is character education related to happiness?
2. How is treating the whole child linked to happiness?
3. Why is the idea of liberal study not valued in society?
4. How is the decline of liberal study related to a decline in academic standards?
5. How is liberal study at odds with cultural studies?

## Is There Common Ground?

Both sides agree that developing the intellectual capabilities of the mind is the primary and focal responsibility of schools. Both sides might also agree that a child is not only a thinking and reasoning organism but also one that is socially motivated and emotionally active. Disagreements between the two sides begin when schools add learning outcomes that are more social (e.g., producing responsible global citizens) and emotional (e.g., becoming caring adults) than cognitive (e.g., academic excellence). What role do schools have in developing the social and emotional aspects of student minds, particularly when academic standards are lowered and practically nonexistent?

I find a great deal of common ground in referring to psychological theories of love and attachment, which was articulated by John Bowlby (1969) and inspired by the Harlow monkey experiment (see videos on Attachment Theory webpage under "Internet Resources"). Applying John Bowlby's attachment theory, one can argue that when children feel safe and view the teacher as a secure base, they are able to explore their educational environment more thoroughly and benefit cognitively. As per Piaget's theory of cognitive development, knowing is tied to exploration of the environment. Thus, it is likely that some schools have to prioritize social and emotional aspects of learning more if they operate in neighborhoods and local regions where crime and poverty rates are high. This is because the functions of the family and other social institutions that help developing persons are absent, and therefore, schools have to pick up additional responsibilities.

Although the "No" side argues convincingly that the aims of schools should be concrete and focused solely on the development of students' intellectual abilities, there may be an implicit assumption that other social institutions are doing their share in developing children's character and providing for their emotional needs. As schools became compulsory and poverty more widespread, schools could not assume this anymore. As college becomes more normative, college faculty can't assume this anymore. As a growing number of the population enrolls in college, reports of declining academic standards may be a reflection of a more diverse (socially disadvantaged) population of students rather than a result of a diluted educational curriculum.

Colleges have long been criticized as institutions that exacerbate social inequality by qualifying the upper classes and excluding the working class (Deresiewicz, 2014). Within this context, why should we prevent any student from enrolling in college? A liberal arts education can be seen as a privileged education, indeed in its most traditional understanding, culture-specific to ancient Greece (Nisbett, 2004). If faculty remain committed to the aims of liberal education, they may have to attend to the social and emotional issues of a socially diverse student body. In many respects, teaching within a liberal studies curriculum is akin to teaching a different cultural view of knowledge, its basis, and the relevance of truth to life.

## References

J. Bowlby, *Attachment. Attachment and Loss: Vol. 1. Loss* (New York: Basic Books, 1969).

W. Deresiewicz, *Excellent Sheep: The Miseducation of the American Elite and the Way to a Meaningful Life* (New York: The Free Press, 2014).

E. Diener, "Subjective well-being," *Psychological Bulletin* (vol. 95, 1984).

M. L. Kamins and C. S. Dweck, "Person versus Process Praise and Criticism: Implications for Contingent Self-worth and Coping," *Developmental Psychology* (vol. 35, 1999).

R. Nisbett, *The Geography of Thought: How Asians and Westerners Think Differently . . . and Why* (New York: The Free Press).

## Additional Resources

T. Cavanagh, "Schooling for Happiness: Rethinking the Aims of Education," *Kairaranga* (vol. 9, 2008).

N. Noddings, *Happiness and Education* (Cambridge, UK; New York: Cambridge University Press, 2003).

P. Roberts, "Happiness, Despair and Education," *Studies in Philosophy & Education* (vol. 32, 2013). doi:10.1007/s11217-012-9325-4

# Internet References . . .

**Attachment Theory**

www.simplypsychology.org/attachment.html

**Happiness in Schools**

www.actionforhappiness.org/about-us/happiness-in-schools

**The Educational Theory of Nel Noddings**

www.newfoundations.com/GALLERY/Noddings.html

**Why I Teach Plato to Plumbers**

www.theatlantic.com/education/archive/2014/04/plato-to-plumbers/361373/

**What Is a 21st Century Liberal Education?**

www.aacu.org/leap/what-is-a-liberal-education

# Unit 2

# UNIT

# Basic Educational Issues

*S*chools in the United States are being asked to do more and more in a world that changes faster and faster. This is a short unit on three basic issues that schools are asked to cope with as they take on more responsibilities. Among the most pressing appears to be how our schools measure up to other nation's schools. Not only must schools meet local and state standards in mathematics and science, but also prepare students for a more interconnected and more globally competitive future. At the same time, schools are desperate to try out anything that can help and brain research has been extremely productive and informative in understanding the complexity of our minds. As a result, many have rushed to apply these new insights in our classrooms and brought about controversy relating to their relevance to teaching. Finally, the schools are asked to narrow the persistent achievement gap of disadvantaged students above all else, but can they? The articles of this section consider the controversies that have arisen as schools have tried to meet the diverse needs of a rapidly changing world of commerce, psychological research, and classroom.

Selected, Edited, and with Issue Framing Material by:
Esther S. Chang, *Soka University of America*

# ISSUE

## Are International Comparisons Helpful?

**YES: OECD**, from "Learning from High-Performing Education Systems," OECD Publishing (2011)

**NO: Anna Dall**, from "Is PISA Counter-Productive to Building Successful Educational Systems?" *Social Alternatives* (2011)

---

### Learning Outcomes

**After reading this issue, you will be able to:**

- Evaluate U.S. performance on international assessments.
- Define the aims and methods of PISA.
- Enumerate the lessons for U.S. education as a result of international comparisons as articulated by PISA.
- Identify weaknesses in international comparisons.
- Define the testing culture and its role in schooling.

---

### ISSUE SUMMARY

**YES:** The OECD argues that if a country is committed to children and their education, the real test of their commitment is how they prioritize education against other commitments, such as youth sports. International comparisons therefore help illuminate why the United States is outperformed by other countries in math, science, and reading.

**NO:** Anna Dall argues that the PISA model is problematic and is counterproductive to building a successful educational system. She critiques the testing culture and believes that there needs to be a paradigm shift away from test performance.

Ever since the Soviets launched Sputnik in 1957 (the first satellite in outer space), American policy makers and big businesses have had to deal with the importance and harsh realities of global competition. One of the consequences of global competition for education was U.S. participation in the First International Mathematics Study (FIMS) in the 1960s, which surveyed 12 countries in mathematics among 13-year-olds. As more data related to U.S. student achievement became available over time, the publication of *A Nation at Risk* (1983), which was researched by the American President Ronald Reagan's National Commission on Excellence in Education, documented the poor performance of U.S. students on numerous national and international tests. Since then, U.S. policy makers have applied a great deal of pressure on the nation's educational system to reform.

Since FIMS, there have been two subsequent tests of international achievement: one is now referred to as the TIMSS (Trends in International Mathematics and Science Study) and the other is the PISA (Program for International Student Assessment). Each battery of tests measures different areas of knowledge and ability among different age/grade groups. TIMSS focuses on 4th and 8th graders whereas PISA focuses on 15-year-olds. TIMSS is more consistent with the school curriculum whereas PISA attempts to measure students' application of knowledge to real-world problems. Although dependent upon how many and which countries participate in the TIMSS, the pattern since the 1990s has been consistent. U.S. students perform about average overall and below average when compared to other countries that are as high as the United States on the Human Development Index. Additional analyses has examined whether the performance of U.S. students varies by type of test or by type of student, such as top-performing vs. average-performing students. However, across the many different types of analyses conducted, U.S. students on average scored significantly lower than the top-performing countries.

Since the selections for this debate refer to the PISA test, it is informative to understand the latest PISA (2012) results. According to the PISA website (see Internet Resources), U.S. 15 year olds performed about average or slightly below average when compared to other countries that are members or partners of the OECD (the Organization for Economic Co-Operation and Development):

- the average performance in reading is 498 points, compared to an average of 496 points in OECD countries.
- the average performance in mathematics is 481 points in mathematics, the main topic of PISA 2012, compared to an average of 494 points in OECD countries.
- the average performance in science literacy is 497 points compared to an average of 501 points in OECD countries.

Results also indicated that Singapore, Hong Kong, Taipei, Korea, Macao, Japan, Liechtenstein, Switzerland, and the Netherlands were the top performers in mathematics; Shanghai-China, Hong Kong, Singapore, Japan, and Korea were the five highest-performing countries in reading; Shanghai-China, Hong Kong, Singapore, Japan, and Finland were the top five performers in science in PISA 2012 (OECD, 2014).

An important issue to address in this debate is what these results mean to Americans and whether we should do anything about them. It has been especially difficult to reach consensus upon the first part of the question, which is to recognize whether there is a problem or not. Much has been published to refute the claims that American students are underperforming given its diversity and size (e.g., Boe and Shin, 2005) whereas others note that this refusal is based in part by the unique ways in which Americans tend to seek and maintain positive illusions about their children (Ozturk and Debelak, 2008). For a long time, we have learned that when compared to Asian parents, U.S. parents have reported higher levels of satisfaction with their child's school and teachers despite significantly lower levels of performance (Stevenson et al., 1993) and have also been found to articulate a sense that their "kids are doing all right" whereas other cultures do not (e.g., Elliott et al., 2001).

Among those who concede that American students underperform, given its international status as a super power and highly advanced economy, the lessons that the United States can learn from international comparisons plagues U.S. policymakers. However, many have identified that some of the sources of underperformance are culturally bound and hard to change with new governmental policies. For example, certain languages can provide more or less advantage for its speakers when referring to and using numbers. English language speakers can be seen to lack an advantage with regard to mathematical skills compared to Chinese language speakers. Cross-cultural research on the automatic processing of numbers has demonstrated the pronunciation of numbers in Chinese language (as well as other East Asian languages that use Chinese characters) helps facilitate its speakers to say numbers faster than English speakers and process numbers more efficiently (e.g., Chen and Stevenson, 1988). Additionally, the ten-based number system in Chinese helps to promote earlier number learning and faster computation.

PISA notes in detail many of the other culturally rooted sources of American underperformance in the "Yes" selection. American cultural values are among the first factors cited as a barrier to student achievement in general. Although PISA in the "Yes" selection assumes that these values can be changed because of our rhetoric emphasizing the importance of educational issues, the reality is that the American preference for entertainment, sports, and free play in daily life is hard for homework to compete with fairly. Comparing life in the rest of the world to life in the United States leaves one to wonder why such international comparisons are useful anyway. Unlike the amount of pressure and competition within countries like Korea and China, American youth enjoy societal conditions that are perceived to offer greater permeability in adulthood (Heckhausen and Chang, 2009). Thus, most will ignore international comparisons by citing that the societal context is simply different. Of course U.S. companies are already prowling the world for the most qualified and work-oriented persons and not limiting themselves to the U.S. population. U.S. businesses are even relocating headquarters outside of the United States to take advantage of the global labor market of highly skilled workers.

The question debated in this issue can require you, as a student of education, to consider and weigh the importance of global competition and the relevance of work-related outcomes but as a student of (cross-cultural) psychology, it should also get you to think about the need to refer to the different social contexts of other nations that are conducive to the academic development of children. In considering these issues, Anna Dall argues in the "No" selection that the results of tests that measure reading, math, and science skills are counterproductive to efforts of building a world-class educational system because it is akin to comparing apples to oranges. In other words, comparison between the United States and other top-performing countries, such as China, Hong Kong, and Korea, is counterproductive because the focus on test results in education has even been criticized within these countries. PISA, on the other hand, believes that cross-national comparisons are insightful for Americans because the differences seen around the world in producing world-class students should convince us that we also have the ability to develop a commitment to education . . . if we *want* to.

## References

E. E. Boe and S. Shin, "Is the United States Really Losing the International Horse Race in Academic Achievement?" *Phi Delta Kappan* (86, 2005).

C. Chen and H. W. Stevenson, "Cross-Linguistic Differences in Digit Span of Preschool Children," *Journal of Experimental Child Psychology* (vol. 46, 1988).

J. G. Elliott, N. R. Hufton, L. Illushin, and W. Willis, "'The Kids Are Doing All Right': Differences in Parental Satisfaction, Expectation and Attribution in St. Petersburg, Sunderland and Kentucky," *Cambridge Journal of Education* (vol. 31, 2002).

J. Heckhausen and E. S. Chang, "How Ambition Can Help Overcome Social Inequality in the Transition to Adulthood," *Research on Human Development* (vol. 6, 2009).

M. A. Ozturk and C. Debelak, "The Unique American Vision of Childhood," *International Review of Education* (vol. 54, 2008).

OECD, *PISA 2012 Results in Focus: What 15-Year-Olds Know and What They Can Do with What They Know* (2014). Available online at www.oecd.org/pisa /keyfindings/pisa-2012-results-overview.pdf

H. W. Stevenson, C. Chen, and S. Y. Lee, "Mathematics Achievement of Chinese, Japanese, and American Children: Ten Years Later," *Science* (vol. 259, 1993).

# YES

## Learning from High-Performing Education Systems

### Developing a Commitment to Education and a Conviction that All Students Can Achieve at High Levels

Many nations declare that they are committed to children and that education is important. The test comes when these commitments are weighed against others. How do they pay teachers compared to the way they pay others with the same level of education? How are education credentials weighed against other qualifications when people are being considered for jobs? Would you want your child to be a teacher? How much attention do the media pay to schools and schooling? When it comes down to it, which matters more, a community's standing in the sports leagues or its standing in the student academic achievement league tables? Are parents more likely to encourage their children to study longer and harder or to want them to spend more time with their friends or playing sports?

In the countries with the highest performance, teachers are typically paid better relative to others, education credentials are valued more, and a higher share of educational spending is devoted to instructional services than is the case in the United States, where parents may not encourage their children to become school teachers if they think they have a chance of becoming attorneys, engineers, doctors or architects. The value placed on education is likely to influence the choices that students make about whether to study or head down to the ball field or hang out with their friends on the corner, and, later, whether the most capable students decide on school teaching, or something with higher social status, as a career. It has an effect on the willingness of the public to honour the views of professional educators or dismiss them.

Some will say that these are cultural matters and not amenable to change, but the preceding chapters suggest that in countries with little in the way of natural resources,

such as Finland, Singapore and Japan, education appears to have a high status at least in part because the public at large has understood that the country must live by its wits and its wits depend on the quality of education. That is, the value that a country places on education depends in part on a country's view of how human capital fits into the way it makes its living. Placing a high value on education may be an underlying condition for building a world-class education system, and it may be that most countries that have not had to live by their wits in the past will not succeed unless their political leaders explain why, though they might not have had to live by their wits in the past, they must do so now.

But placing a high value on education will get a country only so far if the teachers, parents and citizens of that country believe that only some subset of the nation's children can or need to achieve high standards. This volume shows a distribution of attitudes on this point. Brazil inherited a situation in which the people who gained control of it when it was colonised assumed that the people they conquered and the people they enslaved had so little to offer they were not worth educating. Germany is a country in which it was widely assumed until recently that the children of working-class people would themselves get working-class jobs and would not profit from the curriculum offered by the *Gymnasium*. PISA shows these attitudes to be mirrored in the perception of students about their own educational future. While in Germany only a quarter of 15-year-olds in PISA said that they expect to go on to university, fewer than those who actually will, in Japan and Korea, 9 out of 10 students said they expected to do so. The results of these differences can also be seen in the distribution of student performance within each of these countries and in the impact that socio-economic background has on learning.

Furthermore, the writings of some educational psychologists in the United States, from Terman on, have

---

fostered a widespread notion that student achievement is mainly a product of inherited intelligence, not hard work. This is also mirrored in results from the Third International Mathematics and Science Study, where a significant share of American students reported that they needed good luck rather than hard work to do well in mathematics or science, a characteristic that was consistently negatively related to performance. Teachers may feel guilty pressing students who they perceive to be less capable to achieve at higher levels because they think it unfair to the student to do so. Their goal is then likely to enable each student to achieve up to the mean of students in their classrooms rather than, as in Finland, Singapore or Shanghai-China, to achieve high universal standards. A comparison between school marks and performance of American students in PISA also suggests that teachers often expect less of students from lower socio-economic backgrounds even if the students show similar levels of achievement. And those students and their parents may expect less, too. This is a heavy burden for the American education system to bear, and it is unlikely that the United States will achieve performance parity with the best-performing countries until it, too, believes, or behaves as if it believes, that, with enough effort and support, all children can achieve at very high levels.

In contrast, in Finland, Japan, Singapore, Shanghai-China and Hong Kong-China, parents, teachers and the public at large tend to share the belief that all students are capable of achieving high standards and need to do so. This volume provides a wealth of instructive examples for how public policy can support the achievement of universal high standards. One of the most interesting patterns observed among some of the highest-performing countries was the gradual move, in many of them, from a system in which students were streamed into different types of secondary schools, with curricula set to very different levels of cognitive demand, to a system in which all students now go to secondary schools with curricula set to much the same high level of cognitive demand. Those countries did not accomplish this transition by taking the average of the previous levels of cognitive demand and setting the new standards to that level. Instead, they "levelled up," requiring all students to meet the standards that they formerly expected only their elite students to meet. In these top-performing education systems, all students are now expected to perform at the levels formerly thought possible only for their elites.

Recognising that the road to dropping out of high schools starts early, Ontario created the "Student Success Initiative" in high schools. Rather than sending out a team from the ministry, they gave the districts money to hire a Student Success leader to co-ordinate efforts in their district. The ministry also gave money for the district leaders to meet and share strategies. Again, each high school was given support to hire a provincially-funded Student Success teacher and was required to create a Student Success team to track early indicators of academic struggles and design appropriate interventions. The outcomes of this work have changed Ontario's system profoundly, and within a few years the high school graduation rate increased from 68 to 79 percent.

With a different institutional setup, Finland's special teachers fulfil a similar role of early diagnosis and support, working closely with classroom teachers to identify students in need of extra help, and then working individually or in small groups with struggling students to provide the extra help and support they need to keep up with their classmates. It is not left solely to the discretion of the regular classroom teacher to identify a problem and alert the special teacher; every comprehensive school has a "pupils' multi-professional care group" that meets at least twice a month for two hours, and which consists of the principal, the special teacher, the school nurse, the school psychologist, a social worker, and the teachers whose students are being discussed. The parents of any child being discussed are contacted prior to the meeting and are sometimes asked to be present.

Underpinning the entire Singaporean education system is the belief—for students of all ethnic backgrounds and all ranges of ability—that education is the route to advancement and that hard work and effort, not inherited intelligence, is the key to success in school. Singapore, too, had a system of streaming in its elementary schools that it later moderated as it raised its standards. And Singapore uses a wide range of strategies to make sure that student difficulties are diagnosed early and that students who are even just beginning to fall behind are immediately diagnosed properly and given whatever help is needed to get them back on track as quickly as possible. The success of the government's economic and educational policies has brought about immense social mobility that has created a shared sense of national mission and made cultural support for education a near-universal value.

In all these education systems, universal high expectations are not a mantra but a reality and students who start to fall behind are identified quickly, their problem is promptly and accurately diagnosed and the appropriate course of action is quickly taken. Inevitably, this means that some students get more resources than others because the needs of some students are greater; but it is the students with the greatest needs who get the most resources, for that reason.

It has taken most countries time to get from a belief that only a few students can achieve to the point where most educators embrace the proposition that all can do so. It takes a concerted, multifaceted programme of policy making, capacity building and the development of proof points to get to the point at which most educators believe it can be done. But no education system included in this study has managed to achieve sustained high performance without developing a system that is premised, in detail, on the proposition that it is possible for all students to achieve at high levels and necessary that they do so. The importance of recent developments in American federal education policy to set the clear expectation that all students should be taught to the same standards and held to the same expectations cannot be overestimated. The No Child Left Behind Act of 2001 required all schools to make progress towards a state-determined standard of "proficiency" for all students, and the Obama administration has supported the states in their efforts to put in place more rigorous state standards linked to college and career readiness, with an increased focus on the instructional systems and teacher support necessary to ensure that all students are held and taught to these same expectations. The challenge ahead will be to back those expectations up with the kinds of student, parent and school support systems that characterise today's most advanced education systems.

## Establishing Ambitious, Focused and Coherent Education Standards that Are Shared across the System and Aligned with High-Stakes Gateways and Instructional Systems

Fifteen-year-olds in the United States often rate themselves comparatively highly in academic performance in PISA, even if they did not do well comparatively. In part, that may be due to culture, but one interpretation is also that students are being commended for work that would not be acceptable in high-performing education systems. The results from PISA suggest that, across OECD countries, schools and countries where students work in a climate characterised by high performance expectations and the readiness to invest effort, good teacher-student relations, and high teacher morale tend to achieve better results.

One trend across countries over recent years has been for countries to articulate the expectations that societies have in relation to learning outcomes and to translate these expectations into educational goals and standards. All of the high-performing countries profiled in this volume have developed world-class academic standards for their students and their existence tends to be a consistent predictor for the overall performance of education systems. The approaches to standard-setting in OECD countries range from defining broad educational goals up to formulating concise performance expectations in well-defined subject areas. Whatever the approach, such standards shape high-performing education systems by establishing rigorous, focused and coherent content at all grade levels; reducing overlap in curricula across grades; reducing variation in implemented curricula across classrooms; facilitating co-ordination of various policy drivers, ranging from curricula to teacher training; and reducing inequity in curricula across socio-economic groups.

The establishment, by states, of "common core standards" in the United States follows a similar line of reasoning, with the potential to address the current problem of widely discrepant state standards and assessment cut scores that have led to non-comparable results. These non-comparable standards often mean that a school's fate depends more than anything else on in what state the school is located. More important, students across the United States are left on an unequal footing as to how well they are prepared to compete in the United States labour market.

---

**THE OECD** (Organization for Economic Cooperation and Development) is a forum where the governments of 34 democracies and more than 70 partner countries work together to promote economic growth, prosperity, and sustainable development. The OECD conducts the PISA, the Programme for International Student Assessment, which was started in 1997.

Anna Dall

 **NO**

# "Is PISA Counter-Productive to Building Successful Educational Systems?"

## Introduction[1]

Globalisation is a complex concept that has become a household term, uncritically used by economists, politicians, journalists, researchers as well as the general public to explain almost anything and everything. However, for some, globalisation carries the threat of a homogenised world where nations and cultures are neutralised, and for others the hope for a more inclusive and fair world order. It can bring people together in peace and harmony and it can lead to encounters such as 9/11 and AIDS (Ball, 1998; Anleu, 1999; Hirst and Thompson, 1999; World Bank, 2002; Raab et al., 2008). Few would refute though that it is a very real phenomenon affecting economic, political and cultural institutions as well as people's identity, expectations and aspirations. It is even depicted as a natural and inevitable progression of societal development; TINA (There Is No Alternative) has become the established consensus (Sidhu and Matthews, 2005; Rizvi and Lingard, 2010).

When the actual term "globalisation" was coined in the 1980s it initially referred to the economic domain, but quickly came to be applied also in the political and cultural fields, key features being borderless networking by supranational companies and organisations in the promotion of global competition. Highly industrialised countries have moved into high knowledge, high tech production areas, which demand highly skilled workers. At the same time, they aim at keeping social costs down for increased cost efficiency with the intention of attracting international investment (see Ball, 1998; Green, 1999; Henry et al., 1999; Rizvi and Lingard, 2000, 2010; Zambeta, 2005; Spring, 2008). In this market economy, services and ideas are central, and a country's long-term economic growth and prosperity are perceived to depend on how well the education system is aligned with market demands, and how well it is preparing citizens for future study and work in a globalised economy. Competitiveness in the global economy has led to competition in the educational area, since one is assumed to be based on the other. Education has become a commodity and is at present more closely tied to the economic system than ever before (Reynolds et al., 2002; Cheung and Chan 2009; Little and Green, 2009).

According to Carnoy and Rhoten (2002), education is affected by globalisation by way of decentralisation and privatisation, choice and accountability. Efficiency has come to characterise the new epistemology and its focus on performance and achievement outcomes has led to the emergence of a virtual testing culture, both on a national and an international scale. Of major importance is then, of course, who constructs these tests and sets the standards (Ball, 1998; Anleu, 1999; Hirst and Thompson, 1999; World Bank, 2002; Raab et al., 2008).

Since the initiation of the Program for International Student Assessment (PISA) in 2000, the Organisation for Economic Co-operation and Development (OECD) has become a major authority on the quality of educational systems, and proffered policy recommendations have a considerable impact on national education policies (Grek, 2009).

## The PISA Framework

### The Aims:

PISA is an ambitious, collaborative and innovative project conducted by countries consenting to compare the outcomes of their educational systems in an internationally accepted common framework. The surveys are conducted three-yearly, with the focus alternating between reading literacy, mathematical and scientific literacy (in 2003 problem solving was also included), which means that performance can be measured at a certain point in time and also compared over time. Great attention is paid to the construction of tests, so that they are culturally and socially unbiased, all test items are unanimously agreed upon and translation processes are rigorous. For each cycle, an increasing number of nations have taken part, and at present 70 countries are involved (McGaw, 2008; Schleicher, 2009).

PISA is based on the premise that a nation's economic growth is largely dependent on the quality of its human capital; thus PISA can be seen as an expression of globalisation of education. The aim of PISA is to define educational goals relevant for adults in the knowledge society, to set standards and to evaluate how well education systems perform in comparison to each other, with a view to isolating factors that contribute to, or hinder, high achievement outcomes and gender and social equity (OECD, 2001; 2004).

The innovative factor in the PISA surveys is that students are assessed not against their national school curricula but against "how well young adults near the end of compulsory schooling are prepared to meet the challenges of today's knowledge societies and the challenges of adult life in the real world" (OECD, 2001; Kirsch *et al.*, 2002). Thus PISA should reflect what skills and knowledge participating countries deem are required for national and individual success in the global knowledge society, and how education systems can promote these goals in the most effective way.

## Effective Education Systems in PISA Terms

What then characterises an effective education system? Globalised education efficiency has come to be evaluated by performance related to cost. Performance in turn is assessed by testing students against various sets of measurable goals. Thus quantification now defines progress in education. If a variable cannot be measured, no progress can be evidenced. Education takes on an instrumental dimension defined by cognitive abilities that can easily be put to the test (Moutsios, 2010; Rizvi and Lingard, 2010). PISA can be seen as an expression of this trend. In PISA terms, the qualities that prepare students to meet the challenges of today's knowledge societies and the challenges of adult life in the real world are clearly competency in reading, mathematical and scientific literacy. Consequently, effective education systems are defined by how well students are performing in the PISA surveys. Few would argue that high levels of proficiency in these key subjects are essential for the growth of individuals as well as nations. Some would certainly argue though that they merit the sole focus to the detriment of higher order skills. Were the goals different, an effective education system would be different.

## The Testing Culture

Advocates of the testing culture claim that testing is necessary for transparent accountability (Bita, 2009). While formative testing conducted by the individual teacher can be beneficial it has not been shown that frequent, summative, standardised testing improves performance; rather, the opposite. It has been linked to an increase in student drop out, student and teacher cheating and teachers leaving the profession (Sahlberg, 2007; Mitchell *et al.*, 2009; Peters and Oliver, 2009). It creates a fear of failing in teachers and students, and effectively breeds a dislike of schools and learning, thus counteracting the goal of lifelong learning and a learning society promoted by PISA, and others as a cornerstone for the knowledge society (Sahlberg, 2007; Mitchell *et al.*, 2009; Peters and Oliver, 2009). It should also be considered that test results show what students have gained at a superficial level, but not necessarily learned and understood at an abstract level. Finally, tests do not automatically show the efficacy of the educational system—performance can be a result of activities outside of school, such as private tutoring (Sahlberg, 2007).

History is again repeating itself. Welch (1998) relates that as long ago as the 1860s it was suggested that UK schools should be run like businesses and be accountable for results. Thus standards were set for what should be attained by the students, who had to attend school 200 times per year before the test could be taken. Teachers' pay was linked to student attendance and their passing the exams, which led to examples of sick children being forced to school, cheating, a narrowing of the curriculum taught, cramming and rote learning—already then teachers were teaching to the test.

## Is the PISA Model What Is Needed for Future Education?

The view of education and what it means to be educated and to learn have changed. While previously having been a positive in itself, educational value is today measured by what competencies can benefit the individual and the society in the global competition. A different kind of person is sought to be schooled: a person skilled in communication (mother tongue), maths, science, problem solving; a person who is also information literate, globally minded, multilingual, interculturally versed, mobile, adaptable, level headed in crisis, flexible, creative with proper work attitudes and interpersonal skills; and a lifelong learner (Ball, 1998; Spring, 2008; Cheung and Chan, 2009; Rizvi and Lingard, 2010). Thus a paradigm shift in education is required. The linear and static view developed in the industrial era needs to be replaced by meta-cognitive and fluid processes that foster ingenuity and entrepreneurship. The knowledge economy values leadership and team-work. Therefore academic, cognitive intelligence has to share the focus with emotional intelligence of intra-personal and inter-personal skills. A learning society is called for where life-long learning is part of life. Thus students need to develop a love of learning. This can only occur in a classroom where teachers and students feel safe, supported, encouraged to take risks and prepared to make mistakes, where attention is paid to the individual's inherent talents (Sahlberg, 2006; Sahlberg and Oldroyd, 2010).

In Bill Gates' words: "training the workforce of tomorrow with the high schools of today is like trying to teach kids about today's computers on a 50-year-old mainframe. It is the wrong tool for the times" (cited in Sahlberg, 2006).

However, such higher order processes are features that are not easily measured in standardised tests and thus do not fit into the current education efficiency model of transparent accountability and the PISA surveys, which highlights a paradox: a range of higher order processes are seen to be needed for individuals and nations to prosper in the global knowledge society; yet at the same time, PISA is taking on ever increasing importance in evaluating an ever increasing number of education systems. Thus countries that obtain the highest achievement outcomes in the PISA surveys are judged to have world class education systems with students ready to meet real life challenges in the future global world. This PISA governance is leading to an ever increasing consensus that curricula need to be focused (narrowed) and that increased standardised testing is necessary to monitor performance outcomes.

## Narrowed Curricula and the Purpose of Schooling

The pursuit of a more competitive education system and improved PISA rankings motivate many countries to narrow and standardise curricula, a process that some claim is also standardising the students, as not enough attention can be paid to individual talents and potential, with the effect that many students feel they do not fit, and leave school as soon as they can. Standardisation, it is claimed, destroys creativity and system innovation (Peters and Oliver, 2009; Sahlberg and Oldroyd, 2010).

The PISA focus on "real life" skills such as literacy and numeracy promotes a more pragmatic view of the value of education to the exclusion of educational aims concerning, for example, democratic participation, moral and aesthetic development (Sahlberg, 2006; Grek, 2009; Dall, 2010). The

above mentioned higher order skills are commonly referred to as desirable in education for the knowledge economy, but are excluded as they escape quantification.

This leads to the question of what constitutes the main purpose of schooling. Educational goals are typically identified in national steering documents, and in most countries these documents strongly emphasise the students' personal, physical, mental and social development, naming academic performance as only one of a range of goals, but this may well be regarded as politically correct rhetoric if classroom practices are predominantly concerned with academic performance, to better meet testing requirements. If successful schooling does equal fostering independent, socially skilled individuals who can actively participate in, and contribute to a democratic society, studies such as the international civics survey (Torney-Purta *et al.*, 2001) should not go unnoticed and be virtually generally unknown (Dall, 2010).

If effective education systems were measured against these broad national steering documents instead of the narrow PISA focus, the world class education systems thought worthy of being emulated would look totally different.

## The Exception—A Model?

PISA top performers are typically not top performers in the global economy, even though PISA is based on this presumed correlation (OECD, 2001; 2003). However, there is one exception—Finland has continuously, since the PISA inception in 2000, been an overall PISA top achiever and concurrently a top ranked competitive economy (Sahlberg, 2006).

Paradoxically, the Finns do not embrace standardised testing based on competition between individuals and groups and thus favour more quantifiable knowledge and skills. Instead, the Finns adhere to the "culture of trust." Finnish education policies are based on deeply rooted values of equity and equality and school is seen as a place where all students should be able to develop their unique talents, in all areas, to the greatest potential, in an inclusive, holistic and caring school culture. Basically all schools are state funded. There is no streaming or ability tracking. Finnish teachers are rigorously selected and highly educated as all must hold a Masters degree, which means that a primary school teacher studies for a minimum of five years and a subject teacher between six and seven years. Therefore, teachers are highly valued and respected in society, and consequently trusted not only to be able to educate children in an optimal way (in cooperation with principals, parents and the local community), but also to autonomously evaluate and assess their learning without any national, standardised tests. Students are assessed in relation to their individual progress, and extra support is at the ready when needed (Aho *et al.*, 2006; Sahlberg, 2007; Peters and Oliver, 2009; Simola *et al.*, 2009). This "intelligent accountability" may seem unsettling to staunch believers in "transparent accountability." However, the Finns believe this system generates not only higher performance, but also broader and more genuine learning outcomes. The PISA results seem to validate this confidence as the Finnish students obtain high average results combined with small standard deviation, which means that no matter what school the child attends s/he is guaranteed a quality education (OECD, 2004; Aho, *et al.*, 2006; Sahlberg, 2007).

## Conclusion

Is PISA counter-productive to building successful educational systems? The response is open. Education opens the door to tomorrow's society. Today we are faced with the choices.

The main trend at present seems to be to drive down the broad, reductionist PISA highway flanked by narrowed curricula, quantified knowledge and skills easily measured by high-stakes standardised testing, keeping our fingers crossed that what can be learnt on the old mainframe will be enough for our future needs.

The Finland road promises more: signs point to a high performing, holistic and inclusive education culture where equity and quality are combined; knowledge is not quantified for the simplicity of it but higher order processes are alive and well; academic proficiency is valued equally with, for example, creative, aesthetic, athletic, moral and democratic outcomes. However, this road is also intimidating. There is no quick and easy way to get to the destination, and there is the chance of getting lost and never getting there. But no doubt this is the far better alternative.

## References

Aho, E., Pitkänen, K. & Sahlberg, P. 2006 *Policy Development and Reform Principles of Basic and Secondary Education in Finland since 1968*, World Bank, Washington DC.

Anleu, S. R. 1999 'Sociologists confront human rights the problem of universalism', *Journal of Sociology,* 352: 198–212.

Ball, S. J. 1998 'Big Policies/Small World an introduction to international perspectives in education policy', *Comparative Education,* 342: 119–130.

Bita, N. 2009 'Testing foes want happy, uneducated kids Gillard', *The Australian,* 13 November 2009. Retrieved from http://www.theaustralian.com.au/news/nation/testing-foes-want-happy-uneducated-kids-gillard/story-e6frg6nf-1225797124314

Carnoy, M. & Rhoten, D. 2002 'What Does Globalization Mean for Educational Change? A Comparative Approach', *Comparative Education Review,* 461: 1–9.

Cheung, H. & Chan, A. 2009 'Education and competitive economy how do cultural dimensions fit in?' *Higher Education,* 595: 525–541.

Dall, A. 2010 'PISA and reading literacy—comparing apples and oranges?' Paper presented at the 23rd International Congress for School Effectiveness and Improvement Conference, ICSEI 2010.

Green, A. 1999 'Education and globalization in Europe and East Asia convergent and divergent trends', *Journal of Education Policy,* 141: 55–71.

Grek, S. 2009 'Governing by numbers the PISA "effect" in Europe', *Journal of Education Policy,* 241: 23–37.

Henry, M. Lingard, B., Rizvi, F. & Taylor, S. 1999 'Working with/against globalization in education', *Journal of Education Policy,* 141: 85–97.

Hirst, P. & Thompson, G. 1999 *Globalization in Question,* 2nd ed., Polity Press, Cambridge.

Kirsch, I. de Jong, J. Lafontaine, D., McQueen, J., Mendelovits, J. & Monseur, C. 2002 *Reading for Change. Performance and Engagement across Countries. Results from PISA 2000,* OECD, Paris.

Little, A. & Green, A. 2009 'Successful globalisation, education and sustainable development', *International Journal of Educational Development,* 292: 166–174.

McGaw, B. 2008 'The role of the OECD in international comparative studies of achievement', *Assessment in Education Principles, Policy & Practice,* 153: 223–243.

Mitchell, D. Gerwin, D. Schuberth, E. Mancini, M. & Hofrichter, H. 2009 'Assessment without High-Stakes Testing Protecting Childhood and the Purpose of School', *Independent Teacher,* 62. Retrieved from http://www.whywaldorfworks.org/03_NewsEvents/documents/AlternativeAssessment.pdf

Moutsios, S. 2010 'Power, politics and transnational policy-making in education', *Globalisation, Societies and Education,* 81: 121–141.

OECD 2001 *Knowledge and Skills for Life First Results from the OECD Programme for International Student Assessment PISA 2000,* OECD, Paris.

OECD 2004 *Learning for Tomorrow's World, first results from PISA 2003*, OECD, Paris.

Peters, S. & Oliver, L. 2009 'Achieving quality and equity through inclusive education in an era of high-stakes testing', *Prospects*, 393: 265–279.

Raab, M. Ruland, M., Schonberger, B., Blossfeld, H.-P., Hofacker, D., Buchholz, S., et al. 2008 'Global Index A Sociological Approach to Globalization Measurement', *International Sociology*, 234: 596–631.

Reynolds, D. Stringfield, S. Teddlie, C. & Creemers, B. 2002 'The intellectual and policy context' in D. Reynolds, B. Creemers, S. Stringfield, C. Teddlie & G. Schaffer (eds.), World Class Schools. *International Perspectives on School Effectiveness*, Routledge Falmer, London.

Rizvi, F. & Lingard, B. 2000 'Globalization and Education Complexities and Contingencies', *Educational Theory*, 504: 419.

Rizvi, F. & Lingard, B. 2010 Globalizing *Education Policy*, Routledge, London.

Sahlberg, P. 2006 'Education Reform for Raising Economic Competitiveness', *Journal of Educational Change*, 74: 259-287.

Sahlberg, P. 2007 'Education Policies for raising Student Learning; The Finnish Approach', *Journal of Education Policy*, 222: 147-171.

Sahlberg, P. & Oldroyd, D. 2010 'Pedagogy for Economic Competitiveness and Sustainable Development', *European Journal of Education*, 452: 280–299.

Schleicher, A. 2009 'Securing quality and equity in education lessons from PISA', *Prospects*, 393: 251–263.

Sidhu, R. & Matthews, J. M. 2005 'International Education For What? Under What Conditions? The Global Schoolhouse Project', *Social Alternatives*, 244: 6–12.

Simola, H. Rinne, R. Varjo, J. Pitkänen, H. & Kauko, J. 2009 'Quality assurance and evaluation (QAE) in Finnish compulsory schooling—a national model or just unintended effects of radical decentralisation?' *Journal of Education Policy*, 242: 163–178.

Spring, J. 2008 'Research on Globalization and Education', *Review of Educational Research*, 782: 330–363.

Torney-Purta, J. Lehmann, R. Oswald, H. & Schulz, W. 2001 *Citizenship and Education in Twenty-eight Countries Civic Knowledge and Engagement at Age Fourteen*, The International Association for the Evaluation of Educational Achievement, Amsterdam.

Welch, A. R. 1998 'The Cult of Efficiency in Education. Comparative reflections on the reality and the rhetoric', *Comparative Education*, 342: 157–175.

World Bank 2002 Globalization, *Growth, and Poverty Building an Incusive World Economy. A World Bank Policy Research Report*, World Bank, New York.

Zambeta, E. 2005 'The survival of nationalism in a globalized system' in D. Coulby & E. Zambeta (eds) *World Yearbook of Education 2005. Globalization and nationalism in education*, RoutledgeFalmer, London: 59–88.

## Endnote

1. This article is based on a submitted thesis entitled "A crossnational, comparative study of cultural factors underpinning 15-year-old students' performance in reading literacy in Finland, Sweden, Australia and Indonesia." This article is a shortened version of a paper presented at the XVII World Congress of Sociology in Gothenburg, Sweden in 2010. I would like to thank the two anonymous peer reviewers for their valuable comments.

## Author

Anna Dall, BSc. MA, originates from Sweden, where she worked as a senior officer in educational administration, a principal, and also started and ran an international business school. She now lives on the Sunshine Coast and has recently submitted her doctoral thesis at the University of the Sunshine Coast. Anna is a member of the Australian Association for Research in Education, AARE, and the International Sociological Association, ISA.

. . .

ANNA DALL is currently at Satya Wacan Christian University in Indonesia. She is from Sweden, where she worked as a senior officer in educational administration, a principal, and a founder of a business school.

# EXPLORING THE ISSUE

## Are International Comparisons Helpful?

### Critical Thinking and Reflection

1. What lessons identified by PISA are reasonable to institute now?
2. Do Americans care about the quality of their schools?
3. Is there a relation between the test performance of a country and its economic security in the future?
4. Why are many Asian students coming to America for college and university?

### Is There Common Ground?

This debate is able to take place because both sides can acknowledge the results that U.S. students are not the top performers in the world and can even agree (perhaps after some nudging of the "No" side) that U.S. students are actually underperformers given our status as a leader on the world stage. In assessing the usefulness of these results, Anna Dall articulates the feeling of many in this country, which is that international comparisons are uninformative in efforts to build a better system because we begin to teach to the test and value test performance over other educational values. However, what many on the "No" side fail to recognize is that these results are not intended to do that.

As PISA pointed out, what these results really mean is that a comparison between the United States and top-performing countries reveals very interesting insights about the United States. First, top-performing countries pay their teachers more and spend more on instructional costs than the United States (e.g., teachers are among the lowest prestigious jobs in this country and very little is invested in assessment). Although not part of the selection published in this issue, other sections of this PISA publication note that our educational assessments lack quality (i.e., we use multiple choice questions to assess student performance whereas top-performing countries use open-ended qualitative assessments). Second, top-performing countries expect that all students can achieve high standards regardless of social background. For example, those who refute that the United States is not doing well in international comparisons because we have a more diverse student body can be seen to have also assumed that poor and disadvantaged students are not *able* to do well. The implied conclusion is that America does not *really* care about its educational system because if it did, it would respect the job of teaching and expect much more from its children than it does currently. As can be seen around the world, human children can rise to the challenges of education.

Ultimately, the differing rates of student achievement found on international comparisons are valuable and interesting because human groups around the world are not thought to be more or less intelligent from one another. Thus, when some groups flourish whereas others do not, a comparison of the social conditions is deemed helpful to the extent that it allows us to question our own culture. However, these tests and comparisons don't necessarily translate into an accurate assessment of high schools around the world. Much sociological and psychological research has indicated that parents and their social and economic resources have greater influence on student achievement. Thus, the pressure on the educational system to "do something" is unfair if it is not coupled with pressure on parents and governments. It is also a stretch to interpret the lower test performance of U.S. students as a predictor of future economic insecurity. Any research psychologist will tell you that no test is perfect and very few studies in education can be used to draw causal inferences.

### Additional Resources

M. Carnoy and R. Rothstein, "What International Test Scores Tell Us," *Society* (vol. 52, 2015).

D. C. Geary, "International Differences in Mathematical Achievement: Their Nature, Causes, and Consequences," *Current Directions in Psychological Science* (vol. 5, 1996).

S. L. Morgan and E. S. Taylor Poppe, "The Consequences of International Comparisons for Public Support of K-12 Education: Evidence from a National Survey Experiment," *Educational Researcher* (vol. 41, 2012).

H. W. Stevenson, C. Chen, and S. Y. Lee, "Mathematics Achievement of Chinese, Japanese, and American Children: Ten Years Later," *Science* (vol. 259, 1993).

# *Internet References . . .*

**Finnish National Board of Education**

www.oph.fi/english/education_system

**International Data Explorer**

https://nces.ed.gov/surveys/international/ide/

**PISA 2012 Results**

www.oecd.org/pisa/keyfindings/pisa-2012-results.htm

**TIMSS**

https://nces.ed.gov/timss/

Selected, Edited, and with Issue Framing Material by:
Esther S. Chang, *Soka University of America*

# ISSUE

## Do Recent Discoveries About the Brain Have Implications for Classroom Practice?

YES: **Judy Willis**, from "Building a Bridge from Neuroscience to the Classroom," *Phi Delta Kappan* (2008)

NO: **Dan Willingham**, from "When and How Neuroscience Applies to Education," *Phi Delta Kappan* (2008)

---

### Learning Outcomes

---

**After reading this issue, you will be able to:**

- Understand the nature of the questions being asked about the human brain by neuroscientists and the technologies they use to answer those questions.
- Become familiar with examples of the translation of brain science findings into educational practices.
- Understand the potential of brain science to inform educational practice.
- Understand the challenges of translating brain science findings into concrete educational practices.

---

### ISSUE SUMMARY

**YES:** Judy Willis argues that current research on brain function does inform educational practice and she provides some examples from recent brain science findings.

**NO:** Dan Willingham argues that not every finding about how the brain works can or should lead to an accommodation of educational practice.

---

**R**esearch in the brain sciences has proceeded at a rapid pace since the 1970s, due in large measure to the advent of some amazing new technologies, including positron emission tomography (PET), single photon emission computed tomography (SPECT), magnetic resonance imaging (MRI), functional magnetic imaging (fMRI), diffusion tensor imaging (DTI), and high-density event-related potentials (HD-ERP). These technologies provide high-resolution images of the human brain, yielding information about not only structural characteristics but also about how the brain functions "online" as an individual processes perceptual information, solves complex problems, or makes responses as simple as a button press or as complex as planning and producing a sentence. Some of these techniques require sedation, exposure to radiation, and injections and are thus of limited utility with young children. Other techniques, however, are noninvasive, typically requiring

only that the individual whose brain is being "imaged" sit motionless in a special apparatus while performing the cognitive task being studied. Moreover, many of these technologies can be contextualized as games or as involving pretend play, which means that many of these techniques can provide a window into the brains of even very young children.

A few of the findings that have captured the attention of educators (not to mention the news media) in recent years follow:

1. In contrast to what was believed only a few years ago, the structure and function of the human brain is not fixed at birth. It now appears that the brain undergoes dramatic changes in connectedness during infancy. The many neurons (nerve cells) in the baby's brain establish increasing information-exchanging links with each

other. The number of connections, or synapses, increases more than 20 times during the first few months of life.

2. The timing of synaptic development varies across different parts of the human brain, which may account in part for the different behavioral capabilities of children at different ages. For example, at 18 to 24 months, a dramatic increase in synaptic density and changes in the metabolic activity of the brain may help to produce the burst in vocabulary learning normally seen at this time.

3. At the same time that synaptic growth is providing the foundation for new skills and capabilities, it is closing off other avenues of learning. For example, there is evidence that early in infancy neurons in the auditory cortex are responsive to a range of speech sounds. As the infant gains exposure to his or her native language, however, neurons become more specialized, responding only to specific, frequently heard sounds, which leaves them "unresponsive" to unfamiliar speech sounds, such as those included in other languages. This seems to occur by 12 months of age.

4. There is evidence that brain regions that are normally responsible for one function can assume other functions depending on the experiences available to the individual. For example, portions of the temporal lobe that are responsive to sound in individuals with normal hearing are sensitive to visual stimuli in congenitally deaf individuals.

5. Chronic traumatic experiences during periods of rapid brain growth can lead to greatly elevated levels of stress hormones, which then flood the brain, altering its structure and function, with serious long-lasting consequences for subsequent learning and behavior.

6. Individuals with neurodevelopmental disorders, such as autism, appear to process information differently, activating different parts of their brains compared to typically developing individuals performing the same cognitive tasks.

Educators have enthusiastically embraced findings emerging from work in the brain sciences. After all, our understanding of the brain informs us about learning. Presumably, it should follow that our understanding of the brain will inform us about teaching as well. In the first of the following selections, Judy Willis argues that current research on brain function does inform educational practice and she provides some examples from recent brain science findings. Willis cautions, however, that we are truly in the infancy of brain science and the "hard facts" are still scarce. In the second selection, Dan Willingham argues that not every finding about how the brain works can or should lead to an accommodation of educational practice. Morever, Willingham argues that some of the ways in which brain science is conducted, while sensible for learning about the brain and the scientific questions of interest, actually obscure or mislead about the importance of the findings for the classroom.

**Judy Willis**

# Building a Bridge from Neuroscience to the Classroom

*Knowledge of the underlying science, Dr. Willis argues, will enable educators to make good use of all that neuroscientists are learning about our brains, young and old. It is also the best defense against misleading assertions put forth by opportunists.*

**N**euroscience and cognitive science relating to education are hot topics. They receive extensive but simplified coverage in the mass media, and there is a booming business in "brain-booster" books and products, which claim to be based on the research.

Eric Jensen advocates more collaboration among scientists from the full variety of disciplines engaged in brain research. This collaboration, with corresponding evaluations using cognitive and classroom research, can offer educators more coherent knowledge that they can use in teaching. And educators want this knowledge, as shown by a communication I received from Lisa Nimz, a fifth-grade teacher in the Chicago suburb of Skokie, in response to my May 2007 *Kappan* article.

> We know how important it is for relevant research from the scientific community to be shared with and used in the education community. We are anxious for neurological research to become more a part of educators' thinking and wonder how to make it so. There seem to be only a few people in the unique position of being able to understand the research, figure out its implications for the classroom, and use those implications to direct their teaching. We are actively pondering how a sturdy and wide enough bridge can be built between the scientific community and the education community.
>
> There are many obstacles to building such a construct. Reading the primary sources of neurological research can be challenging even for the brightest of us. And even if someone can comprehend these primary sources, there are many highly educated people who don't seem to approach

scientific evidence with the caution and skepticism necessary to make fair judgments about the implications of that evidence. There are also many members of the scientific community and academia who haven't studied pedagogy. We are thankful for books, articles, and presentations that mitigate some of that disconnect.

Ms. Nimz' quandary reflects educators' increasing concern about how to keep up with the exponential growth of the body of information coming from the varied scientific specialties about the structure and function of the brain with regard to learning and memory. Of equal concern is how to interpret the multitude of claims, usually by nonscientists, that the effectiveness of various "brain-based strategies" has been "proven by brain research."

The interdisciplinary collaboration of neuroscientists, molecular geneticists, cellular biologists, cognitive scientists, and education professionals can be the "wide, sturdy bridge" Ms. Nimz seeks to connect scientific knowledge of the human brain to applications of that research in the classroom. But before that bridge is completed, we need to allow some flexibility. In order to help educators make sense of the massive amounts of information, I propose a two-tiered structure in which factual, collaborative brain research is designated as such and educational strategies strongly *suggested* by neuroscientific data are identified as *interpretations* of that research. The resulting structure will change with time because the interpretive tier will become more concrete as initial interpretations are supported or contradicted by subsequent neuroscience.

The first step is to debunk the neuromyths. Even some of the purest, most accurately reported neuroscience research has been misinterpreted. People trying to capitalize on research with their elixirs, books, cure-all learning theories, and curriculum packages have perpetrated much of the damage. Other folks have unintentionally made errors of interpretation when they have been unfairly asked for scientific evidence to support the strategies they have been using successfully for years.

But it is important to understand that some research findings can be applied to education now. For example, a review of neuroplasticity research shows how collaboration across fields, with certain checks and balances, can lead to classroom strategies that can add to teaching success.

Brain research has not yet provided a direct connection between classroom interventions and brain function or structure, but that does not mean it is irrelevant. Its use is akin to the "off-label" uses of medications by doctors. While Food and Drug Administration regulations require that the label information and advertising of a medication indicate the drug's use only for specific, approved conditions, physicians, based on their *knowledge and available current information,* may prescribe a medication for a use not indicated in the approved labeling. In the same way, educators should use their understanding of brain-learning research to evaluate, develop, and use strategies that are neuro-*logical,* based on *knowledge and available current information.*

## Neuromyths

We study history, in part, so that we can learn from the mistakes of the past. Analyzing the errors in interpretation that led to brain-learning myths helps us evaluate the interpretive strengths and limitations of neuroimaging and other current neuroscientific research and avoid misinterpretation.

I go through the research in my fields of neuroscience and education with the goal of finding scientific studies that relate to learning and that adhere to the medical model of limiting the variables and confining interpretation to objective data. Then I seek cognitive testing of the conclusions neuroscientists make from their data. Do the study's data about how the brain responds to a specific input or stimulus correlate with the cognitive test? When I find a valid fit between the neuroscience and the cognitive testing, I go in search of the holy grail: objective evaluation of the effect of the intervention on statistically appropriate numbers of students in their classrooms. To my knowledge, there has not yet been a strategy or intervention that has made it through all three of these filters.

Misinterpreted neuroscientific data have led to beliefs that some people cling to despite objective evidence to the contrary. For example, it has taken more than a decade to debunk the left brain/right brain oversimplification of learning styles, even though neuroimaging studies have, for more than a decade, demonstrated that human cognition is far too complex to be controlled by a single hemisphere. We now know that although parts of the brain are particularly active during certain memory or learning activities, these regions do not work in isolation. There are networks throughout both hemispheres of the brain that constantly communicate, and even these neural networks change in response to genetics and environment throughout our lives.

In the December 1999 *Kappan,* John Bruer reviewed several decades of biological and neuroimaging research and revealed important unconnected dots between laboratory findings and the theories that hitchhiked on the research. For example, Bruer took on the popular assumptions "correlating" synaptic-density growth, high brain metabolism, critical brain-growth periods, and their proposed long-range effects on intelligence and found several weak foundations. He pointed out the flaws in the assumption that critical brain-growth periods of rapid synapse formation are windows of opportunity for instruction geared to those parts of the brain. He reported contradictory research, such as findings that brains build knowledge and store memories with no drop in efficiency long after peak rates of synaptic, axonal, and dendritic growth have leveled off in adolescence.

Bruer also questioned whether increased cortical-glucose metabolism, as measured by PET scans, is direct evidence of rapid growth in synaptic density during the so-called critical periods. This, in turn, called into question the correlations between high metabolic activity measured by neuroimaging and periods of increased potential for learning that were the basis for claims that brain research *proved* that increased environmental stimulation of students during critical brain-growth phases resulted in more learning.

## Neuroplasticity and Pruning

It is important for educators to remember that the absence of a positive correlation between neuroimaging data and environmental stimulation does not mean that stimulating classrooms are not valuable for learning. It is likely that environmental stimulation does influence learning. However, that theory has not yet been proved by brain research. I remain hopeful, as does Bruer, that the indirect evidence from neuroimaging and other neuroscience research has the potential to suggest teaching strategies and environmental stimuli that are valuable for learning. One promising area of ongoing study is neuroplasticity and pruning.

One longtime misconception held that brain growth stops with birth and is followed by a lifetime of brain-cell death. Now we know that, though most of the neurons where information is stored are present at birth, there is lifelong growth of the support and connecting cells that enrich the communication between neurons (axons, dendrites, synapses, glia) and even some brain regions that continue to form new neurons (neurogenesis) throughout life, such as in the dentate nucleus of the hippocampus and the olfactory cortex.[1] Even after the last big spurt of brain growth in early adolescence, neurotrophins (growth-stimulating proteins) appear elevated in the brain regions and networks associated with new learning and memory formation.[2]

Neuroplasticity is the genetically driven overproduction of synapses and the environmentally driven maintenance and pruning of synaptic connections.[3] Once neural networks are formed, it is the brain's plasticity that allows it to reshape and reorganize these networks, at least partly, in response to increased or decreased use of these pathways.[4] After repeated practice, the connections grow stronger, that is, repeated stimulation makes each neuron more likely to trigger the next connected neuron.[5] The most frequently stimulated connections also become thicker with more myelin coating, making them more efficient.[6]

While active cells require blood to bring nourishment and clear away waste, cells that are inactive do not send messages to the circulatory system to send blood. This reduced blood flow means that calcium ions accumulate around the cell and are not washed away. This calcium ion build-up triggers the secretion of the enzyme calpain, which causes cells to self-destruct, in what is called the pruning process.[7] When unused memory circuits break down, the brain becomes more efficient as it no longer metabolically sustains the pruned cells.

As neurological research provides information about various stages of brain maturation through neuroplasticity and pruning, we come full circle to Jean Piaget's theories regarding the developmental stages of the thought processes of children. If neuroplasticity and pruning represent stages of brain maturation, this may be indirect evidence in support of Piaget's theory that, until there is maturation of brain neural networks, children do not have the circuitry to learn specific things or perform certain tasks.[8]

These neuroplasticity findings allow us to consider which strategies and classroom environments promote increased stimulation of memory or strengthening of cognitive neural networks. For example, appealing to a variety of learning styles when we review important instructional information could provide repeated stimulation to multiple neural networks containing this information. Each type of sensory memory is stored in the lobe that receives the input from that sensory system. Visual memory is stored in the occipital lobes, auditory memory is stored in the temporal lobes, and memories of tactile experiences are stored in the parietal lobes. There could be greater potential for activation, restimulation, and strengthening of these networks with practice or review of the information through multi-sensory learning, resulting in increased network efficiency for memory storage and retrieval.

## Off-Label Prescribing

Jensen cautions, "Brain-based education suggests that we not wait 20 years until each of these correlations is proven beyond any possible doubt." The toll of one-size-fits-all education with its teaching to the standardized tests is so high that it calls for a compromise of the pure medical research model. We do need to take some temporary leaps of faith across the parts of the bridge that are not yet sturdy and try interventions before the research is complete.

When a patient has exhausted all the regular treatments for epilepsy or a brain tumor, neurologists try investigative therapies or "off-label" uses of medications. While off-label medications have not completed FDA testing for the condition in question, the physician believes, through experience and knowledge of pharmacology, that the risk is worth taking in order to treat the patient's disease. For students at risk in our schools, we should use a similar strategy, that is, trying new methods even though they are not yet proven.

However, educators need to use these methods prudently. We need to discuss our successes and acknowledge what doesn't work. Our successful strategic interventions may not yet be proven by brain research, but that doesn't mean they are not valuable. Nevertheless, educators need to beware of opportunists who claim that their strategies are proven by brain research.

## Until There Is Hard Evidence

The brain-research evidence for certain instructional strategies continues to increase, but there still is no sturdy bridge between neuroscience and what educators do in the classroom. But educators' knowledge and experience will enable them to use the knowledge gained from brain research in their classrooms. For example, choice, interest-driven investigation, collaboration, intrinsic motivation, and creative problem solving are associated with increased levels of such neurotransmitters as dopamine, as well as the pleasurable state dopamine promotes.[9] Novelty, surprise, and teaching that connects with students' past experiences and personal interests and that is low in threat and high in challenge are instructional strategies that appear to be correlated with increased information passage through the brain's information filters, such as the amygdala and reticular activating system. Lessons in which students are engaged and invested in goals they helped to create have the potential to stimulate and restimulate networks of new memories as students actively process information in the construction of knowledge.[10] These instructional strategies date back to theories developed decades before neuroimaging. But they are consistent with the increasing pool of neuroimaging, behavioral, and developmental psychology.

We can look forward to a time when human brain mapping, correlated with the other areas of neuroscience, will reveal additional brain mechanisms involved in memory and learning to help us define the most successful teaching strategies for the variety of learners we teach. We are likely to have neuroimaging tools to identify presymptomatic students at risk and genetic testing that will isolate the precise genes that predispose children to such conditions as ADHD or the various dyslexias. With these powerful diagnostic tools, cognitive and education professionals will be able to design strategies to provide at-risk children with the interventions needed to strengthen areas of weakness before they enter school and to develop differentiated instruction allowing all learners to achieve to their highest potentials.

University psychology and education departments are already obtaining neuroimaging scanners. This will increase educators' influence on what is studied. Teachers will communicate with researchers about the strategies they find successful, so researchers can investigate what is happening in students' brains when those strategies are used. Researchers will need to make their data accessible to teachers who can develop new strategies that bring the fruits of the research to the students in their classrooms.

With time, collaboration, and greater integration of the neuroscience of learning into schools of education and into professional development, educators who stay on top of the science will play leading roles in designing and implementing curriculum and classroom strategies that are effective and consistent with the discoveries of how the brain learns best.

For now, the most powerful asset we educators have to influence the direction of education policy is our up-to-date knowledge and understanding of the most accurate, collaborative, neuroscientific research. With that knowledge, we can remain vigilant in our scrutiny of any premature or misleading assertions about interventions claimed to be proven by brain research. And we will be ready to create, evaluate, and implement the best, truly brain-based instruction in our classrooms. These will be important

challenges to meet, but the next decade will reward us with extraordinary opportunities. It may not seem like it now, but we are on the brink of the most exciting time in history to be an educator.

# References

1. Peter Eriksson et al., "Neurogenesis in the Adult Human Hippocampus," *Nature Medicine,* vol. 4, 1998, pp. 1313–17.

2. Soo Kyung Kang et al., "Neurogenesis of Rhesus Adipose Stromal Cells," *Journal of Cell Science,* vol. 117, 2004, pp. 4289–90.

3. Dante Cicchetti and W. John Curtis, "The Developing Brain and Neural Plasticity: Implications for Normality, Psychopathology, and Resilience," in Dante Cicchetti and D. J. Cohen, eds., *Developmental Psychopathology: Developmental Neuroscience,* 2nd ed. (New York: Wiley, 2006), p. 11.

4. Jay N. Giedd et al., "Brain Development During Childhood and Adolescence: A Longitudinal MRI Study," *Nature Neuroscience,* vol. 2, 1999, pp. 861–63.

5. Harry Chugani, "Biological Basis of Emotions: Brain Systems and Brain Development," *Pediatrics,* vol. 102, 1998, pp. 1225–29.

6. Nitin Gogtay, "Dynamic Mapping of Human Cortical Development During Childhood Through Early Adulthood," *Proceedings of the National Academy of Sciences,* vol. 101, 2004, pp. 8174–79.

7. Philip Seeman, "Images in Neuroscience: Brain Development, X: Pruning During Development," *American Journal of Psychiatry,* vol. 156, 1999, p. 168.

8. Jean Piaget, "Intellectual Evolution from Adolescence to Adulthood," *Vita Humana,* vol. 15, 1972, pp. 1–12.

9. Panayotics Thanos et al., "The Selective Dopamine Antagonist," *Pharmacology, Biochemistry and Behavior,* vol. 81, 2005, pp. 190–97.

10. Alfie Kohn, "The Cult of Rigor and the Loss of Joy," *Education Week,* 15 September 2004, available at www.alfiekohn.org/articles_subject.htm.

**Judy Willis, MD, MEd,** was a practicing neurologist and more recently an elementary and middle school teacher.

Dan Willingham

 **NO**

# When and How Neuroscience Applies to Education

**I** agree with Eric Jensen on several important points, among them: that neuroscientific data are relevant to educational research, that these data have already proved useful, and that neuroscience alone should not be expected to generate classroom-ready prescriptions. I sharply disagree with him, however, on the prospects for neuroscience to make frequent and important contributions to education.

I set two criteria for a "contribution" to education: the data must tell us something that we did not already know, and that something must hold the promise of helping teachers or students. For example, I expect that most teachers know that students do not learn well if they are hungry or uncomfortably warm. What then does an understanding of the neurobiology of hunger and its effect on cognition add to a teacher's practice?

One might argue that teachers should understand *why* they do what they do, for example, why they ensure that the room is comfortable. I disagree. All of us make use of technologies that we do not understand, and we do so without concern because understanding or ignorance wouldn't change practice. I don't understand what my computer hardware is doing as I type this reply, but if I did, that knowledge would not change how I typed or what I wrote. Thus, while it might be rewarding for a teacher to understand some neurobiology, I argue that education has not moved forward unless that knowledge improves his or her teaching.

So under what conditions do neuroscientific findings improve education? How do we integrate neuroscientific data with educational theory and practice? It's not enough to say that "the brain is intimately involved in and connected with everything educators and students do at school," which is Jensen's premise. That statement is true, but trivially so, because the brain is intimately involved in *anything* related to human affairs. The question is how we leverage what we know about the brain to help us better understand the processes of education. Jensen relies too heavily on his intuition that, because education relies on the brain, knowledge of the brain is *bound* to help.

But knowledge of the brain is not bound to help. This is where the problem of levels of analysis proves vital. Let's set neuroscience aside for a moment and consider how the levels problem plays out in cognitive psychology, using a simple example.

We know that memory is more enduring if you "overlearn" material—that is, continue studying it after you've mastered it.[1] So why not apply that knowledge to the classroom? Why not have students rehearse important facts (for example, multiplication tables) and not quit even when they have mastered them? Any classroom teacher knows that it's not that simple, because continuous practice will be purchased at considerable cost to motivation. So here's the rub: for the sake of simplicity, cognitive psychologists intentionally isolate one component of the mind (e.g., memory or attention) when they study it. But in the classroom, all of the components operate simultaneously. So a principle from the cognitive lab might backfire when it's put into the more complex classroom environment. That's the problem of levels of analysis. Cognitive psychologists study one level—individual components of the mind—but educators operate on a different level—the entire mind of the child. (Or, better put, the mind of the child in the context of a classroom, which complicates things still further.)

Now, how can we add neuroscientific data to this picture? Parts of the brain don't map onto the cognitive system, one for one. There is not a single part of the brain for "learning" and one for "attention." Each of those cognitive functions is served by a network of brain structures. "Memory" relies on the hippocampus, entorhinal cortex, thalamus, and frontal cortex, at the least. Suppose I take an observation about the hippocampus—which I know contributes to memory—and try to draw a classroom application from that. In so doing, I'm assuming that whatever happens in the hippocampus is a reliable guide to what is happening in the memory system as a whole, even though the hippocampus is just one part of that system. And on top of that, I'm still making the other assumption—that

Willingham, Dan. From *Phi Delta Kappan*, February 2008, pp. 421–423. Reprinted with permission of Phi Delta Kappa International. All rights reserved. www.pdkintl.org

if I do something known to benefit memory when the memory system is isolated (as in the laboratory), it will still benefit memory when applied to the mind taken as a whole in the classroom.

But, of course, Jensen never advocated going straight from hippocampus to classroom! He explicitly emphasized that brain-based learning must be multidisciplinary. He's simply arguing that neuroscience should have a place at the table, so to speak. What I argue, in turn, is that the levels-of-analysis problem greatly reduces the likelihood that neuroscience will offer educators much of a payoff. Educators should use these data, by all means, but they should also expect that they won't find occasion to do so very often. As one gets more distant from the desired level of analysis (the child in the classroom), the probability of learning anything useful diminishes. That's true because the interactions between components at one level of analysis make it difficult to predict what's going to happen at the next level of analysis. That is, if you care about whether a child is learning, knowing conditions that make the memory system in isolation operate more efficiently (which is what a cognitive psychologist might contribute) is no guarantee that you will know whether the child in the classroom will learn more quickly. And knowing whether conditions are right for neurogenesis (which is what a neuroscientist might contribute) is no guarantee that you know that the child's memory system will operate more efficiently.

Let's further consider Jensen's example—that exercise is correlated with neurogenesis. It is perfectly plausible that a daily exercise period would benefit learning. But it's just as plausible that exercise would, at the same time, have a negative effect on attention or on motivation. We wouldn't know until we examined the effect of exercise in a real-life school setting. Jensen agrees. And presumably if we couldn't detect a positive effect of exercise on educational outcomes, we would conclude that, neurogenesis notwithstanding, the cognitive system as a whole does not benefit from exercise. Likewise, if careful behavioral research indicated that exercise *did* help in a school setting and neuroscientists protested that it ought not to, we would consider the data from the classroom to be decisive.

So what has neuroscience done for us? In this case, not much, because it's the classroom data that really matter. In principle, neuroscientists might suggest something that we could try in the classroom, and then we would decide—by behavioral (not neuroscientific) measures—whether it works or doesn't work. That would be a valuable contribution, but I don't believe that there will be many such situations—that is, one in which neuroscientists say, "Hey, maybe you should try this at school,"

and educational researchers say, "Never thought of that!" The notion that exercise helps cognition, for example, is hardly new.

Still, there are other, more indirect, ways that neuroscience can illuminate educational theory. Although space limitations preclude a thorough treatment, I will mention three techniques.[2]

First, there are times when two well-developed behavioral theories make very similar predictions, making them difficult to separate with behavioral data. But at the neural level, it might be possible to make different predictions. For example, the nature of dyslexia was, for some time, controversial. Although some behavioral research indicated that it had a phonological basis,[3] other researchers argued that phonology was not the fundamental problem in the disorder. Behavioral data were not conclusive.[4] Brain-imaging data showed dyslexics to have decreased activation in brain regions known to support phonological coding,[5] thus providing support to the phonological theory.

Second, neuroscientific data can show us that there is diversity where there appeared to be unity, or unity where one might suspect diversity. That is, we might discover that what seemed like a single type of behavior (e.g., "learning") is actually supported by two anatomically distinct brain systems. That indicates (but doesn't prove) that what we thought was a single function is in fact two different functions, operating in different ways. The study of learning and memory was revolutionized in the 1980s by such observations.[6] Neuroscientific data might also support the opposite conclusion. That is, we might suspect that two cognitive functions are separate but find that they rely on the same anatomical circuit. For example, although dyslexics show some diversity of behavioral symptoms across cultures and languages, the anatomical locus is quite consistent (at least in alphabetic languages), which indicates that the disorder is the same.[7]

Third, neuroscientific data might prove useful for the diagnosis of some learning disabilities. Researchers know that dyslexic readers show patterns of brain activity on electroencephalograms that differ from those of average readers.[8] Several laboratories are attempting to discern whether abnormal brain activity is measurable *before* reading instruction begins, and there have been some promising results.[9] Early diagnosis would allow early intervention, which could be an enormous advance.

In summary, I agree with Jensen that neuroscientific data can be of use to education. Indeed, they already have been. However, careful specification of how neuroscientific data and theory would actually apply to educational affairs leads to a more sober estimate of their value. The path to the improvement of education has proved steep and thorny. Neuroscience offers an occasional assist, not a significant shortcut.

## References

1. Thomas F. Gilbert, "Overlearning and the Retention of Meaningful Prose," *Journal of General Psychology,* vol. 56, 1957, pp. 281–89.

2. For more details, see Daniel T. Willingham and Elizabeth Dunn, "What Neuroimaging and Brain Localization Can Do, Cannot Do, and Should Not Do for Social Psychology," *Journal of Personality and Social Psychology,* vol. 85, 2003, pp. 662–71; and Daniel T. Willingham and John W. Lloyd, "How Can Brain Imaging Research Help Education?," paper presented at the annual meeting of the American Educational Research Association, Chicago, 2007.

3. Richard K. Wagner and Joseph K. Torgesen, "The Nature of Phonological Processing and Its Causal Role in the Acquisition of Reading Skills," *Psychological Bulletin,* vol. 101, 1987, pp. 192–212.

4. For a review of theories, see Peggy McCardle, Hollis S. Scarborough, and Hugh W. Catts, "Predicting, Explaining, and Preventing Children's Reading Difficulties," *Learning Disabilities Research & Practice,* vol. 16, 2001, pp. 230–39.

5. Judith M. Rumsey et al., "Failure to Activate the Left Temporoparietal Cortex in Dyslexia: An Oxygen 15 Positron Emission Tomographic Study," *Archives of Neurology,* vol. 49, 1992, pp. 527–34.

6. For a review, see Daniel B. Willingham, "Memory Systems in the Human Brain," *Neuron,* January 1997, pp. 5–8.

7. Eraldo Paulesu et al., "Dyslexia: Cultural Diversity and Biological Unity," *Science,* vol. 291, 2001, pp. 2165–67.

8. Gal Ben-Yehudah, Karen Banai, and Merav Ahissar, "Patterns of Deficit in Auditory Temporal Processing Among Dyslexic Adults," *Neuro-report,* vol. 15, 2004, pp. 627–31.

9. Kimberly A. Espy, Dennis L. Molfese, and Victoria J. Molfese, "Development of Auditory Event-Related Potentials in Young Children and Relations to Word-Level Reading Abilities at Age 8 Years," *Annals of Dyslexia,* June 2004, pp. 9–38.

**DAN WILLINGHAM, PHD,** is a professor of psychology at the University of Virginia, Charlottesville.

# EXPLORING THE ISSUE

## Do Recent Discoveries About the Brain Have Implications for Classroom Practice?

### Critical Thinking and Reflection

1. We have discussed whether and how research on brain function informs educational practice. Could the study of classroom practices also inform brain research? Why or why not? Provide examples to support your conclusion.
2. Assume that children with dyslexia (a reading disorder) are born with brains "wired" differently than those of other children. What would this mean for the teaching of reading?
3. Do you think that Willis and Willingham really differ in their views about how to translate brain science findings into educational practices? Or do they differ in the views of specific findings and their implications? Why or why not?

### Is There Common Ground?

Any plausible theory of learning must include the assumption that learning involves the brain. Why, then, is there any controversy about the implications of brain research for educational practice? Doesn't any finding about the brain tell us something useful about how to teach? Unfortunately, it is not always possible to move directly from knowledge about the brain to recommendations for educational practice. This is because learning always involves more than the activity of the brain. Learning results from the interaction of the child (and, of course, his or her brain) with the environment.

Consider, for example, the finding that the "spurt" in children's vocabulary seen at 18 to 24 months of age is associated with a rather dramatic increase in the synaptic density and activity of the brain. This finding is important because it suggests that something may "click" in children's brains at this time that increases their preparedness to learn words. But this finding does not by itself tell us very much about what parents and educators should do during this time to assist children. On the one hand, it may be that children are so prepared at this time that they can pick up words effortlessly from just about any sort of interaction and in any environment. In this case,

there might little we can or should do to help with vocabulary learning. On the other hand, what adults do when children are ready to "spurt" may matter a great deal. In that case, there might need to be a tightly orchestrated match between biology and what parents, teachers, and other people do when they talk to and interact with the child. Deciding between these alternatives is not always clear based on studies of the brain; we need studies of the environment as well.

### Additional Resources

Nancy Frey and Douglas Fisher, "Reading and the Brain: What Early Childhood Educators Need to Know," *Early Childhood Education Journal* (vol. 38, 2010).

Kenneth W. Gasser, "Five Ideas for 21st Century Math Classrooms," *American Secondary Education* (vol. 39 Summer 2011).

Mark H. Johnson, *Developmental Cognitive Neuroscience*, 2nd ed. (Blackwell, 2005).

Robert J. Sternberg, "The Answer Depends on the Question: A Reply to Eric Jensen," *Phi Delta Kappan* (February 2008).

# *Internet References . . .*

**National Institutes of Health**

http://NIH.gov

**Centre for Neuroscience in Education,
Cambridge University**

www.cne.psychol.cam.ac.uk/

**Neuroscience Education Institute**

www.neiglobal.com/

Selected, Edited, and with Issue Framing Material by:
Esther S. Chang, *Soka University of America*

# ISSUE

# Can Schools Close the Achievement Gap between Students from Different Ethnic and Racial Backgrounds?

**YES: Carol Corbett Burris** and **Kevin G. Welner,** from "Closing the Achievement Gap by Detracking," *Phi Delta Kappan* (2005)

**NO: William H. Schmidt, Leland S. Cogan,** and **Curtis C. McKnight,** from "Equality of Educational Opportunity: Myth or Reality in U.S. Schooling?" *American Educator* (2010–2011)

---

## Learning Outcomes

**After reading this issue, you will be able to:**

- Discuss the data regarding racial and ethnic differences in academic achievement in the United States.
- Understand the differences in school experiences of students from different ethnic and racial groups and different economic circumstances.
- Define ability-level tracking and understand its uses and misuses.
- Understand some of the factors that can maintain or close the achievement gap.

---

## ISSUE SUMMARY

**YES:** Carol Burris and Kevin Welner argue that the achievement gap between whites and African American and Latino students can be closed by "detracking" and having similarly high expectations and similar curricular demands on all students.

**NO:** William Schmidt and colleagues argue that minority students are exposed to pervasive and persistent inequalities that make school-based reforms unrealistic.

---

**I**n 2014, the nation will witness the sixtieth anniversary of the U.S. Supreme Court's decision in *Brown v. the Board of Education*, which declared that the segregation of public schools according to race denied African American children the same educational opportunities as white children. Many educators and policymakers, however, do not view this anniversary as an occasion to celebrate, pointing to the continuing gap between the academic achievement of white students, on the one hand, and African American and Hispanic students, on the other hand. Put simply, compared to white students, African American and Hispanic students, on average, score lower on standardized achievement tests and tests of basic skills in mathematics and science, are more likely to leave school before graduating from high school, and are less likely to attend college.

What role do schools play in creating or maintaining this achievement gap? Some critics of public education suggest that schools have created the gap through discriminatory practices and subtle forms of racism perpetrated by teachers, administrators, and support staff, such as having lower expectations for African American and Hispanic students and assigning them to low achieving-track or special education classes at substantially higher rates than their white peers. These critics also point out that the achievement gap actually widens over the school years, with African American and Hispanic students falling further and further behind their white peers as they move through the elementary to the middle and, eventually, the high school years. Critics suggest that this increasing gap is evidence that schools are causing, or at least contributing to, the problem. Indeed, in keeping with this notion, President George W. Bush's controversial No Child Left Behind policy was based on the assumption that any student can succeed if given appropriate educational opportunities.

Many defenders of public education argue that it is not schools that are to blame for the existence of the achievement gap, but rather the broader social and economic conditions that create a wide array of disparities among different ethnic and racial groups. Years of pervasive societal discrimination, it is argued, have led to high rates of poverty among African American and Hispanic families, and thereby to less adequate material resources in homes, including books and other materials, that support academic growth; more limited access to the health care and nutrition necessary to ensure optimal development; and exposure to a variety of hazardous conditions, from lead in paint used in homes to crime and violence, all of which interfere with learning. These defenders of public education point out that children who live in poverty begin school less well prepared (e.g., with fewer preliteracy skills, such as the recognition that print encodes language) than their more affluent peers and thus, wider social forces rather than schooling are to blame for the achievement gap. Thus, it is unreasonable, according to these defenders of public schools, to expect that schools can overcome the pervasive social and economic barriers that exist before an African American or Hispanic child begins school and continue in his or her out-of-school hours.

In the first of the following selections, Carol Corbett Burris and Kevin G. Welner argue that the achievement gap between white students and African American and Hispanic students is a consequence of the overrepresentation of minority students in low-achieving track classes. Thus, for Burris and Weiner, the answer is to detrack schools, and they provide a successful example from a suburban school district in New York State. In the second selection, William H. Schmidt, Leland S. Cogan, and Curtis C. McKnight argue that students in economically disadvantaged neighborhoods, which include an overrepresentation of ethnic and racial minorities, are exposed to less-demanding content and thus achieve less. Moreover, Schmidt and colleagues argue that this economic variation in exposure to learning opportunities is pervasive and persistent in the United States.

# YES

Carol Corbett Burris and Kevin G. Welner

# Closing the Achievement Gap by Detracking

The most recent Phi Delta Kappa/Gallup Poll of the Public's Attitudes Toward the Public Schools found that 74% of Americans believe that the achievement gap between white students and African American and Hispanic students is primarily due to factors unrelated to the quality of schooling that children receive.[1] This assumption is supported by research dating back four decades to the Coleman Report and its conclusion that schools have little impact on the problem.[2] But is the pessimism of that report justified? Or is it possible for schools to change their practices and thereby have a strongly positive effect on student achievement? We have found that when all students—those at the bottom as well as the top of the "gap"—have access to first-class learning opportunities, all students' achievement can rise.

Because African American and Hispanic students are consistently overrepresented in low-track classes, the effects of tracking greatly concern educators who are interested in closing the achievement gap.[3] Detracking reforms are grounded in the established ideas that higher achievement follows from a more rigorous curriculum and that low-track classes with unchallenging curricula result in lower student achievement.[4] Yet, notwithstanding the wide acceptance of these ideas, we lack concrete case studies of mature detracking reforms and their effects. This article responds to that shortage, describing how the school district in which Carol Burris serves as a high school principal was able to close the gap by offering its high-track curriculum to all students, in detracked classes.

## Tracking and the Achievement Gap

Despite overwhelming research demonstrating the ineffectiveness of low-track classes and of tracking in general, schools continue the practice.[5] Earlier studies have argued that this persistence stems from the fact that tracking is grounded in values, beliefs, and politics as much as it is in technical, structural, or organizational needs.[6] Further, despite inconsistent research findings,[7] many parents and educators assume that the practice benefits high achievers. This is partly because parents of high achievers fear that detracking and heterogeneous grouping will result in a "watered-down" curriculum and lowered learning standards for their children.

And so, despite the evidence that low-track classes cause harm, they continue to exist. Worse still, the negative achievement effects of such classes fall disproportionately on minority students, since, as noted above, African American and Hispanic students are overrepresented in low-track classes and underrepresented in high-track classes, even after controlling for prior measured achievement.[8] Socioeconomic status (SES) has been found to affect track assignment as well.[9] A highly proficient student from a low socioeconomic background has only a 50-50 chance of being placed in a high-track class.[10]

Researchers who study the relationship between tracking, race/ethnicity, and academic performance suggest different strategies for closing the achievement gap. Some believe that the solution is to encourage more minority students to take high-track classes.[11] Others believe that if all students are given the enriched curriculum that high-achieving students receive, achievement will rise.[12] They believe that no students—whatever their race, SES, or prior achievement—should be placed in classes that have a watered-down or remedial academic curriculum and that the tracking system should be dismantled entirely.[13] In this article, we provide evidence for the success of this latter approach. By dismantling tracking and providing the high-track curriculum to all, we can succeed in closing the achievement gap on important measures of learning.

## Providing "High-Track" Curriculum to All Students

The Rockville Centre School District is a diverse suburban school district located on Long Island. In the late 1990s, it embarked on a multiyear detracking reform that increased learning expectations for all students. The district began replacing its tracked classes with heterogeneously grouped classes in which the curriculum formerly reserved for the district's high-track students was taught.

This reform began as a response to an ambitious goal set by the district's superintendent, William Johnson, and the Rockville Centre Board of Education in 1993: *By the year 2000, 75% of all graduates will earn a New York State Regents diploma.* At that time, the district and state rates of earning Regents diplomas were 58% and 38% respectively.

To qualify for a New York State Regents diploma, students must pass, at a minimum, eight end-of-course Regents examinations, including two in mathematics, two in laboratory sciences, two in social studies, one in English language arts, and one in a foreign language. Rockville Centre's goal reflected the superintendent's strong belief in the external evaluation of student learning as well as the district's commitment to academic rigor.

Regents exams are linked with coursework; therefore, the district gradually eliminated low-track courses. The high school eased the transition by offering students instructional support classes and carefully monitoring the progress of struggling students.

While the overall number of Regents diplomas increased, a disturbing profile of students who were not earning the diploma emerged. These students were more likely to be African American or Hispanic, to receive free or reduced-price lunch, or to have a learning disability. At the district's high school, 20% of all students were African American or Hispanic, 13% received free and reduced-price lunch, and 10% were special education students. If these graduates were to earn the Regents diploma, systemic change would need to take place to close the gaps for each of these groups.

## Accelerated Mathematics in Heterogeneous Classes

On closer inspection of the data, educators noticed that the second math Regents exam presented a stumbling block to earning the diploma. While high-track students enrolled in trigonometry and advanced algebra in the 10th grade, low-track students did not even begin first-year algebra until grade 10.

In order to provide all students with ample opportunity to pass the needed courses and to study calculus prior to graduation, Superintendent Johnson decided that all students would study the accelerated math curriculum formerly reserved for the district's highest achievers. Under the leadership of the assistant principal, Delia Garrity,

middle school math teachers revised and condensed the curriculum. The new curriculum was taught to all students, in heterogeneously grouped classes. To support struggling learners, the school initiated support classes called math workshops and provided after-school help four afternoons a week.

The results were remarkable. Over 90% of incoming freshmen entered the high school having passed the first Regents math examination. The achievement gap dramatically narrowed. Between the years of 1995 and 1997, only 23% of regular education African American or Hispanic students had passed this algebra-based Regents exam before entering high school. After universally accelerating all students in heterogeneously grouped classes, the percentage more than tripled—up to 75%. The percentage of white or Asian American regular education students who passed the exam also greatly increased—from 54% to 98%.

## Detracking the High School

The district approached universal acceleration with caution. Some special education students, while included in the accelerated classes, were graded using alternative assessments. This 1998 cohort of special education students would not take the first ("Sequential I") Regents math exam until they had completed ninth grade. (We use year of entry into ninth grade to determine cohort. So the 1998 cohort began ninth grade in the fall of 1998.) On entering high school, these students with special needs were placed in a double-period, low-track, "Sequential I" ninth-grade math class, along with low-achieving new entrants. Consistent with the recommendations of researchers who have defended tracking,[14] this class was rich in resources (a math teacher, special education inclusion teacher, and teaching assistant). Yet the low-track culture of the class remained unconducive to learning. Students were disruptive, and teachers spent considerable class time addressing behavior management issues. All students were acutely aware that the class carried the "low-track" label.

District and school leaders decided that this low-track class failed its purpose, and the district boldly moved forward with several new reforms the following year. All special education students in the 1999 cohort took the exam in the eighth grade. The entire 1999 cohort also studied science in heterogeneous classes throughout middle school, and it became the first cohort to be heterogeneously grouped in ninth-grade English and social studies classes.

Ninth-grade teachers were pleased with the results. The tone, activities, and discussions in the heterogeneously grouped classes were academic, focused, and enriched.

Science teachers reported that the heterogeneously grouped middle school science program prepared students well for ninth-grade biology.

Detracking at the high school level continued, paralleling the introduction of revised New York State curricula. Students in the 2000 cohort studied the state's new biology curriculum, "The Living Environment," in heterogeneously grouped classes. This combination of new curriculum and heterogeneous grouping resulted in a dramatic increase in the passing rate on the first science Regents exam, especially for minority students who were previously overrepresented in the low-track biology class. After just one year of heterogeneous grouping, the passing rate for African American and Hispanic students increased from 48% to 77%, while the passing rate for white and Asian American students increased from 85% to 94%.

The following September, the 2001 cohort became the first class to be heterogeneously grouped *in all subjects* in the ninth grade. The state's new multiyear "Math A" curriculum was taught to this cohort in heterogeneously grouped classes in both the eighth and ninth grades.

In 2003, some 10th-grade classes detracked. Students in the 2002 cohort became the first to study a heterogeneously grouped pre-International Baccalaureate (IB) 10th-grade curriculum in English and social studies. To help all students meet the demands of an advanced curriculum, the district provides every-other-day support classes in math, science, and English language arts. These classes are linked to the curriculum and allow teachers to pre- and post-teach topics to students needing additional reinforcement.

## Closing the Gap on Other Measures That Matter

New York's statewide achievement gap in the earning of Regents diplomas has persisted. In 2000, only 19.3% of all African American or Hispanic 12th-graders and 58.7% of all white or Asian American 12th-graders graduated with Regents diplomas. By 2003, while the percentage of students in both groups earning the Regents diploma increased (26.4% of African American or Hispanic students, 66.3% of white or Asian American students), the gap did not close.

In contrast, Rockville Centre has seen both an increase in students' rates of earning Regents diplomas and a decrease in the gap between groups. . . . For those students who began South Side High School in 1996 (the graduating class of 2000), 32% of all African American or Hispanic and 88% of all white or Asian American graduates

earned Regents diplomas. By the time the cohort of 1999 graduated in 2003, the gap had closed dramatically—82% of all African American or Hispanic and 97% of all white or Asian American graduates earned Regents diplomas. In fact, . . . for this 1999 cohort (the first to experience detracking in all middle school and most ninth-grade subjects), the Regents diploma rate for the district's minority students surpassed New York State's rate for white or Asian American students.

In order to ensure that the narrowing of the gap was not attributable to a changing population, we used binary logistic regression analyses to compare the probability of earning a Regents diploma before and after detracking. In addition to membership in a detracked cohort, the model included socioeconomic and special education status as covariates. Those students who were members of the 1996 and 1997 cohorts were compared with members of the 1998–2000 cohorts. We found that membership in a cohort subsequent to the detracking of middle school math was a significant contributor to earning a Regents diploma. . . . In addition, low-SES students and special education students in the 2001 cohort also showed sharp improvement.

These same three cohorts (1998–2000) showed significant increases in the probability of minority students' studying advanced math courses. Controlling for prior achievement and SES, minority students' enrollment in trigonometry, precalculus, and Advanced Placement calculus all grew.[15] And as more students from those cohorts studied AP calculus, the enrollment gap decreased from 38% to 18% in five years, and the AP calculus scores significantly increased. . . .

Finally, detracking in the 10th grade, combined with teaching all students the pre-IB curriculum, appears to be closing the gap in the study of the IB curriculum. This year 50% of all minority students will study IB English and "History of the Americas" in the 11th grade. In the fall of 2003, only 31% chose to do so.

❧

Achievement follows from opportunities—opportunities that tracking denies. The results of detracking in Rockville Centre are clear and compelling. When all students were taught the high-track curriculum, achievement rose for all groups of students—majority, minority, special education, low-SES, and high-SES. This evidence can now be added to the larger body of tracking research that has convinced the Carnegie Council for Adolescent Development, the

National Governors' Association, and most recently the National Research Council to call for the reduction or elimination of tracking.[16] The Rockville Centre reform confirms common sense: closing the "curriculum gap" is an effective way to close the "achievement gap."

## Notes

1. Lowell C. Rose and Alec M. Gallup, "The 36th Annual Phi Delta Kappa/Gallup Poll of the Public's Attitudes Toward the Public Schools," *Phi Delta Kappan,* September 2004, p. 49.
2. James Coleman et al., *Equality of Educational Opportunity* (Washington, D.C.: U.S. Government Printing Office, 1966).
3. Kevin G. Welner, *Legal Rights, Local Wrongs: When Community Control Collides with Educational Equity* (Albany: SUNY Press, 2001).
4. Clifford Adelman, *Answers in the Tool Box: Academic Intensity, Attendance Patterns, and Bachelor's Degree Attainment* (Washington, D.C.: Office of Educational Research, U.S. Department of Education, 1999); . . . Henry Levin, *Accelerated Schools for At-Risk Students* (New Brunswick, N.J.: Rutgers University, Center for Policy Research in Education, Report No. 142, 1988); Mano Singham, "The Achievement Gap: Myths and Realities," *Phi Delta Kappan,* April 2003, pp. 586–91; and Jay P. Heubert and Robert M. Hauser, *High Stakes: Testing for Tracking, Promotion, and Graduation* (Washington, D.C.: National Research Council, 1999).
5. Jeannie Oakes, Adam Gamoran, and Reba Page, "Curriculum Differentiation: Opportunities, Outcomes, and Meanings," in Philip Jackson, ed., *Handbook of Research on Curriculum* (New York: Macmillan, 1992), pp. 570–608.
6. Welner, op. cit.
7. Frederick Mosteller, Richard Light, and Jason Sachs, "Sustained Inquiry in Education: Lessons from Skill Grouping and Class Size," *Harvard Educational Review,* vol. 66, 1996, pp. 797–843; Robert Slavin, "Achievement Effects of Ability Grouping in Secondary Schools: A Best-Evidence Synthesis," *Review of Educational Research,* vol. 60, 1990, pp. 471–500; and James Kulik, *An Analysis of the Research on Ability Grouping: Historical and Contemporary Perspectives* (Storrs, Conn.: National Research Center on the Gifted and Talented, University of Connecticut, 1992).
8. Roslyn Mickelson, "Subverting Swann: First- and Second-Generation Segregation in Charlotte-Mecklenburg Schools," *American Educational Research Journal,* vol. 38, 2001, pp. 215–52; Robert Slavin and Jomills Braddock II, "Ability Grouping: On the Wrong Track," *College Board Review,* Summer 1993, pp. 11–17; and Welner, op. cit.
9. Samuel Lucas, *Tracking Inequality: Stratification and Mobility in American High Schools* (New York: Teachers College Press, 1999).
10. Beth E. Vanfossen, James D. Jones, and Joan Z. Spade, "Curriculum Tracking and Status Maintenance," *Sociology of Education,* vol. 60, 1987, pp. 104–22.
11. John Ogbu, *Black American Students in an Affluent Suburb* (Mahwah, N.J.: Erlbaum, 2003).
12. Levin, op. cit.; and Slavin and Braddock, op. cit.
13. Jeannie Oakes and Amy Stuart Wells, "Detracking for High Student Achievement," *Educational Leadership,* March 1998, pp. 38–41; and Susan Yonezawa, Amy Stuart Wells, and Irene Sema, "Choosing Tracks: 'Freedom of Choice' in Detracking Schools," *American Educational Research Journal,* vol. 39, 2002, pp. 37–67.
14. Maureen Hallinan, "Tracking: From Theory to Practice," *Sociology of Education,* vol. 67, 1994, pp. 79–91; and Tom Loveless, *The Tracking Wars: State Reform Meets School Policy* (Washington, D.C.: Brookings Institution Press, 1999).
15. Carol Corbett Burris, Jay P. Heubert, and Henry M. Levin, "Math Acceleration for All," *Educational Leadership,* February 2004, pp. 68–71.
16. Carnegie Council on Adolescent Development, *Turning Points: Preparing American Youth for the 21st Century* (New York: Carnegie Corporation, 1989); *Ability Grouping and Tracking: Current Issues and Concerns* (Washington, D.C.: National Governors Association, 1993); and National Research Council, *Engaging Schools: Fostering High School Students' Motivation to Learn* (Washington, D.C.: National Academies Press, 2004).

**CAROL CORBETT BURRIS** is the principal of South Side High School in Rockville Centre, New York.

**KEVIN G. WELNER** is a professor and director of the National Education Policy Center at the University of Colorado at Boulder.

## William H. Schmidt, Leland S. Cogan, and Curtis C. McKnight

# Equality of Educational Opportunity: Myth or Reality in U.S. Schooling?

Public schooling is often regarded as "the great equalizer" in American society. For more than 100 years, so the story goes, children all across the country have had an equal opportunity to master the three Rs: reading, writing, and arithmetic. As a result, any student willing to work hard has the chance to go as far as his or her talent allows, regardless of family origin or socioeconomic status.

This assumption regarding opportunity and emphasis on individual talent and effort seems to be a natural offshoot of the rugged individualism and self-reliance that are so much a part of the fabled American character. We have long celebrated our cowboys, entrepreneurs, and standout athletes—but we have also long ignored those who have not succeeded. When success is individual, so is failure. It must result from a lack of effort, talent, motivation, application, or perseverance, not a lack of opportunity. Right?

Not according to our research. Defining educational equality in the most basic, foundational way imaginable—equal coverage of core academic content—we've found that America's schools are far from being the equalizers we, as a nation, want them to be.

So what? Does it really matter that "the great equalizer" is a myth? To our way of thinking, it does. First, as researchers, we believe it is always important to question our assumptions—and that goes for our national assumptions about equality and individualism as well as our personal assumptions. Second, the more we study schools, the more inequity we see. While other researchers have tackled important issues like disparities in teachers' qualifications and in classroom resources, we have focused on the basic question of what mathematics topics are taught. We have been disturbed to see that whether a student is even exposed to a topic depends on where he or she lives. Third, we find that those who don't question basic assumptions draw tragic, unsupportable conclusions. Take, for example, the controversial book *The Bell Curve*,[1] in which Richard J. Herrnstein and Charles Murray wrongly argued that unequal educational outcomes can *only* be explained by the unfortunate but unavoidable distribution of inherited abilities that relegate some students to the low end of the intelligence distribution. As we will show, unequal educational outcomes are clearly related to unequal educational opportunities.

In this article, we explore the extent to which students in different schools and districts have an equal opportunity to learn mathematics. Specifically, we discuss research on (1) the amount of variability in content coverage in eighth grade across 13 districts (or consortia of districts) and 9 states, and (2) the variation in mathematics courses offered by high schools in 18 districts spread across 2 states. We knew we would find some variability in terms of content coverage and course offerings, so our real question had to do with the nature and extent of the differences and whether they seemed to matter in terms of student achievement. Simply put, sometimes differences yield equivalent results, but sometimes differences make a difference.

In the United States, research like this is necessary because our educational system is not one system, but a disparate set of roughly 15,000 school districts distributed among 50 states and the District of Columbia. While states, with varying degrees of focus, rigor, and coherence,[2] have developed academic standards, local districts still maintain *de facto* control of their curriculum—some have written their own standards, some have written their own curriculum, some mandate the use of selected textbooks, and some leave all such decisions up to the schools. Even in states that control the range of textbooks that may be adopted by districts, the districts themselves always control (or choose to allow schools to control) which content within those textbooks will be covered or emphasized.

Leaving the choice of content coverage to individual districts and schools (with very few state controls) makes it possible and even *probable* that schools cannot be the equalizers we would like them to be. With roughly 15,000 school systems, American children simply are not likely to have equal educational opportunities as defined at the most basic level of equivalent content coverage. It is therefore highly questionable and even unfair to assume that differences in student achievement and learning are the sole result of differences in individual students' efforts and abilities. To assert that those who do not achieve at prescribed levels fail to do so because they cannot, or do not, take advantage of the opportunities afforded them is, at best, to mistake part of the story for the whole. The whole story also must consider the radically different opportunities provided by different schools, districts, and states, and acknowledge that which opportunities are provided is determined by socioeconomic factors, housing patterns, community structures, parental decisions, and many other factors that have one thing in common—they are all beyond the control of individual students.

In the research literature, the concept we are exploring is called the "opportunity to learn" (OTL). While it has been defined in many ways, to our way of thinking the specific mathematics content is the defining element of an educational opportunity in mathematics. Of course, many things can and do affect how that content is delivered. But our research focuses on equivalent content coverage because this allows a more precise definition of "equal educational opportunity" as it relates to learning. Without equality in content coverage, there can be no equality in opportunity related to that content, no matter the equality of other resources provided. Ultimately, learning specific content is the goal. The mathematics itself is at the heart of the opportunity to learn and thus is a very salient component in examining equality of educational opportunity. In addition, it is a factor that policymakers can address.

In all, our research aims to answer one question: do all the different mathematics content roads fairly and equally lead to the same high-quality educational outcomes? As we will explain below, they do not.

## Inequality in Eighth Grade

For our research on eighth-grade mathematics, we examined the extent to which students in different districts and states had the same opportunity to learn specific mathematics topics and how that was related to their academic achievement. To do this, we analyzed a unique set of data from a study that replicated the 1995 Third International

Mathematics and Science Study (TIMSS)—the most extensive multinational comparative study ever attempted. In addition to assessing student achievement in over 40 countries, the 1995 TIMSS collected a great deal of other data, including detailed information on the mathematics curricula and classroom content coverage.

The replica study had many components or substudies. The part we are concerned with here is the TIMSS 1999 Benchmarking Study, which was designed to compare—or benchmark—U.S. states and districts against the countries that participated in the 1999 TIMSS. For the benchmarking study we worked with 13 school districts (or consortia of districts) and 9 states, all of which chose (and paid) to participate as we gathered extensive data on their eighth-grade mathematics content coverage and student achievement. A total of 36,654 students in these states and districts took the 1999 TIMSS test and provided a wide array of demographic and socioeconomic data, including age, gender, racial/ethnic group, whether English was spoken in the home, what education-related possessions were in the home (e.g., computer, dictionary, and number of books), parental education level, number of adults in the home, etc. In addition, the students' 1,861 mathematics teachers filled out a questionnaire on the topics they had covered during the school year.

The mathematics topics listed in the teacher questionnaire were based on the mathematics content framework[3] developed for the 1995 TIMSS; it consists of 44 specific mathematics topics (e.g., common fractions, percentages, 3-D geometry, etc.) that cover the full range of K-12 mathematics. On the questionnaire, teachers indicated whether they had taught each topic for 1 to 5 periods, more than 5 periods, or not at all.

Gathering all these data was simply the first step. We didn't just want to know what was being taught in our states and districts; we wanted some sense of how each topic fit into the scope and sequence of mathematics schooling across the grades from an international perspective (hence the benchmarking idea). Using the 1995 TIMSS multinational mathematics curriculum data, we developed an International Grade Placement (IGP) topic index to indicate the grade in which the most countries typically emphasized each topic. We say "emphasized" each topic because we realize that topics are often taught in multiple grades. Nonetheless, we were able to identify the grade in which each topic typically received its greatest instructional focus. Each topic was assigned a value between 1 and 12 indicating an international consensus regarding the grade in which the topic should be emphasized. For example, the first topic, whole numbers, has an IGP value of 1.7. This means that most countries give whole numbers their greatest instructional focus toward the end of first grade.

Given the hierarchical nature of school mathematics (in which addition must come before multiplication, fractions before exponents, etc.), we think it is reasonable to assume that topics receiving their main instructional focus in later grades in most countries are more difficult than those receiving their main focus in earlier grades. Thus, our IGP topic values provide an indication of some international consensus regarding the rigor and appropriate grade level of each topic.

With this IGP topic index and the teacher questionnaire, we developed a measure of students' opportunity to learn mathematics in each of the 1,861 eighth-grade classrooms we were studying. Our opportunity-to-learn measure took into account which topics were taught, how much time was devoted to each topic, and what the IGP value was for each topic. Using this measure, we assigned each classroom a value between 1 and 12 to indicate the average international grade level of all the topics taught (weighted by instructional time). In effect, our opportunity-to-learn measure assigns an International Grade Placement value to each classroom. Averaging all the IGP values for the classrooms in a district, we can then determine each district's IGP value. And, we can do the same for each state.

A classroom that spent a lot of time on fractions (a fourth-grade topic, according to our IGP topic index), and very little time on algebraic expressions or formulas (seventh-grade topics), might have an IGP classroom value of a little more than 5, indicating a content mix that in most TIMSS countries is taught during the fifth grade. In contrast, a classroom that spent the vast majority of its time on geometry and algebra topics would have a value of about 7 to 8, because almost all time was spent on seventh- and eighth-grade topics.

## Students' Opportunity to Learn Mathematics

As we briefly explained in the introduction, school districts have far more influence than states over what content gets taught. So, our discussion focuses on our district-level findings. As for the state-level findings, suffice it to say that we did all the same analyses with our state-level data as with our district-level data, and the findings were very similar. Although variation among states on all opportunity-to-learn indicators was less than that among the districts, this did not alter the pattern or significance of the observed relationships and did not change our conclusions. (The lesser variation at the state level is to be expected as states represent a broader combination of many districts.)

Internationally, the focus of eighth grade for all students in virtually all of the TIMSS countries—except the United States—is algebra and geometry. In our study, not a single district had all of its students focusing mainly on algebra and geometry. This is reflected in the districts' IGP values, which ranged from 6.0 to 6.9. This means that in some districts, eighth-grade teachers (on average) were teaching content typically found at the end of fifth or the beginning of sixth grade internationally, while in other districts, the content came closer to that found at the end of sixth or the beginning of seventh grade. Not only is this a lot of variation in students' opportunity to learn mathematics, it indicates that *all students* were being shortchanged since none of the districts were focusing on eighth-grade (or even seventh-grade) content.

Of course the real question is, does any of this variation in mathematics learning opportunities make any difference in students' achievement? We addressed this issue through a set of analyses that we briefly describe here.

On the basis of decades of findings that students with higher socioeconomic status typically have higher scores on achievement tests,[4] some researchers and policymakers have hypothesized that socioeconomic status has a *greater* impact on achievement than does schooling itself. Some have even gone so far as to conclude that schooling doesn't really matter. Indeed, among our districts, we found a strong relationship between students' mathematics achievement as measured by their TIMSS scores, and the percentage of students' parents who had a college or university degree (a common indicator of socioeconomic status).

Does this mean that all the differences we found in students' opportunity to learn mathematics are not important? Not at all. As IGP value—and, therefore, a more demanding opportunity to learn mathematics—increased, so did achievement. The relationship between students' opportunity to learn and achievement was every bit as strong as the relationship between their socioeconomic status and achievement.

Nonetheless, we still do not have the whole story. Sadly, in our "land of opportunity," students' socioeconomic status is related not only to their achievement, but also to their opportunity to learn. Across the districts we found a strong relationship between the percentage of students' parents with a college or university degree and the district IGP value. This means that the more parents with a college or university degree in a district, the higher the IGP value and the higher the average mathematics achievement. The estimated increase in opportunity to learn was not trivial: the mathematics content coverage in districts in which around 60 percent of students' parents had a college or university degree was about one-half of a grade level ahead of districts in which less than 30 percent of students' parents had a college or university degree.

These results have profound policy implications. The realization of the fundamental vision of public schools as the great equalizers rests on the assumption that content coverage is essentially the same for all children. If some are not taught essential mathematics topics in their schooling, why would we believe they will learn mathematics as well as those who are exposed to all essential content? . . .

Finding that socioeconomic status and opportunity to learn are both independently related to achievement is not surprising; these relationships have been studied previously in various ways with various types of data—both national and international, but not at the district level. In fact, we found such relationships when we analyzed the international TIMSS data.[5] However, what is unique to the United States is the strong estimated relationship between socioeconomic status and opportunity to learn. When high-quality national or regional standards (and/or curricula are in place, as they typically are in other countries, that linkage is essentially minimized if not eliminated.[6]

As a result of its strong correlation between socioeconomic status and opportunity to learn, *the United States has a particularly strong relationship between socioeconomic status and achievement.* Using the 1995 TIMSS data, we found that the correlation between socioeconomic status and achievement was stronger in the United States than in 32 (out of 40) other countries. This raises the issue of equality, given that the lower the income-level composition of a district, the more likely it is that content coverage will be less demanding and that the average mathematics achievement of eighth-graders will be lower. Most other countries have clear, detailed national or regional academic standards and/or curricula that define content coverage and therefore minimize the influence of socioeconomic status on opportunity to learn.[7]

The implication of our conceptual model is that by adopting focused, rigorous, coherent, and common content-coverage frameworks, the United States could minimize the impact of socioeconomic status on content coverage—a goal toward which virtually all our international economic peers are making progress.

Hopefully, the recently developed Common Core State Standards (see www.corestandards.org) will help the United States offer students greater equity in their opportunity to learn. But for now, a burning question remains: which is more important to student learning, socioeconomic status or opportunity to learn? An easy question to pose, but not a simple one to answer due to the complex nature of our U.S. education system. To disentangle these relationships, we analyzed the relationship between socioeconomic status, IGP value, and achievement at the classroom and district levels.

At the classroom level, controlling for socioeconomic status and students' prior achievement, the IGP value was statistically significantly related to achievement (actually, residual gain in achievement), as were our measures of socioeconomic status. For a one grade-level increase in IGP value, the increase in mean achievement at the classroom level was .15 of a standard deviation. That's like a student in the 50th percentile moving to the 56th percentile.

The impact of district-level opportunity to learn on student achievement (controlling for student- and classroom-level variables) was approximately one-third of a standard deviation. So, our best estimate indicates that an increase of one grade-level in IGP value at the district level would move a student from the 50th percentile to roughly the 65th percentile on mathematics achievement. Thus, the answer to our question is that student achievement is significantly related to socioeconomic status, but, *having controlled for this at all three levels (student, classroom, and district), both classroom- and district-level opportunity to learn is also significantly related to student achievement.* Variation in students' opportunity to learn comes from both the classroom and the district. This is both good and bad news. It is good news because opportunity to learn is something districts and teachers can change. The bad news is that districts seem to persist in providing less rigorous content to students with lower socioeconomic status.

The bottom line is that equality of educational opportunity, where opportunity is defined in terms of content coverage, does not exist within or across districts. Just as problematic is our initial finding: for these districts, the typical content covered in these eighth-grade classrooms is considered sixth-grade content internationally. *Other TIMSS countries are typically two grade levels ahead of the United States in terms of the rigor of their curricula.* Fortunately, our research suggests that the achievement of U.S. students would likely increase substantially if we would make our mathematics content more demanding.

Up to this point, we've dealt with the consequences of content variation at the middle school (eighth-grade) level. Do these differences in opportunity to learn persist once students move to high school? We address this in the next section.

## Inequality in High School

As part of a research and development project called Promoting Rigorous Outcomes in Mathematics and Science Education (PROM/SE), we have worked with nearly 60 school districts in two states, Michigan and Ohio (because the work is ongoing, we will not identify the districts). To explore the extent to which high school students have an equal opportunity to learn mathematics, we examined the transcripts of 14,000 seniors in 30 high schools in 18 of our PROM/SE districts. As we explain below, we found a shocking number of mathematics courses and dramatic differences in students' course taking.

Much of the variation we found is the result of the pervasive use of high school tracking (i.e., offering different levels of the same course, such as Basic Algebra, Algebra, and Honors Algebra). While tracking today is typically not as rigid as it used to be (with students in the college, general, or vocational track for all their courses), it still has an impact on students' opportunity to learn.

Most schools and districts in the United States track students because they believe it optimizes students' achievement. Advocates of tracking argue that this type of curricular differentiation facilitates teaching and learning, as it matches students' current knowledge and ability levels to the most suitable curriculum. Tracking theory contends that some students would struggle immensely in a high-level curriculum, while a low-level curriculum would confine others.

Most research on secondary school mathematics tracking, however, has found that it tends to adversely impact students in low-level courses compared with their peers in high-level courses. Students in low-tracked mathematics courses are less likely to expect to go to college, less likely to actually attend college (even after controlling for students' postsecondary expectations), and have lower self-images.[8] Perhaps most salient, though, is that many studies have found that mathematics tracking tends to exacerbate achievement inequalities between high- and low-tracked students.[9]

In order for multiple mathematics tracks to exist, the school must offer multiple mathematics courses. A school that offers four mathematics courses—one corresponding to each grade level—and requires all of its students to take these courses, only offers one possible sequence of courses and thus one track. However, this is highly uncommon. Schools typically offer more than four mathematics courses—often many more—and allow students to choose from numerous possible sequences of courses. These sequences can, and often do, vary by the number of courses taken, the order in which courses are taken, and the types of courses taken.

To find out just how much variability there was in our 30 high schools and 18 districts, we began by counting the number of distinct mathematics courses offered. We treated each new course title as a different course, even in cases like "Formal Geometry" and "Geometry," or

"Applied Algebra" and "Algebra I." Previous research has shown that the covered content in two courses with a similar title can vary wildly.[10] We therefore find it more prudent to assume that if schools choose to give courses different titles, then it is most likely that the content is different, at least to some extent.

In all, we found 270 different mathematics course titles, including 39 focused on mathematics below algebra, 11 on beginning algebra, 9 on geometry, and 9 on advanced algebra. . . .

Of course, what really matters is not all 270 courses, but which courses are offered in each of the 18 districts. We focus on the district rather than the school because the district sets curriculum policies. Of course, high schools in the same district may not offer the exact same number or types of mathematics courses, but we found the variation among schools in the same district to be quite small. In contrast, we found that the number of mathematics courses offered by each district varied considerably. If a district were to offer only one course for each mathematics content category (e.g., beginning algebra, geometry, precalculus, etc.), then there would be fewer than 10 courses offered. Looking across our 18 districts, the number of courses ranges from a low of 10 to a high of 58, with most districts offering close to 30 mathematics courses.

All these courses means that students in each school can arrange the type, number, and order of their courses, and thus vary their exposure to mathematics, in numerous ways. For example, two students in the same school may take substantively different sequences of courses—such as Basic Math, then Algebra, then Geometry; versus Geometry, then Advanced Algebra, then Precalculus—*and* take different versions of these courses—such as Elementary Geometry versus Honors Geometry.

We have, until this point, focused on the total number of courses offered, seeing large variation in both the number and the types of courses. The variation in actual courses taken, however, is not as large as it could be. Many students take similar courses. About 40 percent of the students in our study took Algebra I, Geometry, and Algebra II. Nevertheless, variation in course taking remains significant.

One particular way that students' mathematics course taking varies is in the number of courses they take. We examined the number of mathematics courses taken by each of the 14,000 seniors in our 18 districts. We were dismayed to find that in half the districts, anywhere from 10 to 27 percent of students took just one mathematics course in high school. (In the other districts, anywhere from 0 to 7 percent took just one course.) At the other extreme, in four districts the vast majority of students took four or more mathematics courses. Across districts, variation was common. Most districts had students who took anywhere from one to four or more courses.

Although we began this study well aware that high school students have options in selecting their mathematics courses, we were startled by the differences across districts. Students may attend high school in the same district, but as they graduate there is little commonality in the type or amount of mathematics to which they have been exposed. We do not believe all high school students should take the same courses, but we do believe there should be a high degree of overlap across programs for most students. We certainly do not see any reason for 270 mathematics courses, or for 25 percent of students in one district to take just one mathematics course while more than 90 percent of students in another district take more than four courses.

Most nations endorse the idea that, as public policy, *all* their children should have equal educational opportunities. For the vast majority of 1995 TIMSS countries, intended mathematics content coverage was indeed the same for all their students through what we would call middle school. Even in countries that appear to be creating different tracks, the reality is that basic content is covered by all, with advanced students studying the same topics more deeply.[11] The associated differences among student performance on the TIMSS achievement test were thus far more a matter of individual student ability and effort, combined with differences in teacher quality, than a matter of public policy that supported or even encouraged regional or local differences in students' opportunity to learn.

Sadly, this is not the case in the United States. Not only do we have great variability across districts in eighth grade and high school, but by international standards, our eighth-grade students are exposed to sixth-grade mathematics content. Differences in mathematics achievement are *not* simply the result of differences in student ability and effort, but also matters of chance or social factors such as poverty and housing patterns that influence where a student happens to attend school. There's just no escaping that less opportunity to learn challenging mathematics corresponds to lower achievement.

Though we wish it weren't so, the United States *cannot* be considered a country of educational equality, providing equal educational opportunities to *all* students. This lack of equality in content coverage is not merely an issue for the poor or minorities. Rather, any student in the United States can be disadvantaged simply because of where he or she attends school. In school mathematics at least, the playing field for students is not level. For all students—the lucky few and the unlucky many—educational opportunity depends on factors that cannot be wholly overcome by student ability and effort.

As a nation, we must act to correct these inequities. The solution is not as easy as simply making sweeping changes in course content, but improvement is possible. Although the research we presented here is limited to eighth grade and high school, we suspect changes would need to be made from preschool through high school in mathematics content coverage, textbooks, teacher training, and professional development. Without such changes, the inequality in opportunity to learn mathematics will continue to epitomize the worst sort of playing field: how it tilts depends on where one stands.

# References

1. Richard J. Herrnstein and Charles Murray, *The Bell Curve: Intelligence and Class Structure in American Life* (New York: Free Press, 1994).

2. William H. Schmidt, "What's Missing from Math Standards? Focus, Rigor, and Coherence," *American Educator* 32, no. 1 (Spring 2008): 22–24.

3. David F. Robitaille, William H. Schmidt, Senta Raizen, Curtis McKnight, Edward Britton, and Cynthia Nicol, *Curriculum Frameworks for Mathematics and Science* (Vancouver: Pacific Educational Press, 1993).

4. James S. Coleman, Ernest Q. Campbell, Carol J. Hobson, James McPartland, Alexander M. Mood, Frederic D. Weinfeld, and Robert L. York, *Equality of Educational Opportunity* (Washington, DC: National Center for Educational Statistics, 1966).

5. William H. Schmidt, Curtis C. McKnight, Richard T. Houang, HsingChi Wang, David E. Wiley, Leland S. Cogan, and Richard G. Wolfe, *Why Schools Matter: A Cross-National Comparison of Curriculum and Learning* (San Francisco: Jossey-Bass, 2001).

6. Schmidt et al., *Why Schools Matter*, chapter 4.

7. Schmidt et al., *Why Schools Matter*, chapter 4.

8. Karl L. Alexander, Martha Cook, and Edward L. McDill, "Curriculum Tracking and Educational Stratification: Some Further Evidence," *American Sociological Review* 43, no. 1 (1978): 47–66; Karl L. Alexander and Martha A. Cook, "Curricula and Coursework: A Surprise Ending to a Familiar Story," *American Sociological Review* 47, no. 5 (1982): 626–640; Karl L. Alexander and Bruce K. Eckland,

"School Experience and Status Attainment," in *Adolescence in the Life Cycle: Psychological Change and Social Context,* ed. Sigmund D. Dragastin and Glen H. Elder Jr. (Washington, DC: Hemisphere, 1975), 171–210; Karl L. Alexander and Edward L. McDill, "Selection and Allocation within Schools: Some Causes and Consequences of Curriculum Placement," *American Sociological Review* 41, no. 6 (1976): 963–980; Jeannie Oakes, *Keeping Track: How Schools Structure Inequality* (New Haven, CT: Yale University Press, 1985); James E. Rosenbaum, "Track Misperceptions and Frustrated College Plans: An Analysis of the Effects of Tracks and Track Perceptions in the National Longitudinal Survey," *Sociology of Education* 53, no. 2 (1980): 74–88; and Beth E. Vanfossen, James D. Jones, and Joan Z. Spade, "Curriculum Tracking and Status Maintenance," *Sociology of Education* 60, no. 2 (1987): 104–122.

9. Adam Gamoran, "The Stratification of High School Learning Opportunities," *Sociology of Education* 60, no. 3 (1987): 135–155; Adam Gamoran and Robert D. Mare, "Secondary School Tracking and Educational Inequality: Compensation, Reinforcement, or Neutrality?" *American Journal of Sociology* 94 (1989): 1146–1183; Adam Gamoran, Andrew C. Porter, John Smithson, and Paula A. White, "Upgrading High School Mathematics Instruction: Improving Learning Opportunities for Low-Achieving, Low-Income Youth," *Educational Evaluation and Policy Analysis* 19, no. 4 (1997): 325–338; Maureen T. Hallinan and Warren Kubitschek, "Curriculum Differentiation and High School Achievement," *Social*

*Psychology of Education* 3(1999): 41–62; Thomas B. Hoffer, "Middle School Ability Grouping and Student Achievement in Science and Mathematics," *Educational Evaluation and Policy Analysis* 14, no. 3 (1992): 205–227; Xin Ma, "A Longitudinal Assessment of Antecedent Course Work in Mathematics and Subsequent Mathematical Attainment," *Journal of Educational Research* 94, no. 1 (2000): 16–28; Barbara Schneider, Christopher B. Swanson, and Catherine Riegle-Crumb, "Opportunities for Learning: Course Sequences and Positional Advantages," *Social Psychology of Education* 2 (1998): 25–53; and David Lee Stevenson, Kathryn S. Schiller, and Barbara Schneider, "Sequences of Opportunities for Learning," *Sociology of Education* 67 (1994): 187–198.

10. Leland S. Cogan, William H. Schmidt, and David E. Wiley, "Who Takes What Math and in Which Track? Using TIMSS to Characterize U.S. Students' Eighth-Grade Mathematics Learning Opportunities," *Educational Evaluation and Policy Analysis* 23, no. 4 (2001): 323–341.

11. Schmidt et al., *Why Schools Matter,* chapter 4.

**William H. Schmidt** is a university distinguished professor and codirector of the Education Policy Center at Michigan State University.

**Leland S. Cogan** is a research associate at the Center for the Study of Curriculum at Michigan State University.

**Curtis C. McKnight** is a professor emeritus of the University of Oklahoma.

# EXPLORING THE ISSUE

## Can Schools Close the Achievement Gap between Students from Different Ethnic and Racial Backgrounds?

## Critical Thinking and Reflection

1. Reflect on your experiences in elementary through high school. Can you generate examples of ways in which your racial and ethnic identity (or that of a peer) affected treatment by teachers or other school personnel?
2. Do you think that the detracking discussed by Burris and Welner and the types of curricular changes suggested by Schmidt and colleagues would close the achievement gap? Why or why not?
3. Do you think that schools should have "closing the achivement gap" as a goal?

## Is There Common Ground?

It would appear from the results described by Burris and Welner that the answer to our question should be a resounding "yes." After all, Burris and Welner describe what seem to be substantial improvements in several indicators of the academic achievement of the participating students in the Rockville Centre School District. It is important to recognize, however, that before we fully understand the effects of any educational intervention or curricular change, we must evaluate both the long-term effects and their generalizability. Maintaining the momentum of these curricular changes may be especially difficult because so many of the students may still experience the pernicious effects of ethnic and racial discrimination outside of school. So it will be important to continue to follow the achievement of the students experiencing the curricular change as well as cohorts of students who experience the curriculum in later years to determine the long-term effects of the change. Even if the effects last, we must still be concerned with whether the changes will lead to similar positive results if implemented in other school districts enrolling different types of students, with different resources, and different levels of support from administrators.

It is also important to point out that even if current school-based approaches turn out not to have lasting, transportable effects on the achievement gap, it is possible that more dramatic (i.e., far-reaching) changes could be successful. So, for example, perhaps extending

the school year through the summer would help to reduce the achievement gap when coupled with the sorts of curricular changes described by Burris and Welner. In fact, there is considerable evidence that many of the benefits accrued during the school year by economically disadvantaged African American and Hispanic students are "lost" during the summer, presumably because the pernicious effects of poverty overwhelm the benefits of schooling. Other changes might include having schools provide after-school care for students.

The selection by Schmidt and colleagues identifies many of the same factors as at the root of the achievement gap as does the Burris and Welner selection. Nevertheless, the tone of the former selection is decidedly more pessimistic; hence, our categorization as providing a "no" response to the question: Can schools close the achievement gap between students from different ethnic and racial backgrounds? The difference between the selections lies in part in the fact that whereas Burris and Welner focus on what can be done at the level of an individual school, Schmidt and colleagues take a broader perspective, summarizing the state of affairs in U.S. schools as a whole or at a somewhat more granular level, at the level of the city or school district. This difference in perspective between the selections also provides a valuable lesson: changing a single class or a single school may by possible, but changing the educational system is far more daunting and, more importantly, will probably require different forms of intervention including, perhaps, changes in law.

## Additional Resources

James Gallagher, "Education, Alone, Is a Weak Treatment," *Education Weekly* (July 1998).

Jonathon Kozol, *Savage Inequalities: Children in America's* Schools (Crown, 1991).

Richard Rothstein, "Class and the Classroom," *American School Board Journal* (October 2004).

# *Internet References . . .*

### National Education Association

www.nea.org

### Achievement First: Public Charter Schools

www.achievementfirst.org/

### The Achievement Gap Initiative at Harvard University

www.agi.harvard.edu/

# Unit 3

# Best Practices

*T*his unit investigates best practices in education, ranging from what teachers do (grading, homework) to how classrooms are structured for students with diverse needs (i.e., disabilities, gender). This unit also extends best practices into the home and poses questions relating to how parents can best support children in their education. Whenever possible, empirical articles have been added to challenge students in how to use the results of studies to support a side. Too often, we may give one side more credence by citing "research" or "results." The issues with empirical studies on both sides will offer opportunities to scrutinize research and become better consumers of research. In the end, most research studies are arguments.

Selected, Edited, and with Issue Framing Material by:
Esther S. Chang, *Soka University of America*

# ISSUE

# Does Grading Help Students Learn?

**YES: Kyle Spencer**, from "Standards-Based Grading," *The Education Digest* (2012)

**NO: Alfie Kohn**, from "The Case Against Grades," *Educational Leadership* (2011)

---

## Learning Outcomes

**After reading this issue, you will be able to:**

- Discuss the history and rationale of the grading system typically used in U.S. schools.
- Understand the concept of standards-based grading.
- Recognize the potential benefits and risks of the use of grades to support student learning.

---

### ISSUE SUMMARY

**YES:** Kyle Spencer argues that grades provide useful information if they are linked to standards, or targeted competences to be acquired.

**NO:** Alfie Kohn argues that grades interfere with learning because they subvert one's enjoyment of learning and lead the student to work for grades instead.

**A**ny of us who has grown up in the school system of the United States take for granted that our work will be graded. Concepts such as letters grades, grade point average (GPA), and the like are commonplace. In fact, many of us have found it more than a bit disconcerting if we took a class in which assignments were "checked in" but did not receive a letter grade or numerical rating. Moreover, even advanced professional training and employment options can be influenced by our school grades (e.g., many employers ask for college transcripts and consider GPA in their hiring decisions). But why do we grade? Are grades useful or harmful?

Grading systems can be traced in part to the influence of behaviorism in American psychology in the twentieth century. Although expressed in a number of seemingly distinct theories, the fundamental assumption of behaviorism—namely, that the behavior of any organism is controlled by forces that are external to it—is constant across its many manifestations. In Ivan Pavlov's theory of classical conditioning, a dog reflexively salivates

in response to the sound of a bell that was previously paired with the delivery of food. In B. F. Skinner's theory of operant conditioning, a thirsty rat presses a bar when a light flashes because this results in the delivery of a few drops of water. In these examples, the organism's behavior is controlled by some feature of the world around it—the sound of a bell, the flash of light, the delivery of food or water. Despite its apparent complexity and the addition of a conscious mind, behaviorists have traditionally argued that human behavior, like the behavior of animals, is also controlled by external forces.

The influence of behaviorism has extended far beyond academic psychology to include the American classroom. This influence can be traced most directly to the work of Skinner (1904–1990), who emphasized the role of reinforcement in his theory of operant conditioning. According to Skinner, an event serves as reinforcement if it is contingent on an organism's response to a stimulus and increases the future likelihood of that response. If, for example, a student who is praised consistently by his teacher for completing assignments on time begins to meet deadlines with increasing frequency over time, the teacher's praise would be a reinforcer. It is important to note that, according to Skinner, we cannot know in advance whether praise, a gold star, a good grade, or any other stimulus will be reinforcing. In fact, he argued that we can only know that something is reinforcing if we observe that it leads to an increase in the target behavior. This was a critical point for Skinner. He felt that all too often teachers, parents, and cognitive psychologists expend too much effort "guessing" about what is going on inside a student's head: Is the student motivated? Will the student see my overture as positive or negative? Because we can never know for sure what is going on in another person's mind, Skinner believed that it is far more productive to analyze the consequences of a student's behavior. In short, according to Skinner, we can control a student's behavior by changing its consequences—removing the reinforcement for behaviors we see as negative and providing reinforcement for behaviors we see as positive. In this view, good grades serve to reinforce the behavior that preceded them (e.g., studying) and bad grades serve to punish, or at least not reinforce, the behaviors that preceded them (e.g., skipping class).

Other theories and approaches in psychology and education, however, have also been used to justify grading systems. In many theories of learning in cognitive psychology, grades can be useful for their informational value serving to provide corrective feedback. For example, many theories posit a construct of the mind labeled as the executive function, which is a set of conscious processes involved in planning cognitive activity. Receiving information in the form of grades would allow a student,

through the use of executive function processes, to decide that a poor letter grade indicates the need for more studying, seeking additional assistance, reviewing previously studied material, etc. In short, the grade functions as feedback to change future behavior, presuming that the student is motivated to do well academically. In these theories, grades must be seen as having an informational value and thus are most effective when they are used systematically and coupled with a clear grading rubric or other feedback. If they are seen as arbitrary or assigned based on irrelevant or nontransparent criteria, their value to the learner is diminished.

Despite the different theoretical orientations supporting the use of grades, controversy remains. Grade inflation, variability in grading across classrooms and schools, and more general concerns about student achievement have generated considerable discussion about whether to use grades and if so, how. In the first selection, Kyle Spencer focuses on the potential informational value of grades. Spencer argues that grades provide useful information if they are linked to standards, or targeted competences to be acquired, indicating what competencies the student has mastered and which competences are lagging. Spencer notes that standards-based grading requires more frequent grades than does the traditional approach to grading. In the second selection, Alfie Kohn focuses on the potential motivational effects of grades. Kohn argues that grades interfere with learning because they subvert the student's enjoyment of learning, or intrinsic motivation, instead leading the student to work for the grades rather than to learn. In addition, the focus on grades leads students to avoid intellectually challenging tasks, according to Kohn.

# YES

Kyle Spencer

## Standards-Based Grading

A few years ago, it occurred to Frank Noschese, a physics teacher at John Jay High School in Westchester County, NY, that some of his 11th graders were able to get A's in his class without mastering complex concepts. They could solve exam problems that required them to plug in the right numbers but routinely missed the few questions that tested their understanding of more advanced concepts. Because Noschese's grading system didn't differentiate between those levels of knowledge, there was little incentive for students to focus on harder material.

Noschese wanted a method that would encourage students to move from easy concepts to hard ones and reward them for ultimately obtaining knowledge, no matter how long it took. So he designed a new grading system, inspired by the work of Robert J. Marzano and Jane E. Pollock. Now, every time Noschese's students take a quiz, they don't see one grade but three or four, each indicating whether they have demonstrated their understanding of a pertinent idea. Students who fail to grasp a concept have second and third chances to show they have finally mastered it, by retaking a quiz, conducting a lab experiment, or simply sitting with Noschese at his desk and explaining it.

Noschese is part of a growing band of teachers, schools, and entire districts that have put their faith in standards-based grading, an innovative, albeit complex and sometimes controversial, method that aims to make grades more meaningful. A standards-based report card contains an overall grade for each course but also indicates how well a student has mastered each of the class's several standards. As well, while traditional end-of-course grades are the final products of many factors, including quizzes, homework, behavior, and attendance, with standards-based grading nothing but mastery matters. Standards-based grades account for nonacademic elements very minimally or not at all.

Even if those "process" factors are important aspects of student development, says Ken O'Connor, author of

*A Repair Kit for Grading: Fifteen Fixes for Broken Grades,* report cards need to separate them from academic attainment.

## A Clearer Picture

Grading originally served to determine which students should be promoted to the next level, says Madhabi Chatterji, associate professor at Teachers College, Columbia University. Eventually, it was used as a sorting mechanism that allowed educators to rank students and establish classroom curves and hierarchies. Advocates of standards-based grading contend that traditional grades are often based on vague criteria and therefore unreliable. They can be used to reward or punish students for factors unrelated to competency and don't place enough emphasis on what is truly important: reaching proficiency in a subject so a student can pass state exams and perform well in higher-level classes.

Standards-based grading derives from the idea that teachers ought to have clearly defined academic goals for their students, be able to determine if they've met them, and then communicate that to students and parents. The approach has long been part of life at some elementary schools and was included in the No Child Left Behind Act as a suggested practice.

As states adopt Common Core standards in language arts and math, and as educators move toward a more uniform understanding of what students ought to know, this approach has grown popular among educators at all grade levels.

"There has been a national push to use standards to drive instruction and curricular development," says Kathleen Porter-Magee, a senior director at the Thomas B. Fordham Institute, an education think tank supportive of national standards. "Standards-based grading can seem like a natural extension of that movement," she says. It also "allows for a more nuanced conversation between parents and teachers about where students are strong, where they are weak, and how parents can help them."

Concern over how far American students lag behind other nations has also played a role in encouraging educators to more accurately assess student progress, as has the worry that too many high school graduates are heading to college unprepared.

Standards-based grading is just one of several experimental methods being tested in American classrooms. Another is narrative grading, in which teachers write lengthy reports on student progress. There are also digital badges, where students earn online certificates for accomplishing tasks that are eventually translated into grades. Some educators have moved toward a portfolio system, where students demonstrate progress through a series of projects they assemble and then review with their teachers. And in others there has been a move away from grades altogether.

Some states have encouraged districts to consider standards-based grading. In 2007, state officials in Massachusetts promoted the practice to teachers. The California Department of Education endorsed standards-based grading for improving middle school as early as 2001. And in 2010, Thomas R. Guskey, a professor at the University of Kentucky and coauthor of *Developing Standards-Based Report Cards,* developed a statewide standards-based report card for Kentucky and tested it in 20 schools.

Standards-based grading has become the rule in such districts as Montgomery County, MD; Minnetonka, MN; San Mateo-Foster City, CA; and Quakertown, PA. "There has been a real insurgence in this idea," says Guskey—evident by the proliferation of blogs, software firms, and consultants, all focused on helping schools embrace and adapt to the changes.

## How Standards-Based Grading Works

To understand what standards-based grading means, . . . Like a traditional report card, it includes an overall grade or, for middle and high schoolers, a percentage grade for each class a student is enrolled in. But it goes much further, indicating up to six different marks for each subject, all pertaining to particular strands of learning identified by the Common Core State Standards (which Kentucky has adopted) as well as other national associations, such as the National Science Teachers Association. Rubrics that explain the marks are available online, as are guidelines for using the report cards for students with disabilities and English learners.

An Algebra 1 student, for example, might receive a 4 out of 4 in polynomials and quadratic equations, but only a 2—meaning partial proficiency—in linear equations. Typically, students may take several tries at mastering whatever areas they are weak in, and teachers count just the last or highest assessment.

In a separate box, the teacher can indicate if the student does homework, is punctual, cooperates, and participates. But on Guskey's report card, none of this is included in the student's grade. Shawn Cornally, a biology and calculus teacher at Solon (IA) High School, who uses a similar report card for his students, says separating the learning goals from the other factors is motivating. "It helps them to focus their energy and thoughts on the content of the course rather than the management," he says.

Teasing out topic-by-topic achievement results can be helpful for teachers, and doing so meshes with many districts' embrace of data-based decision making. In the Lindsay Unified School District in Tulare County, CA, which adopted standards-based grading in all of its schools, educators say the new system has changed how students view their time in school and how engaged they become in their mastery of material. This is because Lindsay takes a purist approach to standards-based grading, one that requires high school students to repeat courses until they have earned at least a 3 on their learning objectives.

Tom Blackmon, a world history teacher at Lindsay High School, says the new system has also allowed the school to provide more differentiated instruction, in large part because they track precisely what students know and don't know. Blackmon works with colleagues to group students according to what they've mastered. Through small-group instruction and independent or computer-based learning, students are given the chance to pick up concepts they are struggling with while other students move on.

Detractors of standards-based grading say the time, energy, and even math skills that the system requires can be a big impediment. By its very nature, it requires frequent assessment. Teachers who do this without a school-wide or district-wide initiative must sift through a year's worth of material and decide what the crucial knowledge points are and how to weigh them.

## Overcoming Challenges

Ask proponents what they like about standards-based grading and they are likely to share an anecdote or two about a student who in years past slid by without ever quite mastering the pertinent curricular points. But they can't actually point to research that proves standards-based grading makes students more competent.

In 2004, Susan Pedersen and Doug Williams conducted a small, limited study of 77 7th graders to examine how student motivation was affected by various grading models. But the study's ultimate conclusion—that no matter how the students were graded, they fared more or less the same on the exam—is hardly a ringing endorsement for the need to change long-standing grading practices.

Teachers have acknowledged that instituting a standards-based grading system has its drawbacks. In a survey Guskey conducted in Kentucky during his standards-based grading pilot program, the majority of teachers who were handing out both standards-based report cards and traditional ones reported liking the new ones but not the extra time they took to fill out.

As well, parents have resisted the reform. Some parents in Kennewick, WA, which has been using the system in some middle schools for several years, became so disenchanted with it that they have fought to bring traditional grades back. Their concern: Students lose their motivation to study for tests when they know they will have multiple opportunities to make up for bad scores—something that they may not be able to do in high school and college. Parents have also taken issue with the premise that grading should ignore nonacademic factors, like whether or not children cooperate and do their homework.

And while it's more instructive for a 6th grader, and her parents, to know that she is "partially proficient" in multiplying fractions than that she has a B in math, it can be frustrating to read a report card with dozens of indicators, especially when parents may not know what to do with all that information. In 2005, when Montgomery County, MD, elementary schools piloted a new report card, parents were overwhelmed by the detail. Students had grades in 13 math subcategories—a number that grading experts consider overkill. As well, educators had yet to match up what they were actually teaching with what was on the report card.

The district is now rolling out a revised report card in the upper grades, with four to seven categories per subject and very specific links between classroom work and report card line items.

Educators say the Common Core State Standards have exacerbated this communication problem; many are written in language that seems arcane even to professionals, and there are simply too many to realistically track. Surveys like the one Guskey did in Kentucky discovered that parents respond best to report cards on which the authors have translated jargon-filled standards into language parents can relate to.

Advocates acknowledge that the staggering amount of information that standards-based grading produces, even on well-edited report cards, is really only as good as students' (and, in some ways, parents') ability and willingness to take advantage of it. "This is great for kids who want the chance to improve their grades," Noschese says. For those who are less interested in the challenge of really "getting it," he says, it's not so helpful.

But Douglas Reeves, founder of the Leadership and Learning Center, believes that such a view may be missing the point. Reeves assists educators on their grading practices and has seen that grades are more likely to match up to standardized test scores when schools use standards-based grading. "Standards-based grading makes people more honest," he says.

---

**KYLE SPENCER** is a freelance writer who focuses on educational issues. He is based in New York.

Alfie Kohn

# The Case Against Grades

"I remember the first time that a grading rubric was attached to a piece of my writing. . . . Suddenly all the joy was taken away. I was writing for a grade—I was no longer exploring for me. I want to get that back. Will I ever get that back?"

—Claire, a student (in Olson, 2006)

**B**y now enough has been written about academic assessment to fill a library, but when you stop to think about it, the whole enterprise really amounts to a straightforward two-step dance. We need to collect information about how students are doing, and then we need to share that information (along with our judgments, perhaps) with the students and their parents. Gather and report—that's pretty much it.

You say the devil is in the details? Maybe so, but I'd argue that too much attention to the particulars of implementation may be distracting us from the bigger picture—or at least from a pair of remarkable conclusions that emerge from the best theory, practice, and research on the subject: *Collecting information doesn't require tests, and sharing that information doesn't require grades.* In fact, students would be a lot better off without either of these relics from a less enlightened age.

Why tests are not a particularly useful way to assess student learning (at least the kind that matters), and what thoughtful educators do instead, are questions that must wait for another day. Here, our task is to take a hard look at the second practice, the use of letters or numbers as evaluative summaries of how well students have done, regardless of the method used to arrive at those judgments.

## The Effects of Grading

Most of the criticisms of grading you'll hear today were laid out forcefully and eloquently anywhere from four to eight decades ago (Crooks, 1933; De Zouche, 1945; Kirschenbaum, Simon, & Napier, 1971; Linder, 1940; Marshall, 1968), and these early essays make for

eye-opening reading. They remind us just how long it's been clear there's something wrong with what we're doing as well as just how little progress we've made in acting on that realization.

In the 1980s and '90s, educational psychologists systematically studied the effects of grades. As I've reported elsewhere (Kohn, 1999a, 1999b, 1999c), when students from elementary school to college who are led to focus on grades are compared with those who aren't, the results support three robust conclusions:

- *Grades tend to diminish students' interest in whatever they're learning.* A "grading orientation" and a "learning orientation" have been shown to be inversely related and, as far as I can tell, every study that has ever investigated the impact on intrinsic motivation of receiving grades (or instructions that emphasize the importance of getting good grades) has found a negative effect.

- *Grades create a preference for the easiest possible task.* Impress upon students that what they're doing will count toward their grade, and their response will likely be to avoid taking any unnecessary intellectual risks. They'll choose a shorter book, or a project on a familiar topic, in order to minimize the chance of doing poorly—not because they're "unmotivated" but because they're rational. They're responding to adults who, by telling them the goal is to get a good mark, have sent the message that success matters more than learning.

- *Grades tend to reduce the quality of students' thinking.* They may skim books for what they'll "need to know." They're less likely to wonder, say, "How can we be sure that's true?" than to ask "Is this going to be on the test?" In one experiment, students told they'd be graded on how well they learned a social studies lesson had more trouble understanding the main point of the text than did students who were told that no grades would be involved. Even on a measure of rote recall, the graded group remembered fewer facts a week later (Grolnick and Ryan, 1987).

Research on the effects of grading has slowed down in the last couple of decades, but the studies that are still being done reinforce the earlier findings. For example, a grade-oriented environment is associated with increased levels of cheating (Anderman and Murdock, 2007), grades (whether or not accompanied by comments) promote a fear of failure even in high-achieving students (Pulfrey et al., 2011), and the elimination of grades (in favor of a pass/fail system) produces substantial benefits with no apparent disadvantages in medical school (White and Fantone, 2010). More important, no recent research has contradicted the earlier "big three" findings, so those conclusions still stand.

## Why Grading Is Inherently Problematic

A student asked his Zen master how long it would take to reach enlightenment. "Ten years," the master said. But, the student persisted, what if he studied very hard? "Then 20 years," the master responded. Surprised, the student asked how long it would take if he worked very, *very* hard and became the most dedicated student in the Ashram. "In that case, 30 years," the master replied. His explanation: "If you have one eye on how close you are to achieving your goal, that leaves only one eye for your task."

To understand why research finds what it does about grades, we need to shift our focus from educational measurement techniques to broader psychological and pedagogical questions. The latter serve to illuminate a series of misconceived assumptions that underlie the use of grading.

*Motivation:* While it's true that many students, after a few years of traditional schooling, could be described as motivated by grades, what counts is the nature of their motivation. Extrinsic motivation, which includes a desire to get better grades, is not only different from, but often undermines, intrinsic motivation, a desire to learn for its own sake (Kohn 1999a). Many assessment specialists talk about motivation as though it were a single entity—and their recommended practices just put a finer gloss on a system of rewards and punishments that leads students to chase marks and become less interested in the learning itself. If nourishing their *desire* to learn is a primary goal for us, then grading is problematic by its very nature.

*Achievement:* Two educational psychologists pointed out that "an overemphasis on assessment can actually undermine the pursuit of excellence" (Maehr and Midgley, 1996,

p. 7). That unsettling conclusion—which holds regardless of the quality of the assessment but is particularly applicable to the use of grades—is based on these researchers' own empirical findings as well as those of many others, including Carol Dweck, Carole Ames, Ruth Butler, and John Nicholls (for a review, see Kohn 1999b, chapter 2). In brief: the more students are led to focus on *how well* they're doing, the less engaged they tend to be with *what* they're doing.

It follows that all assessment must be done carefully and sparingly lest students become so concerned about their achievement (how good they are at doing something—or, worse, how their performance compares to others') that they're no longer thinking about the learning itself. Even a well-meaning teacher may produce a roomful of children who are so busy monitoring their own reading skills that they're no longer excited by the stories they're reading. Assessment consultants worry that grades may not accurately reflect student performance; educational psychologists worry because grades fix students' attention *on* their performance.

*Quantification:* When people ask me, a bit defensively, if it isn't important to measure how well students are learning (or teachers are teaching), I invite them to rethink their choice of verb. There is certainly value in *assessing* the quality of learning and teaching, but that doesn't mean it's always necessary, or even possible, to *measure* those things—that is, to turn them into numbers. Indeed, "measurable outcomes may be the least significant results of learning" (McNeil, 1986, p. xviii)—a realization that offers a refreshing counterpoint to today's corporate-style "school reform" and its preoccupation with data.

To talk about what happens in classrooms, let alone in children's heads, as moving forward or backward in specifiable degrees, is not only simplistic because it fails to capture much of what is going on, but also destructive because it may change what is going on for the worse. Once we're compelled to focus only on what can be reduced to numbers, such as how many grammatical errors are present in a composition or how many mathematical algorithms have been committed to memory, thinking has been severely compromised. And that is exactly what happens when we try to fit learning into a four- or five- or (heaven help us) 100-point scale.

*Curriculum:* "One can have the best assessment imaginable," Howard Gardner (1991, p. 254) observed, "but unless the accompanying curriculum is of quality, the assessment has no use." Some people in the field are candid about their relativism, offering to help align your assessment to whatever your goals or curriculum may be. The result is that teachers may become more adept at measuring how well students have mastered a collection of facts and skills whose value is questionable—and never questioned. "If it's not worth teaching, it's not worth teaching well," as Eliot Eisner (2001, p. 370) likes to say. Nor, we might add, is it worth assessing accurately.

Portfolios, for example, can be constructive if they replace grades rather than being used to *yield* them. They offer a way to thoughtfully gather a variety of meaningful examples of learning for the students to review. But what's the point, "if instruction is dominated by worksheets so that every portfolio looks the same"? (Neill et al. 1995, p. 4). Conversely, one sometimes finds a mismatch between more thoughtful forms of pedagogy—say, a workshop approach to teaching writing—and a depressingly standardized assessment tool like rubrics (Wilson, 2006).

## Improving Grading: A Fool's Errand?

> "I had been advocating standards-based grading, which is a very important movement in its own right, but it took a push from some great educators to make me realize that if I wanted to focus my assessment around authentic feedback, then I should just abandon grades altogether."
>
> —New Jersey middle school teacher Jason Bedell (2010)

Much of what is prescribed in the name of "assessing for learning" (and, for that matter, "formative assessment") leaves me uneasy: The recommended practices often seem prefabricated and mechanistic; the imperatives of data collection seem to upstage the children themselves and the goal of helping them become more enthusiastic about what they're doing. Still, if it's done only occasionally and with humility, I think it's possible to assess for learning. But *grading* for learning is, to paraphrase a 1960's-era slogan, rather like bombing for peace. Rating and ranking students (and their efforts to figure things out) is inherently counterproductive.

If I'm right—more to the point, if all the research to which I've referred is taken seriously—then the absence of grades is a necessary, though not sufficient, condition for promoting deep thinking and a desire to engage in it. It's worth lingering on this proposition in light of a variety of efforts to sell us formulas to improve our grading techniques, none of which address the problems of grading, per se.

- It's not enough to replace letters or numbers with labels ("exceeds expectations," "meets expectations," and so on). If you're sorting students into four or five piles, you're still grading them. Rubrics typically include numbers as well as labels, which

is only one of several reasons they merit our skepticism (Wilson, 2006; Kohn, 2006).

- It's not enough to tell students in advance exactly what's expected of them. "When school is seen as a test, rather than an adventure in ideas," teachers may persuade themselves they're being fair "if they specify, in listlike fashion, exactly what must be learned to gain a satisfactory grade . . . [but] such schooling is unfair in the wider sense that it prepares students to pass other people's tests without strengthening their capacity to set their own assignments in collaboration with their fellows" (Nicholls and Hazzard, 1993, p. 77).

- It's not enough to disseminate grades more efficiently—for example, by posting them on-line. There is a growing technology, as the late Gerald Bracey once remarked, "that permits us to do in nanoseconds things that we shouldn't be doing at all" (quoted in Mathews, 2006). In fact, posting grades on-line is a significant step backward because it enhances the salience of those grades and therefore their destructive effects on learning.

- It's not enough to add narrative reports. "When comments and grades coexist, the comments are written to justify the grade" (Wilson, 2009, p. 60). Teachers report that students, for their part, often just turn to the grade and ignore the comment, but "when there's only a comment, they read it," says high school English teacher Jim Drier. Moreover, research suggests that the harmful impact of grades on creativity is no less (and possibly even more) potent when a narrative accompanies them. Narratives are helpful only in the absence of grades (Butler, 1988; Pulfrey et al., 2011).

- It's not enough to use "standards-based" grading. That phrase may suggest any number of things—for example, more consistency, or a reliance on more elaborate formulas, in determining grades; greater specificity about what each grade signifies; or an increase in the number of tasks or skills that are graded. At best, these prescriptions do nothing to address the fundamental problems with grading. At worst, they exacerbate those problems. In addition to the simplistic premise that it's always good to have more data, we find a penchant shared by the behaviorists of yesteryear that learning can and should be broken down into its components, each to be evaluated separately. And more frequent temperature-taking produces exactly the kind of disproportionate attention to performance (at the expense of learning) that researchers have found to be so counterproductive.

The term "standards-based" is sometimes intended just to mean that grading is aligned with a given set of objectives, in which case our first response should be to inquire into the value of those objectives (as well as the extent to which students were invited to help formulate them). If grades are based on state standards, there's particular reason to be concerned since those standards are often too specific, age-inappropriate, superficial, and standardized by definition. In my experience, the best teachers tend to be skeptical about aligning their teaching to a list imposed by distant authorities, or using that list as a basis for assessing how well their students are thinking.

Finally, "standards-based" may refer to something similar to criterion-based testing, where the idea is to avoid grading students on a curve. (Even some teachers who don't do so explicitly nevertheless act as though grades ought to fall into something close to a normal distribution, with only a few students receiving As. But this pattern is not a fact of life, nor is it a sign of admirable "rigor" on the teacher's part. Rather, "it is a symbol of failure—failure to teach well, failure to test well, and failure to have any influence at all on the intellectual lives of students" [Milton, Pollio, & Eison, 1986].) This surely represents an improvement over a system in which the number of top marks is made artificially scarce and students are set against one another. But here we've peeled back the outer skin of the onion (competition) only to reveal more noxious layers beneath: extrinsic motivation, numerical ratings, the tendency to promote achievement at the expense of learning.

If we begin with a desire to assess more often, or to produce more data, or to improve the consistency of our grading, then certain prescriptions will follow. If, however, our point of departure isn't mostly about the grading, but about our desire for students to understand ideas from the inside out, or to get a kick out of playing with words and numbers, or to be in charge of their own learning, then we will likely end up elsewhere. We may come to see grading as a huge, noisy, fuel-guzzling, smoke-belching machine that constantly requires repairs and new parts, when what we should be doing is pulling the plug.

## Deleting—Or at Least Diluting—Grades

"Like it or not, grading is here to stay" is a statement no responsible educator would ever offer as an excuse for inaction. What matters is whether a given practice is in the best interest of students. If it isn't, then our obligation is to work for its elimination and, in the meantime, do what we can to minimize its impact.

Replacing letter and number grades with narrative assessments or conferences—qualitative summaries of student progress offered in writing or as part of a conversation—is not a utopian fantasy. It has already been done successfully in many elementary and middle schools and even in some high schools, both public and private (Kohn, 1999c). It's important not only to realize that such schools exist but to investigate *why* they've eliminated grades, how they've managed to do so (hint: the process can be gradual), and what benefits they have realized.

Naturally objections will be raised to this—or any—significant policy change, but once students and their parents have been shown the relevant research, reassured about their concerns, and invited to participate in constructing alternative forms of assessment, the abolition of grades proves to be not only realistic but an enormous improvement over the status quo. Sometimes it's only after grading has ended that we realize just how harmful it's been.

To address one common fear, the graduates of grade-free high schools are indeed accepted by selective private colleges and large public universities—on the basis of narrative reports and detailed descriptions of the curriculum (as well as recommendations, essays, and interviews), which collectively offer a fuller picture of the applicant than does a grade-point average. Moreover, these schools point out that their students are often more motivated and proficient learners, thus better prepared for college, than their counterparts at traditional schools who have been preoccupied with grades.

In any case, college admission is surely no bar to eliminating grades in elementary and middle schools because colleges are largely indifferent to what students have done before high school. That leaves proponents of grades for younger children to fall back on some version of an argument I call "BGUTI": Better Get Used To It (Kohn, 2005). The claim here is that we should do unpleasant and unnecessary things to children now in order to prepare them for the fact that just such things will be done to them later. This justification is exactly as absurd as it sounds, yet it continues to drive education policy.

Even when administrators aren't ready to abandon traditional report cards, individual teachers can help to rescue learning in their own classrooms with a two-pronged strategy to "neuter grades," as one teacher described it. First, they can stop putting letter or number grades on individual assignments and instead offer only qualitative feedback. Report cards are bad enough, but the destructive effects reported by researchers (on interest in learning, preference for challenge, and quality of thinking) are compounded when students are rated on what they do in school day after day. Teachers can mitigate considerable harm by replacing grades with authentic assessments; moreover, as we've seen, any feedback they may already offer becomes much more useful in the absence of letter or number ratings.

Second, although teachers may be required to submit a final grade, there's no requirement for them to decide unilaterally what that grade will be. Thus, students can be invited to participate in that process either as a negotiation (such that the teacher has the final say) or by simply permitting students to grade themselves. If people find that idea alarming, it's probably because they realize it creates a more democratic classroom, one in which teachers must create a pedagogy and a curriculum that will truly engage students rather than allow teachers to coerce them into doing whatever they're told. In fact, negative reactions to this proposal ("It's unrealistic!") point up how grades function as a mechanism for controlling students rather than as a necessary or constructive way to report information about their performance.

I spoke recently to several middle and high school teachers who have de-graded their classes. Jeff Robbins, who has taught eighth-grade science in New Jersey for 15 years, concedes that "life was easier with grades" because they take so much less time than meaningful assessment. That efficiency came at a huge cost, though, he noticed: Kids were stressed out and also preferred to avoid intellectual risks. "They'll take an easier assignment that will guarantee the A."

Initially Robbins announced that any project or test could be improved and resubmitted for a higher grade. Unfortunately, that failed to address the underlying problem, and he eventually realized he had to stop grading entirely. Now, he offers comments to all of his 125 students "about what they're doing and what they need to improve on" and makes abbreviated notes in his grade book. At the end of the term, over a period of about a week, he grabs each student for a conversation at some point— "because the system isn't designed to allow kids this kind of feedback"—asking "what did you learn, how did you learn it. Only at the very end of the conversation [do] I ask what grade will reflect it . . . and we'll collectively arrive at something." Like many other teachers I've spoken to over the years, Robbins says he almost always accepts students' suggestions because they typically pick the same grade that he would have.

Jim Drier, an English teacher at Mundelein High School in Illinois who has about 90 students ranging "from at-risk to A.P.," was relieved to find that it "really doesn't take that long" to write at least a brief note on students' assignments—"a reaction to what they did and some advice on how they might improve." But he never

gives them "a number or grade on anything they do. The things that grades make kids do are heartbreaking for an educator": arguing with teachers, fighting with parents, cheating, memorizing facts just for a test and then forgetting them. "This is not why I became a teacher."

Without grades, "I think my relationships with students are better," Drier says. "Their writing improves more quickly and the things they learn stay with them longer. I've had lots of kids tell me it's changed their attitude about coming to school." He expected resistance from parents but says that in three years only one parent has objected, and it may help that he sends a letter home to explain exactly what he's doing and why. Now two of his colleagues are joining him in eliminating grades.

Drier's final grades are based on students' written self-assessments, which, in turn, are based on their review of items in their portfolios. He meets with about three-quarters of them twice a term, in most cases briefly, to assess their performance and, if necessary (although it rarely happens) to discuss a concern about the grade they've suggested. Asked how he manages without a grade book full of letters or numbers, Drier replies, "If I spend 18 weeks with them, I have a pretty good idea what their writing and reasoning ability is."

A key element of authentic assessment for these and other teachers is the opportunity for students to help design the assessment and reflect on its purposes—individually and as a class. Notice how different this is from the more common variant of self-assessment in which students merely monitor their progress toward the teacher's (or legislature's) goals and in which they must reduce their learning to numerical ratings with grade-like rubrics.

Points of overlap as well as divergence emerge from the testimonies of such teachers, some of which have been collected by Joe Bower (n.d.), an educator in Red Deer, Alberta. Some teachers, for example, *evaluate* their students' performance (in qualitative terms, of course), but others believe it's more constructive to offer only *feedback*—which is to say, information. On the latter view, "the alternative to grades is description" and "the starting point for description is a plain sheet of paper, not a form which leads and homogenizes description" (Marshall, 1968, pp. 131, 143).

Teachers also report a variety of reactions to de-grading not only from colleagues and administrators but also from the students themselves. John Spencer (2010), an Arizona middle school teacher, concedes that "many of the 'high performing' students were angry at first. They saw it as unfair. They viewed school as work and their peers as competitors. . . . Yet, over time they switch and they calm down. They end up learning more once they aren't feeling the pressure" from grades.

Indeed, research suggests that the common tendency of students to focus on grades doesn't reflect an innate predilection or a "learning style" to be accommodated; rather, it's due to having been led for years to work for grades. In one study (Butler, 1992), some students were encouraged to think about how well they performed at a creative task while others were just invited to be imaginative. Each student was then taken to a room that contained a pile of pictures that other people had drawn in response to the same instructions. It also contained some information that told them how to figure out their "creativity score." Sure enough, the children who were told to think about their performance now wanted to know how they had done relative to their peers; those who had been allowed to become immersed in the task were more interested in seeing *what* their peers had done.

Grades don't prepare children for the "real world"—unless one has in mind a world where interest in learning and quality of thinking are unimportant. Nor are grades a necessary part of schooling, any more than paddling or taking extended dictation could be described that way. Still, it takes courage to do right by kids in an era when the quantitative matters more than the qualitative, when meeting (someone else's) standards counts for more than exploring ideas, and when anything "rigorous" is automatically assumed to be valuable. We have to be willing to challenge the conventional wisdom, which in this case means asking not how to improve grades but how to jettison them once and for all.

# References

Anderman, E. M., & Murdock, T. B., eds. (2007). *Psychology of academic cheating.* Burlington, MA: Elsevier Academic Press.

Bedell, J. (2010, July). Blog post.

Bower, J. (2010, March 28). Blog post.

Bower, J. (n.d.). Blog post. [Grading moratorium list]

Butler, R. (1988). Enhancing and undermining intrinsic motivation: The effects of task-involving and ego-involving evaluation on interest and performance. *British Journal of Educational Psychology, 58,*1–14.

Crooks, A. D. (1933). Marks and marking systems: A digest. *Journal of Educational Research, 27*(4), 259–72.

De Zouche, D. (1945). "The wound *is* mortal": Marks, honors, unsound activities. *The Clearing House, 19*(6), 339–44.

Eisner, E. W. (2001, Jan.). What does it mean to say a school is doing well? *Phi Delta Kappan,* pp. 367–72.

Gardner, H. (1991). *The unschooled mind: How children think and how schools should teach.* New York: Basic Books.

Grolnick, W. S., & Ryan, R. M. (1987). Autonomy in children's learning: An experimental and individual difference investigation. *Journal of Personality and Social Psychology, 52,* 890–98.

Kirschenbaum, H., Simon, S. B., & Napier, R. W. (1971). *Wad-ja-get?: The grading game in American education.* New York: Hart.

Kohn, A. (1999a). *Punished by rewards: The trouble with gold stars, incentive plans, A's, praise, and other bribes.* Rev. ed. Boston: Houghton Mifflin.

Kohn, A. (1999b). *The schools our children deserve: Moving beyond traditional classrooms and "tougher standards."* Boston: Houghton Mifflin.

Kohn, A. (1999c, March). From degrading to degrading. *High School Magazine,* pp. 38–43.

Kohn, A. (2001, Sept. 26). Beware of the standards, not just the tests. *Education Week,* pp. 52, 38.

Kohn, A. (2005, Sept. 7). Getting hit on the head lessons. *Education Week,* pp. 52, 46–47.

Kohn, A. (2006, March). The trouble with rubrics. *Language Arts,* pp. 12–15.

Linder, I. H. (1940, July). Is there a substitute for teachers' grades? *School Board Journal,* pp. 25, 26, 79.

Maehr, M. L., & Midgley, C. (1996). *Transforming school cultures.* Boulder, CO: Westview.

Marshall, M. S. (1968). *Teaching without grades.* Corvallis, OR: Oregon State University Press.

Matthews, J. (2006, Nov. 14). Just whose idea was all this testing? *Washington Post.*

McNeil, L. M. (1986). *Contradictions of control: School structure and school knowledge.* New York: Routledge & Kegan Paul.

Milton, O., Pollio, H. R., & Eison, J. A. (1986). *Making sense of college grades.* San Francisco: Jossey-Bass.

Neill, M., Bursh, P., Schaeffer, B., Thall, C., Yohe, M., & Zappardino, P. (1995). *Implementing performance assessments: A guide to classroom, school, and system reform.* Cambridge, MA: FairTest.

Nicholls, J. G., & Hazzard, S. P. (1993). *Education as adventure: Lessons from the second grade.* New York: Teachers College Press.

Olson, K. (2006, Nov. 8). The wounds of schooling. *Education Week*, pp. 28–29.

Pulfrey, C., Buch, C., & Butera, F. (2011). Why grades engender performance-avoidance goals: The mediating role of autonomous motivation. *Journal of Educational Psychology, 103*, 683–700.

Spencer, J. (2010, July). Blog post.

White, C. B., & Fantone, J. C. (2010). Pass-fail grading: Laying the foundation for self-regulated learning. *Advances in Health Science Education, 15*, 469–77.

Wilson, M. (2006). *Rethinking rubrics in writing assessment.* Portsmouth, NH: Heinemann.

Wilson, M. (2009, Nov). Responsive writing assessment. *Educational Leadership*, pp. 58–62.

---

**ALFIE KOHN** is a writer, lecturer, and commentator who focuses on education, child development, parenting, and human behavior.

# EXPLORING THE ISSUE

## Does Grading Help Students Learn?

## Critical Thinking and Reflection

1. Consider the evidence Kohn cites against the use of grades. Can you use your own experiences in school to support or refute this evidence?
2. From your perspective as a student, do you think the informational value provided by standards-based grading would be more important than the potential "threat" to your intrinsic motivation? Why or why not?
3. Do you think that standards-based grading would be more effective for some types of students than other types? Which students would benefit most? Which would benefit least? Why?

## Is There Common Ground?

Can we use empirical data to decide on whether grades have the detrimental impact on intrinsic motivation claimed by Kohn and other critics? In principle, it should be possible to compare classrooms or schools using traditional grading systems to those eschewing grades in favor of portfolio compilations, narrative assessments, or other more qualitative assessments. It should also be possible to compare classrooms or schools using different variants for traditional grading systems (e.g., those using a grading curve or criterion-based grading). Unfortunately, taking advantage of naturally occurring grading differences involves a correlational approach, which makes interpretation of cause and effect difficult. For example, there are likely to be many differences between a school that uses traditional grades and one using qualitative assessment techniques; thus, if we observe differences in student achievement, those differences may have nothing to do with grading systems but instead may reflect differences in student demographics, curriculum content, or teacher quality. Experiments have been conducted to address these issues, but they have often been quite artificial. In general, though, experiments have supported the idea that grades can diminish motivation when they seem arbitrary or are not linked to transparent criteria that provide useful corrective feedback.

Other issues further complicate the grading story. Some students may find grades motivating for the wrong reason (i.e., they work only for the grades), whereas others are motivated to learn but value the corrective feedback grades can provide. In addition, some students may appreciate the informational value of grades, but if they are not given the opportunity or, more importantly, the assistance needed to learn more effectively after a poor grade, they may become disheartened and lose interest over time. And finally, no system of evaluation can compensate for a poorly structured curriculum or an unskilled or disinterested teacher.

## Additional Resources

C. Pulfrey, D. Buch, and F. Butea, "Why Grades Engender Performance-Avoidance Goals," *Journal of Educational Psychology* (vol. 103, no. 3, 2011).

Thomas R. Guskey, "Five Obstacles to Grading Reform," *Educational Leadership* (November 2011).

Christopher S. Collins, "An Individual or a Group Grade: Exploring Reward Structure for Motivation and Learning," *Journal on Excellence in College Teaching* (vol. 28, 2012).

# *Internet References . . .*

**Center for Teaching—Vanderbilt University**

http://cft.vanderbilt.edu/teaching-guides/

**Teaching & Learning in Higher Ed**

http://teachingandlearninginhighered.org/

**Always Formative**

http://alwaysformative.blogspot.com/

Selected, Edited, and with Issue Framing Material by:
Esther S. Chang, *Soka University of America*

# ISSUE

# Is Full Inclusion Always the Best Option for Children with Disabilities?

**YES: Michael F. Giangreco**, from "Extending Inclusive Opportunities," *Educational Leadership* (2007)

**NO: James M. Kauffman, Kathleen McGee, and Michele Brigham**, from "Enabling or Disabling? Observation on Changes in Special Education," *Phi Delta Kappan* (2004)

---

## Learning Outcomes

**After reading this issue, you will be able to:**

- Define the term "full inclusion."
- Understand the intent of full inclusion.
- Discuss the potential advantages and disadvantages of full inclusion for an individual student with a disability.
- Discuss the potential advantages and disadvantages of full inclusion for an individual student without a disability.

---

### ISSUE SUMMARY

**YES:** Michael F. Giangreco argues that even students with severe disabilities are best served within the "regular" education classroom along with their typically developing peers.

**NO:** James M. Kauffman and colleagues argue that the goal of education for students with disabilities should be to increase their level of competence and independence.

---

**P**ublic Law (P.L.) 94-142, the Education for All Handicapped Children Act (1975), required that all children with disabilities, whatever the nature or severity of their disability, be provided a free and appropriate education within the least restrictive environment possible. Later laws—P.L. 99-457, the 1986 Education of the Handicapped Act, and P.L. 101-476, the 1990 Individuals with Disabilities Education Act (IDEA)—clarified, strengthened, and expanded the 1975 legislation. Before the enactment of these laws, many children with disabilities, especially those with more severe or challenging disabilities, were segregated from their more typically developing peers. Students with disabilities attended special classes in their neighborhood schools, or they attended special schools for those with disabilities. In either case, they had minimal contact with their typically developing peers. Advocates for people with disabilities argued that a separate education denies children with disabilities the same opportunities afforded everyone else.

Rather than being segregated, many children with disabilities are now placed ("mainstreamed") into the regular classroom on at least a part-time basis. Mainstreaming ensures that students with disabilities have contact with their typically developing peers and the regular education curriculum. In recent years, advocates for people with disabilities have successfully argued that simple physical presence in the regular classroom may not lead to full participation in the classroom's intellectual or social life. Advocates, therefore, have argued that schools must move beyond mainstreaming to full inclusion. Full inclusion refers to placement in the regular classroom with appropriate supports and services—such as an interpreter who signs the teacher's talk for a student with impaired hearing—and includes active efforts to ensure participation in the life of the class. Moreover, it is argued that these supports and services must be tailored to the unique needs of each individual as set forth in the Individual Educational Plan (IEP). The IEP is prepared annually by a multidisciplinary team composed of, for example, the school psychologist, a special education teacher, the regular classroom teacher, and a speech-language clinician, all of whom assess the student's current level of functioning and set short- and long-term goals for his or her educational progress.

Although full inclusion may be the ideal, school districts have been granted considerable latitude by the courts to make educational placements. For example, the courts have allowed less than full inclusion if a student is unlikely to derive sufficient academic or nonacademic benefit from inclusion, if a student's placement in the regular classroom is likely to be disruptive, or if the cost of inclusion would be prohibitive for the district. As a result of these constraints, many students experience less than full inclusion—some may have "pull-out" classes, which segregate them from their more typically developing peers for part of the school day; others may be segregated for almost their entire school experience.

Often, the issue of inclusion is most heated in the case of students with severe disabilities, and both of the accompanying selections focus largely on such students. In the first selection, Michael F. Giangreco argues that inclusion of students with even severe disabilities is possible and desirable, and he outlines strategies for accomplishing this. These strategies, which he terms the *multilevel curriculum and curriculum overlapping,* entail adapting the content of the curriculum or level of support provided to the student, but doing so within the shared activities of the classroom. In the second selection, James M. Kauffman and his colleagues argue, first, that the goal of education for students with disabilities is to provide them with the skills needed to increase their independence and bring them as close as possible in terms of functioning to their "mainstream" peers. They then argue that inclusion, with its emphasis on accommodation, thwarts this goal by actually increasing dependence on special assistance, reinforcing maladaptive behaviors, and failing to "push" students to acquire new skills.

# YES

**Michael F. Giangreco**

# Extending Inclusive Opportunities

**M**s. Santos,[1] a 5th grade teacher, had successfully included students with learning disabilities or physical limitations in her classroom for years. Even in years when none of her students had been identified as having disabilities, her students' abilities and needs had varied, sometimes substantially. She regularly taught students whose native languages were not English and students who displayed challenging behaviors or fragile emotional health. The range of her students' reading abilities typically spanned several years.

Ms. Santos had confidently made *instructional* accommodations for all her students, for example, by modifying materials and giving individualized cues—but she had rarely needed to modify her curriculum. Students with and without disabilities in her class worked on the same topics, although sometimes at differing levels and paces. But when a boy who worked far below 5th grade level was assigned to her class, Ms. Santos faced a question that looms large for teachers trying to make inclusion work: How can we achieve true curricular inclusion for students who function substantially below grade level?

## Facing a New Challenge

Last school year, Ms. Santos welcomed Chris into her 5th grade class. A boy new to the school, Chris had a good sense of humor, liked many kinds of music, and had a history of making friends and liking school. Unfortunately, in the eyes of most people, these qualities were overshadowed by the severity of his intellectual, behavioral, sensory, and physical disabilities. Because Chris came to her class functioning at a kindergarten or prekindergarten level in all academic areas, Ms. Santos had trouble conceiving of how he could learn well in a 5th grade class, and she worried about what Chris's parents and her colleagues would expect. By suggesting how a teacher might handle this kind of situation, I hope to assist teachers and other professionals who are attempting to successfully include students with significant disabilities within mainstream classrooms.

## Extending Student Participation

The Individuals with Disabilities Education Improvement Act of 2004 presumes that the first placement option a school system must consider for each student with a disability, regardless of disability category or severity, is the regular classroom. Students with disabilities are entitled to supplemental supports that enable them to meaningfully pursue individually determined learning outcomes—including those from the general education curriculum. The question to be asked is not whether a student is able to pursue the same learning outcomes as his or her age-level peers, but whether that student's needs can be appropriately addressed in the general education setting.

The participation of students with disabilities within general education classes can be broadly characterized along two dimensions: each student's *program* (such as the goals of the student's individualized education program) and each student's *supports*. Supports are anything that the school provides to help the student pursue education goals—for example materials, adaptations, or a classroom aide (Giangreco, 2006).

Within a school day, or even within a single activity, an individual student will sometimes require modifications to the general education program and at other times be able to work within the standard program. Likewise, the number of supports teachers will need to provide for students will fluctuate greatly. In some scenarios, a student with a disability can do the same academic work his or her classmates are doing. These kinds of opportunities help teachers and students interact in a natural way, show classmates that students with learning needs don't always need special help, and allow students to avoid unnecessary supports.

## Setting the Stage for Curricular Modifications

Chris was fortunate that he was assigned a teacher who already had good practices in place for including students with IEPs. Ms. Santos created opportunities for many types

From *Educational Leadership*, February 2007, pp. 34–37. Copyright © 2007 by Michael F. Giangreco. Reprinted by permission of the author.

of instructional interactions through a busy classroom schedule of inquiry-based activities. Her ability to teach students with disabilities grew out of her belief that the core of teaching and learning was the same, regardless of whether a student had a disability label.

Although Ms. Santos was not sure how to meet the challenge of including Chris in her classroom, she asked important questions to clarify her own role as a team member, understand the curricular expectations for Chris, and get a vision for how to teach a class with a wider mix of abilities than she had encountered before. As part of that vision, she drew on the power of relationships, both in drawing Chris into her plans for students and in building a collaborative team of special educators, parents, and others. In her classroom community, she expected students to help one another learn and be responsible for helping the classroom run smoothly. As much as possible, she also planned for Chris to have an active voice in telling his teachers which supports helped him and which did not.

For Chris to be a viable social member of the classroom, he would have to participate in the academic work, not just be physically present or socially accepted. Ms. Santos knew how frustrating and embarrassing it can be for students when curriculum content is over their heads, and she also knew the hazards of underestimating students. She sought ways to adjust the curriculum to an appropriate level of difficulty for Chris, while leaving opportunities for him to surprise her with his capabilities.

## When Curriculum Modifications Are Essential

In many inclusion scenarios, such as the one Ms. Santos faced, modifications to the general education program will be essential. Sometimes the student will need individualized content but will not require specialized supports to work with that content. For example, the teacher might assign a student five new vocabulary words instead of 10, or assign that learner single-digit computation instead of decimals.

In some situations, the classroom teacher will need to both modify the general education program and provide individualized supports. Although students with more severe disabilities may often need both program and support accommodation to succeed in a mainstream class, teachers may not need to alter both the curriculum and the types of support available for all classroom work a student with a disability undertakes. Even a student with significant disabilities, like Chris, rarely needs both an

individualized education program and individualized supports all the time.

## Multilevel Curriculum and Curriculum Overlapping

*Multilevel curriculum* and *curriculum overlapping* are two approaches to adapting curriculum that facilitate participation of students with significant disabilities. In the multilevel curriculum approach, students with disabilities and their peers participate in a shared activity. Each student has individually appropriate learning outcomes that are within the same curriculum area but that may be at grade level or below (or above) grade level (Campbell, Campbell, Collicott, Perner, & Stone, 1988; Peterson & Hittie, 2003). Students of different ability levels may be working on the same or different subject matter within the same academic area. In curriculum overlapping, students with disabilities and nondisabled peers participate together in an activity, but they pursue learning outcomes from different curriculum areas, including such broadly defined curriculum areas as social skills.

### Multilevel Curriculum in Action

Let's go back to Ms. Santos's challenge of including Chris as an academic member of her class and see how she used multilevel curriculum. In class work for a social studies unit, Chris and his classmates studied the Revolutionary War. But Ms. Santos adapted Chris's level of learning outcomes to suit him: His goals were to become familiar with historical people, places, and events, whereas his classmates' goals were to demonstrate knowledge of political and economic factors that led to the war.

To reinforce students' learning, Ms. Santos created a Revolutionary War board game that drew on both the class's grade-appropriate learning goals and Chris's lower-level goals to advance in the game. The game board had colored spaces, and each color a student landed on corresponded to a stack of question cards related to the desired content, with blue cards for historical people, green cards for historical places, and so on. Ms. Santos and a special educator had set aside specially prepared cards for Chris with questions matched to his learning outcomes. The rest of the class drew cards matched to their goals.

Another player read aloud for Chris each question and the multiple-choice answers, which were given both verbally and with images. For example, the question, "What American Revolutionary War hero became the first president of the United States?" might be followed by the labeled images of George Washington and two other famous people. When Chris was learning new content, Ms. Santos made the distracter choices substantially different and included at least one absurd choice (such as George Washington, Abraham Lincoln, and LeBron James). As Chris became more proficient, she used distracter choices that were more difficult to spot. When Chris answered a question correctly, he rolled dice and moved forward. Although this activity focused on social studies, Chris also learned the social skill of taking turns and such math skills as counting.

## Curriculum Overlapping in Action

Curriculum overlapping is a vital strategy for classrooms in which there are substantial differences between the learning outcomes most of the students are pursuing and the outcomes a student with a disability is pursuing.

For example, in a human biology unit, a group of four students might assemble a model of the human cardiovascular system. The primary goal of three students is to learn anatomical structures and their functions. The fourth student, who has significant disabilities, shares the activity, but has learning goals within the curriculum area of communications and social skills, such as learning to follow directions, taking turns, or making requests using a communication device.

One way to start planning for curriculum overlapping with a student who has significant disabilities is to make a simple matrix with the student's individually determined learning outcomes down the side and a list of regularly occurring classes or activities across the top. Team members can then identify where they should focus additional energy to ensure meaningful participation.

Ms. Santos and her team did this. They established cross-lesson routines through which Chris's individual learning outcomes could be embedded within many class activities. For example, Chris had a series of learning objectives involving communication and social skills, including matching to a sample; discriminating between different symbols and photos; following one- and two-step instructions; responding to questions; and describing events, objects, or emotions. Ms. Santos routinely embedded these skills in activities and lessons Chris participated in across different content areas as a form of curriculum overlapping.

While pursuing these learning outcomes, Chris might also work with the actual curricular content. For example, in a geography activity Chris might distinguish between maps of European countries, first discriminating between highly different pairs (a map of Italy paired with an image that is not a map); followed by slightly more similar pairs

(a map of Greece and a map of China); followed by even more similar pairs (maps of France and Germany).

When first using multilevel curriculum and curriculum overlapping, teams often feel that they don't have enough for their student with a significant disability to do within the typical classroom activities. But as they persist in collaborative planning, seek input directly from the student, and involve classmates in problem solving, they find new opportunities for the student's meaningful participation and learning.

Although multilevel curriculum and curriculum overlapping are primarily ways to include students with disabilities, they also enable more meaningful participation for students functioning above grade level. Applying multilevel curriculum allows teachers to stretch their curriculum away from a "middle zone" in which all students share the same curricular content, level, and amount of work. The practices many people associate with differentiated instruction (Tomlinson, 2001) occur within the boundaries of this middle zone. Multilevel curriculum stretches the concept of differentiated instruction. With curriculum overlapping, the boundaries of curriculum planning expand even further to create effective learning situations for students working both far above and far below their peers.

In the interest of access to the general education curriculum, teachers and teams working with students with disabilities should first consider whether the student can pursue the same learning outcomes as classmates or whether multilevel curriculum and instruction will provide enough accommodation before using curriculum overlapping.

## Making It Happen

Implementing either multilevel curriculum and instruction or curriculum overlapping requires time, collaboration, and creativity. But the reward is the authentic inclusion of students who function substantially below grade level. Approaching inclusive education this way contributes to a positive classroom culture, acknowledges differences, promotes acceptance, and provides opportunities for real-life problem solving.

Some claim that inclusion of students with certain disabilities is impossible because in many schools the curriculum is one-size-fits-all and differentiation is minimal or nonexistent. Although it is difficult to include a student with significant disabilities in such classes, this begs the question of whether one-size-fits-all classes are what we want for anyone. Instructional practices such as cooperative learning and differentiated instruction are often beneficial for general education students, too.

Students with disabilities bring educators a challenge to make our teaching practices more inclusive. Meeting the challenge invariably improves the way we teach the broader range of students who don't have disabilities.

## References

Campbell, C., Campbell, S., Collicott, J., Perner, D., & Stone, J. (1988). Individualized instruction. *Education New Brunswick, 3,* 17–20.

Giangreco, M. F. (2006). Foundational concepts and practices for educating students with severe disabilities. In M. E. Snell & F. Brown (Eds.), *Instruction of students with severe disabilities* (6th ed., pp. 1–27). Upper Saddle River, NJ: Pearson Education/Prentice-Hall.

Peterson, J. M., & Hittie, M. M. (2003). *Inclusive teaching: Creating effective schools for all learners.* Boston: Allyn and Bacon.

Tomlinson, C. A. (2001). *How to differentiate instruction in mixed-ability classrooms* (2nd ed.). Alexandria, VA: ASCD.

## Note

1. Ms. Santos is a composite of teachers I have observed who work with students with severe disabilities.

---

**MICHAEL F. GIANGRECO** is professor of education at the University of Vermont.

James M. Kauffman, Kathleen McGee,
and Michele Brigham

 **NO**

# Enabling or Disabling? Observations on Changes in Special Education

Schools need demanding and distinctive special education that is clearly focused on instruction and habilitation.[1] Abandoning such a conception of special education is a prescription for disaster. But special education has increasingly been losing its way in the single-minded pursuit of full inclusion.

Once, special education's purpose was to bring the performance of students with disabilities closer to that of their nondisabled peers in regular classrooms, to move as many students as possible into the mainstream with appropriate support.[2] For students not in regular education, the goal was to move them toward a more typical setting in a cascade of placement options.[3] But as any good thing can be overdone and ruined by the pursuit of extremes, we see special education suffering from the extremes of inclusion and accommodation.

Aiming for as much normalization as possible gave special education a clear purpose. Some disabilities were seen as easier to remediate than others. Most speech and language disorders, for example, were considered eminently remediable. Other disabilities, such as mental retardation and many physical disabilities, were assumed to be permanent or long-term and so less remediable, but movement *toward* the mainstream and increasing independence from special educators were clear goals.

The emphasis in special education has shifted away from normalization, independence, and competence. The result has been students' dependence on whatever special programs, modifications, and accommodations are possible, particularly in general education settings. The goal seems to have become the *appearance* of normalization without the *expectation* of competence.

Many parents and students seem to want more services as they learn what is available. Some have lost sight of the goal of limiting accommodations in order to challenge students to achieve more independence. At the same time, many special education advocates want all services to be available in mainstream settings, with little or no acknowledgment that the services are atypical. Although teachers, administrators, and guidance counselors are often willing and able to make accommodations, doing so is not always in students' best long-term interests. It gives students with disabilities what anthropologist Robert Edgerton called a cloak—a pretense, a cover, which actually fools no one—rather than actual competence.[4]

In this article, we discuss how changes in attitudes toward disability and special education, placement, and accommodations can perpetuate disability. We also explore the problems of ignoring or perpetuating disability rather than helping students lead fuller, more independent lives. Two examples illustrate how we believe good intentions can go awry—how attempts to accommodate students with disabilities can undermine achievement.

*"But he needs resource. . . ."* Thomas, a high school sophomore identified as emotionally disturbed, was assigned to a resource class created to help students who had problems with organization or needed extra help with academic skills. One of the requirements in the class was for students to keep a daily planner in which they entered all assignments; they shared their planner with the resource teacher at the beginning of class and discussed what academic subjects would be worked on during that period.

Thomas consistently refused to keep a planner or do any work in resource (he slept instead). So a meeting was set up with the assistant principal, the guidance counselor, Thomas, and the resource teacher. As the meeting was about to begin, the principal announced that he would not stay because Thomas felt intimidated by so many adults. After listening to Thomas' complaints, the guidance counselor decided that Thomas would not have to keep a planner or show it to the resource teacher and that the resource teacher should not talk to him unless Thomas addressed her first. In short, Thomas would not be required to do any work in the class! When the resource teacher suggested that, under those circumstances, Thomas should perhaps be placed in a study hall, because telling the parents that he was in a resource class would be a misrepresentation, the counselor replied, "But he *needs* the resource class."

"*He's too bright. . . .*" Bob, a high school freshman with Asperger's Syndrome, was scheduled for three honors classes and two Advanced Placement classes. Bob's IEP (individualized education program) included a two-page list of accommodations. In spite of his having achieved A's and B's, with just a single C in math, his mother did not feel that his teachers were accommodating him appropriately. Almost every evening, she e-mailed his teachers and his case manager to request more information or more help for Bob, and she angrily phoned his guidance counselor if she didn't receive a reply by the end of the first hour of the next school day.

A meeting was scheduled with the IEP team, including five of Bob's seven teachers, the county special education supervisor, the guidance counselor, the case manager, the principal, and the county autism specialist. When the accommodations were reviewed, Bob's mother agreed that all of them were being made. However, she explained that Bob had been removed from all outside social activities because he spent all night, every night, working on homework. The accommodation she demanded was that Bob have *no* homework assignments. The autism specialist agreed that this was a reasonable accommodation for a child with Asperger's Syndrome.

The teachers of the honors classes explained that the homework in their classes, which involved elaboration and extension of concepts, was even more essential than the homework assigned in AP classes. In AP classes, by contrast, homework consisted primarily of practice of concepts learned in class. The honors teachers explained that they had carefully broken their long assignments into segments, each having a separate due date before the final project, and they gave illustrations of their expectations. The director of special education explained the legal definition of accommodations (the mother said she'd never before heard that accommodations could not change the nature of the curriculum). The director also suggested that, instead of Bob's sacrificing his social life, perhaps it would be more appropriate for him to take standard classes. What Bob's mother was asking, he concluded, was not legal. She grew angry, but she did agree to give the team a "little more time" to serve Bob appropriately. She said she would "be back with her claws and broomstick" if anyone ever suggested that he be moved from honors classes without being given the no-homework accommodation. "He's too bright to take anything less than honors classes, and if you people would provide this simple

accommodation, he would do just fine," she argued. In the end, she got her way.

## Attitudes Toward Disability and Special Education

Not that many decades ago, a disability was considered a misfortune—not something to be ashamed of but a generally undesirable, unwelcome condition to be overcome to the greatest extent possible. Ability was considered more desirable than disability, and anything—whether a device or a service—that helped people with disabilities to do what those without disabilities could do was considered generally valuable, desirable, and worth the effort, cost, and possible stigma associated with using it.

The disability rights movement arose in response to the widespread negative attitudes toward disabilities, and it had a number of desirable outcomes. It helped overcome some of the discrimination against people with disabilities. And overcoming such bias and unfairness in everyday life is a great accomplishment. But the movement has also had some unintended negative consequences. One of these is the outright denial of disability in some cases, illustrated by the contention that disability exists only in attitudes or as a function of the social power to coerce.[5]

The argument that disability is merely a "social construction" is particularly vicious in its effects on social justice. Even if we assume that disabilities are socially constructed, what should that mean? Should we assume that socially constructed phenomena are not "real," are not important, or should be discredited? If so, then consider that dignity, civil rights, childhood, social justice, and nearly every other phenomenon that we hold dear are social constructions. Many social constructions are not merely near and dear to us, they are real and useful in benevolent societies. The important question is whether the idea of disability is useful in helping people attain dignity or whether it is more useful to assume that disabilities are not real (i.e., that, like social justice, civil rights, and other social constructions, they are fabrications that can be ignored when convenient). The denial of disability is sometimes expressed as an aversion to labels, so that we are cautioned not to communicate openly and clearly about disabilities but to rely on euphemisms. But this approach is counterproductive. When we are able only to whisper or mime the undesirable difference called disability, then we inadvertently increase its stigma and thwart prevention efforts.[6]

The specious argument that "normal" does not exist—because abilities of every kind are varied and because the point at which normal becomes abnormal is arbitrary—leads to the conclusion that no one actually has a disability or, alternatively, that everyone has a disability. Then, some argue, either no one or everyone is due an accommodation so that no one or everyone is identified as disabled. This unwillingness to draw a line defining something (such as disability, poverty, or childhood) is based either on ignorance regarding the nature of continuous distributions or on a rejection of the unavoidably arbitrary decisions necessary to provide special services to those who need them and, in so doing, to foster social justice.[7]

Another unintended negative consequence of the disability rights movement is that, for some people, disability has become either something that does not matter or something to love, to take pride in, to flaunt, to adopt as a positive aspect of one's identity, or to cherish as something desirable or as a badge of honor. When disability makes no difference to us one way or the other, then we are not going to work to attenuate it, much less prevent it. At best, we will try to accommodate it. When we view disability as a desirable difference, then we are very likely to try to make it more pronounced, not to ameliorate it.

Several decades ago, special education was seen as a good thing—a helpful way of responding to disability, not something everyone needed or should have, but a useful and necessary response to the atypical needs of students with disabilities. This is why the Education for All Handicapped Children Act (now the Individuals with Disabilities Education Act) was written. But in the minds of many people, special education has been transformed from something helpful to something awful.[8]

The full-inclusion movement did have some desirable outcomes. It helped overcome some of the unnecessary removal of students with disabilities from general education. However, the movement also has had some unintended negative consequences. One of these is that special education has come to be viewed in very negative terms, to be seen as a second-class and discriminatory system that does more harm than good. Rather than being seen as helpful, as a way of creating opportunity, special education is often portrayed as a means of shunting students into dead-end programs and killing opportunity.[9]

Another unintended negative consequence of full inclusion is that general education is now seen by many as the *only* place where fair and equitable treatment is possible and where the opportunity to learn is extended to all equally.[10] The argument has become that special education is good only as long as it is invisible (or nearly so), an indistinguishable part of a general education system that accommodates all students, regardless of their abilities or disabilities. Usually, this is described as a "unified" (as opposed to "separate") system of education.[11] Special

education is thus something to be avoided altogether or attenuated to the greatest extent possible, regardless of a student's inability to perform in a general setting. When special education is seen as discriminatory, unfair, an opportunity-killing system, or, as one writer put it, "the gold-plated garbage can of American schooling,"[12] then it is understandable that people will loathe it. But this way of looking at special education is like seeing the recognition and treatment of cancer as the cause of the problem.

The reversal in attitudes toward disability and special education—disability from undesirable to inconsequential, special education from desirable to awful—has clouded the picture of what special education is and what it should do for students with disabilities. Little wonder that special education stands accused of failure, that calls for its demise have become vociferous, and that contemporary practices are often more disabling than enabling. An unfortunate outcome of the changing attitudes toward disability and special education is that the benefit of special education is now sometimes seen as freedom from expectations of performance. It is as if we believed that, if a student has to endure the stigma of special education, then the compensation should include an exemption from work.

## Placement Issues

Placing all students, regardless of their abilities, in regular classes has exacerbated the tendency to see disability as something existing only in people's minds. It fosters the impression that students are fitting in when they are not able to perform at anywhere near the normal level. It perpetuates disabilities; it does not compensate for them.

Administrators and guidance counselors sometimes place students in programs for which they do not qualify, even as graduation requirements are increasing and tests are mandated. Often, these students' *testing* is modified although their *curriculum* is not. The students may then feel that they have beaten the system. They are taught that the system is unfair and that the only way to win is by gaming it. Hard work and individual responsibility for one's education are often overlooked—or at least undervalued.

Students who consistently fail in a particular curriculum must be given the opportunity to deal with the natural consequences of that fact as a means of learning individual responsibility. For example, social promotion in elementary and middle school teaches students that they really don't have to be able to do the work to pass. Students who have been conditioned to rely on social promotion do not believe that the cycle will end until it does so—usually very abruptly in high school. Suddenly, no one passes them on, and no one gives them undeserved credit. Many of these students do not graduate in four years. Some never recover, while other find themselves forced to deal with a very distasteful situation.

No one wants to see a student fail, but to alter any standard without good reason is to set that same student up for failure later in life. Passing along a student with disabilities in regular classes, pretending that he or she is performing at the same level as most of the class or that it doesn't really matter (arguing that the student has a legal "right" to be in the class) is another prescription for disappointment and failure in later life. Indeed, this failure often comes in college or on the job.

Some people with disabilities do need assistance. Others do not. Consider Deborah Groeber, who struggled through degenerative deafness and blindness. The Office of Affirmative Action at the University of Pennsylvania offered to intercede at the Wharton School, but Groeber knew that she had more influence if she spoke for herself. Today, she is a lawyer with three Ivy League degrees.[13] But not every student with disabilities can do or should be expected to do what Groeber did. Our concern is that too many students with disabilities are given encouragement based on pretense when they could do much more with appropriate special education.

## Types of Accommodations

Two popular modifications in IEPs are allowing for the use of calculators and granting extended time on tests and assignments. Calculators can be a great asset, but they should be used when calculating complex problems or when doing word problems. Indiscriminate use of a calculator renders many math tests invalid, as they become a contest to see if buttons can be pushed successfully and in the correct order, rather than an evaluation of ability to do arithmetic or use mathematical knowledge.

Extended time on assignments and tests can also be a useful modification, but it can easily be misused or abused. Extended time on tests should mean *continuous* time so that a test is not studied for first and taken later. Sometimes a test must be broken into smaller segments that can be completed independently. However, this could put students with disabilities at a disadvantage, as one part of a test might help with remembering another part. Extensions on assignments need to be evaluated each time they are given, not simply handed out automatically because they are written into an IEP. If a student is clearly working hard, then extensions may be appropriate. If a student has not even been attempting assignments, then more

time might be an avoidance tactic. Sometimes extended time means that assignments pile up and the student gets further and further behind. The result can then be overwhelming stress and the inability to comprehend discussions because many concepts must be acquired in sequence (e.g., in math, science, history, and foreign languages).

Reading tests and quizzes aloud to students can be beneficial for many, but great caution is required. Some students and teachers want to do more than simply read a test. Reading a test aloud means simply reading the printed words on the page *without* inflections that can reveal correct answers and without explaining vocabulary. Changing a test to open-notes or open-book, without the knowledge and consent of the classroom teacher, breaches good-faith test proctoring. It also teaches students dependence rather than independence and accomplishment. Similarly, scribing for a student can be beneficial for those who truly need it, but the teacher must be careful not to add details and to write only what the student dictates, including any run-on sentences or fragments. After scribing, if the assignment is not a test, the teacher should edit and correct the paper with the student, as she might do with any written work. But this must take place *after* the scribing.

## How Misguided Accommodations Can Be Disabling

"Saving" a child from his or her own negative behavior reinforces that behavior and makes it a self-fulfilling prophecy. Well-intentioned guidance counselors often feel more responsibility for their students' success or failure than the students themselves feel. Sometimes students are not held accountable for their effort or work. They seem not to understand that true independence comes from *what* you know, not *whom* you know. Students who are consistently enabled and not challenged are never given the opportunity to become independent. Ann Bancroft, the polar explorer and dyslexic, claims that, although school was a torment, it was disability that forged her iron will.[14] Stephen Cannell's fear for other dyslexics is that they will quit trying rather than struggle and learn to compensate for their disability.[15]

Most parents want to help their children. However, some parents confuse making life *easier* with making life *better* for their children. Too often, parents feel that protecting their child from the rigors of academic demands is in his or her best interest. They may protect their child by insisting on curricular modifications and accommodations in assignments, time, and testing. But children learn by doing, and not allowing them to do something because they might fail is denying them the opportunity to succeed. These students eventually believe that they are not capable of doing what typical students can do, even if they are. Sometimes it is difficult for teachers to discern what a student actually can do and what a parent has done until an in-class assignment is given or a test is taken. At that point, it is often too late for the teacher to do much remediation. The teacher may erroneously conclude that the student is simply a poor test-taker.

In reality, the student may have been "protected" from learning, which will eventually catch up with him or her. Unfortunately, students may not face reality until they take a college entrance exam, go away to college, or apply for a job. Students who "get through" high school in programs of this type often go on to flunk out of college. Unfortunately, the parents of these students frequently blame the college for the student's failure, criticizing the postsecondary institution for not doing enough to help. Instead, they should be upset both with the secondary institution for not preparing the child adequately for the tasks to come and with themselves for their own overprotection.

## The Benefits of Demands

Many successful adults with disabilities sound common themes when asked about their ability to succeed in the face of a disability. Tom Gray, a Rhodes Scholar who has a severe learning disability, claims that having to deal with the hardest experiences gave him the greatest strength.[16] Stephen Cannell believes that, if he had known there was a reason beyond his control to explain his low achievement, he might not have worked as hard as he did. Today, he knows he has a learning disability, but he is also an Emmy Award-winning television writer and producer.[17] Paul Orlalea, the dyslexic founder of Kinko's, believes God gave him an advantage in the challenge presented by his disability and that others should work with their strengths. Charles Schwab, the learning-disabled founder of Charles Schwab, Inc., cites his ability to think differently and to make creative leaps that more sequential thinkers don't make as chief reasons for his success. Fannie Flagg, the learning-disabled author, concurs and insists that learning disabilities become a blessing *only if you can overcome them*.[18] Not every student with a disability can be a star performer, of course, but all should be expected to achieve all that they can.

Two decades ago, special educators thought it was their job to assess a student's achievement, to understand what the student wanted to do and what an average peer could do, and then to develop plans to bridge the gap, if possible. Most special educators wanted to see that each student had the tools and knowledge to succeed as independently as possible. Helping students enter the typical world was the mark of success for special educators.

The full-inclusion movement now insists that *every* student will benefit from placement in the mainstream. However, some of the modifications and accommodations now being demanded are so radical that we are doing an injustice to the entire education system.[19] Special education must not be associated in any way with "dumbing down" the curriculum for students presumed to be at a given grade level, whether disabled or not.

Counselors and administrators who want to enable students must focus the discussion on realistic goals and plans for each student. An objective, in-depth discussion and evaluation must take place to determine how far along the continuum of successfully completing these goals the student has moved. If the student is making adequate progress independently, or with minimal help, special education services might not be necessary. If assistance is required to make adequate progress on realistic goals, then special education may be needed. Every modification and every accommodation should be held to the same standard: whether it will help the student attain these goals—*not* whether it will make life easier for the student. Knowing where a student is aiming can help a team guide that student toward success.

And the student must be part of this planning. A student who claims to want to be a brain surgeon but refuses to take science courses needs a reality check. If a student is unwilling to attempt to reach intermediate goals or does not succeed in meeting them, then special education cannot "save" that student. At that point, the team must help the student revisit his or her goals. Goals should be explained in terms of the amount of work required to complete them, not whether or not the teacher or parent feels they are attainable. When goals are presented in this way, students can often make informed decisions regarding their attainability and desirability. Troy Brown, a university dean and politician who has both a doctorate and a learning disability, studied at home with his mother. He estimates that it took him more than twice as long as the average person to complete assignments. Every night, he would go to bed with stacks of books and read until he fell asleep, because he had a dream of attending college.[20]

General educators and special educators need to encourage all students to be responsible and independent and to set realistic expectations for themselves. Then teachers must help students to meet these expectations in a more and more independent manner. Special educators do not serve students well when they enable students with disabilities to become increasingly dependent on their parents, counselors, administrators, or teachers—or even when they fail to increase students' independence and competence.

## Where We Stand

We want to make it clear that we think disabilities are real and that they make doing certain things either impossible or very difficult for the people who have them. We cannot expect people with disabilities to be "just like everyone else" in what they can do. . . .

In our view, students with disabilities *do* have specific shortcomings and *do* need the services of specially trained professionals to achieve their potential. They *do* sometimes need altered curricula or adaptations to make their learning possible. If students with disabilities were just like "regular" students, then there would be no need whatever for special education. But the school experiences of students with disabilities obviously will not be—*cannot* be—just like those of students without disabilities. We sell students with disabilities short when we pretend that they are no different from typical students. We make the same error when we pretend that they must *not* be expected to put forth extra effort if they are to learn to do some things—or learn to do something in a different way. We sell them short when we pretend that they have competencies that they do not have or pretend that the competencies we expect of most students are not important for them.

Like general education, special education must push students to become all they can be. Special education must countenance neither the pretense of learning nor the avoidance of reasonable demands.

## Notes

1. James M. Kauffman and Daniel P. Hallahan, *Special Education: What It Is and Why We Need It* (Boston: Allyn & Bacon, forthcoming).
2. Doug Fuchs et al., "Toward a Responsible Reintegration of Behaviorally Disordered Students," *Behavioral Disorders*, February 1991, pp. 133–47.
3. Evelyn Deno, "Special Education as Developmental Capital," *Exceptional Children*, November 1970, pp. 229–37; and Dixie Snow Huefner, "The Mainstreaming Cases: Tensions and Trends for School Administrators," *Educational Administration Quarterly*, February 1994, pp. 27–55.
4. Robert B. Edgerton, *The Cloak of Competence: Stigma in the Lives of the Mentally Retarded* (Berkeley, Calif.: University of California Press, 1967); idem, *The Cloak of Competence*, rev. ed. (Berkeley, Calif.: University of California Press, 1993); and James M. Kauffman, "Appearances,

Stigma, and Prevention," *Remedial and Special Education*, vol. 24, 2003, pp. 195–98.
5. See, for example, Scot Danforth and William C. Rhodes, "Deconstructing Disability: A Philosophy for Education," *Remedial and Special Education*, November/December 1997, pp. 357–66; and Phil Smith, "Drawing New Maps: A Radical Cartography of Developmental Disabilities," *Review of Educational Research*, Summer 1999, pp. 117–44.
6. James M. Kauffman, *Education Deform: Bright People Sometimes Say Stupid Things about Education* (Lanham, Md.: Scarecrow Education, 2002).
7. Ibid.
8. James M. Kauffman, "Reflections on the Field," *Behavioral Disorders*, vol. 28, 2003, pp. 205–8.
9. See, for example, Clint Bolick, "A Bad IDEA Is Disabling Public Schools," *Education Week*, 5 September 2001, pp. 56, 63; and Michelle Cottle, "Jeffords Kills Special Ed. Reform School," *New Republic*, 18 June 2001, pp. 14–15.
10. See, for example, Dorothy K. Lipsky and Alan Gartner, "Equity Requires Inclusion: The Future for All Students with Disabilities," in Carol Christensen and Fazal Rizvi, eds., *Disability and the Dilemmas of Education and Justice* (Philadelphia: Open University Press, 1996), pp. 144–55; and William Stainback and Susan Stainback, "A Rationale for Integration and Restructuring: A Synopsis," in John W. Lloyd, Nirbhay N. Singh, and Alan C. Repp, eds., *The Regular Education Initiative: Alternative Perspectives on Concepts, Issues, and Models* (Sycamore, Ill.: Sycamore, 1991), pp. 225–39.
11. See, for example, Alan Gartner and Dorothy K. Lipsky, *The Yoke of Special Education: How to Break It* (Rochester, N.Y.: National Center on Education and the Economy, 1989). For an alternative view, see James M. Kauffman and Daniel P. Hallahan, "Toward a Comprehensive Delivery System for Special Education," in John I. Goodlad and Thomas C. Lovitt, eds., *Integrating General and Special Education* (Columbus, Ohio: Merrill, 1993), pp. 73–102.
12. Marc Fisher, "Students Still Taking the Fall for D.C. Schools," *Washington Post*, 13 December 2001, p. B–1.
13. Elizabeth Tener, "Blind, Deaf, and Very Successful," *McCall's*, December 1995, pp. 42–46.
14. Christina Cheakalos et al., "Heavy Mettle: They May Have Trouble Reading and Spelling, but Those with the Grit to Overcome Learning Disabilities Like Dyslexia Emerge Fortified for Life," *People*, 30 October 2001, pp. 18, 58.
15. Ibid.

16. Ibid.
17. Stephen Cannell, "How to Spell Success," *Reader's Digest,* August 2000, pp. 63–66.
18. Cheakalos et al., op cit.
19. Anne Proffit Dupre, "Disability, Deference, and the Integrity of the Academic Enterprise," *Georgia Law Review,* Winter 1998, pp. 393–473.
20. Cheakalos et al., op cit.

JAMES M. KAUFFMAN is a professor emeritus of education at the University of Virginia in Charlottesville.

KATHLEEN McGEE AND MICHELE BRIGHAM are special education teachers.

# EXPLORING THE ISSUE

## Is Full Inclusion Always the Best Option for Children with Disabilities?

## Critical Thinking and Reflection

1. What are some of the challenges to implementing the multilevel curriculum and curriculum overlapping strategies described by Giangreco?
2. Kauffman and colleagues argue that the goal of education for students with disabilities should be "normalization." Do you agree? Why or why not?
3. Some scholars have argued that the need for inclusion cannot be assessed by research or empirical data. These scholars believe that inclusion hinges on ethical and ideological issues. Do you agree or disagree? Why?

## Is There Common Ground?

It is possible that research on inclusion to date has been inconclusive because researchers have focused on the wrong question. Much of the research in this area seems to have been designed to determine "once and for all" whether students with disabilities have better outcomes in segregated or inclusive educational programs. It is unlikely, however, that inclusion in all its forms will lead to better outcomes for all students and under all conditions. This has led some scholars to encourage researchers to ask more focused questions, such as, what types of students benefit from inclusion? What types of strategies are needed for inclusion to be effective? What types of training and belief systems do teachers need for inclusion to work? What resources are associated with effective inclusive programs? Addressing these questions may help educators to learn more about when and why inclusion is effective or ineffective.

Some scholars have argued that deciding whether or not inclusion is the best option for students with disabilities is an ethical question and, therefore, not answerable by research. See, for example, "Inclusion Paradigms in Conflict," by Peter V. Paul and Marjorie E. Ward, *Theory into Practice* (vol. 35, no. 1, 1996). These scholars argue that segregated education is by its very nature discriminatory because it denies students with disabilities access to the same experiences and opportunities afforded everyone else. Although these scholars see a role for empirical research, that role is not to learn whether inclusion should occur but rather how it should occur.

## Additional Resources

Wayne Sailor and Blair Roger, "Rethinking Inclusion: Schoolwide Applications," *Phi Delta Kappan* (March 2005).

Cindy L. Praisner, "Attitudes of Elementary School Principals toward the Inclusion of Students with Disabilities," *Exceptional Children* (Winter 2003).

Susan Unok Marks, "Self-Determination for Students with Intellectual Disabilities and Why I Want Educators to Know What It Means," *Phi Delta Kappan* (September 2008).

Maury Miller, "What Do Students Think about Inclusion," *Phi Delta Kappan* (January 2008).

# *Internet References . . .*

**Maryland Coalition for Inclusive Education**

www.mcie.org/

**National Dissemination Center for Children with Disabilities**

http://nichcy.org/

**The Association for Persons with Severe Handicaps**

http://tash.org/

Selected, Edited, and with Issue Framing Material by:
Esther S. Chang, *Soka University of America*

# ISSUE

# Are Single-Gender Classes Necessary to Create Equal Opportunities for Boys and Girls?

YES: **Frances R. Spielhagen**, from "How Tweens View Single-Sex Classes," *Educational Leadership* (2006)

NO: **Kelley King and Michael Gurian**, from "Teaching to the Minds of Boys," *Educational Leadership* (2006)

---

## Learning Outcomes

After reading this issue, you will be able to:

- Summarize the achievement differences between male and female students.
- Discuss the views of students who have participated in both single- and mixed-gender classrooms.
- Describe the strategies used to support student learning in single- and mixed-gender classrooms.

---

### ISSUE SUMMARY

YES: Frances Spielhagen argues that single-gender classes are viewed as more conducive to learning than are coeducational classes by students, especially younger students.

NO: Kelley King and Michael Gurian argue that coeducational classrooms can be made to be more accommodating to the learning profiles of both boys and girls.

---

**D**espite changing attitudes and the enactment of laws designed to ensure that males and females are afforded equal educational opportunities, gender-related differences in academic achievement still exist. In reading and language arts, girls score higher on achievement tests and are less likely to be referred for remedial programs than are boys. In math and science, boys maintain an advantage. Although gender differences in academic achievement are relatively small, and certainly less than the differences observed among males or among females, they are important because of their influence on the career paths available to men and women.

Gender-related differences in academic achievement are due, in part, to the beliefs that children bring to school and to their behavior in the classroom. Importantly, there is considerable evidence that differences in academic preparation and behavior are largely the result of the environment rather than of direct biological influences on development.

Parents are an important part of the environment that serves to push boys and girls down different academic paths. The role of the media has also been much debated. Unfortunately, teachers and the culture of most U.S. schools are at fault as well. Consider the following:

1. In preschool and early elementary school years, the physical arrangement of the classroom often segregates boys and girls and reinforces the differences between them. For example, a pretend kitchen and associated role-playing materials are typically used in a different location than are blocks and other building materials.
2. Teachers attend more to boys than to girls, are more likely to ask boys questions (especially open-ended, thought-provoking questions), and give boys more constructive criticism. Such behaviors are especially evident in traditionally male domains, such as science.
3. Teachers are more tolerant of interruptions from boys than from girls and encourage the latter to wait their turn.

4. Teachers are more likely to provide help to girls during difficult academic tasks, including during experiments and other hands-on science activities, while encouraging boys to resolve difficulties on their own.
5. Teachers spend more time with girls during reading and language arts classes but more time with boys during math classes.
6. Teachers are less likely to assign girls than similarly achieving boys to high-math-ability groups. In general, girls are less likely than boys to be identified for inclusion in programs for gifted students.

How can schools be reformed to ensure that they help children to break free of gender stereotypes rather than maintain and even exacerbate achievement differences between boys and girls? Much of the debate surrounding the question of reform has focused on the achievement gaps in math and science, which appear to have the greatest potential for limiting career options. Two approaches to reform have been advocated. In the first, and certainly more popular, approach, scholars and policymakers, assuming that coeducational classrooms are a fact of life, have made suggestions for changing the culture and practices of these classrooms. Proponents of the second, more controversial, approach argue that gender-segregated classes are necessary to allow girls or boys the opportunity to learn in a climate that is suited to their characteristics and needs.

The following two selections weigh in on this issue of gender-segregated classes. In the first, Frances R. Spielhagen presents excerpts from interviews with middle-school students. In general, the students support single-gender classes, seeing them as containing fewer distractions and more supports for learning, although an interest in romantic relationships leads older students to "overlook" the shortcomings of coeducational classrooms. In the second selection, Kelly King and Michael Gurian argue that gender-equitable education is possible within the context of a coeducational classroom provided that the curriculum and pedagogical activities are adapted to meet the unique needs and challenges of students of both genders.

# YES ⤶

**Frances R. Spielhagen**

## How Tweens View Single-Sex Classes

**H**ave you ever heard that saying, 'Time flies when you're having fun?' All-boy classes are fun! James, a 6th grader, cheerfully offered this opinion of the single-sex academic classes at Hudson Valley Middle School.[1] He quickly added, "I will probably want to be with girls when I am in high school."

Melissa, 13, expressed an older adolescent's point of view: "You can say what you want in all-girl classes and not be afraid of being teased, but sometimes we just want to be with the guys."

James and Melissa are part of the majority of students at this middle school in the rural Hudson Valley of upstate New York who have chosen to attend single-sex classes in language arts, math, science, and social studies. Hudson Valley Middle School, a public school whose 600 students come mostly from low-income backgrounds, has offered voluntary single-sex academic classes to its 6th, 7th, and 8th grade students for the last three years. Students remain in mixed groups for nonacademic classes and at lunchtime so they are not isolated from opposite-gender peers. In the first year of this reform, approximately 75 percent of the school's students chose to take single-sex classes; during the last two years, the majority of those students continued with that choice.

As part of my research into single-sex education (Spielhagen, 2005), I interviewed 24 Hudson Valley students a combination of 6th, 7th, and 8th graders who had attended single-sex classes for at least one academic year. Their comments offer insights into the minds of tweens who have sampled single-sex learning. Their perspectives indicate that voluntary single-sex classes can be a viable option for middle school students, but that such arrangements are most effective when classes are designed to address students' developmental needs. The younger students were more likely to find being in a single-sex class a positive experience; as students got older, they expressed more desire to be in mixed classes, even when that choice entailed potential problems.

## Why Try Single-Sex Learning?

Concern over state standardized test scores prompted Hudson Valley Middle School to create voluntary single-sex classes. The school hoped that providing an environment free of the distraction caused by mixed-gender social interaction would lead to higher scores.

In the 19th century, single-sex schools were common, especially in grades 7 through 12. However, because classes for girls did not include academic subjects that would lead to higher education, early feminists urged that schools give *all* students access to the entire academic curriculum. Coeducational schools soon became the preferred model of public education, opening the doors to college enrollment for substantial numbers of girls.

Even then, secondary schools continued to maintain single-sex physical education classes until 1975. In that year, the provisions of Title IX (Tyack & Hansot, 2002) specifically forbade separate-gender physical education classes. According to Salomone (2003), many school districts misunderstood Title IX as a ban on all single-sex classes. Either way, emphasis on coeducational physical education classes quickly led to coeducation as the norm for public schools.

Meanwhile, over the last 20 years, education policy-makers have noted the need to reverse declines in achievement among both boys and girls. Researchers agree that the middle school years are crucial to forming sound study habits (Clewell, 2002), but they have mixed opinions as to whether a return to single-sex classes would enhance the achievement of young adolescents.

For example, in 1995, Sadker and Sadker claimed that coeducational schools shortchange girls. At the same time, the American Association of University Women (AAUW) endorsed single-sex arrangements as a means of promoting female achievement, particularly in mathematics and science. Within a few years, however, the AAUW (1998) reversed its stance and concluded that single-sex classes could lead to programming decisions that discriminated

From *Educational Leadership*, April 2006, pp. 68–69, 71–72. Copyright © 2006 by ASCD. Reprinted by permission. The Association for Supervision and Curriculum Development is a worldwide community of educators advocating sound policies and sharing best practices to achieve the success of each learner. To learn more, visit ASCD at www.ascd.org.

against girls. In terms of boys, Sommers (2002) believes that single-sex arrangements are advantageous for boys who lag in academic areas, particularly reading and writing.

## Listening to Student Voices

From ages 9 through 13, young adolescents experience tremendous physical, emotional, and cognitive development, so it is not surprising that the responses of students with whom I talked varied according to their ages. I asked students about their classroom choices, their perceptions of the classroom environment in single-sex as compared with mixed-gender groups, and their satisfaction level. The majority of the students had positive feelings about single-sex classes, with 62 percent stating that they could focus better without the opposite sex present. In general, the younger the student, the more enthusiastic the praise of the single-sex arrangement.

### The 6th Grade Perspective

Sixth grade students' comments revealed a pre-adolescent viewpoint that the behavior of the other sex was a problem. Both boys and girls in 6th grade referred to their opposite-gender peers as "noisy" and "annoying."

James, a slightly built 11-year-old, responded energetically to questions about being in all-boy classes. He admitted that his favorite class was gym "because you get to play games using your skills," but noted that he didn't pay much attention to the girls in the mixed gym classes because he and his friends (all boys) liked to be on teams together. James also said that he felt "more challenged" in his all-boy classes because he enjoyed the competition with other boys:

> I want to try to beat them. I didn't try to beat the girls [when I was in mixed classes] because I didn't think I could beat the top girls, so why bother?

The comments of 6th grade girls reinforced the conventional wisdom that girls experience more freedom in single-sex academic classes, particularly math and science. Alison, 11, said she "loves all-girl classes," especially math classes, because she's "good at math." She emphasized that in all-girl classes, "you don't have to worry about boys making fun of you." Twelve-year-old Becky echoed Alison's concerns about intellectual safety in mixed classes. When asked why she chose all-girl classes, she replied,

> The boys always picked on me because I am smarter than they are. In all-girl classes, the teachers word things better and say them differently. In mixed classes, they say things more simply for the boys.

She added that all-girl classes are fun and the students get more accomplished, even though the girls "get loud and ask too many questions."

### 7th and 8th Grade Perspectives

Although by 7th grade many students' attitudes had begun to shift toward typically adolescent emotional and social concerns, 7th graders consistently remarked on their ability to focus better in their single-sex classes. Mary, a 13-year-old 7th grader, reported that she had meant to try all-girl classes for just a year but had decided to stay with the arrangement. She reported a definite improvement in her grades, noting that "I can concentrate better. I am not afraid to raise my hand."

Another 7th grader, Nancy, reported that

> In mixed classes, you are too nervous to ask a question and be wrong and the boys might laugh at you. We get higher grades because we pay attention more and don't get distracted.

On the other hand, Heather, 13, complained that she was in an all-girl class because "my mom decided to torture me." Heather went along with her mother's choice because she was curious. She conceded that she liked the all-girl classes because they made it easier to relate to her girlfriends but added that the situation allowed girls to "help each other with guy problems." Heather was clearly becoming more interested in mixed-gender social pairing. She offered another adolescent insight, noting,

> In some ways it's really nice to be with your friends, but sometimes the girls get catty, and it is hard to get space away from them.

The 7th and 8th grade boys were less enthusiastic than the girls about single-sex classes. Bullying seemed to become more of a problem with only boys present. Danny, 13, noted that he had been curious about all-boy classes, but that after two years in such classes, he planned to choose mixed-gender classes for 8th grade. In the all-boy classes, Danny reported, he could talk more about sports with his friends and "just hang out," but that "boys try to act tougher" in that environment. Eighth grader Jim, also 13, admitted that he had been picked on by other boys in mixed classes in 7th grade, but that mistreatment was worse in the all-boy classes. He explained, "The guys who pick on us would be more interested in impressing the girls" in a mixed-gender group. Jim added that he missed being with his female friends.

## What Are the Students Telling Us?

From these tweens' perspective, single-sex classes can clearly contribute to a comfortable yet intellectually challenging middle school experience. Such arrangements work as long as students can choose whether or not to participate.

Students in all grades reinforced the importance of emotional, intellectual, and physical safety perennial concerns in the middle grades. The problem of bullying reared its head among the 7th and 8th grade boys, but the students did not agree on which arrangement might be less bully-prone. However, caution dictates that schools take measures to ensure that a *Lord of the Flies* scenario does not emerge from a policy that keeps boys in the same single-sex grouping during all three years of middle school. Sorting students into different all-male configurations for different years might address this problem.

The overwhelmingly positive responses from the girls in this study suggest that single-sex classes are particularly beneficial to middle school girls. Even 8th grade girls supported the notion that greater concentration is possible in all-girl classes. As the girls grew older, they became more assertive about their interest in boys. Unlike the boys, however, they expressed a feeling of bonding with their female classmates and enjoyed discussing issues about boys together.

Students experienced the distraction presented by the opposite gender in different ways as they grew older. Younger kids complained about the noisiness of their opposite-sex peers, whereas older students simply referred to the social distractions of having the opposite sex in their classrooms. However, older students loudly and clearly stated their preference for facing those distractions.

## Offering Multiple Options

*Turning Points 2000* (Jackson & Davis, 2000), a landmark document on middle school reform, recommended that middle schools organize learning climates that promote intellectual development and shared academic purpose. According to the students in my study, single-sex classes in public middle schools support these goals. *Turning Points 2000* also called for middle schools to offer multiple options to students. Hudson Valley Middle School displays innovative programming by restricting single-sex classes to the academic core courses so that students can experience the benefits of both single-sex classes and day-to-day interaction with students of the other sex. Offering subject-specific single-sex classes in each grade might

provide even more flexibility, as long as the curriculum remains identical for both genders.

Providing optional single-sex environments for young adolescents with the existing public middle school framework would offer cost-effective school choice for parents, involving them as stakeholders in the education of their children. For many tweens, single-sex classes provide an enviable situation in which learning time flies because students are having fun.

## Note

1.  All names in this article are pseudonyms.

## References

American Association of University Women. (1998). *Separated by sex: A critical look at single-sex education for girls*. Washington, DC: Author.

Clewell, B. (2002). Breaking the barriers: The critical middle school years. In E. Rassen, L. Iura, & P. Berkman (Eds.), *Gender in education* (pp. 301–313). San Francisco: Jossey-Bass.

Jackson, A., & Davis, G. (2000). *Turning points 2000: Educating adolescents in the 21st century*. New York: Carnegie Corporation.

Sadker, M., & Sadker, D. (1995). *Failing at fairness: How our schools cheat girls*. New York: Simon & Schuster.

Salomone, R. (2003). *Same, different, equal: Rethinking single-sex schooling*. New Haven, CT: Yale University Press.

Sommers, C. (2002). Why Johnny can't, like, read and write. In E. Rassen, L. Iura, & P. Berkman (Eds.), *Gender in education* (pp. 700–721). San Francisco: Jossey-Bass.

Spielhagen, F. (2005). *Separate by choice: Single-sex classes in a public middle school*. Unpublished manuscript.

Tyack, D., & Hansot, E. (2002). Feminists discover the hidden injuries of coeducation. In E. Rassen, L. Iura, & P. Berkman (Eds.), *Gender in education* (pp. 12–50). San Francisco: Jossey-Bass.

**Frances R. Spielhagen** is an associate professor of education at Mount Saint Mary College.

Kelley King and
Michael Gurian

# Teaching to the Minds of Boys

**B**oys who don't read or write as well as we'd like come in all kinds. There's Garrett, who's perpetually in motion, his fingers drumming the desk. He's not focusing on his reading and pokes the student in front of him. He's becoming a discipline problem. There's Jared, who stares into space, failing to fill more than a few short lines with words. There's Dan, who turns in rushed and sloppy work and receives failing grades. When it comes to fulfilling the kinds of assignments that we call "literacy," boys are often out of their chairs rather than in them.

At Douglass Elementary School, in Boulder, Colorado, a significant literacy gap existed among the 470 students. On the 2005 Colorado State Assessment Program (CSAP), boys attending Douglass underperformed the girls in grades 3–5 (the boys' scores ranged from 6–21 points lower, with a 13-point gap overall). Because boys represented at least half the student population at every grade level—and 75 percent of the special education population—it was clear that the gender gap had powerful implications for the school as a whole and for the futures of the students.

In looking closely at these statistics, the staff suspected that Douglass was not alone in facing classrooms full of boys who were not learning to read and write as well as the girls were. In fact, all over the world boys are struggling in school, with lower grades, more discipline problems, more learning disabilities, and more behavior disorders than girls (Gurian & Stevens, 2005). As experienced teachers of boys, as parents of sons, and as professionals charged with solving a specific and compelling problem, the educators at Douglass went to work. They discovered that recent brain research backed up many of their intuitions about gender and learning styles (see Gurian, Henley, & Trueman, 2001).

By introducing more boy-friendly teaching strategies in the classroom, the school was able to close the gender gap in just one year. At the same time, girls' reading and writing performance improved.

On the Colorado State Assessment Program, Douglass Elementary students experienced an overall net percentage gain of 21.9, which was the highest achievement gain of any school in the Boulder Valley School District. Moreover, Douglass reversed the typical trend of girls outperforming boys: The boys experienced a 24.4 percentage point gain in reading and writing; the girls a 19 percentage point gain, which constituted three times the gain of girls in other district elementary schools. Most remarkably, Douglass special education students achieved 7.5 times the average gain for this population of students in the district, coming in with a 50-point gain.

## A Look into Boy-Friendly Classrooms

How did Douglass manage these successes? Using a theory developed by one of the authors (Gurian et al., 2001; Gurian & Stevens, 2005), the school analyzed the natural assets that both girls and boys bring to learning (see "The Brain: His and Hers," p. 59). Douglass realized that its classrooms were generally a better fit for the verbal-emotive, sit-still, take-notes, listen-carefully, multitasking girl. Teachers tended to view the natural assets that boys bring to learning—impulsivity, single-task focus, spatial-kinesthetic learning, and physical aggression—as problems. By altering strategies to accommodate these more typically male assets, Douglass helped its students succeed, as the following vignettes illustrate.

## Increasing Experiential and Kinesthetic Learning Opportunities

Today's assignment in Mrs. Hill's 4th grade class is to arrange words and punctuation marks into a sentence that makes sense and is grammatically correct. Instead of relying on worksheets or the overhead, which might have bored students like Alexander, the teacher directs the students to arrange cards representing the sentence parts across the classroom floor. The task-oriented discussion and interaction, the physical movement, and the orientation in space access the boys' neurological strengths, keeping them energized and attentive. Alexander and his group are working hard to complete their grammatical challenge before the other groups do.

These male-friendly elements have also energized the girls. Many of them like a good debate, competition, and moving around.

## Supporting Literacy Through Spatial-Visual Representations

Across the hall in Mrs. Johnston's 3rd grade classroom, the students are writing. Timothy has great ideas and is always trying to please, but at the beginning of the year, he had great difficulty writing even a single paragraph. Formulating his ideas into well-organized thoughts, coupled with sitting still and the fine-motor task of writing, often overwhelmed him. His mother testified to his frequent meltdowns at home.

Realizing the need for nonverbal planning tools, especially in males, to help bridge the gap between what students are thinking and what they're able to put down on paper, Mrs. Johnston now asks Timothy and his classmates to create storyboards, a series of pictures with or without words that graphically depict a story line. The pictures on the storyboard prompt the brain to remember relevant words, functioning for these learners as first-stage brainstorming. Now when Timothy writes, he describes what he has previously drawn and then adds to that foundation. His spatial-visual assets are helping him to write.

## Letting Boys Choose Topics That Appeal to Them

Although parents and educators are quick to point out to students the more practical relevance of reading—you need to read to get through high school and college so you can get a job—this kind of reasoning works more readily for girls than for boys. Said one 6th grade boy, "The only reading that's a *must* is reading what's on the computer or in a football manual. There's no point to reading a book for pleasure."

Many teachers are familiar with this kind of response. Boys often seem to think that what they read in language arts class is irrelevant. Mrs. Vanee decided to innovate in this area. In her 2nd grade classroom, most of the boys read and write about such topics as NASCAR racing, atomic bombs, and football or about such situations as a parrot biting a dad through the lip. Many of the girls write about best friends, books, mermaids, and unicorns.

When asked why he thought he was writing about superheroes whereas Brittany was writing about her best friend, 8-year-old Luke replied, "Because boys have more R-rated minds than girls do," with "R-rated" referring to a preference for aggression scenarios, competition, action, and superhero journeys. Brittany concurred as she rolled her eyes in a "Yes."

Although Mrs. Vanee is aware of the potential for excess here, she now understands how relevant this focus on action and heroism is to males, and she sees that letting boys write on these topics has improved their papers. It has also provided her with numerous opportunities to teach lessons on character, nonviolence, and civility. Moreover, giving students greater choice in what they read and write has improved writing among both boys and girls.

## Helping Boys with Homework

One of the primary reasons that some boys get Ds and Fs in school is their inattention to homework. This was true for 5th grader Todd, who generally did his homework in a shoddy way—or not at all.

Douglass teachers now request that parents sign homework assignments. Homework with no signature requires an explanation. This way, the school gets parents involved, encouraging them to supervise homework and cut out distractions that their children may be experiencing, such as TV and video games, until the homework is completed. This policy also keeps parents apprised of the quality of the homework that their child is turning in.

Todd's grades have improved since this policy was started. He's now getting Bs instead of Ds on his language arts assignments. His teacher, Mrs. Steposki, is especially vigilant, meeting with him regularly to see whether he's gotten his homework signed and supporting his parents in keeping him focused. Although Todd still doesn't enjoy a lot of his homework—much of it feels like busywork to him—he does feel pride in getting a B. "Things are better now," he says.

## Offering Single-Gender Learning Environments

One of the innovations that teachers can use in targeted ways in coeducational classes is single-gender grouping. Mrs. Holsted has decided to divide her 2nd grade class today to give the students a choice in reading material. The girls choose several *American Girls* doll books; the boys choose Lynne Reid Banks's *The Indian in the Cupboard* (HarperTrophy, 1999).

Soon the girls are on the floor with a giant piece of chart paper and markers. They label each of three circles of a Venn diagram with the name of a female book character and then they write down adjectives to describe that character. Meanwhile, in the boys' group, Ryan and David are writing lines for a play about the novel they've chosen, happy to be able to act out the battle scene. A lot of what these students need to learn "sticks" because of this approach. Tomorrow, the students will return to their coed groupings, and some will note that they like being back together.

## Making Reading and Writing Purposeful

Quite often, boys do their best work when teachers establish authentic purpose and meaningful, real-life connections. In his 4th grade classroom, Mr. Hoyt talks to 10-year-old Clayton about his narrative fiction piece. Clayton doesn't feel the need to do any more work on his D+ paper. When Mr. Hoyt asks who his audience is, Clayton replies, "Just the class and you." "What if you were reading this to someone else?" asks Mr. Hoyt. "Say, a high school basketball player you like?" Clayton ponders this. "Think about an older guy you respect," Mr. Hoyt suggests. "Write this for him to read." Clayton thinks of just the right person—his older brother—and starts the paper over again.

Garrett sits across the room. His real-life project is to draw to scale a map of the school and playground and then annotate it. From there, he'll develop a proposal for a new playground layout and present it to the school's landscape design architect and the playground revitalization committee.

Meanwhile, Greg is designing a Web site on which students can post their writing projects for others to read. In fact, to create a greater sense of the importance of writing, Mr. Hoyt suggested that Douglass Elementary start providing opportunities for all students to share their writing in front of large audiences—at monthly school assemblies, for example. Competition and the opportunity to earn public respect have helped motivate many undermotivated students—especially the boys.

## Seeking Out Male Role Models

Douglass Elementary recognizes the special insight and impact of teachers like Mr. Hoyt, who serve as valuable role models for boys. The school actively encourages men to visit classrooms to share their own writing and speak about their favorite books. This is an area in which the school successfully partnered with parents. Several of the students' fathers write professionally as journalists, screenwriters, authors, or lyricists. Appealing to fathers to be role models for literacy has yielded many special guest speakers and several weekly "regulars" in the classroom.

## Getting Serious About Gender Learning

There's nothing revolutionary about the strategies that we have suggested. Teachers have already used many of them in their classrooms, but perhaps they haven't used them in an organized and scientific way. Teacher training at Douglass, which focused on the gender learning work conducted by the Gurian Institute, connected brain science to classroom practice. Teachers learned that good science supported many of their personal observations about how boys and girls learn.

By incorporating new theories from gender science into classroom practice, teachers *can* close gender gaps and significantly improve learning. Douglass Elementary school provided the action research that proves just that. But to bring about these improvements, teachers need to ask themselves some key questions:

- As teachers, do we fully understand the challenges that boys face in education today?
- Do we realize that there is a scientific basis for innovating on behalf of both girls and boys as disaggregated groups?
- Does my school incorporate boy-friendly and girl-friendly learning innovations in full knowledge of how essential they are in accommodating the structural and chemical gender differences built into the human brain?
- Do the educators in my school realize that many behaviors typical of either boys or girls are neurologically based?

Although tackling these questions is challenging, acting on what we have learned can lead to rewards for everyone—for teachers, parents, communities, and especially our students.

## References

Blum, D. (1997). *Sex on the brain: The biological differences between men and women.* New York: Viking.

Havers, F. (1995, March 2). Rhyming tasks male and female brains differently. *The Yale Herald.*

Gurian, M. (1996). *The wonder of boys.* New York: Tarcher/Putnam.

Gurian, M., Henley, P., & Trueman, T. (2001). *Boys and girls learn differently: A guide for teachers and parents.* San Francisco: Jossey–Bass.

Gurian, M., & Stevens, K. (2005). *The minds of boys: Saving our sons from falling behind in school and life.* San Francisco: Jossey-Bass.

Rich, B. (Ed.). (2000). *The Dana brain daybook*. New York: The Charles A. Dana Foundation.

Sax, L. (2005). *Why gender matters*. New York: Doubleday.

Taylor, S. (2002). *The tending instinct*. New York: Times Books.

**KELLEY KING** is the former principal of Douglass Elementary School in the Boulder Valley School District, Boulder, Colorado.

**MICHAEL GURIAN** is a marriage and family counselor in private practice, author, and cofounder of the Gurian Institute, which is nonprofit foundation supporting educational research and training.

# EXPLORING THE ISSUE

## Are Single-Gender Classes Necessary to Create Equal Opportunities for Boys and Girls?

### Critical Thinking and Reflection

1. Summarize the findings from Spielhagen's study of same-sex middle-school classrooms. What are the strengths of the study? What are its weaknesses or limitations?
2. Briefly summarize King and Gurian's suggestions for ensuring a boy-friendly classroom. Do you think that the accommodations suggested for boys may put girls at a disadvantage? Why?
3. Imagine that you are the teacher for an all-boys math class. How would you organize and conduct the class? How would it be similar to and different from the class described by King and Gurian? Why?

### Is There Common Ground?

Can we rely on empirical research to decide whether or not single-gender classes ensure that boys and girls have equal chances to succeed in all academic fields? In principle, the answer is yes. It should be possible, for example, to compare the math or science achievement of girls enrolled in girls-only classes to that of girls enrolled in coeducational classes. Do the former have higher achievement than the latter? Does their achievement equal that of boys? In fact, several studies suggest that achievement is higher for girls in single-gender classes than in coeducational classes. See "The Effects of Sex-Grouped Schooling on Achievement: The Role of National Context," by David P. Baker, Cornelius Riordan, and Maryellen Schaub, *Comparative Education Review* (November 1995).

Unfortunately, interpreting such comparisons is often not a straightforward matter because researchers have been content largely with comparisons of "naturally occurring" classes, that is, classes over which they had little or no control in terms of the assignment of students and teachers to classes or the curriculum. As a result, the classes that were compared may have differed in many ways, including in parental beliefs about innate differences between boys and girls, the motivation of the students to master the subject in question, the intensity and content of the instruction, and the extent to which single-gender classes are perceived to have high status or prestige by the community. This makes it difficult to determine whether differences in achievement between girls in girls-only classes and girls in coeducational classes are due to the gender composition of the classes (and the associated differences in climate) or to one or more of these "confounding" factors. Controlled experiments are needed to show the full impact of single-gender classes on the achievement of girls and boys.

### Additional Resources

Dara E. Babinski, Margaret H. Sibley, J. Megan Ross, & William E. Pelham, "The Effects of Single Versus Mixed Gender Treatment for Adolescent Girls with ADHD," *Journal of Clinical Child & Adolescent Psychology* (2013, 42:2, 243–250, DOI: 10.1080/15374416.2012.756814).

Christy Belcher, Andy Frey, and Pamela Yankeelov, "The Effects of Single-Sex Classrooms on Classroom Environment, Self-Esteem, and Standardized Test Scores," *School Social Work Journal* (Fall 2006).

Deborah A. Garrahy, "Three Third-Grade Teachers' Gender-Related Beliefs and Behavior," *The Elementary School Journal* (vol. 102, 2001).

Marlon C. James., "Never Quit: The Complexities of Promoting Social and Academic Excellence at a Single-Gender School for Urban African American Males," *Journal of African American Males in Education* (vol. 1, no. 3, 2010).

# Internet References . . .

**The Gurian Institute**

http://gurianinstitute.com/

**American Association of
University Women**

www.aauw.org/

**The Myra Sadker Foundation**

www.sadker.org/

Selected, Edited, and with Issue Framing Material by:
Esther S. Chang, *Soka University of America*

# ISSUE

# Does Homework Improve Student Achievement?

**YES: Swantje Dettmers et al.**, from "Homework Works if Homework Quality Is High: Using Multilevel Modeling to Predict the Development of Achievement in Mathematics," *Journal of Educational Psychology* (2010)

**NO: Harris Cooper et al.**, from "Relationships Among Attitudes About Homework, Amount of Homework Assigned and Completed, and Student Achievement," *Journal of Educational Psychology* (1998)

| Learning Outcomes |
| --- |
| **After reading this issue, you will be able to:** |
| • Identify the ways in which homework has been operationalized in educational psychology. |
| • Describe what the multilevel problem and common cause confounder is in educational research. |
| • Understand the reasons why homework has been found to benefit only some students. |

## ISSUE SUMMARY

**YES:** On the basis of a one-year, two-time point, longitudinal study of a nationally representative German sample of high school students in Grade 9, Swantje Dettmers and colleagues demonstrated that high homework quality fosters motivation to do homework, which in turn leads to higher achievement over time among high school students.

**NO:** Although advocates of homework in general, Harris Cooper and colleagues conducted a study of parents, teachers, and students at lower and upper grades and found that the amount of homework assigned was associated with negative student attitudes weakly related to student grades.

In the educational research literature, there are two widely cited studies documenting the positive influence of homework on achievement—both papers are reviews by Cooper and colleagues (H. Cooper [1989, November], "Synthesis on Research of Homework," *Educational Leadership*, 47(3), pp. 85–91, and H. Cooper, J. C. Robinson, and E. A. Patall [2006], "Does Homework Improve Academic Achievement? A Synthesis of Research 1987–2003," *Review of Educational Research*, 76(1), pp. 1–62). Both are important syntheses of the existing research literature of the time and both were designed to find out what the evidence was about the effects of homework on academic achievement. Overall, the reviews have led to the general conclusion and conventional wisdom that on balance there is an overall net positive association between homework and academic achievement.

But there have been popular press critiques of the reviews (see critiques by Alfie Kohn in which he argues [poorly] from an almost ad-hominen position that Cooper and colleagues approached the problem from an "establishment" perspective and were deliberately trying to find evidence supporting homework). There has also been a sense among the practice community (teachers, school administrators) that while the burden of homework has increased, it is less clear that there is corresponding academic gain, and there is concern that there may well be detrimental effects for some student groups as well as families (see, for example, E. Kralovec and John Buell [2000], *The End of Homework: How Homework Disrupts Families, Overburdens Children, and Limits Learning*, Boston: Beacon).

The most common metric is "time spent on homework." But what if the metric was changed and the question concerned homework frequency (how often assigned), or homework type (of problems), or homework study tactics, or homework effort? Similarly, there are other individual (student) factors that increasingly are recognized as affecting the relationship between homework and achievement including positive/negative homework emotions, motivation, and the subject area and student's interest in it. The net effect of considering definitional differences, measurement differences, and different variables considered in different analytic models is that the answer about whether homework leads to improved student achievement seems to be a nuanced qualified "yes." Yes, but it depends. It has long been recognized that there are age/student level differences such that the associations between homework and achievement are stronger in the secondary grades than primary or middle school. But, even here, there are qualified conclusions—with much of the variability in outcome possibly related to positive or negative homework emotions and amount of effort required as much as the conventional "time spent on homework" metric.

Aside from the general critiques of the previous syntheses, it is a fair question to ask how good is the research evidence from individual studies? There are two really "thorny" issues (see Trautwein and colleagues for an excellent overview and recommended reading). One is referred to as the "multilevel analysis problem" and the other might best be called the "common cause confounder." The multilevel analysis problem refers to the fact that there are at least three levels of analysis that are possible— at the class level (comparing between classes), at the inter-individual level (comparing between students), and at the intra-individual level (comparing within a student; e.g., gains before and after homework). Each of the levels requires a specific and separate analysis model and each can lead to different inferences about the effects of homework on achievement. The "common cause confounder" refers to overlooking potential confounding variables that may better explain the relationship between homework and academic achievement. For example, imagine a study that included in the sample elite math classes/elite schools with students from privileged backgrounds in which teachers required more homework and a strong positive association between homework and achievement is found. The effect is more likely explained by the "common cause" of a high-quality school or related variables rather than the homework, per se. Similarly, there is a "chicken/egg" problem lurking, in that the majority of studies are correlational, relying on a single time point for measurement often without prior educational achievement controlled

for making the "directionality" of the relationship difficult to disentangle—does homework time cause improved achievement or does high prior achievement affect homework time?

Perhaps the best "takeaway" regarding the issue— whether homework leads to improved academic achievement—is to remember the old adage about analytic models—all models are wrong but some are more useful than others. Rather than a simple model (more homework = improved achievement), it seems that a more nuanced view reflecting the complexity of the relation—although less convenient to capture in a "sound bite"—may better reflect reality. For example, homework effort does seem positively associated with achievement outcomes, but it is less clear that there is a uniform positive relation between homework time and achievement outcomes. In fact, homework time combined with negative homework emotions negatively predicts achievement. Conversely, high achievement is positively associated with less homework time but also with homework effort and lower levels of negative homework emotions. Perhaps the next generation of homework research will consistently consider both sides of the equation; "homework" definition/ measurement and student performance factors (emotions, academic interests, levels of support) to more accurately reflect the nature of the relation between homework and achievement providing a better road map for school policy and classroom practice.

The empirical article selected for the "Yes" side is a good example of how psychological science has addressed the "multilevel analysis problem" and the "common cause confounder" in educational research. Swantje Dettmer and colleagues modeled different levels at the same time: the student and class level. Their study design was also extremely sophisticated because the data was large, nationally representative, and included two time points of high schools students from Grade 9 to Grade 10. Their evidence supports the "Yes" side more than the "No" side but you will see that there are many situational requirements for a consistent positive effect. The "No" side article selected for this issue is conducted by an advocate of homework and the first author of two major meta-analyses mentioned above. Although Harris Cooper and his co-authors discuss how homework can be beneficial for students of all ages at the end of the study, the results reveal more pitfalls than promises of homework overall. The unique contribution of this study to the debate question is the consideration of teachers and parents. (Introduction by L. Abbduto and F. Symons.)

# YES

Swantje Dettmers, Ulrich Trautwein, Oliver Lüdtke, Mareike Kunter, and Jürgen Baumert

# Homework Works if Homework Quality Is High: Using Multilevel Modeling to Predict the Development of Achievement in Mathematics

Does homework enhance school effectiveness? More precisely, under which conditions does homework effectively supplement inschool learning? In most countries around the world, homework accounts for a substantial proportion of study time (Cooper, 1989; Cooper, Lindsay, Nye, & Greathouse, 1998; Xu, 2005). At the same time, the effectiveness of homework is a topic of much discussion, and studies investigating the relationship between homework and achievement have produced mixed results. Most previous homework research has focused on homework time and analyzed the relationship between homework and achievement (Cooper, Robinson, & Patall, 2006). However, according to Corno (1996), homework is a complex process influenced by a variety of factors. Much empirical research fails to reflect the complexity of the variables involved in homework assignment and homework completion (see Cooper, 1989), and the methodological shortcomings of many studies make it difficult to draw firm conclusions about the strength of the homework–achievement relationship (Trautwein, 2007).

The present article builds on the homework model proposed by Trautwein, Lüdtke, Schnyder, and Niggli (2006). The model predicts that homework motivation, homework behavior, and achievement are influenced by characteristics including homework quality (i.e., well prepared and adequately challenging assignments). To date, however, empirical research on homework quality has been sparse. For instance, it was only a peripheral issue in Cooper et al.'s (2006) state-of-the art review of homework studies. This paucity of research is surprising, given that homework quality has been a subject of lively debate among teachers, parents, and students for decades now. To address this research deficit, this article examines how homework quality is associated with homework motivation, homework behavior, and mathematics achievement.

## Homework as an Opportunity to Learn

Homework is defined as "tasks assigned to students by school teachers that are meant to be carried out during non-school hours" (Cooper, 1989, p. 7). Homework involves different actors (teachers, students, and parents), serves different purposes (e.g., enhancing student performance and self-regulation), impacts the organization of lessons (e.g., discussing, checking, and grading homework), and involves tasks at different levels of challenge (e.g., routine vs. complex tasks). Thus, homework is a complex issue that warrants investigation within a broad theoretical framework derived from research on learning and instruction (Trautwein & Köller, 2003).

Models of school learning (e.g., Bloom, 1976; Carroll, 1963, 1989) propose that time is an important determinant of degree of learning. Homework contributes substantially to time on task in core subjects and thus provides an additional opportunity to learn. One of the main reasons for assigning homework is thus to increase the total study time (Paschal, Weinstein, & Walberg, 1984; Walberg & Paschal, 1995). Indeed, most homework studies investigate out-of-school learning as a function of time or quantity of homework (e.g., Cooper et al., 2006). Studies conducted in the United States point to a positive overall association between homework time and achievement,

Dettmers, Swantje et al., "Homework Works if Homework Quality Is High: Using Multilevel Modeling to Predict the Development of Achievement in Mathematics," *Journal of Educational Psychology*, Vol 102(2) May 2010, 467–482. No further reproduction or distribution is permitted without written permission from the American Psychological Association.

but methodological shortcomings in most of these studies have been noted (Cooper et al., 2006; Trautwein, 2007). Major criticisms include the lack of control for other important predictors of achievement, the failure to adequately model the multilevel structure inherent in homework studies, the reliance on cross-sectional data, uncertainty about the reliability of the homework measures used, and the absence of a theoretical model of homework assignment and homework behavior (Cooper, 1989; Trautwein & Köller, 2003).

In an attempt to overcome some of the limitations of prior homework research, Trautwein and colleagues (for a detailed description, see Trautwein, Lüdtke, Kastens, & Köller, 2006; Trautwein, Lüdtke, Schnyder, & Niggli, 2006) proposed a theoretical model that combines elements of expectancy–value theory (Eccles, 1983; Eccles & Wigfield, 2002), self-determination theory (Deci & Ryan, 2002; Grolnick & Slowiaczek, 1994; Ryan & Deci, 2000), and research on learning and instruction (Brophy & Good, 1986; Weinert & Helmke, 1995a, 1995b). The model takes into account the three protagonists in the homework process (students, teachers, and parents) and covers six major groups of variables (achievement, homework behavior, homework motivation, student characteristics, parental behavior, and the learning environment). The model predicts that the effort students spend on their homework assignments (i.e., doing their best to solve the tasks assigned) is positively related to their achievement. In line with expectancy–value theory, homework effort is conceptualized as strongly influenced by expectancy and value beliefs, representing two aspects of homework motivation. The expectancy component reflects a student's belief in being able to complete a given homework assignment successfully (Bandura, 1998; Pintrich, 2003). The value component describes students' reasons for doing a task (Eccles & Wigfield, 2002; Pintrich, 2003; Pintrich & De Groot, 1990) in terms of the importance of succeeding in a specific domain, the enjoyment of engaging in the activity, the utility of the activity, and the costs associated with it. The model further predicts that family characteristics and the quality of parental homework assistance are associated with homework expectancy and value beliefs and with homework effort. Furthermore, student characteristics such as prior knowledge, cognitive abilities, and conscientiousness are predicted to affect homework motivation (expectancy and value beliefs) and effort. Finally, the model comprises core characteristics of homework, including homework frequency, homework length, homework control, and homework quality. Homework quality is at the core of the present investigation.

# Homework Quality, Homework Motivation, Homework Behavior, and Achievement

Based on Astleitner (2007), homework can be regarded as a set of tasks or problems that are supposed to support learning (e.g., by activating prior knowledge, intensifying comprehension, or applying knowledge to new tasks or problems). High homework quality thus requires the careful selection and preparation of appropriate and, to some extent, interesting tasks that reinforce classroom learning (Trautwein & Lüdtke, 2007). Further, homework assignments must be cognitively challenging but not overtaxing. Homework assignments of low cognitive challenge simply require students to recall information, whereas challenging tasks require them to synthesize ideas, for example, or to combine strategies or knowledge areas.

In stark contrast to research on general instructional quality (Kunter & Baumert, 2006a; Weinert, Schrader, & Helmke, 1989), research on the relationship between homework quality and student achievement is—as noted above—surprisingly scarce. Instead, the clear focus of homework research has been on homework quantity (Warton, 2001). Yet the time needed to learn a given criterion is, in part, a function of the quality of instruction and of the students' ability to understand that instruction (Gettinger, 1989). Warton (2001) argued that "the quality and type of homework tasks vary to such an extent both within and between subject areas, ability, and grade level that to focus on time variables alone seems an oversimplification" (p. 157).

The few empirical studies to date that have included homework quality variables indicate beneficial effects of homework quality. For instance, using structural equation modeling, Keith and Cool (1992) found that high-quality instruction (in terms of average student ratings of quality of instruction, school reputation, and teachers' interest in students) was positively associated with a higher motivation, which led to more academic coursework, which in turn was positively related to achievement. Moreover, the authors found that higher quality of instruction and higher motivation resulted in higher homework times.

Trautwein and colleagues (Trautwein & Lüdtke, 2007, 2009; Trautwein, Lüdtke, Schnyder, & Niggli, 2006) used student reports about the quality of their homework assignments as predictors of homework expectancy beliefs, homework value, and homework effort. The homework quality items used in these studies covered several aspects of homework assignments, such as teachers' advance preparation of assignments, integration in lessons, and difficulty level.

Higher self-reported homework expectancy and value beliefs and higher homework effort were found among students who had a more favorable perception of homework quality than their classmates (student-level effect) and in classes where the aggregated perception of homework quality was higher than in other classes (class-level effect). Unfortunately, achievement was not considered in these studies. Although it did not target homework quality directly, a study by Trautwein, Niggli, Schnyder, and Lüdtke (2009) is also of relevance in the present context. The authors asked teachers about their homework attitudes and behaviors. Overall, they found a relatively low emphasis on drill and practice tasks and a high emphasis on motivation was associated with favorable developments in students' homework effort and achievement.

Cooper (1989) distinguished between homework containing same-day tasks and homework including elements of practice and or preparation. The former is cognitively less demanding, consisting primarily of repetitive exercises. Practice or preparation homework is cognitively more demanding, involving material that has not been covered fully in class or material dealt with previous lessons. Reviewing eight studies, Cooper found an average effect size of $d = 0.14$ favoring cognitively more demanding homework assignments. Lipowsky, Rakoczy, Klieme, Reusser, and Pauli (2004) analyzed the predictive power of homework assignments for mathematics achievement. They found that students in classes where homework was perceived to be cognitively demanding ("Our math teacher sets homework tasks that make us think about new things") showed greater achievement gains than their peers in other classes.

Overall, the few available studies indicate that homework quality matters. More research is necessary, however. In particular, the link between homework quality and later achievement is far from established, despite the intuitive assumption that homework quality matters. Moreover, research would benefit from a deeper understanding of different facets of quality and whether they can be reliably measured. The present study is a step in this direction. We focused on two indicators of homework quality, which were collected via student reports. The first, *homework selection,* taps the selection of appropriate and interesting homework tasks. Do the tasks selected by teachers enhance students' understanding? Are they interesting? Is homework well integrated into lessons? The homework task selection indicator reflects students' general evaluation of homework quality. The measure has similarities to scales used in previous research (e.g., Trautwein & Lüdtke, 2009), the findings of which generally point to positive associations with homework motivation and behavior.

The second indicator, *homework challenge,* measures students' perceptions of the cognitive challenge inherent in the homework tasks. Are they easy to solve or do they require mental effort? This indicator targets the individually perceived difficulty level of homework. Cognitively activating instruction has been found to be positively associated with student achievement at the class level (Kunter & Baumert, 2006b), whereas repetitive tasks and easy homework assignments have been found in some studies to be negatively related to student achievement (Cooper, 1989; Trautwein, Köller, Schmitz, & Baumert, 2002).

## Assessing Homework Quality Using Student Reports

The focus of the present study is on homework quality as a characteristic of the learning environment. At least three data sources are regularly used to assess classroom environments (Anderson, 1982; Fraser, 1991; Turner & Meyer, 2000): observer ratings, teacher ratings, and student ratings. Each perspective has specific methodological and theoretical advantages and disadvantages. Observer ratings are very cost and labor intensive. Teachers, who can be considered experts on different instructional approaches and are responsible for guiding the instructional process, might seem to be the ideal source of information. However, self-serving strategies and teaching ideals may compromise the validity of their ratings. In the present study, student ratings were used to assess homework quality. Students can also be considered experts on the learning environment. They are exposed to a variety of teachers in different subjects and thus have the opportunity to compare different teaching styles. From a phenomenological point of view, students' ratings are the most appropriate source of data for assessing the learning environment: A given student's behavior is likely to be more affected by his or her interpretation of the classroom context than by any objective indicator of that context. At the same time, given the idiosyncratic nature of students' perceptions of their learning environment, the reliability of student report data has been questioned (Aleamoni, 1999; Marsh & Roche, 1997; but see also Marsh, 2001; Marsh & Roche, 2000). Conceptual and methodological challenges therefore need to be addressed before student ratings can properly be used to gauge the effects of characteristics of the learning environment (see Lüdtke, Robitzsch, Trautwein, & Kunter, 2009).

Most important, perceived homework quality can be conceptualized at two different levels: the student and the class level. At the student level, ratings represent individual perceptions of homework quality that may differ across the students in a class, depending, for instance, on their prior knowledge. At this level, the focus of interest is whether individual students' perceptions of their classroom or teacher are related to individual differences in motivational, cognitive, and behavioral outcomes. Conversely, data aggregated at the class level yield a measure of the shared perception of the learning environment; idiosyncrasies in individual perceptions tend to be canceled out by the averaging process.

The literature on multilevel modeling (e.g., Raudenbush & Bryk, 2002; Robinson, 1950) has clearly demonstrated that relations between variables often vary across the different levels of analysis. The associations found at a higher, aggregate level (e.g., class level) do not allow conclusions to be drawn about relationships at the lower level of analysis (e.g., student level), and vice versa. The main reason for differential effects at different levels of analysis is that entirely different factors might operate at the individual and the group level. Such diverging patterns of associations are highly interesting from a theoretical and practical point of view, and one of the main accomplishments of multilevel analyses is to document them. Prominent examples of differential relations at different levels of analysis in educational research are effects of ability grouping (e.g., the big-fish-little-pond

effect; Trautwein, Lüdtke, Marsh, Köller, & Baumert, 2006; Trautwein, Lüdtke, Marsh, & Nagy, 2009) and the amount of time spent on homework (Trautwein, 2007).

In the present study, we looked at two analytical levels: the student level and the class level. At the student level, we were interested in interindividual differences between students' perceptions of their homework assignments in the same class and their associations with different outcome variables. At the class level, which reflects the shared environment, we aimed at analyzing the overall effect of the quality of the homework assigned to a class. Recent studies have confirmed that class-mean ratings provide a reliable indicator of homework quality, with multilevel models showing that between 12% and 21% of the total variance in students' perceptions of homework quality was located between classes (Trautwein & Lüdtke, 2009; Trautwein, Lüdtke, Schnyder, & Niggli, 2006).

## The Present Study

The present study examined whether homework quality predicts homework motivation (homework expectancy and value beliefs), homework behavior (time on homework and homework effort), and achievement in mathematics (see Figure 1 for a graphical illustration). We used data obtained from a nationally representative sample of

*Figure 1*

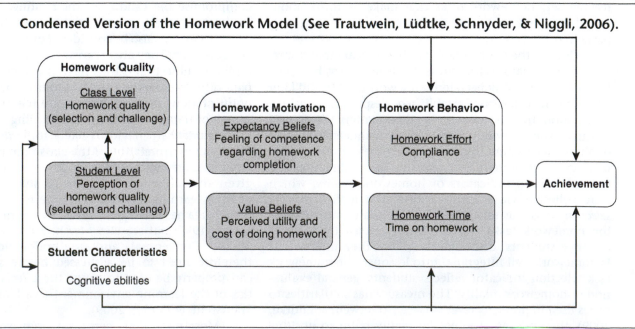

Condensed Version of the Homework Model (See Trautwein, Lüdtke, Schnyder, & Niggli, 2006).

3,483 high school students at two points of measurement over the course of a year in the context of the German extension to the PISA 2003 study (Prenzel, Carstensen, Schöps, & Maurischat, 2006).

We investigated four research questions: two concerning relationships at the student level and two pertaining to the class level. Our first research question addressed the predictive power of perceived homework selection at the student level. Generally, we expected to find a positive association between homework task selection and the outcome variables. More specifically, at the student level, we expected high ratings of homework selection to predict high homework expectancy and value beliefs, homework effort, and time spent on homework. Moreover, we expected students who perceived that homework was well selected and interesting to show greater achievement gains than their peers.

Our second research question concerned the role of homework challenge. A student who reports a high level of homework challenge relative to his or her classmates may feel overtaxed by the homework assignments and exhibit less favorable outcomes. We thus hypothesized that homework challenge is negatively related to homework expectancy beliefs at the student level. Moreover, because individual perceptions of homework challenge depend to some extent on students' cognitive abilities and prior achievement, we expected high homework challenge ratings to negatively predict mathematics achievement. No specific hypotheses were formulated for the association between homework challenge and homework value beliefs, homework time, and homework effort. According to Good and Brophy (1990), homework assignments must be of appropriate difficulty for students to perceive them as valuable. Assignments that are either too easy or too difficult may be perceived as a waste of time. According to expectancy–value theory, low value beliefs are likely to result in low effort.

Our third research question concerned the role of homework task selection at the class level. We hypothesized a positive association between aggregated homework selection ratings and homework motivation (expectancy and value beliefs) and homework behavior (time spent on homework and homework effort). In addition, we expected to find greater achievement gains in classes in which the mean perception of homework selection was comparatively high.

The fourth research question addressed the role of homework challenge at the class level. The meaning of this variable might be quite different at the student and the class level. At the class level, a high level of perceived challenge might indicate that the teacher considers it important to assign cognitively challenging tasks. Paralleling our hypotheses at the student level, we expected the relationship between homework challenge and homework expectancy beliefs to be negative. No specific hypotheses were formulated for the relationship between homework challenge and homework value beliefs, homework time, and homework effort. However, we expected to find differential associations with mathematics achievement at the student and the class level. The aggregated perceived level of challenge is a proxy of how cognitively challenging homework assignments are perceived to be within a class. In line with research on instructional quality (Kunter & Baumert, 2006a), which has found cognitively activating elements of instruction to be positively associated with student achievement, we assumed that perceived level of challenge positively predicts mathematics achievement at the class level.

# Methods

## Data Source and Sample

The Programme for International Student Assessment (PISA) was initiated by the Organisation for Economic Cooperation and Development (OECD) to study and compare student achievement in the OECD and in some non-OECD countries (Organisation for Economic Cooperation and Development [OECD], 2004a). The analyses reported are part of the PISA-I-Plus study, the German extension to the 2003 cycle of the PISA study. The study was conducted during the school years 2003 (when students were in Grade 9) and 2004 (when students were in Grade 10). The German PISA extension study focused on intact classes in schools participating in the international PISA 2003 study. The main goal of this extension study was to examine effects of variables at the student, parent, teacher, and school level on learning gains in mathematics (Prenzel, Drechsel, Carstensen, & Ramm, 2004). A multistage sampling procedure was implemented to ensure high representativeness of the data. The full dataset consisted of 4,567 students in 194 classes. The dataset used in the analyses reported here was restricted in two respects: to students participating at both measurement points and to classes with the same mathematics teacher at both measurement points. Thus, the final data set consisted of 3,483 students (56.8% female; mean age at first measurement point: 15.1 years) in 155 classes (average class size: 22.47 students). The students participating in the PISA-I-Plus study were administered additional tests the day after the international PISA assessment.

## Instruments

With the exception of the second mathematics achievement test, all instruments analyzed in the present study were administered in Grade 9 (T1). Further, all homework instruments referred specifically to homework assignments in mathematics.

*Variables at the student level.* In sum, the following eight variables and four control variables were analyzed at the student level.

*T1 achievement.* We used students' Grade 9 mathematics literacy and reading literacy scores in the international PISA 2003 assessment to control for prior achievement.

*T2 mathematics achievement.* Mathematics achievement at T2 was assessed by a test covering the standard content stipulated in the federal states' curricula for Grade 10 mathematics (see Baumert et al., in press). The test was administered to all students in the present sample. The correlation between the national and the international test was .92. Mathematics test scores were generated using item response theory techniques (for details, see Prenzel et al., 2006). The resulting test score distribution had a mean of $M = 500$ ($SD = 100$); test reliability was $r = .79$ (T2). Because PISA used a multimatrix design to assess mathematics achievement, each individual score is based on a small sample of tasks. It was therefore not possible to estimate Cronbach's alpha. Instead, we report reliability in terms of the correlation between independent plausible value draws (Adams & Wu, 2002; OECD, 2004b).

*Homework behavior.* Homework effort was measured by five items (e.g., "I do my best in my mathematics homework"; "I always try to do my complete mathematics homework"). Students scoring high on this scale do their homework assignments carefully and to the best of their ability. A 4-point Likert response scale (from 1 = *totally disagree* to 4 = *totally agree*) was used. Internal consistency (Cronbach's alpha) was $\alpha = .69$. Homework time was assessed using one open-ended item that required students to state how much time (in hours) they spent on mathematics homework per week (see Baumert et al., 2006).

*Homework motivation.* Two scales assessed the *expectancy component* ("If I make an effort, I can do all my mathematics homework"; three items; $\alpha = .66$) and the *value component* ("Our mathematics homework takes a lot of time and is of little use to me" [reverse scored]; two items; $\alpha = .72$). A 4-point Likert response scale (from 1 = *totally disagree* to 4 = *totally agree*) was used. Students who score high on homework expectancy beliefs are optimistic about their capability to work successfully on the task assigned. The items tapping the value component focused on the facets of utility and cost (see Baumert et al., 2006).

*Homework quality.* Two scales were used to describe homework quality. *Perceived quality of homework task selection* was measured by five items (e.g., "Our mathematics teacher almost always chooses homework assignments really well"; $\alpha = .83$). The scale assesses how well-prepared and interesting homework assignments were perceived to be. *Perceived homework challenge* was measured by four items (e.g., "Our mathematics homework assignments are often too easy" [reverse scored]; $\alpha = .74$). The scale assesses the extent to which homework assignments are perceived to be cognitively challenging. Both homework quality scales are reported in the appendix. In both cases, a 4-point Likert response scale (from 1 = *totally disagree* to 4 = *totally agree*) was used (see Baumert et al., 2006).[1]

*Control variables.* Four variables, which were specified in the individual background model used in Baumert et al. (in press), were included in the multilevel models to control for possible confounds at the student level. First, we included a measure of basic cognitive abilities. The Figure Analogies subscale of the Cognitive Ability Test 4−12 + R (Heller & Perleth, 2000), a German version of Thorndike and Hagen's (1993) Cognitive Abilities Test, was used. Because the Figure Analogies subscale taps highly g-loaded ability components (Carroll, 1993), it is frequently used as a parsimonious test of cognitive abilities. Second, we controlled for students' socioeconomic status (SES), assessed using the International Socio-Economic Index (ISEI) developed by Ganzeboom, de Graaf, Treiman, and de Leeuw (1992). We used the highest ISEI score in the family in our analyses. Third, we created six dummy variables to control for the parental educational background.[2] Fourth, we controlled for the sex of the students.

*Variables at the class level.* At the class level, we included two measures of homework quality and school track as a control variable in our models.

*Homework quality.* The two homework quality scales, perceived quality of homework task selection and perceived homework challenge, were aggregated at the class level to give a measure of homework quality effects.

*Control variables.* At the class level, we controlled for *school track.* After completing primary school (at the age of 10 or, in some states, 12), students in Germany are typically assigned to either a comprehensive school or to one of three secondary tracks: *Gymnasium,* the highest track; *Realschule,* the intermediate track; or *Hauptschule,* the least academically demanding track. Because *Hauptschule* students graduate after Grade 9, they were not analyzed in the present study. Some German states have a combined *Mittelschule* (catering for *Realschule* and *Hauptschule* students). Thus, four school types are included in the following analyses (*Gymnasium, Realschule, Mittelschule,* and comprehensives). Dummy variables were created for each track to control for effects of school type. *Realschule* was used as the reference category.

## Statistical Analyses

**Analyzing hierarchical data.** As in most research conducted in school settings, students in this study were nested within classes. Students within a class are typically more similar to each other than are two students randomly selected from the whole sample. For the present research, it is important to note that the meaning of a variable at the student level may not bear any straightforward relation to its meaning at the class level. Whenever major variables represent different levels of analysis, it is important to use a statistical method that takes the nested structure into account. Multilevel modeling provides a powerful framework for analyzing data collected in the school context by accounting for nonindependence of the observations (Raudenbush & Bryk, 2002). A detailed description of multilevel modeling is beyond the scope of the present investigation and is available elsewhere (e.g., Goldstein, 1995; Hox, 2002; Raudenbush & Bryk, 2002; Snijders & Bosker, 1999).

When aggregated individual data are used to assess effects of group characteristics, the observed group average score (e.g., aggregated student ratings of homework quality) may be a rather unreliable measure of the unobserved "true" group mean. As has been shown, the reliability of these aggregated ratings depends on the number of students per class and the extent to which students' ratings vary across classes (Lüdtke, Trautwein, Kunter, & Baumert, 2006; Raudenbush & Bryk, 2002). We adopted the multilevel latent covariate approach (MLC) implemented in Mplus to control for the unreliability of aggregated student ratings of their learning environment (Lüdtke et al., 2008; Muthén & Muthén, 1998–2007). The MLC approach corrects for the unreliable assessment of the group mean when estimating group effects by taking into account that only a finite number of students provided ratings of the quality of their homework. Lüdtke et al. (2008) suggested that research designs involving student ratings of the learning environment are ideally suited to the MLC approach, because each student's perception of homework quality reflects a construct at the class level (i.e., quality of the homework assigned to a class). Thus, variation within each

class can be regarded to some extent as unreliability in the measurement of homework quality. In the present study, a series of multilevel models were specified using Mplus 5.1 (Muthén & Muthén, 1998–2007) to predict homework motivation, homework behavior, and mathematics achievement. Correlations and residual correlations were freely estimated; thus, all models were saturated.

**Centering student-level predictor variables.** One critical issue in multilevel modeling is the centering of student-level predictor variables (see Enders & Tofighi, 2007; Kreft, de Leeuw, & Aiken, 1995). Student ratings of the learning environment can be adjusted either to the cluster to which the student belongs (groupmean centering) or to the mean ratings of the whole sample (grand-mean centering). The decision to center student-level predictors at the group mean or the grand mean can affect the interpretation of the parameters estimated (Enders & Tofighi, 2007) and must be driven by the research questions addressed. In the present study, individual and aggregated ratings of the learning environment (e.g., homework selection, homework challenge) were entered simultaneously as predictors in the multilevel models (see Lüdtke et al., 2009). Grand-mean centering would control for interindividual differences in student ratings among classes and would thus eliminate an essential component of the aggregated student ratings. Because we were primarily interested in the effects of homework selection and homework challenge as features of the learning environment, we treated both classroom features as classlevel variables and decided to center student ratings at their group mean. This approach allows us to differentiate between-class from within-class variation in perceived homework characteristics (e.g., Karabenick, 2004). The other Level 1 predictor variables, which are primarily defined at the individual level (e.g., value and expectancy beliefs), were centered at the grand mean. Thus, interindividual differences among students are taken into account when estimating effects of homework assignment at the class level.

**Missing values.** The present analyses are part of a larger assessment, the PISA-I-Plus study. Due to time constraints, the students in a class were randomly administered different versions of the questionnaire. All students were administered the items tapping homework motivation and homework behavior, but the homework selection and homework challenge items were administered in only one of two booklets. Thus, approximately 50% of the homework selection and homework challenge data are missing by design. Planned missing data designs (Graham, Taylor, Olchowski, & Cumsille, 2006) are well established as a research strategy and have been applied in several large-scale assessment studies to increase cost effectiveness and design efficiency (Graham et al., 2006). The average percentage of missing data was otherwise 3.5%.

In the methodological literature on missing data (Peugh & Enders, 2004; Schafer & Graham, 2002), there is growing consensus that multiple imputation of missing data is superior to traditional pairwise and listwise deletion methods. Even when 50% of the data are missing by design, methods such as multiple imputation allow researchers to obtain reliable parameter estimates and standard errors. In multiple imputation, missing values are predicted from the observed values of each participant, with random noise added to maintain a correct amount of variability in the imputed data (Schafer & Graham, 2002). According to Schafer and Graham (2002), estimation of five values provides highly sufficient estimates for a moderate amount of missing data; increasing the number of estimations increases the accuracy only marginally. We therefore produced five data sets in which missing data were replaced with values estimated by the PAN algorithm implemented in the R software (Schafer, 2008). The PAN algorithm was developed to impute multivariate panel data or clustered data. PAN uses a multivariate extension of a two-level linear regression model commonly applied to multilevel data (Schafer, 2001). Each imputed data set was analyzed separately, and the resulting estimates were combined using the formulas given by Rubin (1987) and implemented in the Mplus software.

## Results

### Descriptives and Zero-Order Correlations

Table 1 presents means, standard deviations, and missing values for the variables analyzed. Students' average ratings of homework effort were close to the scale midpoint. On average, students reported typically spending 2.60 hr per week on their mathematics homework assignments. Homework motivation ratings were moderately above the scale midpoint (expectancy: $M = 2.96$; value: $M = 3.04$), indicating rather high motivation levels. Finally, the students perceived their mathematics homework assignments as somewhat difficult (homework challenge: $M = 2.25$) and the quality of homework selection of middle to high quality (homework selection: $M = 2.69$).

Table 2 presents zero-order correlations among the variables analyzed. To take the multilevel structure into account, we estimated all correlations using the Mplus option "type = complex." As shown in Table 2, we

*Table 1*

**Means, Standard Deviations, and Percentage of Missing Values**

| Variable | N | M | SD | % Missing |
|---|---|---|---|---|
| Class level | | | | |
| Gymnasium[a] | 155 | 36.77 | 0.49 | 0.00 |
| Mittelschule[a] | 155 | 11.61 | 0.31 | 0.00 |
| Realschule[a] | 155 | 43.87 | 0.50 | 0.00 |
| Comprehensive schools | 155 | 7.74 | 0.24 | 0.00 |
| HW selection | 155 | 2.69 | 0.34 | 0.00 |
| HW challenge | 155 | 2.25 | 0.31 | 0.00 |
| Student level | | | | |
| Achievement T1[b] | 3,462 | 0.23 | 0.87 | 0.60 |
| Achievement T2[b] | 3,324 | 571.22 | 79.44 | 4.57 |
| Reading achievement | 1,831 | 0.35 | 1.12 | 47.43 |
| Cognitive abilities | 3,436 | 0.26 | 1.35 | 1.35 |
| Socioeconomic status | 3,407 | 52.83 | 15.96 | 2.18 |
| Immigration status | 3,483 | 0.80 | 0.40 | 0.00 |
| Male | 3,483 | 0.43 | 0.50 | 0.00 |
| HW time | 3,390 | 2.60 | 1.84 | 2.67 |
| HW effort | 3,408 | 2.69 | 0.63 | 2.15 |
| HW value | 3,407 | 3.04 | 0.83 | 2.18 |
| HW expectancy | 3,408 | 2.96 | 0.70 | 2.15 |
| HW selection | 1,864 | 2.69 | 0.68 | 46.48 |
| HW challenge | 1,854 | 2.25 | 0.70 | 46.77 |

*Note.* HW = homework.

[a]Means are based on dummy coded school indicators. The means refer to the population of students in the specific school track.

[b]Means are above the midpoint because students attending the academically least demanding track were excluded from all analyses.

found differential associations between the homework characteristics and the achievement indicators. Homework selection was positively associated with homework expectancy and value beliefs, homework effort, and homework time. Moreover, there was a positive correlation with achievement at T2. Homework challenge was negatively associated with homework expectancy and value beliefs, homework effort, and mathematics achievement at both points of measurement.

### Homework Quality: A Class-Level Variable?

One major precondition for using student ratings of the classroom environment is that the aggregated ratings

*Table 2*

### Intercorrelations Among All Variables

| Variable | 1 | 2 | 3 | 4 | 5 | 6 | 7 | 8 | 9 | 10 | 11 | 12 | 13 | 14 | 15 | 16 |
|---|---|---|---|---|---|---|---|---|---|---|---|---|---|---|---|---|
| 1. *Mittelschule* (lower track) | — | | | | | | | | | | | | | | | |
| 2. *Gymnasium* (highest track) | −0.27 | — | | | | | | | | | | | | | | |
| 3. Comprehensive schools | −0.09 | −0.20 | — | | | | | | | | | | | | | |
| 4. Achievement T1 | −0.16 | 0.43 | −0.19 | — | | | | | | | | | | | | |
| 5. Achievement T2 | −0.16 | 0.43 | −0.17 | 0.49 | — | | | | | | | | | | | |
| 6. Reading achievement | −0.18 | 0.33 | −0.17 | 0.27 | 0.25 | — | | | | | | | | | | |
| 7. Cognitive abilities | −0.14 | 0.36 | −0.17 | 0.36 | 0.39 | 0.19 | — | | | | | | | | | |
| 8. SES | −0.16 | 0.35 | −0.10 | 0.06 | 0.09 | 0.04 | 0.03 | — | | | | | | | | |
| 9. Migration status | −0.07 | −0.11 | 0.06 | −0.05 | −0.04 | −0.10 | −0.0[a] | −0.18 | — | | | | | | | |
| 10. Male | 0.03 | −0.01 | 0.03 | 0.16 | 0.20 | 0.00[a] | 0.07 | 0.06 | −0.03 | — | | | | | | |
| 11. HW time | −0.07 | −0.05 | −0.02 | −0.14 | −0.19 | −0.06 | −0.13 | −0.06 | 0.04 | −0.18 | — | | | | | |
| 12. HW effort | −0.01[a] | −0.05 | −0.02 | 0.17 | 0.11 | 0.13 | 0.07 | 0.00[a] | −0.01[a] | −0.06 | 0.15 | — | | | | |
| 13. HW value | −0.06 | 0.01 | −0.01 | −0.01[a] | −0.05 | 0.01[a] | −0.03 | −0.02[a] | 0.04 | −0.08 | 0.14 | 0.26 | — | | | |
| 14. HW expectancy | 0.00[a] | −0.04 | 0.02 | 0.20 | 0.12 | 0.07 | 0.10 | 0.05 | 0.01[a] | 0.11 | −0.03 | 0.29 | 0.17 | — | | |
| 15. HW selection | −0.01[a] | −0.04 | −0.01 | 0.03 | −0.02 | 0.00[a] | −0.02[a] | −0.04 | 0.06 | 0.00[a] | 0.10 | 0.20 | 0.40 | 0.28 | — | |
| 16. HW challenge | 0.00[a] | −0.05 | −0.02 | 0.26 | 0.24 | 0.16 | 0.20 | 0.06 | −0.03 | 0.15 | −0.17 | 0.24 | 0.07 | 0.37 | 0.15 | — |

*Note.* $N = 3,483$. The Mplus option "type = complex" was used to correct for clustering effects. All items and variables were z-standardized before the correlations were calculated. Correlations $> .023$ are statistically significant at $p < .05$. SES = socioeconomic status; HW = homework.

[a]Nonsignificant correlations.

must be sufficiently reliable. In multilevel modeling, the reliability of aggregated individual student judgments is estimated by the intraclass correlation coefficients $ICC_1$ and $ICC_2$ (Bliese, 2000; Raudenbush & Bryk, 2002). The $ICC_1$ reflects the proportion of variance attributable to differences between classes; the higher the $ICC_1$, the more similar are the ratings of the students in a given class. The $ICC_1$ for homework selection was .18; that for homework challenge was .11. Thus, 18% of the variance in homework selection and 11% of the variance in homework challenge was located between classes. These findings are consistent with those of prior studies based on students' ratings of their learning environment (e.g., Frenzel, Pekrun, & Goetz, 2007; Kunter, Baumert, & Köller, 2007). The somewhat lower $ICC_1$ for homework challenge indicates larger differences in individual perceptions of this variable than of homework selection. Perceptions of homework challenge may be more dependent on interindividual differences in, for instance, cognitive abilities or prior knowledge. Whereas the $ICC_1$ indicates the reliability of an individual student's rating, the $ICC_2$ provides an estimate of the reliability of the class-mean rating. It is calculated by applying the Spearman-Brown prophecy formula (Nunnally, 1978) to the $ICC_1$. A satisfactory $ICC_2$ is a necessary precondition for detecting associations between variables at the class level (see Bliese, 2000; Lüdtke et al., 2006). Drawing on the classical test theory literature, we regarded .70 as a reasonable lower bound for acceptable reliability of aggregated ratings. The $ICC_2$ for homework selection was .83; that for homework challenge was .74, indicating satisfactory reliability of the class-mean ratings.

In addition, we examined the agreement among the students in each class on homework selection and challenge. The average deviation index ($AD_M$) proposed by Burke, Finkelstein, and Dusig (1999) and Burke and Dunlap (2002) indicates individual students' deviation from the class mean. A cutoff point of .73 has been proposed for a 4-point Likert scale with more than 20 raters per cluster, with lower values indicating better agreement (see Smith-Crowe & Burke, 2003). Averaging the single $AD_M$ indices across classes indicated sufficient agreement between students within classes on homework selection ($M = 0.63$; mean $AD_M$ value across classes) and homework challenge ($M = 0.69$). In sum, computation of the $ICC_1$, $ICC_2$, and $AD_M$ confirmed the reliability and within-group agreement of the aggregated student perceptions of the learning environment, indicating that it is appropriate to use the aggregated data as class-level variables.

# Predicting Homework Motivation, Homework Behavior, and Mathematics Achievement

Using Mplus 5.1, we specified several multilevel models to test our hypotheses. Tables 3 to 5 present the results. In all models, we controlled for potential confounding variables and mathematics achievement at T1. M1 models present the relationships between homework motivation (expectancy and value beliefs), homework behavior (effort and time spent on homework), and mathematics achievement. M2 models additionally include the homework characteristics task selection and challenge (both class-mean centered) but exclude the mediator variables homework expectancy and value beliefs (Tables 4 and 5). M3 models include all variables, allowing us to investigate the mediating role of homework motivation (Tables 4 and 5). The results are presented in two sections. First, we present the results for homework expectancy and value beliefs, homework effort, and homework time; second, we describe the findings for mathematics achievement.

**Predicting homework motivation and homework behavior.** In a first step (see Table 3), we specified multilevel models predicting homework expectancy beliefs (first two columns of Table 3) and homework value beliefs (last two columns of Table 3). We first describe our findings for homework expectancy beliefs. We expected homework

*Table 3*

## Predicting Homework Expectancy and Homework Value: Results From Multilevel Modeling

| Variable | HW Expectancy (*B*) | | HW Value (*B*) | |
|---|---|---|---|---|
| | M1 | M2 | M1 | M2 |
| **Level 2: Classes** | | | | |
| School type (Reference category: middle track) | | | | |
| *Mittelschule* (lower track) | 0.01 | −0.01 | −0.21* | −0.14 |
| *Gymnasium* (highest track) | −0.24*** | −0.10 | −0.03 | −0.01 |
| Comprehensives | 0.07 | 0.06 | −0.08 | 0.00 |
| HW selection | | 0.10* | | 0.48*** |
| HW challenge | | −0.35*** | | 0.03 |
| **Level 1: Students** | | | | |
| Male | 0.19*** | 0.11*** | −0.16*** | −0.18*** |
| SES | 0.01 | 0.00 | −0.01 | −0.02 |
| Cognitive abilities | 0.06** | 0.04 | −0.01 | 0.00 |
| Achievement T1 | 0.06** | 0.02 | −0.02 | −0.02 |
| Reading achievement T1 | 0.02 | −0.01 | 0.04 | 0.02 |
| Immigration status | 0.14 | 0.07 | 0.18 | 0.03 |
| PEB 1 | 0.03 | −0.01 | −0.08 | −0.07 |
| PEB 2 | 0.06 | 0.04 | 0.03 | −0.01 |
| PEB 3 | 0.01 | −0.01 | 0.04 | 0.00 |
| PEB 5 | 0.17** | 0.12 | 0.04 | 0.03 |
| PEB 6 | −0.07 | −0.02 | −0.05 | −0.05 |
| HW selection | | 0.24*** | | 0.43*** |
| HW challenge | | −0.32*** | | −0.03 |
| $R^2$ Level 2 | 0.00 | 52.94 | 9.72 | 65.28 |
| $R^2$ Level 1 | 3.02 | 18.73 | 1.39 | 17.70 |

*Note.* $N = 3,483$. M1 = models without homework characteristics; M2 = models with homework characteristics; HW = homework; SES = socioeconomic status; PEB = parental educational background (reference category: PEB 4); PEB 1 = no apprenticeship, with or without *Hauptschule* certificate (lowest parental educational background); PEB 2 = apprenticeship, with or without *Hauptschule* certificate; PEB 3 = apprenticeship and *Realschule* certificate; PEB 4 = *Hauptschule* or *Realschule* certificate and technical college; PEB 5 = technical college or *Gymnasium* certificate, no higher education; PEB 6 = degree qualification (highest educational background).
* $p < .05$. ** $p < .01$. *** $p < .001$.

*Table 4*

## Predicting Homework Time and Homework Effort: Results from Multilevel Modeling

| Variable | HW time T1 ($B$) | | | HW effort T1 ($B$) | | |
|---|---|---|---|---|---|---|
| | M1 | M2 | M3 | M1 | M2 | M3 |
| **Level 2: Classes** | | | | | | |
| School type (Reference category: middle track) | | | | | | |
| *Mittelschule* (lower track) | −0.30*** | −0.27*** | −0.26*** | −0.02 | −0.04 | −0.01 |
| *Gymasium* (highest track) | 0.05 | −0.06 | −0.06 | −0.21*** | −0.21*** | −0.20*** |
| Comprehensive schools | −0.28* | −0.23 | −0.24* | −0.03 | 0.00 | −0.02 |
| HW selection | | 0.23** | 0.16 | | 0.28*** | 0.19** |
| HW challenge | | 0.34*** | 0.39*** | | −0.10 | −0.02 |
| **Level 1: Students** | | | | | | |
| Male | −0.27*** | −0.26*** | −0.25*** | −0.17*** | −0.21*** | −0.20*** |
| SES | −0.01 | −0.01 | −0.01 | −0.03 | −0.04 | −0.03 |
| Cognitive abilities | −0.07*** | −0.06** | −0.06** | 0.00 | 0.00 | −0.01 |
| Achievement T1 | −0.14*** | −0.12*** | −0.12*** | 0.08** | 0.06** | 0.06** |
| Reading achievement T1 | −0.03 | −0.02 | −0.02 | 0.08*** | 0.07*** | 0.07*** |
| Migration status | 0.08 | 0.06 | 0.06 | 0.09 | 0.11 | 0.09 |
| PEB 1 | 0.05 | 0.06 | 0.07 | 0.22*** | 0.19* | 0.20** |
| PEB 2 | −0.04 | −0.05 | −0.05 | 0.02 | 0.03 | 0.03 |
| PEB 3 | 0.06 | 0.05 | 0.05 | 0.09 | 0.08 | 0.08 |
| PEB 5 | −0.05 | −0.03 | −0.03 | 0.11* | 0.12* | 0.09 |
| PEB 6 | −0.06 | −0.09 | −0.09 | 0.06 | 0.06 | 0.07 |
| HW selection | | 0.12*** | 0.07** | | 0.19*** | 0.06* |
| HW challenge | | 0.13*** | 0.14*** | | −0.20*** | −0.13*** |
| Value | 0.13*** | | 0.11*** | 0.23*** | | 0.20*** |
| Expectancy | −0.01 | | 0.03 | 0.26*** | | 0.20*** |
| $R^2$ Level 2 | 29.41 | 47.06 | 50.00 | 51.43 | 54.29 | 62.86 |
| $R^2$ Level 1 | 8.21 | 9.06 | 10.02 | 15.38 | 10.29 | 17.05 |

*Note.* $N = 3,483$. M1 = models without homework characteristics; M2 = models without homework expectancies and homework value; M3 = complete models; HW = homework; SES = socioeconomic status; PEB = parental educational background (reference category: PEB 4); PEB 1 = no apprenticeship, with or without *Hauptschule* certificate (lowest parental educational background); PEB 2 = apprenticeship, with or without *Hauptschule* certificate; PEB 3 = apprenticeship and *Realschule* certificate; PEB 4 = *Hauptschule* or *Realschule* certificate and technical college; PEB 5 = technical college or *Gymnasium* certificate, no higher education; PEB 6 = degree qualification (highest educational background).

* $p < .05$. ** $p < .01$. *** $p < .001$.

selection to positively predict expectancy beliefs at the student and the class level. Moreover, we expected to find a negative association between homework challenge and expectancy beliefs at both analytical levels. As shown in Table 3, homework expectancy beliefs were associated with T1 mathematics achievement and gender. At the class level, relative to the reference category *Realschule*, we found *Gymnasium* students to report lower expectancy beliefs (*Gymnasium*: $M = 2.92$, $SD = 0.72$; *Realschule*: $M = 2.99$, $SD = 0.70$; *Mittelschule*: $M = 2.96$, $SD = 0.67$;

comprehensive school: $M = 3.02$, $SD = 0.59$). Explained variance[3] was low at both the class level (0.00%) and the student level (3.02%; M1). In the next step (M2), homework characteristics were included in the model. As shown in Table 3, at the student level a high rating of the quality of homework selection was indeed associated with high homework expectancy beliefs. This result is in line with recent findings of a positive relationship between homework quality and homework motivation (see Trautwein, Lüdtke, Schnyder, & Niggli, 2006). Moreover, in line with

*Table 5*

### Predicting Mathematics Achievement: Results from Multilevel Modeling

| Variable | Achievement ($B$) | | |
| --- | --- | --- | --- |
| | M1 | M2 | M3 |
| **Level 2: Classes** | | | |
| School type (reference category: middle track) | | | |
| *Mittelschule* (lower track) | −0.07 | −0.01 | −0.04 |
| *Gymasium* (highest track) | 0.33*** | 0.20*** | 0.26*** |
| Comprehensive schools | −0.23* | −0.16* | −0.20* |
| HW selection | | 0.21*** | 0.19* |
| HW challenge | | 0.25*** | 0.27** |
| **Level 1: Students** | | | |
| Male | 0.10*** | 0.09*** | 0.09*** |
| SES | −0.01 | −0.01 | −0.01 |
| Cognitive abilities | 0.18*** | 0.17*** | 0.17*** |
| Achievement T1 | 0.35*** | 0.35*** | 0.34*** |
| Reading achievement T1 | 0.13*** | 0.13*** | 0.13*** |
| Migration status | −0.08 | −0.06 | −0.07 |
| PEB 1 | −0.04 | −0.04 | −0.05 |
| PEB 2 | −0.02 | 0.00 | −0.01 |
| PEB 3 | 0.06 | 0.07 | 0.06 |
| PEB 5 | 0.07 | 0.07 | 0.06 |
| PEB 6 | 0.04 | 0.05 | 0.04 |
| HW selection | | 0.01 | −0.02 |
| HW challenge | | −0.10*** | −0.06*** |
| Value | −0.01 | | −0.01 |
| Expectancy | 0.08*** | | 0.07*** |
| HW time | −0.03* | | −0.02 |
| HW effort | 0.07*** | | 0.06*** |
| $R^2$ Level 2 | 87.77 | 91.85 | 89.95 |
| $R^2$ Level 1 | 32.19 | 30.99 | 32.48 |

*Note.* $N = 3,483$. M1 = models without homework characteristics; M2 = models without homework expectancies and homework value; M3 = complete models; HW = homework; SES = socioeconomic status; PEB = parental educational background (reference category: PEB 4); PEB 1 = no apprenticeship, with or without *Hauptschule* certificate (lowest parental educational background); PEB 2 = apprenticeship, with or without *Hauptschule* certificate; PEB 3 = apprenticeship and *Realschule* certificate; PEB 4 = *Hauptschule* or *Realschule* certificate and technical college; PEB 5 = technical college or *Gymnasium* certificate, no higher education; PEB 6 = degree qualification (highest educational background).
* $p < .05.$ ** $p < .01.$ *** $p < .001.$

parts of our second hypothesis, homework challenge was negatively related to homework expectancy beliefs at the student level. Hence, students who perceived their homework assignments to be demanding had less belief in being able to complete them than did other students. At the class level, we found homework selection ratings to be positively related to homework expectancy beliefs, whereas homework challenge was negatively related to homework expectancy beliefs. Hence, students in classes with higher average perceptions of homework demands had lower homework expectancy beliefs than did students in other classes. Inclusion of homework task selection and homework challenge in the model considerably increased the amounts of variance explained at the class level (52.94%) and moderately increased the amounts explained at the student level (18.73%).

The next two columns in Table 3 present the results for the prediction of homework value beliefs. We expected to find a positive association between homework selection and value beliefs at the student and the class level. No specific hypotheses were formulated for the predictive power of homework challenge. In Model 1, we found that male students reported higher value beliefs than other students. Moreover, *Mittelschule* students reported lower value beliefs than *Realschule* students (*Gymnasium*: $M = 3.04$, $SD = 0.78$; *Realschule*: $M = 3.06$, $SD = 0.85$; *Mittelschule*: $M = 2.90$, $SD = 0.89$; comprehensive school: $M = 3.03$, $SD = 0.86$). Explained variance was low at both the class level (9.27%) and the student level (1.39%; M1). The last column in Table 3 presents the results after the inclusion of homework selection and homework challenge into the model. Consistent with parts of our first and third hypotheses, students who perceived that their homework assignments were well selected reported higher value beliefs than did other students. Furthermore, students in classes where homework was generally perceived to be well selected scored higher on the value beliefs scale than did students in other classes. Finally, no statistically significant association was found between homework challenge and value beliefs. The variance explained increased in Model 2 at both the class (65.28%) and the student level (17.70%).

Table 4 presents the results for predicting homework time and homework effort; we first describe the findings for homework time. In Model 1, being male, having high cognitive abilities, and having high achievement at T1 negatively predicted time on homework. Conversely, high value beliefs were positively related to homework time. At the class level, *Mittelschule* and comprehensive school students reported statistically significantly shorter homework times than did *Realschule* students (*Gymnasium*: $M = 2.49$, $SD = 1.76$; *Realschule*: $M = 2.79$, $SD = 1.86$; *Mittelschule*: $M = 2.26$, $SD = 1.19$; comprehensive school: $M = 2.45$, $SD = 1.86$). The amount of variance explained was low at the student level (8.21%) and moderate at the class level (29.41%). When homework expectancy and value beliefs were replaced by the two homework characteristics in Model 2, homework selection was—as expected—positively associated with homework time at both levels of analysis. Moreover, homework challenge was likewise positively associated with homework time at both levels. Thus, students who perceived their homework assignments to be well selected and cognitively demanding spent more time completing their homework than did other students. In Model 2, the variance explained increased at the class level (47.06%) but remained almost the same at the student level (9.06%). When the mediator

variables (expectancy and value beliefs) were reintroduced in Model 3, the regression coefficient for homework selection decreased at the student and the class level, revealing the mediating role of homework motivation.

In terms of homework effort, in addition to several control variables, homework motivation (expectancy and value beliefs) positively predicted homework effort at the student level (M1). Moreover, on average, *Gymnasium* students reported less homework effort than did *Realschule* students (*Gymnasium*: $M = 2.65$, $SD = 0.64$; *Realschule*: $M = 2.74$, $SD = 0.64$; *Mittelschule*: $M = 2.67$, $SD = 0.56$; comprehensive school: $M = 2.66$, $SD = 0.56$). The variables in Model 1 explained 15.38% of the variance at the student level and 51.43% of the variance at the class level. In line with parts of our first and third hypotheses, Model 2 showed a strong association between homework selection and homework effort at the student and the class level. Hence, students who perceived that their homework was well selected reported investing more effort in homework completion than did other students. Moreover, students in classes with high average perceptions of homework selection put more effort into homework completion than did students in other classes. Furthermore, as indicated by the decreased regression coefficient for homework selection ($B = 0.06$), the association between homework selection and homework effort was largely mediated by homework expectancy and value beliefs. With respect to homework challenge, however, we found that students who perceived their homework assignments to be cognitively demanding put less effort into homework completion than other students ($B = -0.20$). This result may be attributable to low expectancy beliefs. Indeed, inclusion of the mediator variables homework expectancy and value beliefs in Model 3 resulted in a decreased regression coefficient for homework challenge. The variance explained increased slightly at the class level (54.29%) but decreased at the student level (10.29%) in Model 2, emphasizing the role of homework expectancy and value beliefs for homework effort at the student level. In Model 3, the variance explained increased moderately at the student level (17.05%) and at the class level (62.86%).

In sum, we found homework selection and homework challenge to be strongly related to homework motivation and homework behavior. Including the two variables in the multilevel models increased the amounts of variance, providing further support for the view that student ratings of the classroom environment should be analyzed within a multilevel framework.

**Predicting mathematics achievement.** Table 5 presents our results for mathematics achievement. Controlling for potential confounding variables and achievement at T1, we found homework expectancy beliefs and homework effort to positively predict mathematics achievement at the student level (M1). Hence, students who were confident in their ability to complete their homework assignments successfully and students who did their best to complete their assignments scored higher in the mathematics achievement test than did other students. In contrast, homework time proved to be a negative predictor of student achievement, indicating that long homework times might reflect inefficient study habits. *Gymnasium* students showed greater achievement gains in mathematics than did other students (*Gymnasium*: $M = 613.63, SD = 68.79$; *Realschule*: $M = 550.79, SD = 72.47$; *Mittelschule*: $M = 535.83, SD = 67.75$; comprehensive school: $M = 512.12, SD = 84.36$). The variance explained was 32.19% at the student level and 87.77% at the class level. In Model 2, homework task selection and homework challenge were introduced as predictor variables. Contrary to our first hypothesis, homework selection did not positively predict mathematics achievement at the student level. In line with our second hypothesis, however, homework challenge was negatively related to mathematics achievement at the student level to a statistically significant degree.[4] Thus, students who perceived homework assignments to be cognitively challenging showed lower achievement gains than did other students. In line with our third and fourth hypotheses, both homework quality indicators positively predicted mathematics achievement at the class level. Students in classes with higher average perceptions of homework selection showed greater achievement gains than did students in other classes ($B = 0.19$), as did students in classes with higher average perceptions of homework challenge ($B = 0.27$).[5] Thus, in general, high homework quality was positively related to mathematics achievement. The amount of variance explained in Model 2 increased slightly at the class level (91.85%) and remained stable at the student level (30.99%). The inclusion of the mediator variables in Model 3 led to a decreased regression coefficient for homework challenge at the student level, pointing to the mediating role of homework motivation and homework behavior. Finally, we tested for cross-level interactions between student characteristics (gender, cognitive abilities, socioeconomic status, achievement at T1, reading achievement, homework challenge, homework selection, homework value, homework expectancy, and homework effort) and homework challenge. These additional analyses revealed a statistically significant cross-level interaction between students' cognitive abilities and homework challenge ($B = -0.10$, $p < .05$). Hence, challenging homework

assignments are less important for highly intelligent students than for their classmates.

## Discussion

### Homework Works

The primary aim of the present study was to analyze the effects of homework quality on students' learning and homework behavior. Two indicators of homework quality were examined. Replicating the results of recent studies (Trautwein & Lüdtke, 2007, 2009; Trautwein, Lüdtke, Schnyder, & Niggli, 2006), we found the first indicator, homework selection, to be positively associated with homework motivation (expectancy and value beliefs) and homework behavior (effort and time). Moreover, we found first evidence for a positive relationship between high-quality homework selection and mathematics achievement at the class level. The second indicator, homework challenge, proved to be negatively related to homework expectancy beliefs and homework effort (the latter only at the student level). We found students in classes with higher average perceptions of homework challenge showed greater achievement gains than students in other classes, even when prior knowledge was controlled. Finally, we found differential effects for homework selection and homework challenge at the student and the class level, indicating that different factors might operate at the individual and the class level. In the following, we outline the main contributions of the study to homework research and describe possible educational implications. Finally, we identify the limitations of the present study and make recommendations for future research.

### Contribution of the Present Study to Homework Research

Our findings supplement the existing research in several respects. First, our study was based on a large, nationally representative sample of 3,483 students from 155 classes. Second, homework quality was measured on two scales: one assessing the quality of homework selection and one assessing how cognitively demanding homework assignments were perceived to be. Although we found higher student agreement on homework selection, both homework quality scales proved to be reliable indicators of the learning environment and can thus be used as student-level and as class-level variables. The homework selection scale shares similarities with scales used in prior research (see Trautwein & Lüdtke, 2009); to our knowledge, however, the present study is the first to address the role of perceived challenge of homework assignments. Third, we examined the predictive power of the two homework quality scales for mathematics achievement. Most previous studies have focused on the role of homework quality for homework motivation and behavior (see Trautwein & Lüdtke, 2007, 2009; Trautwein, Lüdtke, Schnyder, & Niggli, 2006). We were able to confirm the importance of homework selection and homework challenge for student achievement at the class level, even when controlling for prior knowledge and potential confounding variables. Hence, students in classes given well-chosen and challenging homework assignments learn more than their peers in other classes (teacher-or class-level effect).

A different picture emerges at the student level. We found no statistically significant association between homework selection and mathematics achievement. Moreover, we found that students with high homework challenge ratings showed lower achievement gains than other students. At first glance, these results seem somewhat counterintuitive. However, it is well established in the literature on multilevel modeling that variables can show different relations at different levels of analysis (Raudenbush & Bryk, 2002). For example, Trautwein and colleagues (e.g., Trautwein et al., 2002; Trautwein & Lüdtke, 2007) have found time spent on homework to be negatively related to achievement at the student level but positively related at the class level. A plausible explanation is that measures of homework time typically conflate total time and active time. Thus, an individual student's report of high homework time is not necessarily a sign of great studiousness but may reflect problems of motivation or concentration. At the class level, however, reports of high homework time indicate that the teacher sets frequent or long homework assignments. In a similar vein, student ratings of homework challenge can be interpreted in two ways: First, students' individual perceptions of homework challenge can be assumed to be affected by their prior knowledge and cognitive abilities. In other words, they are not only a function of the homework assigned by the teacher, but also reflect individual differences among students. Second, at the class level, the class-average response can be interpreted as students' shared perception of homework challenge, in which individual idiosyncrasies are averaged out. Class-average ratings of homework challenge thus reflect differences among classes in the homework assigned. In sum, the differential effects found at the student and the class level underline the importance of analyzing homework quality data within a multilevel framework. Had we not differentiated between the student and the class level, the two effects would have been confounded, producing different results.

Fourth, student achievement was measured by a highly reliable and valid assessment of mathematics achievement. Many previous studies have used school grades as an indicator of student achievement. Grades seem problematic as outcome measures, however, because they partly reflect individual student effort. Research that relies on class grades as outcomes might thus overestimate the influence of homework (Cooper, 1989).

## Educational Implications

What are the implications of our findings for homework practice? Our study provides strong evidence that interesting and well-selected homework assignments are associated with higher expectancy and value beliefs and with higher homework effort and that they are effective for learning. Teachers may thus be able to improve the effectiveness of their instruction by optimizing the homework assignments they set, and it may well be worth focusing more on the quality of homework assignments in teacher training. However, the picture that emerges for homework challenge is more complex. We found that challenging homework assignments were negatively related to homework expectancy beliefs and homework effort and found differential effects for mathematics achievement. In our view, the complexity of our results reflects the difficulties teachers face in their daily routine: What is the ideal balance between cognitively activating instruction (i.e., challenging homework assignments) and instruction that caters for the low-achieving students in the class?

Given these results, how should homework assignments be designed to enhance homework motivation, homework effort, and achievement? Achievement motivation research suggests that tasks of moderate difficulty are most likely to enhance student motivation (Astleitner, 2007). Likewise, Good and Brophy (1990) suggested that only homework assignments perceived as adequately difficult elicit high value beliefs and high effort. From the constructivist point of view, however, highly complex tasks can be expected to be effective for learning (Astleitner, 2007)—provided that students are adequately instructed (e.g., through scaffolding; Anghileri, 2006). This hypothesis is in line with the homework challenge effect we found at the class level, which showed that challenging homework assignments generally foster achievement. In sum, the current literature suggests that teachers should assign adequately difficult tasks to improve students' motivation and effort and challenging but well-structured tasks to foster students' performance.

But how should teachers go about designing homework tasks that are both adequately difficult and challenging? One possibility may be to assign individualized homework tasks that challenge but do not overtax individual students. Moreover, assigning homework tasks that match individual students' interests may help to increase motivation and homework effort and, at the same time, enhance achievement. Such individualized assignments are rare in the German school system, however (Rossbach, 1995; Schoenbrunn, 1989). Individualized assignments make intensive demands on teachers' time and resources. Moreover, they may in fact increase within-class differences in achievement (see Trautwein & Köller, 2003). A further possibility would be to assign tasks that can be solved by various methods of differing levels of complexity. Such tasks have the potential to challenge— but not overchallenge— most of the students in a class, depending on the approach chosen.

## Limitations and Future Research

Several limitations of the present research must be mentioned. First, student reports were our sole source of information, even on shared aspects of the learning environment. Empirical studies assessing characteristics of the learning environment may draw on external observers, teacher reports, student reports, or a combination of data sources (Anderson, 1982; Fraser, 1991; Turner & Meyer, 2000). Each perspective can be assumed to assess at least slightly different aspects of the construct in question. A combination of methods might provide deeper insights into the effects of homework quality for homework motivation, homework behavior, and achievement in future research (De Jong & Westerhof, 2001; Kunter & Baumert, 2006b).

Second, we were not able to address the issue of causation satisfactorily. The homework model implies that teachers' homework practices affect students' homework motivation, homework behavior, and achievement. However, we cannot rule out the possibility that further confounding variables were omitted from the present study: Unobserved predictor variables may also impact homework behavior, homework motivation, and achievement. The only way of addressing causality would be a carefully designed intervention study in which teachers were assigned to different treatments. To date, few studies have systematically evaluated homework intervention programs (e.g., Perels, Gürtler, & Schmitz, 2005; Zimmerman, Bonner, & Kovach, 1996). Intervention studies could complement the present research, providing

valuable insights into the mechanisms of homework and its influence on homework motivation, homework behavior, and achievement.

Third, it might be worthwhile for future research to assess further aspects of homework quality. More specifically, items tapping the opportunity for students to apply and combine different strategies or to generate new ideas and items assessing the variation in tasks and their potential to challenge beliefs might help to shed light on the association between the perceived level of challenge and value beliefs. However, it is unclear to what extent students are able to evaluate such complex constructs.

Fourth, the generalizability of our results remains uncertain. Our results apply specifically to ninth graders and to mathematics. Previous research has identified differences in the homework–achievement relationship across grades (Cooper, 1989). Future studies should therefore analyze homework quality effects in different grade levels and in different subjects. It is also possible that cultural differences affect the results. Cross-cultural studies are thus also necessary to test the generalizability of the effects found in the current study.

To conclude, the present study added to prior research by demonstrating the importance of homework quality for student achievement. Moreover, it confirmed the predictive power of homework challenge as a further indicator of the learning environment. In sum, the findings extend the scientific understanding of the circumstances under which students invest effort in homework completion and of how homework assignments can enhance student achievement in mathematics.

## Notes

1 We also conducted a confirmatory factor analysis with the five homework scales (value, expectancy, effort, selection, and challenge). This model revealed an acceptable fit, with $\chi^2(3) = 1,007.31$, root-mean-square error of approximation = .043, and CFI = .929. On average, the standardized factor loadings were .52 (effort), .64 (value), .76 (expectancy), .70 (selection), and .55 (challenge). Two of the scales (homework effort and perceived homework challenge) included both positively and negatively worded items, potentially leading to method factors. For instance, a negative-item effect occurs if there are systematic residual covariations among the responses to the negatively worded items and if this so-called correlated uniqueness cannot be explained by

the postulated latent factor. We thus included a total of three correlated uniquenesses among two pairs of negatively worded items and one pair of positively worded items to address this issue (see Marsh, 1996).

2 The six dummy variables were Parental Educational Background (PEB) 1 (no apprenticeship, with or without *Hauptschule* certificate; lowest educational background), PEB 2 (apprenticeship, with or without *Hauptschule* certificate), PEB 3 (apprenticeship and *Realschule* certificate), PEB 4 (*Hauptschule* or *Realschule* certificate and technical college), PEB 5 (technical college/*Gymnasium* certificate, no higher education), PEB 6 (degree qualification; highest educational background). PEB 4 (intermediate educational background) served as the reference category.

3 Explained variance was computed using the variance components of the unconditional means model and the residual variances estimated by Mplus.

4 It might be hypothesized that the relationship between homework challenge and achievement is nonlinear, with an optimum level of homework challenge. However, an additional analysis did not reveal a statistically significant nonlinear relationship between the two variables.

5 In some additional analyses, we transformed the two homework quality indicators (selection and challenge) to obtain results based on grand-mean centering. For homework challenge, the resulting beta coefficient was $\beta = 0.33$; for homework selection we found a beta coefficient of $\beta = 0.21$. Hence, the direction of results for the present data did not change; on the contrary, the beta coefficients increased slightly, indicating a rather stronger relationship between the two homework quality variables and mathematics achievement with grand-mean centering. These results show that our findings are not sensitive to the centering decision. We further tested whether this result might be due to the different school tracks. Using the Mplus software with a multiple group multilevel model, we examined whether the association between homework challenge and school track was of the same magnitude in each track. The chi-square test did not reveal a statistically significant difference in the relationship across the school tracks.

# References

Adams, R., & Wu, M. (2002). *PISA 2000: Technical report.* Paris, France: Organisation for Economic Cooperation and Development.

Aleamoni, L. M. (1999). Student rating myths versus research facts from 1924 to 1998. *Journal of Personnel Evaluation in Education, 13,* 153–166.

Anderson, C. S. (1982). The search for school climate. *Review of Educational Psychology, 52,* 368–420.

Anghileri, J. (2006). Scaffolding practices that enhance mathematics learning. *Journal of Mathematics Teacher Education, 9,* 33–52.

Astleitner, H. (2007). Theory: Designing task-based learning sequences. A categorical model of task attributes. In H. Astleitner & H.-J. Herber (Eds.), *Task-and standard-based learning: An instructional psychology perspective* (pp. 9–34). Frankfurt am Main, Germany: Lang.

Bandura, A. (1998). *Self-efficacy: The exercise of control.* New York, NY: Freeman.

Baumert, J., Blum, W., Neubrand, M., Klusmann, U., Brunner, M., Jordan, A., . . . Löwen, K. (2006). *Professionswissen von Lehrkräften, kognitiv aktivierender Matehmatikunterricht und die Entwicklung von mathematischer Kompetenz (COACTIV): Dokumentation der Erhebungsinstrumente* [Professional competence of teachers, cognitively activating instruction, and the development of students' mathematical literacy (COACTIV): Documentation of the instruments]. Berlin, Germany: Max Planck Institute for Human Development.

Baumert, J., Kunter, M., Blum, W., Brunner, M., Voss, T., Jordan, A., . . . Tsai, Y. (in press). Teachers' mathematical knowledge, cognitive activation in the classroom, and student progress. *American Educational Research Journal.*

Bliese, P. D. (2000). Within-group agreement, nonindependence, and reliability: Implications for data aggregation and analysis. In K. J. Klein & S. W. Kozlowski (Eds.), *Multilevel theory, research, and methods in organizations* (pp. 349–381). San Francisco, CA: Jossey-Bass.

Bloom, B. S. (1976). *Human characteristics and school learning.* New York, NY: McGraw-Hill.

Brophy, J., & Good, T. (1986). Teacher behavior and student achievement. In M. C. Wittrock (Ed.),

*Handbook of research on teaching* (3rd ed., pp. 328–375). New York, NY: Macmillan.

Burke, M. J., & Dunlap, W. P. (2002). Estimating interrater agreement with the average deviation index: A user's guide. *Organizational Research Methods, 5,* 159–172.

Burke, M. J., Finkelstein, L. M., & Dusig, M. S. (1999). On average deviation indices for estimating interrater agreement. *Organizational Research Methods, 2,* 49–68.

Carroll, J. B. (1963). A model of school learning. *Teachers' College Record, 64,* 723–733.

Carroll, J. B. (1989). The Carroll model: A 25-year retrospective and prospective view. *Educational Researcher, 18,* 26–31.

Carroll, J. B. (1993). *Human cognitive abilities: A survey of factor-analytic studies.* Cambridge, England: Cambridge University Press.

Cooper, H. (1989). *Homework.* White Plains, NY: Longman.

Cooper, H., Lindsay, J. J., Nye, B., & Greathouse, S. (1998). Relationships among attitudes about homework, amount of homework assigned and completed, and student achievement. *Journal of Educational Psychology, 90,* 70–83.

Cooper, H., Robinson, J. C., & Patall, E. A. (2006). Does homework improve academic achievement? A synthesis of research, 1987–2003. *Review of Educational Research, 76,* 1–62.

Corno, L. (1996). Homework is a complicated thing. *Educational Researcher, 25,* 27–30.

Deci, E. L., & Ryan, R. M. (Eds.). (2002). *Handbook of self-determination research.* New York, NY: University of Rochester Press.

De Jong, R., & Westerhof, K. J. (2001). The quality of student ratings of teacher behavior. *Learning Environments Research, 4,* 51–85.

Eccles, J. S. (1983). Expectancies, values, and academic choice: Origins and changes. In J. Spence (Ed.), *Achievement and achievement motivation* (pp. 87–134). San Francisco, CA: Freeman.

Eccles, J. S., & Wigfield, A. (2002). Motivational beliefs, values, and goals. *Annual Review of Psychology, 53,* 109–132.

Enders, C. K., & Tofighi, D. (2007). Centering predictor variables in cross-sectional multilevel models: A new look at an old issue. *Psychological Methods, 12,* 121–138.

Fraser, B. J. (1991). Two decades of classroom environment research. In B. J. Fraser & H. J. Wahlberg (Eds.), *Educational environments: Evaluation, antecedents and consequences* (pp. 3–27). London, England: Pergamon.

Frenzel, A., Pekrun, R., & Goetz, T. (2007). Perceived learning environment and students' emotional experiences: A multilevel analysis of mathematics classrooms. *Learning and Instruction, 17,* 478–493.

Ganzeboom, H. B. G., de Graaf, P. M., Treiman, D. J., & de Leeuw, J. (1992). A standard international socio-economic index of occupational status. *Social Science Research, 21,* 1–56.

Gettinger, M. (1989). Effects of maximizing time spent and minimizing time needed for learning on pupil achievement. *American Educational Research Journal, 26,* 73–91.

Goldstein, H. (1995). *Multilevel statistical models.* London, England: Arnold.

Good, T. L., & Brophy, J. E. (1990). *Educational psychology: A realistic approach.* White Plains, NY: Longman.

Graham, J. W., Taylor, B. T., Olchowski, A. E., & Cumsille, P. E. (2006). Planned missing data designs in psychological research. *Psychological Methods, 11,* 323–343.

Grolnick, W. S., & Slowiaczek, M. L. (1994). Parents' involvement in children's schooling: A multidimensional conceptualization and motivational model. *Child Development, 65,* 237–252.

Heller, K. A., & Perleth, C. (2000). *Kognitiver Fähigkeitstest für 4.-12. Klassen, Revision (KFT 4–12 +R)* [Cognitive Abilities Test, Revised Version (KFT 4–12 + R)]. Göttingen, Germany: Hogrefe.

Hox, J. (2002). *Multilevel analysis: Techniques and applications.* Mahwah, NJ: Erlbaum.

Karabenick, S. A. (2004). Perceived achievement goal structure and college student help seeking. *Journal of Educational Psychology, 96,* 569–581.

Keith, T. Z., & Cool, V. A. (1992). Testing models of school learning: Effects of quality of instruction, motivation, academic coursework, and homework on academic achievement. *School Psychology Quarterly, 7,* 207–226.

Kreft, I. G. G., de Leeuw, J., & Aiken, L. S. (1995). The effect of differing forms of centering in hierarchical linear models. *Multivariate Behavioral Research, 30,* 1–21.

Kunter, M., & Baumert, J. (2006a). Linking TIMSS to research on learning and instruction: A re-analysis of the German TIMSS and TIMSS video data. In S. J. Howie & T. Plomp (Eds.), *Contexts of learning mathematics and science: Lessons learned from TIMSS* (pp. 335–351). London, England: Routledge.

Kunter, M., & Baumert, J. (2006b). Who is the expert? Construct and criteria validity of student and teacher ratings of instruction. *Learning Environments Research, 9,* 231–251.

Kunter, M., Baumert, J., & Köller, O. (2007). Effective classroom management and the development of subject-related interest. *Learning and Instruction, 17,* 494–509.

Lipowsky, F., Rakoczy, K., Klieme, E., Reusser, K., & Pauli, C. (2004). Hausaufgabenpraxis im Mathematikunterricht: Ein Thema für die Unterrichtsqualitätsforschung? [Homework practice in mathematics instruction: A topic for instructional quality research?]. In J. Doll & M. Prenzel (Eds.), *Bildungsqualität von Schule: Lehrerprofessionalisierung, Unterrichtsentwicklung und Schülerförderungen als Strategien derq Ualitätsverbesserung* (pp. 250–266). Münster, Germany: Waxmann.

Lüdtke, O., Marsh, H. W., Robitzsch, A., Trautwein, U., Asparouhov, T., & Muthén, B. (2008). The multilevel latent covariate model: A new, more reliable approach to group-level effects in contextual studies. *Psychological Methods, 13,* 203–229.

Lüdtke, O., Robitzsch, A., Trautwein, U., & Kunter, M. (2009). Assessing the impact of learning environments: How to use student ratings of classroom characteristics in multilevel modeling. *Contemporary Educational Psychology, 34,* 120–131.

Lüdtke, O., Trautwein, U., Kunter, M., & Baumert, J. (2006). Reliability and agreement of student ratings of the classroom environment: A reanalysis of TIMSS data. *Learning Environments Research, 9,* 215–230.

Marsh, H. W. (1996). Positive and negative global self-esteem: A substantively meaningful distinction or artifacts? *Journal of Personality and Social Psychology, 70,* 810–819.

Marsh, H. W. (2001). Distinguishing between good (useful) and bad workload on students' evaluations of teaching. *American Educational Research Journal, 38,* 183–212.

Marsh, H. W., & Roche, L. A. (1997). Making students' evaluations of teaching effectiveness effective: The critical issues of validity, bias, and utility. *American Psychologist, 52,* 1187–1197.

Marsh, H. W., & Roche, L. A. (2000). Effects of grading leniency and low workloads on students' evaluations of teaching: Popular myth, bias, validity or innocent bystanders? *Journal of Educational Psychology, 92,* 202–228.

Muthén, L. K., & Muthén, B. O. (1998 –2007). *MPlus user's guide.* Los Angeles, CA: Muthén & Muthén.

Nunnally, J. C. (1978). *Psychometric theory* (2nd ed.). New York, NY: McGraw-Hill.

Organisation for Economic Cooperation and Development. (2004a). *Learning for tomorrow's world: First results from PISA 2003.* Paris, France: Author.

Organisation for Economic Cooperation and Development. (2004b). *PISA 2003 technical report.* Paris, France: Author.

Paschal, R. A., Weinstein, T., & Walberg, H. J. (1984). The effects of homework on learning: A quantitative synthesis. *Journal of Educational Research, 78,* 97–104.

Perels, F., Gürtler, T., & Schmitz, B. (2005). Training of self-regulatory and problem-solving competence. *Learning and Instruction, 15,* 123–139.

Peugh, J. L., & Enders, C. K. (2004). Missing data in educational research: A review of reporting practices and suggestions for improvement. *Review of Educational Research, 74,* 525–556.

Pintrich, P. R. (2003). A motivational science perspective on the role of student motivation in learning and teaching contexts. *Journal of Educational Psychology, 95,* 667–686.

Pintrich, P. R., & De Groot, E. V. (1990). Motivational and self-regulated learning components of classroom academic performance. *Journal of Educational Psychology, 82,* 33–40.

Prenzel, M., Carstensen, C., Schöps, K., & Maurischat, C. (2006). Die Anlage des Längsschnitts bei PISA 2003 [The longitudinal design of the PISA 2003 study]. In M. Prenzel, J. Baumert, W. Blum, R. Lehmann, D. Leutner, M. Neubrand, . . . U. Schiefele (Eds.), *PISA 2003. Untersuchungen zur Kompetenzentwicklung im Verlauf eines Schuljahres [PISA 2003: Analyses of literacy development over a school year]* (pp. 29–62). Münster, Germany: Waxmann.

Prenzel, M., Drechsel, B., Carstensen, C. H., & Ramm, G. (2004). PISA 2003: Eine Einführung [PISA 2003:

An introduction]. In M. Prenzel, J. Baumert, W. Blum, R. Lehmann, D. Leutner, M. Neubrand, . . . U. Schiefele (Eds.), *PISA 2003. Der Bildungsstand der Jugendlichen in Deutschland—Ergebnisse des zweiten internationalen Vergleichs [PISA 2003: The educational attainment of young people in Germany—Results of the second international comparison]* (pp. 13–46). Münster, Germany: Waxmann.

Raudenbush, S. W., & Bryk, A. S. (2002). *Hierarchical linear models* (2nd ed.). Thousand Oaks, CA: Sage.

Robinson, W. S. (1950). Ecological correlations and the behavior of individuals. *American Sociological Review, 15,* 351–357.

Rossbach, H.-G. (1995). Hausaufgaben in der Grundschule [Homework in primary schools]. *Die Deutsche Schule, 87,* 103–112.

Rubin, D. B. (1987). *Multiple imputation for nonresponse in surveys.* New York, NY: Wiley.

Ryan, R. M., & Deci, E. L. (2000). Self-determination theory and the facilitation of intrinsic motivation, social development, and well-being. *American Psychologist, 55,* 68–78.

Schafer, J. L. (2001). Multiple imputation with PAN. In L. M. Collins & A. G. Sayer (Ed.), *New methods for the analysis of change* (pp. 357–377). Washington, DC: American Psychological Association.

Schafer, J. L. (2008). *The PAN package.* Retrieved from http://cran.r-project.org/web/packages/pan/pan.pdf

Schafer, J. L., & Graham, J. W. (2002). Missing data: Our view of the state of the art. *Psychological Methods, 7,* 147–176.

Schoenbrunn, G. (1989). Hausaufgaben in der paedagogischen Diskussion [Homework in the educational debate]. *Der Mathematikunterricht, 35,* 5–21.

Smith-Crowe, K., & Burke, M. J. (2003). Interpreting the statistical significance of observed AD interrater agreement values: Correction to Burke and Dunlap (2002). *Organizational Research Methods, 6,* 129–131.

Snijders, T. A. B., & Bosker, R. J. (1999). *Multilevel analysis: An introduction to basic and advanced multilevel modeling.* London, England: Sage.

Thorndike, R. L., & Hagen, E. (1993). *The Cognitive Abilities Test: Form 5.* Itasca, IL: Riverside.

Trautwein, U. (2007). The homework–achievement relation reconsidered: Differentiating homework time, homework frequency, and homework effort. *Learning and Instruction, 17,* 372–388.

Trautwein, U., & Köller, O. (2003). The relationship between homework and achievement: Still much of a mystery. *Educational Psychology Review, 15,* 115–145.

Trautwein, U., Köller, O., Schmitz, B., & Baumert, J. (2002). Do homework assignments enhance achievement? A multilevel analysis in 7th grade mathematics. *Contemporary Educational Psychology, 27,* 26–50.

Trautwein, U., & Lüdtke, O. (2007). Students' self-reported effort and time on homework in six school subjects: Between-students differences and within-student variation. *Journal of Educational Psychology, 99,* 432–444.

Trautwein, U., & Lüdtke, O. (2009). Predicting homework motivation and homework effort in six school subjects: The role of person and family characteristics, classroom factors, and school track. *Learning and Instruction, 19,* 243–258.

Trautwein, U., Lüdtke, O., Kastens, C., & Köller, O. (2006). Effort on homework in Grades 5–9: Development, motivational antecedents, and the association with effort on classwork. *Child Development, 77,* 1094–1111.

Trautwein, U., Lüdtke, O., Marsh, H. W., Köller, O., & Baumert, J. (2006). Tracking, grading, and student motivation: Using group composition and status to predict self-concept and interest in ninth-grade mathematics. *Journal of Educational Psychology, 98,* 788–806.

Trautwein, U., Lüdtke, O., Marsh, H. W., & Nagy, G. (2009). Withinschool social comparison: How students' perceived standing of their class predicts academic self-concept. *Journal of Educational Psychology, 101,* 853–866.

Trautwein, U., Lüdtke, O., Schnyder, I., & Niggli, A. (2006). Predicting homework effort: Support for a domain-specific multilevel homework model. *Journal of Educational Psychology, 98,* 438–456.

Trautwein, U., Niggli, A., Schnyder, I., & Lüdtke, O. (2009). Between teacher differences in homework assignments and the development of students' homework effort, homework emotions, and achievement. *Journal of Educational Psychology, 101,* 176–189.

Turner, J. C., & Meyer, D. K. (2000). Studying and understanding the instructional contexts of classrooms: Using our past to forge the future. *Educational Psychologist, 35,* 69–85.

Walberg, H. J., & Paschal, R. A. (1995): Homework. In L. W. Anderson (Ed.), *International Encyclopaedia of Teaching and Teacher Education* (pp. 268–271). Oxford, England: Elsevier.

Warton, P.-M. (2001). The forgotten voices in homework: Views of students. *Educational Psychologist, 36,* 155–165.

Weinert, F. E., & Helmke, A. (1995a). Interclassroom differences in instructional quality and interindividual differences in cognitive development. *Educational Psychologist, 30,* 15–20.

Weinert, F. E., & Helmke, A. (1995b). Learning from wise Mother Nature or Big Brother instructor: The wrong choice as seen from an educational perspective. *Educational Psychologist, 30,* 135–142.

Weinert, F. E., Schrader, F.-W., & Helmke, A. (1989). Quality of instruction and achievement outcomes. *International Journal of Educational Research, 3,* 895–914.

Xu, J. (2005). Purposes for doing homework reported by middle and high school students. *Journal of Educational Research, 99,* 46–55.

Zimmerman, B. J., Bonner, R., & Kovach, R. (1996). *Developing self-regulated learners: Beyond achievement to self-efficacy.* Washington, DC: American Psychological Association.

# Appendix

## Homework Selection Scale

Our mathematics teacher often sets interesting homework assignments.

Our mathematics teacher knows what homework to set to help us understand the material covered in the lesson.

Our mathematics homework assignments really help us to understand our mathematics lessons.

Our mathematics teacher almost always chooses homework assignments really well.

Our mathematics homework assignments are always well integrated into the lessons.

## Homework Challenge Scale

Our mathematics homework assignments are often quite difficult and really make us think.

Our mathematics homework assignments are often too easy.

Our mathematics homework assignments are often too difficult.

Our mathematics homework assignments are usually fairly easy.

First author, **SWANTJE DETTMERS,** is a research associate at the University of Hagen in the teaching field of educational psychology in Germany. His co-authors are former colleagues and mentors at the Max Planck Institute for Human Development and University of Tuebingen.

**Harris Cooper, James J. Lindsay,
Barbara Nye, and Scott Greathouse**

# Relationships Among Attitudes About Homework, Amount of Homework Assigned and Completed, and Student Achievement

**H**omework, defined as tasks assigned to students by school teachers that are meant to be performed during non-school hours (Cooper, 1989, p. 7), is a pervasive teaching strategy. The National Assessment of Educational Progress found that two thirds of students in 4th, 8th, and 11th grades reported doing homework and the percentage was increasing over time (Anderson et al, 1986). Among 8th graders, the average amount of time spent on homework is about 1 hour each day (Walberg, 1991).

## Relationship Between Homework and Achievement

The reason most often cited for giving homework is that it can improve students' retention and understanding of the covered material. However, some educators point out that any activity can remain rewarding for only so long. Thus, if students are required to spend too much time on academic material, they are bound to grow bored with it, and achievement will decline.

Researchers have been far from unanimous in their assessments of the strengths and weaknesses of homework as an instructional technique. The conclusions of more than a dozen reviews of the homework literature conducted between 1960 and 1989 varied greatly (cf. Keith, 1987; Knorr, 1981). Their assessments ranged from homework having positive effects, no effects, or complex effects to the suggestion that the research was too sparse or poorly conducted to allow trustworthy conclusions.

Cooper (1989) presented an exhaustive meta-analysis of research on the effects of homework. The review covered nearly 120 empirical studies of homework and the ingredients of successful homework assignments. Two types of studies were used to help answer the general question of whether homework improves students' achievement. The first type compared achievement of students given homework assignments with that of students given no homework or any other treatment to compensate for the lack of required home study. Of 20 independent samples, 14 produced effects favoring homework, whereas 6 favored no homework. Most interesting was a dramatic influence of grade level on homework's effectiveness. These studies revealed that the average high school student in a class doing homework would outperform 75% of the students in a no-homework class. In junior high school, the average homework effect was half this magnitude. In elementary school, homework had very little effect on achievement gains.

For the second type of evidence, 50 studies correlated the amount of time students reported spending on homework with achievement levels. Many of these correlations came from statewide surveys or national assessments. In all, 43 correlations indicated mat students who did more homework had better achievement test scores or class grades, whereas only 7 indicated the opposite. Again, a strong grade-level interaction appeared. For students in Grades 3 through 5, the correlation between amount of homework and achievement was nearly zero; for students in Grades 5 through 9, .07; and for high school students, .25.

Several correlational studies using large databases have been conducted since the meta-analysis appeared. Keith et al. (1993) used data from the National Educational Longitudinal Study to create a structural equation model predicting student achievement. Eighth-grade student ($N = 21,814$) reports of time spent on homework were significantly related to a composite achievement measure based on standardized test scores in reading, math, science, and social studies (beta = .187).

Cooper, Harris, Lindsay, James J., Nye, Barbara, Greathouse, Scott, "Relationships Among Attitudes About Homework, Amount of Homework Assigned and Complete, and Student Achievement," *Journal of Educational Psychology*, Vol 90(1) March 1998, 70–83. No further reproduction or distribution is permitted without written permission from the American Psychological Association.

Keith and Cool (1992) performed a similar analysis, but this time the data were from the 1980 and 1982 High School and Beyond Longitudinal Studies involving students when they were sophomores and again as seniors ($N = 25,875$). They found that the zero-order correlation between time spent on homework and a composite achievement measure was .297, and the direct path from homework to achievement with measures of ethnicity, family background, motivation, and course work also in the model had a beta value of .055.

Using younger students from Grades 3 and 6 ($N = 7,690$) chosen as a stratified random sample from 51 school districts in Indiana, Bents-Hill et al. (1988) correlated both the number of days parents reported their children did homework and their total homework time with competency tests scores, achievement test scores, and teacher-assigned grades. For third graders, the correlations were negative, ranging on subtests from $-.22$ to $-.09$. For sixth graders, the correlations between measures of amount of homework and competency or achievement were positive but weak, ranging from .00 to .15. Thus, these more recent studies are consistent with the meta-analysis finding that the relation between homework and achievement is moderated by grade level.

In addition to grade level differences, another obvious question is whether homework is more effective for some subject areas than for others. Cooper (1989) found no clear pattern indicating an influence for subject matter.

## Weaknesses in Previous Research

Correlational studies have the advantage of allowing large samples of data to be collected across populations of students that vary in individual characteristics, social circumstances, and educational treatment. These data sets can then be analyzed using modeling procedures that permit the study of complex relationships that mirror real-world processes (see Keith, 1996).

Of course, the major weakness of correlational studies is their inability to permit inferences about causal relations. However, when both experimental and broad-based correlational research examines the same process, their complementary types of information can lead to the greatest understanding.

One weakness specific to correlational research relating homework to achievement is that no distinction has been made between how achievement relates to (a) amount of homework teachers assign and (b) proportion of assigned homework completed by students, instead, previous largescale correlational research almost uniformly related a measure of achievement to students'

self-reports of the amount of time they spend doing homework. (Bents-Hill et al., 1988, used reports by parents, but no distinction was made between the amount of homework assigned and the amount completed.)

Another weakness of many studies is that they typically measure achievement using either a standardized achievement test or teacher-assigned grades. Rarely are both measures taken on the same students (again, Bents-Hill et al., 1988, is the exception). If both measures are taken, it is possible to investigate not only the simple correlations between each achievement measure and homework (and how they might differ) but also the relation between grades and homework while controlling for standardized achievement test scores.

The correlational study reported next included measures of both the amount of homework assigned by the teacher and the amount completed by the student. Further, these homework measures were obtained from teachers, students, and one of the students' parents. Finally, both standardized test scores and teacher-assigned grades were obtained as measures of student achievement.

## Attitudes Concerning Homework

Considerable evidence demonstrates that attitudes play an important role in determining behavior (Kraus, 1995), and attitudes about homework should be no different. However, at different times during the last century, the prevailing public attitude toward homework has shifted from positive to negative and back again.

Early in the 20th century, homework was believed to be an important means of disciplining children's minds (Brink, 1937). The mind was viewed as a muscle, and memorization not only led to knowledge acquisition but was also good mental exercise. Because memorization could be accomplished easily at home, homework was a key schooling strategy.

By the 1940s, a reaction against homework set in. Developing problem-solving ability, as opposed to learning through drill, became a central task of education. The use of homework as punishment or to enhance memorization skills was questioned. Greater emphasis was placed on developing student initiative and interest in learning. Also, the life adjustment movement viewed home study as an intrusion on students' time to pursue other private, at-home activities (LaConte, 1981).

The trend toward less homework was reversed in the late 1950s after the Russians launched the Sputnik satellite. Americans became concerned that a lack of rigor in the educational system was leaving children unprepared to face a complex technological future and to compete against our ideological adversaries. Homework was viewed as a means for accelerating the pace of knowledge acquisition.

By the mid-1960s, the cycle again reversed itself. Homework came to be seen as a symptom of too much pressure on students to achieve (Wildman, 1968). Contemporary learning theories were again cited that questioned the value of most approaches to homework. Yet again, the possible detrimental mental health consequences of too much homework were brought to the fore.

Today, views of homework have again shifted toward a more positive assessment (National Commission on Excellence in Education, 1983). In the wake of increasing concern for achievement test scores and America's global competitiveness, the general perception of the value of homework has undergone its third renaissance in the past 50 years.

Perhaps surprisingly, Cooper (1989) could find no study that examined whether teacher, student, or parent attitudes about homework served as a significant predictor of homework behavior and student achievement. Further, homework is often the source of considerable friction between teacher and student, child and parent, and teacher and parent. Many pediatricians and family practitioners indicate that problems with homework are a frequent source of concern when children report medical problems (Cooper, 1991). Therefore, it seems important to know whether or not the three participants in the homework process hold consistent beliefs and attitudes about homework assignments. Although past research has assumed that beliefs about homework are an important influence on achievement, the present study is the first to incorporate attitudes into an analysis of the homework-achievement link.

## Research Questions

The study reported here used a newly developed questionnaire: the Homework Process Inventory (HPI). The HPI was meant to assess numerous aspects of homework practices and procedures. Different versions were constructed for students, parents, and teachers at different grade levels. The questionnaire was administered to a large number of students, parents, and teachers. This report presents only a portion of the study's results.

The first questions guiding our analyses asked whether teachers, students, and parents differed in their beliefs about the amount of homework assigned by teachers and the proportion completed by students. Next, we asked whether teachers, students, and parent attitudes about homework were consistent and related to one another. A third set of questions asked whether different

relationships existed between the two types of achievement measures and homework behaviors reported by different actors in the homework process. Specifically, we related teacher, student, and parent reports of the amount of homework teachers assigned and the proportion of homework students completed to the students' standardized test scores and class grades. A fourth set of questions asked whether teachers' and students' attitudes about homework were related to reports of the amount of homework assigned and completed. A fifth set of questions asked whether relationships existed between teacher and student attitudes toward homework and achievement. Finally, to summarize the data, we developed a path diagram to guide a series of multiple regression analyses that included all of the variables incorporated in the research questions. All of the analyses were carried out separately for different grade levels.

## Method
### Sample Size and Composition

To have a usable data unit, we had to obtain complete data from a teacher, at least one student in that teacher's class, and one parent of that student. We referred to this unit of data as a "triad." Within any class, there could be as many usable triads as there were students.

When the data were analyzed, a total of 709 complete triads were available associated with the 82 teachers. However, for any given analysis, the sample size could be smaller because of a missing response on the questionnaire, missing class grades, or missing standardized test scores.

*Response rate.* A total of 103 teachers in Grades 2, 4, 6, 7, 8, 10, 11, and 12 were contacted and initially agreed to take part in the study. Of these, 82 (80%) returned at least one usable triad. The number of usable triads associated with a particular teacher ranged from 1 to 27. The median number of complete triads per teacher was 9. The median number of students on a class roster was 26. Therefore, the average response rate per class was about 35%.

The 35% response rate is somewhat lower than that obtained in other homework studies that required parents to complete and return questionnaires. For example, Epstein (1988) obtained responses from 59% of parents, and Bents-Hill et al. (1988) achieved a 56% parent response rate. There may be several reasons for our lower response rate. First, and most important, our questionnaire was considerably longer than those used in previous research and, therefore, required parents to commit more time to complete and return it. Second, our response rate is based on complete triads. Thus, unlike other studies, our response rate is lowered if either the parent or the student could or did not participate. Of course, in most instances triads were lost to the sample because parents did not return their questionnaire along with the accompanying consent form for their child. However, other triads were lost because the student was absent on the day questionnaires were administered (32 absences were reported) or because the student wished not to take part (eight high school students refused to give assent).

Finally, the two previous studies involving parent-completed homework questionnaires had response rates that benefited from (a) preselection of teachers who were identified as emphasizing parent involvement in learning activities at home (44% of the sample in Epstein, 1988) or (b) prescreening to eliminate students without current home addresses (Bents-Hill et al., 1988). Neither technique was used in the present study.

The low response rate raises the legitimate concern that respondents may have more positive attitudes toward homework and better homework practices than nonrespondents. This must be kept in mind as the results are interpreted. However, this study appears to warrant no greater concern for selection bias, based on response rates and sampling procedures, than other similar studies that rely on the cooperation of parents. Although we would have liked to pursue nonresponding parents beyond the second mailing procedure described next, doing so was beyond the resources of our study.

*School districts.* Three school districts agreed to take part in the research:

1. A large metropolitan public school district in the state of Tennessee. The district serves nearly 65,000 students. About 58% of students are White and 39% are African American. About 45% of students receive free lunch. Seven teachers provided usable triads. A total of 65 complete triads were returned from class rosters including 153 students, for a response rate of 42%. The participating teachers were drawn from one elementary school, two middle schools, and one high school.
2. A suburban school district Adjacent to the urban district the suburban district serves about 12,000 predominantly White (94%) middle-class families (6.5% of students qualify for free lunch). Forty-four teachers in two elementary schools, two middle schools, and three high schools returned usable triads. There were a total of 369 complete returns of apossible 1,195, foraresponse rate of 31%.
3. A rural school district. This district serves about 2,200 students, 90% of whom are White and 25%

of whom are eligible for free lunch. The rural district had 31 teachers participate from five schools serving kindergarten through Grade 8 and one high school. A total of 275 triads of a possible 780 (for a response rate of 35%) were returned.

*Teachers.* The vast majority of teachers in our sample were White women, and more than half had greater than 10 years teaching experience. About half of the teachers in lower grades and three quarters of those in the upper grades had advanced degrees (master's level or beyond).

*Students and parents.* In 85% of cases, the student's mother completed the parent questionnaire. Students, parents, and teachers were sampled primarily from 2nd ($n = 95$), 4th ($n = 190$), 6th ($n = 124$), 8th ($n = 112$), 10th ($n = 117$), and 12th ($n = 55$) grades, with a few students in 7th and 11th grades. A total of 285 students constituted the lower-grade sample (Grades 2–5) and 424 students constituted the upper-grade sample (Grades 6–12).

Table 1 presents the percentage of students in the lower-grade and upper-grade samples according to their gender, racial or ethnic group, type of residence, and whether they were eligible for free lunch. When the school district descriptions were compared with the characteristics of respondents, it was clear that respondents were not a random sample drawn from the districts. For example, just over 90% of respondents were White, but only about 64% of patrons of the three school districts were White. Similarly, only about 12% of respondents were eligible for free lunch, whereas about 40% of all school district students were eligible.

The differences in respondent backgrounds are probably related to their attitudes toward homework and homework practices. Therefore, care must be taken in generalizing our results to populations containing percentages of Whites and disadvantaged families that differ markedly from our sample statistics. However, it should also be kept in mind that minorities and families of low socioeconomic status were already somewhat overrepresented in the three school districts compared with national statistics.

## Instruments

*The homework questionnaire.* The HPI was developed explicitly for this study. The questionnaire is a multi-item survey that has six different versions, one each for lower- and upper-grade students, their teachers, and their parents. The different versions include parallel questions so that consistency of responses across the six versions can be examined.

The HPI was pilot tested with small but heterogenous samples of students, teachers, and parents before

*Table 1*

## Characteristics of Student Participants

| Student characteristic | Lower grades (%) | Upper grades (%) |
|---|---|---|
| Sex | | |
| Girls | 58 | 53 |
| Boys | 42 | 47 |
| Race or ethnic group | | |
| White | 92 | 93 |
| African American | 3 | 5 |
| Other | 5 | 2 |
| Type of residence | | |
| Apartment | 4 | 4 |
| House | 86 | 92 |
| Trailer | 10 | 4 |
| Lunch | | |
| Free | 16 | 7 |
| Other | 84 | 93 |

*Note.* For lower grades, $n \approx 285$ and for upper grades, $n \approx 424$.

the actual data collection began. These testings led to revisions in wording and the addition of questions. The instrument was also examined by consultants from the Academic Resource Center at the University of Missouri.

For Grades 2 through 5, the HPI was completed with reference to homework in general without regard to subject area. At these grade levels, students in the study had a single teacher and probably could not give reliable estimates of the amount of homework they were given or completed in multiple different subject areas. Likewise, we surmised that parents might be able to judge how much time their child spent on homework in general but not be able to distinguish reliably between homework in different subject areas.

At Grade 6 and above, the questionnaire was completed by teachers and students for individual subject areas. Parents still completed it for school in general. An attempt was made to ensure that these upper-level students and teachers completed the survey for one class only so that responses would be independent at the classroom level. About 58% of upper-level students completed the HPI with reference to math homework (e.g., basic math, algebra, geometry) and 42% with reference to English or literature homework.

One question on the HPI asked teachers, students, and parents how much homework the teacher typically assigned each night. Possible responses were *none* (scored 1), *0 to 15 min* (scored 2), *15 to 30 min* (scored 3), *30 to 60 min*

(scored 4), and *more than 1 hr* (scored 5). However, although the question was the same, the HPI referred to different circumstances for different groups of respondents. In lower grades, the question referred to all homework received by the student, because these students only had one teacher. In contrast, the HPI referred to a specific class for upper-grade students and teachers. For upper-grade parents, the questions referred to all classes, because we believed it was unlikely that parents could estimate their child's amount of homework in specific subject areas. Because of the differences, we could not compare responses to this question by upper-grade parents and upper-grade students or teachers.

The HPI also included a question that asked students and their parents how much of their assigned homework the student typically finished. Possible responses were *none* (scored 1), *some* (scored 2), *about half* (scored 3), *most* (scored 4), and *all* (scored 5). Teachers were not asked this question because it would have been too burdensome to have them respond for each student in their class.

Using responses to the questions regarding how much homework was assigned and completed, we could construct an approximate measure of the amount of time students spent on homework. For students, this was done by (a) converting each student's responses to the question about the amount of homework assigned by the teacher to the midpoint of minutes associated with each scale value ( 1 = 0 min, 2 = 8 min; 3 = 23 min, 4 = 45 min, and 5 = 68 min), (b) converting the portion of homework completed responses to percentages (0 = 0%, 2 = 25%, 3 = 50%, 4 = 75%, and 4 = 100%), and (c) finding the product of the two newly scaled responses. Although this is only a crude measure of time spent on homework, we created the measure for comparison purposes because it would most closely correlate with the self-report measure of homework obtained in most previous studies. We also calculated a similar measure using parents' responses to the same two questions.

Five questions on the HPI asked teachers, parents, and uppergrade students about their beliefs and affective reactions to homework. One question asked "In general, how do you feel about homework?" and had the following possible responses: *don't like it at all* (scored 0); *dislike it some* (scored 1); *neither like nor dislike it* (scored 2); *like it some* (scored 3); *like it very much* (scored 4). A second question asked "Do you think homework increases or decreases students' interest in school?" and had the following possible responses: *decreases it a lot* (scored 0); *decreases it some* (scored 1); *does not make a difference* (scored 2); *increases it some* (scored 3); *increases it a lot* (scored 4). Three questions measured the respondents' beliefs about some possible positive effects of homework. The three questions asked whether respondents thought homework helps students "learn," "develop study skills," and "learn how to manage their time." All three questions had three possible responses: *does not help at all* (scored 0); *helps a little* (scored 1); *helps very much* (scored 2).

When we examined the interrelations between responses to these questions by students we found the interitem correlations ranged from .31 to .58. The raw alpha coefficient for a scale composed of all five questions was .77. Therefore, in the results described next, a single "homework attitudes scale" was used that combined both a cognitive and an affective component to measure attitudes (cf. Rajecki, 1990). Scale scores could range from 0 (*very negative attitude toward homework*) to 14 (*very positive attitude toward homework*).

Students in lower grades were asked only the question "Do you think homework helps you learn?" This served as their measure of attitude toward homework.

In addition to the questions on the amount of homework and homework attitudes, the HPI also included sections on characteristics of assignments, initial classroom factors, involvement of others, home-community factors, and classroom follow-up as well as background information on the respondent. Results involving these sections are examined in separate research reports.

*Measures of achievement.* To minimize the time and expense needed to collect data and the inconvenience to classrooms, we did not administer measures of achievement for the particular purposes of this study. Instead, we used achievement measures that were collected as part of the participating districts' and classes' typical testing schedule.

The state of Tennessee administers a standard achievement test, called the Tennessee Comprehensive Assessment Program (or TCAP) to all students in the 2nd through 8th and 10th grades. The TCAP includes both a norm-referenced and a criterion-referenced component. The norm-referenced part of the test consisted of the fourth edition of the Comprehensive Test of Basic Skills (CTBS/4; CTB, 1988). The CTBS/4 was developed using widely accepted test development procedures for selection of item content and review and was nationally normed in 1988. For the level of aggregation used in this study, Kuder-Richardson estimates of CTBS/4 internal consistencies were all greater than .80 at every grade level. The criterion-referenced component of the TCAP was developed by CTB but is customized for the Tennessee curriculum.

For students in Grades 2 and 4, separate TCAP raw scores were obtained for word analogies (Grade 2 only),

vocabulary, reading comprehension, language mechanics, and spelling. For students in Grades 6 through 10, TCAP raw scores were available for vocabulary, reading comprehension, language expression, language mechanics, spelling, math comprehesion, math calculation, science, social studies, and study skills.

For this study, we developed our own standardized raw score measures of achievement. First, we formed an achievement measure for each student on the basis of TCAP raw scores. For Grades 2 and 4, we used each student's total TCAP score. For Grades 6 through 10, we used the student's cumulative TCAP raw score on all math-related subtests if the course that the homework responses related to involved math skills, or we used the cumulative score on all language-related subtests if the course involved language skills. These choices ensured that the achievement measures related most directly to the homework questions. However, it was also the case that total TCAP and subject-related TCAP scores were very highly correlated for Grades 6 through 10 (range, .59 −.97).

Next, we standardized the raw scores within each grade level and subject matter (total tests for lower grades, math or English for upper grades). In this way, our scores should be highly correlated with standard scores or grade level equivalent measures within each subject area. Our scores would also be combinable across grade levels and subject matters because each student's score was expressed as a departure, in standard deviation units, from the grade level and subject matter sample mean. Because they were standardized, the mean of the TCAP scores was set to 0 and the standard deviation to 1. The scores ranged from −3.68 to 2.10.

In addition, we used teacher-assigned grades as a second measure of achievement. That is, teachers were asked to provide the class grade each participating student would receive if the class ended on the day they completed the questionnaires. For lowerlevel students, teachers provided a single overall grade, not grades in individual subjects. For upper-level students, the grade was specific to the subject matter of the course. In most instances (especially at upper-grade levels), teachers provided grades as percentages. In those instances in which letter grades were provided, the letter grade was converted to an equivalent percentage (e,g., A = 92%, B = 82%). The mean grade gives by all teachers was 88.74 (*SD* = 7.96). In all grade level groups, teacher-assigned grades were moderately correlated with TCAP scores—for Grades 2 through 4, $r(273) = .48$, $p < .0001$; for Grades 6 through 10, $r(269) = .50$, $p < .0001$—but not so highly correlated that similar relations with other variables could be assumed.

## Procedure

*Recruitment of schools and teachers.* In October 1994, a meeting was held between the primary investigators and administrative personnel from each of the three participating school districts. At the meeting, the background and nature of the study were explained.

After this meeting, each of the district administrators asked school principals whether they were interested in allowing the study to be conducted in their schools. Names and addresses of consenting principals were then forwarded to the research staff, and a letter of consent was sent to each principal.

Principals then sent to the research staff lists of teachers in their school who had agreed to learn more about the study. A letter describing the study and a consent form were then sent to each interested teacher. A $20 honorarium was offered to each teacher who agreed to participate.

*Questionnaire administration.* Students, (heir teachers, and parents completed the HPI in February, March, and April 1995.

Materials for completion by parents or guardians of lower-grade students were sent home with die child. Materials for parents or guardians of upper-grade students were sent to the students' homes by U.S. mail. The mailed packet contained the HPI, a no. 2 lead pencil inscribed with the words "Thank you from The Homework Study," and a stamped and self-addressed return envelope.

About 4 weeks after the initial contact, new surveys were sent to parents who had not returned the survey. Parents who did not respond to the second contact were lost to the study.

To minimize expenses and disruption in classes, school personnel administered the HPI to students. However, a standard, written, procedural description was developed that included a list of students whose parents had agreed to let them participate and instructions for HPI administration and how to respond to student queries. The procedural description was meant to reduce the variability in how instructions were given and how much time students were given to answer.

After administering the HPI, teachers completed an administration survey that asked (a) the name of the administrator, (b) the name of the classroom teacher, (c) the date, (d) how nonparticipating students were treated, (e) whether or not the instructions were read aloud, (f) which questions, if any, prompted questions by students, (g) the approximate time it took for students to complete the questionnaire, (h) whether all participating students completed the questionnaire, and (i) when the participating teacher completed the questionnaire.

In about 90% of classrooms, the teacher administered the questionnaire. Students required an average of approximately 20 minutes to complete the HPI. In about three quarters of classes, participating students completed the questionnaire while other students performed other activities. More than half of the classrooms, primarily at lower grades, had the HPI read aloud to them by the teacher. About 72% of teachers completed the HPI after students, whereas about 15% completed it while administering it to students.

Participating teachers completed the HPI at approximately the same time the survey was administered to their students. Teachers who taught multiple class sections were asked to complete the HPI specifically in reference to the section participating in the study.

*Achievement data collection.* The TCAP was administered to students in April 1995, roughly concurrent with the completion of the homework surveys. Teacher-assigned grades were collected at the same time.

## Statistical Analyses

Analyses that involved teacher responses used the teacher-classroom as the unit of analysis. That is, the teacher's response and the mean classroom responses of students and parents served as data. These analyses were conducted using within-classroom designs with respondent (the teacher and either the student or parent) as a repeated measures factor.

Analyses conducted on student and parent responses used the student or parent as unit of data. Therefore, there can be slight differences in student and parent mean responses when they are compared with one another as opposed to when they are compared with teacher responses, because of different weighting caused by the creation of classroom means.

Also, there are differences in power to detect significant relationships between analyses involving teachers and those involving only students or their parents or both. The power characteristics of the sample sizes are quite good for analyses involving students and parents but somewhat weak for teachers (see Cohen, 1988). For this reason, we pay attention to the magnitude of relations as well as their significance when we interpret our findings.

All results are reported by grade level. We also conducted all analyses separately for upper-grade math and English. However, we found very few instances in which a relation differed markedly on the basis of subject matter, and these occurred in analyses associated with small sample sizes (e.g., the 15 math teachers). Therefore, because the data reporting became much more cumbersome if the two subject areas were broken out, we chose not to report the separate math and English results. We do report when subject matter was formally tested as a main effect and interacting variable in certain regression analyses.

The particular statistical testing strategy and units of analysis varied depending on the research question. Therefore, the rationale for each strategy is presented along with the results.

## Results

### Differences in Estimates of Homework

#### Assigned and Completed

The first questions guiding our analyses asked whether respondents differed in their beliefs about the amount of homework assigned by teachers and the proportion completed by students. Table 2 presents the means, standard deviations, and sample sizes associated with teachers', students', and parents' estimates of these homework behaviors.

*Amount assigned by teachers.* The means revealed that most responses concerning the amount of homework teachers assigned centered around the middle of the scale (scored 3), or "15 to 30 min" each night, except for parents of upper-grade students, whose responses were closer to "30 to 60 min" (scored 4). This difference is understandable in that these parents were estimating homework across all subjects, not just homework in math or English. Across all respondents, responses were roughly normally distributed and revealed no ceiling or floor effects. Only

1.1% of parents, 4.0% of students, and 1.3% of teachers reported that teachers gave no homework, whereas 16.7% of parents, 6.4% of students, and 0% of teachers reported teachers gave "more than 1 hr" of homework a night.

Planned comparisons between pairs of means indicated that, for lower grades (Grades 2 and 4), teachers reported assigning more homework than the average of their students' reports said teachers assigned (teacher $M = 3.07$, student $M = 2.78$), $t(27) = 2.17$, $p < .039$. Students also reported being assigned less homework than their parents thought they were assigned (student $M = 2.84$, parent $M = 3.30$), $t(284) = 6.75$, $p < .0001$. Teacher reports and average parent reports did not differ (parent $M = 3.24$), $t(27) = 1.63$, ns.

Also for lower grades, the correlation between the teachers' reports of the amount of homework they assigned and the average of their students' reports approached significance, $r(27) = .36$, $p < .07$, whereas that between teacher reports and average parent reports was positive but not significant, $r(27) = .23$, ns. The correlation between student and parent reports of the amount of assigned homework was weaker than those involving teachers, but it did reach significance because of greater power, $r(284) = .16$, $p < .008$.

For upper grades, teacher and average student reports of assigned homework did not differ (teacher $M = 3.02$, student $M = 3.09$), $t(51) = .44$, ns. Teacher and average student reports also were positively correlated but not significantly so, $r(51) = .23$, ns.

*Portion completed by students.* Reports of how much homework students completed revealed a more skewed

*Table 2*

**Means for Homework Variables by Teachers, Students, and Parents at Each Grade Level**

| Homework variable | Lower grades | | | Upper grades | | |
|---|---|---|---|---|---|---|
| | Teachers | Students | Parents | Teachers | Students | Parents |
| Teacher assigned | | | | | | |
| M | 3.07 | 2.84 | 3.30 | 3.02 | 3.06 | 3.89 |
| SD | 0.72 | 0.97 | 0.81 | 0.61 | 0.90 | 0.87 |
| n | 28 | 285 | 285 | 52 | 422 | 423 |
| Portion completed | | | | | | |
| M | — | 4.79 | 4.81 | — | 4.31 | 4.58 |
| SD | — | 0.64 | 0.51 | — | 0.91 | 0.74 |
| n | — | 283 | 285 | — | 423 | 423 |
| Attitude toward | | | | | | |
| M | 11.08 | 1.48 | 9.03 | 10.15 | 6.42 | 9.30 |
| SD | 2.15 | 0.65 | 3.08 | 2.35 | 3.15 | 2.78 |
| n | 26 | 282 | 279 | 52 | 414 | 416 |

distribution. Among parents, about 75% reported that their child completed all homework. Among students, 65% reported completing all homework.

For lower grades, the planned comparisons revealed no difference between the portion of homework students and parents said students completed (student $M = 4.79$, parent $M = 4.81$), $t(282) = 0.55$, ns. The correlation between student and parent reports of how much homework was completed was weak but significant, $r(282) = .16$, $p < .008$. For upper grades, student reports referred to homework in one subject, whereas parent reports referred to all homework, making it inappropriate to compare the means directly.

*Time spent by students.* Our measure of the time students spent on homework, created from the assigned and completed homework measures, revealed that the average lower-grade student reported doing about 22 min of homework per night ($SD = 17.5$), whereas their parents reported an average of about 29 min per night ($SD = 15.6$). At upper grades, students reported about 22 min of either math or English homework ($SD = 15.2$). Their parents reported at least 39 min of total homework ($SD = 18.2$).

### Differences in Attitudes Toward Homework

Our next set of questions asked whether teachers', students', and parents' attitudes about homework were consistent and related to one another. Table 2 also displays the teacher, student, and parent homework attitude ratings.

In general, respondents expressed positive attitudes toward homework. The homework scale for all respondents except lower-grade students could range from 0 to 14, with a midpoint of 7. Teacher and parent responses are well above the midpoint, whereas upper-grade student responses are somewhat below. Lower-grade student responses could range from 0 to 2. Thus, their mean response was quite positive, falling between "homework helps me learn some" (scored 1) and "homework helps me learn very much" (scored 2).

For lower grades, teachers expressed more positive attitudes toward homework ($M = 11.08$) than did the average parent of students in their class ($M = 9.06$), $t(25) = 4.02$, $p < .0005$. For upper grades, teacher attitudes ($M = 10.15$) were also more positive than parent attitudes ($M = 9.30$), $t(51) = 2.22$, $p < .04$, which were in turn more positive than student attitudes ($M = 6.36$), $t(51) = 9.93$, $p < .0001$.

For both lower-and upper-grade students, we found significant positive correlations between student and parent homework attitudes; for lower grades, $r(277) = .15$, $p < .015$; for upper grades, $r(406) = .23$, $p < .0001$. Teacher attitudes were not significantly related to their average student's rating—for lower grades, $r(25) = .15$, ns; for upper grades, $r(51) = .18$, ns—but the magnitude of these correlations was similar to that between students and parents. Teacher attitudes and average parent ratings revealed correlations near zero; for lower grades, $r(25) = .01$, ns; for upper grades, $r(51) = .02$, ns.

## Relationships Between Homework

### Behaviors and Achievement

The next questions we asked concerned whether relationships existed between homework behaviors and students' achievement. Results of these analyses are summarized in Table 3.

*Amount assigned by teachers.* For Grades 2 and 4, positive but nonsignificant relationships were found between the amount of homework teachers said they assigned and the average student achievement in their class; for TCAP scores, $r(27) = .12$, ns; for teacher-assigned grades, $r(27) = .19$, ns. However, student reports of teacherassigned homework were negatively, but not significantly, correlated with TCAP scores, $r(276) = -.04$, ns, and significantly negatively correlated with grades, $r(279) = -.22$, $p < .0002$. Significant negative relations also were found for correlations involving parent reports of the amount of homework assigned by teachers and students' achievement; for TCAP scores, $r(276) = -.12$, $p < .05$; for grades, $r(279) = -.22$, $p < .0002$.

For upper grades, negative but nonsignificant relations were found between the amount of homework teachers said they assigned and the average student achievement in their class; for TCAP scores (Grades 6–10), $r(38) = -.27$, $p < .10$; for teacher-assigned grades (Grades 6–12), $r(43) = -.09$, ns. For students, reports of the amount of teacherassigned homework were not significantly related to achievement and were near zero; for TCAP scores, $r(319) = -.05$, ns; for grades, $r(357) = .05$, ns. Parents' reports of teacher-assigned homework were correlated near zero for TCAP scores, $r(320) = .03$, ns, but were positively correlated with their students' grades, $r(357) = .12$, $p < .03$.

*Portion students completed.* At both grade levels, student and parent reports of the portion of homework assignments completed by students were positively correlated with both measures of achievement. At lower grades, student correlations did not reach significance— for TCAP scores, $r(274) = .07$, ns; for grades, $r(274) = .10$, $p < .09$—but parent correlations did reach significance— for TCAP scores, $r(277) = .22$, $p < .0003$; for grades, $r(279) = .31$, $p < .0001$. At upper grades, correlations were significant for both student reports—for TCAP

*Table 3*

### Correlations Between Homework Behavior and Achievement

| Homework variable | Lower grades | | | Upper grades | | |
|---|---|---|---|---|---|---|
| | Teachers | Students | Parents | Teachers | Students | Parents |
| Standardized test scores | | | | | | |
|    Teacher assigned | .12 | −.04 | −.12* | −.27 | −.05 | .03 |
|    Portion completed | — | .07 | .22*** | — | .14* | .26*** |
|    Time spent | — | −.04 | −.06 | — | .00 | .14** |
| Grades | | | | | | |
|    Teacher assigned | .19 | −.22*** | −.22*** | −.09 | .05 | .12* |
|    Portion completed | — | .10 | .31**** | — | .31**** | .36**** |
|    Time spent | — | −.19** | −.13* | — | .17** | .24**** |

*$p < .05$. **$p < .01$. ***$p < .001$. ****$p < .0001$.

scores, $r(320) = .14$, $p < .02$; for teacher-assigned grades, $r(358) = .31$, $p < .0001$—and parents reports—TCAP scores, $r(320) = .26$, $p < .0001$; for grades, $r(358) = .36$, $p < .0001$.

*Time spent.* At lower grades, the composite measure of the amount of time students spent on homework was not significantly correlated with TCAP scores for either students, $r(276) = −.04$, ns, or parents, $r(276) = −.06$, ns. However, teacher-assigned grades were significantly negatively correlated with time spent on homework for both students, $r(279) = −.19$, $p < .002$, and parents, $r(279) = −.13$, $p < .03$.

At upper grades, the composite measure of the amount of time students spent on homework was generally positively correlated with achievement measures. For TCAP scores, the correlation was not significant for students' estimates of time on homework, $r(321) = .00$, ns, but was significant for parents' estimates, $r(319) = .14$, $p < .01$. For teacherassigned grades, both correlations were significant; for students, $r(358) = .17$, $p < .002$; for parents, $r(356) = .24$, $p < .0001$.

*Portion completed with amount assigned controlled.* To examine further the relation between homework and achievement, we next ran three hierarchical multiple regressions. These analyses were conducted (a) to determine whether student reports of how much homework they completed were significantly related to achievement when the amount of homework teachers assigned was statistically controlled and (b) to test for interactions involving grade level and subject matter.

Using the student as the unit of analysis, we entered the following variables in the given order as predictors of TCAP scores and teacher-assigned grades: grade level, subject matter (total, math, English), amount of homework

assigned by the teacher (entered as a categorical variable so as to remove any variance, not just linear variance, associated with amount assigned), amount of homework students' reported completing, the interaction of grade level and amount completed, and the interaction of subject matter and amount completed. Only the last three sources of variance are of substantive interest in this analysis.

We found significant positive relations between the amount of homework students said they finished and both achievement measures when we controlled for all the preceding factors; for TCAP $F(1, 583) = 6.88$, $p < .009$; for grades, $F(1, 624) = 40.22$, $p < .0001$. These were the only significant effects.

To examine these relations further, we residualized the achievement measures using the amount of homework assigned by the teacher as the control variable and then correlated the residual scores with students' reports of how much homework they typically completed. This analysis revealed no relation at the lower grades for TCAP scores, $r(274) = .07$, ns, but a nonsignificant trend between completed homework and residualized teacher-assigned grades, $r(277) = .11$, $p < .07$. For the upper grades, portion of completed homework was related to both residualized TCAP scores, $r(319) = .13$, $p < .02$, and residualized teacher-assigned grades, $r(358) = .32$, $p < .0001$.

*Portion completed with grading controlled.* The difference for lower-grade and upper-grade students in the relation between residualized teacher-assigned grades and portion of completed homework raised the possibility that grades on homework assignments might have a larger direct effect on the overall class grades given by teachers to upper-level students than lower-level students, rather than homework influencing knowledge acquisition, which, in turn, affected grades. Evidence that this might be the case was found when we examined the difference in teachers' responses to a question we asked about how much of a role homework played in determining students' grades. The mean response for teachers of Grades 2 and 4 was "between 1% and 10%," whereas for teachers of Grades 6 through 12 it was "above 11% to 20%."

However, when we residualized students' class grades so that they were no longer influenced by the teachers' reported use of homework in determining grades (linear effect only), we found a nonsignificant positive relation at the lower grades, $r(277) = .08$, $ns$, and a significant positive relation at the upper grades, $r(358) = .27$, $p < .0001$. Thus, at least for students in Grades 6 through 12, completing more homework has a positive relation to class grades even when its direct effect on grades is controlled.

## Relationships Between Homework

### Behaviors and Attitudes

Next we asked a series of questions concerning whether teacher and student attitudes about homework were related to the homework behaviors. Here, we restricted our analyses to teacher and student responses only. Results are displayed in Table 4.

For lower grades, we found a nonsignificant positive correlation between the amount of homework teachers reported assigning and teachers' attitudes toward homework, $r(25) = .10$, $ns$. However, there was a significant negative relation between the amount of homework teachers said they assigned and the average attitude toward homework expressed by students in the teacher's class, $r(27) = -.38$, $p < .05$.

Lower-grade student reports of the amount of homework assigned, the portion completed, and the composite measure of time spent on homework all produced near-zero correlations with student attitudes; for amount assigned, $r(281) = .00$, $ns$; for portion completed, $r(279) = .04$, $ns$; for time spent, $r(281) = .00$, $ns$.

For upper grades, the relation between the amount of homework teachers reported assigning and their homework attitudes was positive and significant, $r(51) = .41$, $p < .003$. However, neither the teachers' nor the students' report of amount of homework assigned was significantly correlated with the students' attitudes; for teachers, $r(51) = .12$, $ns$; for students, $r(412) = .00$, $ns$. Upper-grade students' attitudes toward homework were significantly positively correlated with both their reports of the portion of homework they completed, $r(412) = .31$, $p < .0001$, and the composite measure of time spent on homework, $r(412) = .10$, $p < .05$.

## Relationships Between Homework

### Attitudes and Achievement

Next, we explored relationships between homework attitudes and achievement. These results are displayed in Table 5.

For lower grades, we found a sizable but nonsignificant negative correlation, indicating that teachers who had more positive homework attitudes also had students who averaged poorer scores on the TCAP, $r(25) = -.24$, $ns$. A significant negative correlation was found between lower-grade students' homework attitudes and their TCAP scores, $r(273) = -.19$, $p < .002$, along with a similar trend for grades, $r(276) = -.10$, $p < .09$. A near-zero correlation was found for teacher attitudes and teacher-assigned grades, $r(25) = -.01$, $ns$.

For upper grades, we found negative but nonsignificant relations between teacher attitudes and both their

*Table 4*

**Correlations Between Homework Behaviors and Attitudes**

| Respondent | Behavior | Attitude holder | Lower | Upper |
|---|---|---|---|---|
| Teacher | Amount assigned | Teacher | .10 | .41** |
| Teacher | Amount assigned | Student | −.38* | .12 |
| Student | Amount assigned | Student | .00 | .00 |
| Student | Portion completed | Student | .04 | .31**** |
| Student | Time spent | Student | .00 | .10* |

*$p < .05$. **$p < .01$. ****$p < .0001$.

*Table 5*

**Correlations Between Teachers' and Students' Attitudes Toward Homework and Measures of Students' Achievement**

| Achievement measure/Attitude holder | Lower | Upper |
|---|---|---|
| Standardized tests | | |
| Teacher | −.24 | −.08 |
| Student | −.19** | −.06 |
| Grades | | |
| Teacher | −.01 | −.13 |
| Student | −.10 | .11* |

*$p < .05$. **$p < .01$.

average student's TCAP score, $r(38) = -.08$, ns, and the average grade they assigned, $r(43) = -.13$, ns. A nonsignificant negative relation also was found between student homework attitudes and TCAP scores, $r(311) = -.06$ ns, whereas a significant positive relation was found between student attitudes and teacher-assigned grades, $r(352) = .11$, $p < .05$.

### Path Analysis Summary

As a final means for summarizing the data, we developed a path diagram to help guide a series of multiple regression analyses that included many of the variables and relations examined previously as well as some as yet untested relations.

First, we treated the students' standardized test scores (TCAP) and parent and teacher attitudes toward homework as exogenous variables. These three variables were used to predict the amount of homework teachers said they assigned. For lower grades, $R^2(247) = .02$; for upper grades, $R^2(311) = .32$. All four variables were then used to predict student attitudes toward homework. For lower grades, $R^2(244) = .16$; for upper grades, $R^2(297) = .03$. Next, all five variables were used to predict the portion of assignments students completed. For lower grades, $R^2(241) = .03$; for upper grades, $R^2(295) = .16$. Last, all prior variables were used to predict the students' class grades. For lower grades, $R^2(236) = .28$; for upper grades, $R^2(250) = .34$.

Figure 1 presents those standardized regression coefficients that proved to be statistically significant, using the student as the unit of analysis, separately for lower and upper grades. For lower grades, the teachers' attitudes were the only significant predictor of the amount of homework they assigned (beta = .13, $p < .04$). Student attitudes were positively related to parent attitudes (beta = .18, $p < .003$) and negatively related to TCAP scores (beta = $-.21$, $p < .0008$) and the amount of homework the teacher assigned (beta = $-.27$, $p < .0001$). The amount of homework completed by students had no significant predictors. Finally, die students' class grades were positively related to both their standardized test scores (beta = .47, $p < .0001$) and the amount of homework they completed (beta = .13, $p < .02$).

For upper grades, the amount of homework assigned by teachers was positively related to the teachers' attitudes toward homework (beta = .51, $p < .0001$) and negatively related to their students' TCAP scores (beta = $-.20$, $p < .0001$). Students' attitudes toward homework were predicted only by parent attitudes (beta = .16, $p < .006$). The amount of homework students completed was positively related to their attitudes (beta = .30, $p < .0001$) and negatively related to the amount of homework the

teacher assigned (beta = $-.19$, $p < .005$), Finally, students' class grades were positively related to their TCAP scores (beta = .45, $p < .0001$), portion of completed homework (beta = .22, $p < .0001$), and their parents' homework attitude (beta = .12, $p < .02$).

## Discussion

### Differences in Estimates of Homework

#### Assigned and Completed

The results of this study indicated that lower-grade students said they received less homework than either their teachers or parents indicated that the students received. Teachers and parents did not differ in their estimates. Lower-grade students and parents did not differ in how much homework they said the student completed. Upper-grade students reported a similar amount of assigned homework to that reported by their teachers. Generally, correlations between reports were positive but weak, ranging from .15 to .36.

Cooper, Lindsay, Nye, and Greathouse (1997), in a companion piece to this article, suggested three socially related cognitive reasons for inconsistency in homework behavior reports. First, teachers, students, and parents may hold different expectations about homework, and these may influence how they collect and interpret information. Second, each respondent is exposed to a different part of the homework process. For example, teachers are not exposed to what happens at home and parents are not exposed to school activities. Finally, respondent estimates may be influenced by a desire to present their own role in the homework process in the most favorable light.

About 75% of parents reported that their child completed all homework, whereas 65% of students reported completing all homework. Interpreting this result is somewhat like describing a glass of water as half empty or half full; although it may be a cause for concern that about one third of students say they typically do not finish their homework, it would also be improper to conclude that students in general neither work hard nor accomplish much in school.

#### Homework Behaviors and Achievement; Relating the Current Findings to Previous Research

In Cooper's (1989) meta-analysis, the correlation between the amount of homework students reported doing each night and their achievement was .02 for lower grades (3–5) and .14 for middle grades (6–9). The meta-analysis also found that the relationship was of similar strength for both standardized tests and teacher-assigned grades.

*Figure 1*

**Path Diagrams of Significant Multiple Regression Results Relating Homework Attitudes and Practices and Student Achievement. Entries Are Standardized Regression Coefficients Significant At *p* < .05 or Lower.**

A. Lower Grades

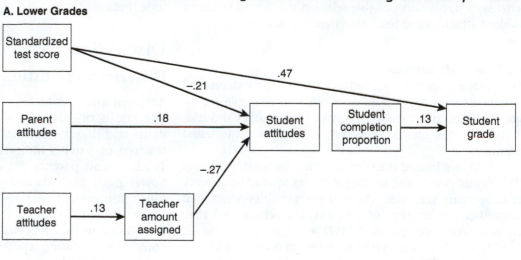

B. Upper Grades

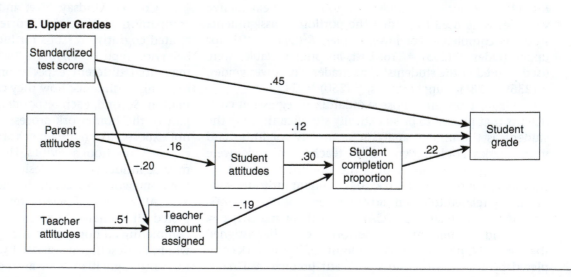

In this study, Grade 2 and 4 students' composite measure of time spent on homework also was correlated near zero with a standardized measure of achievement (*r* = −.04) but was significantly negatively correlated with class grades (*r* = −.19). Students in Grades 6 through 10 revealed no relation between time on homework and standardized test scores (*r* = .00), but those in Grades 6 through 12 showed a significant positive relation with grades (*r* = .17). Thus, the present results are not inconsistent with past research but also suggest more differentiation of relationships based on whether achievement was measured by standardized tests or teacher-assigned grades.

Our results are also consistent with those of Bents-Hill et al. (1988), who found that parent reports of time on homework were negatively correlated with achievement in lower grades but positively correlated with achievement in upper grades.

The present study differed from most past studies in that we distinguished between the amount of homework teachers assigned and the proportion that students completed. The added distinction proved to be an important one. The results relating to student reports of how much homework the teacher assigned were generally unrelated to achievement, but student reports of how much homework they completed were very consistent with the results of the meta-analysis.

Also, unlike past studies, this study obtained estimates of homework behavior from three sources. We found (nonsignificant) evidence that teachers' reported assigning more homework to better achieving classes in lower grades and less homework to better achieving classes in upper grades. Opposite relations were exhibited by student and parent reports.

One possible explanation for the difference in relationships could be that respondents disagree about how much homework actually was assigned, as discussed previously. Another possible explanation might be that teachers estimated the time on homework for their entire class, whereas student and parent estimates were influenced not only by class averages but also by the individual student's variations around these averages. Thus, it might be that all three respondents are giving roughly accurate estimates, but they pertain to relations operating at different levels of aggregation (Burstein, 1980).

Also, it cannot be determined from the data whether student test scores influence the amount of homework assigned by the teacher, whether assigned homework causes test scores, whether bidirectional causal mechanisms are operating, or whether both homework practices and achievement are the result of third factors. We suspect that bidirectional and third-factor influences are the best description of nature. However, when unidirectional models must be constructed and, therefore, preponderance of causal influence is at issue, we suggest that standardized test scores are best viewed as determinants of homework practices because of their high correlation with stable abilities. This causal ordering is more defensible at lower grades because homework is typically minimal during the first years of school. Choosing a unidirectional causal ordering for standardized tests and homework at upper grades is more problematic.

Teacher-assigned grades, on the other hand, are more likely to be influenced by specific classroom achievements and efforts. Therefore, they are more appropriately viewed as influenced by homework practices, and such a causal ordering is probably legitimate at both lower and upper grades.

In sum, this study's results indicated generally weak relations between reports of the amount of homework teachers assigned and student achievement. There was some evidence that teachers in Grades 2 and 4 reported assigning more homework to classes with lower achievement, but students and parents reported that teachers assigned more homework to higher achieving students, especially when grades were the measure of achievement.

Further, the findings suggested positive relations between the portion of homework assignments students complete and their achievement. This relation is stronger at upper than lower grades and stronger for teacher-assigned grades than standardized tests. The relations held even when the amount of homework the teacher assigns or the use by the teacher of homework in determining grades was statistically controlled.

### Role of Attitudes in the Homework Process

In lower grades, students who expressed poorer attitudes toward homework had teachers who said they assigned more homework. Also at lower grades, students with poorer achievement test scores held more positive homework attitudes. Teachers of poorer achieving students also expressed more positive attitudes toward homework but not significantly so. In upper grades, more positive teacher attitudes toward homework were associated with more assigned homework. More positive student attitudes were associated with more completed homework and higher class grades.

As discussed, these findings make the most sense if we assume that poorer standardized test scores are a determinant of positive attitude ratings and not vice versa. From this perspective, both students with lower standardized test scores and their teachers viewed homework as a more useful strategy for improving performance.

### Path Diagram Summary

Our final summary of the data is captured in the path diagrams of multiple regression results (see Figure 1). They indicate that most of our conclusions based on the simple bivariate correlations withstand analyses that control for other variables in the homework process. They also bring more coherence to our picture of the homework process by imposing an assumed causal ordering on our correlational data.

Most notably, the regressions serve to underscore the importance of completion of homework by students as a positive factor in achievement even when other influences are controlled.

The path diagrams also suggest that two relatively independent homework processes may be at work in lower grades. Teachers may determine the amount of homework they assign young students based on their own attitude toward homework. Lower test scores and parents with more positive attitudes may influence students to hold more positive attitudes toward homework. Perhaps most interesting, at lower grades more homework assigned by teachers may cause poorer attitudes in students.

However, none of these factors predicted how much homework is completed by young students. A different model involving variables not measured in this study may be needed to understand completion rates among young students. Alternatively, the means relating to the portion of homework completed and to respondent attitudes both were positively skewed, serving to underscore our concern that this sample may represent families that take a more positive attitude toward homework than exists in the population at large. This lack of variation may contribute to why attitudes and completion rates were unrelated in lower grades.

As students grow older, a more integrated model seems to emerge. The path diagrams highlight the finding that as students grow older their own attitudes about homework and those of their parents play an increasingly important role in how much homework they complete and in their class grades. Again, however, positive teacher attitudes toward homework may affect students negatively but indirectly. Positive teacher attitudes may cause longer homework assignments, which, in turn, cause lower completion rates and then poorer grades.

Both path diagrams clearly indicate that parents' attitudes about homework have direct, positive effects on their children's attitudes and, at upper grades, on their children's classroom achievements. Of course, examining the importance of parents in the educational process is a topic that has generated considerable previous research. Epstein (1992) provided a broad overview of perspectives on and types of partnerships between schools and families that can serve to improve student motivation and achievement. Casanova (1996), alternatively, provided some cautions concerning (a) parents becoming overly involved in the schooling process (largely for political purposes) and (b) educators assuming that a lack of visible parental involvement is a sign of disinterest. Our findings should be acceptable to both perspectives. They demonstrate that attitudes may be transmitted from parent to child and that even this simplest form of involvement has implications for educational outcomes.

Differences in the path diagrams can be understood if we view homework as largely an effortful and individual activity. As students mature, their motivation and ability to perform self-regulated learning should influence the importance of attitudes toward homework in the achievement process. Thus, it is not surprising to find that research on self-regulation of homework reveals that students in Grade 2 reported being reminded by another about homework more often than students in Grade 6. In contrast, sixth graders were three times more likely than second graders to say their homework behavior was self-regulated (e.g., "It's my responsibility") versus other regulated (e.g., "So my mom does not get angry"; Warton, 1993). Further, research indicates that students who are more proficient at using self-regulatory behaviors such as cognitive and meta-cognitive strategies and effort management behaviors (e.g., setting goals and managing time) are also more likely to enhance their own learning and to improve academic achievement (cf. Schunk & Zimmerman, 1994).

### Suggestions for Future Research

First, future investigators need to find ways to involve families that are typically underrepresented in homework studies. We pointed out that this study, along with many conducted before it, relied on the voluntary participation of parents. Voluntary response rates are low, suggesting that parents who do respond are more likely to be positively involved in their children's education. Responding parents are also more likely to be White and less likely to represent low-income families. Future research would be of greater value if it focused on families for which homework is either devalued or for whom obstacles exist that make it difficult to complete homework assignments.

More substantively, we encourage future homework studies to continue to make the distinction between the amount of homework teachers assign and the portion students report completing. Doing so may not only improve our ability to predict student achievement but may also help us understand how the effectiveness of homework can best be influenced by changes in teaching practices or changes in student and parent behavior. Especially, researchers need to look at how homework assignments can promote cognitive and motivational strategies and behaviors in students.

To accomplish this last objective, it is also important for future research to examine the causal links between the attitudes of all role players and student achievement. Of course, studies that attempt to affect change in attitudes and then track their consequences will be costly and will require both ample time for strong interventions and proper measurement intervals.

Finally, as all these data suggest, future research ought to broaden the nature of the criteria used to evaluate the effectiveness of homework. Rather than viewing achievement outcomes as the sole criteria for "success," certain intermediate outcomes, such as appropriate cognitive strategies, improved motivation, and effective study habits ought to be used to gauge the impact of homework, especially in younger students.

### Practical Implications

Several lessons relating to good homework practices can be learned from this study. First, in the past, some educational leaders have recommended that homework be abandoned for young children because the evidence has shown no relation between the amount of homework a child does and achievement (Stern, 1993). Our results suggest that the benefits of homework for young children may not be immediately evident but exist nonetheless. First, by examining complex models and distinguishing between homework assigned and homework completed, we were able to show that, as early as the second and fourth grades, the frequency of completed homework assignments predicts grades, even when controlling for standardized test differences, amount assigned, and teacher, student, and parent attitudes. Further, to the extent that homework helps young students develop effective study habits, our results suggest that homework in early grades can have a long-term developmental effect that reveals itself as an even stronger relationship between completion rates and grades when the student moves into secondary school. Thus, we suggest that the present study supports the assignment of homework in early grades, not necessarily for its immediate effects on achievement but rather for its potential long-term impact. The impact of early-grade homework is mediated, through time, by its facilitation of the development of proper study skills, which, in turn, influence grades.

However, a caution is in order as well. We found a negative relation between the amount of homework teachers assign and students' attitudes at lower grades and between amount assigned and completion rates at upper grades. This suggests that teachers should ensure that assignments are of a proper length for the developmental level of their students. Teachers should avoid lengthy homework assignments that lead to fatigue and the extinction of interest in the covered material.

Further, our construction of homework's role in early grades points to some suggestions about what constitutes a proper homework assignment for young students. Specifically, in addition to the academic component, homework for young children may be especially beneficial if it includes explicit lessons on how to study.

A second practical implication of this study derives from its demonstration of the significant and stable role that parental attitudes play in shaping students' attitudes toward homework and on the grades of older students. School teachers and educational policymakers should interpret these results to mean that efforts to improve parent attitudes toward homework are likely to pay off. The lack of positive effect of homework for some students may be due, in part, to attitudes toward homework held by parents that impede, or at least do not support, their children's full participation, persistence, or commitment to completing assignments. If teachers are not aware that parent beliefs are linked to student homework performance, they may draw unwarranted inferences about the lack of value of particular assignments or about homework in general.

Improved parent attitudes are most likely to result from the clear communication of homework's goals (e.g., fostering study skills in young children, reinforcing or enriching academic skills in all students) and through proper involvement of parents in the homework process itself (cf. Wieinstein & Mignano, 1993). Indeed, our results can be used by educators to demonstrate to parents directly and empirically the importance of the role they play.

# References

Anderson, B., Mead, N., & Sullivan, S. (1986). *Homework: What do national assessment results tell us?* Princeton, NJ: Educational Testing Service.

Bents-Hill, C, Boswell, R., Byers, J., Cohen, N., Cummings, J., & Leavitt, B. (1988, April). *Relationship of academic performance to parent estimate of homework time.* Paper presented at the annual meeting of the National Association of School Psychologists, Chicago, IL.

Brink, W. G. (1937). *Direct study activities in secondary schools.* New York: Doubleday.

Burstein, L. (1980). The analysis of multilevel data in educational research and evaluation. In D. Berliner (Ed.), *Review of research in education, Vol. 8.* Washington, DC: American Educational Research Association.

Casanova, U. (1996). Parent involvement: A call for prudence. *Educational Researcher, 25,* 30–32.

Cohen, J. (1988). *Statistical power analysis for the behavioral sciences.* Hillsdale, NJ: Erlbaum.

Cooper, H. (1989). *Homework.* White Plains, NY: Longman.

Cooper, H. (1991). Homework. *Feelings and the Medical Significance, 33*(2), 7–10.

Cooper, H., Lindsay, J. J., Nye, B., & Greathouse, S. (1997). *Similarities and differences between student, teacher, and parent descriptions of homework.* Manuscript submitted for publication.

CTB. (1988). *Comprehensive test of basic skills: Technical Report* (4th ed.)-New York: Macmillan/McGraw-Hill.

Epstein, J. L. (1988). *Homework practices, achievements, and behaviors of elementary school students* (Center for Research on Elementary and Middle Schools Rep. No. 26). Baltimore, MD: Johns Hopkins University.

Epstein, J. L. (1992). School and family partnerships. In M. Alkin (Ed.), *Encyclopedia of educational research* (pp. 1139–1151). New York: Macmillan.

Keith, T. Z. (1987). Children and homework. In A. Thomas & J. Grimes (Eds.), *Children's needs: Psychological perspectives*. Washington, DC: National Association of School Psychologists.

Keith, T. Z. (1996). Structural equation modeling in school psychology. In C. R. Reynolds & T. B. Gutkin (Eds.), *Handbook of school psychology* (3rd ed.). New York: Wiley.

Keith, T. Z., & Cool, V. A. (1992). Testing models of school learning: Effects of quality of instruction, motivation, academic coursework, and homework on academic achievement *School Psychology Quarterly, 1,* 209–226.

Keith, T. Z., Keith, P. B., Troutman, G. C, Bickley, P. G., Trivette, P. S., & Singh, K. (1993). Does parental involvement affect eighth-grade student achievement? Structural analysis of national data. *School Psychology Review, 22,* 474–496.

Knorr, C. L. (1981, January). *A synthesis of homework research and related literature* (ERIC Document Reproductive Service No. ED 199 933). Paper presented at the Lehigh Chapter of Phi Delta Kappa, Bethlehem, PA.

Kraus, S. J. (1995). Attitudes and the prediction of behavior: A meta-analysis of the empirical research. *Personality and Social Psychology, 21,* 58–75.

LaConte, R. T. (1981). *Homework as a learning experience. What research says to the teacher.* (ERIC Document Reproduction Service No. ED 217

022). Washington, DC: National Education Association.

National Commission on Excellence in Education. (1983). *A nation at risk: The imperative for educational reform.* Washington, DC: U.S. Department of Education.

Rajecki, D. W. (1990). *Attitudes* (2nd ed.). Sunderland, MA: Sinauer.

Schunk, D. H., & Zimmerman, B. J. (1994). *Self-regulation of learning and performance.* Hillsdale, NJ: Erlbaum.

Stern, G. (1993, October 11), Kids' homework may be going the way of the dinosaur. *The Wall Street Journal,* pp. Bl, B6.

Walberg, H. J. (1991). Does homework help? *School Community Journal, 7*(1), 13–15.

Warton, P. M. (1993, March). *Responsibility for homework: Children's ideas about self-regulation.* Paper presented at the meeting of the Society for Research in Child Development, New Orleans, LA.

Weinstein, C. F, & Mignano, A. J., Jr. (1993). *Elementary classroom management.* New York: McGraw-Hill.

Wildman, P. R. (1968). Homework pressures, *Peabody Journal of Education, 45,* 202–204.

First author, **HARRIS COOPER** is the Hugo L. Blomquist Professor and Faculty Network Member of Duke Institute for Brain Sciences. From 1977 to 2003, he was on the faculty at the University of Missouri. In 2003, he moved to Duke University where he is a professor and chair of the Department of Psychology & Neuroscience. Dr. Cooper has been a Visiting Scholar at Stanford University, the University of Oregon, and the Russell Sage Foundation in New York City.

# EXPLORING THE ISSUE

## Does Homework Improve Student Achievement?

## Critical Thinking and Reflection

1. What, in your opinion, is the major issue with regard to homework effects and the difficulty in clearly understanding them?
2. In what way should the nature of the evidence be used to help frame a school district's policy discussion about whether or not to change their policy about homework?
3. If you were a building-level school principal, what kind of conversation should you have with your teaching staff regarding homework? How would this conversation differ if your school was an elementary school versus a high school?

## Is There Common Ground?

Both articles are successful attempts to provide evidence that homework *causes* or produces behaviors and cognitions that are promotive of student learning and achievement. However, both articles also reveal significant qualifications relating the different aspects of homework. Thus, in seeking common ground, one must admit there is a positive association both longitudinally and cross-sectionally but the answer is accompanied by a resounding "BUT." The "Yes" side article authored by Dettmers et al. (2010) indicated that the perceived quality of homework task selection ("Our mathematics teacher almost always chooses homework assignments really well") mattered quite a bit. Thus, quality mattered a great deal. It was positively related to homework motivation and behaviors at the level of the individual and the class (see Tables 3 and 4). Homework selection was also positively and significantly related to achievement at the class level but not at the individual level, indicating a group-level influence not seen on the individual level, which is very interesting. An aspect of homework that showed inconsistent effects was amount of homework challenge. Therefore, we can conclude with much confidence that for early high school students, high-quality homework can improve student achievement.

Although this would appear to conclude the debate in favor of "Yes," the issues brought up by the "No" study by Cooper et al. (1998) remind us of the values we wish students to internalize against the other costs of homework. First, the results remind educators that although the association between the amount of homework completed and grades is positive, it is not huge (refer to the standardized regression coefficients of the arrows pointing to student grades in Figure 1). This comparison was possible because their study included these factors whereas the Dettmers study did not. Second, the results indicated in both the lower and upper grades that the greater the amount of homework, the more negative students' attitudes toward homework (see Figure 1 again). Thus, it appears that while an important contributor to students' academic development, it is not the biggest contributor, and with some costs to consider.

## Additional Resources

C. H. Brock, D. Lapp, J. Flood, D. Fisher, and K. T. Han, "Does Homework Matter?: An Investigation of Teacher Perceptions about Homework Practices for Children from Nondominant Backgrounds," *Urban Education* (vol. 42, 2007).

H. Cooper and J. C. Valentine, "Using Research to Answer Practical Questions about Homework," *Educational Psychologist* (vol. 36, 2001).

P. Rosário, J. C. Núñez, G. Vallejo, J. Cunha, T. Nunes, R. Mourão, and R. Pinto, "Does Homework Design Matter? The Role of Homework's Purpose in Student Mathematics Achievement," *Contemporary Educational Psychology* (2015).

U. Trautwein and O. Köller, "The Relationship between Homework and Achievement—Still Much of a Mystery," *Educational Psychology Review*, (no. 2, 2003).

# *Internet References . . .*

### Does Homework Improve Learning?

www.alfiekohn.org/homework-improve-learning/

### The Case For and Against Homework

www.ascd.org/publications/educational-leadership
/mar07/vol64/num06/The-Case-For-and-Against
-Homework.aspx

### What Research Says about the Value of Homework?

www.centerforpubliceducation.org/Main-Menu
/Instruction/What-research-says-about-the-value-of
-homework-At-a-glance

**Selected, Edited, and with Issue Framing Material by:**
Esther S. Chang, *Soka University of America*

# ISSUE

# Is Parental Involvement in Education Critical for Student Achievement?

**YES: Nancy E. Hill and Diana F. Tyson,** from "Parental Involvement in Middle School: A Meta-Analytic Assessment of the Strategies That Promote Achievement," *Developmental Psychology* (2009)

**NO: Cecilia S. S. Cheung and Eva M. Pomerantz,** from "Value Development Underlies the Benefits of Parents' Involvement in Children's Learning: A Longitudinal Investigation in the United States and China," *Journal of Educational Psychology* (2015)

---

## Learning Outcomes

**After reading this issue, you will be able to:**

- Define what parental involvement in education is in each empirical study (i.e., how is parental involvement in education measured).
- Describe why parental involvement in education is promotive of student achievement (i.e., processes underlying the benefits of parental involvement for student achievement).
- Define academic socialization.
- Understand what a meta-analysis is and the advantages of conducting one.
- Understand what a longitudinal study is and the advantages of conducting one.

---

### ISSUE SUMMARY

**YES:** Nancy Hill and Diana Tyson conducted a meta-analysis and found a positive and significant association for most types of parental involvement even after considering publication biases.

**NO:** Cecilia S. S. Cheung and Eva M. Pomerantz demonstrated that the association between parental involvement and students' academic achievement could be explained by the parent–child transmission of values placed on academics.

**A**s evidenced by learning partnership agreements that are mandatory for parents to sign at some charter schools, policy officials and leaders in education, and perhaps many teachers, assume that parental involvement in their children's education is critical for student achievement. Among psychologists, however, the assumption that what parents do for their child's education is directly related to their levels of achievement has been a difficult empirical question. According to traditional theories of social learning, parental involvement in children's education would directly cause higher achievement because children are assumed to be passive recipients of active parental investment. Although intuitively appealing, the research careers of the authors selected for the "Yes" and "No" articles have flourished in search of concrete answers to this sometimes elusive *correlation*.

The main questions posed in the research literature on parental involvement in education reflect the unique contributions of psychological research methods to any practical real-world question: measurement and a critical analysis of study design. Psychology begins the task of problem solving by asking the most basic question related to measurement of the constructs under question. This is one of the contributions of the "Yes" article selected for this issue (i.e., definition of parental involvement in education). Nancy Hill and Diana Tyson effectively review the most valuable ways in which scholars have measured and conceived parental involvement in education, and they provide an excellent list of references for further study. Furthermore, since their studies were on middle school youth, they also provide a summary of how parents are involved during the critical middle school years.

It is relevant to mention, in short, that the results of decades of research has thus far indicated that parental involvement in education consists of many factors, or dimensions, that are useful and valid. Yet, it lacks a universal framework for understanding the various factors across developmental stage and/or culture. Thus, parental involvement in education is not simply volunteering in the classroom or communicating with the teacher. It is multidimensional in nature, meaning that it consists of more than one factor or dimension of experience. For example, parents can be involved at school or at home, and this distinction is rather important because these distinct types of behaviors have unique sources of origin and perhaps different functions since the correlations with academic outcomes are not in the same direction. School-based parental involvement (e.g., volunteering in classrooms, attending book fairs, etc.) has been found to be more consistently associated with higher levels of student achievement whereas home-based parental involvement (e.g., doing homework together, going to the library, etc.) has had mixed results (refer to a review by Pomerantz, Moorman, & Litwack, 2007 for details). The beneficial influence of a particular parenting behavior is also thought to differ depending upon age/development. For example, parents are more likely to be involved by doing homework with elementary school children at home. However, by middle school, parental involvement in getting their child's homework completed may not only decline but may also interfere with youth autonomy (Hill & Taylor, 2009).

Most people perusing the literature on parental involvement in education do not necessarily discriminate the difference between studies that are based upon young children versus studies that use adolescents. Since middle schools are larger and more complicated in structure than the one-classroom in elementary school and because youth in middle school are more autonomous and competent, Hill and Taylor (2009) conducted a meta-analysis to examine any differences in the type and function of parenting involvement during the middle school years exclusively. A meta-analysis is a review of all studies published within a certain period time, which is defined by authors and which investigated both parental involvement and student achievement during the middle school years. While reading how they select their studies, note the study designs of the articles that were included for study. Among their important results is articulating new way of describing parental involvement during the middle school years. They found it necessary to identify this new conceptualization of parental involvement and find that this definition is positively correlated with middle school students' academic achievement.

Given the declines in student achievement during the middle school years, one may believe that more parental involvement in education will stave off any achievement declines or reverse the declining trend altogether. However, previous research has found that "more is not always better"—even among younger children. This is because the parenting climate or emotional tone of parental involvement behaviors may not always be promotive of positive affect and should not assumed to be (Pomerantz et al., 2007). In particular, when one is encouraging more homework among students with authoritarian parents, who tend to be less responsive to the needs of their child, any potential benefits will most likely be lost due to the increases in negative affect during homework time. Thus, there is a need for more sophisticated research designs (not just measurement) if we are inclined to design policy and interventions that attempt collaborations between the school and family.

After psychologists have a good measure of parental involvement that is valid and useful, the next step is to use these measures in a study designed to confirm or disconfirm a hypothesis. For the psychologist, the gold standard for knowing the truth relating to parental involvement is to conduct an experiment. This would involve an attempt to randomly assign parents and students with each other and to create different conditions of the study, which would ideally vary in the control, the type of parental involvement in type, timing, and dose over the observation period. Since this is not feasible or desirable, we critique nonexperimental studies against the gold standard in order to weather our excitement over results that confirm our ideas.

The next best study design, after experimental studies, would be longitudinal studies that follow a sample over time. Longitudinal studies allow us to test whether measurements of our independent variable (i.e., parental involvement in education), which was measured at an earlier time point, is related to increases in the dependent variable (i.e., student achievement), which was measured at a later time point (often after controlling for earlier levels of achievement). This is the study design that is applied by Cheung and Pomerantz

(2015) who studied seventh and eighth graders four times over two years in two countries/cultures. Although not perfect (because it is not a true experiment), this is an extremely sophisticated study design compared to the typical cross-sectional study that relies on one-time point of data within a single culture.

## Reference

E. M. Pomerantz, E. A. Moorman, and S. D. Litwack, "The How, Whom, and Why of Parents' Involvement in Children's Academic Lives: More Is Not Always Better," *Review of Educational Research* (vol. 77, 2007).

# YES

Nancy E. Hill and Diana F. Tyson

# Parental Involvement in Middle School: A Meta-Analytic Assessment of the Strategies That Promote Achievement

Early adolescence and entry into middle school reflect change on multiple levels. The middle school years coincide with key changes in adolescent development, including biological and cognitive growth, social development, and renegotiations of family relationships, especially the parent–adolescent relationship (Adams & Berzonsky, 2003; Grolnick, Price, Beiswenger, & Sauck, 2007; Keating, 2004; Lerner & Steinberg, 2004; Smetana, Campione-Barr, & Daddis, 2004; Steinberg & Silk, 2002). Further, the middle school context reflects a significant change compared to elementary school, including a larger, more bureaucratic system with many more teachers, peers, and curricular choices (Dauber & Epstein, 1989; Eccles & Harold, 1996; Hill & Chao, 2009). In the context of such changes and development, adolescents' academic performance often declines (Barber & Olsen, 2004; Eccles, 2004; Gutman & Midgley, 2000), while at the same time, the long-term implications of achievement for educational and occupational attainment increase (Eccles & Harold, 1993). The confluence of these developmental and contextual changes at early adolescence increases the risk that students may not reach their potential and heightens the need to identify sources of support.

In promoting achievement across elementary and secondary school levels, theories, research, and policies have identified the significant role of families, family–school relations, and parental involvement in education (Fan & Chen, 2001; Hill & Chao, 2009; Seginer, 2006). Indeed, family–school relations and parental involvement in education have been identified as a way to close demographic gaps in achievement and maximize students' potential (Dearing, Kreider, Simpkins, & Weiss, 2006; Hampton, Mumford, & Bond, 1998; Hara, 1998). As such, federal policies like the No Child Left Behind Act (NCLB; 2002) mandate parental involvement in education

and family–school relations across elementary and secondary school levels. Despite consensus about the importance of families and schools working together across developmental stages, extant theories of parental involvement in education have been based on elementary school students and elementary school contexts and do not account for the changes associated with middle school and early adolescent development (Hill & Taylor, 2004; Hill, Tyson, & Bromell, 2009). Indeed, some research has demonstrated that the strength of the relation between parental involvement and achievement declines between elementary and middle schools (e.g., Singh et al., 1995). Whereas some aspects of parental involvement in education may decline in amount or in effectiveness during middle school, like involvement at school (Singh et al., 1995; Stevenson & Baker, 1987), other aspects of involvement that are not accounted for in extant frameworks may increase in significance (Chao, Kanatsu, Stanoff, Padmawidjaja, & Aque, 2009). Therefore, it is imperative to identify the extent to which parental involvement in education is positively related to achievement for middle school students and which types of involvement are most effective.

In the last two decades, the amount of research on parental involvement in education, especially for middle school, has increased exponentially, but it has produced often competing findings. For example, some research has demonstrated that parental involvement in education is positively associated with adolescents' academic outcomes throughout middle and high school (e.g., Catsambis, 2001; Hill et al., 2004). However, other research found that parental involvement is not related to achievement (e.g., Balli, Wedman, & Demo, 1997; Bronstein, Ginsberg, & Herrera, 2005). This growing but disaggregated body of research has used a variety of methods, making it difficult to draw firm conclusions for middle school. Although recent meta-analyses have focused on parental involvement

Hill, Nancy E. and Tyson, Diana F., "Parental Involvement in Middle School: A Meta-Analytic Assessment of the Strategies That Promote Achievement" *Developmental Psychology*, Vol 45(3) May 2009, 740–763. No further reproduction or distribution is permitted without written permission from the American Psychological Association.

(e.g., Fan & Chen, 2001; Jeynes, 2003, 2005), these meta-analyses did not consider the developmental stage of students as a unique factor in their analyses. These studies collapsed across research from prekindergarten through high school. Further, whereas Jeynes (2007)focused on secondary schools, this meta-analysis collapsed across middle and high schools and was limited to urban contexts. Unlike the high school years, when parents have gained experience with supporting more autonomous adolescents and larger, more bureaucratic schools, the middle school years reflect a renegotiation for schools, families, and students. Therefore, identifying the most effective strategies in middle school will guide programs and policies so that they can promote the most effective strategies (Hill et al., 2009). To this end, we conducted a meta-analysis of the existing research on parental involvement in middle school and situate our findings within existing theories and frameworks and within the developmental context of early adolescence. This meta-analysis addressed two broad questions. First, what is the strength of the relation between parental involvement in education and achievement during middle school? Second, which types of involvement have the strongest positive relation with achievement?

## Parental Involvement in Education: Definitions and Frameworks

Although there are numerous definitions of parental involvement in education, we define it as "parents' interactions with schools and with their children to promote academic success" (Hill et al., 2004, p. 1491). This is somewhat broader than the definition articulated in the NCLB, which is "the participation of parents in regular, two-way, and meaningful communication involving student academic learning and other school activities" (No Child Left Behind Act, 2002, §9101). Consistently included in the extant theories, frameworks, and assessments are home-based and school-based involvement strategies (e.g., Kohl, Lengua, McMahon, & the Conduct Problems Prevention Research Group, 2000; Seginer, 2006). Further, such a distinction is useful as it distinguishes policy-relevant realms—home and school. The most widely cited among existing frameworks is Epstein's (1987; Conners & Epstein, 1995; Epstein & Sanders, 2002), which includes *school-based involvement* strategies (e.g., volunteering at school, communication between parents and teachers, and involvement in school governance); *home-based involvement* strategies, including engaging in educational activities at home; school support for parenting (e.g., parent training programs); and involvement between

the school and community agencies. Second, the framework undergirding Comer's (1995) School Development Program has also informed research in this field. Comer's framework also includes *school-based involvement*—such as parent–teacher conferences, volunteering and being present in the school, and participation in school governance—and *home-based involvement*, such as parental reinforcement of learning at home. Finally, Grolnick and Slowiaczek (1994) articulated a three-pronged framework: First, *behavioral involvement* includes both home-based and school-based involvement strategies, such as active connections and communication between home and school, volunteering at school, and assisting with homework. Second, *cognitive–intellectual involvement* reflects home-based involvement and includes parental role in exposing their children to educationally stimulating activities and experiences. Finally, *personal involvement* includes attitudes and expectations about school and education and conveying the enjoyment of learning, which reflects parental socialization around the value and utility of education.

Within an elementary school context, school-based involvement is associated with children's achievement, because such involvement is likely to include visits to the classroom and interactions with children's teachers. Such interactions and exposure increase parents' knowledge about the curriculum, enhance social capital, and increase the effectiveness of involvement at home (Comer, 1995; Epstein, 2001; Hill & Taylor, 2004). Further, interactions between parents and teachers may increase mutual respect and increase teachers' perceptions about how much parents value education (Comer, 1995; Epstein, 2001). However, in middle school, school-based involvement has been shown to change from assisting in the classroom to attendance at school activities (Seginer, 2006). This latter type of school-based involvement is less likely to provide middle school parents with information about pedagogy and classroom content or the opportunity to create mutual respect between parents and teachers. Therefore, its relation with academic outcomes may be weaker.

Home-based involvement has been advocated because it affirms the knowledge and instruction received at school (Comer, 1995), provides assistance and clarification with homework (Cooper, 1989), provides structure for free time and homework time (Fan & Chen, 2001), includes visiting museums and other educational venues (Reynolds & Gill, 1994), and enhances and encourages motivations (Hoover-Dempsey & Sandler, 1995). In addition, as part of home-based involvement, parents can supplement instruction through educationally based, cognitively stimulating activities (Chao, 2000; Grolnick & Slowiaczek, 1994). However, by middle school, many parents feel less able to assist with homework or provide activities and experiences that increase their adolescents' knowledge or achievement (Dauber & Epstein, 1993). Therefore, the amount and type of home-based involvement that is effective may be reduced during the middle school years (Seginer, 2006). Yet another reason why parental involvement might change in significance is that aspects of the middle school structure do not support home- and school-based involvement strategies in the same way as in elementary school.

## Middle School Context and Parental Involvement

The middle school context presents a number of challenges that may undermine parents' ability to be effectively involved in their adolescents' education and work productively with schools (Dauber & Epstein, 1989; Hill & Chao, 2009; Sanders & Epstein, 2000). First, middle schools are large and complex, often making it difficult for parents to figure out how to become effectively involved. Second, middle school teachers instruct a large number of students, making it difficult for teachers to develop and maintain productive relations with the parents of each student. Further, the departmentalization or specialization of instruction by academic subject results in teachers having fewer interactions with individual students (Dornbusch & Glasgow, 1996; Eccles & Harold, 1996). Third, and in conjunction with the previous point, the increase in the number of teachers each student has across subjects makes it difficult for parents to know whom to contact to obtain information about their adolescents' progress. Fourth, the complexity of curricular choices and the often obscured nature of course tracking in middle school further complicate parental involvement (Hill & Taylor, 2004). Not only does the middle school context impact the types of involvement that matter, adolescents' development itself impacts how parents can maintain involvement and its effectiveness (Hill & Chao, 2009).

## Early Adolescent Development and Parental Involvement in Education

The types of parental involvement used and the nature of the relation between parental involvement and achievement may be influenced by characteristics of early adolescent development and family dynamics during adolescence. As has been outlined extensively elsewhere (Adams & Berzonsky, 2003; Lerner & Steinberg, 2004), adolescence is marked by dramatic cognitive development

and the development of conceptualizations of the self as an autonomous, efficacious individual. Cognitively, adolescents have an increased ability to consider multiple dimensions of problems simultaneously when making decisions (Keating, 2004). In addition, adolescents have an increased ability to anticipate the results and consequences of their actions and decisions (Halpern-Felsher & Cauffman, 2001), learn from their successes and failures and apply that knowledge to future problem solving, and strategically coordinate the pursuit of multiple goals (Byrnes, Miller, & Reynolds, 1999).

Each of these abilities enables adolescents to play a more active role in their education and educational decisions. These cognitive changes may increase adolescents' sense of efficacy, ability to make decisions about course selection, and ability to understand how courses and extracurricular activities are related to goals and aspirations in the immediate time frame and for the future and thereby decrease their need for direct parental involvement. That is, more direct involvement strategies, such as school-based involvement and direct homework assistance, may be needed less and thus are less effective (Seginer, 2006). Indeed, students' increased sense of autonomy is associated with their desire to not have their parents visit the school (Stevenson & Baker, 1987). Often parents interpret students' desire for autonomy as a cue to reduce more direct forms of parental involvement, such as home- and school-based involvement (Prescott, Pelton, & Dornbusch, 1986).

In addition to cognitive development, parent-adolescent relationships undergo a transformation and renegotiation during adolescence as they become less hierarchical and are characterized by increased bidirectional communication (Collins & Laursen, 2004; Steinberg & Silk, 2002). Early adolescence is marked by the need for a realignment of roles and expectations as adolescents question their parents' authority (Grolnick et al., 2007; Smetana et al., 2004) and as parents attempt to set boundaries and communicate expectations while promoting healthy independence. Parental influence often becomes more indirect. Parents' beliefs about adolescents' abilities, skills, and potential shape adolescents' own beliefs, which influence their performance (Bleeker & Jacobs, 2004; Jones & Schneider, 2009).

As parental influence becomes more indirect and promotes the use of adolescents' developing decision-making skills, strategies for involvement in education should change as well. For early adolescence, parental involvement may entail communicating parental expectations for education and its value or utility, linking schoolwork to current events, fostering educational and occupational aspirations, discussing learning strategies with children, and making preparations and plans for the future—that is, *academic socialization*. We hypothesize that involvement that scaffolds adolescents' burgeoning decision-making and problem solving skills and elucidates linkages between their schoolwork and future goals may be more strongly linked to achievement in middle school than is home- or school-based involvement. Parental involvement in education that reflects academic socialization allows parents to maintain their involvement while also affirming adolescents' autonomy, independence, and advancing cognitive abilities.

In this meta-analysis, we examine the relative association between three types of parental involvement in education and academic achievement. *Home-based involvement* includes strategies like communication between parents' and children about school, engagement with school work (e.g., homework help), taking children to events and places that foster academic success (i.e., museums, libraries, etc.), and creating a learning environment at home (e.g., making educational materials accessible, such as books, newspapers, educational toys). *School-based involvement* includes visits to school for school events (e.g., PTA meetings, open houses, etc.), participation in school governance, volunteering at school, and communication between parents and school personnel. Finally, *academic socialization* includes communicating parental expectations for education and its value or utility, linking school-work to current events, fostering educational and occupational aspirations, discussing learning strategies with children, and making preparations and plans for the future.

## Ethnic Variations in Parental Involvement in Education

In addition to outlining types of parental involvement strategies, prior research has demonstrated ethnic differences in mean levels of parental involvement strategies (Baker & Stevenson, 1986; Kohl et al., 2000), parents' beliefs about involvement (Lareau, 1987; Lynch & Stein, 1987), and the relations between parental involvement and academic outcomes (e.g., Hill et al., 2004; Hill & Craft, 2003). African Americans, in particular, have had a long and tumultuous history with American schools (Cross, 2003; Spencer, Cross, Harpalani, & Goss, 2003). Whereas African American cultural heritage has placed an emphasis on the value and utility of education, discrimination and bias experienced at school by many African Americans has resulted in a mistrust of school and teachers by many

African American parents (Lareau, 1987; Ogbu, 1978). These historical and contemporary experiences may influence the nature of parental involvement and its influence. This is heightened during adolescence, because it is a time when African American students are grappling with their own ethnic identity (Hughes et al., 2006).

Prior research on ethnic differences in parental involvement has been mixed. Some research found that the relation between involvement and achievement is stronger for African Americans than European Americans (Hill et al., 2004), whereas others found that the relation is weaker (e.g., Seyfried & Chung, 2002). In a meta-analysis across prekindergarten to 12th grade, ethnicity had a negligible effect (Fan & Chen, 2001). Another meta-analysis found that the relation was positive for ethnic minorities (i.e., collapsing across African Americans, Latinos, and Asian Americans), but the strength of the relation was not compared across ethnicity (Jeynes, 2007). Although much has been written about ethnic differences in levels and types of involvement, it is unclear whether to expect the relation between involvement and achievement to vary across ethnicity.

## The Meta-Analysis

The current investigation used meta-analytic techniques to synthesize the results of the existing empirical literature to determine the extent to which parental involvement is positively associated with achievement outcomes in middle school and which types of involvement have the strongest relation. We expect that involvement characterized as academic socialization will have the strongest positive relation with achievement outcomes as it empowers adolescents to act semiautonomously and understand the consequences and purposes of their actions; home-based and school-based involvement will have smaller relations. To assess the empirical evidence of ethnic variations in the relation between parental involvement and achievement, we examined differences between African Americans and European Americans in an exploratory manner.

## Method

### Extant Literature

To limit the potential cohort effects, we restricted our review of the literature to those studies published between 1985 and 2006. The exhaustive search of the extant literature published since 1985 produced 50 empirical reports (or articles). This set of reports represents 127 correlations and 82 beta coefficients for the relation between different types of parent involvement and an array of achievement outcomes. These reports represent three types of studies:

1. Naturalistic longitudinal and cross-sectional studies that included correlations between parental involvement and achievement ($n = 27$). These 27 articles and unpublished data sets represented 32 different samples and 92 separate correlations (see Table 1). Table 2 shows the studies that included partial correlations that controlled for demographic or other variables ($N = 1$). Table 3 shows those studies that were longitudinal in design, which may provide some evidence of the direction of effect ($N = 2$).
2. Studies that reported on the effects of interventions designed to enhance parental involvement ($N = 5$; see Table 4).
3. Articles that reported on data from public-access, nationally representative datasets (e.g., the National Education Longitudinal Study 1988 [NELS-88], the Longitudinal Study of American Youth [LSAY], and the National Longitudinal Survey of Youth [NLSY]; $N = 13$; see Tables 5, 6, and 7).

When multiple articles use the same dataset, they pose the risk of lack of independence and overrepresentation of the data in the meta-analysis. When they provided enough information to calculate an effect size, these effect sizes were averaged using the shifting unit of analysis approach across all effect sizes and included in the meta-analysis. In addition, there were 5 studies that included middle school students and either older or younger students and 1 study that used regression analyses but did not include correlations (see Table 8).

## Literature Search Procedures

To conduct a comprehensive review of the literature, we searched the major databases that catalogue research abstracts. These included PsychInfo, ERIC, Dissertation Abstracts International, and Sociological Abstracts. Due to the paucity of literature focusing solely on parental involvement in middle school as a primary emphasis, extensive hand searches were also conducted for the following journals to identify articles that included parental involvement in education as a secondary focus and thereby might have been missed in the database search. The following journals were hand searched: *American Education Research Journal, Child Development, Developmental Psychology, Journal of Educational Psychology, Journal of Family Psychology, Journal for Research on Adolescence,* and *Review of Education Research.*

The searches were conducted by combining terms reflecting middle school populations with terms reflecting parental involvement in education. The following terms and phrases were used to reflect parental involvement in education: parent involvement, parent-school partnership, parent–school relation*, family–school partnership, family–school involvement, *parental involvement in education, parenting involvement in school, family–school relation*, family–school involvement, and family involvement in education* (the asterisk indicates that all forms of that stem were included; e.g., *relation** includes *relations, relationship,* and *relationships*). The search was later expanded to include terms such as *parent risk factors,* as the initial search demonstrated that many articles examining achievement outcomes in middle school focused on parental influences on non-normative developmental trajectories for middle school students. To identify studies of middle school samples, we used the following search terms: *middle school**, middle school education, *middle school transition, junior high, junior high school*, junior high students, junior high transitions,* and *early adolescence.* We combined each middle school term with a parental involvement term and then examined each study to determine whether an achievement outcome was included. Achievement outcomes included grades, course or class grades, grade point averages (GPA), test scores, and placement in advanced courses.

In addition, descendant searches were conducted on major papers in the field. Using the Social Sciences Citation Index, we located articles that cited seminal articles, such as publications outlining the major theories in the field (e.g., Comer, 1995; Conners & Epstein, 1995; Eccles & Harold, 1996; Epstein, 1987; Epstein & Sanders, 2002; Grolnick & Slowiaczek, 1994). In addition, we conducted descendent searches on papers by authors who appeared in our search at least twice. We conducted backward or ancestry searches by examining the reference lists of all papers that resulted from our search. Further, we identified key researchers in the field (defined as having two or more papers in our database; $n = 11$), contacted them, and requested relevant new work in press and unpublished findings. We received responses with data from 4 of the 11 researchers contacted. To maximize our sample size, we also contacted 4 authors of recent papers that included middle school students combined with other age groups to request correlations for just the middle-school-age sample. We received one response with correlations for the middle-school-age sample for the data reported in Sirin and Rogers-Sirin (2004).

*Table 1*

## Studies Including Bivariate Correlations for the Relationship Between Parent Involvement and Achievement (25 studies, 32 Independent Samples)

| Author (year) and publication type | Sample size | Grade | Type of parent involvement | Category for meta-analysis | Outcome measure | | |
|---|---|---|---|---|---|---|---|
| | | | | | Reading | Math | GPA |
| Baker & Stevenson (1986) Journal article | 40 | 8th | Knowledge of child's schooling (knows the names of homeroom and other teachers, know how child performance compares to previous year, saw last report card) | Academic socialization | | | +.24 |
| | | | Contact w/school (number of conferences attended, contact teacher about specific school problem) | School-based | | | +.10 |
| | | | Homework help (used a strategy to find out about homework assignments, number of strategies used) | Home-based | | | −0.5 |
| | | | General academic strategies (used a tutor, used sanctions in reaction to school grades) | General involvement | | | −.35 |
| | | | High school course selection (selecting college preparatory course for high school) | Academic socialization | | | +.73 |
| Balli et al. (1997) Journal article | 74 | 6th | Homework help | Home-based | Reading achievement: −.24 | | +.60 |
| Bandura et al. (1996) Journal article | 279 | 6th & 7th; cross-sectional | Communicating career aspirations | Academic socialization | | | −.49 |
| Bronstein et al. (2005) Journal article | 77 | 7th | Homework surveillance ("What percentage of the time do you **remind** your child to do his/her homework?") | Home-based | Total battery of Stanford achievement: −.35 | | −.27 |
| | | | Homework surveillance ("What proportion of the time do you **insist** that your child do his/her homework?") | | Total battery of Stanford achievement: −.20 | | |
| Driessen et al. (2005) Journal article | 12,000 | 8th | Homework help<br>Parents ask for information about school matters | Home-based<br>School-based | Language: −.12<br>Language: −.01 | −.21<br>−.02 | |
| | | | Leisure involvement (go to exhibitions, museums) | Home-based | Language: +.13 | +.10 | |
| Garcia Bacete & Ramirez (2001) Journal article | 150 | 7th (in Spain) | Meetings with teacher<br>Attending school events | School-based<br>School-based | | | +.39<br>+.43 |
| Grolnick & Slowiaczek (1994) Journal article | 302 | 6th, 7th, & 8th; cross-sectional | Mother behavioral involvement (attending parent-teacher conferences, open houses, open school nights, and other events) | School-based | | | +.30 |
| | | | Mother personal involvement (knowing what happens at school, when the report card comes out) | Academic socialization | | | +.17 |

*Table 1 (continued)*

| Author (year) and publication type | Sample size | Grade | Type of parent involvement | Category for meta-analysis | Outcome measure | | |
|---|---|---|---|---|---|---|---|
| | | | | | Reading | Math | GPA |
| | | | Mother cognitive involvement (encouraging reading newspapers and books, talking about current events, taking child to the library or museum) | Home-based | | | +.14 |
| | | | Father behavioral involvement | School-based | | | +.19 |
| | | | Father personal involvement | Academic socialization | | | +.17 |
| | | | Father cognitive involvement | Home-based | | | +.14 |
| Grolnick et al. (2000) Journal article | 60 | 6th | School involvement (includes participating in events at child's school) | School-based | +.33 | +.29 | |
| | | | Cognitive involvement (intellectually stimulating activities, going to the library, discussing current events) | Home-based | +.42 | +.42 | |
| | | | Personal involvement (parent knows classmates, knows when report card comes out) | Academic socialization | +.35 | +.27 | |
| Gutman & Eccles (1999) Journal article | 617 | 7th; two waves (longitudinal) | Classroom volunteer | School-based | | | +.14 |
| | | | Open house attendance | School-based | | | +.25 |
| | | | PTA attendance | School-based | | | +.10 |
| Gutman & Midgley (2000) Journal article | 62 | 5th (students pre- and post transition to middle school) | General involvement (checking homework, working as a school program supporter, chaperoning field trips, discussing assignments) | General involvement | | | +.07 |
| Gutman et al. (2002) Journal article | 837 | 7th | Parent school involvement (parent serves on school staff, advocate, decision maker) | School-based | | Standardized test scores: +.07 | +.10 |
| Harris (1990) Dissertation | 76 | 8th | Homework help (estimate of the extent of parental awareness and support of homework, frequency of assignments that requested parent help) | Home-based | Test scores: +.18 Language test scores: −.03 | Test scores: −.02 | |
| | | | Communicating with teacher | School-based | Test scores: −.01 Language test scores: −.28 | Test scores: −.23 | |
| Hawes & Plourde (2005) Journal article | 48 | 6th | General parent involvement (time spent helping with homework or reading, time spent conferencing with teachers) | General involvement | Reading comprehension test: +.13 | | |
| Hughes et al. (2006) Unpublished data | 90 European American | 6th; correlations provided by ethnicity | School involvement | School-based | | | +.19, +.18 |
| | | | Home involvement | Home-based | | | +.26, +.01 |
| | | | Parents' academic expectations | Academic socialization | | | +.31, +.06 |

*Table 1 (continued)*

| Author (year) and publication type | Sample size | Grade | Type of parent involvement | Category for meta-analysis | Reading | Math | GPA |
|---|---|---|---|---|---|---|---|
| Hughes et al. (2006) Unpublished data | 183 African American | | School involvement | School-based | | | +.16, +.17 |
| | | | Home involvement | Home-based | | | −.02, +.12 |
| | | | Parents' academic expectations | Academic socialization | | | +.39, −.11 |
| | 183 Chinese American | | School involvement | School-based | | | −.07, −.31 |
| | | | Home involvement | Home-based | | | +.28, +.26 |
| | | | Parents' academic expectations | Academic socialization | | | +.23, +.10 |
| | 161 Hispanic | | School involvement | School-based | | | +.27, +.11 |
| | | | Home involvement | Home-based | | | −.22, +.12 |
| | | | Parents' academic expectations | Academic socialization | | | +.19, +.03 |
| Jodl et al. (2001) Journal article | 444 | 7th | Academic activity involvement (help with homework, asking how the child did at school) | Home-based | | Academic ability (i.e., "How good is your child in math/how well do you think your child will do in math?") | |
| | | | | | | Mother | +.09 |
| | | | | | | Father | +.13 |
| | | | School involvement (PTA, class trips, etc.) | School-based | | Mother | +.19 |
| | | | | | | Father | +.06 |
| | | | Parents' value of education ("What are the chances your child will do well in junior high, high school, and college?") | Academic socialization | | Mother | +.59 |
| | | | Educational expectations/aspirations for youth ("How far would you like your child to go in school?") | Academic socialization | | Father | +.60 |
| | | | | | | Mother | +.35 |
| | | | | | | Father | +.42 |
| Juang & Silbereisen (2002) Journal article | 641 | 6th (German sample) | Parent involvement (educational encouragement and stimulation, interest in adolescent's schooling) | Academic socialization | | | +.52 |
| Latendresse (2005) Dissertation | 309 | 6th | Parent expectations (parents expect excellence and have high expectations for children) | Academic socialization | | | +.19 |

*Table 1 (continued)*

| Author (year) and publication type | Sample size | Grade | Type of parent involvement | Category for meta-analysis | Outcome measure | | |
|---|---|---|---|---|---|---|---|
| | | | | | Reading | Math | GPA |
| Marchant et al. (2001) Journal article | 230 | 5th & 6th; cross-sectional | Parent values and attitudes about the importance of academic success | Academic socialization | | | +.25 |
| | | | School involvement (attending school events and functions) | School-based | | | +.26 |
| Reynolds & Gill (1994) | 729 | 6th; longitudinal | School involvement (participation in school activities, talks to teacher about child progress, PTA) | School-based | Standardized test scores: +.12 | Standardized test scores: +.11 | |
| Seidman et al. (2003) Journal article | 500 | 6th & 7th; longitudinal | Going to the museum, zoo | Home-based | +.10 | | +.07 |
| | | | Leisure time involvement (participating in social, cultural, and athletic events) | Home-based | | +.10 | |
| Seyfried & Chung (2002) Journal article | 372 European American | 5th grade | Expectations/career aspirations | Academic socialization | | | +.53 |
| | 195 African American | | | | | | +.29 |
| Sirin & Rogers-Sirin (2004) Journal article | 75 | 7th & 8th; cross-sectional | Communicating the value of education; obtained through email | Academic socialization | | | +.06[a] |
| Useem (1992) Journal article | 88 | 6th | Parent knowledge of the mathematics tracking system | Academic socialization | | | +.56 |
| | | | Parent integration (involvement in volunteer activities at the school or informal school networks) | School-based | | | +.57 |
| | | | Parent intervention (acting on behalf of child with teachers to change or "customize" the educational experience) | Academic socialization | | | +.43 |
| Xu & Corno (2003) Journal article | 118 | 6th | Help with homework | Home-based | | | −.03 |

[a] Correlation obtained from S. R. Sirin via a separate analysis conduted for 7th and 8th grade students only (article collapses across middle and high school).

*Table 2*

### Studies Estimating the Effect of Parent Involvement Using Partial Correlations

| Author (year) and publication type | Sample size | Grade | Type of parent involvement | Category for meta-analysis | Outcome measure | Correlation |
|---|---|---|---|---|---|---|
| Kim (2002) Journal article | 245 Korean adolescents | 6th–12th | General parent involvement | General involvement | GPA | Partial correlations controlling for age and parent level of education: $+.16, +.25$ |

*Note.* GPA = grade point average.

*Criteria for inclusion.* The criteria for inclusion of an article in this meta-analysis were threefold. First, the report had to include a measure of parental involvement and academic achievement. Because the focus of this meta-analysis was the relation between parental practices and academic outcomes, we limited the set of research reports to those that measured academic outcomes. Second, the identified research reports needed to be based on middle school samples, which are typically defined as Grades 6 through 8. However, in an attempt to comprehensively account for middle school populations, we used explicit identification as well. For example, when fifth or ninth grade students were included in a study and the authors identified the population as middle school students, these reports were included (e.g., Gutman & Midgley, 2000; Marchant, Paulson, & Rothlisberg, 2001). Third, the report needed to include correlations (Pearson's $r$), $d$ indexes, or sufficient information to calculate an estimate of the effect size. This included means and standard deviations to calculate the $d$ index as outlined by Rosenthal (1991). Studies that used a wide variety of statistical analyses were included, such as studies that used structural equation

*Table 3*

### Studies Estimating the Long-Term Effect of Parent Involvement (Longitudinal Only)

| Author (year) and publication type | Sample size | Grade | Type of parent involvement | Category for meta-analysis | Outcome measure Reading | Math | GPA |
|---|---|---|---|---|---|---|---|
| Hill et al. (2004) Journal article | 463 | 7th grade students tested at four waves (7th grade parent involvement correlated with 9th grade scores) | General involvement | General involvement | | | |
| | | | | Mother report | Grade: +.13 Standard test: +.11 | Grade: +.09 Standard test: −.00 | |
| | | | | Student report | Grade: +.06 Standard test: +.04 | Grade: +.11 Standard test: −.01 | |
| | | | | Teacher report | Grade: +.08 Standard test: +.14 | Grade: +.06 Standard test: +.14 | |
| Melby & Conger(1996) Journal article | 347 | 7th grade students tested at four waves | General involvement (setting standards for behavior, such as completing schoolwork) | General involvement | | | +.22 |
| | | 8th grade parent involvement predicting11th grade GPA | | | | | +.27 |

*Note.* GPA = grade point average.

*Table 4*

**Interventions**

| Author (year) and publication type | Sample size | | Grade | Type of parent intervention | Category for meta-analysis | Outcome measure | Pearson's $r$[a] |
| --- | --- | --- | --- | --- | --- | --- | --- |
| | Treatment | Control | | | | | |
| Balli et. al (1998) Journal article | 22 | 25 | 6th | Epstein's TIPS intervention (Epstein et al., 1995) used in math classes | Home-based | 40-item mathematics posttest | $r = .29$ |
| Keisner (1997) Dissertation | 11 | 12 | 6th–8th | Parents received instruction for supervising math homework | Home-based | Math achievement test | $r = -.06$ |
| | | | | | | Cumulative math achievement test | $r = -.26$ |
| | | | | | | Class grades | $r = -.67$ |
| Rillero & Helgeson (1995) Conference presentation | 101 | 99 | 6th | Quasi-experimental study: SPLASH(Student-Parent Laboratories Achieving Science at Home) intervention where students were given homework assignments that required parent participation | Home-based | Science homework | None provided; results reported as significant, entered as $r = .20$[b] |
| Tamayo (1992) Dissertation | 16 | 15 | 7th | Parents received instruction for monitoring math homework; control group parents received no instruction | Home-based | Math grade | $r = -.07$ |
| | | | | | | Homework Stanford achievement test | $r = -.06$ $r = -.08$ |
| Van Voorhis (2003) Journal article | 146 | 107 | 6th & 8th | TIPS intervention (Epstein et al.,1995) used in science classes | Home-based | Homework grades | $r = .15$ |
| | | | | | | Science class grades | $r = .15$ |

[a] For consistency of data presentation, the $d$ indexes for the quasi-experimental studies have been converted to Pearson's $rs$. [b] Study reported the effect size as significant but did not provide an effect size. Therefore, we used the formula $r = Z/\sqrt{N}$, where $Z = 1.96$ and $N$ is the sample size for the study.

modeling, hierarchical linear modeling, regression, and other statistical techniques, provided that the article also included information from which effect sizes could be calculated. Reports were not included in the meta-analysis if they did not include such information and it was not available from the author. However, their findings and the directions of effects were coded to determine whether they provided additional support to the general results of the meta-analysis.

*Criteria for exclusion.* We eliminated studies that used a broad conceptualization of parental involvement, such as reports that included assessments of general monitoring,

parenting styles (i.e., authoritative vs. authoritarian), or discipline in their conceptualization of parental involvement, as this meta-analysis focused on the specific strategies parents use to foster achievement on their own and in collaboration with school. In addition, one central goal of this meta-analysis was to determine whether parental involvement in education, as defined by the prevailing theories of parental involvement and family-school relations, was related to achievement among middle school students. Studies were also eliminated if they combined middle-school-age students with other age groups, as the focus of this meta-analysis was on early

*Table 5*

### Studies Using the National Education Longitudinal Study (NELS)

| Author (year) and publication type | Sample characteristics | Modeling technique | Predictor variables | Outcome variable | Regression coefficient | Size and significance |
|---|---|---|---|---|---|---|
| Desimone (1999)[a] Journal article | 19,386 NELS 8th grade students; 13,483 European American[b] | Multiple regression | Discussion with child about high school | GPA | $\beta = .03$ | $p = .050$ |
| | | | Talk w/parents about post-high school plans | | $\beta = .05$ | $p = .001$ |
| | | | Volunteering or fundraising | | $\beta = .11$ | $p = .001$ |
| | | | Rules about homework, GPA, and chores | | $\beta = -.11$ | $p = .001$ |
| | | | PTO involvement | | $\beta = .08$ | $p = .001$ |
| | | | Parent attends PTO meetings | | $\beta = .00$ | $ns$ |
| | | | Rules about TV, friends, & chores | | $\beta = .03$ | $p = .001$ |
| | | | Parents check homework | | $\beta = -.06$ | $p = .001$ |
| | | | Contact school about academics | | $\beta = -.19$ | $p = .001$ |
| | | | Discussion with parents about school | | $\beta = .18$ | $p = .001$ |
| | | | Talk with father about planning high school programs | | $\beta = .02$ | $ns$ |
| | | | Social capital: knowing parents of child's friends | | $\beta = .03$ | $p = .001$ |
| | 2,334 African American | | Discussion with child about high school | | $\beta = -.06$ | $p = .057$ |
| | | | Talk w/parents about post-high school plans | | $\beta = .05$ | $p = .030$ |
| | | | Volunteering or fundraising | | $\beta = .03$ | $ns$ |
| | | | Rules about homework, GPA, and chores | | $\beta = -.06$ | $ns$ |
| | | | PTO involvement | | $\beta = .30$ | $p = .001$ |
| | | | Parent attends PTO meetings | | $\beta = -.09$ | $ns$ |
| | | | Rules about TV, friends, and chores | | $\beta = .05$ | $p = .017$ |
| | | | Parents check homework | | $\beta = -.09$ | $p = .001$ |
| | | | Contact school about academics | | $\beta = -.05$ | $p = .005$ |
| | | | Discussion with parents about school | | $\beta = .08$ | $p = .001$ |
| | | | Talk with father about planning high school programs | | $\beta = .07$ | $p = .002$ |
| | | | Social capital: knowing parents of child's friends | | $\beta = .02$ | $p = .007$ |
| | 2,368 Hispanic | | Discussion with child about high school | | $\beta = -.00$ | $ns$ |
| | | | Talk w/parents about post-high school plans | | $\beta = .02$ | $ns$ |
| | | | Volunteering or fundraising | | $\beta = -.04$ | $ns$ |
| | | | Rules about homework, GPA, and chores | | $\beta = .00$ | $ns$ |
| | | | PTO involvement | | $\beta = .16$ | $p = .051$ |
| | | | Parent attends PTO meetings | | $\beta = -.02$ | $ns$ |
| | | | Rules about TV, friends, and chores | | $\beta = .05$ | $p = .013$ |
| | | | Parents check homework | | $\beta = -.06$ | $p = .001$ |
| | | | Contact school about academics | | $\beta = -.12$ | $p = .001$ |
| | | | Discussion with parents about school | | $\beta = .19$ | $p = .001$ |
| | | | Talk with father about planning high school programs | | $\beta = .03$ | $ns$ |
| | | | Social capital: knowing parents of child's friends | | $\beta = -.00$ | $ns$ |
| | 1,201 Asian | | Discussion with child about high school | | $\beta = -.06$ | $ns$ |
| | | | Talk w/parents about post-high school plans | | $\beta = -.04$ | $ns$ |
| | | | Volunteering or fundraising | | $\beta = .05$ | $ns$ |
| | | | Rules about homework, GPA, and chores | | $\beta = .12$ | $p = .029$ |
| | | | PTO involvement | | $\beta = -.04$ | $ns$ |
| | | | Parent attends PTO meetings | | $\beta = .10$ | $ns$ |
| | | | Rules about TV, friends, and chores | | $\beta = .05$ | $ns$ |
| | | | Parents check homework | | $\beta = -.09$ | $p = .001$ |
| | | | Contact school about academics | | $\beta = -.08$ | $p = .005$ |
| | | | Discussion with parents about school | | $\beta = .08$ | $p = .010$ |
| | | | Talk with father about planning high school programs | | $\beta = .09$ | $p = .045$ |
| | | | Social capital: knowing parents of child's friends | | $\beta = -.03$ | $p = .015$ |

*Table 5 (continued)*

| Author (year) and publication type | Sample characteristics | Modeling technique | Predictor variables | Outcome variable | Regression coefficient | Size and significance |
|---|---|---|---|---|---|---|
| Hao & Bonstead-Bruns (1998)Journal article | 25,000 NELS 8th grade students | HLM | Parent expectations for schooling | HLM estimate<br>Math<br>Reading<br>GPA | <br>3.92<br>3.74<br>0.33 | <br>$p < .01$<br>$p < .01$<br>$p < .01$ |
| Kelly (2004) Journal article | 13,548 NELS (Parent involvement in 8th grade predicting math track placement in 9th grade) | Logit models | Block One<br>  Parental education<br>  Parental income<br>  Parental occupation<br><br>Block Two<br>  Skipped a grade<br>  Held back a grade<br>  Parent decides which courses student takes<br>  Parent requested current math course<br>  Number of times parent contacted school about academic program<br>  Neutral contact with school (volunteer, fundraising)<br>  Involvement in PTO activities<br>  Discussion about school<br>  Talking about school<br>  Parent knows parents of student's friends | Math track placement | <br><br><br><br><br>0.27<br>−0.32<br>0.0074<br>0.42<br>−0.049<br><br>−0.15<br><br>0.11<br>0.021<br>0.029<br>−0.0037 | <br><br><br><br><br><br>$p < .001$<br><br>$p < .05$<br><br><br>$p < .01$<br><br>$p < .005$ |
| McNeal (1999)[c] Journal article | 11,401 NELS(8th grade parent involvement predicting achievement in 10th grade) | Not specified | (Controlling for GPA, hours worked, hours of homework, having been retained a grade in school, and gender)<br>Black<br>Hispanic<br>Asian<br>SES<br>Base-achievement<br>Single-headed household<br>Social capital<br>  Parent–child discussion<br>  PTO involvement<br>  Monitoring<br>  Educational support strategies | | <br><br><br><br><br><br><br><br>0.150<br>−0.115<br>−0.071<br>−0.014 | <br><br><br><br><br><br><br><br>$p < .01$<br>$p < .01$<br>$p < .10$ |
| Muller (1995) Journal article | 13,881 NELS students (analysis of 8th grade test scores) | Hierarchical multiple regression | Block One<br>Family income, parents' highest education, gender, single mother,mother/stepfather, Asian American,Hispanic, African American, Catholic,other religious school, independent private, urban, suburban, 8th grade math grades, part-time, not in labor force, number of children home<br>Block Two<br>Talk about school experiences<br>Talk about high school program w/father<br>Talk about high school program w/mother<br>Parents check homework<br>Parents restrict TV<br>Child enrolled in extra music class<br>Time unsupervised after school<br>Number of friends' parents know<br>PTO participation<br>Parents contact school<br>Parent volunteers at school | 8th grade mathematics achievement test score | <br><br><br><br><br><br><br><br><br>$b = -1.053$<br><br><br><br><br>$b = -0.231$<br>$b = -0.653$<br>$b = 0.058$ | <br><br><br><br><br><br><br><br><br>$p < .001$<br><br><br><br><br>$p < .01$<br>$p < .001$<br>ns |

*Table 5 (continued)*

| Author (year) and publication type | Sample characteristics | Modeling technique | Predictor variables | Outcome variable | Regression coefficient | Size and significance |
|---|---|---|---|---|---|---|
| Peng & Wright (1994) Journal article | 24,599 NELS (overlap: includes 8th–10th grade) | Multiple regression | Asian vs. Hispanic | Achievement test scores | | |
| | | | Asian vs. Black | | | |
| | | | Asian vs. White | | | |
| | | | Asian vs. Indian | | | |
| | | | School control | | | |
| | | | Parental education | | | |
| | | | Family income | | | |
| | | | Family composition | | | |
| | | | Homework | | | |
| | | | Television | | | |
| | | | Educational activity | | | |
| | | | Outside classes | | | |
| | | | Educational aspirations | | $\beta = .25$ | $p < .01$ |
| | | | Discuss school | | $\beta = -.03$ | $p < .01$ |
| | | | Assist in homework | | $\beta = -.17$ | $p < .01$ |
| Sui-Chi & Willms (1996) Journal article | 25,000 NELS (8th grade) | Hierarchical linear modeling | Adjusted school mean SES, family and student background, parent involvement factors | Achievement test scores | | |
| | | | Home discussion (talks with parents, discusses school activities) | Reading Math | $\beta = .124$ $\beta = .124$ | $p < .01$ $p < .01$ |
| | | | Home supervision (monitor homework, limits TV time, home after school) | Reading Math | $\beta = .009$ $\beta = .033$ | ns $p < .01$ |
| | | | School communication (school contacts parents, parents contact school) | Reading Math | $\beta = -.051$ $\beta = -.056$ | $p < .01$ $p < .01$ |
| | | | School participation (volunteer at school, PTO) | Reading Math | $\beta = .030$ $\beta = .026$ | $p < .01$ $p < .01$ |

*Note.* GPA = grade point average; PTO = parent-teacher organization; HLM = hierarchical linear modeling; SES = socioeconomic status. [a] Actual report examines GPA, reading, and math scores as a function of ethnicity and SES in multiple regressions. For the purposes of this analysis, only GPA is reported by ethnicity. [b] Results are presented by ethnicity and SES in the article. [c] Actual report also includes a breakdown by ethnicity. However, for the purposes of this report, we used results that were collapsed across ethnic groups.

adolescence and middle school as a unique developmental stage and context. Finally, studies were eliminated that demonstrated a lack of overall face validity (e.g., indicated that their focus was on parental involvement but did not assess parental involvement as defined by the prevailing theories). These criteria for inclusion resulted in 50 articles, reflecting 127 separate correlations.

## Coding and Information Retrieved From Research Reports

*Coding.* The coding scheme was developed to extract information about the characteristics of the sample, type of publication, theories used, conceptualization and measurement of parental involvement and academic outcomes, and results (i.e., effect sizes, information to calculate effect

sizes, and general magnitude and direction of the relation between parental involvement and academic outcomes). Each research report was coded by two coders. The primary coder was a developmental psychology graduate student with expertise in parental involvement in education, academic motivation, and academic achievement. The secondary coder was an advanced undergraduate research assistant who received extensive training on the theories and research related to parental involvement in education and the goals of the meta-analysis. After retrieving abstracts from the databases, each coder examined each abstract to determine its relevance. If either coder deemed an abstract was relevant, the full article was retrieved for further coding. Research reports received through communications with key researchers in the field were also included in this round of coding. Both coders

*Table 6*

#### Studies Using National Education Longitudinal Study (NELS) and Structural Equation Modeling

| Author (year) and publication type | Sample characteristics | Modeling technique | Predictor variables | Outcome variable | Regression coefficient | Size and significance |
|---|---|---|---|---|---|---|
| Keith et al. (1993) Journal article | 21,814 NELS 8th grade students | SEM | Parent involvement composite | GPA | $\beta = .29$ | Not mentioned |
| Keith & Lichtman (1994) Journal article | 1,714 NELS Mexican American 8th grade students | SEM | Parent involvement composite | Overall GPA<br>Reading<br>Math<br>Science<br>Social studies | $\beta = .12$<br>$\beta = .12$<br>$\beta = .08$<br>$\beta = .10$<br>$\beta = .12$ | $p < .05$<br>$p < .05$<br>$p < .05$<br>$p < .05$<br>$p < .05$ |
| Singh et al. (1995) Journal article | 25,000 NELS 8th grade students | SEM | Parent aspirations<br>Participation at school<br>Home environment | GPA | $\beta = .28$<br>$\beta = -.02$<br>$\beta = -.10$ | Not mentioned |

*Note.* SEM = structural equation modeling; GPA = grade point average.

extracted information from each report selected for inclusion. Any discrepancies between coders were discussed until consensus was reached. If agreement could not be reached, the disagreement was resolved by Nancy E. Hill. This method of discussing discrepancies until consensus is reached, as a way of assuring intercoder reliability, is consistent with the meta-analysis methodology presented in Rosenthal (1991). This meta-analysis focused on three types of involvement (home-based involvement, school-based involvement, and academic socialization). Studies were coded for these types of involvement. In addition, several studies created measures of parent involvement that combined several types of involvement into a single construct. The code "general involvement" was used when the report did not specify a specific type of involvement or used a unidimensional construct of parental involvement. In the meta-analysis, the construct *general involvement* was created for all reports by combining across all indicators of involvement.

## Information Retrieved from Research Reports

The main information coded for each article included characteristics of the publication, the independent variables, the sample characteristics, and the outcomes measures of interest.

*Characteristics of the publication.* First, the authors of the research report and the date of publication were recorded. Next, information about the type of publication or report was recorded. These included peer-reviewed journal articles, dissertations, private reports (i.e., the

author provided correlations not originally included in a publication), government reports, conference papers, and unpublished datasets. In addition, the type of study was coded; that is, whether the study was a naturalistic correlational study, controlled for a third variable, used advanced statistics and did not include correlations (i.e., structural equation modeling, hierarchical linear modeling), was an intervention trial, or used public-access datasets.

*Characteristics of the sample.* Demographic information about samples was gathered and coded, including sample size, ethnic or racial background of the sample, gender of the target child, specific grade levels or ages of adolescents included in the study, socioeconomic status of the families (including parental education level), and any labels that were given to the samples (e.g., "at risk," "exceptional students").

*Characteristics of the independent variables.* Studies were coded and correlations gathered for each type of involvement, along with the effect size for the overall relation between parental involvement and achievement (i.e., general involvement). As mentioned previously, if the research report did not allow for distinctions between the types of involvement, they were coded as having an assessment of general parental involvement.

*Characteristics of the dependent variables.* The main outcome of interest for this meta-analysis was academic achievement, conceptualized as class grades, GPA, standardized test scores, track placement, and other tests designed to measure achievement.

*Information to calculate an effect size.* Effect sizes were ascertained from each research report for each relation

*Table 7*

### National Datasets Other Than the National Education Longitudinal Study (NELS)

| Author (year) and publication type | Sample characteristics | Modeling technique | Predictor variables[a] | Outcome variable | Regression coefficient | Size and significance |
|---|---|---|---|---|---|---|
| Eamon (2005) Journal article | 388 Latino youth from the NLSY, ages 10–14 | Hierarchical multiple regression | Block 1 Ethnicity, gender, age, | Reading achievement | β = .09 | p < .05 |
| | | | Block 2 Youth's English language problem, mother's age at 1st birth, mother's years of education, mother's AFQT score, no English language problem, mother born in U.S., average adult–child ratio, proportion of youth's lives poor Block Three School environment, neighborhood quality Block Four Cognitive stimulation, parent-youth conflict, *academic involvement* | Math achievement | β = .11 | p < .05 |
| Ma (1999) Journal article | 3,116 students from the LSAY (longitudinal analysis, 7th–12th grade) | Logistic survival analysis/event history analysis | *Parent expectations* *Parent college planning* *Volunteering* | Participation in advanced math from Grades 8–12 | [b]Parent expectations and college planning linked to increased achievement. [b]Students of parents who volunteer were 9 times more likely to take advanced mathematics in Grade 12. | |
| Shumow & Miller (2001) Journal article | 1,670 seventh and 8th grade students from the LSAY[c] | Hierarchical multiple regression | Block 1 Parent gender, child gender, pasts school adjustment, parent education level | | | |
| | | | Block 2 *Parent involvement at home* (parental assistance with homework including writing, mathematics, and special projects) | GPA Achievement test scores | β = −.10 β = −.14 | p < .001 p < .001 |
| | | | *Parent involvement at school* (school visits, level of parent-teacher organization membership, attentiveness to school issues) | GPA Achievement test scores | β = .05 β = .02 | p < .01 ns |

*Note.* NLSY = National Longitudinal Survey of Youth; LSAY = Longitudinal Study of Adolescent Youth; GPA = grade point average; AFQT = Armed Forces Qualification Test Score. [a]Predictor variables in italics are the parent involvement variables; regression coefficients for each parent involvement predictor available are listed. [b] No effect size reported. [c] 11.3% African American; 3.9% Asian American; 10.3% Hispanic American; 67.7% Caucasian American.

*Table 8*

### Studies Including Bivariate Correlations for the Relationship Between Parent Involvement and Achievement Where There Is an Age-Group Overlap

| Author (year) and publication type | Sample size | Grade | Type of parent involvement | Category for meta-analysis | Outcome measure | Correlation |
|---|---|---|---|---|---|---|
| Deutscher & Ibe (n.d.) Web-based article | 400 | 7th–11th | Volunteering at school | School-based | California Standards Test | |
| | | | | | English | + .19 |
| | | | | | Math | + .23 |
| Pelegrina et al. (2003) Journal article | 323 | Adolescents, 11–15 years old | Reading school newsletter | Home-based | Math | − .29 |
| | | | Checking student planner | Home-based | Math | + .28 |
| | | | Grolnick & Slowiaczek (1994): Parent involvement scale, combined as general involvement | General involvement | GPA (math, language, and science) | + .29 |
| Salazar et al. (2001) Journal article | 400 | 7th–12th | Parent involvement (general) | General involvement | Student involvement (measure of effort, persistence, and interest in various subjects) | + .28 |
| Shumow & Lomax (2002) Journal article | 929 students (677 mothers, 322 fathers) | 10-to 17-year-old students from the Survey of Parents and Children (1990) | Parent involvement (attending events and activities, talking to teachers, attending PTA meetings) | School-based | GPA (overall) | + .21 |
| Stevenson & Baker (1987) Journal article | 179 | 5–17 years old: 5–8, 21.2% 9–11, 25.8% 12–14, 26.2% 15–17, 26.8% | Parental involvement in school activities (teacher report of the extent to which parents participate in PTO and conferences) | School-based | GPA European Americans | + .21 |
| | | | | | GPA African Americans | + .24 |
| | | | | | GPA Latinos | + .16 |
| | | | | | Child performance (i.e.how well is the student performing relative to his/her ability, rated on as cale from 1 to 5) | + .34 |

*Note.* GPA = grade point average; PTO = parent–teacher organization.

between a type of parental involvement and the outcomes. A single article could provide more than one effect size if multiple dimensions of parental involvement or multiple outcomes were included. If effect sizes were not included in the research report, information that could be used to calculate an effect size was gathered and input into the Comprehensive Meta-Analysis program (CMA; Version 2.0; Biostat, Englewood, NJ) to calculate the appropriate effect size (e.g., correlations and Cohen's $d$ index). In calculating the effect size, we incorporated the shifting unit of analysis approach to account for independence assumptions among the variables. According to this approach, all study effect sizes are coded as independent events (Cooper, 1998). Then, when the overall result for the meta-analysis was generated, the effect sizes were weighted in CMA so that each study contributed to the overall finding on the basis of its sample size and other characteristics. The shifting unit of analysis approach takes into account the fact that one study can contribute multiple effect sizes (Cooper, 1998). For example, Marchant et al. (2001) contributed two effect sizes from the same sample: one for the relationship between academic socialization and GPA and one for the relationship between school involvement and GPA. As such, the shifting unit of analysis approach takes the average of these correlations and contributes one effect size for the purposes of examining the relation between general parental involvement and achievement. However, when conducting moderator analyses, the study effect sizes are only examined across the separate categories of the moderator (Cooper, 1998). When analyses of each type of involvement are considered separately, this approach counts one effect size per category. Thus, in the case of Marchant et al. (2001), when the impact of different forms of parent involvement is examined, each of the two correlations counts independently in the analysis.

## Data Integration and Meta-Analysis Plan

We used meta-analytic techniques to calculate the relations between parental involvement and achievement and the 95% confidence interval. A random effects model was used, which extrapolates to the entire possible pool of studies that may potentially examine the relation between parent involvement and achievement. Thus, random effects models make the current meta-analysis generalizable to all possible studies. This is important because it attempts to account for unpublished studies or studies not published in peer-reviewed journals and book chapters. In addition to determining whether the relation between parental involvement and achievement was significantly different from zero, we examined the heterogeneity of the distribution

of the effect sizes using the $Q$ statistic (Rosenthal, 1991). Heterogeneity may be due to the inclusion of outliers, multiple underlying dimensions within the distribution, or sampling error. We used the significance of the $Q_w$ to determine the appropriateness of conducting the moderator analyses. We conducted moderator analyses using meta-analytic strategies to compare the strength of the relations between parental involvement and achievement across the three types of involvement (i.e., school-based, home-based, and academic socialization), which were our planned comparisons. The $Q_B$ statistic was used to determine whether the groups of effect sizes for each type of parental involvement differed from each other. Due to potential violations of independence at the sample and item level, studies that used public-access datasets were grouped together. These studies did not include correlation matrices, likely due to the large sample sizes. Rather, authors used a variety of modeling techniques (i.e., multiple and hierarchical regression) to examine the relation between parent involvement and achievement. We examined and reported the range of the betas for these studies, which included an array of control variables in addition to parent involvement items. Finally, we conducted exploratory meta-analyses to examine variations in the relation between parental involvement and achievement between African Americans and European Americans.

## Results

### Overall Relation Between General Parental Involvement and Achievement

Overall, the meta-analysis of the correlational studies demonstrated a positive relation between general parental involvement and achievement in middle school. The correlations ranged from $-.49$ to $.73$; the average weighted correlation across the 32 independent samples was $r = .18$, 95% confidence interval (CI) $= .12, .24, Q(31) = 1,581.10, p < .0001$. . . . Because the confidence interval does not include zero, we concluded that the relation between general parental involvement and academic achievement is positive and significantly different from zero. However, due to the size and the significance of the $Q$ statistic, which is an assessment of the heterogeneity of the distribution of correlations, there is likely more than one underlying construct of parental involvement with differing associations with academic outcomes.

When a meta-analysis is conducted, one common concern is publication bias. That is, the field often has a bias against publishing null results, which may render a meta-analysis based on published studies biased in favor

*Table 9*

**Moderator Analyses: Examining the Correlation Between Parent Involvement and Academic Achievement**

| Analysis | k | r | 95% CI Low estimate | 95% CI High estimate | $Q_w$ |
|---|---|---|---|---|---|
| Overall | 32 | .04** (.18) | .04 (.12) | .05 (.24) | 1,581.10** |
| Moderators | | | | | $Q_b$ |
| Type of parent involvement | | | | | 1,206.92** (38.10)** |
| School-based | 21 | .19** | .10 | .21 | |
| Home-based | 19 | .03, ns | −.02 | .11 | |
| Academic socialization | 16 | .39** | .26 | .44 | |
| Type of home-based involvement | | | | | 937.81** (7.61)* |
| Help with homework | 6 | −.11** | −.04 | −.25 | |
| Activities at home | 5 | .12** | .05 | .19 | |
| Ethnicity | | | | | 32.67** (1.80), ns |
| African American | 7 | .11** | .05 | .17 | |
| European American | 11 | .19** | .09 | .29 | |

*Note.* Random effects Q values and point estimates are presented in parentheses. CI = confidence interval.
$*p < .005.$ $**p < .0001.$

of statistical significance. To prevent this, we attempted to obtain unpublished data from key researchers in the field. However, this is not always possible. To obtain an estimate of the publication bias, the "trim and fill" technique was used to impute potentially missing studies (Duval, 2005; Taylor & Tweedie, 2000). The trim and fill technique is based on the assumption that the full set of possible studies on a topic will be distributed symmetrically around a true mean. To estimate the number of plausibly missing studies, the trim and fill method "trims" the outlying studies that do not have a counterpart on the other side of the mean. The mean effect is recalculated, often resulting in a more conservative effect size; the outlying studies are returned, and their counterparts are estimated based on the new mean level effect size. Using this method, we estimated that 11 studies were potentially missing. These imputed studies were each below the mean and had a negative correlation between parental involvement and achievement.

Next, we conducted moderator analyses to determine whether the strength of the relation between parental involvement and achievement varied among the three types of involvement.

## Are All Types of Involvement Equally Effective?

All but six samples provided separate correlations for specific types of parental involvement (i.e., they only included assessments of general forms of parental involvement or collapsed across the different types of involvement). To determine the extent to which each type of involvement was similarly related to achievement, we first examined whether the simple relation between each type of involvement and achievement was significantly different from zero. Second, we compared the magnitudes of the relations across type of involvement using the $Q_B$ statistic to determine whether one type of involvement was more strongly related to achievement than another.

Average weighted correlations between parental involvement and achievement were positive and significantly different from zero for school-based involvement and academic socialization (See Table 9). For home-based involvement, the relation was not significant. The 95% CI included zero, indicating that we could not rule out that the relation between home-based involvement and achievement was not significantly different from zero.

In comparing the strength of the relations across types of parental involvement, we found that the average weighted correlation for each type of involvement and achievement was significantly different, $Q_B(2) = 38.10$, $p < .0001$. Three planned contrasts were conducted to examine the differences between types of involvement. These included a comparison between academic socialization and home-based involvement, between academic socialization and school-based involvement, and between home- and school-based involvement. Academic socialization was more strongly related to achievement than was home-based involvement. The average weighted correlation between academic socialization and achievement and between home-based involvement and achievement were $r = .39$ and $.03$, respectively; $Q_B(1) = 36.68, p < .0001$. For the comparison between academic socialization and school-based involvement and their relation to achievement outcomes, the relation was also stronger for academic socialization. Whereas the average weighted correlation for academic socialization and achievement was $.39$, it was $.19$ for school-based involvement and achievement, $Q_B(1) = 13.30, p < .0001$. Finally, the average weighted correlation between school-based involvement and achievement was stronger than the average weighted correlation between home-based involvement and achievement, $Q_B(1) = 12.30, p < .0001$. In summary, parental involvement in education is positively associated with academic outcomes during middle school. Further, among the types of parental involvement, academic socialization emerged as a critical component of parental involvement in middle school that had the strongest positive relation with achievement.

As further evidence of the differences in the strength of the relations between the types of involvement and achievement, the range of the beta weights were examined for the studies using the public-access dataset (e.g., NELS-88, NLSY, LSAY) that could not be included in the meta-analysis. Indeed, the examination of the range suggests that the relation is stronger and more positive for academic socialization (betas ranged from $.00$ to $.42$ for studies using the NELS-88 and $.11$ for the study using the NLSY), compared to school-based involvement (betas ranged from $-.06$ to $.11$ for studies using the NELS-88 and $-.02$ to $.05$ for studies using the LSAY) and home-based involvement (betas ranged from $-.17$ to $.08$ for studies using the NELS-88 and $-.14$ to $-.11$ for studies using the LSAY).

The relation between home-based involvement and achievement was not significant, and it was weaker than the relation between other types of involvement and achievement. The $Q$ statistics for home-based involvement suggest that there may be subtypes of home involvement. Because prior research had suggested that home-based involvement should be positively related to achievement, we attempted to identify which types of home involvement were positively related to achievement and whether some types of involvement had a negative relation.

## Are There Subtypes of Home Involvement?

To examine potential multidimensionality among studies of home-based involvement, we examined the types of home-based involvement that were assessed. Prior research suggested that helping with homework is the most controversial type of home-based involvement. Homework help has been shown to both accelerate and interfere with achievement (Cooper, 1989, 2007; Wolf, 1979). The negative relation may be due to parental interference with students' autonomy, to excessive parental pressure, or to differences between parents and schools in how they present the material. Further, help with homework may be elicited by poor school performance, also resulting in a negative relation between homework help and achievement. Other types of home-based involvement—such as providing educationally enriching activities at home, making books and other educational materials available, and taking children to museums, libraries, the zoo, and other educational outlets—have been shown to have a more consistent positive relation with achievement (Reynolds & Gill, 1994). Therefore, we coded the studies into these two types of home-based involvement and tested the relations with achievement using meta-analytic techniques. There were five correlations representing involvement in activities at home and six correlations representing homework help.

Consistent with our post hoc hypothesis, help with homework was negatively related to achievement, whereas other types of involvement at home were significantly and positively related to achievement. The average weighted correlation between activities at home and achievement was $.12$ (95% CI = $.05, .19$), whereas involvement in homework produced a significant but negative average weighted correlation with achievement ($r = -.11$; 95% CI = $-.25, -.04$). These average weighted correlations were significantly different from each other, $Q_B(1) = 7.61, p < .006$. Overall, among the types of home involvement, educationally enriching activities were positively related to achievement, but helping with homework was associated with lower levels of performance.

In summary, parental involvement is positively related to achievement in middle school. Further, parental involvement characterized as academic socialization has the strongest and most positive relation and helping with homework has the strongest negative association with achievement. Other types of home-based and school-based involvement demonstrated significant positive relations with achievement. However, the strength of these relations was more moderate. Our final two questions were whether the relations between parental involvement and achievement varied across ethnicity and whether any evidence on the direction of effect can be ascertained from the results of the five intervention studies and the two longitudinal studies.

*Ethnic differences in the relation between involvement and achievement.* Although most studies did not provide separate correlations for each ethnic group, 15 studies did provide such information for African Americans and European Americans. Six studies and 7 samples provided data from African American participants, and 9 studies with 11 samples provided data for European Americans. The overall weighted correlations suggested similarities across ethnicities in the strength of the relation. For African Americans, the average weighted correlation was .11 (95% CI = .05, .17); for European Americans, it was .19 (95% CI = .09, .29). Whereas each was positive and significantly different from zero, they were not significantly different from each other, $Q_B(1) = 1.80$, *ns*, suggesting that the strength of the relation is similar between African Americans and European Americans.[1]

*Attempts at discerning directions of effect and causality from longitudinal and intervention studies.* Much debate in psychological research has focused on the ability to discern directions of effects (e.g., Duncan, Magnusson, & Ludwig, 2004). Duncan et al. suggested that research capitalize on natural experiments, use longitudinal designs, and use quasi-experimental designs as a way to attempt to establish causality and directions of effect. Longitudinal and experimental studies are presented in Tables 3 and 4. As can be seen, longitudinal studies show a moderate positive relation between parental involvement at Time 1 and achievement at Time 2. Further, five studies employed an experimental design that attempted to increase parental involvement in education—specifically, involvement in homework—and in turn, increase adolescents' school performance.

The studies that used experimental designs to examine the impact of parent training for homework were evaluated using meta-analytic techniques to determine the nature of the relation. The weighted mean *d* index was .21 and was not statistically different from zero (95% CI = −.54, .98). The weighed mean correlations is .11 (95% CI = −.26, .44). However, the test of the distribution of *d* indexes was very large and significant, $Q_w(3) = 15,074.48$, $p < .0001$. Part of the heterogeneity may be due to the fact that these studies were extremely different in terms of design. Ideally, moderator analyses could be conducted to determine whether there were subtypes of homework help that were differently related to achievement, given the heterogeneity in the distribution of correlations; however, three of the five intervention studies explicitly stated that parents were given multiple types of instructions, precluding our ability to examine subtypes. Based on the intervention studies, parental involvement in homework shows a minor effect on achievement, according to the *d* index.

## Overall Summary

Overall, parental involvement during middle school is positively related to achievement. However, the types of involvement in which parents engage matter. Among the types of involvement, parental involvement that creates an understanding about the purposes, goals, and meaning of academic performance; communicates expectations about involvement; and provides strategies that students can effectively use (i.e., academic socialization) has the strongest positive relation with achievement. Involvement pertaining to homework assistance and supervising or checking homework was the only type of involvement that was not consistently related with achievement. Whereas school-based involvement—including visiting the school, volunteering at school, and attending school events—was moderately positive in its association with achievement, our evidence suggests that the most salient type of parental involvement is involvement that relates to achievement, results in socialization around the goals and purposes of education, and provides adolescents with useful strategies that they can use in semiautonomous decision making.

## Discussion

In the face of declines in academic achievement during middle school and increased barriers associated with maintaining parental involvement with adolescents (who are increasingly autonomous and independent) and in middle schools (that are larger and more bureaucratic), the synthesis of the extant literature confirms that parental involvement is positively associated with achievement. Moreover, through this meta-analysis, we identified a specific type of involvement, namely academic socialization, that has the strongest positive relation with achievement during middle school. School-based involvement was also positively related to achievement, but less strongly so. Finally, the results for home-based involvement were mixed. Involvement that entailed assisting with homework was not consistently associated with achievement, whereas other types of home-based involvement were positively related to achievement.

Academic socialization includes parents' communication of their expectations for achievement and value for education, fostering educational and occupational aspirations in their adolescents, discussing learning strategies with children, and making preparations and plans for the future, including linking material discussed in school with students' interests and goals. An adolescent's ability to engage in logical and analytic thinking, problem solving, planning, and decision making increase during adolescence (Halpern-Felsher & Cauffman, 2001; Keating, 2004). Further, it is during adolescence that goals, beliefs, and motivations are internalized and such inner processes shape adolescents' academic performance and course selection (Wigfield, Byrnes, & Eccles, 2006). Academic socialization includes the types of strategies that will scaffold adolescents' burgeoning autonomy, independence, and cognitive abilities. In addition, this type of involvement represents developmentally appropriate strategies of involvement, as it fosters and builds upon the development of internalized motivation for achievement, focuses on future plans, provides a link between school work and future goals and aspirations, and is consistent with the needs of middle school students. Further, it provides young adolescents with the tools to make semiautonomous decisions about their academic pursuits.

In addition to being developmentally appropriate for adolescents, academic socialization strategies are developmentally appropriate for middle school contexts. One of the largest challenges for middle school teachers in their attempts to involve parents is the large number of parents with whom they must develop relationships. Middle school teachers instruct many more students than elementary school teachers. Moreover, because students have multiple teachers, it is difficult for parents to develop productive relationships with their adolescent's teachers (Hill & Chao, 2009). Academic socialization as a parental involvement strategy is adaptive for middle school contexts because it is not dependent on the development of deep, high-quality relationships with each teacher— a goal that is often not feasible even for the most motivated teacher. It is dependent on parents' knowledge about how to navigate the middle school context, which is information that can more easily be provided to parents through communications between the school and home and through electronic communications (e.g., Bouffard, 2009), and builds upon the relationship between the adolescent and the parent. This type of involvement can be more easily solicited by adolescents as they assess their own needs and direct their interests and trajectories. Further, students' academic promise may elicit this level of involvement and planning from parents.

School-based involvement was also positively related to achievement, although the relation was weaker than the relation for academic socialization. Whereas prior research and theory have demonstrated the positive effect of school-based involvement (Comer, 1995; Epstein & Sanders, 2002; Grolnick & Slowiaczek, 1994; Hill, 2001; Hill & Craft, 2003; Lareau, 1987), it is possible that the processes through which school-based involvement has its effect

(e.g., increasing social capital or knowledge) are more difficult to realize in middle school. School-based involvement during middle school is less likely to entail involvement directly in one's child's classroom. It is more likely to entail assisting teachers with preparation (e.g., bulletin boards, setting up classrooms), fundraising, administrative duties in the office, or committee work. Whereas this type of involvement is important for the functioning of the school, it often does not directly provide parents with knowledge about instructional styles and course content that will facilitate their involvement with their students' schoolwork. Further, because students have multiple teachers in middle school, parents would need to spend a considerable amount of time at school to build relations with each teacher and spend time in each classroom. Finally, as adolescents become more independent, they do not want their parents to visit the school (Stevenson & Baker, 1987); they want to be trusted that they will manage their responsibilities. That is, adolescents often indicate that they want their parents' help but do not want their parents to visit the school (Collins & Laursen, 2004; Grotevant, 1998). Given adolescents' increased sense of efficacy, autonomy, and problem-solving skills, they may have a greater role in soliciting the type of involvement they need from their parents, which would make active school-based involvement less effective than other types of involvement.

Home-based involvement entails a range of activities from supporting achievement by providing appropriate structure and intellectually engaging materials in the home to monitoring and checking homework. The provision of an educationally supportive home environment consistently has been shown to be positively related to achievement (Chao et al., 2009; Reynolds & Gill, 1994). In contrast, helping with homework has been shown to both accelerate and interfere with achievement (Cooper, 1989, 2007; Wolf, 1979). The negative relation may be due to parental interference with students' autonomy, to excessive parental pressure, or to differences in how parents and schools present the material. On the contrary, supporting a student who is having trouble completing or understanding homework can deepen and further the student's understanding of the material. The meta-analysis of the extant literature demonstrated that, on the whole, parental assistance with homework is not consistently associated with achievement. It is plausible that, rather than undermining achievement, parental engagement in homework is elicited by poor school performance, which also results in a negative relation between homework help and achievement.

Attempts at disentangling the direction of effect are futile with correlational research. Longitudinal, natural, and experimental designs provide the best context for social scientists to infer causality or direction of effect (Duncan et al., 2004). The synthesis of interventions designed to increase the amount and quality of parental involvement in homework demonstrated only a weak association between homework help and achievement, and in some cases a negative effect. Whereas in some cases parents' direct involvement in homework may rescue a failing student, the provision of support and structure that enable middle school students to function semiautonomously, understand the value and utility of education for their future, and understand how the knowledge gained at school links to their interests, talents, and current events seems most significant.

In the context of these consistent findings showing that parental involvement in education is positively associated with achievement during middle school (with the exception of homework help), there are a number of limitations to the existing literature that give us some pause in the confidence we have in our conclusions and provide fruitful ground for future research. First, we have attempted to be careful in our discussion of the findings to refrain from making causal inferences. Whereas most theories suggest that parental involvement improves achievement, there is also a growing body of literature that points to the motivating effect of prior achievement in increasing or decreasing levels of parental involvement (Eccles, 2007; Hoover-Dempsey, Ice, & Whitaker, 2009). For example, the negative relation between parental homework help and achievement may reflect parents' appropriate response for children who are not performing well, rather than demonstrating that parental homework help undermines achievement. Further, adolescents' increased cognitive abilities, sense of efficacy, and confidence may result in soliciting advice and involvement from parents, which also impacts our understanding of the nature of the dynamic relation between involvement and achievement. Second, the studies included in this meta-analysis reflect incredible heterogeneity in measurement and study design. Indeed, based on our review of the literature, there is not a standard measure of involvement that is used consistently in studies of middle school families. Rarely does one see the same measure used across studies (Hill & Tyson, 2005). The most consistently used measure is from Steinberg et al. (1992; five items). Three studies cited it; however, two studies modified it. Even when researchers used the same national datasets (e.g., NELS-88), different items were used to assess parent involvement across studies. Although such heterogeneity might undermine our ability to identify consistent patterns in the relation between parental involvement and achievement, the

meta-analysis still points to the conclusion that parental involvement that reflects academic socialization has the strongest positive relation with achievement.

Finally, the state of the extant literature did not permit a thorough examination of ethnic and socioeconomic variations in involvement and their relation with academic outcomes. The findings suggested that there is no difference in the strength of the relation between involvement and achievement for European Americans compared to African Americans when considering the findings from the random effects models, which extrapolate to the broader literature (i.e., random-effects design). However, the fixed effect models demonstrated that the relation was positive for both African American and Euro-American families, but stronger for European Americans. Some research suggests that parental involvement has different meanings and motivations across ethnicity (Hill & Craft, 2003; Lynch & Stein, 1987), and those from varying economic background engage in parental involvement with different levels of social capital (i.e., resources, knowledge; Hill et al., 2004; Lareau, 2003; Lareau & Horvat, 1999). It is possible that seemingly ethnic differences are ultimately the result of differences in economic resources. Thus, ethnic differences found in the fixed effects model may be due to the potential confounding of ethnicity and other contextual factors in the studies in this meta-analysis. Supporting this contention, Jeynes's (2005) meta-analysis found no statistical differences in the strength of the relation between studies reflecting "mostly ethnic minority" samples and Euro-American samples when socioeconomic indicators were controlled. Similarly, Fan and Chen (2001) did not find ethnicity to be a significant moderator in their meta-analysis. It is also possible that ethnic differences in beliefs, practices, and processes are not related to involvement as defined in this study. For example, prior research has found that African American parents' involvement has entailed monitoring the school and teachers rather than forming partnerships with them (Lareau & Horvat, 1999), and African American parents of high achievers have indicated that they are involved at school, in part, to demonstrate to school personnel their commitment to education.

Other than with African Americans, the body of literature on parental involvement in middle school does not include sufficient studies of other sizable ethnic groups, such as Latinos or Asian Americans. Although there is evidence that Asian American students have the highest average achievement levels, their parents are the least involved in education as defined by the prevailing theories (Chao, 2000). Given current demographic trends that predict that Latinos will become the largest ethnic minority group in the United States, it is imperative that psychologists conduct research to understand how Latino families and schools work together most productively. In addition, it is important to identify the types of involvement strategies used by Asian American families. This is particularly important because academic socialization as a parental involvement strategy is more dependent on parents' knowledge and resources and schools' ability to provide such information to parents than are other types of involvement.

In the current policy climate—one that requires schools to maintain policies and support parental involvement in education—it is imperative that the scientific field identify developmentally appropriate practical strategies for middle schools. Although the NCLB Act (2002) requires parental involvement in education, largely defined as accountability and communication between families and schools, the results of this meta-analysis suggest that programs and policies need to consider a broader range of involvement strategies. In their mandates, policies such as the NCLB should carefully consider the specific needs of middle school students, including the provision of information about tracking and placement as it effects college access, the ways in which curriculum can be linked to students' interests and current events, and linkages between the middle school curriculum and students' long term goals. Lack of guidance was the primary reason that academically able students did not attend postsecondary institutions after high school (Catsambis & Garland, 1997; Conners & Epstein, 1995; Jordan & Plank, 2000). In the current context of increased demand for parental involvement in education (e.g., school choice, tracking, course selection), without effective parental involvement, adolescents' opportunities are often foreclosed, leading to lost potential, unrealized talent, diminished educational and vocational attainment, and widening demographic gaps in achievement.

## Note

1   Based on the fixed effects model, which does not generalize to the broader literature but reflects the current set of studies, the average weighted correlation was .07 (95% CI = .04, .11) for African Americans and .20 (95% CI = .17, .23) for European Americans. These average weighted correlations were significantly different from each other ($Q(1) = 32.67\ p < .001$), suggesting that the relation between parental involvement and achievement is stronger for European Americans, albeit positive and significant for both groups.

# References

References marked with an asterisk indicate studies included in the meta-analysis.

Adams, G. R., & Berzonsky, M. D. (Eds.). (2003). *Blackwell handbook of adolescence*. Malden, MA: Blackwell.

*Baker, D. P., & Stevenson, D. L. (1986). Mothers' strategies for children's school achievement: Managing the transition to high school. *Sociology of Education, 59*, 156–166.

*Balli, S. J., Demo, D. H., & Wedman, J. F. (1998). Family involvement with children's homework: An intervention in the middle grades. *Family Relations, 47*, 149–157.

*Balli, S. J., Wedman, J. F., & Demo, D. H. (1997). Family involvement with middle-grades homework: Effects of differential prompting. *Journal of Experimental Education, 66*, 31–48.

*Bandura, A., Barbaranelli, C., Caprara, G. V., & Pastorelli, C. (1996). Multifaceted impact of self-efficacy beliefs on academic functioning. *Child Development, 67*, 1206–1222.

Barber, B. K., & Olsen, J. A. (2004). Assessing the transition to middle and high school. *Journal of Adolescent Research, 19*, 3–30.

Bleeker, M. M., & Jacobs, J. E. (2004). Achievement in math and science: Do mothers' beliefs matter 12 years later? *Journal of Educational Psychology, 96*, 97–109.

Bouffard, S. M. (2009). Tapping into technology: Using the Internet to promote family–school communication. In N. E. Hill & R. K. Chao (Eds.), *Families, schools, and the adolescent: Connecting research, policy, and practice* (pp. 147–161). New York: Teachers College Press.

*Bronstein, P., Ginsburg, G. S., & Herrera, I. S. (2005). Parental predictors of motivational orientation in early adolescence: A longitudinal study. *Journal of Youth and Adolescence, 34*, 559–575.

Byrnes, J. P., Miller, D. C., & Reynolds, M. (1999). Learning to make good decisions: A self-regulation perspective. *Child Development, 70*, 1121–1140.

Catsambis, S. (2001). Expanding knowledge of parental involvement in children's secondary education: Connections with high school seniors' academic success. *Social Psychology of Education, 5*, 149–177.

Catsambis, S., & Garland, J. E. (1997). *Parental involvement in students' education during middle and high school* (Report No. 18). Baltimore, MD: Johns Hopkins University, Center for Research on the Education of Students Placed at Risk.

Chao, R. K. (2000). Cultural explanations for the role of parenting in the school success of Asian American children. In R. W. Taylor & M. C. Wang (Eds.), *Resilience across contexts: Family, work, culture, and community* (pp. 333–363). Mahwah, NJ: Erlbaum.

Chao, R. K., Kanatsu, A., Stanoff, N., Padmawidjaja, I., & Aque, C. (2009). Diversities in meaning and practice: The parental involvement of Asian immigrants. In N. E. Hill & R. K. Chao (Eds.), *Families, schools, and the adolescent: Connecting research, policy, and practice* (pp. 110–125). New York: Teachers College Press.

Collins, W. A., & Laursen, B. (2004). Parent–adolescent relationships and influences. In R. M. Lerner & L. Steinberg (Eds.), *Handbook of adolescent psychology* (2nd ed., pp. 331–362). Hoboken, NJ: Wiley.

Comer, J. P. (1995). *School power: Implications of an intervention project*. New York: Free Press.

Conners, L. J., & Epstein, J. L. (1995). Parents and school partnerships. In M. H. Bornstein (Ed.), *Handbook of parenting* (Vol. 4, pp. 437–458). Hillsdale, NJ: Erlbaum.

Cooper, H. (1989). *Homework*. New York: Longman.

Cooper, H. (1998). The data analysis stage. In H. Cooper (Ed.), *Synthesizing research* (Vol. 2, pp. 104–156). Thousand Oaks, CA: Sage Publications.

Cooper, H. (2007). *The battle over homework: Common ground for administrators, teachers, and parents*. Thousand Oaks, CA: Corwin.

Cross, W. E. (2003). Tracing the historical origins of youth delinquency and violence: Myths and realities about black culture. *Journal of Social Issues, 59,* 67–82.

Dauber, S. L., & Epstein, J. L. (1989). *Parents' attitudes and practices of involvement in inner-city elementary and middle schools* (Report No. 33). Baltimore, MD: Johns Hopkins University, Center for Research on Elementary and Middle Schools.

Dauber, S. L., & Epstein, J. L. (1993). Parents' attitudes and practices of involvement in inner-city elementary and middle schools. In N. F. Chavkin (Ed.), *Families and schools in a pluralistic soceity* (pp. 53–71). Albany, NY: State University of New York.

Dearing, E., Kreider, H., Simpkins, S., & Weiss, H. B. (2006). Family involvement in school and low-income children's literacy: Longitudinal association between and within families. *Journal of Educational Psychology, 98,* 653–664.

*Desimone, L. (1999). Linking parent involvement with student achievement: Do race and income matter? *Journal of Educational Research, 93,* 11–30.

*Deutscher, R. & Ibe, M. (n.d.). Relationships between parental involvement and children's motivation. Retrieved in May 2007 from the Lewis Center for Educational Research website, http://www.lewiscenter.org/research/relationships.pdf

Dornbusch, S. M., & Glasgow, K. L. (1996). The structural context of family–school relations. In A. Booth & J. F. Dunn (Eds.), *Family–school links: How to affect educational outcomes* (pp. 35–44). Mahwah, NJ: Erlbaum.

*Driessen, G., Smit, F., & Sleegers, P. (2005). Parental involvement and educational achievement. *British Educational Research Journal, 31,* 509–532.

Duncan, G. J., Magnuson, K. A., & Ludwig, J. (2004). The endogeneity problem in developmental studies. *Research in Human Development, 1*(1 & 2), 59–80.

Duval, S. (2005). The trim and fill method. In H. R. Rothstein, A. J. Sutton, & M. Borenstein (Eds.), *Publication bias in meta-analysis: Prevention, assessment and adjustments* (pp. 127–144). Hoboken, NJ: Wiley.

*Eamon, M. K. (2005). Social-demographic, school, neighborhood, and parenting influences on the academic achievement of Latino young adolescents. *Journal of Youth and Adolescence, 34,* 163–174.

Eccles, J. S. (2004). Schools, academic motivation, and stage– environment fit. In R. M. Lerner & L. D. Steinberg (Eds.), *Handbook of adolescent psychology* (2nd ed., pp. 125–153). New York: Wiley.

Eccles, J. S. (2007). Families, schools, and development achievementrelated motivations and engagement. In J. E. Grusec & P. D. Hastings (Eds.), *Handbook of socialization: Theory and research* (pp. 665–691). New York: Guilford.

Eccles, J. S., & Harold, R. D. (1993). Parent–school involvement during the early adolescent years. *Teachers College Record, 94,* 568–587.

Eccles, J. S., & Harold, R. D. (1996). Family involvement in children's and adolescents' schooling. In

A. Booth & J. F. Dunn (Eds.), *Family–school links: How do they affect educational outcomes* (pp. 3–34). Mahwah, NJ: Erlbaum.

Epstein, J. L. (1987). Toward a theory of family–school connections: Teacher practices and parent involvement. In K. Hurrelman, F. X. Kaufman, & F. Losel (Eds.), *Social intervention: Potential and constraints* (pp. 121–136). Berlin, Germany: de Gruyer.

Epstein, J. L. (2001). *School, family, and community partnerships: Preparing educators and improving schools.* Boulder, CO: Westview.

Epstein, J. L., Salinas, K. C., & Jackson, V. E. (1995). *Manual for teachers and prototype activities: Teachers Involve Parents in Schoolwork (TIPS) language arts, science/health, and mathematics interactive homework in the middle grades* (Rev. ed.). Baltimore: Johns Hopkins University, Center on School, Family, and Community Partnerships.

Epstein, J. L., & Sanders, M. G. (2002). Family, school, and community partnerships. In M. H. Bornstein (Ed.), *Handbook of parenting: Vol. 5. Practical issues in parenting* (pp. 507–437). Mahwah, NJ: Erlbaum.

Fan, X., & Chen, M. (2001). Parental involvement and students' academic achievement: A meta-analysis. *Educational Psychology Review, 13*(1), 1–22.

*Garcia Bacete, F. J., & Ramirez, J. R. (2001). Family and personal correlates of academic achievement. *Psychological Reports, 88*, 533–547.

*Grolnick, W. S., Kurowski, C. O., Dunlap, K. G., & Hevey, C. (2000). Parental resources and the transition to junior high. *Journal of Research on Adolescence, 10*, 465–488.

Grolnick, W. S., Price, C. E., Beiswenger, K. L., & Sauck, C. C. (2007). Evaluative pressure in mothers: Effects of situation, maternal, and child characteristics on autonomy supportive versus controlling behavior. *Developmental Psychology, 43*, 991–1002.

*Grolnick, W. S., & Slowiaczek, M. L. (1994). Parents' involvement in children's schooling: A multidimensional conceptualization and motivational model. *Child Development, 65*, 237–252.

Grotevant, H. S. (1998). Adolescent development in family contexts. In W. Damon & N. Eisenberg (Eds.), *Handbook of child psychology: Vol. 3. Social, emotional, and personality development* (5th ed., pp. 1097–1150). New York: Wiley.

*Gutman, L. M., & Eccles, J. S. (1999). Financial strain, parenting behaviors, and adolescents' achievement: Testing model equivalence between African American and European American single- and two-parent families. *Child Development, 70*, 1464–1476.

*Gutman, L. M., & Midgley, C. (2000). The role of protective factors in supporting the academic achievement of poor African American students during the middle school transition. *Journal of Youth and Adolescence, 20*, 223–248.

*Gutman, L. M., Sameroff, A. S., & Eccles, J. S. (2002). The academic achievement of African American students during early adolescence: An examination of risk, promotive, and protective factors. *American Journal of Community Psychology, 30*, 376–399.

Halpern-Felsher, B. L., & Cauffman, E. (2001). Costs and benefits of a decision: Decision-making competence in adolescents and adults. *Journal of Applied Developmental Psychology, 22*, 257–276.

Hampton, F. M., Mumford, D. A., & Bond, L. (1998). Parental involvement in inner city schools: The Project FAST extended family approach to success. *Urban Education, 33*, 410–427.

*Hao, L., & Bonstead-Bruns, M. (1998). Parent–child differences in educational expectations and the academic achievement of immigrant and native students. *Sociology of Education, 71*, 175–198.

Hara, S. R. (1998). Parent involvement: The key to improved student achievement. *School Community Journal, 8*(2), 9–19.

*Harris, A. (1990). Students' perceptions and attitudes toward parent involvement in academic homework and its relationship to academic achievement. (Doctoral dissertation, Florida State University). *Dissertation Abstracts International, 51*, p. 4018.

*Hawes, C. A., & Plourde, L. A. (2005). Parental involvement and its influence on the reading achievement of 6th grade students. *Reading Improvement, 42*, 47–57.

Hill, N. E. (2001). Parenting and academic socialization as they relate to school readiness: The role of ethnicity and family income. *Journal of Educational Psychology, 93*, 686–697.

*Hill, N. E., Castellino, D. R., Lansford, J. E., Nowlin, P., Dodge, K. A., Bates, J. E., & Pettit, G. S. (2004). Parent academic involvement as related to school behavior, achievement, and aspirations: Demographic variations across adolescence. *Child Development, 75*, 1491–1509.

Hill, N. E. & Chao, R. K. (2009). *Families, schools, and the adolescent: Connecting research, policy, and practice*. New York: Teachers College Press.

Hill, N. E., & Craft, S. A. (2003). Parent–school involvement and school performance: Mediated pathways among socioeconomically comparable African American and Euro-American families. *Journal of Educational Psychology, 95,* 74–83.

Hill, N. E., & Taylor, L. C. (2004). Parental school involvement and children's academic achievement: Pragmatics and issues. *Current Directions in Psychological Science, 13,* 161–164.

Hill, N. E., & Tyson, D. F. (2005, February). *Family–school involvement: Developmental and demographic variations during the transition to middle school*. Paper presented at the Carolina Consortium on Human Development: Series on School Transitions, Chapel Hill, NC.

Hill, N. E., Tyson, D. F., & Bromell, L. (2009). Parental involvement in middle school: Developmentally appropriate strategies across SES and ethnicity. In N. E. Hill & R. K. Chao (Eds.), *Families, schools, and the adolescent: Connecting research, policy, and practice* (pp. 53–72). New York: Teachers College Press.

Hoover-Dempsey, K. V., Ice, C. L., & Whitaker, M. C. (2009). "We're way past reading together": Why and how parental involvement in adolescence makes sense. In N. E. Hill & R. K. Chao (Eds.), *Families, schools, and the adolescent: Connecting research, policy, and practice* (pp. 19–36). New York: Teachers College Press.

Hoover-Dempsey, K. V., & Sandler, H. M. (1995). Parent involvement in children's education: Why does it make a difference. *Teachers' College Record, 97,* 310–331.

Hughes, D., Rodriguez, J., Smith, E. P., Johnson, D. J., Stevenson, H. C., & Spicer, P. (2006). Parents' ethnic–racial socialization practices: A review of research and directions for future study. *Developmental Psychology, 42,* 747–770.

*Hughes, D. (2004). [Data from the Center on Research, Culture, Development and Education on a multiethnic sample of middle school students]. Unpublished raw data.

Jeynes, W. H. (2003). A meta-analysis: The effects of parental involvement on minority children's academic achievement. *Education and Urban Society, 35,* 202–218.

Jeynes, W. H. (2005). A meta-analysis of the relation of parental involvement to urban elementary school student academic achievement. *Urban Education, 40,* 237–269.

Jeynes, W. H. (2007). The relationship between parental involvement and urban secondary school student academic achievement: A meta-analysis. *Urban Education, 42,* 82–110.

*Jodl, K. M., Michael, A., Malanchuk, O., Eccles, J. S., & Sameroff, A. (2001). Parents' roles in shaping early adolescents' occupational aspirations. *Child Development, 72,* 1247–1265.

Jones, N. & Schneider, B. (2009). Rethinking the role of parenting: Promoting adolescent academic success and emotional well-being. In N. E. Hill & R. K. Chao (Eds.), *Families, schools, and the adolescent: Connecting research, policy, and practice* (pp. 73–90). New York: Teachers College Press.

Jordan, W. J., & Plank, S. B. (2000). Talent loss among high-achieving poor students. In M. G. Sanders (Ed.), *Schooling students placed at risk: Research policy and practice in the education of poor and minority adolescents* (pp. 83–108). Mahwah, NJ: Erlbaum.

*Juang, L. P., & Silbereisen, R. K. (2002). The relationship between adolescent academic capability beliefs, parenting and school grades. *Journal of Adolescence, 25,* 3–18.

Keating, D. P. (2004). Cognitive and brain development. In R. M. Lerner & L. Steinberg (Eds.), *Handbook of adolescent psychology* (2nd ed., pp. 45–84). Hoboken, NJ: Wiley.

*Keisner, J. W. (1997). The effects of a parental homework monitoring intervention on school engagement of high risk middle school students. (Doctoral dissertation, University of Oregon, 1997). *Dissertation Abstracts International, 58,* 0980.

*Keith, P. B., & Lichtman, M. V. (1994). Does parental involvement influence the academic achievement of Mexican-American eighth graders? Results from the National Education Longitudinal Study. *School Psychology Quarterly, 9,* 256–273.

*Keith, T. Z., Keith, P. B., Troutman, G. C., & Bickley, P. G. (1993). Does parental involvement affect eighth-grade student achievement? Structural analysis of national data. *School Psychology Review, 22,* 474–496.

*Kelly, S. (2004). Do increased levels of parental involvement account for social class differences in track placement? *Social Science Research, 33,* 626–659.

*Kim, E. (2002). The relationship between parental involvement and children's educational achievement in the Korean immigrant family. *Journal of Comparative Family Studies, 33*, 529–563.

*Kim, K., & Rohner, R. P. (2002). Parental warmth, control, and involvement in schooling: Predicting academic achievement among Korean American adolescents. *Journal of Cross-Cultural Psychology, 33*, 127–140.

Kohl, G. O., Lengua, L. J., McMahon, R. J., & the Conduct Problems Prevention Research Group. (2000). Parent involvement in school: Conceptualizing multiple dimensions and their relations with family and demographic risk factors. *Journal of School Psychology, 38*, 501–538.

Lareau, A. (1987). Social class differences in family–school relationships: The importance of cultural capital. *Sociology of Education, 60*, 73–85.

Lareau, A. (2003). *Unequal childhoods: Class, race and family life.* Berkeley, CA: University of California.

Lareau, A., & Horvat, E. M. (1999). Moments of social inclusion and exclusion: Race, class, and cultural capital in family–school relationships. *Sociology of Education, 72*, 37–53.

*Latendresse, S. (2005). Perceptions of parenting among affluent youth: Exploring antecedents of middle school adjustment trajectories. [Doctoral dissertation]. *Dissertation Abstracts International, Session B: The Sciences and Engineering, 65*, 3746.

Lerner, R. M., & Steinberg, L. D. (Eds.). (2004). *Handbook of adolescent psychology* (2nd ed.). New York: Wiley.

Lynch, E. W., & Stein, R. C. (1987). Parent participation by ethnicity: A comparison of Hispanic, Black and Anglo families. *Exceptional Children, 54*(2), 105–111.

*Ma, X. (1999). Dropping out of advanced mathematics: The effects of parental involvement. *Teachers College Record, 101*, 60–81.

*Marchant, G. J., Paulson, S. E., & Rothlisberg, B. A. (2001). Relations of middle school students' perceptions of family and school contexts with academic achievement. *Psychology in the Schools, 38*, 505–519.

*McNeal, R. B. (1999). Parental involvement as social capital: Differential effectiveness on science achievement, truancy, and dropping out. *Social Forces, 78*, 117–144.

*Melby, J. N., & Conger, R. D. (1996). Parental behaviors and adolescent academic performance: A longitudinal analysis. *Journal of Research on Adolescence, 6*, 113–137.

Miller, J. D., Kimmel, L., Hoffer, T., & Nelson, C. (2001). *Longitudinal study of American youth: User's manual.* Chicago: International Center for the Advancement of Scientific Literacy at Northwestern University.

*Muller, C. (1995). Maternal employment, parent involvement, and mathematics achievement among adolescents. *Journal of Marriage & the Family, 57*, 85–100.

*National Education Longitudinal Study of 1988* [Data file]. Washington, DC: National Center for Education Statistics.

*National Longitudinal Survey of Youth,* 1997 [Data file]. Washington, DC: Bureau of Labor Statistics.

No Child Left Behind Act of 2001, Pub. L. No. 107–110, 114 Stat. 1425 (2002). Retrieved February 26, 2009, from http://www.ed.gov/policy/ elsec/leg/esea02 /107–110.pdf

Ogbu, J. U. (1978). *Minority education and caste: The American system in cross-cultural perspective.* New York: Academic Press.

*Pelegrina, S., García-Linares, M., & Casanovam, P. F. (2003). Adolescents and their parents' perceptions about parenting characteristics. Who can better predict the adolescent's academic competence? *Journal of Adolescence, 26*, 651–665.

*Peng, S. S., & Wright, D. (1994). Explanation of academic achievement of Asian American students. *Journal of Educational Research, 87*, 346–352.

Prescott, B. L., Pelton, C. L., & Dornbusch, S. M. (1986). Teacher perceptions of parent–school communication: A collaborative analysis. *Teacher Education Quarterly, 13*, 67–83.

*Reynolds, A. J., & Gill, S. (1994). The role of parental perspectives in the school adjustment of inner-city Black children. *Journal of Youth and Adolescence, 23*, 671–695.

*Rillero, P., & Helgeson, S. L. (1995, April). *An evaluation of the use of hands-on science homework assignments by sixth grade students and their parents.* Paper presented at the annual meeting of the National Association for Research in Science Teaching, San Francisco, CA.

Rosenthal, R. (1991). *Meta-analytic procedures for social research* (Rev. ed.). Newbury Park, CA: Sage.

*Salazar, L. P., Schuldermann, S. M., Schuldermann, E. H., & Huynh, C. M. (2000). Filipino adolescents' parental socialization for academic achievement in the United States. *Journal of Adolescent Research, 15,* 564–586.

Sanders, M. G., & Epstein, J. L. (2000). Building school–family–community partnerships in middle and high schools. In M. G. Sanders (Ed.), *Schooling students placed at risk: Research, policy, and practice in the education of poor and minority adolescents* (pp. 339–361). Mahwah, NJ: Erlbaum.

Seginer, R. (2006). Parents' educational involvement: A developmental ecological perspective. *Parenting: Science and Practice, 6,* 1–48.

*Seidman, E., Allen, L., Aber, J. L., Mitchell, C., & Feinman, J. (1994). The impact of school transitions in early adolescence on the self-system and perceived social context of poor urban youth. *Child Development, 65,* 507–522.

*Seidman, E., Lambert, L. E., Allen, L., & Aber, J. L. (2003). Urban adolescents' transition to junior high school and protective family transactions. *Journal of Early Adolescence, 23,* 166–193.

*Seyfried, S. F., & Chung, I. J. (2002). Parent involvement as parental monitoring of student motivation and parent expectations predicting later achievement among African American and European American middle school age students. *Journal of Ethnic & Cultural Diversity in Social Work, 11,* 109–131.

*Shumow, L., & Lomax, R. (2002). Parental efficacy: Predictor of parenting behavior and adolescent outcomes. *Parenting: Science and Practice, 2,* 127–150.

*Shumow, L., & Miller, J. D. (2001). Parents' at-home and at-school academic involvement with young adolescents. *Journal of Early Adolescence, 21,* 68–91.

*Singh, K., Bickley, P, Trivette, P., Keith, T. Z., Keith, P. B., & Anderson, E. (1995). The effects of four components of parental involvement on eighth grade student achievement: Structural analysis of NELS-88 data. *School Psychology Review, 24,* 299–317.

*Sirin, S. R., & Rogers-Sirin, L. (2004). Exploring school engagement of middle-class African American adolescents. *Youth & Society, 35,* 323–340.

Smetana, J. G., Campione-Barr, N., & Daddis, C. (2004). Longitudinal development of family decision making: Defining healthy behavioral autonomy for middle class African American adolescents. *Child Development, 75,* 1418–1434.

Spencer, M. B., Cross, W. E., Harpalani, V., & Goss, T. N. (2003). Historical and developmental perspectives on Black academic achievement: Debunking the "acting White" myth and posing new directions for research. In C. C. Yeakey & R. D. Henderson (Eds.), *Surmounting all odds: Education, opportunity, and society in the new millennium* (pp. 273–303). Greenwich, CT: Information Age.

Steinberg, L., Lamborn, S. D., Dornbusch, S. M., & Darling, N. (1992). Impact of parenting on adolescent achievement: Authoritative parenting, school involvement, and encouragement to succeed. *Child Development, 63,* 1266–1281.

Steinberg, L., & Silk, J. S. (2002). Parenting adolescents. In M. H. Bornstein (Ed.), *Handbook on parenting* (Vol. 1, pp. 103–134). Mahwah, NJ: Erlbaum.

*Stevenson, D. L., & Baker, D. P. (1987). The family–school relation and the child's school performance. *Child Development, 58,* 1348–1357.

*Sui-Chi, H. E., & Willms, D. J. (1996). Effects of parental involvement on eighth-grade achievement. *Sociology of Education, 69,* 126–141.

*Survey of Parents and Children, 1990* [Data file]. Ann Arbor, MI: Inter-University Consortium for Political and Social Research. doi:10.3886/ICPSR09595

*Tamayo, L. F. (1992). Hispanic parent monitoring of seventh grade mathematics homework assignments and relationship with achievement and self-esteem. (Doctoral dissertation, University of Massachusetts, 1992). *Dissertation Abstracts International, 53,* 1805.

Taylor, S., & Tweedie, R. (2000). Trim and fill: A simple funnel plot based method of testing and adjusting for publication bias in meta-analysis. *Biometrics, 56,* 455–463.

*Toney, L. P., Kelley, M. L., & Lanclos, N. F. (2003). Self- and parental monitoring of homework in adolescents: Comparative effects on parents' perceptions of homework behavior problems. *Child and Family Behavior Therapy, 25,* 35–51.

*Useem, E. L. (1992). Middle schools and math groups: Parents' involvement in children's placement. *Sociology of Education, 65,* 263–279.

*Van Voorhis, F. (2003). Interactive homework in middle school: Effects on family involvement and science achievement. *Journal of Educational Research, 96,* 323–338.

Wigfield, A., Byrnes, J. P., & Eccles, J. S. (2006). Development during early and middle adolescence.

In P. A. Alexander & P. H. Winne (Eds.), *Handbook of educational psychology* (2nd ed., pp. 87–113). Mahwah, NJ: Erlbaum.

Wolf, R. M. (1979). Achievement in the United States. In H. J. Walberg (Ed.), *Educational environments and effects* (pp. 313–330). Berkeley, CA: McCutchan.

*Xu, J., & Corno, L. (2003). Family help and homework management reported by middle school students. *Elementary School Journal, 103,* 503–517.

First author, **NANCY E. HILL**, holds two appointments at Harvard University. She is the Suzanne Young Murray Professor at the Radcliffe Institute for Advanced Study and Professor at the Graduate School of Education. Additionally, she is the Distinguished Faculty Fellow of the William T. Grant Foundation. Diana F. Tyson, the co-author, completed her graduate studies focusing on the transition into adolescence and middle school.

## Cecilia Sin-Sze Cheung and Eva M. Pomerantz

**NO**

# Value Development Underlies the Benefits of Parents' Involvement in Children's Learning: A Longitudinal Investigation in the United States and China

A wealth of research supports the idea that parents' involvement in children's learning enhances children's academic functioning (for reviews, see Grolnick, Friendly, & Bellas, 2009; Pomerantz, Kim, & Cheung, 2012): Children whose parents are involved on the school (e.g., attending parent-teacher conferences) and home (e.g., discussing school with children) fronts often exhibit enhanced engagement (e.g., use of self-regulated strategies), skills (e.g., phonological awareness), and achievement (e.g., grades). Notably, parents' involvement plays a role in children's academic functioning even when aspects of children's home environment such as parents' income and education are taken into account (e.g., Dearing, Kreider, Simpkins, Weiss, 2006; Jeynes, 2005, 2007). The effects of parents' involvement are also not accounted for by other dimensions of parenting such as supporting children's autonomy (e.g., C. S. Cheung & Pomerantz, 2011; Deslandes, Bouchard, & St.-Amant, 1998).

Research focusing on why parents' involvement in children's learning benefits children's academic functioning identifies the development of children's actual and perceived competencies as important (e.g., Dearing et al., 2006; Senechal & LeFevre, 2002). However, it has also been argued that parents' involvement leads children to view doing well in school as valuable, which fosters children's engagement in school, enhancing their achievement (e.g., Epstein, 1988; Grolnick & Slowiaczek, 1994). Unfortunately, such a value development model has not been tested. The goal of the current research was to address this gap by evaluating whether the effect of parents' involvement on children's engagement and grades in school is due in part to the development of children's values in regard to school achievement. Drawing on prior theory and research on value transmission (i.e., children's adoption of parents' values; e.g., Grusec & Goodnow, 1994; Knafo & Schwartz, 2009) as well as parents' involvement in children's learning (e.g., Hill & Tyson, 2009), we hypothesized two pathways by which parents' involvement facilitates children valuing achievement in school.

## The Perception-Acceptance Value Development Pathway

Grusec and Goodnow (1994) proposed a two-step process model by which parents transmit their values to children. First, children must be aware of parents' values such that they perceive them accurately. Second, children must accept parents' values as their own. Both steps are considered key in effective transmission of values from generation to generation (e.g., Barni, Ranieri, Scabini, & Rosnati, 2011; Knafo & Schwartz, 2009). Grusec and Goodnow focused on how the type of discipline parents use with children contributes to value transmission by shaping children's perceptions of parents' values. Several other dimensions of interactions between parents and children, such as parents' discussion of their values with children (e.g., Knafo & Schwartz, 2004; Okagaki & Bevis, 1999) and the quality of children's relationships with parents (Barni et al., 2011), have also received attention. As a commitment of resources (e.g., time, energy, and financial provisions) to children in the academic arena (Grolnick & Slowiaczek, 1994), parents' involvement in children's learning may be a key mechanism by which parents convey to children that they view school as important. When parents take the time and trouble to participate in school events, children may view parents as placing importance on learning. Parents' involvement on the home front may have similar consequences—for example, when parents ask children about what they are learning in school or provide children with learning resources (e.g., books), they may communicate that they see doing well in school as useful.

When children see parents as valuing achievement in school, they may come to value it themselves (e.g., Eccles et al., 1983; Grolnick, Ryan, & Deci, 1997). Grusec and Goodnow (1994) argued that once children are aware of the values parents hold their acceptance of such values as their own is facilitated in the context of a warm relationship with parents (see also Barni et al., 2011). The commitment of resources characteristic of parents' involvement may signal to children that parents care about them. Moreover, in the context of their involvement, parents may provide emotional support for children (e.g., by reacting to children's frustration with homework with soothing words), thereby creating a sense of trust in children that may facilitate their adoption of parents' values (e.g., C. S. Cheung & Pomerantz, 2012; Grolnick & Slowiaczek, 1994; Grusec, 2002). Parents' involvement in children's learning may be a particularly unique dimension of parenting in that it simultaneously communicates the value parents place on doing well in school (Step 1 of Grusec and Goodnow's model), while also leading children to take on this value as their own (Step 2 of Grusec and Goodnow's model). Thus, parents' involvement may enhance children's achievement via a *perception-acceptance pathway*: Parents' involvement leads children to perceive parents as valuing school achievement, thereby heightening the value children themselves place on it.

## The Experience Value Development Pathway

The perception-acceptance pathway may be accompanied by what we label an experience pathway that directly fosters the value children place on achievement in school. Although parents' involvement in children's learning likely conveys the value parents' place on children's school endeavors, it may not always lead children to value school achievement via children's awareness of parents' values (Eccles et al., 1983). When parents become involved in children's learning, they may create experiences for children that directly heighten the value children place on school achievement. For example, when parents discuss school with children, children may generate reasons for its utility, leading them to see doing well in school as valuable (Hill & Tyson, 2009). In a somewhat different vein, drawing from Bem's (1967, 1972) Self-Perception Theory, practices such as helping children to sustain their effort on

their homework until it is finished may lead children to conclude that they value doing well in school given how much time they invest in it. In the *experience pathway*, parents' involvement creates experiences that lead children to place value on school achievement, regardless of their perceptions of parents' values.

## The Role of Values in Academic Functioning

Whether the value children place on achievement in school ensuing from parents' involvement develops via a perception-acceptance pathway or an experience pathway, prior theory and research (e.g., Eccles et al., 1983; Wang & Pomerantz, 2009) indicates it supports children's academic functioning. In their Expectancy-Value Theory, Eccles et al. (1983) made the case that when children value achievement in school, they become more engaged in school, which enhances their achievement. Indeed, the more children view doing well in school as important, the more engaged they are—for example, they use heightened self-regulated learning strategies, such as monitoring and planning their learning (e.g., Pintrich, 1999; Wang & Pomerantz, 2009). Notably, heightened value as well as engagement predicts improved achievement among children over time (e.g., Alexander, Entwisle, & Dauber, 1993; Kenney-Benson, Pomerantz, Ryan, & Patrick, 2006; Wang & Pomerantz, 2009).

## Value Development Pathways in the United States and China

Over the last several years, there has been a call to extend the understanding of psychological processes beyond Western populations (e.g., Arnett, 2008; Henrich, Heine, Norenzayan, 2010a, 2010b). In the case of parents' involvement in children's learning, this may be of import when it comes to China because Chinese parents are involved differently in children's learning than are their American counterparts (for a review, see Pomerantz, Ng, Cheung, & Qu, in press). For one, Chinese (vs. American) parents are more involved compared to American parents (e.g., Chen & Stevenson, 1989; Ng, Pomerantz, & Lam, 2007). Consequently, both the perception-acceptance and experience value development pathways may be stronger in China than the United States as such heightened involvement may convey more clearly that parents value school achievement and create more experiences that directly heighten the value children place on school achievement. Moreover, the amplified commitment of resources reflected in parents' involvement may enhance children's adoption of parents' values.

Chinese parents' involvement in children's learning, however, is more controlling than that of American parents with greater attention to children's mistakes (e.g., C. S. Cheung & Pomerantz, 2011; Ng et al., 2007). This along with the tendency for Chinese (vs. American) children to feel less close to parents during adolescence (e.g., Pomerantz, Qin, Wang, & Chen, 2009) may undermine value transmission. Although it is unclear if parents' involvement similarly fosters value development in China and United States, prior examination of the effects of parents' involvement on children's engagement and grades yields similar effects in the two countries (C. S. Cheung & Pomerantz, 2011).

## Overview of the Current Research

To examine whether parents' involvement in children's learning enhances children's academic functioning by heightening the value children place on school achievement in the United States and China, the current research evaluated the hypothesis that two value-development pathways underlie the benefits of parents' involvement. In the *perception-acceptance pathway*, parents' involvement signals to children that parents value school achievement, leading children to value it, which in turn enhances children's achievement. In the *experience pathway*, parents' involvement develops the value children place on school achievement not through the messages it conveys about parents' values, but rather directly through the experiences it creates. Comparisons between the United States and China for both pathways were made to evaluate their generalizability.

In testing the value transmission pathways, we focused on children in the middle school years because parents' involvement may offset the devaluing of school that often occurs among children during this phase of development (for a review, see Wigfield & Wagner, 2005). Children in the United States and China reported four times over the seventh and eighth grades on parents' involvement in their learning, their perceptions of the value parents place on school achievement, and the value they themselves place on it. Children's academic functioning was assessed with children's reports and school records. The four-wave design allowed for the examination of the sequence of effects posited. Because each construct was assessed at each wave, autoregressive effects could be taken into account, which permitted identification of the direction of effects.

We investigated two dimensions of children's academic functioning that have important implications for children's lives. First, children's *engagement* in school is not only predictive of their achievement over time (e.g., M.-T. Wang & Fredricks, 2014; Q. Wang & Pomerantz, 2009) but also appears to protect children against internalizing and externalizing problems (e.g., M.-T. Wang & Fredricks, 2014; M.-T. Wang & Peck, 2013). Children reported on two forms of their engagement—their use of self-regulated learning strategies and the time they spend on schoolwork outside of school. Second, children's *grades* in school are a significant reflection of their achievement (Duckworth & Seligman, 2005; Grolnick et al., 1997) with implications for subsequent opportunities (e.g., placement in enrichment activities) as well as success later in life (e.g., Geiser & Santelices, 2007). There is sizeable evidence documenting the importance of parents' involvement in children's learning for both children's engagement and grades (e.g., C. S. Cheung & Pomerantz, 2011; Grolnick & Slowiaczek, 1994).

With the exception of grades, children provided reports for all the constructs under study. This is of particular concern when it comes to parents' involvement in children's learning. Children's reports of such involvement are only modestly associated with teachers and parents' reports (e.g., Bakker, Denessen, & Brus-Laeven, 2007; Hill et al., 2004; Reynolds, 1992). However, because children, teachers, and parents' reports of parents' involvement each predict unique variance in children's achievement, it has been argued that each captures unique aspects of parents' involvement (Reynolds, 1992). Children's reports reflect their *perceptions* of parents' involvement. This is significant because children must notice parents' involvement to draw conclusions about parents' values (C. S. Cheung & Pomerantz, 2012; Grolnick & Slowiaczek, 1994). However, each reporter may also bring a unique set of biases to their reports. In the current context, the value children view parents placing on school achievement or that they themselves place on it may bias their reports, such that effects reflect children's perceptions of parents' values or their own values rather than parents' involvement. To rule out this possibility, we tested alternative pathways—for example, the value children place on school achievement predicts their reports of parents' involvement over time.

## Method

### Participants

The University of Illinois U.S.-China Adolescence Study began when children entered a new school in seventh grade and concluded at the end of eighth grade in the United States and China (e.g., Pomerantz et al., 2009; Wang & Pomerantz, 2009). Participants were 374 American children (187 boys; *M* age = 12.78 years in the fall of seventh grade) and 451 Chinese children (240 boys; $M$ age = 12.69 years in the fall of seventh grade). In each country, children attended public school in primarily working- or middle-class areas. The American children attended one of two public schools consisting of the seventh and eighth grades in the suburbs of Chicago. Chicago is a city with high population density (12,750 people per square mile at the time of the research) with a median yearly family gross income of $61,182 at the time of the research; 30% of the population over the age of 25 possessed at least a college degree at the time of the research (U.S. Census Bureau, 2007). The median family income of the two selected suburbs was $60,057 and $72,947, with 21% and 26% of the population over the age of 25 possessing a college degree. Reflecting the ethnic composition of these areas, participants were predominantly European American (88%) with 9% Hispanic American, 2% African American, and 1% Asian American. Seventy-nine percent of participating children reported living with two parents.

The Chinese children attended one of two public schools in the suburbs of Beijing; one school consisted of the seventh to ninth grades and the other of the seventh to 12th grades. According to the Beijing Municipal Bureau of Statistics (2005), Beijing is a densely populated city (13,386 people per square mile at the time of the research) with an annual discretionary income per capita of $15,638 RMB at the time of the research; 13% of the population over the age of 6 had at least a college degree at the time of the research. In the two selected suburbs, 9% and 28% of the population over the age of 6 had a college degree. Over 95% of the residents in these areas were of the *Han* ethnicity (Beijing Municipal Bureau of Statistics, 2005), which is slightly above the 92% for the country as a whole (China Population and Development Research Center, 2001). Eighty-six percent of the participating children reported living with two parents. An opt-in consent procedure was used in which parents provided permission for children to participate. Sixty-four percent of parents in the United States and 59% of parents in China allowed their children to participate.

## Procedure

Children completed a set of questionnaires during two 45-min sessions at four times approximately 6 months apart: fall of seventh grade (Wave 1), spring of seventh grade (Wave 2), fall of eighth grade (Wave 3), and spring of eighth grade (Wave 4). Instructions and items were read aloud to children in their native language in the classroom during regular class time by trained native research staff. Children received a small gift (e.g., a calculator) as a token of appreciation at the end of each session. The average attrition rate over the entire study was 4% (2% in the United States and 6% in China). More than 85% of the children had data at all four waves of the study for all of the analyses, with more than 98% having data at two or more waves for all of the analyses. At Wave 1, children with complete data differed from those without complete data only in that their grades were better, $t(818) = 2.01$, $p < .05$. The Institutional Review Boards of the University of Illinois and Beijing Normal University approved the procedures.

## Measures

The measures were originally written in English. Standard translation and back-translation procedures (Brislin, 1980) were employed with repeated discussion among American and Chinese members of the research team to modify the wording of the items to ensure equivalence in meaning between the English and Chinese versions (Erkut, 2010). Equivalence was also established statistically. A series of confirmatory factor analyses (CFAs) was conducted in the context of two-group nested structural equation modeling (SEM) to examine the metric invariance of the measures between the United States and China over the four waves of the study; metric invariance is essential and sufficient in making valid comparisons of the associations (e.g., Little, 1997), as was done in the current research (see below).

In each set of CFAs, an unconstrained model was compared to a constrained (i.e., metric invariance) model. The unconstrained models consisted of the same latent construct repeatedly assessed over the four waves yielding a total of four latent constructs. These constructs were allowed to correlate with one another; errors of the same indicators over time were also allowed to correlate when suggested by modification indexes from the CFAs conducted on the sample with no missing data (Keith, 2006; McDonald & Ho, 2002). The parameters in the unconstrained models were freely estimated without any between-country or across-time equality constraints. In the constrained models, the factor loadings of the same indicators were forced to be equal between the two countries and across the four waves. Monte Carlo studies indicate that a decrease from the unconstrained to the corresponding constrained model in the comparative fit index (CFI) of no more than .01, supplemented by an increase in the root-mean-square error of approximation (RMSEA) of no more than .015, is reflective of invariance (Chen, 2007). Although chi-square difference tests are considered appropriate for hypothesis testing purposes, the current consensus is that they are not appropriate for evaluating measurement invariance (e.g., Chen, 2007; G. W. Cheung & Rensvold, 2002; Little, 1997).

Prior analyses on these data, using two parcels of items (or two items in the case of time spent on homework outside of school) to represent each latent construct indicated that the measures of parents' involvement in children's learning, the value children place on school, and children's engagement have metric invariance between countries and over time (C. S. Cheung & Pomerantz, 2011; Wang & Pomerantz, 2009). The use of parcels allowed us to build parsimonious models based on solid and meaningful indicators, enhancing the likelihood of replication in future research (Little, Cunningham, Shahar, & Widaman, 2002; Little, Rhemtulla, Gibson, & Schoemann, 2013). Parsimony was of particular concern in the current research given the sizeable number of items comprising each scale and the complexity of the models, which can strain the number of free parameters that can be estimated (e.g., Kline, 1998), despite our sample size of 825. In such a case, the use of parcels is desirable (Little et al., 2013). Importantly, principal components analysis (PCA) on each set of items comprising each parcel indicated that each set formed a single factor; the parcels were also each internally reliable on their own ($\alpha$s = .73 to .88).

Metric invariance of children's perceptions of the value parents place on school achievement has not been evaluated in prior analyses; thus, it was tested for the current research. The latent construct was represented by two parcels of items: Items about the importance of doing well were aggregated in one parcel, which PCA indicated formed a single factor ($\alpha$s = .80 to .93; see item descriptions below), and items about the importance of not doing poorly were aggregated in another, which PCA indicated form a single factor as well ($\alpha$s = .84 to .92). Both the unconstrained, $\chi^2(df = 9) = 26.10$, CFI = .95, Tucker–Lewis index (TLI) = .92, RMSEA = .08, and constrained, $\chi^2(df = 13) = 38.12$, CFI = .95, TLI = .92, RMSEA = .07, models fit the data adequately, with differences between the CFIs and RMSEAs of no more than .01.

**Parental involvement in child learning.** Parents' involvement in children's learning was assessed with 10 items (e.g., "My parents help me with my homework when I ask." "My parents try to get to know the teachers at my school." "My parents purchase extra workbooks or outside materials related to school for me.") adapted from prior research (Chao, 2000; Kerr & Stattin, 2000; Kohl, Lengua, McMahon, & The Conduct Problems Prevention Research Group, 2000; Stattin & Kerr, 2000). In line with Grolnick and Slowiaczek's (1994) definition of parents' involvement, the items characterize a variety of practices

(e.g., attendance of parent-teacher conferences, discussion of school with children, and assistance with homework) reflecting parents' commitment of resources to children in the academic arena. Children indicated the extent to which each of the statements was true (1 = *not at all true*, 5 = *very true*). The 10 items were combined, with higher numbers reflecting greater involvement as reported by children ($\alpha$s = .83 to .85 in the United States and .77 to .83 in China).

**Child perceptions of parental value.** To assess children's perceptions of the value their parents place on school achievement, children indicated how important (1 = *not at all important*, 7 = *very important*) it is to parents that they do well (e.g., "How important is it to your parents that you do well in language arts?") and avoid doing poorly (e.g., "How important is it to your parents that you avoid doing poorly in math?") on four core subjects (language arts, math, science, and social studies in the United States; language arts, math, biology, and English in China) for which children received grades. The eight items were combined, with higher numbers reflecting perceptions of greater parental value ($\alpha$s = .93 to .96 in the United States and .87 to .91 in China).

**Child value.** The value children themselves place on school achievement was assessed with a modified version of Pomerantz, Saxon, and Oishi's (2000) measure. Paralleling the measure of children's perceptions of the value parents place on school achievement, for each of the four core subjects, children indicated how important (1 = *not at all important*, 7 = *very important*) it was for them to do well (e.g., "How important is it to you to do well in math?") and avoid doing poorly (e.g., "How important is it to you to avoid doing poorly in language arts?"). The eight items were combined, with higher numbers reflecting greater value ($\alpha$s = .91 to .94 in the United States and .88 to .91 in China).

**Child engagement.** Two forms of children's engagement in school were assessed. The 30-item Dowson and McInerney (2004) Goal Orientation and Learning Strategies Survey assessed children's use of *self-regulated learning strategies*. Three scales assess children's metacognitive strategies: Six items assess monitoring (e.g., "I check to see if I understand the things I am trying to learn"), six assess planning (e.g., "I try to plan out my schoolwork as best as I can"), and six assess regulating (e.g., "If I get confused about something at school, I go back and try to figure it out"). Two scales assess children's cognitive strategies: Six items assess rehearsal (e.g., "When I want to learn things for school, I practice repeating them to myself") and six assess elaboration (e.g., "I try to understand how the things I learn in school fit together with each other"). Children indicated the extent to which each of the 30 statements was true of them (1 = *not at all true*, 5 = *very true*). The metacognitive and cognitive strategies scales were combined, with higher numbers representing greater school engagement ($\alpha$s .96 to .97 in the United States and .93 to .96 in China).

The *time children spend on schoolwork outside of school* was assessed with a modified version of the scale used by Fuligni, Tseng, and Lam (1999). Children indicated how much time they spend on their schoolwork outside of school on a typical weekday and weekend (1 = *less than 1 hr*, 6 = *more than 5 hr*). Their responses for a typical weekday were weighted by five and combined with those of each day for a typical weekend weighted by two. Higher numbers reflect more time spent on schoolwork outside of school ($rs$ = .48 to .64 in the United States and .41 to .52 in China).

**Child grades.** Children's grades in the four core subjects were obtained from schools. Grades in the American schools were originally in letters and were converted to numbers. Because there were 13 steps in the ladder of grades used in the American schools, grades were converted to numbers with a range of 0 (i.e., a grade of F) to 12 (i.e., a grade of A+) with a 1-point increment between each step in the grades (e.g., B– = 7, B = 8, B+ = 9, A– = 10). Such conversion has been used in prior research (e.g., Coe, Pivarnik, Womack, Reeves, & Malina, 2006; Schwartz, Kelly, & Duong, 2013; Wood & Locke, 1987). Moreover, simulation research indicates that the treatment of discrete categories as continuous is unlikely to result in biased parameter estimates when the number of categories is more than six as is the case in the current research (Rhemtulla, Brosseau-Liard, & Savalei, 2012). In the Chinese schools, grades were originally numerical, ranging from 0 to 100 in one school and from 0 to 120 in the other. In both countries, grades were standardized within school to take into account differences in the grading systems of the schools. The four subjects were combined, with higher numbers reflecting better grades.

## Results

Overall, the measures in the current research were approximately normally distributed. In both the United States and China across the four waves of assessment, the indexes for skewness and kurtosis were less than 1, with only one exception—the index for skewness was 1.47 and the kurtosis index was 2.28 for the avoidant dimension of the value children place on school achievement at Wave 1 in the United States. Hence, across the six measures at each of the four waves there was no indication of serious violation of the normality assumption.

As shown in Table 1, in both the United States and China, parents' involvement in children's learning—as reported by children—was positively associated with children's perceptions of the value parents place on school achievement ($rs$ = .25 to .43, $ps$ < .001) as well as the value children themselves place on it ($rs$ = .25 to .39, $ps$ < .001) at each wave. Children's perceptions of the value parents place on school achievement were positively associated at each wave with the value children place on it ($rs$ = .28 to .55, $ps$ < .001). The value children place on school achievement was also associated with their engagement ($rs$ = .30 to .58 for self-regulated learning strategies and .13 to .21 for time spent on school schoolwork outside of school; $ps$ < .05) as well as grades ($rs$ = .22 to .38, $ps$ < .001) at each wave in the United States and China. Although such associations are suggestive of the viability of both the perception-acceptance and experience value development pathways, they do not provide insight into the direction of effects. Evaluation of the direction of effects requires analyses accounting for the autoregressive effects.

The central analyses took such effects into account. These analyses were conducted within a latent SEM framework using Mplus 7.0 (Muthén & Muthén, 1998–2012), which employs full information maximum likelihood (FIML) estimation in the presence of missing data; FIML provides more reliable standard errors to handling missing data under a wider range of conditions than does not only list- and pairwise deletion but also mean-imputation (Arbuckle, 1996; Wothke, 2000). To identify differences between the United States and China, two-group nested model comparisons were employed: The unconstrained models were compared to more parsimonious models with constraints of equal coefficients imposed between the two countries on the effects of interest; for each set of models, the constraints were imposed one by one and then simultaneously. A significant difference ($\Delta\chi^2$) between an unconstrained model and a more parsimonious constrained model indicates a country difference. The same two parcels or items used in the CFAs conducted to establish measurement invariance (see the Method section) were employed for the latent constructs in the model; for grades, the four subjects were each used as indicators of the latent construct. A separate set of models was conducted for each dimension of academic functioning.

Prior research using this data set already established the total effects of parents' involvement on children's engagement and grades over time. C. S. Cheung and

*Table 1*

## Means and Correlations Among the Central Constructs

| Variable | 1 | 2 | 3 | 4 | 5 | 6 | 7 | 8 | 9 | 10 | 11 | 12 | 13 | 14 | 15 | 16 |
|---|---|---|---|---|---|---|---|---|---|---|---|---|---|---|---|---|
| **Parental involvement** | | | | | | | | | | | | | | | | |
| 1. Wave 1 | — | .50 | .54 | .46 | .25 | .24 | .25 | .27 | .27 | .24 | .18 | .19 | .01 | .04 | .07 | .10 |
| 2. Wave 2 | .64 | — | .59 | .55 | .26 | .35 | .29 | .26 | .26 | .32 | .26 | .28 | .04 | .05 | .06 | .06 |
| 3. Wave 3 | .51 | .60 | — | .63 | .15 | .27 | .34 | .26 | .16 | .28 | .25 | .27 | .07 | .10 | .11 | .12 |
| 4. Wave 4 | .48 | .45 | .48 | — | .15 | .29 | .26 | .33 | .12 | .26 | .24 | .27 | .05 | .05 | .09 | .11 |
| **Perceived parental value** | | | | | | | | | | | | | | | | |
| 5. Wave 1 | .31 | .27 | .21 | .28 | — | .39 | .38 | .34 | .51 | .28 | .28 | .21 | .05 | .03 | .10 | .12 |
| 6. Wave 2 | .34 | .43 | .27 | .22 | .41 | — | .53 | .48 | .32 | .43 | .39 | .41 | .11 | .12 | .16 | .15 |
| 7. Wave 3 | .30 | .32 | .38 | .29 | .39 | .52 | — | .57 | .33 | .44 | .55 | .50 | .12 | .16 | .17 | .17 |
| 8. Wave 4 | .21 | .16 | .24 | .38 | .34 | .36 | .54 | — | .31 | .40 | .46 | .49 | .09 | .12 | .12 | .13 |
| **Child value** | | | | | | | | | | | | | | | | |
| 9. Wave 1 | .38 | .30 | .28 | .21 | .28 | .28 | .33 | .24 | — | .49 | .43 | .37 | .28 | .26 | .24 | .30 |
| 10. Wave 2 | .44 | .39 | .36 | .26 | .28 | .41 | .43 | .30 | .67 | — | .61 | .59 | .36 | .38 | .31 | .39 |
| 11. Wave 3 | .38 | .33 | .35 | .27 | .22 | .36 | .47 | .38 | .58 | .73 | — | .67 | .27 | .33 | .29 | .31 |
| 12. Wave 4 | .31 | .32 | .34 | .33 | .20 | .31 | .46 | .41 | .55 | .65 | .75 | — | .27 | .28 | .27 | .32 |
| **Grades** | | | | | | | | | | | | | | | | |
| 13. Wave 1 | .09 | .13 | .22 | .14 | −.03 | .01 | .12 | .13 | .28 | .20 | .20 | .31 | — | .91 | .82 | .88 |
| 14. Wave 2 | .12 | .15 | .22 | .16 | −.01 | .05 | .11 | .13 | .28 | .22 | .27 | .33 | .92 | — | .86 | .91 |
| 15. Wave 3 | .11 | .15 | .22 | .15 | .03 | .07 | .14 | .12 | .26 | .24 | .31 | .35 | .82 | .87 | — | .88 |
| 16. Wave 4 | .12 | .15 | .20 | .16 | .00 | .10 | .13 | .16 | .30 | .27 | .35 | .38 | .80 | .84 | .92 | — |
| Mean (U.S.) | 3.61 | 3.44 | 3.43 | 3.37 | 6.38 | 6.14 | 6.09 | 6.10 | 5.65 | 5.29 | 5.35 | 5.29 | | | | |
| SD (U.S.) | 0.71 | 0.80 | 0.76 | 0.76 | 0.79 | 1.07 | 1.05 | 1.11 | 1.10 | 1.18 | 1.25 | 1.29 | | | | |
| Mean (China) | 3.79 | 3.69 | 3.67 | 3.64 | 6.00 | 6.10 | 6.08 | 6.05 | 5.91 | 5.82 | 5.78 | 5.74 | | | | |
| SD (China) | 0.62 | 0.71 | 0.68 | 0.68 | 0.94 | 0.92 | 0.94 | 0.94 | 0.88 | 1.08 | 1.08 | 1.13 | | | | |

*Note.* Results are based on the observed, rather than latent, variables. Correlations for the American sample are presented in the lower triangle; those for the Chinese sample are presented in the upper triangle. Correlations with absolute values greater than .10 are significant ($p < .05$). Grades were standardized within schools with means equal to zero and standard deviationss equal to one; the other dimensions of academic functioning were not included given space limitations, but information on them may be obtained by contacting the first author (see also the Results section).

Pomerantz (2012) conducted sets of two-group nested SEM analyses examining if parents' involvement is predictive of children's academic functioning over the four waves (see also C. S. Cheung & Pomerantz, 2011): The effect of parents' involvement at Wave 1 on children's academic functioning (i.e., engagement and grades) at Wave 4 was evaluated, taking into account residual variance by adjusting for children's earlier (Wave 1) academic functioning as well as allowing the variance of parents' involvement and children's academic functioning at Wave 1 to correlate. The unconstrained, $\chi^2$s($df > 5$) $< 3.91$, CFIs $> .96$, TLIs $> .95$, RMSEAs $< .05$, and constrained, $\chi^2$s($dfs = 4$) $= 1.67$, CFIs $> .96$, TLIs $> .96$, RMSEAs $= .04$, models fit the data well, with the effects similar in the United States and China, $\Delta\chi^2$s($df = 1$) $< 1.5$. The more involved parents were in children's learning, the more children were engaged ($\gamma = .15$ for self-regulated learning strategies and .08 for time spent on schoolwork; $ts > 2.66$, $ps < .01$), and the better their grades ($y = .07$; $t = 3.01$, $p < .01$) 2 years later over and above their earlier engagement and grades.

In the current report, we used two-group nested SEM analyses to identify the role of the two value development pathways (i.e., the perception-acceptance and experience pathways) in explaining the effects of parents' involvement on children's academic functioning. . . . children's reports of parents' involvement at Wave 1 were specified to predict children's perceptions of the value parents place on school achievement (i.e., the first step of the perception-acceptance pathway) and the value children themselves place on school (i.e., the first step of the experience pathway) at Wave 2. For the perception-acceptance pathway, children's perceptions of parents' values at Wave 2 were specified to predict their own values at Wave 3, which in turn were specified to predict children's academic functioning at Wave 4. For the experience pathway, the value children place on school achievement at Wave 2 was specified to predict the maintenance of such value at Wave 3, which in turn was specified to predict their academic functioning at Wave 4.

The mediating roles of the two pathways were simultaneously evaluated to assess the unique effects of each. Residual variance for each of the downstream constructs was taken into account. Specifically, corresponding constructs assessed 6 months prior to each of the constructs specified in the pathways were included to take into account autoregressive effects. Concurrent associations between constructs were also taken into account by allowing the variances (Wave 1) or error variances (Wave 2, 3, and 4) of the constructs to correlate within each wave. Because children's residence in single-headed household as well as their gender are associated with children's achievement during middle school (e.g., Downey, 1994; Dwyer & Johnson, 1997; Entwisle, 1997), children's reports of whether they reside with both parents in the same household (1 = *not residing with both parents*, 2 = *residing with both parents*) and their gender (1 = *boys*, 2 = *girls*) were included as covariates by specifying them to predict children's grades at Wave 4.

The unconstrained models (i.e., individual models for self-regulated learning strategies, time spent on schoolwork outside of school, and grades) fit the data adequately, $\chi^2$s($df$s > 319) = 1080, CFIs > .94, TLIs > .92, RMSEAs < .08. Two-group nested model

comparisons indicated that the links comprising both the perception-acceptance and experience pathways were similar in the United States and China, $\Delta\chi^2$s($df$s = 1) < 2.2, $ns$; thus, all such effects were constrained to be equal between the two countries in the final constrained models, $\chi^2$s($df$s > 314) > 1069, CFIs > .96, TLIs > .94, RMSEAs < .07. As shown in Table 2, there was support for the perception-acceptance pathway. Children's reports of parents' involvement at Wave 1 predicted children's perceptions of the value parents place on school achievement at Wave 2 taking into account children's earlier (Wave 1) perceptions ($t$s = 2.96, $p$s < .01). In turn, the more children perceived parents as valuing school achievement at Wave 2, the more they themselves valued it at Wave 3 taking into account the earlier (Wave 2) value children placed on school achievement ($t$s = 2.02, $p$s < .05). The value children placed on school achievement at Wave 3 predicted enhanced engagement ($t$s > 3.10, $p$s < .01) and grades ($t$s = 4.92, $p$s < .001) among children at Wave 4 over and above their earlier (Wave 1) engagement and grades. Notably, at Wave 3, neither parents' involvement nor children's perceptions of the value parents place on school achievement uniquely predicted children's engagement or grades ($t$s < 1). Thus, although the value children placed on school achievement predicted their subsequent perceptions of the value parents place on it, this was not a viable pathway by which parents' involvement benefits children's academic functioning.

There was also support for the experience pathway (see Table 2). Parents' involvement as reported by children at Wave 1 predicted the value children themselves placed on school achievement at Wave 2 taking into account children's earlier (Wave 1) value ($t$s = 2.08, $p$s < .05). The value children placed on school achievement was maintained over time—that is from Wave 2 to 3 ($t$s = 6.28,

*Table 2*

### Summary of Model Fit and Parameter Estimates for the Value Development Models

| Dimension of academic functioning | Model fit | | | Estimates | | | Delta coefficient | |
|---|---|---|---|---|---|---|---|---|
| | CFI | TLI | RMSEA | Involvement → Parent Value | Parent Value → Child Value | Child Value → Adjustment | Perception-Acceptance Pathway | Experience Pathway |
| Grades | .95 | .94 | .07 | .15** | .11** | .16*** | 2.08* | 3.38** |
| SRL | .96 | .94 | .07 | .24*** | .17** | .19*** | 2.21* | 5.48*** |
| Time on schoolwork | .94 | .94 | .07 | .23*** | .19** | .10** | 1.81† | 4.55*** |

*Note.* CFI = comparative fit index; TLI = Tucker–Lewis index; RMSEA = root-mean-square error of approximation; SRL self-regulated learning. Based on the chi-square difference tests, all paths comprising the indirect pathways were constrained to be equal between the United States and China. Estimates from the final constrained models are reported.
† $p$ < .06. * $p$ < .05. ** $p$ < .01. *** $p$ < .001.

$p$s < .01), which, as reported above, predicted children's engagement and grades at Wave 4.

The total effects of parents' involvement (Wave 1) on children's academic functioning (Wave 4) were no longer evident in either country ($\gamma$s < .03) with the inclusion of the value development pathways, which resulted in a reduction of at least 65% of the total effect for each of the three dimensions of children's academic functioning. Mplus's delta method indicated that the two-step perception-acceptance pathway was significant in the United States and China in explaining the role of involvement in children's engagement as reflected in their self-regulated learning strategies ($z$s > 2.21, $p$s < .05) and grades ($z$s > 2.08, $p$s < .05). For engagement, as reflected in children's time spent on schoolwork outside of the school, the perception-acceptance pathway was marginal ($z$s = 1.81, $p$s < .06). The one-step experience pathway was evident across all three dimensions of children's academic functioning ($z$s > 3.38, $p$s < .01). These results are consistent with those yielded by analyses using bootstrap resampling techniques. For example, in the model focusing on grades as the final outcome, the estimate of the perception-acceptance pathway via perceptions of parental value and child value using 5,000 bootstrap resamples was .004 (95% CI = .001, .009), and that of the experience pathway was .017 (95% CI = .001, .042).

The model examined also allowed us to test the viability of alternative pathways—for example, the possibility that the value children place on school achievement leads them to report parents as more involved over time, which in turn leads children to view parents as more invested in their achievement, thereby enhancing children's academic functioning. To examine these alternative explanations, we evaluated the role of all possible pathways in the link between parents' involvement and children's academic functioning, including the value development pathways, simultaneously in the same model. The unconstrained, $\chi^2$s ($df$s > 360) = 1203, CFIs > .92, TLIs > .90, RMSEA = .08, and constrained, $\chi^2$s ($df$s > 350) > 1191, CFIs > .92, TLIs > .90, RMSEAs < .08, models fit the data adequately. When simultaneously evaluated in the model with the two value development pathways, none of the alternative pathways (out of six possible pathways) was evident ($z$s < 1.10, $ns$). However, the two value development pathways remained significant ($z$s > 2.10, $p$s < .05), reflecting their uniqueness. Although none of the alternative pathways were evident, one link comprising one of them was: In both countries, children's value at Wave 2 was predictive of their perceptions of parents' value at Wave 3, adjusting for children's earlier perceptions ($\gamma$s = .25–.28, $t$s > 2.78, $p$s < .05).

# Discussion

The current research is the first empirical test of one of the most frequently proposed pathways—that is, value development—argued to underlie the benefits of parents' involvement in children's learning (e.g., Epstein, 1988; Grolnick & Slowiaczek, 1994). Consistent with the two-step value transmission model put forth by Grusec and Goodnow (1994), there was evidence for a *perception-acceptance pathway*: The more involved parents were—as reported by children—the more children perceived them as placing heightened value on school achievement; this, in turn, was predictive of children coming to value school achievement more over time. In line with ideas that parents' involvement may create experiences that foster value development among children (e.g., Hill & Tyson, 2009), there was also evidence that parents' involvement contributes directly to the value children place on school achievement (i.e., the *experience pathway*). Both pathways uniquely accounted for the beneficial effect of parents' involvement on children's later academic functioning (i.e., engagement and grades).

The effects of the two value development pathways were robust in that they remained even when alternative pathways were taken into account (e.g., the more children value school achievement, the more they see parents as valuing it, which heightens children's reports of parents' involvement, thereby enhancing their achievement); the value development pathways were also not due to children's gender or residence with both (vs. one) parent, which have been linked to children's achievement (e.g., Downey, 1994; Dwyer & Johnson, 1997; Entwisle, 1997). Although comparable to those of prior research using stringent statistical controls to identify indirect pathways over time (e.g., Davies, Woitach, Winter, & Cummings, 2008; NICHD Early Child Care Research Network, 2003), the effects of the value development pathway were modest—perhaps because value development has been underway for some time once children reach adolescence with only incremental change occurring at this time. Even modest effects, however, may be critical to offsetting the devaluing of school that often occurs among children over adolescence (for a review, see Wigfield & Wagner, 2005). Moreover, incremental change can be meaningful as it may accumulate over time (Pomerantz, Qin, Wang, & Chen, 2011). Moderation may also contribute to the modest effects. For example, drawing from Grusec and Goodnow (1994), when children have poor relationships with parents, parents' involvement in their learning may be less likely to lead them to take on parents' values as their own.

Increasingly research has focused on understanding the processes underlying the benefits of parents' involvement in children's learning for children's academic functioning (for a review, see Pomerantz et al., 2012). In this vein, children's actual and perceived competencies have been identified as important mechanisms (e.g., Dearing et al., 2006; Senechal & LeFevre, 2002). Although it is possible that such mechanisms are distinct from the value development pathways identified in the current research, it is also possible that they work together. Value development may establish the foundation for growth in children's competencies: Once children come to see achievement in school as personally important, they may be more receptive to parents' instruction, which may develop their competencies, thereby allowing them to feel confident. Other mechanisms may also be a part of the value development pathways. For example, C. S. Cheung and Pomerantz (2012) found that the effect of parents' involvement on children's achievement was due in part to children adopting parent-oriented reasons (e.g., to meet parents' expectations) for school achievement; such motivation may be particularly likely to develop once children see parents as valuing school achievement, ultimately leading children to view achievement as personally important so that they may do well to satisfy parents who have committed substantial resources to their learning.

Despite differences in the quantity and quality of American and Chinese parents' involvement in children's learning (for reviews, see Chao & Tseng, 2002; Pomerantz, Ng, & Wang, 2008), the value development pathways were similarly evident in the United States and China. Although Chinese parents tend to accompany their involvement in children's learning with control more than do American parents (e.g., C. S. Cheung & Pomerantz, 2011), the more parents were involved, the more children viewed them as valuing school achievement and valued it themselves in both the United States and China. Moreover, children's perceptions of the value parents place on school achievement were similarly predictive over time of the value children themselves placed on it in the two countries. Thus, it appears that regardless of the quantity or quality, parents' involvement in children's learning may be a unique dimension of parenting in that it conveys parents' values while also having characteristics such as emotional support that may increase the accuracy of children's perceptions of such values as well as their acceptance of them.

The current research was guided by Grusec and Goodnow's (1994) two-step process model by which parents transmit their values to children. However, it diverged from the model in that the actual value parents place on school achievement was not directly assessed, but rather assumed to be reflected in parents' involvement in children's learning. Although parents' values likely drive their involvement, so do other forces—for example, children's invitations to be involved, parents' beliefs about their capacity to support children's learning, and whether parents see it as their role to be involved (for a review, see Hoover-Dempsey & Sandler, 1997). The current research did not examine the *accuracy* of value transmission, but rather what parents' involvement conveyed to children about the value parents' place on achievement in school. It is of note that the value parents place on children's school achievement may not be conveyed if parents are not involved. Hence, simply valuing school achievement may not reap the same benefits as being involved.

## Limitations

Several limitations should be considered in interpreting the results. Perhaps most significantly, with the exception of grades, children served as the sole reporters. To rule out informant bias, our model controlled for the concurrent associations between the child-reported constructs as well as the stability of each over time as both these links are likely to contain informant bias. Given such controls, the value development pathways are unlikely to contain informant bias. However, we went further in ruling out the possibility of other pathways that could result in bias due to children's reports—for example, we ensured that the effects were not simply due to children's values driving their reports of parents' values and involvement. Despite the merits of using multiple informants, it was crucial that children report on both their perceptions of the value parents place on school as well as the value they themselves place on school given that these constructs represent children's beliefs to which they likely have the best access. Yet, because children's reports of parents' involvement are only modestly associated with parents and teachers' reports (e.g., Bakker et al., 2007; Hill et al., 2004; Reynolds, 1992), it will be important for future research to examine the value development pathways using parents and teachers' reports.

The current research also did not distinguish between mothers and fathers' involvement, asking children instead to report on involvement as practiced by parents as a single entity. It is quite possible that mothers and fathers are differentially involved reflecting differences in their time and values. For example, Roest, Dubas, Gerris, and Engels (2009) reported only modest correspondence between Dutch mothers and fathers' values in terms of such things as the importance of pursuing happiness and working hard. Research in the United States indicates that mothers and fathers' involvement in children's learning does not necessarily overlap—for example, mothers are often more likely than fathers to attend school events and assist children with homework (Nord & West, 2001). Future research should examine if mothers and fathers' involvement differentially guides value development among children. Attention should also be given to the moderating role of the consistency between mothers and fathers in their values and involvement because when there is more agreement between parents in their values, children often have more accurate perceptions of parents' values (Knafo & Schwartz, 2004).

Given their homogeneity (e.g., the American sample was mainly of European descent and the Chinese sample was mainly of *Han* descent), the samples used in the current research do not represent the diversity of the United States and China. Thus, questions remain concerning within-culture variations in the role of value development in the effect of parents' involvement in children's learning. Within the United States, there is some evidence that how parents are involved varies demographically (e.g., Hill & Taylor, 2004; Snyder & Dillow, 2012). For example, the more educated parents are, the more they take part in events at children's school (Snyder & Dillow, 2012). It is possible that different types of involvement convey different messages about the value parents' place on school (e.g., those that children see as taking more time and energy indicate most that parents view school as important). Of additional concern, is that urban areas such as Beijing in China have been increasingly exposed to Western values in the past few decades. Thus, it is possible that the Chinese children in the current research interpret parents' involvement more similarly to American children than do Chinese children residing in rural areas.

## Conclusions

Despite these limitations, the current research is of import in providing empirical support for a value development model of the effects of parents' involvement in children's learning: Such involvement appears to benefit children in part because it leads children to view school achievement as valuable, which heightens their engagement in school, ultimately enhancing their grades. Via a perception-acceptance pathway, when parents become involved in children's learning, children perceive parents as placing heightened value on achievement in school; such perceptions in turn foreshadow children viewing achievement in school as personally important. In an experience pathway, parents' involvement foreshadows children placing heightened value on school achievement presumably due to the experiences created by parents' involvement (e.g., discussion about school allows

children to generate reasons for its utility), which in turn predicts enhanced academic functioning among children. These value development pathways were similarly evident in the United States and China where the quantity and quality of parents' involvement differ.

## References

Alexander, K. L., Entwisle, D. R., & Dauber, S. L. (1993). First-grade classroom behavior: Its short- and long-term consequences for school performance. *Child Development, 64,* 801–814. doi:10.2307/1131219

Arbuckle, J. L. (1996). Full information estimation in the presence of incomplete data. In G. A. Marcoulides & R. E. Schumacker (Eds.), *Advanced structural equation modeling: Issues and techniques* (pp. 243–277). Mahwah, NJ: Erlbaum.

Arnett, J. J. (2008). The neglected 95%: Why American psychology needs to become less American. *American Psychologist, 63,* 602–614. doi:10.1037/0003-066X.63.7.602

Bakker, J., Denessen, E., & Brus-Laeven, M. (2007). Socio-economic background, parental involvement and teacher perceptions of these in relation to pupil achievement. *Educational Studies, 33,* 177–192. doi: 10.1080/03055690601068345

Barni, D., Ranieri, S., Scabini, E., & Rosnati, R. (2011). Value transmission in the family: Do adolescents accept the values their parents want to transmit? *Journal of Moral Education, 40,* 105–121. doi:10.1080/ 03057240.2011.553797

Beijing Municipal Bureau of Statistics. (2005). *Beijing statistical yearbook 2005.* Retrieved from http://www .bjstats.gov.cn/tjnj/2005-tjnj/

Bem, D. J. (1967). Self-perception: An alternative interpretation of cognitive dissonance phenomena. *Psychological Review, 74,* 183–200. doi: 10.1037/h0024835

Bem, D. J. (1972). Self-perception theory. In L. Berkowitz (Ed.), *Advances in experimental social psychology* (Vol. 6, pp. 1–62). New York, NY: Academic Press.

Brislin, R. W. (1980). Translation and content analysis of oral and written materials. In H. C. Triandis & J. W. Berry (Eds.), *Handbook of crosscultural psychology: Vol. 2. Methodology* (pp. 389–444). Boston, MA: Allyn & Bacon.

Chao, R. K. (2000). The parenting of immigrant Chinese and European American mothers: Relations between parenting styles, socialization goals, and parental practices. *Journal of Applied Developmental Psychology, 21*, 233–248. doi:10.1016/S0193-3973(99)00037-4

Chao, R., & Tseng, V. (2002). Parenting of Asians. In M. H. Bornstein (Ed.), *Handbook of parenting: Vol. 4 Social conditions and applied parenting* (2nd ed., pp. 59–93). Mahwah, NJ: Erlbaum.

Chen, C. S., & Stevenson, H. W. (1989). Homework: A cross-cultural examination. *Child Development, 60*, 551–561. doi:10.2307/1130721

Chen, F. F. (2007). Sensitivity of goodness of fit indexes to lack of measurement invariance. *Structural Equation Modeling, 14*, 464–504. doi:10.1080/10705510701301834

Cheung, C. S., & Pomerantz, E. M. (2011). Parents' involvement in the United States and China: Implications for children's academic and emotional adjustment. *Child Development, 82*, 932–950. doi:10.1111/j .1467-8624.2011.01582.x

Cheung, C. S., & Pomerantz, E. M. (2012). Why does parents' involvement enhance children's achievement? The role of parent-oriented motivation. *Journal of Educational Psychology, 104*, 820–832. doi:10.1037/a0027183

Cheung, G. W., & Rensvold, R. B. (2002). Evaluating goodness-of-fit indexes for testing measurement invariance. *Structural Equation Modeling, 9*, 233–255. doi:10.1207/S15328007SEM0902_5

China Population and Development Research Center. (2001). *Major figures of the 2000 census*. Retrieved from http://www.cpirc.org.cn/en/ e5cendata1.htm

Coe, D. P., Pivarnik, J. M., Womack, C. J., Reeves, M. J., & Malina, R. M. (2006). Effect of physical education and activity levels on academic achievement in children. *Medicine and Science in Sports and Exercise, 38*, 1515–1519. doi:10.1249/01.mss.0000227537.13175.1b

Davies, P. T., Woitach, M. J., Winter, M. A., & Cummings, E. M. (2008). Children's insecure representations of the interparental relationship and their school adjustment: The mediating role of attention difficulties. *Child Development, 79*, 1570–1582. doi:10.1111/j.1467-8624.2008.01206.x

Dearing, E., Kreider, H., Simpkins, S., & Weiss, H. B. (2006). Family involvement in school and low-income children's literacy performance: Longitudinal associations between and within families. *Journal of Educational Psychology, 98*, 653–664. doi:10.1037/0022-0663.98.4.653

Deslandes, R., Bouchard, P., & St.-Amant, J. (1998). Family variables as predictors of school achievement: Sex differences in Quebec adolescents. *Canadian Journal of Education, 23*, 390–404. doi:10.2307/ 1585754

Downey, D. (1994). The school performance of children from singlemother and single-father families: Economic or interpersonal deprivation? *Journal of Family Issues, 15*, 129–147. doi:10.1177/ 019251394015001006

Dowson, M., & McInerney, D. M. (2004). The development and validation of the Goal Orientation and Learning Strategies Survey (GOALS-S). *Educational and Psychological Measurement, 64*, 290–310. doi: 10.1177/0013164403251335

Duckworth, A. L., & Seligman, M. E. P. (2005). Self-discipline outdoes IQ in predicting academic performance of adolescents. *Psychological Science, 16*, 939–944. doi:10.1111/j.1467-9280.2005.01641.x

Dwyer, C., & Johnson, L. (1997). Grades, accomplishments, and correlates. In W. Willingham & N. Cole (Eds.), *Gender and fair assessment* (pp. 127–156). Mahwah, NJ: Erlbaum.

Eccles, J. S., Adler, T. F., Futterman, R., Goff, S. B., Kaczala, C. M., Meece, J. L., & Midgley, C. (1983). Expectancies, values, and academic behaviors. In J. T. Spence (Ed.), *Achievement and achievement motives: Psychological and sociological approaches* (pp. 75–146). San Francisco, CA: Freeman.

Entwisle, D. R. (1997). *Children, schools, and inequality*. Boulder, CO: Westview Press.

Epstein, J. L. (1988). How do we improve programs for parental involvement? *Educational Horizons, 66*, 75–77.

Erkut, S. (2010). Developing multiple language versions of instruments for intercultural research. *Child Development Perspectives, 4*, 19–24. doi: 10.1111/j.1750-8606.2009.00111.x

Fuligni, A. J., Tseng, V., & Lam, M. (1999). Attitudes toward family obligation among American adolescents with Asian, Latin American, and European American backgrounds. *Child Development, 70*, 1030–1044. doi:10.1111/1467-8624.00075

Geiser, S., & Santelices, M. V. (2007). *Validity of high-school grades in predicting student success beyond the freshman year: High-school record vs standardized tests as indicators of four-year college outcomes*. Berkeley, CA: Center for Studies in Higher Education, University of California, Berkeley.

Grolnick, W. S., Friendly, R., & Bellas, V. (2009). Parenting and children's motivation at school. In K. Wentzel & A. Wigfield (Eds.), *Handbook of motivation at school* (pp. 279–300). Mahwah, NJ: Erlbaum.

Grolnick, W. S., Ryan, R. M., & Deci, E. L. (1997). Internalization in the family: The self-determination perspective. In J. E. Grusec & L. Kuczynski (Eds.), *Parenting and children's internalization of values* (pp. 135–161). New York, NY: Wiley.

Grolnick, W. S., & Slowiaczek, M. L. (1994). Parents' involvement in children's schooling: A multidimensional conceptualization and motivational model. *Child Development, 65,* 237–252. doi:10.2307/1131378

Grusec, J. E. (2002). Parenting socialization and children's acquisition of values. In M. H. Bornstein (Ed.), *Handbook of parenting: Vol. 5: Practical issues in parenting* (pp. 143–167). Mahwah, NJ: Erlbaum.

Grusec, J. E., & Goodnow, J. J. (1994). Impact of parental discipline methods on the child's internalization of values: A reconceptualization of current points of view. *Developmental Psychology, 30,* 4–19. doi: 10.1037/0012-1649.30.1.4

Henrich, J., Heine, S. J., & Norenzayan, A. (2010a). Most people are not WEIRD. *Nature, 466,* 29. doi:10.1038/466029a

Henrich, J., Heine, S. J., & Norenzayan, A. (2010b). The weirdest people in the world. *Behavioral and Brain Sciences, 33,* 61–83. doi:10.1017 / S0140525X0999152X

Hill, N. E., Castellino, D. R., Lansford, J. E., Nowlin, P., Dodge, K. A., Bates, J. E., & Petit, G. S. (2004). Parent-academic involvement as related to school behavior, achievement, and aspirations: Demographic variations across adolescence. *Child Development, 75,* 1491–1509. doi: 10.1111/j.1467-8624.2004.00753.x

Hill, N. E., & Taylor, L. C. (2004). Parental school involvement and children's academic achievement: Pragmatics and issues. *Current Directions in Psychological Science, 13,* 161–164. doi:10.1111/j.0963- 7214.2004.00298.x

Hill, N. E., & Tyson, D. (2009). Parental involvement in middle school: A meta-analytic assessment of the strategies that promote achievement. *Developmental Psychology, 45,* 740–763. doi:10.1037/a0015362

Hoover-Dempsey, K. V., & Sandler, H. (1997). Why do parents become involved in their children's education? *Review of Educational Research, 67,* 3–42. doi:10.3102/00346543067001003

Jeynes, W. H. (2005). A meta-analysis of the relation of parental involvement to urban elementary school student academic achievement. *Urban Education, 40,* 237–269. doi:10.1177/0042085905274540

Jeynes, W. H. (2007). The relationship between parental involvement and urban secondary school student academic achievement: A meta-analysis. *Urban Education, 42,* 82–110. doi:10.1177/0042085906293818

Keith, T. Z. (2006). *Multiple regression and beyond.* Boston, MA: Allyn & Bacon.

Kenney-Benson, G., Pomerantz, E. M., Ryan, A., & Patrick, H. (2006). Sex differences in math performance: The role of how children approach school. *Developmental Psychology, 42,* 11–26. doi:10.1037/0012-1649.42.1.11

Kerr, M., & Stattin, H. (2000). What parents know, how they know it, and several forms of adolescent adjustment: Further support for a reinterpretation of monitoring. *Developmental Psychology, 36,* 366–380. doi: 10.1037 /0012-1649.36.3.366

Kline, R. B. (1998). *Principles and practice of structural equation modeling.* New York, NY: Guilford Press.

Knafo, A., & Schwartz, S. H. (2004). Identity formation and parent–child value congruence in adolescence. *British Journal of Developmental Psychology, 22,* 439–458. doi:10.1348/0261510041552765

Knafo, A., & Schwartz, S. H. (2009). Accounting for parent–child value congruence: Theoretical considerations and empirical evidence. In U. Schönpflug (Ed.), *Culture and psychology* (pp. 240–268). New York, NY: Cambridge University Press. doi:10.1017 /CBO9780511804670.012

Kohl, G. O., Lengua, L. J., McMahon, R. J., & The Conduct Problems Prevention Research Group. (2000). Parent involvement in school: Conceptualizing multiple dimensions and their relations with family and demographic risk factors. *Journal of School Psychology, 38,* 501–523. doi:10.1016 /S0022-4405(00)00050-9

Little, T. D. (1997). Mean and covariance structures (MACS) analyses of cross-cultural data: Practical and theoretical issues. *Multivariate Behavioral Research, 32,* 53–76. doi:10.1207/ s15327906mbr3201_3

Little, T. D., Cunningham, W. A., Shahar, G., & Widaman, K. F. (2002). To parcel or not to parcel: Exploring the question, weighing the merits. *Structural Equation Modeling, 9,* 151–173. doi:10.1207/S15328007SEM0902_1

Little, T. D., Rhemtulla, M., Gibson, K., & Schoemann, A. M. (2013). Why the items versus parcels controversy needn't be one. *Psychological Methods, 18,* 285–300. doi:10.1037/a0033266

McDonald, R. P., & Ho, M.-H. R. (2002). Principles and practice in reporting structural equation analyses. *Psychological Methods, 7,* 64–82. doi:10.1037/1082-989X.7.1.64

Muthén, L. K., & Muthén, B. O. (1998–2012). *Mplus user's guide* (7th ed.). Los Angeles, CA: Muthén & Muthén.

Ng, F. F., Pomerantz, E. M., & Lam, S. F. (2007). European American and Chinese parents' responses to children's success and failure: Implications for children's responses. *Developmental Psychology, 43,* 1239–1255. doi:10.1037/0012-1649.43.5.1239

NICHD Early Child Care Research Network. (2003). Do children's attention processes mediate the link between family predictors and school readiness? *Developmental Psychology, 39,* 581–593. doi:10.1037/0012-1649.39.3.581

Nord, C. W., & West, J. (2001). *Fathers and mothers' involvement in their children's schools by family type and resident status.* Washington, DC: National Center for Educational Statistics.

Okagaki, L., & Bevis, C. (1999). Transmission of religious values: Relations between parents' and daughters' beliefs. *The Journal of Genetic Psychology: Research and Theory on Human Development, 160,* 303–318. doi:10.1080/00221329909595401

Pintrich, P. R. (1999). The role of motivation in promoting and sustaining self-regulated learning. *International Journal of Educational Research, 31,* 459– 470. doi:10.1016/S0883-0355(99)00015-4

Pomerantz, E. M., Kim, E. M., & Cheung, C. S. (2012). Parents' involvement in children's learning. In K. R. Harris, S. Graham, T. C. Urdan, S. Graham, J. M. Royer, & M. Zeidner (Eds.), *APA educational psychology handbook* (pp. 417–440). Washington, DC: American Psychological Association. doi:10.1037/13274-017

Pomerantz, E. M., Ng, F. F., Cheung, C. S., & Qu, Y. (in press). How to raise happy children who succeed in school: Lessons from China and the United States. *Child Development Perspectives.* doi:10.1111/cdep.12063

Pomerantz, E. M., Ng, F. F., & Wang, Q. (2008). Culture, parenting, and motivation: The case of East Asia and the United States. In M. L. Maehr, S. A. Karabenick, & T. C. Urdan (Eds.), *Advances in motivation and achievement: Social psychological perspectives* (Vol. 15, pp. 209–240). Bingley, England: Emerald Group. doi:10.1016/S0749-7423 (08)15007-5

Pomerantz, E. M., Qin, L., Wang, Q., & Chen, H. (2009). American and Chinese early adolescents' inclusion of their relationships with their parents in their self-construals. *Child Development, 80,* 792–807. doi: 10.1111/j.1467-8624.2009.01298.x

Pomerantz, E. M., Qin, L., Wang, Q., & Chen, H. (2011). Changes in early adolescents' sense of responsibility to their parents in the United States and China: Implications for their academic functioning. *Child Development, 82,* 1136–1151. doi:10.1111/j.1467-8624.2011.01588.x

Pomerantz, E. M., Saxon, J. L., & Oishi, S. (2000). The psychological trade-offs of goal investment. *Journal of Personality and Social Psychology, 79,* 617–630. doi:10.1037/0022-3514.79.4.617

Reynolds, A. J. (1992). Comparing measures of parental involvement and their effects on academic achievement. *Early Childhood Research Quarterly, 7,* 441–462. doi:10.1016/0885-2006(92)90031-S

Rhemtulla, M., Brosseau-Liard, P., & Savalei, V. (2012). When can categorical variables be treated as continuous? A comparison of robust continuous and categorical SEM estimation methods under sub-optimal conditions. *Psychological Methods, 17,* 354–373. doi:10.1037/ a0029315

Roest, A. M. C., Dubas, J. S., Gerris, J. R. M., & Engels, R. C. M. E. (2009). Value similarities among fathers, mothers, and adolescents and the role of a cultural stereotype: Different measurement strategies reconsidered. *Journal of Research on Adolescence, 19,* 812–833. doi: 10.1111/j.1532-7795.2009.00621.x

Schwartz, D., Kelly, B. M., & Duong, M. T. (2013). Do academicallyengaged adolescents experience social sanctions from the peer group? *Journal of Youth and Adolescence, 42,* 1319–1330. doi:10.1007/s10964-012-9882-4

Sénéchal, M., & LeFevre, J. (2002). Parental involvement in the development of children's reading skill: A five year longitudinal study. *Child Development, 73,* 445– 460. doi:10.1111/1467-8624.00417

Snyder, T. D., & Dillow, S. A. (2012). *Digest of education statistics 2011* (NCES 2012– 001). Washington, DC: National Center for Education Statistics, Institute of Education Sciences, U.S. Department of Education.

Stattin, H., & Kerr, M. (2000). Parental monitoring: A reinterpretation. *Child Development, 71,* 1072–1085. doi:10.1111/1467-8624.00210

U.S. Census Bureau. (2007). *Census 2000 Summary File 1 and 3.* Retrieved January 4, 2010, from http://factfinder.census.gov/servlet/DatasetMainPageServlet?_lang=en&_ts=235058466046&_ds_name=DEC_2000_SF3_U&_program=

Wang, M.-T., & Fredricks, J. (2014). The reciprocal links between school engagement and youth problem behavior during adolescence. *Child Development, 85,* 722–737. doi:10.1111/cdev.12138

Wang, M.-T., & Peck, S. (2013). Adolescent educational success and mental health vary across school engagement profiles. *Developmental Psychology, 49,* 1266–1276. doi:10.1037/a0030028

Wang, Q., & Pomerantz, E. M. (2009). The motivational landscape of early adolescence in the United States and China: A longitudinal study.

*Child Development, 80,* 1272–1287. doi:10.1111/j.1467-8624.2009.01331.x

Wigfield, A., & Wagner, A. L. (2005). Competence, motivation, and identity development during adolescence. In A. Elliott & C. Dweck (Eds.), *Handbook of competence and motivation* (pp. 222–239). New York, NY: Guilford Press.

Wood, R. E., & Locke, E. A. (1987). The relation of self-efficacy and grade goals to academic performance. *Educational and Psychological Measurement, 47,* 1013–1024. doi:10.1177/0013164487474017

Wothke, W. (2000). Longitudinal and multigroup modeling with missing data. In T. D. Little, K. U. Schnabel, & J. Baumert (Eds.), *Modeling longitudinal and multilevel data: Practical issues, applied approaches, and specific examples* (pp. 219–240). Mahwah, NJ: Erlbaum.

First author, Cᴇᴄɪʟɪᴀ S.-S. Cʜᴇᴜɴɢ, is currently an assistant professor of psychology at UC-Riverside. She studied with Eva M. Pomerantz, the co-author, who is a professor of psychology at the University of Illinois at Urbana-Champagne. Professor Pomerantz is also a Fellow of the Association for Psychological Science and an Editorial Consultant for *Child Development.*

# EXPLORING THE ISSUE

## Is Parental Involvement in Education Critical for Student Achievement?

## Critical Thinking and Reflection

1. Why is there a publication bias in studies of parental involvement in education?
2. What are the potential third variables that can be driving the positive correlation that Hill and Tyson (2009) found?
3. How different are the measures of parental involvement in education and student achievement in the two studies?
4. What were the significant predictors of student grades in the Cheung and Pomerantz (2015) study?
5. According to the Cheung and Pomerantz (2015) study, what role does parental involvement have in socializing youth in education?

## Is There Common Ground?

Both studies in this issue focus on the middle school population and set out to confirm the positive benefits of parental involvement in education on student achievement. Hill and Tyson (2009)'s study set out to improve our definition of parental involvement behaviors and confirmed that a positive correlation between the two variables (parental involvement in education and student achievement) has existed in the studies published in the past 30 years. A strength of their study is that they considered publication bias and factored into their analysis those studies that were "missing." Their study also contributes to research progress because it is a necessary requirement to perfect measurement and confirm the existence of a significant correlation between two variables before moving on to theorize a casual chain of events. However, correlations give us very little confidence that parental involvement is the critical factor in student achievement. Many third variables are possible.

Indeed, Cheung and Pomerantz (2015) did not set out to disconfirm the proposed positive benefits of parental involvement on student achievement. The two authors may be appalled that this study was used to debate the "No" side because their interest was in testing a value development pathway to describe the processes through which parental involvement has positive (indirect) effects on student achievement. The focus on process is a huge contribution to any field of study and their study technically should be part of the "Yes" part of this debate. Their theory points to parental involvement as the ultimate

reason why students do well because youth see these behaviors as indicators of their parents' values and internalize them as a result. Nonetheless, I decided to use the Cheung and Pomerantz (2015) study for the "No" side in order to show that their results indicated that parental involvement (measured in the fall of their eighth grade year) did not have statistically significant direct associations with student grades in both cultural contexts among middle school students by the end of the eighth grade. Because this study was longitudinal in design, we were able to observe the independent variables at a time prior to the dependent variable.

Thus, the most important, critical factor in student achievement remains to be the student, not the parent. In this study, it was the extent to which youth perceive and internalize educational values. When student grades are the criterion, what parents do and even what they perceive their parents think is important are directly unrelated to increases in grades. Of course parents may have been the ultimate reason why youth do well in school or they do not, but not the proximal reason for understanding variation in student grades.

## Additional Resources

J. Eccles-Parsons, T. Adler, R. Futterman, S. Goff, C. Kaczala, J. Meece, and C. Midgley, "Expectations, Values, and Academic Behaviors." In J. T. Spence (Ed.), *Achievement and Achievement Motivation*, 77–146. (New York: Freeman, 1983).

J. L. Epstein and S. L. Dauber, "School Programs and Teacher Practices of Parent Involvement in Inner-City Elementary and Middle Schools," *Elementary School Journal. Special Issue: Educational Partnerships: Home, School, Community* (vol. 91, 1991).

W. S. Grolnick and M. L. Slowiaczek, "Parents' Involvement in Children's Schooling: A Multidimensional Conceptualization and Motivational Model," *Child Development* (vol. 65, 1994).

L. C. Taylor, J. D. Clayton, and S. J. Rowley, "Academic Socialization: Understanding Parental Influences on Children's School-Related Development in the Early Years," *Review of General Psychology* (vol. 8, 2004).

# *Internet References . . .*

**NEA Reviews of the Research on Best Practices in Education**

www.nea.org/tools/17360.htm

**Involvement in My Child's Education**

www2.ed.gov/parents/academic/involve/edpicks.jhtml

**Helping Your Child**

www2.ed.gov/parents/academic/help/hyc.html?src=rt

**19 Proven Tips for Getting Parents Involved at School**

www.edutopia.org/groups/classroom-management/783266

Selected, Edited, and with Issue Framing Material by:
Esther S. Chang, *Soka University of America*

# ISSUE

# Should We Be "Tiger" Parents?

**YES: Ruth K. Chao and Christine Aque**, from "Interpretations of Parental Control by Asian Immigrant and European American Youth," *Journal of Family Psychology* (2009)

**NO: Su Yeong Kim, et al.**, from "Does 'Tiger Parenting' Exist? Parenting Profiles of Chinese Americans and Adolescent Developmental Outcomes," *Asian American Journal of Psychology* (2013)

## Learning Outcomes

**After reading this issue, you will be able to:**

- Define the four different parenting styles.
- Compare and contrast tiger parenting to other parenting constructs (e.g., parenting styles, guan, etc.).
- Identify the difference between behavioral control and psychological control and which is typically related to higher academic achievement.
- Articulate the cultural explanation of the positive association between authoritarian parenting and student achievement.

## ISSUE SUMMARY

**YES:** Ruth Chao and Christine Aque argue that parental control can be viewed as a virtue, especially in Asian-influenced cultures. They conduct a cross-sectional study that demonstrates that Asian youth report lower levels of anger on average in reaction to parental strictness and limit setting compared to European Americans, and that parental control will be effective as long as it does not make youth angry.

**NO:** Su Yeong Kim and colleagues found that tiger parenting was not common perhaps because it is maladaptive. They conducted a 3-point longitudinal study spanning 8 years to demonstrate that tiger parenting existed among Chinese immigrant families in the United States but did not have beneficial influences over time.

$A$my Chua published a parenting memoir entitled the *Battle Hymn of the Tiger Mother* in 2011 and unintentionally started a somewhat bitter nationwide discussion about parenting, children's achievement, and culture. She has an academic appointment at Yale Law School and has an impressive educational and occupational history, but she stated that she never intended the book to be a manual for parenting. Nevertheless, many believed that the Chinese-influenced parenting practices she described to have used in raising her daughters were implied to be superior. Of course, it did not help that the *Wall Street Journal* article that described her book was entitled, "Why Chinese mothers are superior" (8 January, 2011).

According to Amy Chua's personal website, she graduated from Harvard College (1984) and soon after from Harvard Law School (1987). She clerked at the U.S. Court of Appeals and practiced at a prominent Wall Street firm before assuming an academic appointment at Duke University and eventually at Yale University. She has published two bestseller books in her field of expertise and her memoir on childrearing has been translated into at least 30 languages and coined the now popular term "tiger mother." In her memoir, she described how she restricted her daughters by not allowing them to go to sleepovers, participate in school plays, watch TV, or play computer games. She expected her daughters to be the #1 student in every subject except gym and drama. The way that she described how she pushed her daughters to practice piano horrified many Americans who deemed her methods to be hostile and akin to child abuse. Specifically, to be a tiger mom is to have high academic expectations of your children and to exert a high level of strictness and control to ensure their focus. For parents who allow for some TV and video gaming, this debate asks whether we should be more like the tiger mother. Her two daughters did go to Harvard University and children do lack wisdom and control.

Fortunately, much psychological research has been invested in the search for optimal parenting practices and particularly into the question of parental control. Unfortunately, much of the concepts that have been developed were based on Western European families of the upper middle class. The most widely used parenting concept is Diana Baumrind's parenting styles model, which is a hybrid of psychodynamic and social learning theories of children's development. Parenting styles represent a macro-level construct reflective of a parent's typical response to a childrearing situation, or a general attitude toward the child (Darling & Steinberg, 1993). The two dimensions that differentiate the four parenting styles are parental responsiveness and parental control. I will focus on two particular parenting styles that are both high in parental control but differ in levels of responsiveness to the child. Authoritative parents, which many White middle-class youth describe their parents as, are highly responsive to their child and supportive of their autonomy. Authoritarian parenting, which many Asian and other minority youth describe their parents as, are low in responsivity to their child. The concept of tiger parent overlaps a great deal with the latter style of parenting.

Although parental control has been seen to be an important component of parenting because it socializes children to be respectful, prosocial, and emotionally stable, it is believed to be effective when matched by parental warmth and support for child's self-esteem. Thus, a growing conclusion among socialization researchers has been that authoritative parenting is optimal for children's development. However, there was an interesting puzzle. In a well-cited study, Dornbusch et al. (1987) reported that Asian Americans in their sample had the highest grades although their parents were the least authoritative. Thus, the parenting styles model did little to explain the high levels of Asian American achievement, as authoritarian parenting was the strongest predictor of grades. Additionally, Hispanics and African Americans reported more authoritative parents than Asians, but had the lowest average grades in school.

It was proposed that measures of authoritarian parenting do not have construct validity within the Chinese family context (Chao, 1994). Though Chinese parents generally score higher in control and lower in warmth than their European American counterparts, the context of Chinese parenting does not assume cruel domination over children inherent in authoritarian parenting but an organizational type of control for the purposes of child "training," also known as "childrearing" in Chinese. The concept of training, *chiao shun*, is indigenous to the Chinese and refers to teaching children appropriate behaviors, including the readiness to perform well in school (as reflected in its emphasis on hard work, self-discipline, and obedience). "Training" children is argued to have roots in Confucian ideology and functions to promote relational harmony (which is comparable to warmth) within families and society. Thus, its purpose is to assure the integrity of the family rather than to express ambivalence or hostility toward the child (Chao, 1994). A key question that remained unanswered was whether youth of Chinese or East Asian parents feel that their parents' efforts to control them are intrusive. In the "Yes" selection, Chao and Aque (2009) examine not only the extent to which parental control is adaptive for different ethnic groups but also the extent to which youth from different ethnic backgrounds are angry when their parents use controlling strategies. Their findings help support the "Yes" side of this debate because their results reveal the extent to which parental control can be adaptive.

Since "tiger parenting" did not emerge from the literature but from mainstream popular culture, Su Yeong Kim and colleagues set out to discover if and to what extent "tiger parenting" was present among a sample of Chinese American mothers and fathers. Moreover, they hypothesize that if a tiger parenting profile emerges from the data, it should be highly correlated to academic achievement. Kim et al. (2013) used a sophisticated study design, using reports from adolescents, mothers, and fathers. They also tracked the same families three times over 8 years and tested to examine which parenting style was related to student achievement over time. This article was selected to represent the "No" side because their results suggest that what is adaptive for European American families may also be adaptive for Chinese living in America. Therefore, it would not be wise to be a tiger parent, particularly with the element of harshness that Chua described in her memoir.

# YES

**Ruth K. Chao and Christine Aque**

# Interpretations of Parental Control by Asian Immigrant and European American Youth

Researchers have begun demonstrating sociocultural differences, including ethnic and immigrant group membership, in the effects of parenting on adolescent outcomes (Chao, 1994, 2001; Chen, Dong, & Zhou, 1997; Dornbusch, Ritter, Leiderman, Roberts, & Fraleigh, 1987; Steinberg, Lamborn, Dornbusch, & Darling, 1992). For example, Chao (1994, 2001) has discussed the importance of culture-specific definitions of parental control for Asian immigrants in the United States defined by the notion of *guan*, a Chinese character that, when translated, means both "to govern" as well as "to love." This more positive connotation of parental control highlights the possibility that there may be important differences in the parental control of Asian Americans—particularly recent immigrants—and European Americans. Control and discipline are regarded as important parental responsibilities in many Asian societies, according to Confucian traditions (Ho, 1986, 1996). European Americans, on the other hand, may view excessive parental control as an intrusion upon their children's autonomy. Hence, how adolescents view or interpret parental control may differ for European Americans compared with other ethnic groups, especially those that include recent immigrants.

In fact, Mason, Walker-Barnes, Tu, Simons, and Martinez-Arrue (2004) have shown that adolescent interpretations of parental control do vary by ethnicity, with African American youth associating parental control more with feelings of being loved and cared for, and less with anger, than did White or Hispanic youth. Their study was the first to consider the youth's affective meaning of parental control, which they defined as the emotional reaction a child feels toward specific parental control behaviors (Mason et al., 2004).

There is little research examining specific affective interpretations of parental control across ethnic groups, especially among Asian American youth. Although many studies have shown differences in the effects of certain types of parental control on outcomes across ethnic groups, few have been able to explain the processes underlying these ethnic differences. To further explain possible ethnic and sociocultural differences in the effects of parental control on adolescent outcomes, this study, in the same vein as Mason et al. (2004), considers adolescents' affective interpretations regarding both behavioral and psychological control. Specifically, this study first examines whether there are differences in the effects of behavioral and psychological control between European Americans and three ethnic groups of Asian immigrants (Chinese, Koreans, and Filipinos). Ultimately, this study examines whether adolescents' feelings of anger may moderate the relationship between parental control and adolescents' behavioral adjustment for European American and each Asian immigrant group.

## Distinctions Between Behavioral and Psychological Control and Their Effects

Previous research has distinguished between two types of parental control: behavioral and psychological. Behavioral control consists of setting rules and limits and administering punishments or consequences for misbehavior (Barber, 1996), which is considered necessary for the development of behavioral regulation and social competence in adolescents (Steinberg, 1990). Studies have also found behavioral control to be associated with decreases in adolescents' externalizing symptoms (e.g., antisocial behavior, school deviance, and delinquency) and, to a smaller extent, internalizing problems (Barber, Olsen, & Shagle, 1994; Barber, Stoltz, & Olsen, 2005; Gray & Steinberg, 1999; Walker-Barnes & Mason, 2004), as well as higher levels of academic achievement (Bean, Bush, McKenry, & Wilson, 2003; Steinberg,

Chao, Ruth; Aque, Christine, "Interpretations of Parental Control by Asian Immigrant and European American Youth," *Journal of Family Psychology*, vol. 23, no. 3, June 2009, pp. 342–354. No further reproduction or distribution is permitted without written permission from the American Psychological Association.

Elmen, & Mounts, 1989). Psychological control, on the other hand, refers to more intrusive control of the child's thoughts and emotions through anxiety or guilt induction, shaming, and love withdrawal (Barber & Harmon, 2002). This type of control is positively associated with internalizing problems such as depression and anxiety, as well as with externalizing problems including delinquency, antisocial behavior, and substance use; it is also associated with lower self-esteem, self-reliance, and academic achievement (Barber et al., 2005; Bean et al., 2003; Doyle & Markiewicz, 2005; Gray & Steinberg, 1999; Pettit, Laird, Dodge, Bates, & Criss, 2001; Rogers, Buchanan, & Winchell, 2003; Walker-Barnes & Mason, 2004).

Very few studies have directly examined differences between European Americans and Asians in the effects of either behavioral or psychological control. A few studies with Asian samples have found that psychological control had no association with internalizing and externalizing symptoms or, specifically, with self-esteem and school grades (Olsen et al., 2002; Rudy & Halgunseth, 2005). Another study, focusing on unilateral parental decision making, found negative associations with deviance and academic competence for European Americans but not for Asian Americans (Lamborn, Dornbusch, & Steinberg, 1996).

However, other scholars did not find any ethnic group differences in the effects of parental control, specifically between European Americans and Asians (Hasebe, Nucci, & Nucci, 2004; Mantzicopoulos & Oh-Hwang, 1998). Hence, findings regarding the differential effects of parental control appear to be mixed. More comparative studies of the unique effects of behavioral and psychological control on adolescents are sorely needed.

## Affective Interpretations of Parental Control

Although parental control may be perceived as normal or appropriate in more interdependent cultures, high levels of parental control might be perceived as hostile and rejecting by individualist cultures such as the United States, particularly among European Americans (Kağitçibaşi, 1996). The aforementioned study by Mason et al. (2004) of European Americans and African Americans included youth ratings of parents' behavioral and psychological control that were based on the widely used Child-Rearing Practices Behavioral Inventory (CRPBI; Schludermann & Schludermann, 1988), as well as ratings of their own feelings (i.e., hurt, angry, controlled, loved, cared for) with respect to parents' use of each type of control. Even with behavioral control, which is related

to positive outcomes, European American youth reported feeling more hurt, angry, and controlled than African American youth.

Additionally, the study by Mason et al. (2004) found that European American youth also reported feeling less loved and cared for with psychological control than African American youth. Although studies have consistently found that psychological control has negative consequences for European American youth, there have been no studies that have examined whether adolescents' own interpretations or feelings about such control may influence the associations between control and adolescents' well-being. Likewise, youth interpretations or feelings about parents' behavioral control may also affect the effect that this control may have on their well-being. Specifically, feeling anger toward parents' use of psychological control may actually mitigate the negative effects of such control for European Americans. That is, adolescents' ability to feel angry in reaction to parents' use of psychological control may reflect their psychological or internal rejection of such strategies. When parents engage in shaming or inducement of guilt, feeling angry at parents may help youth to distance themselves from such negativity and may thus be less likely to lead to problem behaviors in these youth than for those who do not feel angry.

On the other hand, for European American youth, rejecting or feeling angry about control behaviors that are more likely to benefit youth (e.g., behavioral control and, specifically, monitoring) may diminish their positive effects. With behavioral control that sets limits on potentially destructive behaviors, angry reactions from youth may amplify these behaviors or else lead to the youth's rebellion. This may not be the case for Asian immigrant youth, however. Not only may these youth view parental control in a more positive light than European American youth, as mentioned earlier, but they may also regard the expression of negative emotions such as anger as inappropriate. Although the expression of anger is somewhat tolerated in European American families, it is highly discouraged among Asians (Lai & Linden, 1993; Matsumoto et al., 1988) and is considered unnecessary or serving no useful purpose (Markus & Kitayama, 1991). Studies (Yau & Smetana, 1996, 2003) that have explicitly examined parent–adolescent conflict among Chinese, however, have reported moderate levels, albeit lower than those found among their European American counterparts. Rothbaum, Pott, Azuma, Miyake, and Weisz (2000) have maintained that, in European American families, conflict and tension are typical, and parents expect noncompliance from their children, considering it part of the healthy development of the child's individuality and relationship skills.

Because Asian immigrant youth may feel less angry about parental control compared with European American youth, even control that is more intrusive, the consequences of control are not moderated by their feelings of anger as they are for European American youth. Thus, feelings of anger toward psychological control may mitigate its negative effects for European American youth but not for Asian immigrant youth. Likewise, feeling anger toward control that is beneficial (i.e., behavioral control) has been shown to have no moderating effect for Asian immigrant youth.

However, there may also be important differences among Asian immigrant youth, and some groups of Asian immigrants may differ more from European Americans in their parenting than others. Although the studies reviewed earlier focused more on immigrant Chinese families, some of the findings for these families may also apply to Korean immigrants. Both Chinese and Koreans share Confucian-based heritages, with an emphasis on filial piety affording a great deal of authority and respect to parents (Chao & Tseng, 2002). Similar to Chinese parents, Korean parents view their high levels of control as a demonstration of their love and interest in their children (Kim, 2005).

On the other hand, although Filipinos do not share such Confucian influences, they may place an even greater emphasis on parental authority and control or the use of such authority for controlling the behavior of their adolescents, particularly girls. Fuligni (1998) has found that both Filipino and Chinese youth from immigrant families were more accepting of parental authority and less willing to disagree with their parents than were European American youth. In comparisons of Chinese Americans and Filipino Americans, Blair and Qian have shown that Catholicism, in particular, has particular salience for Filipino American youth in that it predicted higher school performance for these youth but not for Chinese American youth (Blair & Qian, 1998). Espiritu (1995, 2001, 2003) has argued that parental control of daughters is rooted in the influences of Catholicism and in the consequences of the U.S. military presence in the Philippines (i.e., prostitution). These historical influences have shaped parents' roles as protectors of their daughters by restricting their independence and autonomy. Thus, it may be that Filipino American youth, from immigrant families in particular, view their parents as controlling more than European American youth, and perhaps even more than Chinese and Korean youth from immigrant families. However, cultural and sociohistorical influences have shaped Filipino youths' views of parental authority so that they are less likely than European American youth to feel anger toward their parents.

The purpose of this study is to investigate possible differences in the meaning ascribed to parenting by examining adolescents' affective interpretations or anger with different types of parental control (i.e., behavioral and psychological). Asian immigrant and European American adolescents may interpret parenting on the basis of their divergent sociocultural scripts for defining parenting, with these scripts reflected in adolescents' emotional reactions to parental control. These differing interpretations for both types of control may explain why some studies have found ethnic group differences in the effects of each type on adolescent outcomes (Bean et al., 2003; Olsen et al., 2002; Walker-Barnes & Mason, 2004). We begin the study by examining whether there are across-group differences in the associations between each type of control and adolescent wellbeing, comparing each of the three Asian immigrant groups with European Americans. Next, we investigate within each ethnic group whether these associations are moderated by how angry the youth feel about the control.

Although all three groups of Asian immigrants will report higher levels of parental control than European Americans, they will also report lower levels of feeling angry about parental control, compared with European American adolescents. The effects of parental control will also vary between European American and Asian immigrant adolescents, particularly between Filipino immigrants and European Americans. Finally, the following hypotheses for the moderating effects of anger were proposed: The effects of parental control on adolescent problem behaviors will vary according to the levels of feeling angry about control for European Americans, but not for any of the three Asian immigrant groups. That is, for European Americans only, the effects of psychological control on adolescents' behavioral problems will be less deleterious (i.e., the associations will be less positive), the angrier the youth feel; whereas the effects of behavioral control will be less beneficial (i.e., the associations will be less negative), the angrier the youth feel.

# Method

## Participants

The study included 484 Asian immigrant (197 Chinese, 174 Korean, 113 Filipino) and 601 European American ninth graders from eight high schools in the greater Los Angeles area, with at least 10% Asian Americans in their student body. The Asian immigrant youth were drawn from a larger sample (over 1,700) of Asian American youth with immigrant parents (with the first-generation immigrant youth identified as those born outside the United States). The sample was drawn from the first wave of a longitudinal study with data collected for three cohorts of ninth graders (i.e., those who began in the fall of 2002, 2003, and 2004). The mean age of all adolescents was 14.8 years (14.7 years for Chinese, 15.0 years for Koreans, 14.9 years for Filipinos, and 14.8 years for European Americans). Just over 49% of the overall sample was comprised of females (53% with 1 missing among the Chinese; 49% among the Koreans; 43% among the Filipinos; and 48% with 6 missing among the European Americans). The Asian adolescents immigrated to the United States at an average age of 8.0 years (7.7 years for Chinese, 8.9 years for Koreans, and 7.5 years for Filipinos). The European American adolescents were of at least third-generation descent; that is, both adolescents and parents were born in the United States. The mean parental education level was 7.4 years for the entire sample (7.2 years for Chinese, 7.6 years for Koreans, 7.7 years for Filipinos, and 7.3 years for European Americans), with 7 as "finished 4-year college" and 8 as "finished graduate school." The proportion of youth whose parents owned their own homes was 71% for Chinese, 53% for Koreans, 53% for Filipinos, and 79% for European Americans. Also, the proportion of youth living in single-parent households was 14% for Chinese, 19% for Koreans, 10% for Filipinos, and 24% for European Americans. The proportion of youth who identified their mothers as the primary caregiver was 85% for Chinese, 81% for Koreans, 71% for Filipinos, and 79% for European Americans. On the basis of a chi-square analysis or one-way analysis of variance (ANOVA), followed by post hoc Tukey analyses, no significant differences were found on parental education, $F(3, 1081) = 0.468$, $p = .70$. However, a greater proportion of European-American youth were from single-parent households than were Chinese, Korean, and Filipino immigrant youth, $\chi^2(3) = 18.59$, $p = .00$. Also, a greater proportion of immigrant Chinese youth reported their mothers as their primary caregivers than did Filipino immigrant youth, $\chi^2(3) = 8.45$, $p = .04$; and Chinese and European American adolescents reported higher rates of owning their home than did Korean and Filipino adolescents, $\chi^2(3) = 67.11$, $p = .00$.

## Procedure

On the basis of the procedures and measures described later, approval for the use of human subjects was acquired through the internal review board of the University of California, Riverside. Parental and adolescent consent was obtained before students' participation in the study. Consent forms were mailed beforehand to all parents of ninth-grade students to request their children's participation. Parents mailed back consent forms only if they did not want their children to participate in the study. All parents received copies of consent letters in English, Chinese, and Korean, along with a postage-paid, self-addressed envelope. Adolescents were also provided with an assent statement on the cover page of their survey. Adolescents completed these paper-and-pencil surveys, consisting of the following measures, during one of their class periods.

### Parental Control

Parental behavioral control was measured with the Firm Control/Lax Control scale of the Children's Report on Parent Behavior Inventory (CRPBI-30) adapted by Schludermann and Schludermann (1988) for adolescents (Youth Self-Report). This is the same measure used by Mason et al (2004) and is a very well-established measure of parenting practices, including behavioral and psychological control (Barber, Stolz, & Olsen, 2005). The scale includes 10 items involving setting standards and expectations, as well as enforcing rules (e.g., "insists that I do exactly as I'm told"). Parental psychological control was measured with Barber's (1996) revised scale of psychological control from the CRPBI-30 containing 8 items (e.g., "brings up past mistakes when s/he criticizes me").

For both scales, responses to the items were measured on a 5-point Likert-type scale ranging from 1 (*not at all like*) to 5 (*a lot like*). Next, to determine whether the parental control scales would remain as one scale or form separate subscales, we conducted separate factor analyses for each group (Chinese, Koreans, Filipinos, and European Americans) with a varimax rotation, using Guadagnoli and Velicer's (1988) criteria that all items load at .40 or higher. For the behavioral control items, a two-factor structure was found. The first factor, labeled Strictness consisted of the following six items: (a) is very strict with me, (b) gives hard punishments when I misbehave, (c) insists that I do exactly as I am told, (d) believes in having a lot of rules and sticking with them, (e) is easy with me (reverse-coded), and (f) lets me off easy when I do something wrong (reverse-coded). These items had good internal consistencies (Cronbach's alphas), with 0.77 for the whole sample, and ranges from 0.71 to 0.79 for the ethnic groups. The second factor, labeled Provides Structure consisted of the following four items, all reverse-coded: (a) lets me go any place I want without asking, (b) gives me as much freedom as I want, (c) lets me do anything I like to do; and (d) lets me go out any evening I want. These items also had good internal consistencies ($\alpha = 0.78$ for the overall sample; range $= 0.75 - 0.80$ for ethnic groups). With the psychological control measure, all the items loaded on one factor, with good internal consistencies ($\alpha = 0.80$ for the whole sample; range $= 0.71 - 0.82$ for ethnic groups). On the basis of these factor structures, we created scale scores by calculating the mean of the items in each scale.

On the basis of Pearson's correlations, we also conducted bivariate associations among the three parental control scales with the associations between (a) Strictness and Provides Structure, (b) Strictness and psychological control, and (c) Provides Structure and psychological control at .51, .51, and .06, respectively, among Chinese immigrants; .48, .42, and .15, respectively, among Korean immigrants; .66, .40, and .19, respectively, among Filipino immigrants; and .42, .33, and −.02, respectively, among European Americans. All correlations were significant at $p < .05$, with the exception of those between Provides Structure and psychological control. It is interesting that the associations between Strictness and psychological control were of similar magnitude as those between Strictness and Provides Structure. Moreover, as the magnitude of associations between Strictness and Provides Structure was not consistently high or over .50 for all the ethnic groups, the decision was made to treat these as separate scales.

*Affective Interpretations of Anger Toward Parental Control*
We measured affective interpretations of anger toward control by presenting the same items described earlier (i.e., 10 items for behavioral control and 8 items for psychological control) and then asking adolescents how angry they would feel if their parent acted accordingly (e.g., "if my parent . . . [is very strict with me], then I would feel . . ."). This was very similar to the measure used by Mason and colleagues (2004) involving youth ratings of their feelings (e.g., loved, hurt, angry).

The responses were scored on a 4-point Likert-type scale ranging from 1 (*not angry*) to 4 (*very angry*). Exploratory factor analysis again revealed a similar two-factor solution as reported earlier for the items measuring behavioral control, angry–Strictness (six items) and angry–Provides Structure (four items). The internal consistencies were adequate for angry–Strictness (.75 overall; range = .68 −.77 for the ethnic groups) and excellent for angry–Provides Structure (.90 overall; range = .84 −.91 for the ethnic groups). Exploratory factor analysis for feeling angry–psychological control resulted in all eight items loading on one factor, with $\alpha$s that were excellent (.87 overall; range = .84 −.88 for ethnic groups).

*Behavioral Adjustment*
Adolescents' behavioral adjustment was measured with the Internalizing and Externalizing scales from the Youth Self-Report of the Child Behavioral Checklist (CBCL; Achenbach, 1991). The Internalizing scale has 31 items with three subscales measuring depression–anxiety (e.g., "I cry a lot"), somatic complaints (i.e. "I feel overtired"), and withdrawal symptoms ("I am too shy or timid"). The

Externalizing scale has 32 items with two subscales measuring delinquency (i.e. "I lie or cheat") and aggression (i.e., "I am mean to others"). All items were scored on a 3-point Likert-type scale ranging from 0 (*not true*) to 2 (*very true or often true*). The $\alpha$s for the Internalizing scale were 0.90 for the whole sample (range = 0.89−0.92 for ethnic groups); $\alpha$s for the Externalizing scale were 0.90 overall (range = 0.86−0.91 for the ethnic groups).

We evaluated adolescents' drug use using items from the National Youth Survey and revised by Huizinga, Menard, and Elliott (1989). The scale, ranging from 0 (*0 days*) to 4 (*20–30 days*), consisted of six items assessing the number of days in the past month during which youth have used alcoholic beverages, cigarettes, marijuana, cocaine, inhalants, and other illegal drugs. The scale had good internal consistencies overall ($\alpha = 0.85$), but these differed for each ethnic group. Specifically, the alphas were similarly strong for Filipinos and European Americans ($\alpha = 0.86$), marginal for Koreans ($\alpha = 0.63$), and poor for Chinese ($\alpha = 0.50$). Thus, the findings for drug use involving Chinese adolescents should be interpreted with caution.

# Results

## Mean Level Differences in Parental Control and Affective Interpretations of Anger

To test for differences in mean levels between Asian immigrant and European American youth, we conducted univariate analyses of variance (ANOVAs) followed by Tukey post hoc tests. Means and standard deviations are presented in Table 1. With behavioral control, significant ethnic differences were found so that Chinese immigrant adolescents reported higher levels of strictness for their parents than did the European American adolescents, $F(3, 1078) = 5.2, p = .00$. Chinese, Korean, and Filipino immigrant adolescents also reported significantly higher levels of psychological control than did European American adolescents, $F(3, 1078) = 13.42, p = .00$. Chinese immigrant adolescents reported significantly lower levels of feeling angry with parental strictness, $F(3, 992) = 4.35, p = .00$. Immigrant Chinese, Korean, and Filipino adolescents also reported lower levels of feeling angry with psychological control than European American adolescents did, $F(3, 987) = 22.56, p = .00$.

## Effects of Parental Control on Adolescent Outcomes

First, bivariate associations (Pearson's correlations) between the three aspects of control with the adolescent outcomes are presented in Table 2. Additional bivariate

*Table 1*

### Means (and Standard Deviations) for All Variables

#### n, M (and SD) for participants

| Variable | Whole sample | Chinese | Korean | Filipino | European American | Differences across groups |
|---|---|---|---|---|---|---|
| Strictness | $n = 1{,}082$, 3.05 (0.73) | $n = 196$, 3.23 (0.77) | $n = 172$, 3.04 (0.74) | $n = 113$, 3.10 (0.69) | $n = 601$, 2.99 (0.72) | E < C |
| Provides structure | $n = 1{,}077$, 3.65 (0.81) | $n = 196$, 3.69 (0.80) | $n = 170$, 3.56 (0.78) | $n = 112$, 3.56 (0.82) | $n = 599$, 3.67 (0.82) | |
| Psychological control | $n = 1{,}082$, 2.30 (0.75) | $n = 196$, 2.48 (0.69) | $n = 172$, 2.38 (0.72) | $n = 113$, 2.51 (0.64) F | $n = 601$, 2.17 (0.78) | E < C, K, F |
| Strictness–feeling angry | $n = 996$, 2.36 (0.69) | $n = 183$, 2.21 (0.67) | $n = 151$, 2.33 (0.67) | $n = 109$, 2.40 (0.74) | $n = 553$, 2.42 (0.70) | C < E |
| Provides structure–feeling angry | $n = 973$, 3.59 (0.62) | $n = 172$, 3.66 (0.58) | $n = 146$, 3.59 (0.60) | $n = 109$, 3.60 (0.61) | $n = 546$, 3.57 (0.65) | |
| Psychological control–feeling angry | $n = 991$, 2.80 (0.70) | $n = 180$, 2.61 (0.67) | $n = 151$, 2.64 (0.66) | $n = 109$, 2.54 (0.68) | $n = 551$, 2.96 (0.69) | C, K, F < E |

*Note.* The findings for the across-group differences were based on an alpha level of .05. C = Chinese; K = Korean; F = Filipino; and E = European American.

*Table 2*

### Bivariate Associations (R) Between Parental Control (Strictness, Provides Structure, Psychological Control) and Affective Interpretation of Anger (Feeling Angry), and Adolescent Outcomes

| | Internalizing | | | | Externalizing | | | | Drug use | | | |
|---|---|---|---|---|---|---|---|---|---|---|---|---|
| Variable | Chinese | Korean | Filipino | European American | Chinese | Korean | Filipino | European American | Chinese | Korean | Filipino | European American |
| Gender (male) | −.09 | −.18* | −.14 | −.14** | .14 | .07 | .00 | .15** | −.06 | .15* | .05 | .09 |
| Homeowner Status | .07 | .00 | −.19 | −.01 | .09 | .00 | .04 | −.03 | .01 | .10 | .15 | .00 |
| Parental education | −.05 | .01 | −.13 | .06 | −.01 | −.07 | −.03 | .05 | −.04 | .01 | −.05 | .06 |
| Single-parent household | .10 | .03 | .08 | .08* | .00 | .03 | .07 | .14** | .03 | .04 | −.06 | .13** |
| Primary caregiver (mother) | −.06 | .03 | −.02 | −.05 | .00 | −.06 | .01 | −.09* | −.03 | .13 | −.14 | −.06 |
| Strictness | .29** | .03 | .26** | .12** | .24** | .10 | .26** | .06 | .03 | .07 | .04 | .03 |
| Provides structure | .03 | .00 | .17 | −.02 | −.04 | .02 | .17 | −.15** | −.24*** | −.11 | .05 | −.13** |
| Psychological control | .45** | .27** | .32** | .38** | .44** | .17* | .28** | .38** | .29** | .09 | .07 | .24** |
| Strictness–feeling mad | .16* | .32** | .29** | .18** | .22** | .24** | .41** | .24** | .27** | .11 | .03 | .07 |
| Provides structure–feeling mad | .08 | −.17* | −.11 | −.03 | .08 | .07 | −.05 | .03 | .07 | .02 | −.20* | −.04 |
| Psychological control–feeling mad | .11 | .12 | .21* | .14** | .15* | .12 | .27** | .01 | .11 | .01 | −.03 | −.09* |

$^*p < .05.$ $^{**}p < .01.$

associations were also conducted among the three outcomes with the associations between (a) internalizing and externalizing, (b) internalizing and drug use, and (c) externalizing and drug use at .54, .21, and .39, respectively, among Chinese immigrants; .53, .09, and .41, respectively, among Korean immigrants; .55, .13, and .35, respectively, among Filipino immigrants, and .55, .23, and .53, respectively, among European Americans.

Then we conducted regression analyses to examine whether there were ethnic group differences in the associations between the types of control and adolescent adjustment. As shown in Table 3, separate regression analyses, which were conducted for each type of parental control, included the main effects for control and ethnicity (four dummy-coded variables, i.e., Chinese, Korean, Filipino, and European American, with the latter omitted) and two-way interactions between each ethnic group and control (with the interaction term for European Americans omitted as the reference or comparison group). Thus, in Table 3, the main

effects for parental control represent the effect for European Americans (e.g., .054 for Strictness), and the interactions terms represent the difference in the effect of control for each Asian immigrant group relative to the effect found for European Americans. By adding the coefficients for the interaction terms to the coefficient representing the effect for European Americans, the effects for each of the Asian immigrant groups can be derived. For example, the effects for Strictness would be .001 for Chinese, .010 for Koreans, and −.016 for Filipinos. Adolescents' gender, single-parent status, parental education, homeowner status, and mother as primary caregiver were included as covariates in all of the analyses. For interactions that were significant, we tested the significance of the slopes for the simple regression lines using Cohen, Cohen, Aiken, and West's (2003) test.

Although we first conducted three-way interactions between ethnicity, parental control, and feelings of anger, these were not significant; this is not surprising, given that such complex interactions require a great deal of power.

*Table 3*

**Relationship Between Each Type of Control (Strictness, Provides Structure, and Psychological Control) and Each Outcome (Internalizing Behaviors, Externalizing Behaviors, and Drug Use)**

| Type of control | Internalizing behaviors | | Externalizing behaviors | | Drug use | |
|---|---|---|---|---|---|---|
| | B | SE | B | SE | B | SE |
| Strictness | .054** | .018 | .021 | .016 | .015 | .026 |
| Ethnicity (Chinese) × Strictness | .055 | .034 | .038 | .030 | −.008 | .049 |
| Ethnicity (Korean) × Strictness | −.044 | .037 | .014 | .034 | .016 | .054 |
| Ethnicity (Filipino) × Strictness | .070 | .045 | .088* | .040 | .014 | .064 |
| | $n = 1,004$, $R^2 = .09$, $F(12, 991) = 8.09$, $p = .00$ | | $n = 1,004$, $R^2 = .25$, $F(12, 991) = 5.55$, $p = .00$ | | $n = 977$, $R^2 = .04$, $F(12, 964) = 3.17$, $p = .00$ | |
| Provides structure | −.007 | .016 | −.044** | .014 | −.079** | .022 |
| Ethnicity (Chinese) × Provides Structure | .002 | .032 | .030 | .029 | .046 | .047 |
| Ethnicity (Korean) × Provides Structure | .008 | .034 | .057† | .030 | .072 | .049 |
| Ethnicity (Filipino) × Provides Structure | .084* | .038 | .111* | .034 | .122* | .054 |
| | $n = 999$, $R^2 = .07$, $F(12, 986) = 5.83$, $p = .00$ | | $n = 999$, $R^2 = .06$, $F(12, 986) = 5.33$, $p = .00$ | | $n = 973$, $R^2 = .05$, $F(12, 960) = 4.33$, $p = .00$ | |
| Psychological control | .148** | .015 | .141** | .014 | .158** | .023 |
| Ethnicity (Chinese) × Psychological Control | .037 | .033 | −.011 | .030 | −.106* | .050 |
| Ethnicity (Korean) × Psychological Control | −.043 | .036 | −.088** | .032 | −.130* | .054 |
| Ethnicity (Filipino) × Psychological Control | .043 | .044 | −.019 | .040 | −.111† | .066 |
| | $n = 1,004$, $R^2 = .19$, $F(12, 991) = 19.80$, $p = .00$ | | $n = 1,004$, $R^2 = .17$, $F(12, 991) = 16.33$, $p = .00$ | | $n = 977$, $R^2 = .08$, $F(12, 964) = 7.36$, $p = .00$ | |

*Note.* All regression analyses included main effects for ethnicity (Chinese, Korean, and Filipino, with European Americans as the omitted group) as well as the control variables.

† $p < .10$. * $p < .05$. * $p < .01$.

Thus, the two sets of analyses for the two-way interactions were pursued, with the first set (described earlier) testing for ethnic differences in the effects of parental control in the sample overall and the second set (described later), for the interactions involving parental control and feelings of anger within each ethnic group.

Strictness was related to higher externalizing for Filipinos, more so than for European Americans. Although the test of simple slopes for European Americans was not significant, it was for Filipinos, $b = 0.11$, $t(991) = 2.97$, $p = .00$. There were no other significant ethnic group differences found for the other outcomes.

Provides Structure was related to lower internalizing and externalizing symptoms, and also drug use for European Americans, whereas it was related to increases in these outcomes for Filipinos. For internalizing, the test of simple slopes showed that Provides Structure had a positive association with Filipino adolescents' internalizing symptoms, $b = 0.08$, $t(986) = 2.20$, $p = .03$; but no significant association was found for European Americans. For externalizing, a similar interaction was found as that with internalizing in that Provides Structure was positively associated with externalizing for Filipinos, $b = 0.07$, $t(986) = 2.15$, $p = .03$; but was negatively associated for European Americans, $b = -3.14$, $t(986) = -3.14$, $p = .00$. Finally, with drug use, the simple slopes test revealed that Provides Structure had a negative association for European Americans, $b = -0.08$, $t(960) = -3.59$, $p = .00$; whereas it was not significant for Filipinos.

Psychological control, on the other hand, was related to higher externalizing symptoms and drug use more for European Americans than Chinese, Koreans, and Filipinos. For European Americans, the test of simple slopes indicated a strong, positive relationship, $b = 0.14$, $t(991) = 10.07$, $p = .00$, between psychological control and externalizing symptoms; and only a marginally significant relationship for Koreans, $b = 0.05$, $t(991) = 1.83$, $p = .07$. With drug use, no associations were found for Chinese, Koreans, and Filipinos, whereas positive associations were found for European Americans, $b = 0.16$, $t(964) = 6.87$, $p = .00$. Last, there were no ethnic differences in the association between psychological control and internalizing symptoms.

## Effects of Affective Interpretations of Anger (Feeling Angry) Toward Control in the Association Between Parental Control and Adolescent Outcomes

For those specific ethnic groups in which differences in the effects of parental control were found, we conducted further analyses within these groups to address the hypotheses for the moderating effects of adolescents' feelings about parental control. That is, for each ethnic group, separate regression analyses were performed for each parental control construct, with its counterpart feelings of anger together in the models. Two-way interactions between parental control (b1), and feeling angry (b2) were used to test whether the associations between each type of parental control and adolescent outcomes differed at varying levels of feeling angry. The five covariates listed earlier (i.e., adolescents' gender, single-parent status, parental education, homeowner status, and mother as primary caregiver), along with the main effects for parental control and feeling angry, were entered first, followed by the interaction term (Parental Control × Feeling Angry). In addition, the analyses for each of the Asian immigrant groups also included the covariate of age at immigration. All predictors were centered at the overall sample mean. The interaction terms were created with these centered variables. The unstandardized coefficients, standard errors, and tests of significance for the overall models are displayed in Table 4, Table 5, and Table 6.

### Strictness

On the basis of the differences found between Filipinos and European Americans in the effects of strictness on externalizing, we examined the moderation between strictness and feeling angry within these groups, but no interactions were found among either the Filipinos or European Americans (see Table 4).

### Provides Structure

As differences in the effects of Provides Structure were found between European Americans and Filipinos on all outcomes, and between European Americans and Koreans on externalizing, further withingroup analyses focus on these groups (see Table 5). With the outcome of internalizing symptoms, a significant twoway interaction was observed between Provides Structure and feeling angry for European Americans, whereas no interaction was found among Filipinos. This interaction for the European Americans is graphically displayed in Figure 1 (with high levels of feeling angry, and of Provides Structure, defined as 1 standard deviation above the mean, medium levels at the mean, and low levels at 1 standard deviation below the mean). The interaction for European Americans suggests that the association between Provides Structure and internalizing behaviors becomes less negative at high levels of feeling angry than at low levels. On the basis of the test of simple slopes, Provides Structure was negatively associated with internalizing symptoms only at low levels of feeling angry,

*Table 4*

**Multiple Regressions of Family Characteristics, Strictness, Feeling Angry, and Interaction Terms for Strictness and Feeling Angry on Externalizing: Centered Coefficients and *SE (B)***

| Variable | European American | | Filipino | |
|---|---|---|---|---|
| | B | SE | B | SE |
| Age immigrated | — | — | .007 | .006 |
| Gender (male) | .086** | .025 | .062 | .050 |
| Homeowner | .008 | .032 | .048 | .051 |
| Parental education | .010** | .003 | −.044† | .022 |
| Single parent | .010** | .030 | .015 | .080 |
| Primary caregiver (mother) | −.034 | .031 | .015 | .053 |
| Strictness | .046* | .018 | .096** | .034 |
| Feeling angry | .109** | .018 | .186** | .045 |
| Strictness × Feeling Angry | −.012 | .021 | −.004 | .053 |
| | $n = 520, R^2 = .13$, $F(8, 511) = 9.27$, $p = .00$ | | $n = 100, R^2 = .26$, $F(9, 91) = 3.49$, $p = .00$ | |

† $p < .10$. * $p < .05$. ** $p < .01$.

*Table 5*

**Multiple Regressions of Family Characteristics, Provides Structure, Feeling Angry, and Interaction Terms for Provides Structure and Feeling Angry on Internalizing, Externalizing, and Drug Use (Centered Coefficients & *SE (B)*)**

| Variable | Internalizing | | | | Externalizing | | | | | | Drug use | | | |
|---|---|---|---|---|---|---|---|---|---|---|---|---|---|---|
| | European Americans | | Filipinos | | European Americans | | Filipinos | | Koreans | | European Americans | | Filipinos | |
| | B | SE | B | SE | B | SE | B | SE | B | SE | B | SE | B | SE |
| Age immigrated | — | — | .008 | .009 | — | — | .001 | .007 | .000 | .005 | — | — | .019 | .012 |
| Gender (male) | −.078** | .026 | .012 | .071 | .081** | .026 | .071 | .057 | −.004 | .041 | .063 | .047 | .009 | .096 |
| Homeowner | .006 | .034 | −.071 | .073 | .003 | .033 | .047 | .058 | −.034 | .041 | .032 | .059 | .176† | .009 |
| Parental education | .004 | .003 | −.035 | .031 | .007* | .003 | −.028 | .025 | −.003 | .005 | .011 | .006 | −.032 | .042 |
| Single parent | .062† | .032 | .123 | .115 | .097** | .031 | .086 | .091 | .069 | .051 | .167** | .056 | −.026 | .155 |
| Primary caregiver (mother) | −.031 | .033 | −.037 | .076 | −.033 | .032 | .019 | .060 | −.070 | .052 | −.028 | .058 | −.077 | .102 |
| Provides structure | −.014 | .016 | .086† | .044 | −.038* | .016 | .075* | .035 | .013 | .029 | −.067* | .029 | .034 | .060 |
| Feeling angry | −.019 | .020 | −.006 | .056 | .011 | .020 | −.013 | .045 | .007 | .035 | −.024 | .038 | −.101 | |
| Provides Structure × Feeling Angry | .057** | .022 | −.096 | .091 | .067** | .021 | −.038 | .072 | −.013 | .043 | .109** | .038 | .001 | .123 |
| | $n = 514, R^2 = .05$, $F(8, 505) = 3.05$, $p = .00$ | | $n = 99, R^2 = .12$, $F(9, 90) = 1.20$, $p = .30$ | | $n = 514, R^2 = .09$, $F(8, 505) = 6.35$, $p = .00$ | | $n = 99, R^2 = .08$, $F(9,90) = .84$, $p = .58$ | | $n = 130, R^2 = .04$, $F(9, 121) = .589$, $p = .80$ | | $n = 510, R^2 = .06$, $F(8, 501) = 4.25$, $p = .00$ | | $n = 99, R^2 = .08$, $F(8, 92) = 0.961$, $p = .47$ | |

† $p < .10$. * $p < .05$. ** $p < .01$.

$b = -0.05$, $t(510)_{low} = -2.47$, $p = .01$. On the other hand, among the Filipino immigrants, Provides Structure was positively related to internalizing behaviors, regardless of how angry they felt.

With the outcome of externalizing symptoms, an interaction was found among European Americans but not among Korean or Filipino immigrants. Similar to the interaction described earlier, the relationship between Provides

*Table 6*

**Multiple Regressions of Family Characteristics, Psychological Control, Feeling Angry, and Interaction Terms for Psychological Control and Feeling Angry on Externalizing Behaviors and Drug Use: Centered Coefficients and SE (B)**

| | Externalizing | | | | Drug use | | | | | | | |
|---|---|---|---|---|---|---|---|---|---|---|---|---|
| | European American | | Korean | | European American | | Filipino | | Koreans | | Chinese | |
| Variable | B | SE | B | SE | B | SE | B | SE | B | SE | B | SE |
| Age immigrated | — | — | −.003 | .005 | — | — | .021† | .012 | −.010* | .004 | .002 | .003 |
| Gender (male) | .073** | .024 | .007 | .039 | .052 | .045 | −.011 | .096 | .064 | .035 | .005 | .019 |
| Homeowner | −.006 | .031 | −.031 | .039 | .017 | .057 | .172† | .096 | .021 | .035 | .007 | .021 |
| Parental education | .008** | .003 | −.003 | .005 | .011* | .005 | −.039 | .042 | .000 | .018 | .000 | .002 |
| Single parent | .078** | .029 | .065 | .049 | .123* | .054 | −.061 | .154 | .048 | .044 | .000 | .026 |
| Primary caregiver (mother) | −.040 | .029 | −.054 | .050 | −.060 | .055 | −.128 | .102 | .082† | .045 | −.005 | .019 |
| Psychological control | .148** | .018 | .092** | .030 | .186** | .029 | .050 | .069 | .055* | .027 | .055** | .013 |
| Feeling angry | .031† | .018 | .058† | .029 | −.051 | .033 | −.020 | .069 | .019 | .026 | .019 | .014 |
| Psychological Control × Feeling Angry | −.051* | .021 | .077† | .044 | −.178** | .039 | .054 | .094 | .061 | .040 | .032† | .019 |

$n = 519$, $R^2 = .20$, $F(8, 510) = 16.21$, $p = .00$; $n = 40$, $R^2 = .12$, $F(9, 131) = 2.01$, $p = .04$; $n = 515$, $R^2 = .13$, $F(8, 506) = 9.23$, $p = .00$; $n = 100$, $R^2 = .09$, $F(9, 91) = .997$, $p = .45$; $n = 139$, $R^2 = .13$, $F(9, 130) = 2.10$, $p = .03$; $n = 171$, $R^2 = .13$, $F(9, 162) = 2.64$, $p = .01$

† $p < .10$. * $p < .05$. ** $p < .01$.

*Figure 1*

**The interactive effect of the factor Provides Structure and feeling angry on internalizing behaviors as reported by European American adolescents.**

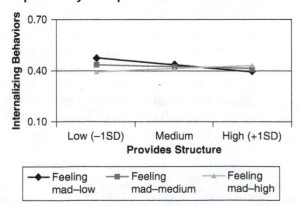

Legend: ◆ Feeling mad–low   ■ Feeling mad–medium   ▲ Feeling mad–high

Structure and externalizing symptoms was less negative at high levels of feeling angry than at low levels. On the basis of the test of simple slopes, Provides Structure was negatively associated with internalizing symptoms at low and medium levels of feeling angry, $b = -0.08$, $t(505)_{\text{low}} = -4.02$, $p = .00$; and $b = -0.04$, $t(505)_{\text{medium}} = -2.38$, $p = .02$. On the other hand, Provides Structure was positively related to externalizing behaviors among Korean and Filipino immigrants, regardless of how angry these youth felt.

Finally, with the outcome of drug use, an interaction similar to that described earlier for the outcomes of internalizing and externalizing behaviors was found for European Americans, so that the association between Provides Structure and drug use was less negative at high levels of feeling angry than at low levels. On the basis of the test of simple slopes, Provides Structure was only associated with drug use at low and medium levels of feeling angry, $b = -0.14$, $t(501)_{\text{low}} = -3.74$, $p = .00$; and $b = -0.07$, $t(501)_{\text{medium}} = -2.31$, $p = .02$. On the other hand, no significant interactions were found for Filipino immigrants.

### Psychological Control

As ethnic group differences in the effects for psychological control were found for the outcomes of externalizing symptoms (involving Korean immigrants only) and drug use involving all the Asian immigrant groups, further analyses focus on these groups for the outcomes given earlier (see Table 6). With externalizing symptoms, a significant two-way interaction for European Americans was found. The interaction for European Americans is displayed in Figure 2.

*Figure 2*

**The interactive effect of psychological control and feeling angry on externalizing behaviors as reported by European American adolescents.**

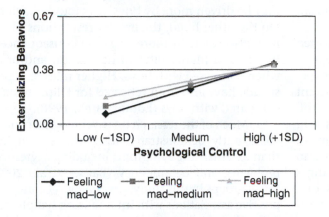

*Figure 3*

**The interactive effect of psychological control and feeling angry on drug use as reported by European American adolescents.**

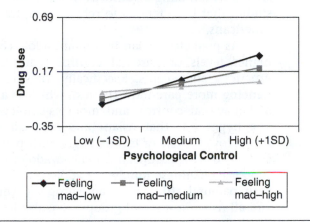

That is, the angrier European American adolescents felt about parents' use of psychological control, the less positive the association was between psychological control and externalizing symptoms. On the basis of the tests of simple slopes, for all levels of feeling angry, psychological control was positively associated with externalizing symptoms, $b = 0.18$, $t(510)_{low} = 8.48$, $p = .00$; $b = 0.15$, $t(510)_{medium} = 9.25$, $p = .00$; and $b = 0.11$, $t(510)_{high} = 5.22$, $p = .00$. However, for Korean immigrants, psychological control was related to increases in externalizing symptoms, regardless of their feelings of anger.

With the outcome of drug use, an interaction was found among European Americans, but not among any of the Asian immigrant groups. As displayed in Figure 3, the interaction suggests that the relationship between psychological control and drug use was less negative at higher levels of feeling angry, compared with low levels. On the basis of the test of simple slopes, psychological control was associated with drug use at low and medium levels of feeling angry, $b = 0.31$, $t(506)_{low} = 7.80$, $p = .00$; and $b = 0.19$, $t(506)_{medium} = 6.41$, $p = .00$.

Additional moderation effects for control and feeling angry were also tested among all the groups. However, this interaction was of a different pattern than that found for European Americans. That is, for Chinese Americans, the associations between Provides Structure and drug use became more negative as their levels of anger increased. On the basis of the test of simple slopes, Provides Structure was negatively associated with drug use only at medium and high levels of feeling angry, $b = -0.04$, $t(157)_{medium} = -2.77$, $p = .01$; and $b = -0.08$, $t(157)_{high} = -5.15$, $p = .00$.

## Discussion

This study provided an understanding of the sociocultural processes underlying how parenting influences the wellbeing of Asian immigrant and European American youth. The study first demonstrated, in across-group analyses, that there were differential effects of behavioral and psychological control on behavioral adjustment between Asian immigrant youth (especially Filipino immigrants) and European American youth. These ethnic differences in the effects of parental control on adolescent outcomes may be explained by how adolescents interpret their parents' control strategies. Behavioral and psychological control may have different consequences for Asian immigrant and European American youth because of the moderating effect of their affective interpretations (i.e., anger) regarding control. Indeed, in analyses conducted within groups, support was found for the hypotheses that, for European Americans, the associations between control and adjustment depended upon their feelings about control. More specifically, European American adolescents experienced a decrease in the deleterious consequences of psychological control as the anger they felt increased, whereas Asian immigrant youth did not. Additionally, the beneficial effects of behavioral control—namely, Provides Structure—were reduced for European American adolescents at higher levels of feeling angry, whereas no such effect was found for Asian immigrant youth.

Evidence of possible differences in cultural processes was initially demonstrated by the fact that the items for the scale measuring behavioral control separated into two factors for the three Asian immigrant groups as well as the European Americans. Although this has not been found (or even examined) in some studies relying on the CRPBI, when samples of Asian immigrant youth are included, this scale does not hang together as well as it may have in past studies that have tended to rely on samples of European Americans. . . .

As predicted, Asian immigrant adolescents reported higher levels of parental control than did European American adolescents. Specifically, they reported experiencing more parental strictness, which is a component of behavioral control, and more psychological control. The hypothesis that Asian immigrant adolescents will report lower levels of feeling angry with parental control compared with European American adolescents was also supported. Chinese immigrant adolescents felt less anger with parental strictness than European Americans did, and all Asian immigrant groups were also less angry with psychological control than European Americans were.

The prediction that there will be differences in the effects of parental control on adolescent outcomes between Asian immigrants and European Americans was also supported. As part of behavioral control, Provides Structure was more negatively associated with problem behaviors for European Americans than it was for Asian immigrants, particularly Filipino immigrants. In fact, for Filipino immigrant youth, this type of control was related to increases in both internalizing and externalizing symptoms. In addition, Strictness was also found to be more deleterious for Filipino immigrant youth than European American youth in that it was related to higher externalizing symptoms for the Filipino immigrants. These negative effects for both types of behavioral control may reflect that there are different processes at work for Filipino immigrants than there are for European Americans.

One possible explanation is that Filipino parents may only exert more of this type of control as they need to or as adolescents begin showing behavioral problems. Perhaps, for this group, parenting is driven by youth's behaviors, rather than the other way around. These effects for behavioral control need to be tested with additional time points of data, controlling for previous levels of youth's behavioral problems. These possible explanations for Filipinos deserve further attention, as studies also indicate that these youth have higher rates of depression, suicidal thoughts, and lower self-esteem than other ethnic Asian immigrants and nativeborn European Americans (David & Okazaki, 2006; Espiritu & Wolf, 2001; Rumbaudt, 1996).

In addition, future studies involving larger samples are needed to test for possible gender differences in these effects. As mentioned earlier, Espiritu (1995, 2001, 2003)

has reported not only on the restrictions placed on girls but also on the greater freedom that boys are afforded by parents. Thus, it may be that the positive associations between both types of behavioral control and problem behaviors may be found more for boys than for girls and may be driven more by boys' previous behavior problems. On the other hand, the greater restrictions placed on girls may also result in more negative consequences for them in terms of higher rates of depression and/or acting out, when compared with boys. Higher rates of depression and suicide have also been reported for Filipino American girls compared with boys (Edman et al., 1998).

Much of the research on psychological control has more consistently demonstrated associations with internalizing than externalizing symptoms including aggression, conduct problems, and delinquency (Barber et al., 2005). Indeed, for all groups in this study, psychological control had similar positive associations with internalizing symptoms. However, with other outcomes, such as externalizing and drug use, this study found that psychological control had more deleterious consequences for European Americans than Chinese and Korean immigrants. Thus, the ubiquitous negative effects for psychological control apply more to internalizing symptoms but not necessarily to "acting out" behaviors.

The primary hypothesis addressed whether, for European Americans, the effects of control on adolescent problem behaviors will vary according to their levels of anger. The results showed that they did vary, most often for European Americans. For Asian immigrant adolescents, as expected, there was largely no moderating effect of feeling angry on the associations between the types of control and adolescents' problem behaviors. In fact, in additional tests for all possible moderation effects between parental control and feeling angry, regardless of whether there were initial group differences in effects of parental control, no additional moderation effects were found for any of the groups (other than those already reported on in Results). However, there was one exception to this overall finding. A significant interaction was found for immigrant Chinese. This interaction, however, was in the opposite direction from that of the European Americans.

Specifically, for European Americans, the beneficial effects of behavioral control are most evident at low to moderate levels of anger, whereas high levels of anger protect youth against the adverse effects of psychological control. For these youth, although feeling angry may serve as an important defensive reaction to control that is more manipulative, it also serves as an impediment to the effectiveness of more regulatory types of control. For immigrant Chinese youth, the beneficial effects of behavioral control were not mitigated as their anger increased.

In fact, the opposite was found in that behavioral control was most beneficial for youth when they felt more anger over this type of control. This latter finding is contrary to the argument that anger for Asian adolescents is irrelevant to how parental control affects their well-being. However, the pattern of results may suggest different processes underlying how control is experienced by these immigrant youth, compared with European American youth, and deserves further investigation. It may be that these youth feel more anger toward parents who use this type of control but may still feel that this control is legitimate. Some caution, however, is in order regarding this interaction in that the internal consistencies of the drug use scale were very poor for Chinese ($\alpha = 0.50$).

There are also limitations to the study that warrant further caution to the findings reported earlier. Limitations of the study was the reliance on youth self-report and, as mentioned earlier, on only one time point of data. With regard to the former issue, although stronger associations among variables are usually found due to shared method variance, it is unlikely that the shared method variance would affect one ethnic group more than another. Additionally, as mentioned above, longitudinal data would allow us to examine whether adolescents' behaviors are actually driving parenting rather than the other way around, or alternatively that both have reciprocal influences on one another. A more salient concern is the fact that all surveys were administered in English, which probably created greater difficulties in understanding and also in completing the survey items for those immigrants who have most recently arrived to the United States. One consequence of their greater difficulty may be higher missing or noncompletion rates for these recent immigrants. Their greater missing rates, however, would likely mean that ethnic differences in the effects of parental control, and in the moderation effects of feeling angry, were somewhat attenuated or perhaps not detected due to overrepresentation in the sample of immigrants who are more fluent in English and more acculturated.

These findings underscore the need for culturally sensitive clinical practices in working with Asian immigrant families and adolescents. Although developmentally adolescents may require more autonomy, it is often unclear how parents balance this need with the control, guidance, and monitoring that adolescents also require. Moreover, this process may differ for Asian immigrant families compared with European American families, as Asian immigrants may feel that providing control and guidance is more paramount than providing autonomy. Asian adolescents from immigrant families may themselves regard parents' use of control as a necessary part of parenting or of showing care and concern. Thus, their feelings about parental control may not affect how parental control affects their well-being as these feelings do for European American youth. Clinicians need to be cognizant of how all family members, including youth, experience the parenting practices used in their homes, and that youth's own feelings or reactions may affect the effectiveness of such strategies in different ways

# References

Achenbach, T. M. (1991). *Manual for the Child Behavior Checklist/4–18 and 1991 profile*. Burlington: University of Vermont, Department of Psychiatry.

Barber, B. K. (1996). Parental psychological control: Revisiting a neglected construct. *Child Development, 67*, 3296–3319.

Barber, B. K., & Harmon, E. L. (2002). Violating the self: Parental psychological control of children and adolescents. In B. K. Barber (Ed.), *Intrusive parenting: How psychological control affects children and adolescents* (pp. 15–52). Washington, DC: American Psychological Association.

Barber, B. K., Olsen, J. E., & Shagle, S. C. (1994). Associations between parental psychological and behavioral control and youth internalized and externalized behaviors. *Child Development, 65*, 1120–1136.

Barber, B. K., Stoltz, H. E., & Olsen, J. A. (2005). Parental support, psychological control, and behavioral control: Assessing relevance across time, culture, and method. *Monographs of the Society for Research in Child Development, 70*, 1–137.

Bean, R. A., Bush, K. R., McKenry, P. C., & Wilson, S. M. (2003). The impact of parental support, behavioral control, and psychological control on the academic achievement and self-esteem of African American and European American adolescents. *Journal of Adolescent Research, 18*, 523–541.

Blair, S. L., & Qian, Z. (1998). Family and Asian students' educational performance: A consideration of diversity. *Journal of Family Issues, 19*, 355–374.

Chao, R., & Tseng, V. (2002). Parenting of Asians. In M. H. Bornstein (Ed.), *Handbook of parenting. Vol. 4: Social conditions and applied parenting* (2nd ed., pp. 59–93). Hillsdale, NJ: Erlbaum.

Chao, R. K. (1994). Beyond parental control and authoritarian parenting style: Understanding Chinese parenting through the cultural notion of training. *Child Development, 65*, 1111–1119.

Chao, R. K. (2001). Extending research on the consequences of parenting style for Chinese Americans and European Americans. *Child Development, 72,* 1832–1843.

Chen, X., Dong, Q., & Zhou, H. (1997). Authoritative and authoritarian parenting practices and social and school performance in Chinese children. *International Journal of Behavioral Development, 21,* 855–873.

Cohen, J., Cohen, P., Aiken, L. S., & West, S. G. (2003). *Applied multiple regression/correlation analysis for the behavioral sciences* (3rd ed.). Hillsdale, NJ: Erlbaum.

David, E. J. R., & Okazaki, S. (2006). Colonial mentality: A review and recommendation for Filipino psychology. *Cultural Diversity and Ethnic Minority Psychology, 12,* 1–16.

Dornbusch, S. M., Ritter, P. L., Leiderman, P. H., Roberts, D. F., & Fraleigh, M. J. (1987). The relation of parenting style to adolescent school performance. *Child Development, 58,* 1244–1257.

Doyle, A. B., & Markiewicz, D. (2005). Parenting, marital conflict and adjustment from early- to mid-adolescence: Mediated by adolescent attachment style? *Journal of Youth and Adolescence, 34,* 97–110.

Edman, J. L., Andrade, N. N., Glipa, J., Foster, J., Danko, G. P., Yates, A., Johnson, R. C., McDermott, J. F., & Waldron, J. A. (1998). Depressive symptoms among Filipino American adolescents. *Cultural Diversity and Mental Health, 4,* 45–54.

Espiritu, Y. L. (1995). *Filipino American lives.* Philadelphia: Temple University Press.

Espiritu, Y. L. (2001). "We don't sleep around like White girls do": Family, culture, and gender in Filipina American lives. *Journal of Women in Culture and Society, 26,* 415–440.

Espiritu, Y. L. (2003). *Home bound: Filipino American lives across cultures, communities, and countries.* Berkeley, CA: University of California Press.

Espiritu, Y. L., & Wolf, D. (2001). The paradox of assimilation: Children of Filipino immigrants in San Diego. In R. Rumbaut & A. Portes (Eds.), *Ethnicities: Children of immigrants in America* (pp. 157–186). Thousand Oaks, CA: Sage.

Fuligni, A. J. (1998). Authority, autonomy, and parent–adolescent conflict and cohesion: A study of adolescents from Mexican, Chinese, Filipino, and European backgrounds. *Developmental Psychology, 34,* 782–792.

Gray, M. R., & Steinberg, L. (1999). Unpacking authoritative parenting: Reassessing a multidimensional construct. *Journal of Marriage and Family, 61,* 547–587.

Guadagnoli, E., & Velicer, W. (1988). Relation of sample size to the stability of component patterns. *Psychological Bulletin, 103,* 265–275.

Hasebe, Y., Nucci, L., & Nucci, M. S. (2004). Parental control of the personal domain and adolescent symptoms of psychopathology: A cross-national study in the United States and Japan. *Child Development, 75,* 3, 815–828.

Ho, D. Y. (1986). Chinese patterns of socialization: A critical review. In M. H. Bond (Ed.), *The psychology of the Chinese people* (pp. 31–37). Hong Kong: Oxford University Press.

Ho, D. Y. (1996). Filial piety and its psychological consequences. In M. H. Bond (Ed.), *The handbook of Chinese psychology* (pp. 143–154). Hong Kong: Oxford University Press.

Huizinga, D. H., Menard, S., & Elliott, D. S. (1989). Delinquency and drug use: Temporal and developmental patterns. *Justice Quarterly, 6,* 419–455.

Kağitçibaşi, Ç. (1996). *Family and human development across cultures: A view from the other side.* Mahwah, NJ: Erlbaum.

Kim, E. (2005). Korean American parental control: Acceptance or rejection? *Ethos, 3,* 347–366.

Lai, J., & Linden, W. (1993). The smile of Asia: Acculturation effects on symptom reporting. *Canadian Journal of Behavioral Science, 25,* 303–313.

Lamborn, S. D., Dornbusch, S. M., & Steinberg, L. (1996). Ethnicity and community context as moderators of the relations between family decision making and adolescent adjustment. *Child Development, 67,* 283–301.

Mantzicopoulos, P. Y., & Oh-Hwang, Y. (1998). The relationship of psychosocial maturity to parenting quality and intellectual ability for American and Korean adolescents. *Contemporary Educational Psychology, 23,* 195–206.

Markus, H. R., & Kitayama, S. (1991). Culture and the self: Implications for cognition, emotion, and motivation. *Psychological Review, 98,* 224–253.

Mason, C. A., Walker-Barnes, C. J., Tu, S., Simons, J., & Martinez-Arrue, R. (2004). Ethnic differences in the affective meaning of parental control behaviors. *The Journal of Primary Prevention, 25, 1,* 59–79.

Matsumoto, D., Kudoh, T., Schere, K., & Wallbott, H. (1988). Antecedents of and reactions to emotions in the United States and Japan. *Journal of Cross-Cultural Psychology, 19,* 267–286.

Olsen, S. F., Yang, C., Hart, C. H., Robinson, C. C., Wu, P., Nelson, D. A., et al. (2002). Maternal psychological control and preschool children's behavioral outcomes in China, Russia, and the United States. In B. K. Barber (Eds.), *Intrusive parenting: How psychological control affects children and adolescents* (pp. 235–262). Washington, DC: American Psychological Association.

Pettit, G. S., Laird, R. D., Dodge, K. A., Bates, J. E., & Criss, M. M. (2001). Antecedents and behavior-problem outcomes of parental provides structure and psychological control in early adolescence. *Child Development, 72,* 583–598.

Rogers, K. N., Buchanan, C. M., & Winchell, M. E. (2003). Psychological control during early adolescence: Links to adjustment in differing parent/adolescent dyads. *Journal of Early Adolescence, 23,* 349–383.

Rothbaum, F., Pott, M., Azuma, H., Miyake, K., & Weisz, J. (2000). The development of close relationships in Japan and the United States: Paths of symbiotic harmony and generative tension. *Child Development, 71,* 1121–1142.

Rudy, D., & Halgunseth, L. C. (2005). Psychological control, maternal emotion and cognition, and child outcomes in individualist and collectivist groups. *Journal of Emotional Abuse, 5,* 237–264.

Rumbaudt, R. G. (1996). The crucible within: Ethnic identity, self-esteem, and segmented assimilation among children of immigrants. In A. Portes (Ed), *The new second generation* (pp. 119–170). New York: Sage.

Schludermann, E. H., & Schludermann, S. M. (1988). *Children's report on parent behavior (CRPBI-108, CRPBI-30) for children and older adolescents* (Technical report). Winnipeg, Manitoba, Canada: University of Manitoba, Department of Psychology.

Steinberg, L. (1990). Autonomy, conflict, and harmony in the family relationship. In S. S. Feldman & G. R. Elliott (Eds.), *At the threshold: The developing adolescent* (pp. 255–276). Cambridge, MA: Harvard University Press.

Steinberg, L., Elmen, J. D., & Mounts, N. S. (1989). Authoritative parenting, psychosocial maturity, and academic success among adolescents. *Child Development, 60,* 1424–1436.

Steinberg, L., Lamborn, S. D., Dornbusch, S. M., & Darling, N. (1992). Impact of parenting practices on adolescent achievement: Authoritative parenting, school involvement, and encouragement to succeed. *Child Development, 63,* 1266–1281.

Walker-Barnes, C. J., & Mason, C. A. (2004). Delinquency and substance use among gang-involved youth: The moderating role of parenting practices. *American Journal of Community Psychology, 34,* 235–250.

Yau, J., and Smetana, J. G. (1996). Adolescent-parent conflict among Chinese adolescents in Hong Kong. *Child Development, 67,* 1262–1275.

Yau, J., and Smetana, J. G. (2003). Adolescent-parent conflict in Hong Kong and Shenzhen: A comparison of youth in two cultural contexts. *International Journal of Behavioral Development, 27(3),* 201–211.

**RUTH K. CHAO** was professor of psychology at University of California, Riverside. She served on the editorial boards of leading journals, including *Developmental Psychology* and the *Journal of Research on Adolescence*. **CHRISTINE AQUE** was a PhD student in developmental psychology at the time of publication.

**Su Yeong Kim et al.**

# Does "Tiger Parenting" Exist? Parenting Profiles of Chinese Americans and Adolescent Developmental Outcomes

There is a common perception that Asian American parents are authoritarians when it comes to schoolwork and extracurricular activities, and exceedingly demanding of their children both academically and at home. Recently, these parents have been termed *tiger parents* (Chua, 2011) for the ferocity with which they discipline their children and for their emphasis on the importance of family obligation and academic achievement. They are also viewed as displaying relatively less warmth and affection towards their children, and as running households that do not exhibit democratic values. The spotlight on tiger parenting has caused the public to question whether the control these parents exert over their children is appropriate, and whether their parenting practices positively or negatively affect children's development. Studies have yet to find empirical evidence to support or refute these concerns. The current study uses longitudinal data from Chinese American adolescents and their parents to examine the parenting profiles that may exist specifically within this group, and the adolescent outcomes that may be associated with each emerging parenting profile.

## Parenting in Asian Americans

"All decent parents want to do what's best for their children. The Chinese just have a totally different idea of how to do that" (Chua, 2011, p. 63). Chua's book, in which she presents a personal account of her own parenting practices, stirred parents and experts nationwide. She claims to be a tiger mother herself, and argues that the methods she used to raise her daughters are aligned with the Chinese cultural emphasis on academic achievement and family obligation–two means by which adolescents bring honor to the family (Chao, 1994). This is in contrast to European American

practices, which emphasize the importance of children's self-esteem and personal growth (Chao & Tseng, 2002). These differences between the motivations of Asian and European-American parents may mean that western-derived parenting profiles are not as applicable to Asian Americans.

## Parenting Dimensions and Profiles

Research on parenting styles originated with Baumrind's research on parental control, which identified three parenting styles: authoritative, authoritarian, and permissive (Baumrind, 1966). Maccoby and Martin expanded on Baumrind's work by reassessing parenting profiles using two dimensions, responsiveness (warmth) and demandingness (control), which allowed them to identify an additional parenting profile: negligent (Maccoby & Martin, 1983). Authoritative parenting is viewed as supportive, with parents granting autonomy and encouraging communication (Darling & Steinberg, 1993). This style is correlated with positive academic outcomes and increased competence. Authoritarian parenting is viewed as harsh, with parents using fear to elicit behavioral compliance (Darling & Steinberg, 1993); parents may also use power and control to produce desired behaviors in their children (Baumrind, 1966). These methods are correlated with increased depressive symptoms and lower self-esteem (Nguyen, 2008). While both of these parenting profiles are characterized by the use of control, the type of control (power) differs. Authoritative parents employ confrontive power, which is open to negotiation and reasoning, while authoritarian parents use coercive power, which is aimed at maintaining the hierarchical structure of the parent-child relationship (Baumrind, 2012). A negligent parenting profile characterizes parents who exert low levels of control and who are largely unresponsive to their children.

Kim, Su Yeong; Wang, Yijie; Orozco-Lapray, Diana; Shen, Yishan; Murtuza, Mohammed, "Does 'Tiger Parenting' Exist? Parenting Profiles of Chinese Americans and Adolescent Development Outcomes," *Asian American Journal of Psychology*, vol 4, no. 1, March 2013, pp. 7–18. No further reproduction or distribution is permitted without written permission from the American Psychological Association.

In contrast, a permissive parenting profile characterizes parents who are more responsive, maintain low levels of control, are nonpunitive, and low in demandingness (Baumrind, 1966). While these parenting profiles have become widely accepted in the literature, they were initially identified using a population of toddlers and young children in well-functioning, European American families (Baumrind, 1966; Maccoby & Martin, 1983). Scholars are increasingly recognizing the need to assess parental profiles using expanded dimensions to accommodate ethnic populations and different developmental periods (Steinberg, Lamborn, Dornbusch, & Darling, 1992).

Previous research on parenting practices in ethnic minority groups indicates that cultural values and practices may impact parenting styles such that the western-derived profiles established by Baumrind (1966) and expanded by Maccoby and Martin (1983) are not as applicable to these groups. Working from the hypothesis that ethnic minorities' parenting practices may differ from those evinced in the classic profiles, Domenech Rodriguez, Donovick, and Crowley (2009) found the classic parenting styles did indeed have less relevance in the case of ethnic minority families. Studies conducted on ethnic minority parents have found that these parents exhibit lower levels of parental sensitivity, use culturally specific types of parental control, and exhibit higher levels of protectiveness (Chao, 1994; Mesman, van Ijzendoorn, & Bakermans-Kranenburg, 2012; Domenech Rodriguez et al., 2009). Overall, these studies question whether the classic parenting styles accurately capture parenting practices in ethnic minorities such as Asian Americans.

Previous studies on Asian parents have employed classic labels, but have added caveats such as, "authoritative and psychologically controlling" (Chan, Bowes, & Wyver, 2009, p. 849) to the classic authoritarian label. Such parenting may be an example of tiger parenting, even though the term is relatively new. Recently, the term *tiger parent* was popularized, and is colloquially understood to refer to Asian American parents (Chua, 2011). The hypothesized tiger parenting profile may be characterized by high levels of both authoritativeness and authoritarianism among Asian parents, and may be viewed as the culturally salient merger of the classic authoritative and authoritarian parenting profiles (Chan et al., 2009; Xu et al., 2005). In addition to the tiger parenting profile, we expect to find additional parenting profiles in our sample. For example, a profile in which parents are supportive may be similar to the classic authoritative profile; a profile in which parents are characterized as harsh may be similar to the classic authoritarian profile; and a profile in which parents are easygoing may be similar to the classic negligent and/or permissive parenting profiles.

Contemporary scholars are increasingly recognizing the importance of using multiple dimensions, both positive and negative, to define parenting profiles (Nelson, Padilla-Walker, Christensen, Evans, & Carroll, 2011). Accordingly, the current study conceptualizes its potential parenting profiles as reflecting varying levels of eight different parenting dimensions. The classic dimension of warmth is expanded to include both positive (parental warmth) and negative (parental hostility) dimensions in an effort to distinguish between the mere lack of warmth and the presence of actual hostility. The classic dimension of control is expanded to include the multiple facets of control–specifically, positive control is measured by parental monitoring and democratic parenting; negative control is measured by psychological control and punitive parenting. Additionally, inductive reasoning, which is a measure of parents' effective communication with their children, is included as part of the fourth dimension, along with shaming, which has been shown to play a significant role in the socialization of Chinese-origin children (Fung, 1999). Fung (1999) notes that Asian parents actively pressure their children to internalize feelings of shame for not conforming to norms or for failing to perform as parents expect. These expanded dimensions allow for a more comprehensive measurement of control and warmth than can be identified using the classic profiles.

A possible "supportive" parenting profile emergent in this study would score high on positive measures (parental warmth, democratic parenting, parental monitoring, and inductive reasoning) and low on negative measures (parental hostility, psychological control, punitive parenting, and shaming). Another possible profile, one characterized as "harsh," would score low on positive measures and high on negative measures. A profile characterized as "easygoing" may score low on both positive and negative measures. Finally, a profile characterized as "tiger parenting" may score high on both positive and negative measures.

## A Variable-Centered Versus a Person-Centered Approach

In a variable-centered approach to studying parenting, each parenting dimension is examined in isolation. The disadvantage of this approach is that the effect of individual parenting dimensions may differ depending on the parenting styles compiled from multiple dimensions (Kerr, Stattin, & Ozdemir, 2012). For example, high levels of control may be perceived differently when accompanied by high levels of warmth than when they are accompanied by low levels of warmth (Keijsers, Frijns, Branje, & Meeus, 2009). Although parenting is multifaceted, empirical studies that create profiles have relied on arbitrary cutoffs or a median split approach in order to create parenting styles using two dimensions. For example, Chao (2001) and Berge, Wall, Loth, and Neumark-Sztainer (2010) identified the four traditional parenting profiles by placing subjects rated as high (above the median) or low (below the median) in two dimensions into a four-tier parenting classification system. One notable limitation in this type of analysis is the researcher may misclassify subjects by artificially placing an equal number of participants into each of the four profiles, which may not accurately depict the prevalence of each profile in the sample. In addition, by focusing on only two dimensions, this approach precludes the inclusion of other important dimensions used to define parenting profiles, such as autonomy granting/communication (Darling & Steinberg, 1993).

The current study uses multiple parenting dimensions in a latent profile analysis to create the clusters that define parenting profiles in a sample of Chinese Americans. Nelson, and colleagues (2011) also examined eight dimensions of parenting using a person-centered approach. The advantage of a person-centered approach, such as latent profile analysis, is that it allows the data to determine the optimal number of solutions (profiles) and can provide the probability of a participant belonging to one of the profiles. A person-centered approach eliminates any presumed bias towards a specified number of solutions, and is advantageous for its applicability to multidimensional models (Weaver & Kim, 2008).

## Parenting Profiles Across Adolescent Developmental Periods and Across Reporters

In the current study, parenting profiles are assessed during early, middle, and late adolescence. It may be possible for parenting profiles emergent at one developmental period to differ from those at another developmental period. Nelson, et al. (2011) examined parenting during young adulthood and concluded that, while classical parenting styles were applicable to their sample, other parenting styles may be more relevant during emerging adulthood. The current study allows for an examination of parenting styles at developmental periods from early adolescence to emerging adulthood, and addresses whether the tiger parenting profile is evident throughout adolescence or only during specific developmental periods by a specific parent in the family.

The common adage "strict father, kind mother" (Chao & Tseng, 2002) in Chinese families suggests that the mother may be responsible for daily upbringing and emotional guidance, while the father may be responsible for discipline and socialization outside the home. At this time, little research has yet examined whether mothers and fathers may take on the roles of disciplinarian and compassionate parent to varying degrees at different times during a child's development. If the tiger parenting profile does exist, it may be more evident during a particular time period, since parenting practices may be influenced by what mothers and fathers deem most appropriate for meeting the developmental needs of their children at any given time (Costigan & Dokis, 2006; Inman, Howard, Beaumont, & Walker, 2007). For example, mothers may be tiger parents during the earlier years, when they are more responsible for children's socialization in the home, up until their children's transition into adolescence. Fathers, on the other hand, might take on the tiger parenting role as adolescents gain more autonomy and independence during emerging adulthood.

In addition to parents' reports on their own parenting styles, adolescents' perspectives on their parents' parenting is also important to assess. Parents and adolescents may not agree about which style of parenting is practiced in the home. Indeed, there is a high level of mismatch between the parenting practices Chinese American adolescents experience and those they deem to be examples of ideal parenting, suggesting a large discrepancy between parent and adolescent reports of parenting practices (Wu & Chao, 2011).

## Parenting Profiles and Adolescent Outcomes

This study evaluates multiple domains of adolescent outcomes associated with each parenting profile that emerged in a Chinese American sample. Assessing multiple adolescent outcomes can provide a better understanding of how parenting profiles affect overall adjustment across the developmental periods of early adolescence, middle adolescence, and emerging adulthood. The outcomes include academic achievement, educational attainment, academic pressure, depressive symptoms, parent-child alienation and family obligation. Previous studies have evaluated the role of parenting profiles in relation to a single outcome, such as academic achievement or depressive symptoms. By examining these and other outcomes together, the current study may be able to address how parenting profiles relate to the "achievement/adjustment paradox" wherein

Asian American students have high levels of academic achievement, but low levels of psychological adjustment (Qin, 2008). This paradox may be most evident among Asian American adolescents whose parents fit into the tiger parenting profile.

Previous research has identified authoritative parenting as positively correlated and authoritarian parenting as negatively correlated with GPA (measure of academic achievement) (Steinberg, et al., 1992). Chao and Tseng (2002) emphasize that Chinese parents measure success by their children's performance in school and their children's adherence to familial responsibilities, which means that children may feel a strong sense of academic pressure and family obligation. It is also important to assess adolescent adjustment by measuring outcomes such as parent-child alienation and depressive symptoms. Research has found that unsupportive parenting behaviors decrease parent-child bonding, leading adolescents to develop an increased sense of alienation from their parents (S. Y. Kim, Chen, Wang, Shen, & Orozco-Lapray, 2012). In addition, authoritarian-like parenting practices may also increase adolescents' depressive symptoms (Nguyen, 2008).

We expect that if tiger parenting does indeed emerge as a parenting profile, it may be the most likely of the profiles to relate to the achievement/adjustment paradox, given that tiger parenting's emphasis on high academic achievement and strong sense of family obligation may go hand-in-hand with high academic pressure and heightened adolescent depressive symptoms. This study will also explore whether the achievement/adjustment paradox is evident in other profiles specific to Chinese American parenting that may emerge.

## Current Study

Chua's book (2011) instigated a need to assess parenting profiles using an expanded model of parenting dimensions that may better reflect the parenting practices of a sample of Chinese Americans. First, this study aims to identify parenting profiles for Chinese American mothers and fathers separately, and to determine if a tiger parenting profile emerges, by using both parent self-reports and adolescent reports of parenting practices (warmth, parental monitoring, democratic parenting, inductive reasoning, hostility, psychological control, shaming, and punitive parenting). Second, this study will evaluate various adolescent outcomes (academic achievement, educational attainment, academic pressure, depressive symptoms, parent-child alienation and family obligation) associated with each parenting profile across three distinct developmental periods: early adolescence, middle adolescence and emerging adulthood.

# Method

## Participants

Participants were Chinese American families participating in a three-wave longitudinal study, with data gathered every 4 years. Adolescents were initially recruited from seven middle schools in Northern California. There were 444 families in Wave 1, 350 families in Wave 2 and 330 families in Wave 3. Slightly over half of the adolescent sample is female ($n = 246$, 54%). The age of the adolescents in the initial wave ranges from 12 to 15 ($M = 13.03$, $SD = 0.73$) years old. Median family income is in the range of $30,001 to $45,000 across all three waves. Median parental education level is some high school education for both fathers and mothers. Most (75%) of the adolescents were born in U.S., whereas 91% of the mothers and 88% of the fathers were born outside the U.S. Most of the participants originally came from Hong Kong or southern provinces of China. Fewer than 10 families hailed from Taiwan. The occupational status of immigrant parents is wide-ranging, from those in professional occupations (e.g., banker or computer programmer) to unskilled laborers (e.g., construction worker or janitor). The majority speaks Cantonese; less than 10% of the families speak Mandarin as their home language.

## Procedure

Participants were initially recruited from seven middle schools in major metropolitan areas of Northern California. With the aid of school administrators, Chinese American students were identified, and all eligible families were sent a letter describing the research project in both Chinese and English. The 47% of these families that returned parent consent and adolescent assent received a packet of questionnaires for the mother, father, and target adolescent in the household. Participants were instructed to complete the questionnaires alone and not to discuss answers with friends and/or family members. They were also instructed to seal their questionnaires in the provided envelopes immediately following the completion of their responses. Within approximately 2–3 weeks after sending the questionnaire packet, research assistants visited each school to collect the completed questionnaires during the students' lunch periods. Among the families who agreed to participate, 76% returned surveys. Four years after the initial wave, families were asked to participate in the second wave, and after another 4 years had passed, they were asked to participate in the third wave of data collection. Families who returned questionnaires were compensated a nominal amount of money ($30 at Wave 1, $50 at Wave 2, and $130 at Wave 3) for their participation.

Questionnaires were prepared in English and Chinese. The questionnaires were first translated to Chinese and then back-translated to English. Any inconsistencies with the original English version scale were resolved by bilingual/bicultural research assistants with careful consideration of culturally appropriate meanings of items. Around 71% parents used the Chinese language version of the questionnaire and the majority (85%) of adolescents used the English version.

Attrition analyses were conducted at Waves 2 and 3 to compare families who participated with those who did not on the demographic variables measured at Wave 1 (i.e., parental education, family income, parent and child generational status, parent and child age). Only one significant difference emerged: boys were less likely than girls to have continued participating ($\chi^2$ (1) = 7.20 to 10.41, $p < .01$). Adolescent sex is included as a covariate for all analyses.

## Measures

### Parenting Dimensions

Adolescents, mothers and fathers all responded to questions about eight parenting dimensions: parental warmth, inductive reasoning, parental monitoring, democratic parenting, parental hostility, psychological control, shaming, and punitive parenting. The internal consistency for each parenting dimension was from acceptable to high across waves and informants ($\alpha$ = .65 to .91), except for mother report of democratic parenting at Wave 1 ($\alpha$ = .59).

Parental warmth, inductive reasoning, parental monitoring, and parental hostility were assessed through measures adapted from the Iowa Youth and Families Project (Conger, Patterson, & Ge, 1995; Ge, Best, Conger, & Simons, 1996). Parental warmth was measured with eight items about an affective dimension of parenting on a 7-point scale. Some examples of the items are "act loving, affectionate, and caring," "listen carefully," and "act supportive and understanding." Using a 5-point scale, participants also rated four items assessing *inductive reasoning* (e.g., give reasons for decisions; ask for the target child's opinion before making decisions; and discipline by reasoning, explaining or talking), as well as three items assessing parental monitoring (e.g., know whereabouts of the target child; know who the target child is with; know when the target child comes home). Parental hostility was assessed using seven items about parents' hostile behavior toward their children on a 7-point scale. Some examples of the items are "shout or yell," "get angry," and "insult or swear" at the target child.

Democratic parenting and punitive parenting were assessed through two subscales of the Parenting Practices Questionnaire (Robinson, Mandleco, Olson, & Hart, 1995) using a five-point scale. Democratic parenting was measured with five items about parents' autonomy granting (e.g., encourage the target child to freely express himself/herself, allow the target child to give input into family rules, and take into account the target child's preferences). Punitive parenting was measured with four items about parents' use of punitive discipline (e.g., punish the target child by taking privileges away with little or no explanation, discipline first and ask questions later, and use threat of punishment with little or no explanation).

Psychological control was assessed through a measure of psychological control adapted by Barber (1996) from the Child's Report of Parental Behavior Inventory (Schaefer, 1965). Using a 3-point scale, all participants rated eight items about parents' attempts to regulate children's psychological experience (e.g., change the subject whenever the target child has something to say, avoid looking at the target child if disappointed, and become less friendly when the target child does not see things in the parent's way).

*Shaming* was assessed through an unpublished measure developed by Ruth K. Chao at the University of California, Riverside. Using a 3-point scale, participants rated five items about parents' attempts to socialize their children by inducing feelings of shame. The five items are: "Teach my child what not to do by using examples of bad behavior in other youths," "Teach my child by pointing out other youths that I think are successful," "Tell my child to consider my wishes or expectations in his or her actions or behaviors," "Tell my child that his or her actions should bring respect and honor to the family," and, "Tell my child that his or her actions should not bring shame to me."

### Adolescent Adjustment

Adolescent adjustment was measured using six indicators: academic achievement, education attainment, academic pressure, depressive symptoms, parent-child alienation, and family obligation. The internal consistency of each outcome was high across waves and informants ($\alpha$ = .72 to .89). The internal consistency for academic achievement and educational attainment was not computed because they were measures with a single item.

Academic achievement was measured at Waves 1 and 2 using unweighted Grade Point Average (GPA, without physical education courses) from school records. In Wave 3, adolescents reported their current education attainment using a scale ranging from (1) *high school dropout* to (5) *currently in graduate school (medical, law, Master's Degree, etc.).*

Academic pressure was measured at Waves 1 and 2 using a scale developed by the first author. On a 5-point scale, adolescents rated three items about the pressure they felt to succeed in school. The three items are: "Feel pressure from my parents to do well in school," "Get annoyed when my parents remind me about the importance of getting good grades," and "Stressed out about getting good grades." Adolescent *depressive symptoms* were assessed using the Center for Epidemiologic Studies of Depression Scale (CES-D) (Radloff, 1977). Using a 4-point scale, adolescents, fathers, and mothers each rated 20 items about adolescents' depressed mood. Parent-child alienation was assessed through the alienation subscale of the Inventory of Parent and Peer Attachment (Armsden & Greenberg, 1987). Using a 5-point scale, adolescents, fathers, and mothers each rated eight items on adolescents' feeling of alienation from their parents (e.g., do not get much attention at home, have to rely on oneself when having a problem to solve, and get upset a lot more than parents know about). The measure of family obligation was adapted from a scale developed by Fuligni, Tseng and Lam (1999). Using a 5-point scale, adolescents rated 13 items about family obligation (e.g., providing assistance to the family as a child, do well for the sake of the family, and make sacrifices for the family).

### Demographic Information

At all three waves, adolescents answered questions on their sex, age, and whether they were born in the U.S. At all three waves, fathers and mothers answered questions on their age, highest level of education attained and whether they were born in the U.S. These variables were included as covariates when examining the differences in adolescent adjustment among the various parenting profiles.

## Results

### Analysis Plan

All the analyses were conducted separately for adolescent report of maternal parenting, adolescent report of paternal parenting, mother report of own parenting and father report of own parenting, and also separately for Waves 1, 2 and 3. Data analyses proceeded in two steps. First, parenting profiles indicated by the eight parenting dimensions were explored using Latent Profile Analyses (LPA). LPA assumes there are subpopulations in the sample, with distinct profiles comprised of multiple indicators, and attempts to identify these subpopulations. To determine the optimal number of profiles, a series of models were fitted to estimate between two to five parenting profiles

sequentially. Each model was compared with its previous model (i.e., $n$ class model compared to $n-1$ class model) on multiple fit indices to determine whether estimating one more class improved model fit. The best fitting model was chosen when there was no further improvement by adding more classes. Indices included Bayesian information criterion (BIC), the sample size adjusted BIC (ABIC), and a log-likelihood based test (i.e., Lo-Mendel-Rubin (LMR) test) (Nylund, Asparouhov, & Muthén, 2007). Smaller BIC and ABIC values indicated better model fit, and a significant LMR test indicated that a given model significantly improved model fit compared to the previous model. Using a combination of multiple model fit indices strengthens the reliability of class enumeration (B. Muthén, 2003). The number of random starts was increased to ensure that the final model converged at a stable solution (Hipp & Bauer, 2006).

Second, the effect of parenting profiles on adolescent adjustment was examined using path analyses. All the outcome variables were included as dependent variables in the same model, and dichotomous variables representing the parenting profiles were treated as the independent variables. In each model, when there were $n$ parenting profiles, $n-1$ dichotomous variables were created, with the last parenting profile as the reference group. The coefficient estimation for each dichotomous variable indicated how each separate parenting profile was associated with adolescent adjustment relative to the reference parenting profile. The reference group was rotated to obtain all possible comparisons among parenting profiles. Demographic variables were controlled for, including adolescents' sex, age, and birth place, as well as parents' age, birth place, and highest education level attained.

All the analyses were conducted in Mplus 6.12 (Muthén & Muthén, 1998–2011). Mplus handles missing data with full-information maximum likelihood (FIML) by default. FIML uses all the available information in its estimates and is therefore recommended among the current methods of handling missing data (Graham, 2009).

### Parenting Profiles

Our first research question focused on whether there were different parenting profiles based on the eight parenting dimensions. For all the chosen optimal solutions derived from latent profile analyses, BIC and ABIC were the lowest, or the decline in BIC and ABIC between two adjacent models began to level off. In addition, the LMR test was significant, or marginally significant, between the optimal solution and its previous model, but not significant among any following models. The optimal solutions of parenting profiles are displayed in Table 1. In the discussion that follows, the number of parenting profiles in each optimal solution is described, then each parenting profile is labeled, and finally, the prevalence of each parenting profile in the current sample is examined.

The optimal solutions were stable over time for adolescent-reported maternal parenting (four profiles across three waves), most differentiated in middle adolescence for adolescent-reported paternal parenting (four profiles at Wave 2 compared to three profiles at Waves 1 and 3), less differentiated over time for mother-reported maternal parenting (four, three, and two profiles from Waves 1 to 3), and most differentiated in emerging adulthood for father-reported paternal parenting (three profiles at Wave 3 compared to two profiles at Waves 1 and 2). Solutions with the same number of profiles show a similar pattern of mean levels on the eight parenting dimensions. Examples of mean levels for the eight parenting dimensions in a four-profile, a three-profile, and a two-profile solution are displayed in Figures 1, 2 and 3, respectively.

When the optimal solution was four profiles, each parenting profile was labeled according to its relative mean values compared to those of the other profiles on the four positive parenting dimensions (parental warmth, inductive reasoning, parental monitoring and democratic parenting) and the four negative parenting dimensions (parental hostility, psychological control, shaming and punitive parenting). Specifically, the parenting profile that scored relatively high on the positive parenting dimensions and low on the negative parenting dimensions was labeled as *supportive parenting*; the parenting profile that scored relatively high on both the positive and negative parenting dimensions was consistent with our operationalization of *tiger parenting* and was labeled accordingly; the parenting profile that scored relatively low on both the positive and negative parenting dimensions was labeled as *easygoing parenting*; and the parenting profile that scored relatively low on the positive parenting dimensions but high on the negative parenting dimensions was labeled as *harsh parenting*. The same labeling scheme was applied when the optimal solution was three or two profiles.

Table 1 also shows the group size of each parenting profile. In general, supportive parenting was the largest group, followed by tiger parenting and/or easygoing parenting, and harsh parenting was the smallest group. Comparing adolescent and parent reports, the percentage of the sample classified as supportive tended to be smaller in the adolescent reports than in the parent reports. On the other hand, the percentage of the sample classified as tiger or harsh tended to be larger in the adolescent reports than in the parent reports. Regarding the changes in group size across waves, although

*Table 1*

### Classification Estimation from Parenting Latent Profile Analyses

| | Classes | | | | |
|---|---|---|---|---|---|
| | 1 | 2 | 3 | 4 | |
| | Supportive $n$ (%) | Tiger $n$ (%) | Easygoing $n$ (%) | Harsh $n$ (%) | Total |
| W1 Maternal parenting (A) | 199 (45.0%) | 123 (27.8%) | 86 (19.5%) | 34 (7.7%) | 442 |
| W2 Maternal parenting (A) | 139 (40.3%) | 66 (19.1%) | 97 (28.1%) | 43 (12.5%) | 345 |
| W3 Maternal parenting (A) | 136 (42.4%) | 59 (18.4%) | 109 (34.0%) | 17 (5.3%) | 321 |
| W1 Paternal parenting (A) | 272 (63.4%) | 80 (18.6%) | 77 (17.9%) | — | 429 |
| W2 Paternal parenting (A) | 131 (39.8%) | 91 (27.7%) | 77 (23.4%) | 30 (9.1%) | 329 |
| W3 Paternal parenting (A) | 179 (58.3%) | 85 (27.7%) | 43 (14.0%) | — | 307 |
| W1 Maternal parenting (M) | 142 (34.8%) | 55 (13.5%) | 182 (44.6%) | 29 (7.1%) | 408 |
| W2 Maternal parenting (M) | 239 (77.3%) | 52 (16.8%) | 18 (5.8%) | — | 309 |
| W3 Maternal parenting (M) | 210 (70.7%) | — | 87 (29.3%) | — | 297 |
| W1 Paternal parenting (F) | 276 (72.4%) | — | 105 (27.6%) | — | 381 |
| W2 Paternal parenting (F) | 208 (74.3%) | — | 72 (25.7%) | — | 280 |
| W3 Paternal parenting (F) | 188 (69.6%) | 52 (19.3%) | 30 (11.1%) | — | 270 |

*Note.* W = wave; A = adolescent report; M = mother report; F = father report; the sample sizes in Waves 1, 2, and 3 are 444, 350, and 330, respectively.

*Figure 1*

**Four Parenting Profiles Estimated from Adolescents' Report of Maternal Parenting Practices at Wave 1**

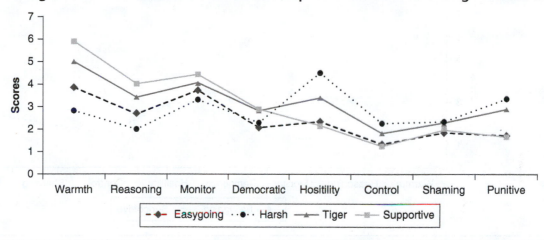

there were no clear patterns for supportive, easygoing or harsh parenting, a pattern did emerge for tiger parenting. Specifically, the percentage of the sample that fit the profile for tiger parenting decreased among mothers but increased among fathers according to both adolescent and parent reports.

## Parenting Profiles and Adolescent Adjustment

Our second research question was how parenting profiles were associated with adolescent adjustment. The coefficient estimates from path analyses are displayed in Table 2,

indicating each parenting profile's association with adolescent adjustment relative to the reference parenting profile. For each type of report, there were significant associations between parenting profiles and each developmental outcome in at least one of the three waves, with one exception: father-reported paternal parenting profiles were not significantly related to adolescent-reported academic pressure.

In general, supportive parenting was associated with best developmental outcomes, followed, in order, by easygoing parenting, tiger parenting and harsh parenting. This pattern was consistent for both adolescent and parent reports. Specifically, when being compared to the other

*Figure 2*

**Three Parenting Profiles Estimated from Mothers' Report of Maternal Parenting Practices at Wave 2.**

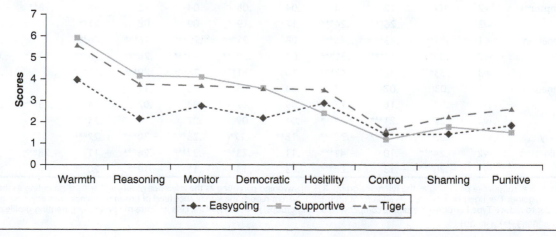

*Figure 3*

### Two Parenting Profiles Estimated from Fathers' Report of Paternal Parenting Practices at Wave 1.

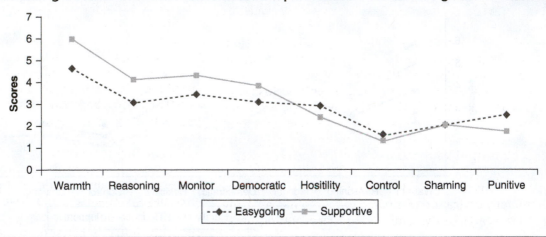

*Table 2*

### Coefficients Estimates from Path Analyses on the Relationship Between Parenting Profiles and Adolescent Adjustment

| | | Adolescent report maternal parenting | | | | | | Adolescent report paternal parenting | | | | | |
| | | R_S | | | R_E | | R_T | R_S | | | R_E | | R_T |
| Variable | Wave | E | T | H | T | H | H | E | T | H | T | H | H |
|---|---|---|---|---|---|---|---|---|---|---|---|---|---|
| GPA | w1 | −.06 | −.18*** | −.04 | −.11 | .00 | .07 | −.05 | −.10 | | −.05 | | |
| | w2 | −.13 | −.25*** | −.13 | −.13 | −.04 | .08 | −.17** | −.28*** | −.06 | −.09 | .05 | .11 |
| Attainment | w3 | −.15 | −.15 | −.24*** | −.02 | −.17** | −.16 | −.11 | −.19** | | −.05 | | |
| Academic | w1 | .11 | .30*** | .24*** | .17** | .16** | .06 | .02 | .27*** | | .26*** | | |
| Pressure | | | | | | | | | | | | | |
| (A) | w2 | .16** | .33*** | .26*** | .19** | .14 | −.02 | .13 | .16** | .21*** | .03 | .12 | .10 |
| Depressive | w1 | .24*** | .30*** | .30*** | .03 | .14** | .12 | .13** | .28*** | | .15 | | |
| Symptoms | w2 | .12 | .25*** | .40*** | .15 | .31*** | .19** | .20*** | .22*** | .25*** | .00 | .11 | .11 |
| (A) | w3 | .13 | .35*** | .21*** | .24*** | .15** | .01 | .05 | .27*** | | .20 | | |
| Depressive | w1 | .13 | .18*** | .13** | .03 | .04 | .03 | .07 | .12 | | .04 | | |
| Symptoms | w2 | .09 | .12 | .14 | .04 | .08 | .04 | .13 | .08 | .18** | −.05 | .09 | .13 |
| (P) | w3 | .11 | .26*** | .24*** | .17** | .19** | .09 | .08 | .21** | | .11 | | |
| Alienation | w1 | .31*** | .43*** | .46*** | .08 | .25*** | .20*** | .16*** | .46*** | | .30*** | | |
| (A) | w2 | .30*** | .33*** | .51*** | .07 | .29*** | .23*** | .26*** | .26*** | .43*** | −.01 | .26*** | .27*** |
| | w3 | .33*** | .37*** | .47*** | .10 | .31*** | .26*** | .29*** | .45*** | | .08 | | |
| Alienation | w1 | .03 | .07 | .08 | .04 | .06 | .03 | .11 | .04 | | −.07 | | |
| (P) | w2 | .07 | .16 | .17** | .09 | .12 | .04 | .07 | .14 | .25*** | .07 | .21** | .16 |
| | w3 | .22*** | .21*** | .19*** | .04 | .09 | .07 | .11 | .24*** | | .10 | | |
| Family | w1 | −.32*** | −.18*** | −.38*** | .18** | −.17** | −.28*** | −.30*** | −.27*** | | .04 | | |
| Obligation | w2 | −.24*** | −.10 | −.41*** | .11 | −.23*** | −.32*** | −.26*** | −.11 | −.28*** | .16 | −.11 | −.21*** |
| (A) | w3 | −.20*** | −.13 | −.23*** | .03 | −.13 | −.15 | −.19** | −.20*** | | .05 | | |

*Note.* R_S = supportive parenting as the reference group; R_E = easygoing parenting as the reference group; R_T = tiger parenting as the reference group; E = easygoing; T = tiger; H = harsh; A = adolescent report; P = parent report; the significance level of group differences was adjusted using Bonferroni Correction in order to reduce Type I error from multiple comparisons among groups, *p* < .0083; blank cells indicate the particular parenting profile did not emerge.

** *p* < .0083. *** *p* < .001.

three groups, supportive parenting profile, as reported by either adolescents or parents, was associated with higher GPA ($\beta$ = .13 to .28, $p$ <= .007) and educational attainment ($\beta$ = .18 to .24, $p$ <= .002); a lower level of academic pressure ($\beta$ = −.33 to −.16, $p$ <= .003), depressive symptoms ($\beta$ = −.40 to −.13, $p$ <= .006) and feelings of alienation from their parents ($\beta$ = −.51 to −.16, $p$ <= .007); and a stronger sense of family obligation ($\beta$ = .14 to .41, $p$ <= .008). In addition, compared to easygoing parenting, tiger parenting was associated with higher levels of academic pressure ($\beta$ = .17 to .26, $p$ <= .005), depressive symptoms ($\beta$ = .17 to .24, $p$ <= .008) and feelings of alienation from their parents ($\beta$ = .16 to .30, $p$ <= .001). The only exception was that tiger parenting among mothers as reported by adolescents at Wave 1 was significantly related to higher family obligation compared to easygoing parenting ($\beta$ = .18, $p$ = .001). Lastly, compared to tiger parenting, harsh parenting was associated with higher levels of depressive symptoms ($\beta$ = .19, $p$ = .001), higher levels of alienation from their parents ($\beta$ = .20 to .27, $p$ < .001) and lower levels of family obligation ($\beta$ = −.32 to −.21, $p$ < .001).

# Discussion

The current study identifies parenting profiles within a Chinese American sample using multiple dimensions of parenting practices. More importantly, the current study provides empirical support for the existence of Chua's (2011) concept of tiger parenting. Up to four parenting profiles are identified: supportive parenting, easygoing parenting, tiger parenting and harsh parenting, with supportive parenting making up the largest proportion, tiger parenting and easygoing parenting making up the second or third largest proportion, depending on the developmental period and the informant, and harsh parenting making up the smallest proportion. In most cases, of the various aspects of adolescents' developmental outcomes investigated, supportive parenting is associated with the best outcomes, easygoing parenting is associated with similar or better outcomes than tiger parenting, and harsh parenting is associated with similar or worse outcomes than tiger parenting. As expected, tiger parenting is associated with high academic pressure.

| | Mother report maternal parenting | | | | | | Father report paternal parenting | | |
| --- | --- | --- | --- | --- | --- | --- | --- | --- | --- |
| | R_S | | | R_E | | R_T | R_S | | R_E |
| E | T | H | T | H | H | E | T | T |
| −.07 | −.15** | −.08 | −.10 | −.04 | .04 | −.13** | | |
| .03 | −.07 | | −.12 | | | .06 | | |
| −.14 | | | | | | −.09 | −.18** | −.07 |
| .08 | .16** | .12 | .11 | .08 | .00 | −.03 | | |
| .02 | .03 | | .00 | | | −.13 | | |
| .13 | .18** | .16** | .09 | .09 | .03 | .01 | | |
| .01 | .04 | | .03 | | | −.00 | | |
| .08 | | | | | | −.03 | .19** | .22 |
| .26** | .29*** | .33*** | .11 | .19*** | .11 | .24*** | | |
| .14 | .13 | | −.09 | | | .15 | | |
| .21*** | | | | | | .08 | .29*** | .18 |
| .09 | .18** | .18** | .12 | .13 | .05 | .04 | | |
| .07 | .12 | | .00 | | | −.05 | | |
| .16** | | | | | .04 | .20** | .14 | |
| .28*** | .35*** | .27*** | .16** | .13** | .01 | .29*** | | |
| .23*** | .22*** | | −.15 | | | .22*** | | |
| .31*** | | | | | | .23*** | .41*** | .12 |
| −.10 | −.07 | −.14** | .00 | −.09 | −.09 | −.08 | | |
| −.04 | −.03 | | .03 | | | −.16** | | |
| −.01 | | | | | | −.11 | −.05 | .08 |

The current study takes a person-centered approach by conducting a latent profile analysis to identify parenting profiles within a sample of Chinese Americans. A person-centered approach is more advantageous than a variable-centered approach because the impact of parenting practices is examined in the context of parenting styles, which represent a combination of different levels of various parenting practices (Kerr et al., 2012). A classic person-centered approach to parenting studies is the median-split analysis, which has several shortcomings (Berge et al., 2010). First, the number of profiles is predetermined. Second, models with multiple dimensions can be extremely complicated. For example, with eight dimensions, the number in our study, a median-split approach would lead to 256 profiles. Third, all profiles are presumed to consist of equal number of participants, which is not realistic. Latent profile analysis, on the other hand, allows for the identification of different numbers of profiles–three to five in our study–and selects the optimal solution based on the model fit to the data. In addition, the group size varied among all the parenting profiles, which enabled us to compare the prevalence of each profile in the current sample.

The profiles identified in the current study are similar to the classic parenting styles in that warmth and control are the general criteria for distinguishing profiles. For example, supportive parenting is akin to the classic authoritative parenting style, with high scores on both parental warmth and positive control, while harsh parenting is akin to the authoritarian parenting style, with low scores on parental warmth and high scores on negative control. However, our parenting dimensions are more nuanced and comprehensive than the two classic parenting dimensions of warmth and control, which means that the parenting profiles that emerge in this study are distinct from the classic parenting styles. For example, in order to capture the multifaceted nature of parental control, the classic dimension has been parceled into multiple dimensions across both positive (parental monitoring and democratic parenting) and negative (psychological control and punitive control) constructs. The classic dimension of parental warmth has been expanded to include not only warmth, but also hostility. Considering warmth and hostility as separate dimensions, rather than as two extreme poles of a single dimension, allowed us to distinguish tiger parenting (high warmth, high hostility) from easygoing parenting (low warmth, low hostility).

Our profiles also included the dimension of inductive reasoning, because reasoning and explanation provide an avenue for better parent-child communication, which is considered to be an important component of authoritative

parenting (Darling & Steinberg, 1993). Inductive reasoning is also key for distinguishing between confrontive control of authoritative parenting from coercive control of authoritarian parenting (Baumrind, 2012). Finally, a culturally specific dimension of shaming has been included to create culturally meaningful parenting profiles. The results show that supportive parenting, which is most beneficial for adolescent adjustment, includes higher extent of shaming than easygoing parenting, although not as high as the level of shaming in tiger or harsh parenting. Our results suggest that the use of shaming is an important component of being a supportive and successful parent in Chinese culture, but the dimension of shaming is completely absent in the classic authoritative parenting style. Thus, the culturally specific parenting profiles that emerged in this study are not merely interchangeable with the classic parenting styles.

Whereas most of the existing research on this topic uses either a cross-sectional or a short-term longitudinal design only, covering one or two specific developmental periods, the current study goes beyond these studies by using a longitudinal design that covers three developmental periods (early adolescence, middle adolescence and emerging adulthood) and gathers data from multiple informants. This allows for an examination of whether or not parenting styles remain consistent across different developmental periods, as parenting may vary according to children's changing developmental needs (Nelson et al., 2011). Indeed, our results consistently show that the proportion of tiger mothers tends to decrease or disappear across waves, whereas the proportion of tiger fathers tends to increase or emerge, and this is so regardless of informant.

Traditional Chinese parents are supposed to be, as the adage goes, "strict father and kind mother," meaning that the father exerts restrictive control and the mother manifests warmth (Chao & Tseng, 2002). However, our results suggest that the roles of mothers and fathers change over time in a way that is tied to the development of their children. It appears that mothers gradually relinquish their role as the tiger parent to fathers over the period of time from early adolescence to emerging adulthood. The reason for this phenomenon is not known yet, but one possible explanation may have to do with the role Asian American parents play in the socialization of their children. In Asian American families, mothers are responsible for the socialization of young children at home (Inman et al., 2007), while fathers are responsible for the socialization of children outside of the home (Costigan & Dokis, 2006). Therefore, tiger parenting, as a culturally rooted parenting style, may be more likely to be used by mothers during earlier periods of adolescence, when adolescents' social interactions are more likely to occur within the family. As children move into later periods of adolescence and emerging adulthood, and begin to interact more with the wider society, fathers may become more responsible for disciplining the child, and thus may begin to take over the role of tiger parent.

Unlike many previous studies, which have relied on adolescent self-reports about their parents' practices, this study uses reports from both adolescents and their parents, for both maternal and paternal parenting practices. This allows for a comparison between adolescent reports and parents' self-reports of parenting. The results suggest that, compared to their parents' self-reports, adolescents are less likely to categorize their parents as supportive and more likely to categorize them as harsh or tiger parents. Previous research has shown that Chinese American adolescents are more likely than their European American counterparts to experience a salient mismatch between their ideals and perceptions of the parent-adolescent relationship (Wu & Chao, 2011). Because of this mismatch, which may deepen the typical parent-child generational gap, Chinese American adolescents are more likely than their parents to report negative parenting practices. The current study provides additional empirical evidence for a discrepancy in the perceptions of adolescents and parents within Chinese American families, and emphasizes the importance of comparing reports from target adolescents and their parents.

The current study also compares the developmental outcomes associated with each emerging parenting profile for both mothers and fathers, and across different periods of adolescence. Despite the widely accepted notion of an "achievement/adjustment paradox" in Asian Americans, particularly in the children of tiger parents, the current study findings do not seem to support the existence of such a paradox. Regardless of the parenting profile, high academic achievement and high educational attainment are always accompanied by high levels of psychological adjustment, and low academic achievement and low educational attainment are accompanied by low levels of psychological adjustment. The widely agreed-upon paradox may be operative when comparing Asian American adolescents to their non-Asian peers, but within the current sample of Chinese American adolescents, levels of achievement and adjustment are found to go hand in hand.

Tiger parenting, which owes its existence to the belief that "academic achievement reflects successful parenting" (Chua, 2011), ironically does not result in the best educational attainment or the best academic achievement; instead, it results in children experiencing a level of academic pressure that is as high as that associated with harsh parenting. It is actually supportive parenting, not tiger parenting, which is associated with the best developmental outcomes: low academic pressure, high GPA, high educational attainment, low depressive symptoms, low parent-child alienation, and high family obligation. These results are to some extent consistent with the literature on the authoritative parenting style within European American samples (Steinberg, Elmen, & Mounts, 1989). Easygoing parenting is associated with similar or better developmental outcomes than tiger parenting, with the exception of Wave 1 family obligation for the adolescent-reported maternal parenting profiles. Harsh parenting is associated with similar or worse developmental outcomes than tiger parenting, which reflects findings in the literature on authoritarian parenting (Nguyen, 2008). These differences are consistent across parent and adolescent reports.

There are some limitations of this study. First, the sample is selected from an area with a dense Chinese American population. Students in the initial sample were recruited from schools with a sizable proportion (>20%) of Asians in the student population, which is four times higher than the 5.6% that the Asian population represents in the United States (Hoeffel, Rastogi, Kim, & Shahid, 2010). Because families function in the context of the larger community, and because tiger parenting is a culturally specific construct, other studies may not be able to replicate our results. Tiger parenting may not emerge in other areas of the U.S. where the Chinese American population is smaller, or it may emerge but not be associated with the same developmental outcomes as in the current study. Second, the current study, as one of the first attempts to investigate Asian American parenting profiles, uses a sample of only Chinese American families, the largest ethnic group of Asian Americans in the U.S. (Hoeffel et al., 2010). It is not known whether the study findings are applicable to other Asian ethnic groups who share similar collectivistic values that may also emphasize children's academic achievement as a way to bring honor to the family (B. S. Kim, Atkinson, & Yang, 1999). Third, due to the culturally specific measures used (e.g., shaming), the new parenting profiles created in the current study may not be applicable to non-Asian racial or ethnic groups, such as European Americans. This is because the mean values that represent the various parenting profiles within a Chinese American sample may not be similar to those of other groups, such as European Americans, who generally show higher mean values on parental warmth and lower mean values on parental control. In other words, it may be that the parents identified as supportive in the current study would no longer be identified as supportive if they were part of a sample that included European American families.

There are at least two future research directions to consider. First, the effect of parenting practices may depend on the child's own characteristics. Chua's (2011) book shows that tiger parenting may not result in the same developmental outcomes in different children, even when they are siblings with the same tiger parent. Studies that compare the developmental outcomes of siblings can be conducted in the future to see how each child's specific characteristics can affect the way tiger parenting and other parenting profiles relate to adolescent outcomes. Second, results of the current study suggest that the parenting practices that comprise parenting profiles are not permanent, but vary over time. It may be that parenting practices fluctuate on a daily basis. Future studies could use a daily diary approach to investigate the changes in parenting practices and their relation to adolescents' developmental outcomes in a short-term intensive longitudinal study.

This study represents an initial effort at documenting and evaluating tiger parenting, which is oftentimes perceived by the public as distinctively Chinese or Asian American way of parenting. As controversial as tiger parenting has been, it is relatively understudied. The current study suggests that tiger parenting does exist in Chinese American families, but it is not the most common parenting profile, nor is it associated with optimal developmental outcomes in adolescents.

# References

Armsden, G. C., Greenberg, M. T. (1987). The Inventory of Parent and Peer Attachment: Individual differences and their relationship to psychological well-being in adolescence. *Journal of Youth and Adolescence, 16*, 427–454. doi: 10.1007/BF02202939

Barber, B. K. (1996). Parental psychological control: Revisiting a neglected construct. *Child Development, 67*, 3296–3319. doi:10.2307/1131780

Baumrind, D. (1966). Effects of authoritative parental control on child behavior. *Child Development, 37*, 887–907. doi:10.2307/1126611

Baumrind, D. (2012). Differentiating between confrontive and coercive kinds of parental power-assertive disciplinary practices. *Human Development, 55*, 35–51. doi:10.1159/000337962

Berge, J. M., Wall, M., Loth, K., & Neumark-Sztainer, D. (2010). Parenting style as a predictor of adolescent weight and weight-related behaviors. *Journal of Adolescent Health, 46*, 331–338. doi:10.1016/j.jadohealth.2009.08.004

Chan, S. M., Bowes, J., & Wyver, S. (2009). Chinese parenting in Hong Kong: Links among goals, beliefs and styles. *Early Child Development and Care, 179*, 849–862. doi:10.1080/03004430701536525

Chao, R. K. (1994). Beyond parental control and authoritarian parenting style: Understanding Chinese parenting through the cultural notion of training. *Child Development, 65*, 1111–1119. doi:10.2307/1131308

Chao, R. K. (2001). Extending research on the consequences of parenting style for Chinese Americans and European Americans. *Child Development, 72*, 1832–1843. doi:10.1111/1467-8624.00381

Chao, R. K., & Tseng, V. (2002). Parenting of Asians. In M. H. Bornstein (Ed.), *Handbook of parenting* (Vol. 4, pp. 59–93). Mahwah, NJ: Erlbaum.

Chua, A. (2011). *Battle hymn of the tiger mother*. New York, NY: Penguin Press.

Conger, R. D., Patterson, G. R., & Ge, X. (1995). It takes two to replicate: A mediational model for the impact of parents' stress on adolescent adjustment. *Child Development, 66*, 80–97. doi:10.2307/1131192

Costigan, C. L., & Dokis, D. P. (2006). Relations between parent–child acculturation differences and adjustment within immigrant Chinese families. *Child Development, 77*, 1252–1267. doi:10.1111/j.1467-8624.2006.00932.x

Darling, N., & Steinberg, L. (1993). Parenting style as context: An integrative model. *Psychological Bulletin, 113*, 487–496. doi:10.1037/0033-2909.113.3.487

Domenech Rodriguez, M. M., Donovick, M. R., & Crowley, S. L. (2009). Parenting styles in a cultural context: Observations of "protective parenting" in first-generation Latinos. *Family Process, 48*, 195–210. doi: 10.1111/j.1545-5300.2009.01277.x

Fuligni, A. J., Tseng, V., & Lam, M. (1999). Attitudes towards family obligations among American adolescents with Asian, Latin American, and European backgrounds. *Child Development, 70*, 1030–1044. doi: 10.1111/1467-8624.00075

Fung, H. (1999). Becoming a moral child: The socialization of shame among young Chinese children. *Ethos, 27*, 180–209. doi:10.1525/eth.1999.27.2.180

Ge, X., Best, K. M., Conger, R. D., & Simons, R. L. (1996). Parenting behaviors and the occurrence and co-occurrence of adolescent depressive symptoms and conduct problems. *Developmental Psychology, 32,* 717–731. doi:10.1037/0012-1649. 32.4.717

Graham, J. W. (2009). Missing data analysis: Making it work in the real world. *Annual Review of Psychology, 60,* 549–576. doi:10.1146/annurev.psych. 58.110405.085530

Hipp, J. R., & Bauer, D. J. (2006). Local solutions in the estimation of growth mixture models. *Psychological Methods, 11,* 36 –53. doi: 10.1037/1082-989X. 11.1.36

Hoeffel, E. M., Rastogi, S., Kim, M. O., & Shahid, H. (2010). *The Asian population: 2010.* Washington, DC: U. S. Census Bureau.

Inman, A. G., Howard, E. E., Beaumont, R. L., & Walker, J. A. (2007). Cultural transmission: Influence of contextual factors in Asian Indian immigrant parents' experiences. *Journal of Counseling Psychology, 54,* 93–100. doi:10.1037/0022-0167.54.1.93

Keijsers, L., Frijns, T., Branje, S. J. T., & Meeus, W. (2009). Developmental links of adolescent disclosure, parental solicitation, and control with delinquency: Moderation by parental support. *Developmental Psychology, 45,* 1314–1327. doi:10.1037/ a0016693

Kerr, M., Stattin, H., & Ozdemir, M. (2012). Perceived parenting style and adolescent adjustment: Revisiting directions of effects and the role of parental knowledge. *Developmental Psychology,* Advance online publication. doi:10.1037/a0027720

Kim, B. S., Atkinson, D. R., & Yang, P. H. (1999). The Asian values scale: Development, factor analysis, validation, and reliability. *Journal of Counseling Psychology, 46,* 342–352. doi:10.1037/0022-0167. 46.3.342

Kim, S. Y., Chen, Q., Wang, Y., Shen, Y., & Orozco-Lapray, D. (2012). Longitudinal linkages among parent child acculturation discrepancy, parenting, parent–child sense of alienation, and adolescent adjustment in Chinese immigrant families. *Developmental Psychology,* Advance online publication. doi:10.1037/a0029169

Maccoby, E. E., & Martin, J. A. (1983). Socialization in the context of the family: Parent-child interaction. In P. H. Mussen (Series Ed.) & E. M. Hetherington (Vol. Ed.), *Handbook of child psychology: Vol. 4. Socialization, personality, and social development* (4th ed., pp. 1–101). New York, NY: Wiley.

Mesman, J., van Ijzendoorn, M. H., & Bakermans-Kranenburg, M. J. (2012). Unequal in opportunity, equal in process: Parental sensitivity promotes positive child development in ethnic minority families. *Child Development Perspectives, 6,* 239–250. doi:10.1111/j.1750-8606.2011 .00223.x

Muthén, B. (2003). Statistical and substantive checking in growth mixture modeling: Comment on Bauer and Curren (2003). *Psychological Methods, 8,* 369–377. doi:10.1037/1082-989X.8.3.369

Muthén, L. K., & Muthén, B. O. (1998 –2011). *Mplus user's guide* (6th ed.). Los Angeles, CA: Muthén & Muthén.

Nelson, L. J., Padilla-Walker, L. M., Christensen, K. J., Evans, C. A., & Carroll, J. S. (2011). Parenting in emerging adulthood: An examination of parenting clusters and correlates. *Journal of Youth and Adolescence, 40,* 730–743. doi:10.1007/ s10964-010-9584-8

Nguyen, P. V. (2008). Perceptions of Vietnamese fathers' acculturation levels, parenting styles, and mental health outcomes in Vietnamese American adolescent immigrants. *Social Work, 53,* 337–346. doi: 10.1093/sw/53.4.337

Nylund, K., Asparouhov, T., & Muthén, B. O. (2007). Deciding on the number of classes in latent class analysis and growth mixture modeling: A Monte Carlo simulation study. *Structural Equation Modeling: A Multidisciplinary Journal, 14,* 535–569. doi:10.1080/ 10705510701575396

Qin, D. B. (2008). Doing well vs. feeling well: Understanding family dynamics and the psychological adjustment of Chinese immigrant adolescents. *Journal of Youth and Adolescence, 37,* 22–35. doi:10.1007/ s10964-007-9220-4

Radloff, L. S. (1977). The CES-D Scale: A self-report depression scale for research in the general population. *Applied Psychological Measurement, 1,* 385–401. doi:10.1177/014662167700100306

Robinson, C. C., Mandleco, B., Olson, S. F., & Hart, C. H. (1995). Authoritative, authoritarian, and permissive parenting practices: Development of a new measure. *Psychological Reports, 77,* 819–830. doi: 10.2466/pr0.1995.77.3.819

Schaefer, E. S. (1965). A configurational analysis of children's reports of parent behavior. *Journal of Consulting Psychology, 29,* 552–557. doi: 10.1037/ h0022702

Steinberg, L., Elmen, J. D., & Mounts, N. S. (1989). Authoritative parenting, psychosocial maturity, and academic success among adolescents. *Child Development, 60,* 1424–1436. doi:10.2307/1130932

Steinberg, L., Lamborn, S. D., Dornbusch, S. M., & Darling, N. (1992). Impact of parenting practices on adolescent achievement: Authoritative parenting, school involvement, and encouragement to succeed. *Child Development, 63,* 1266–1281. doi:10.2307/1131532

Weaver, S. R., & Kim, S. Y. (2008). A person-centered approach to studying the linkages among parent– child differences in cultural orientation, supportive parenting, and adolescent depressive symptoms in Chinese American families. *Journal of Youth and Adolescence, 37,* 36–49. doi:10.1007/s10964-007-9221-3

Wu, C., & Chao, R. K. (2011). Intergenerational cultural dissonance in parent and adolescent relationships among Chinese and European Americans. *Developmental Psychology, 47,* 493–508. doi:10.1037/a0021063

Xu, Y., Farver, J. M., Zhang, Z., Zeng, Z., Yu, L., & Cai, B. (2005). Mainland Chinese parenting styles and parent–child interaction. *International Journal of Behavioral Development, 29,* 524–531. doi:10.1177/01650250500147121

. . .

**Su Yeong Kim** is associate professor in the Department of Human Development and Family Sciences at University of Texas at Austin. Yijie Wang is a postdoctoral fellow in the Department of Psychology at Fordham University. Diana Orozco-Lapray and Yishan Shen are doctoral students of human development and family sciences at University of Texas at Austin. Mohammed Murtuza is a doctoral student of Medicine at Texas A&M University.

# EXPLORING THE ISSUE

## Should We Be "Tiger" Parents?

### Critical Thinking and Reflection

1. Why do tiger parents motivate Asian American children (when they do)?
2. Based on the results of the two articles, which aspects of tiger parenting can be adaptive and which aspects can be maladaptive?
3. What feelings do you think accompany "provides structure" that can explain its negative relation to externalizing behaviors and drug use?

## Is There Common Ground?

When the tiger mother, Amy Chua, appeared on TV morning shows, many accused her of child abuse and the attention eventually focused on the main characters of her parenting memoir. Both of her daughters have been subsequently interviewed and studied by the public. Both have also been outspoken about their support for their mother. Sophia Chua-Rubenfield was quoted in an interview: "You need to have this chip on your shoulder to get ahead, but you also need to have no doubt that you can do it." In a separate article published by the *New York Post* (January 18, 2011), she also submitted her own letter to the public about her mother and admitted:

> Having you as a mother was no tea party. There were some play dates I wish I'd gone to and some piano camps I wish I'd skipped. But now that I'm 18 and about to leave the tiger den, I'm glad you and Daddy raised me the way you did. Here's why.

First, she points to her own role in her mother's parenting: "Early on, I decided to be an easy child to raise . . . . I didn't rebel, but I didn't suffer all the slings and arrows of a Tiger Mom, either." Socialization researchers are intensely focused on the parents' role in parenting for all of the obvious reasons but it is not acknowledged enough that children are part of parenting as well. Children differ in their personalities, unique needs, and desires. Some are easygoing and others are not, just like parents. In Sophia's case, she decided to allow her mother to be her mother.

As can be seen in the Chao and Aque (2009) study, children differ in their reactions to strictness and structure both within and between cultures. Asian children

of immigrants are less likely (not all) to be angered by parental strictness and even parental intrusiveness perhaps because of their Confucian-influenced family values. Their results also indicate that this difference makes all the difference for parenting success. Tiger parents can take advantage of this situation and attempt to maximize their children's achievement by setting high expectations:

> Everybody's talking about the birthday cards we once made for you, which you rejected because they weren't good enough. Funny how some people are convinced that Lulu and I are scarred for life. Maybe if I had poured my heart into it, I would have been upset. But let's face it: The card was feeble, and I was busted. It took me 30 seconds; I didn't even sharpen the pencil. That's why, when you rejected it, I didn't feel you were rejecting me. If I actually tried my best at something, you'd never throw it back in my face.

In the context of Chinese culture, this is an expression of love and commitment to the child. The parent expresses expectations that the child can do better. Yet, we all differ in actual ability, opportunity, income, family size, and family interdependence. The challenge for parents is to seek a balance between striving for achievement and well-being for both the parent and child. Many settle for well-being (see results of study of China and the United States in Wang, Pomerantz, & Chen, 2007).

According to the results of Kim et al. (2013), most Chinese immigrant families are supportive or authoritative with their child. Although tiger parents were relatively frequent (less than supportive type but more than harsh and easy going types), their impact on their child's achievement over time was not positive. Thus, it appears that regardless of culture, parenting is not a one size fits all. What we learn from tiger parents is that children will not "scarred for life" if you give them honest feedback so long as one is not a hostile and rejecting parent.

## References

Ruth K. Chao, "Beyond parental control; authoritarian parenting style: Understanding Chinese parenting through the cultural notion of training," *Child Development* (vol. 45, 1994).

A. Chua, *Battle Hymn of the Tiger Mother* (Penguin Press, 2011).

S. M. Dornbusch, P. L. Ritter, P. H. Leiderman, D. F. Roberts, and M. J. Fraleigh, "The relation of parenting style to adolescent school performance," *Child Development* (vol. 58, 1987).

L. Steinberg, S. M. Dornbusch, and B. B. Brown, "Ethnic differences in adolescent achievement," *American Psychologist* (vol. 47, 1992).

## Additional Resources

X. Chen, Q. Dong, and H. Zhou, "Authoritative and authoritarian parenting practices and social and school performance in Chinese children," *International Journal of Behavioral Development* (vol. 21, no. 4, 1997).

A. S. Fu, and H. R. Markus, "My mother and me: Why tiger mothers motivate Asian Americans but not European Americans," *Personality & Social Psychology Bulletin* (vol. 40, 2014).

Q. Wang, E. M. Pomerantz, and H. Chen, "The role of parents' control in early adolescents' psychological functioning: A longitudinal investigation in the United States and China," *Child Development* (vol.78, no. 5, 2007).

# *Internet References . . .*

**Amy Chua—The Battle Hymn of the Tiger Mother**

http://amychua.com

**On Tiger Moms**

http://thepointmag.com/2012/examined-life/on-tiger-moms

**Traditional Chinese Parenting**

www.parentingscience.com/chinese-parenting.html

**Why Chinese Mothers Are Superior**

www.wsj.com/articles/SB10001424052748704111504576059713528698754

**What Is "Tiger" Parenting? How Does It Affect Children?**

http://www.apadivisions.org/division-7/publications/newsletters/developmental/2013/07/tiger-parenting.aspx

# Unit 4

# Educational Interventions

*T*he last unit of this volume highlights the effectiveness of educational interventions, which tests our psychological theories of student behavior (i.e., cash incentives) and economic theories of institutional behavior (i.e., charter schools). In addition, a wide range of popular (i.e., class size reduction) and controversial educational interventions (i.e., abstinence-only sex education) are included, which should help students think about the complex politics involved in education and how psychological science can or cannot mediate competing interests. Finally, the prevention of bullying on school campuses speaks to the type of community we all wish to create and recreate for the rest of our lives, and this issue in particular reminds us that adults have as much to learn as students at our schools.

**Selected, Edited, and with Issue Framing Material by:**
Esther S. Chang, *Soka University of America*

# ISSUE

# Should Schools Use Cash Incentives to Promote Educational Goals?

**YES: W. David Pierce, et al.**, from "Positive Effects of Rewards and Performance Standards on Intrinsic Motivation," *Psychological Record* (2003)

**NO: Roy F. Baumeister,** from "Choking Under Pressure: Self-Consciousness and Paradoxical Effects of Incentives on Skillful Performance," *Journal of Personality and Social Psychology* (1984)

---

## Learning Outcomes

**After reading this issue, you will be able to:**

- Apply cognitive evaluation theory to understand the positive and negative effects of rewards.
- Apply social cognitive theory to understand the effects of rewards.
- Understand intrinsic motivation and describe how psychological research typically measure it.
- Understand the processes related to "choking" under pressure.
- Explain the positive and negative messages associated with money.

---

### ISSUE SUMMARY

**YES:** W. D. Pierce and colleagues demonstrated that cash rewards can promote intrinsic motivation, particularly if the rewards are used progressively (i.e., after work is completed, more work is given to individuals after cash is given) compared to when rewards were not used and/or given work constantly. Thus, rewarding individuals with cash followed by giving them more work communicates positive messages that significantly enhance intrinsic motivation.

**NO:** Roy Baumeister conducted a classic series of experiments that underscore how situations that demand performance, including the use of cash incentives, cause the individual to "choke"—or fail—due to increased self-consciousness. The role of cash in this study was to communicate "pressure."

*"When I was young I thought that money was the most important thing in life; now that I am old, I know that it is."*

—Oscar Wilde

*"Money often costs too much."*

—Ralph Waldo Emerson

**D**espite the role of money in our daily lives and despite the fact that most students will eventually work for monetary rewards at their future job positions, there may not be a bigger controversy than that of schools paying students to come to school or for doing well on a report card. Nevertheless, it is common for principals to give a class a pizza party for the "best" decorated pumpkin in the school, giving candy for winning a game in class, the chance to be principal for the day if you have perfect attendance, and even *fake* money for good behavior. However, if you substitute any number of real dollar bills as the reward in all of these examples, a great deal of moral soul searching will likely result. Why? It's almost common practice for parents to pay kids for an A. Some parents may even joke that it's the best dollar they ever spent. Why is it different when schools and teachers do the same? This debate is not only about the use of cash in educational contexts but it is also about the use of any reward in education.

Roland Fryer, an economist and professor at Harvard University, is best known for his scholarship on racial inequality, and the achievement gap in education is among his top concerns in research. Accordingly, as he started to experiment with financial incentives (others would call it "bribing") among socially and economically disadvantaged students, he was celebrated and condemned for it. Roland Fryer tested a program that paid students for good grades or test scores in select schools in Chicago, DC, NYC, Dallas, and Houston (Allan & Fryer, 2011). He hypothesized that paying kids cash would yield learning gains at a lower cost than other educational reforms that have been hard to institute and were ambiguous in evaluating for the desired outcome. The results of his studies indicated that when cash incentives were based on student learning processes, such as $2 for reading a book or $2 a math objective, learning gains were found to be significantly positive over time. When incentives were based on outcomes, such as $250 per report card grades or $250 for test results, no gains were registered. However, the most important lesson was that it was possible to get children who were otherwise disenfranchised from learning to learn . . . with cash. One problem remained however about what they learned and whether they learned.

Education is indeed a busy crossroads for many disciplines. When an economist steps in to test an educational innovation, he or she risks inadvertently stepping into a hotly debated topic in another discipline with vastly different goals and interests. This is exactly what happened with Fryer's research, which gained a great deal of media attention when he began arriving at public schools with his offers of cash. Although from an economic standpoint it is momentous that a few cash incentive programs can produce desirable outcomes apparently at a cheaper cost than other hotly debated programs (e.g., charter schools, teacher merit pay), the question from a psychological perspective is whether students internalized the learning goals of the program or intervention. It is an educational institution after all and not a business seeking to watch its bottom line. In short, the economic interest is in the effective distribution of scarce resources in education, which is an important concern, but the psychological interest is in the effective learning and motivation of students.

In thinking about the potential effects of rewards on human behavior, psychological research has been more focused on the general question of the use of rewards than the use of cash as a particular kind of reward. Despite the widespread use of rewards, the empirically demonstrated usefulness of rewards within school and home contexts has been hotly debated for decades among social and motivational psychologists. According to social cognitive theory (Bandura, 1986), rewards for improved performance can help humans become more interested and therefore more motivated in a task. Many of the studies in this field of research are of a particular design. In order to determine whether a reward has any effect on participants' intrinsic motivation, a social psychologist would first ask participants to engage in a task (e.g., do a puzzle) and then give them a reward or not give them a reward depending upon which condition the participant was randomly assigned. Experimenters would then leave the participant alone and observe to see if the participant engages in the task of interest spontaneously in what is often referred to as a free-choice period. Since the participants do not think that they are being watched, the researchers can conclude that the participants were intrinsically motivated if they were more likely to engage in the task. The reason why participants were intrinsically motivated would depend upon the condition or group the participant was assigned: i.e., the reward or no reward condition. In reviewing several of these types of studies to assess their average finding, researchers early on argued and provided evidence that rewards do not harm one's intrinsic motivation (Cameron & Pierce, 1996). This implied that educators should feel free to use rewards in the classroom if they need to, including cash since cash was not singled out as a taboo reward.

The article by Pierce, Cameron, Banko, and So (2003), which is selected to argue the "Yes" side of the debate, represents a classic study design and results display that was reported more recently. The strength in reviewing the Pierce et al. (2003) study is that they supplemented their study by adding self-reported measures of competence (e.g., self-efficacy), autonomy, ratings of task interest and enjoyment, as well as ratings of task difficulty and anxiety. An examination of these ratings is important considering the competing perspective.

A competing theory was articulated by other researchers, who proposed that rewards can be more harmful than helpful—and they can also be both—depending upon how rewards enhance or undermine one's basic need to feel competent and self-determining (Deci & Ryan, 1980).

This theory, cognitive evaluation theory, assumed that humans are more complex in nature than the humans in social cognitive theory. It was argued that human motivation is driven by complex cognitive processes whereby information is not processed at face value. Instead, we interpret our environment and all its contingencies actively in order to pursue our own goals. Thus, to the extent that a reward conveyed *information* about one's ability and work orientation to students, then the reward would foster intrinsic motivation. It was argued that rewards typically convey feelings of being *controlled*, and because this counters the need to be self-determining, rewards generally do not foster intrinsic motivation. They have found that a re-analysis of the same data indicated that tangible rewards (such as pizza, lollipops, and cash) were all harmful to one's intrinsic motivation (Deci, Koestner, & Ryan, 1999, 2001). It should be noted that it would follow logically that if you have a problem with giving cash to children for reading a book, you shouldn't give stars, pizza, or lollipops either.

The Baumeister experiment (1984) is a series of six studies, of which Study 5 is the most relevant to the "No" side of the debate. Studies 1 through 4 provide the background for Study 5, and Study 6 was conducted to convince the critical reader of the results reported in Study 5. Study 5 was designed with two basic conditions: a cash and a no-cash group, but it should be noted that their outcome variable was performance, not intrinsic motivation. The advantage of discussing this classic series of studies is to involve concepts, such as "choking under pressure," which is particularly important in a high-stakes testing environment. It is also useful for students in educational psychology to think about how arguments in social psychology are effectively made with the series of studies.

# YES

W. David Pierce et al.

## Positive Effects of Rewards and Performance Standards on Intrinsic Motivation

For over thirty years, researchers in social psychology have argued that rewarding people for doing activities produces detrimental effects. The claim is that when individuals are rewarded for performing a task, they will come to like the task less and spend less time on it once the rewards are no longer forthcoming. Rewards are said to destroy people's intrinsic motivation. A recent meta-analytic review of experiments on the topic, however, shows that under some conditions, rewards actually enhance people's motivation and performance (Cameron, Banko, & Pierce, 2001). Specifically, when people are offered a tangible reward (e.g., money) to meet a designated performance level, studies show increases in measures of intrinsic motivation. The present study is designed to determine how rewards affect motivation and performance when the rewards are tied to meeting increasingly demanding performance standards.

Since the 1970s, more than 140 experiments have examined the effects of reward on intrinsic motivation. A number of meta-analyses have been conducted on the experimental studies. Some researchers argue that negative effects of rewards are pervasive (Deci, Koestner, & Ryan, 1999); others contend that negative effects are limited (Cameron & Pierce, 1994, 2002; Eisenberger & Cameron, 1996). The major area of disagreement in the various meta-analyses concerns what has been termed "performance-contingent" rewards. According to Deci et al. (1999), performance-contingent rewards are those "given specifically for performing the activity well, matching some standard of excellence, or surpassing some specified criterion" (p. 628). In their analysis of this reward contingency, Deci et al. found that performance-contingent rewards, on average, led to decreased intrinsic motivation.

In a recent meta-analysis on the topic, Cameron et al. (2001) suggested that the category "performance-contingent" was too broad and that distinct reward procedures that produce positive effects were being combined with those that produce negative effects. Cameron and her associates demonstrated that when studies are organized according to the actual procedures used in experiments, rather than by any theoretical orientation, negative, positive, and no effects of performance-contingent reward are detected (see also Eisenberger, Pierce, & Cameron, 1999). Negative effects of performance-contingent reward occurred when the rewards signified failure or were loosely tied to level of performance. In contrast, intrinsic motivation was maintained or enhanced when the rewards were offered for meeting a specific criterion or for surpassing the performance level of others.

In the few studies that have shown positive effects of tangible rewards on intrinsic motivation (e.g., Harackiewicz, Manderlink, & Sansone, 1984), experimental participants were offered a reward to meet or exceed a certain score on a task (absolute standard) or to do better than a specified norm (normative standard). For example, in a study by Eisenberger, Rhoades, and Cameron (1999), undergraduate students worked on a "find-the-difference" task. The task involved finding six differences in two drawings that were otherwise identical. Participants were asked to find one difference on a first set of drawings, two on the second, three on the third, and four on the fourth. Half the participants were required to exceed a performance level greater than 80% of their classmates and half were required to meet an absolute standard of performance. The participants were told they had met the performance standard when they had found four differences on the last set of drawings. Half the participants in each group were offered and delivered a reward (pay); the other half was assigned to a no-reward condition. The results indicated that participants in reward conditions had higher levels of intrinsic motivation than those in nonreward groups, suggesting that rewards based on exceeding a normative standard or an absolute standard have positive effects. Although participants in the study of Eisenberger et al. (1999) were required to meet a progressively demanding standard of performance over the trials, reward was not tied to the increasing demands.

To date, no studies have examined the effects of rewards on measures of intrinsic motivation when the rewards are offered for achieving increasingly higher standards of performance. The present study focused on the effects of rewards when rewards were tied to meeting an unchanging absolute standard (constant standard) or to a progressively demanding performance criterion (progressive standard).

Several theoretical views are important for understanding how rewards could affect intrinsic motivation when reward is tied to meeting a constant or progressive standard. One account, social cognitive theory (Bandura, 1986, 1997), asserts that rewards given for achievement of challenging performance standards can result in high task interest (see Harackiewicz & Sansone, 2000, for a similar theoretical analysis). According to social cognitive theory, feedback from rewards based on progressive accomplishments increases self-efficacy (i.e., the belief that one can cope and succeed at a given level of an activity, task, or problem). Enhanced self-efficacy, in turn, contributes to increased task interest. Social cognitive theory proposes that rewards given for progress and graded achievements are likely to act as positive feedback for judgments of self-efficacy and, in doing so, increase interest. Perceived self-efficacy mediates the effects of rewards on interest and motivation from a social cognitive perspective. Considering rewards given for attainment of a constant versus a progressive performance standard, social cognitive theory would predict that perceived self-efficacy will be greatest when rewards are tied to meeting progressively challenging accomplishments. Furthermore, the increase in perceived self-efficacy should result in greater intrinsic motivation.

Cognitive evaluation theory (CET), in contrast, offers an alternative theoretical account of the effects of rewards on intrinsic motivation (Deci et al., 1999). A requirement of the theory is that the activity or task be of moderate to high initial interest. Rewards can only undermine intrinsic motivation when people are initially interested in the task. CET has typically focused on negative effects of rewards; however, there are circumstances in which CET points to possible positive effects. Specifically, Deci et al. (1999) discuss the controlling versus informational aspects of rewards. Rewards that are closely tied to performance standards are said to be perceived as controlling and tend to undermine perceptions of self-determination, leading to a reduction in intrinsic motivation. However, rewards linked to achievement can also provide information about competence that affects the cognitive evaluation process (Deci et al., 1999, pp. 628–629). When people succeed at attaining a performance standard, the rewards convey competence information that is positively evaluated; this evaluation may offset some of the controlling aspects of rewards and enhance intrinsic motivation. The competing tendencies of the controlling and competence-affirmation aspects of rewards must be considered in predicting the results of the present study.

Based on a consideration of CET, rewards given for achieving a constant standard (constant reward) could enhance intrinsic motivation because of their informational value. According to CET, typically, these rewards would reduce intrinsic motivation because of their controlling nature. However, the positive informational value could offset this control. Relative to a no-reward group, CET would predict that rewarding achievement of a constant standard could mitigate the negative effects of rewards. Using a similar analysis, rewards given for attainment of a progressively increasing performance standard (progressive reward) would further enhance competence affirmation. This increased perceived competence would lead to higher levels of intrinsic motivation relative to no-reward conditions. The progressive reward condition would also be expected to show higher intrinsic motivation than the constant reward group.

Attribution theory and the overjustification hypothesis (Lepper, Greene, & Nisbett, 1973) provide still another explanation. As with CET, the focus here has been on the negative effects of rewards; rewards tied to performance are said to decrease intrinsic motivation by altering people's attribution of causation for their behavior. When rewards are given for performance, people are said to discount the internal causes of their actions (intrinsic interest) and to focus on the external incentives (rewards). This shift in attribution from internal to external causes results in a loss of intrinsic motivation. Lepper, Keavney, and Drake (1996) have also extended the attributional framework to account for positive effects of rewards. The important condition for enhanced motivation is that rewards are given for successful performance. When individuals are rewarded for success, perceptions of competence increase. We suggest that the increase in perceived competence directs attributions of causation toward self. This leads individuals to attribute their behavior to internal causes rather than external ones and intrinsic motivation for an activity is enhanced. This extended attributional account would predict that rewards based on achievement will increase perceptions of competence, lead people to internal attributions, and increase intrinsic motivation for an activity. Based on the attributional framework, rewards given for attainment of constant and progressive performance standards should both lead to enhanced intrinsic motivation relative to no-reward groups.

When rewards are given for achievement of performance standards, Eisenberger (1992) suggests that people learn a general level of industriousness. Eisenberger's (1992) theory of learned industriousness is built upon the concept of effort. When individuals are rewarded for expending a large amount of effort on one activity, the sensation of high effort acquires secondary reward properties, thereby increasing people's readiness to expend high effort on a subsequent task. In contrast, rewards given for low effort on a task condition sensations of low effort with secondary reward value and people expend little effort on later tasks.

In an extension of Eisenberger's (1992) theory of learned industriousness, rewards linked to meeting progressively demanding performance standards lead people to choose challenging tasks and activities. When rewards are tied to achieving a graded level of performance, people's sensations of rising effort are paired with mounting levels of reward. Based on this conditioning, intensifying sensations of effort could take on secondary reward value. People with this kind of reward history would evoke these sensations of effort when they choose challenging tasks over less demanding ones. In contrast, when rewards are tied to an unchanging, moderate level of performance, people would not experience the satisfying effects of increasing effort. In this case, people would prefer less demanding activities and spend less time on them.

The present study investigated the effects of rewarding the attainment of constant versus progressively demanding performance standards on measures of intrinsic motivation. . . . Specifically, we expected that the progressive reward condition would show higher intrinsic motivation than the other conditions. Social cognitive theory predicts that progressive reward enhances intrinsic motivation through increases in perceived self-efficacy. CET posits perceived competence as a mediator of higher intrinsic motivation in the progressive reward condition. Attribution theory states that rewards based upon accomplishment affect perceived competence and lead people to attribute their behavior to internal causes. This shift in attribution would enhance intrinsic motivation. Finally, the theory of learned industriousness points to differences in effort and perceived task difficulty as the basis for changes in performance. These different theoretical accounts were assessed in this study.

## Method

### Participants

Participants ($N = 75$) were recruited from introductory sociology classes at a Canadian university. . . .

## Procedure

The experiment was a $2 \times 2$ factorial design with two levels of reward (reward or no reward) and two levels of performance standard (constant or progressive). Participants were randomly assigned to one of the four experimental conditions ($N = 15$ per condition) and run individually.

When participants arrived at the laboratory, they were taken to an experimental room and seated at a table. All participants were informed that the session was being videotaped. Participants were told that the study concerned learning and puzzle solving. Participants were shown a sample of the task, a challenging commercial game called Set™ (Set Enterprises Incorporated, Fountain Hills, AZ) and asked if they had ever played it. Participants who answered "no" were given a page of instructions for the game. The basic instructions were as follows (see www.setgame.com):

> The object of the task is to identify a "set" of three cards from the puzzle that is made up of 12 numbered cards. There are six possible sets in this puzzle. Each card has four features that can vary as follows: (1) symbols (ovals, squiggles, or diamonds), (2) color of symbols (red, green, or purple), (3) number of symbols (one, two, or three), and (4) shading of symbols (solid, striped, or open). To complete a set, each feature must be the *same* or *different* on all three cards. All features must separately satisfy this rule. You are to write down the card numbers that make up a set.

Included with the instructions was an example of a set and a description of how each feature on the three cards satisfied the "same or different" rule. In the example, all three cards in the set contained only one diamond indicating that the shape feature (diamond) and the number of symbols feature (one) were the same across the cards. The symbols on each of the cards were different colors (on one card the symbol was red, on another card the symbol was green, and on the third card the symbol was purple (indicating that the color feature was different across the cards). Finally, the shading of the symbol was different across the cards (one was solid, one other was open, and the third was striped).

After going through the instructions, participants completed a series of scales that assessed initial task interest and self-efficacy. Participants were then presented with a different puzzle in random order on each of three trials (training phase). During the three trials, participants were treated differently by experimental condition. Participants assigned to the constant performance standard were asked to find three sets on each of the trials. Those assigned to the progressive performance standard were asked to find one, three, and five sets respectively over the three trials. Thus, in total, all participants were required to find nine sets during the training phase. Participants were told that there was no time limit to find correct sets and that they could take as much time as they wanted. Participants recorded their answers until they met the predetermined criterion for their condition.

Once a puzzle was presented, the researcher entered an adjoining room and returned when participants called out that they had found the required number of sets for that trial. The experimenter verified the solutions, thereby providing corrective feedback. Participants who found the required number of sets moved to the next trial; those who did not meet the criterion were asked to continue to find sets. Participants in the reward conditions were offered and given $1 for each correct set; the money was given to them after each trial (total of $9). Those in the no-reward conditions did not expect or receive any money during the training phase but they were paid ($9) once the experiment was over.

Following the training phase, participants completed a questionnaire that assessed task interest, task difficulty, competence, and self-efficacy. The questionnaire also asked participants to rate their feelings about autonomy and anxiety, their reasons for doing the task, and their attributions of performance. Participants in reward conditions completed an additional set of items that asked them to rate their feelings about receiving money.

At this point, participants were given a timed test using two new puzzles (test phase). For each puzzle, participants had 5 minutes to find as many sets as possible. A free-choice period followed the test (free-choice phase). Across all conditions, participants were told that another person had arrived and it would take a few minutes to get the new participant going on the puzzles in another room. The researcher told them that they could read magazines while they were waiting, do more set puzzles, or just wait. When the experimenter returned, participants filled out a final questionnaire of task interest. Finally, all participants were debriefed.

The dependent measure for initial task interest (reliability alpha = .85) was composed of four bipolar items (interesting/boring, exciting/dull, enjoyable/unpleasant, and entertaining/tedious), each measured on a 5-point scale and later coded as 2, 1, 0, −1, −2 (partial-interval, Osgood, Suci, & Tannenbaum, 1957, p. 74). For each item, the first descriptor in the pair was coded with positive numbers and the mean of the four items made up the task interest scale.

Five-point bipolar scales were also used to measure initial task difficulty (challenging/not challenging, complex/simple, and difficult/easy; alpha = .84) and competence (confident/unsure, competent/incompetent, and capable/unable; alpha = .89). These same scales were used to assess interest, task difficulty, and competence following the training phase.

Measures of self-efficacy also were obtained following the instructions and after the training phase. Participants were asked to indicate how confident they were about finding sets in a 5-min period. On six separate scales with 10-point increments ranging from 0 to 100, participants indicated their certainty (in percentage) in finding 1 out of 6 sets, 2 out of 6 sets, 3, 4, etc. For example, if participants felt 100% confident that they could find 1 out of 6 sets, they circled 100 on that scale; if they felt 80% confident of finding 2 out of 6, they circled 80 on that scale, and so on. Overall self-efficacy was measured as the mean percentage over the six scales (a similar type of self-efficacy measure was used in a different context and reported in Symbaluk, Heth, Cameron, & Pierce, 1997).

We also took other measures after the training phase. Measures of autonomy (at ease/intimidated, easygoing/overwhelmed, self-controlled/pressured, and free/constrained; alpha = .86) and anxiety (calm/anxious, and relaxed/nervous; alpha = .78) were assessed on 5-point bipolar scales. Using 7-point Likert scales, task motivation and attributed causes of performance also were measured. Participants rated how much they were motivated by enjoyment of the game, pleasing the researcher, concern about evaluation, and performing well. In terms of attributed causes of performance, participants rated how much of their performance was due to effort, time pressure, skill, situational pressure, interest, feedback from the researcher, and luck or chance. In addition, participants in the reward conditions rated how they felt about receiving the money. Responses to 7-point scales measured how much participants felt (a) controlled by the money, (b) enjoyment from receiving it, (c) pressured from receiving it, (d) that the money provided performance feedback, (e) that the money distracted attention from the task, (f) that the money motivated them to perform well, and (g) that the money decreased their interest in the task.

Performance measures for the training and test phases were also obtained. There were two measures of performance for the training phase: the time (minutes) to identify nine sets over the three trials (time to criterion) and the number of incorrect sets. Performance measures for the test phase were the number of correct and incorrect sets found on the two timed puzzle tests.

For the free-choice phase, one measure of intrinsic motivation was the time (minutes) participants spent on puzzles, beginning when the experimenter left the room and ending after 10 minutes. The time measure was calculated from the videotapes; an assistant blind to the experimental conditions observed the tapes and recorded time on task during the free-choice period. A second measure of intrinsic motivation was participants' self-reported game enjoyment (7-point scale) measured at the end of the free-choice period.

## Results

The results of the experiment are presented to highlight the major findings. At first, we establish that participants initially rated the puzzle-solving task as interesting, meeting the test requirements of cognitive evaluation theory. Next, we show the positive effects of rewards tied to progressive performance standards on free-choice measures of intrinsic motivation. Finally, we outline additional results for each phase of the experiment.

### Initial Task Interest

A multivariate analysis of variance on initial task interest measures (interesting/boring, enjoyable/unpleasant, exciting/dull, entertaining/tedious) did not indicate any significant main effects of performance standard, $F(4, 53) = .13$, $p > .05$; reward, $F(4, 53) = 1.36$, p = .26; or an interaction effect, $F(4, 53) = .86$, $p > .05$. Inspection of the means for each measure showed that the ratings were above the midpoint of zero for interesting ($M = .73$, $SD = .86$), enjoyable ($M = .50$, $SD = .89$), exciting ($M = .28$, $SD = .99$), and entertaining ($M = .30$, $SD = .93$). These results indicate that the task was of moderate to high initial interest to the participants.

### Time and Interest for the Free-Choice Phase

Figure 1 depicts the interaction between reward and performance standard on the free-time (minutes) measure of intrinsic motivation. Inspection of the figure shows that, as expected, free time spent on set puzzles increased under the progressive reward condition. A planned contrast between constant ($M = 4.69$) and progressive ($M = 3.38$) no-reward conditions was not significant, $t(56) = .90$, $p > .05$. Based on this finding, a complex contrast was performed comparing the mean of the progressive reward condition ($M = 7.79$) with the mean of all other conditions combined ($M = 4.43$); results from this contrast indicated a significant effect, $t(56) = 2.84$, $p = .006$.

*Figure 1*

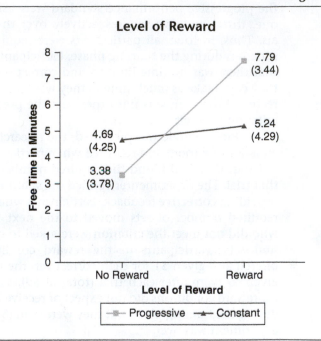

The effects of performance standard and reward on free-time (minutes) intrinsic motivation. Means and standard deviations (brackets) are shown for each codition.

Once the planned contrasts were completed, we examined the analysis of variance for additional effects. inspection of the results revealed a significant main effect of reward, $F(1, 56) = 5.90$, $p = .018$. Participants in the reward conditions spent more time ($M = 6.51$, $SD = 4.04$) on puzzles in the free-choice phase than those in the no-reward group ($M = 4.03$, $SD = 4.01$).

We conducted planned contrasts on the free-choice measure of interest (enjoyment of the game), but none of the contrasts was statistically significant. Inspection of the analysis of variance indicated no significant effects of reward, $F(1, 56) = .27$, $p = .608$, performance standard, $F(1, 56) = .10$, $p = .758$, and no significant interaction of the factors, $F(1, 56) = .27$, $p = .608$. For the entire sample, participants rated the game as enjoyable ($M = 5.08$, $SD = 1.23$).

. . .

### Measures Following the Training Phase

Following the training phase, measures of task interest, self-efficacy, task difficulty, perceived competence, control, and anxiety were obtained. Table 1 presents the means and standard deviations for each scale by experimental

*Table 1*

## Means and Standard Deviations for Scale Measures Taken After Training Phase

| Condition | Task Interest M | Task Interest SD | Self-Efficacy M | Self-Efficacy SD | Task Difficulty M | Task Difficulty SD | Competence M | Competence SD | Autonomy M | Autonomy SD | Anxiety M | Anxiety SD |
|---|---|---|---|---|---|---|---|---|---|---|---|---|
| Reward | | | | | | | | | | | | |
| Constant | .65 | .77 | 66.1 | 22.3 | .56 | .85 | .80 | .84 | .04 | .81 | .17 | .72 |
| Progressive | .53 | .49 | 68.4 | 20.5 | .89 | .67 | .35 | 1.06 | .16 | 1.03 | .04 | .99 |
| No Reward | | | | | | | | | | | | |
| Constant | .75 | .66 | 75.2 | 10.9 | .29 | .67 | 1.02 | .51 | .82 | .74 | .70 | .72 |
| Progressive | .95 | .47 | 69.4 | 13.3 | .75 | .62 | .82 | .73 | .40 | .94 | .37 | 1.18 |

*Note.* Means for task interest, task difficulty, competence, autonomy and anxiety can range from −2 to 2. For the anxiety measure, positive values indicate that participants reported feeling calm and relaxed. Self-efficacy means are based on percentages.

condition. Across conditions, Table 1 shows that participants' ratings of task interest, task difficulty, competence, and autonomy were always in the positive direction (above zero) indicating that participants generally found the task interesting and difficult and they perceived themselves as competent and autonomous. On the anxiety scale, the positive values indicate that participants reported themselves as calm and relaxed. Additionally, participants showed moderate to high self-efficacy.

To assess differences among conditions, for each measure, a 2 × 2 analysis of variance was conducted with two levels of reward (reward, no reward) and two levels of performance standard (constant, progressive). There were no significant main or interaction effects for task interest, self-efficacy, perceived competence, and anxiety. For task difficulty, there was a significant main effect of performance standard, $F(1, 56) = 4.73$, $p = .03$. Participants in the progressive conditions rated the task as more difficult ($M = .82$, $SEM = .13$) than those in the constant conditions ($M = .42$, $SEM = .13$). There was also a significant main effect of reward on perceived autonomy, $F(1, 56) = 4.92$, $p = .03$; participants in the no-reward conditions indicated more autonomy ($M = .61$, $SEM = .16$) than those in the reward conditions ($M = .10$, $SEM = .16$). In order to evaluate the results further, a series of multivariate analyses were conducted on the measures used following the training phase.

. . .

### *Ratings of Monetary Reward*

Participants in the reward conditions were asked to rate the monetary reward in terms of control, enjoyment, pressure, feedback, distraction, motivation, and interest (see Method section). A multivariate analysis of variance on these ratings (two missing cases) indicated a marginal effect of performance standard on ratings of the money, $F(7, 20) = 2.30$, $p = .068$. Univariate tests revealed a significant effect of performance standard only on ratings of feedback, $F(1, 26) = 4.71$, $p = .039$. Participants in the progressive standard condition indicated that the money provided more feedback ($M = 3.23$, $SD = 1.92$) than those in the constant standard group ($M = 1.80$, $SD = 1.57$). Regardless of performance standard, participants in reward conditions rated the money as low in control ($M = 2.29$, $SD = 1.58$), enjoyable ($M = 4.71$, $SD = 1.84$), low in pressure ($M = 2.79$, $SD = 2.01$), low distracting ($M = 2.04$, $SD = 1.43$), low motivating ($M = 3.29$, $SD = 2.17$), and low in terms of decreasing their interest ($M = 2.07$, $SD = 1.41$).

## Performance During the Test Phase

Analyses of variance were conducted on the number of correct and incorrect puzzle solutions during the test phase of the experiment. For both measures, there were no main or interaction effects of reward and performance standard. For the entire sample, participants averaged almost nine correct solutions ($M = 8.5$, $SD = 1.6$) and about one incorrect ($M = .97$, $SD = 1.5$).

## Discussion

The major finding from this experiment is that people who are rewarded for meeting progressively demanding performance standards on an activity spend more time on the activity in a free-choice situation than those who are rewarded for attaining a constant level of performance or than those who are not rewarded for meeting performance standards. In other words, rewarding individuals for meeting a graded level of performance increases their intrinsic motivation.

Another basis for this effect could involve the variable (changing) nature of the progressive reward procedure. That is, aspects of the reward schedule itself may account for the greater free time on task shown by participants in the progressive reward conditions. Our study did not specifically investigate properties of reward schedules; instead it was designed to test theoretical accounts of rewards and intrinsic motivation. However, one way to address the effects of reward schedules would be to design an experiment where the rewards are progressive, regressive ($5, $3, to $1) and constant. If the progressive and regressive reward conditions enhance intrinsic motivation, this would be evidence that a variable reward schedule is responsible for the effects we observed. Another possibility is that the most recent payoff influences free time on task. That is, people would be more likely to choose puzzle solving if they had just received a $5 payoff (progressive reward) than if they had received a constant $3 payoff. If this were so, a regressive reward procedure would lead to the least amount of free time on task when compared with progressive and constant reward procedures.

. . .

A theoretical analysis may be useful for understanding the finding that free-choice intrinsic motivation was highest for participants who were rewarded for meeting a progressively demanding performance standard. Social cognitive theory and CET predict a rise in intrinsic motivation for the progressive reward condition. The basis of this prediction for social cognitive theory is that rewards tied to progressively demanding standards of performance convey information about self-efficacy. From a CET perspective, rewards based on meeting a progressively challenging standard enhance intrinsic motivation if people infer greater competence. One problem for these theories is that our results do not show differences in perceived self-efficacy or competence by experimental conditions. Thus, there is no direct evidence that the higher level of intrinsic motivation exhibited by the progressive reward group is mediated by feelings of greater self-efficacy or perceived competence. As previously mentioned, there were no performance differences between groups; the lack of performance variation may have prevented us from detecting differences in feelings of self-efficacy and competence.

Several aspects of our experiment explicitly address cognitive evaluation theory (CET). One requirement of CET is that participants have high initial interest in the task or activity. According to the theory, the negative effects of rewards on intrinsic motivation can occur only if people are initially interested in the task or activity. In the present experiment, we measured participants' initial interest in the puzzle-solving task. Generally, participants across all conditions rated the task as interesting; thus, cognitive evaluation theory is relevant to our findings. A major question is why do rewards tied to meeting progressively demanding standards of performance enhance (rather than undermine) intrinsic motivation?

From the perspective of CET, rewards are generally experienced as controlling and this contributes to their general negative effect on intrinsic motivation. Our experimental procedures, however, may actually have activated perceptions of autonomy and enhanced the informational value of rewards. These two effects would lead to a rise in intrinsic motivation in the progressive reward condition.

Perceptions of autonomy were measured with four indicators (at ease/intimidated, easy going/overwhelmed, self-controlled/pressured, free/constrained). Results based on the autonomy scale showed a significant main effect of reward. That is, following the training phase, participants who received a reward for meeting a standard (either constant or progressive) reported less autonomy than nonrewarded participants. Further analysis of the separate items from the autonomy scale showed an effect of reward only on the at ease/intimidated item. Participants in no-reward conditions rated themselves as more at ease than those who received rewards. Although this finding deals with an aspect of control, participants were not intimidated by the offer of reward. Participants who received rewards also reported that they did not feel pressured, controlled, or distracted by the money. In fact, participants in reward conditions indicated that they enjoyed receiving the reward. Overall, the pattern of findings shows that the rewards were not perceived as controlling.

From a CET perspective, the rewards did not undermine intrinsic motivation because they were not perceived as controlling. This finding, of itself, does not account for the higher intrinsic motivation evidenced by participants in the progressive reward condition. A rise in intrinsic motivation could occur. If the rewards provided information about accomplishment. That is, the rewards given for meeting a progressively challenging standard of performance could have indicated that participants were improving at the task. This feedback would be valued even though participants did not infer greater competence. In fact, our results indicate that participants in the progressive reward condition reported that rewards provided more feedback than did participants in the constant reward condition. The low control and the high informational value of the rewards in the progressive reward condition provide an explanation for the increase of intrinsic motivation from a CET perspective.

Our results are also relevant to the overjustification account of reward and intrinsic motivation. From this perspective, rewards are said to shift the attribution of causation for an activity from internal to external sources. Analyses of internal and external attributions of performance in the present study, as well as reasons for doing the task, did not reveal any differences by experimental conditions. One possibility for the lack of evidence for a shift in attribution could be the informational value of the rewards that we have described. When extrinsic rewards convey information about personal accomplishments, people may not make an internal to external shift in attribution because their attention is focused on themselves rather than the external context.

Our findings are most consistent with an extension of learned industriousness theory (Eisenberger, 1992). In this account, when rewards are linked to increasingly challenging levels of performance, people's sensations of rising effort are associated with increasing amounts of reward. This pairing of reward and effort conditions sensations of effort with secondary reward value. Once increasing sensations of effort acquire reward value, people evoke these sensations when they choose more challenging tasks over less demanding ones. In terms of our study, participants in the progressive reward condition spent more free time on the puzzle task than those in the other conditions. From a learned industriousness perspective, the rewards were linked to increasing sensations of effort, the sensations of effort acquired secondary reward value, and participants generated these sensations of effort by spending more free time on the task when extrinsic rewards were withdrawn.

Further support for a learned industriousness account of our findings comes from the analysis of participants' perceptions of task difficulty. Analysis of the task difficulty scale showed that participants in the progressive standard conditions rated the task as more difficult than those in the constant standard conditions. Additional analyses of the difficult/easy item indicated that perceptions of task difficulty increased in the progressive standard condition from pretraining to posttraining. In contrast, participants in the constant standard groups reported that the task was less difficult from pretraining to posttraining. One interpretation of this finding is that task difficulty is correlated with sensations of effort. That is, when participants had to solve more and more problems to attain the reward, the task became more difficult and underlying sensations of effort were generated. Assuming that increasing sensations of effort were evoked for all participants in progressive conditions (reward and no reward), these sensations only acquired secondary reward value when tied to monetary incentive. Once the extrinsic reward was withdrawn, participants in the progressive reward condition showed a preference for the challenging puzzle task because of the secondary reward value of effort. Although the evidence is indirect, a learned industriousness account of rewards and intrinsic motivation may help to specify when and under what conditions rewards have positive effects.

Overall, the findings from this experiment indicate that rewards can be used to enhance people's intrinsic motivation. In school, work, and family settings, tying rewards to meeting progressively demanding and attainable standards is one way to increase preference for challenging activities (also, see Schunk, 1983, 1984). Flora and Flora (1999) examined the effects of parental pay for reading, as well as participation in the "Book It" reading program sponsored by Pizza Hut. The program involved over 22 million children in Australia, Canada, and the United States. The children set reading goals and were rewarded for coupons redeemable for pizzas if they met their objectives. The findings indicated that neither offers of money or pizzas negatively affected reading or intrinsic motivation for reading in everyday life. Our findings suggest that reward programs can actually enhance motivation when rewards are linked to meeting progressively demanding and achievable standards.

# References

BANDURA, A. (1986). *Social foundations of thought & action: A social cognitive theory*. Englewood Cliffs, NJ: Prentice Hall.

BANDURA, A. (1997). *Self-efficacy: The exercise of control*. New York: W. H. Freeman and Company.

CAMERON, J., BANKO, K. M., & PIERCE, W. D. (2001). Pervasive negative effects of rewards on intrinsic motivation: The myth continues. *The Behavior Analyst, 24*, 1–44.

CAMERON, J., & PIERCE, W. D. (1994). Reinforcement, reward and intrinsic motivation: A meta-analysis. *Review of Educational Research, 64*, 363–423.

CAMERON, J., & PIERCE, W. D. (2002). *Rewards and intrinsic motivation: Resolving the controversy*. Westport, CT: Bergin & Garvey.

DECI, E. L., KOESTNER, R., & RYAN, R. M. (1999). A meta-analytic review of experiments examining the effects of extrinsic rewards on intrinsic motivation. *Psychological Bulletin, 125*, 627–668.

EISENBERGER, R. (1992). Learned industriousness. *Psychological Review, 99*, 248–267.

EISENBERGER, R., & CAMERON, J. (1996). The detrimental effects of reward: Myth or reality? *American Psychologist*, 51, 1153–1166.

EISENBERGER, R., PIERCE, W. D., & CAMERON, J. (1999). Effects of reward on intrinsic motivation—Negative, neutral, and positive: Comment on Deci, Koestner, and Ryan (1999). *Psychological Bulletin*, 125, 677–691.

EISENBERGER, R., RHOADES, L., & CAMERON, J. (1999). Does pay for performance increase or decrease self-determination and intrinsic motivation? *Journal of Personality and Social Psychology*, 77, 1026–1040.

FLORA, S. R., & FLORA, D. B. (1999). Effects of extrinsic reinforcement for reading during childhood on reported reading habits of college students. *The Psychological Record*, 49, 3–14.

HARACKIEWICZ, J. M., MANDERLINK, G., & SANSONE, C. (1984). Rewarding pinball wizardry: effects of evaluation and cue value on intrinsic interest. *Journal of Personality and Social Psychology*, 47, 287–300.

HARACKIEWICZ, J. M., & SANSONE, C. (2000). Rewarding comptence: The importance of goals in the study of intrinsic motivation. In C. Sansone & J. M. Harackiewicz (Eds.), *Intrinsic and extrinsic motivation: The search for optimal motivation and performance* (pp. 79–103). San Diego, CA: Academic Press.

LEPPER, M. R., GREENE, D., & NISBETT, R. E. (1973). Undermining children's intrinsic interest with extrinsic reward: A test of the "overjustification" hypothesis. *Journal of Personality and Social Psychology*, 28, 129–137.

LEPPER, M. R., KEAVNEY, M., & DRAKE, M. (1996). Intrinsic motivation and extrinsic rewards: A commentary on Cameron and Pierce's meta-analysis. *Review of Educational Research*, 66, 5–32.

OSGOOD, C. E., SUCI, G. I., & TANNENBAUM, P. H. (1957). *The measurement of meaning*. Urbana, IL: University of Illinois Press.

SCHUNK, D. H. (1983). Reward contingencies and the development of children's skills and self-efficacy. *Journal of Educational Psychology*, 75, 511–518.

SCHUNK, D. H. (1984). Enhancing self-efficacy and achievement through rewards and goals: Motivational and informational effects. *Journal of Educational Research*, 78, 29–34.

SYMBALUK, D., HETH, C. D., CAMERON, J., & PIERCE, W. D. (1997). Social modeling, monetary incentives, and pain endurance: The roles of self-efficacy and pain perceptions. *Personality and Social Psychology Bulletin*, 23, 258–269.

**W. DAVID PIERCE** is professor of social psychology in the Department of Sociology at the University of Alberta. Judy Cameron is professor emerita of educational psychology at the University of Alberta. Katherine M. Banko and Sylvia So were graduate students of psychology at the University of Alberta at the time of publication.

**Roy F. Baumeister**

# Choking Under Pressure: Self-Consciousness and Paradoxical Effects of Incentives on Skillful Performance

*Note to readers: Only Experiments 3 and 5 are reported below.*

"Choking under pressure" is a metaphorical expression used to describe the occurrence of inferior performance despite individual striving and situational demands for superior' performance. *Pressure* may be defined as any factor or combination of factors that increases the importance of performing well on a particular occasion. *Choking* refers to performance decrements under pressure circumstances. The terms are most commonly used in connection with competition, but their usage does extend to noncompetitive performances.

Although pressure per se has received little direct research attention, research on related topics suggests a model of how it could lead to choking. Competition, which is one type of pressure situation, is generally regarded as arousing. Wankel (1972) identified rivalry, audience presence, and the presence of coactors as the three motivational components of competition, and each of these has been associated with increased arousal and drive (Martens & Landers, 1972; Paulus & Cornelius, 1974; Paulus, Shannon, Wilson, & Boone, 1972; Steigleder, Weiss, Balling, Wenninger, & Lombardo, 1980; Steigleder, Weiss, Cramer, & Feinberg, 1978; Zajonc, 1965). Wegner and Giuliano (1980) provided evidence that arousal helps focus one's attention on oneself. Indeed, the presence of an audience has been shown to be a cue that focuses attention on oneself (Carver & Scheier, 1978). Finally, Kimble and Perlmuter (1970), Langer (1978), and Langer and Imber (1979) have noted that heightened self-awareness may disrupt the performance of well-learned or "overlearned" skills. More generally, Martens and Landers (1972) suggested that focusing evaluative attention on the *process* of performance may impair the performance more than focusing such attention on the performance *outcome*. Their results were not confined to an overlearned task. Thus, competition is arousing; arousal heightens self-consciousness; and self-consciousness disrupts performance of some tasks.

The present research was based on a model holding that pressure increases self-consciousness, possibly by means of heightened arousal, and that this focus of attention disrupts skillful performances. Under pressure, a person realizes consciously that it is important to execute the behavior correctly. Consciousness attempts to ensure the correctness of this execution by monitoring the process of performance (e.g., the coordination and precision of muscle movements); but consciousness does not contain the knowledge of these skills, so that it ironically reduces the reliability and success of the performance when it attempts to control it. To use the familiar example of typing (Langer & Imber, 1979), the attempt to ensure accuracy by conscious monitoring of one's finger movements (necessitated, perhaps, by the pressure of having run out of correction fluid) is often counterproductive.

It must be emphasized, however, that choking is not restricted to well-learned or "overlearned" skills. Past research has defined the distinction between learning and performing in several different ways. One can call it *performing* when the learning has asymptoted, that is, stabilized. One can call it *performing* when the correct response has become dominant (see especially Zajonc, 1965). Finally, one can call it *performing* when the situation defines it as such (instead of as *learning*). The present research is based on the third understanding of the distinction between learning and performing. In other words, the distinction between learning and performing is under stood here as determined by the structure of the situation and the intentionality of the subject, not by the intrinsic level of the performance. Although this differs from the traditional

Baumeister, Roy F. "Choking Under Pressure: Self-Consciousness and Paradoxical Effects of Incentives on Skillful Performance," *Journal of Personality and Social Psychology*, vol 46, no. 3, March 1984, pp. 610–620. No further reproduction or distribution is permitted without written permission from the American Psychological Association.

(first and second) views, it has some practical justification. A high school athlete or introductory-level student cannot be said to have mastered anything, but such a person will be quite sensitive to the difference between practice and competition (or test), and he or she may certainly choke. My analysis of the concept of pressure emphasizes that it focuses on a particular trial. On that trial, the subject tries to do the best he or she can; learning is incidental. I use *choking* to describe a failure to perform up to whatever level of skill and ability the person has at that time.

An alternative derivation of the present model can be based on Sartre (1974/1934), who argued that human behavior is free and not subject to causal determinism. His reasoning and examples apply only to conscious choices. Consciousness, in that view, frees behavior from certain causal factors; consciousness reduces the automatic or instinctive quality of behavior (cf. also Kimble & Perlmuter, 1970; Langer & Saegert, 1977). Hefferline, Keenan, and Harford (1959) showed that the operation of the laws of operant conditioning on a covert muscle response could be undermined by making the person increasingly conscious of the behavioral process by which reinforcement was obtained even when the individual was consciously trying to help (facilitate) the process. Insight psychotherapy presumably relies on a similar principle: By making unconscious material conscious, the therapist frees the neurotic of its determining effects on his or her behavior. Thus, there are several indications that increased consciousness makes behavior less lawful and less pre dictable. In skillful performance, however, the optimum is for behavior to proceed reliably as a causally ineluctable sequence of events. To the extent that consciousness undermines this causal reliability, consciousness would tend to be detrimental to performance, as in the Hefferline et al. study.

The role of self-consciousness in this model brings up an issue that is central to Experiments 3, 4, and 5, namely, dispositional self-consciousness. If self-consciousness is bad for performance, then in the absence of pressure persons who are habitually low in self-consciousness should outperform those who are high in it. However, if pressure causes self-consciousness, then pressure may affect persons differentially as a function of trait self-consciousness. Persons who are habitually self-conscious should find it easier to cope with situations that engender self-consciousness because they are accustomed to performing while self-conscious. Thus, the increment in self-consciousness caused by going from a non-pressure to a pressure situation may be greater for a person who is dispositionally low (rather than high) in self-consciousness, and it may be reflected in greater choking among persons low in self-consciousness rather than high in it.

The measure of dispositional self-consciousness (Fenigstein, Scheier, & Buss, 1975) contains subscales for private and public self-consciousness. The present investigation was oriented toward using full-scale self-consciousness scores because the theory was formulated in terms of self-consciousness in general and because on an a priori basis it seemed plausible that both subscales could contribute to choking. Specifically, the increased awareness of one's performance process seems to denote a private self-consciousness, but public self-consciousness may increase one's sensitivity to some situational manipulations of pressure (e.g., audience or coactor presence). Results of the present studies therefore emphasize the full-scale self-consciousness scores but will report the effects of the subscales as a way of getting additional insight.

The six experiments here are organized according to the following plan. Experiment 3 sought to verify that performance decrements are caused by increased awareness of the performance process. Experiments 4 and 5 sought to show that pressure causes performance decrements (i.e., choking)—indeed, decrements similar to the ones caused by the attentional manipulations in Experiments 1, 2, and 3. Experiments 4 and 5 are therefore the most important ones, for they are concerned with the situational and dispositional causes of choking. Finally, Experiment 6 sought to verify that choking is an actual decrement in performance (by using a within-subjects demonstration of choking), to show that it occurs among people who are already good at the task, and to demonstrate choking in a field setting.

The same task was used in Experiments 1 through 5. (Experiment 6 used a popular video game instead.) The task was chosen as an analog to the skillful aspects of athletic performance. Other factors that aid athletic performance (strength, reaction time, stamina) are largely irrelevant to this task. It is described prior to Experiment 1.

## Task and General Procedure

The task used in the first five experiments was the commercially available "roll-up" game. A picture and description of the apparatus were given by Martens and Landers (1972). Two rods are attached to a vertical board at one end and the subject holds the other ends in his or her hands. A metal ball rests on the rods. By moving the rods horizontally, the subject attempts to cause the ball to roll along the rods, which is *up* a slight incline. Points are scored by moving the rods apart so that the ball drops into one of the holes in the platform beneath the rods. The object is to roll the ball as far as possible from the starting point (the vertical board to which the rods are attached) toward the subject and to drop it in the hole farthest from the starting point. The task thus requires motor and visual-motor coordination.

Subjects practiced the task for 5 min. The experimenter came over and observed the final minute, recording the subject's total score for that minute. This constituted the subject's "practice trial" score. The manipulations were then introduced, and the subject performed two 1-min trials. Subjects were always informed of what they had scored.

## Experiment 1 (Pilot)

Half of the subjects were told to be aware of their hands while performing the task. The rest heard similar instructions and explanations regarding the ball. The model predicted that increased attention to performance process ("hands" condition) would result in poorer performance than in the "ball" condition. This prediction was supported. Analysis of covariance using baseline (practice trial) scores as the covariate revealed a significant difference, $F(1, 21) = 8.20$, $p < .01$.

Experiment 1 provided results consistent with the hypothesis that skillful performance is disrupted by increased awareness of one's movements and efforts. If pressure produces similar attentional shifts, then these shifts could help account for choking.

The lack of a no-manipulation control group in Experiment 1 made an alternative explanation plausible—specifically, that performance was improved by the instructions to be aware of the ball. Experiment 2 was de signed to rule out this alternative interpretation.

## Experiment 2 (Pilot)

Experiment 2 substituted a control group, in which there was no manipulation of awareness, for the ball condition in Experiment 1. The subjects in the hands condition tended to perform worse than the control subjects, but the result did not reach significance, $F(1, 24)$ 2.00, $p = .17$. Still, the mean of the control subjects was quite close to the mean of the ball condition in Experiment 1. Taken together, Experiments 1 and 2 seem to indicate that increased awareness of one's internal performance processes can hamper skillful performance.

## Experiment 3

Experiment 3[1] replicated Experiment 2 with the addition of a measure of dispositional self-consciousness (Fenigstein et at., 1975). The implication of Experiments 1 and 2 was that directing attention to performance process could

disrupt performance; it seemed plausible that people who are habitually unaware of their internal states and processes (i.e., those low in dispositional self-consciousness) would be especially vulnerable to the deleterious effects of the instructions to attend to these processes.

## Method

### Subjects

Twenty-five undergraduate students from Case Western Reserve University participated in the experiment. The data from 1 subject were discarded because a brief discussion of performance pressure between her and the experimenter took place just before her performance.

### Procedure

The procedure replicated that of Experiment 2, except that subjects filled out a questionnaire measure of self-consciousness (Fenigstein et al., 1975) prior to the practice period.

## Results and Discussion

Analysis on the performance scores (combined for both trials), using practice scores as covariate, revealed a significant main effect for focus of attention, $F(1, 19) = 8.51$, $p < .01$. Other effects were not significant. Simple analysis of variance (ANOVA) on these performance scores similarly showed a significant main effect of attentional focus, $F(1, 20) = 5.01$, $p < .05$; the main effect for level of self-consciousness and the interaction between focus and self-consciousness were both marginally significant, unlike in the analysis of covariance. Table 1 shows the adjusted means from the covariance analysis.

The disruption of performance by the attentional instructions appeared most clearly in the subjects low in self-consciousness, $t(19) = 2.97$, $p < .05$, for the adjusted means. Among subjects high in self-consciousness, the effect of the instructions was weak, $t(19) = 1.32$, ns.

The subscales for public and private self-consciousness were scored and subjects were classified as high or low in each of these by median splits. A $2 \times 2 \times 2$ analysis of

*Table 1*

### Mean Performance Scores: Experiment 3

| Self-consciousness | Focus | |
|---|---|---|
| | Hands | Control |
| High | 49.4 | 59.6 |
| Low | 52.2 | 71.7 |

*Note.* The numbers are adjusted means from analysis of covariance. High scores represent good performance.

covariance (ANCOVA) using both subscales as independent variables revealed three significant effects. The main effect for focus of attention obtained, $F(1, 15) = 10.57$, $p = .005$. A main effect for *private* self-consciousness reflected the consistently superior performance of persons low in that trait over persons high in it, $F(1, 15) = 8.15$, $p = .012$. Finally, an interaction between *public* self-consciousness and focus of attention, $F(1, 15) = 10.75$, $p = .005$, showed the greater vulnerability of persons low in that trait (than of people high in that trait) to performance decrements caused by the attention instructions.

Experiments 4 and 5 were designed to investigate whether situational manipulations of pressure could effect performance decrements similar to those caused by attentional refocusing in the first three experiments.

# Experiment 4

Experiment 4 used Wankel's (1972) three components of competition—rivalry, coaction, and audience—to generate pressure. In this study, the competition and the pressure were implicit; Experiment 5 used an explicit manipulation of pressure.

In competition, one source of pressure is the relative score of the contestants. Pressure was previously defined as the importance of performing well on a particular occasion. Given that the object of competition is to win (i.e., to outperform one's opponent), the score is an important determinant of how well one will have to perform in order to achieve this success. If one is far ahead, one can afford some errors without losing; pressure is minimal. If one has only a slight lead, the pressure is increased, although an occasional or minor error will keep the contest still undecided (unless perhaps it is nearly over). Pressure would seem to be greatest if one is slightly to moderately behind. In that situation, one retains the possibility of success only if one performs very well; any further mistakes or setbacks may end one's chance of winning. If one is far behind, pressure is presumably diminished. Performing well becomes irrelevant when one has already effectively lost the contest. (This reasoning is consistent with the findings of Seta, 1982).

The present experiment selected two of these situations to compare with a control (no competition) condition. Subjects performed the task in alternation with a confederate who did either moderately better or moderately worse than the subject. It was predicted that pressure would be greater and choking would be more common in the former condition than in the latter.

Rather than have the subject and the confederate compete explicitly for some prize or reward, the present study relied on self-presentational concerns to generate implicit pressure. The contribution of self-presentational concerns to pressure derives from the individual's belief that others will evaluate him or her unfavorably if he or she performs poorly (Baumeister, 1982).

# Method

## Subjects

Forty-five male undergraduates at Case Western Reserve University participated in the experiment in connection with general course requirements. Three subjects turned around to watch the confederate perform the task; data from these 3 subjects were not included in the analyses. Data from 2 additional subjects were unusable because their unusual form of experimentation during the practice period rendered the baseline (practice trial) data meaningless. Subjects were randomly assigned among treatments, as always.

## Procedure

The subject signed up for an experiment on "Personality and Game Performance." Upon arrival, he was given two questionnaires to fill out, which contained the Self-Consciousness Scale (Fenigstein et al., 1975) and the Bern Sex Role Inventory (Bern, 1974).[2] Subjects were run individually.

## Control Condition

When control subjects completed their questionnaires, they were moved to the other table and put through the practice period and performance trials just as were the control subjects in Experiment 2.

## Pressure Conditions

Shortly after the subjects in the experimental condition began working on the questionnaire, there was a knock on the door. The experimenter answered it. A female student (the confederate) stood there. She explained that she had been scheduled to do the experiment that morning but had been unable to show up. After a brief discussion, the experimenter somewhat reluctantly "decided" that it would be feasible to run 2 subjects at once.

The experimenter pretended to decide that the best plan was for the 2 subjects to alternate turns at the roll-up task, each returning to the questionnaire while the other was doing the task. The confederate went first. During the subject's practice period, the experimenter asked him and then the confederate if they had .played the game before; the confederate gave the same answer the subject did.

After the subject's practice period, the experimenter gave the instructions for the two performance trials (how the scoring worked, the importance of doing one's best, etc.). Ostensibly to demonstrate scoring, the subject was told what his score "would have been" had the last minute of his practice period been a performance trial. The subject was then returned to his questionnaire (seated with his back to the table with the roll-up) and the confederate performed her first trial.

The experimenter pretended to record her performance. However, when she completed the 1-min trial, the experimenter announced a score for her that was computed based on the subject's practice trial score. Later, the confederate's apparent score on the second trial was computed based on the subject's first trial. In the high-pressure conditions, her scores were 13 and 11 points above what the subject had just scored. In the low-pressure conditions, she apparently scored 7 and 9 points below the subject's previous score.[3] Thus, the subject clearly heard that the confederate had scored definitely better or worse than he had. As the subject prepared to start his second trial, the confederate interrupted to say she had finished the questionnaire and to ask permission to watch the subject perform. The experimenter said "Sure," as if it were unimaginable that her surveillance would affect the subject's performance. She sat on the table next to the subject (on the other side from the experimenter). She made no comment or reaction; when the subject finished, she left. The subject then finished his questionnaire and was debriefed.

## Results

### Manipulation Check

During the debriefing, the experimenter asked subjects whether they had noticed the discrepancy between their own performance level and the confederate's. Nearly all subjects reported that they had. A few said they had paid no attention, but such statements could have been face-saving gestures rather than accurate reports.

### Performance Data

Table 2 shows the mean. (adjusted for covariance) performance scores. Scores are based on the combined scores of the two performance trials. Both measures showed significant interactions between pressure and dispositional self-consciousness. An ANCOVA (using the practice trial scores as covariate) revealed a significant interaction, $F(2, 33) = 3.99$, $p < .05$, as well as a significant main effect for pressure, $F(2, 33) = 4.47$, $p < .02$.

The pattern of means largely supported the predictions. Persons low in self-consciousness performed significantly better than those high in self-consciousness in the control condition, $t(33) = 2.40$, $p < .05$. However,

**Table 2**

**Mean Performance Scores: Experiment 4**

| Self-consciousness | High pressure | Low pressure | control |
|---|---|---|---|
| High | 74.0 | 80.1 | 67.2 |
| | (77.5) | (84.8) | (70.7) |
| Low | 65.1 | 83.3 | 81.2 |
| | (61.3) | (81.7) | (74.7) |

*Note.* Numbers in parentheses are for analysis using private self-consciousness instead of the full scale. The other numbers are adjusted means from analysis of covariance. High scores represent good performance.

persons low in self-consciousness were the ones who choked under pressure. Persons low in self-consciousness performed much worse in the high-pressure situation than in the control situation, $t(33) = 2.56$, $p < .02$, whereas persons high in self-consciousness showed a nonsignificant improvement. Under high pressure, persons low in self-consciousness were marginally worse than those high in it, $t(33) = 1.62$, $p < .12$.

Both high- and low-self-consciousness subjects performed well under low pressure. In fact, highly self-conscious persons performed significantly better under low pressure than they did in the control condition, $t(33) = 2.07$, $p < .05$. This result suggests that a little situational pressure combined with favorable feedback may facilitate performance. Perhaps when one is successful one does not feel the need to pay increased attention to one's performance process, so that the self-defeating attentional shift is avoided. Such an explanation is consistent with the finding that persons with low dispositional self-consciousness choked only when they needed to improve in order to avoid being outperformed by the confederate; when they were already doing better than she, these subjects performed quite well, $t(33) = 3.29$, $p < .005$, for the subjects low in self-consciousness in the two pressure conditions.

The predictions regarding the subscales of the self-consciousness scale were also supported. Private self-consciousness did interact with pressure, $F(2, 33) = 3.68$, $p < .05$, on the ANCOVA on the combined scores, with practice score as covariate. The pattern of means resembled that of the analysis that used full scale self-consciousness scores (see Table 2). The difference between the performance of the two self-consciousness groups in the control condition did not reach significance when private self-consciousness was used to differentiate the groups. However, the difference between the performance of the subjects who were high and low in private self-consciousness in the high-pressure condition was highly significant, $t(33) = 3.18$, $p < .01$; subjects high in self-consciousness performed better. Private self-consciousness does seem to be closely related to choking.

The interaction between public self-consciousness and pressure was not significant, $F(2, 33) = 1.41$, $ns$, as predicted. Public self-consciousness did, however, contribute to predicting the effect of being watched by the confederate while performing the second trial. A repeated-measures ANCOVA revealed a significant interaction between trial, public self-consciousness, and pressure, $F(2, 34) = 9.02$, $p < .001$. In the high-pressure condition, subjects performed about the same on the first trial regardless of their level of public self-consciousness; but when watched by the confederate on the second trial, persons with high public self-consciousness improved, whereas those with low public self-consciousness got worse. This is consistent with. the general interpretation here that situational increases in self-consciousness disrupt performance less among individuals who are habitually self-conscious than among those who are not.

The possibility that the results were mediated by differential effort was explored by considering the number of times the subject let the ball drop as a rough measure of effort. Most subjects typically dropped the ball two or three more times during a performance trial than during the practice, which is consistent with increased effort. However, an ANOVA on the number of times the ball dropped revealed no significant effects, interactions, or differences.

One last finding may deserve mention. As a measure of consistency of performance, the absolute value of the difference between the two performance trial scores was computed for each subject. An ANOVA on these scores revealed a marginally significant main effect for self-consciousness, $F(1, 34) = 2.87$, $p = .10$, and a significant interaction between (fulls cale) self-consciousness and pressure, $F(2, 34) = 8.43$, $p < .001$. The high-self-consciousness group in the low-pressure condition was exceptional. Their performances were significantly more inconsistent than those of low-self-consciousness persons in the same condition, $t(34) = 3.11$, $p < .01$. Although this effect was not predicted, it may warrant further investigation.

## Discussion

The results of Experiment 4 were consistent with the predictions based on the model of choking as mediated by attention to self (i.e., to one's internal processes involved in the performance). In the absence of situational pressure, high dispositional self-consciousness hampered skillful performance. Persons who were habitually unaccustomed to being self-conscious were, however, the ones who choked (i.e., who showed performance decrements in the situation that called strongly for performance increments). Persons with high dispositional self-consciousness seemed better able to avoid the performance-inhibiting effects of situational pressure.

Several qualifications must be made. The pressure in this situation was implicit; that is, it is only by inference that one can assume greater pressure to perform well when in danger of being outperformed than when performing alone or performing at a level comfortably superior to that of the coactor. Experiment 5 was designed to remedy this weakness by using an explicit manipulation of situational pressure.

Moreover, the pressure conditions differed from the control condition in the presence of the coactor. The additional observer may have contributed to social facilitation effects (Zajonc, 1965). Experiment 5 was also designed to avoid confounding pressure with the presence of additional persons in the room.

The negligible correlation $(r = -.08)$ between practice trial score and change score (performance minus practice) would seem to disconfirm a suggestion that the results of this experiment may have been influenced by ceiling or floor ability effects. In particular, the Hull-Spence notion that increased drive would facilitate performance for those with high initial skills but inhibit performance for those with poor initial skills was not in evidence.

## Experiment 5

The goal of Experiment 5 was to demonstrate choking with an explicit and unconfounded manipulation of pressure, in the sense of the importance of performing well on a given occasion. Subjects were offered an incentive in the form of cash if they would perform at a certain level. The level was computed based on the subject's baseline (practice trial) performance according to reasoning similar to that in the high-pressure condition of Experiment 4. That is, it was set within the subject's presumed reach, but he or she would have to perform quite well (for his or her ability level) in order to achieve it. The improvement necessary was the highest mean change score among the six cell means of Experiment 4.[4]

It was predicted that subjects low in self-consciousness would perform worse in the incentive condition than in the control condition, in which no money was used. Based on the results of Experiment 3, a statistically weak trend toward choking was predicted for subjects high in dispositional self-consciousness.

# Method

## Subjects

Thirty-seven male and female undergraduates at Case Western Reserve University took part in this experiment under the same terms as in Experiment 4. (No subject participated in both experiments.)

## Procedure

Each subject was greeted by the experimenter and given the same initial explanation as in Experiment 4. The subject was given only the Self-Consciousness Scale to fill out. When he or she completed it, the experimenter asked him or her to move to the performance table. The practice trial was conducted the same as in the previous experiments.

The procedure for the control condition was identical to that of Experiments 2, 3, and 4.

The procedure for the pressure condition diverged from that of the control condition at the end of the practice period. Just before the beginning of the first performance trial, the experimenter took two dollar bills from the pocket of his sport coat and laid them on the table. He said that in order to motivate the subject to perform well, he was offering subjects one dollar for each trial in which the subject's performance exceeded the criterion "that we're using." He named a criterion 14 points above the subject's practice trial score. However, the experimenter acted as if the same absolute criterion was used for all subjects; the subject was not made aware that the criterion had been computed in relation to his own practice score.

The two trials were then performed, with an interval of 1 min between them. Subjects were then debriefed. Subjects who had won money were paid accordingly.

# Results

An ANCOVA on the combined performance trial scores, using practice score as a covariate, revealed marginally significant main effects for both variables, $F(1, 32) = 2.62$, $p < .12$, for pressure, and $F(1, 32) = 3.15$, $p < .10$, for self-consciousness. The interaction between them was not significant, $F(1, 32) < 1$, $ns$. The main effects indicated superior performance in the control (no money) condition and for subjects low in self-consciousness, respectively.

Several subjects in the cash (pressure) condition appeared to choke on the first trial but approached or reached the criterion for success on the second trial. When asked about the discrepancy, they said that they had "given up" on reaching the criterion after the failure on the first trial; that is, they had dissociated themselves from the performance pressure by choosing to disregard the incentive.

*Table 3*

### Mean Adjusted Scores: Experiment 5

| Trial | Cash | | Control | |
|---|---|---|---|---|
| | HSC | LSC | HSC | LSC |
| 1 | 27.3 | 29.4 | 31.8 | 35.4 |
| 2 | 32.5 | 33.9 | 30.8 | 37.4 |

*Note.* HSC denotes high self-consciousness, LSC, low selfconsciousness. The numbers are adjusted means from analysis of covariance. High scores represent good performance.

The pressure manipulation may have thus lost some of its impact on the second trial. To explore that possibility, a repeated-measures ANCOVA was conducted, separating the two trial scores. The main effect for trial was highly significant, $F(1, 33) = 8.05$, $p < .01$, showing substantially superior performance on the second trial over that on the first trial. That this effect obtained mainly in the cash conditions was confirmed by a significant interaction between trial and pressure, $F(1, 33) = 5.31$, $p < .05$. Table 3 shows the means.

On the first performance trial, the low-self-consciousness subjects appeared to choke; they performed worse in the cash than in the control condition, $t(33) = 2.26$, $p < .05$. The high-self-consciousness subjects showed a weaker trend toward choking, $t(33) = 1.51$, $.10 < p < .15$. The predictions were thus supported for the first trial. They did not receive support on the second trial.

# Discussion

Subjects of both levels (high and low) of self-consciousness showed signs of choking in Experiment 5, although the effect was stronger for those low in self-consciousness. Thus, offering a reward for improved performance paradoxically caused subjects to perform worse.

The fact that choking appeared on the first trial and not the second suggests some caution in interpreting the results. However, if the subjects' self-reports were accurate, they lend further support to the model. If "giving up" on reaching the criterion resulted in improved performance, then the pressure of the criterion was indeed a factor that was hampering performance. The fact that subjects could avoid the effects of pressure by internally abandoning the goal also implies that the situation alone does not create pressure—rather, some internal acceptance of the importance by the performing individual may be necessary in order for choking to occur. The possibility that a private cognitive reorientation by the individual may help prevent choking calls for further research.

# Experiment 6

Experiment 6 was an attempt to provide a clear demonstration of choking in a field setting on a reasonably well-learned task. Although Experiments 1 through 5 showed that various situational and dispositional factors affect performance levels, two facts suggest reservations .about interpreting them. First, the task was new to some subjects, and 5-min practice may not have overcome the novelty. Second, there was no proof that each individual subject who supposedly choked could actually have performed better in a different situation. Practice trial scores were sometimes higher than performance scores, but the cell means rarely reflected an average decrease in score from practice level. Although the weight of the between-subjects analyses suggests that subjects who choked would have done better in different circumstances, it is still somewhat plausible that the manipulations facilitated performance in some conditions instead of hampering it in others. Experiment 6 was designed to alleviate these interpretive problems.

## Method

### Subjects

Subjects were customers at a video game arcade in a shopping mall. They were recruited by being offered a free game at the game they were playing. Potential subjects were excluded on the basis of any of the following: failure to reach a minimum cutoff score in their own ("practice") previous game, which signified a lack of ability at the task; failure to have played the same game on at least several previous days (in answer to direct questioning); or age below 13. Thirteen subjects took part.

### Procedure

Potential subjects were observed surreptitiously while playing either of two popular video games, "Pac Man" or "Ms. Pac Man." If the subject reached the criterion score, the experimenter approached the subject upon completion of his or her game and said, "I'd like to give you a free game, if you have a minute. I'm doing research on these video games." No subject declined to participate. The experimenter verified that the subject had played the game on previous occasions.

Pressure was manipulated by self-presentational concerns. The experimenter asked the subject's name and age and recorded these. (The experimenter also quietly recorded the subject's previous score, which was displayed on the screen, and which served as a "practice" score.) The experimenter then said "I want you to get the best score you possibly can, OK? I can only give you one chance, so make it the best you can do." The experimenter then

observed the subject's performance, pretending to time it with a stopwatch. The subject's score was recorded and the subject was thanked.

## Results

Percentage of change scores were used in this study because of the interest in demonstrating actual decrements in performance and because the two different games gave different levels of scores. Therefore, for each subject, the adjusted change score equaled the performance score minus the practice score, divided by the practice score.

The average change was a 25% drop in performance from the previous (practice) trial to the pressure (performance) trial. This was significantly below zero, $t(12) = 2.91$, $p < .02$, indicating that it was a definite decrement in performance.

## Discussion

A verbal instruction emphasizing the importance of doing well on that particular trial, combined with enhanced self-presentational concerns created by getting the subject's name and by overt surveillance of the subject's performance, resulted in performance inferior to what the subject had just done on the same game. In Experiment 6, situational pressure clearly resulted in choking.

The use of a performance criterion ensured that all subjects were good at the task. Indeed, the practice scores of the subjects were from three to seven times as high as those of obvious beginners. Although the subjects perhaps cannot be said to have totally mastered the game (in part because total mastery of one of these games is hard to define: No one stays on forever), they all can be said to have achieved substantial skill prior to the experiment.

# General Discussion

The present series of experiments was based on a model of choking as mediated by attentional shifts. According to this model, situational demands for excellent performance (i.e., pressure) cause the individual to attend consciously to his or her internal process of performance, and this consciousness disrupts that process and harms the performance. The results of the experiments were generally consistent with that model. Performance of a skill task was lowered by directing the individual's attention to his or her internal performance process and by dispositional self-consciousness. Similar performance decrements were obtained by competitive pressure and by a cash incentive offered for improved performance.

Experiments 1, 2, and 3 suggested that self-consciousness harms performance. Experiments 4, 5, and 6 suggested that pressure harms performance similarly. The present experiments did not provide direct evidence that pressure causes increased attention to one's own internal performance process, although there was ample indirect evidence of relationships between pressure and such self-consciousness. Further research is needed to substantiate that relationship.

This model would not apply directly to performance based on strength, stamina, or perseverance because such performances are not based on the execution of automatically learned response sequences. However, self-consciousness could mediate choking on such tasks by increasing the person's awareness of bodily fatigue, pain, and stress, so that he or she decides to reduce the effort. Pennebaker and Lightner (1980) provided results suggestive of that hypothesis, although their subjects were never instructed to try to perform well.

The relevance of self-consciousness to impaired cognitive performance has also been suggested. Wine (1971) cited the focus of attention on oneself as an important feature of test anxiety. In persons high in test anxiety, reduction of "self-preoccupation" has been associated with improved performance (e.g., Sarason, 1981). It is plausible that the performance decrements of test-anxious individuals follow from processes similar to those that mediated choking in the present experiments.

Moreover, the relation of performance expectancies to choking under pressure deserves investigation. Past research has suggested that expectancies can help bring about poor performance (Aronson & Carlsmith, 1962; Baumeister, Cooper, & Skib, 1979; House & Perney, 1974; Zanna, Sheras, Cooper, & Shaw, 1975). Zanna et al. suggested that the combination of internal and external expectancies of success could backfire and lead to choking. It is plausible that the performance decrements in Experiments 4 and 5 (although not those in Experiments 1, 2, and 3) were mediated by expectancies formed by the subject during the experiment and never expressed overtly. Such an explanation would, of course, need to account for the influences of dispositional self-consciousness on performance, either by differential expectancy formation or differential impact of expectancies as a function of self-consciousness.

A final possible interpretation deserves mention. It could be suggested that attention to oneself decreases one's attention to the task, so that performance decrements are due to overlooking information necessary to perform the task. Essential to this interpretation is the view that self-consciousness and attention to anything else (other than oneself) are mutually exclusive. This view was suggested by Duval and Wicklund (1972) but contradicts other theorists who have regarded self-awareness as superimposed on awareness of external circumstances (e.g., Kant, 1956/1787). This controversy awaits definitive empirical resolution. Still, it must be noted that performance decrements cannot be equated with lack of awareness of task matters; Hefferline et al. (1959), Kimble and Perlmutter (1970), and Langer and Imber (1979) have all indicated that increased attention to certain tasks can impair performance.

## Notes

1 The six experiments were performed in the sequence in which they are reported here, except that Experiment 3 was actually performed fifth. The author is grateful to James Pennebaker for suggesting that Experiment 2 be replicated with the inclusion of the Self-Consciousness Scale in order to make that study resemble Experiments 4 and 5, as well as for his other suggestions and comments.

2 The BSRI was included as a possible means of identifying "macho" (ultra-masculine) males who might be unusually susceptible to competition with a female. However, the sample of men in that category was too small to permit a reasonable test.

3 Scores below 5 are simply implausible, so if the subject scored extremely low, the confederate's score was given as closer to it than the formula specified, although of course it was still below the subject's score.

4 The highest mean change score in Experiment 4 was 27, which is for two trials. For one trial, then, an improvement of 14 was required to meet the criterion.

## References

Aronson, E., & Carlsmith, J. M. (1962). Performance expectancy as a determinant of actual performance. *Journal of Abnormal and Social Psychology, 65,* 178–182.

Baumeister, R. F. (1982). A self-presentational view of social phenomena. *Psychological Bulletin, 91,* 3–26.

Baumeister, R. F., Cooper, J., & Skib, B. A.(1979). Inferior performance as a selective response to expectancy: Taking a dive to make a point. *Journal of Personality and Social Psychology, 37,* 424–432.

Bem, S. (1974). The measurement of psychological androgyny. *Journal of Consulting and Clinical Psychology, 42,* 155–162.

Carver, C., & Scheier, M. (1978). Self-focusing effects of dispositional self-consciousness, mirror presence, and audience presence. *Journal of Personality and Social Psychology, 36,* 324–332.

Duval, S., & Wicklund, R. (1972). *A theory of objective self-awareness.* New York: Academic Press.

Fenigstein, A., Scheier, M. F., & Buss, A. H.(1975). Public and private self-consciousness: Assessment and theory. *Journal of Consulting and Clinical Psychology, 43,* 522–527.

Hefferline, R., Keenan, B., & Harford, R. (1959). Escape and avoidance conditioning in human subjects without their observation of the response. *Science, 130,* 1338–1339.

House, W., & Perney, V. (1974). Valence of expected and unexpected outcomes as a function of locus of goal and type of expectancy. *Journal of Personality and Social Psychology, 29,* 454–463.

Kant, I. (1956). *Kritik der reinen Vernunft [Critique of Pure Reason].* Frankfurt, West Germany: Meiner (Raymund Schmidt, Ed.). (Original work published 1787.)

Kimble, G., & Perlmuter, L. (1970). The problem of volition. *Psychological Review, 77,* 361–384.

Langer, E. (1978). Rethinking the role of thought in social interaction. In J. Harvey, W. Ickes, & R. Kidd (Eds.), *New directions in attribution research* (Vol. 2, pp. 35–58). Hillsdale, NJ: Erlbaum.

Langer, E. J., & Imber, L. G. (1979). When practice makes imperfect: Debilitating effects of overlearning. *Journal of Personality and Social Psychology, 37,* 2014–2024.

Langer, E., & Saegert, S. (1977). Crowding and cognitive control. *Journal of Personality and Social Psychology, 35,* 175–182.

Martens, R., & Landers, D. M. (1972). Evaluation potential as a determinant of coaction effects. *Journal of Experimental Social Psychology, 8,* 347–359.

Paulus, P. B., & Cornelius, W. L. (1974). Analysis of gymnastic performance under conditions of practice and operative observation. *Research Quarterly, 45,* 56–63.

Paulus, P. B., Shannon, V. C., Wilson, D. L., & Boone, T. D. (1972). The effects of operator presence on gymnastic performance in a field situation. *Psychonomic Science, 29,* 88–90.

Pennebaker, J. W., & Lightner, J. M. (1980). Competition of internal and external information in an exercise setting. *Journal of Personality and Social Psychology, 39,* 165–175.

Sarason, I. (1981). Test anxiety, stress, and social support. *Journal of Personality, 49,* 101–114.

Sartre, J.P. (1974). *Being and nothingness.* Secaucus, NJ: Citadel. (Original work published 1934)

Seta, J. J. (1982). The impact of comparison processes on coactors' task performance. *Journal of Personality and Social Psychology, 42,* 281–291.

Steigleder, M. K., Weiss, R. F., Balling, S. S., Wenninger, V. L., & Lombardo, J. P. (1980). Drivelike motivational properties of competitive behavior. *Journal of Personality and Social Psychology, 38,* 93–104.

Steigleder, M. K.; Weiss, R. F., Cramer, R. E., & Feinberg, R. A. (1978). The motivating and reinforcing functions of competitive behavior. *Journal of Personality and Social Psychology, 36,* 1291–1301.

Wankel, L. M. (1972). Competition in motor performance: An experimental analysis of motivational components. *Journal of Experimental Social Psychology, 8,* 427–437.

Wegner, D. M., & Giuliano, T. (1980). Arousal-induced attention to self. *Journal of Personality and Social Psychology, 38,* 719–726.

Wine, J. (1971). Test anxiety and direction of attention. *Psychological Bulletin, 76,* 92–104.

Zajonc, R. B. (1965). Social facilitation. *Science, 149,* 269–274.

Zanna, M., Sheras, P., Cooper, J., & Shaw, C. (1975). Pygmalion and Galatea: The interactive effects of teacher and student expectancies. *Journal of Experimental Social Psychology, 11,* 279–287.

**Roy F. Baumeister** is currently the Eppes Eminent Professor of Psychology at Florida State University. He is a fellow of the American Psychological Society and has received their William James Fellow Award for lifetime contributions to psychological science. He has a total of 540 publications, many of which are widely cited and of the highest impact.

# EXPLORING THE ISSUE

## Should Schools Use Cash Incentives to Promote Educational Goals?

### Critical Thinking and Reflection

1. Think of a reward that would foster information and be acceptable according to cognitive evaluation theory.
2. Would the study results be different if cash was not used?
3. How can educators prevent "choking under pressure"?
4. Are there other rewards we use that can make students choke under pressure?

### Is There Common Ground?

The issue obviously remains to be open for debate (although it may be trending toward the feeling that rewards are harmful). The two studies selected are both from the traditions of social psychology. Both are experiments with four different conditions and both use cash incentives as an experimental condition. The "Yes" study provides evidence that the use of cash rewards can enhance motivation. The "No" study provides evidence that the use of cash rewards can elicit feelings of pressure. Since the two results are in contradiction about the usefulness of cash rewards in educational contexts, it is useful to review the details of each study's design.

The Pierce et al. study compared intrinsic motivation in the classic free choice period between four groups that differed in whether they received work progressively (do 1, 3, and then 5) versus constantly (do 3 at a time) and whether they were rewarded with cash or not: Progressive—Cash, Progressive—No cash, Constant—Cash, Constant—No cash. The results indicated that when participants were in the Progressive—Cash condition, they exhibited the highest levels of intrinsic motivation (see Figure 1). The rationale for why builds a bridge between the two sides conceptually (i.e., between Cameron & Pierce, 1996 and Deci et al., 1999). As the authors explained, cognitive evaluation theory can be used to explain both the potentials and the disadvantages of rewards on motivation. In this particular case, it was used to explain the potential of using money. Thus, one might be quick to conclude that money can enhance motivation when used within a specific context that considers the feelings of self-competence.

However, in addition to deleterious effects of cash rewards on motivation often cited by cognitive evaluation

theory (Deci et al., 2001), the Baumeister study argued that the use of rewards, such as cash, conveys a message of pressure and can interfere with student learning. It was explained that students, particularly those who are usually low in self-consciousness, become more aware of the learning process (not so much with outcome) and this self-consciousness leads to "choking under pressure." The role of money in this study was in inducing "pressure."

The reality is that money is valued in society and therefore the stakes can be made to be higher than necessary when using it to reward anyone. This points to the interesting communication powers of money. Other studies have also shown that reminders of money activate behaviors related to self-sufficiency (e.g., reduced help seeking from others), but also reduced helpfulness to others (e.g., Vohs, Mead, & Goode, 2006). Thus, money can be for better and for worse. For self-development and self-focus, money can foster independence and the pursuit of individual goals. However, it may be at the expense of educational goals related to societal development.

### References

B. M. Allan and R. G. Fryer, *The Powers and Pitfalls of Education Incentives in the Hamilton Project* (The Hamilton Project, 2011).

A. Bandura, *Social Foundations of Thought and Action: A Social Cognitive Theory* (Prentice-Hall, 1986).

J. Cameron and W. D. Pierce, "The debate about rewards and intrinsic motivation: Protests and accusations do not alter the results," *Review of Educational Research* (vol. 66, 1996).

E. L. Deci, R. Koestner, and R. M. Ryan, "A meta-analytic review of experiments examining the effects of extrinsic rewards on intrinsic motivation," *Psychological Bulletin* (vol. 125, 1999).

E. L. Deci, R. Koestner, and R. M. Ryan, "Extrinsic rewards and intrinsic motivation in education: Reconsidered once again," *Review of Educational Research* (vol. 71, 2001).

E. L. Deci and R. M. Ryan, "The empirical exploration of intrinsic motivational processes." In L. Berkowitz (Ed.), *Advances in Experimental Social Psychology* (vol. 13, pp. 39–80) (Academic Press, 1980).

K. D. Vohs, N. L. Mead, and M. R. Goode, "The psychological consequences of money," *Science* (vol. 314, 2006).

## Additional Resources

S. E. Bonner and G. B. Sprinkle, "The effects of monetary incentives on effort and task performance: theories, evidence, and a framework for research," *Accounting, Organizations and Society* (2002).

E. L. Deci, R. Koestner, and R. M. Ryan, "A meta-analytic review of experiments examining the effects of extrinsic rewards on intrinsic motivation," *Psychological Bulletin* (vol. 125, 1999).

U. Gneezy, S. Meier, and P. Rey-Biel, "When and why incentives (don't) work to modify behavior," *Journal of Economic Perspectives* (vol. 25, 2011).

E. A. Hanushek, "Moving beyond spending fetishes," *Educational Leadership* (vol. 53, 1995).

E. A. Hanushek, "Applying performance incentives to schools for disadvantaged," *Education & Urban Society* (vol. 29, 1997).

# *Internet References . . .*

**Discuss: Should We Be Paying Students?**

http://learningmatters.tv/blog/web-series/discuss
-should-we-be-paying-students/7769

**The Education Innovation Laboratory at Harvard University (Roland Fryer)**

http://edlabs.harvard.edu

**The Problem with Financial Incentives— And What to Do About It**

http://knowledge.wharton.upenn.edu/article/the
-problem-with-financial-incentives-and-what-to-do
-about-it

**Self-Determination Theory: An Approach to Human Motivation and Personality**

www.selfdeterminationtheory.org/authors
/edward-deci

**Why Incentive Plans Cannot Work**

https://hbr.org/1993/09/why-incentive-plans
-cannot-work

Selected, Edited, and with Issue Framing Material by:
Esther S. Chang *Soka University of America*

# ISSUE

# Is There Anything Good about Abstinence-Only Sex Education?

**YES: Elaine A. Borawski, et al.,** from "Effectiveness of Abstinence-Only Intervention in Middle School Teens," *American Journal of Health Behavior* (2005)

**NO: Kathrin F. Stanger-Hall and David W. Hall,** from "Abstinence-Only Education and Teen Pregnancy Rates: Why We Need Comprehensive Sex Education in the U.S.," *PLoS One* (2011)

---

## Learning Outcomes

**After reading this issue, you will be able to:**

- Define abstinence-only or abstinence-until-marriage sex education.
- Be able to identify the advantages and disadvantages for an abstinence-only curriculum.
- Be able to identify the advantages and disadvantages for a comprehensive sex education curriculum.
- Design a field experiment that would prove the effectiveness of one educational curriculum over another.

---

### ISSUE SUMMARY

**YES:** Elaine Borawski and colleagues tested an abstinence-only sex education curriculum against a matched control group of middle school students in seven schools. They demonstrated that an abstinence-until-marriage curriculum can positively influence abstinence as well as reduce the frequency of sex among sexually experienced youths.

**NO:** Kathrin Stanger-Hall and David Hall argue that as a matter of policy an abstinence-only curriculum is ineffective in reducing teen sex. They show that the more the states emphasized abstinence in sex education programs, the higher their teen pregnancy and birth rates.

---

**S**ex sells and perhaps that is why sex is everywhere. Sex is pervasive, accessible, and free on the Internet. Sex is a common activity on highly rated movies and TV dramas, and its value is implicit in erectile dysfunction and Viagra pharmaceutical commercials during early evening network news broadcasts. Needless to say, there are movies that youth see and rate as "better than porn." The problem with the pervasiveness of "sexy media" is that it oftentimes gives a false image of what sex really is and many teens are exposed to it unintentionally (e.g., prominent roadside billboard advertisements for the TV series "Jane the Virgin") and/or drawn to see it in a variety of unrealistic Hollywood-inspired contexts.

Although there is debate regarding the proper role of schools in the area of morality and character building of the child, the reality has been that high teenage pregnancy rates and the spread of sexually transmitted diseases (STDs) become societal burdens, both in terms of money and health. When schools remain as bystanders, they may wonder if they are part of the problem. An examination of the responses to the 2002 National Survey of Family Growth, which surveyed more than 2,000 nationally representative adolescents, found that receiving formal sex education from school, church, or a community organization was associated with lower rates of sexual intercourse. Moreover, the researchers found that males who received formal sex education at school were more likely to report using birth control the first time they had sex (Mueller, Gavin, & Kulkarni, 2008). Of course, we don't know if the type of sex education they had was abstinence-only or comprehensive. However, these over-all correlations are promising because according to the Centers for Disease Control and Prevention (CDC), 47 percent of U.S. high school students have had sexual intercourse in 2013 and 41 percent did not use a condom the last time they had sex (see Internet Resources for more information at the CDC website). Other facts the CDC has on its website is that almost half of the 20 million new STDs diagnosed each year were among young people between the ages of 15 and 24 and that approximately 273,000 babies were born to teen girls aged 15–19 years in 2013. Based simply on this brief and cursory peek at the numbers, it can easily be concluded that it appears that there needs to be more help available for teens with regard to their sex-related decisions. Therefore, sex education in schools may be the only sound information source available for many adolescents, particularly the most vulnerable and early developing youth.

Most people agree that abstinence is the safest choice an adolescent can make regarding sexual activity. It is the only 100 percent effective way to avoid pregnancy and the hundreds of STDs that are epidemic in our society. However, as can be seen by the numbers reported by the CDC, adolescents are having sex. The problem is that parents and educators cannot agree on the best way to teach children and adolescents about the implications of premarital sex. One group believes that the best approach is through comprehensive sex education, which encourages abstinence but also provides information on birth control, protection against STDs, and the emotional aspects of engaging in sex. The other group promotes abstinence-only sex education, which provides information on the hazards of sex (i.e., pregnancy, STDs, broken hearts, etc.) and sometimes includes information on self-esteem, life goals, and dealing with peer pressure to have premarital sex. Advocates for comprehensive sex education argue that many adolescents will have premarital sex; as a consequence, adolescents need to be taught about birth control methods and STD prevention techniques. Those supporting abstinence-only sex education believe that teaching about birth control methods and STD prevention sends mixed messages about premarital sex. It could give teens the impression that teachers and parents accept that adolescents cannot help themselves from having sex, which is contrary to the pro-abstinence movement's goals.

To intensify the debate, the government established a federal entitlement program for "abstinence-only-until-marriage" education (2006, 2007). When schools

and other agencies accept these grants, they must adhere to the program's rules, which include requiring schools to teach little about sexuality but instead to send a strong message that sexual activity outside of marriage is psychologically and physiologically harmful. Therefore, teaching about or discussing premarital sex should be avoided when accepting these grants. This is worrisome to advocates of comprehensive sex education because they believe that education about sexuality is the best way to empower adolescents to make sound decisions regarding premarital sex. In fact, among academic circles, the words "abstinence only" elicits negative reactions largely due to accumulating evidence that abstinence-only programs have been ineffective but continuously restored with federal funding (see review of policy in Stanger-Hall & Hall, 2011).

Many questions should be considered when deciding on a sex education curriculum. It appears fair to allow the results of science to decide, such as program evaluations of different types of sex education curriculums that students are randomly assigned to and complete successfully compared to students who are not exposed to any sex education. The comparison to a control group that receives nothing in terms of sex education remains important and can often be ignored among the many who may rush to emphasize comprehensive sex education.

Are abstinence-only programs all failures when compared to comprehensive programs or no program? The "Yes" side article reports upon a relatively large middle school sample drawing from seven schools and was sophisticated in its design for program evaluation. It tracked two groups of students who were (not randomly) assigned to two possible groups: the intervention (i.e., the abstinence-only sex education class) or the control (no sex education). Overall, they find that the program is *effective* when compared to control. Thus, the argument that students must consider is whether abstinence-only education is better than doing nothing in terms of attempting some formal education on sex. The "No" side takes issue with the assumption that abstinence-only will be better than doing nothing. This study primarily provides evidence to argue that the more the state policies in the United States focused on abstinence, the more of a problem it had with teen pregnancy and birth rates.

## Acknowledgments

*The author would like to acknowledge the contributions of Kourtney Vaillancourt from New Mexico State University in helping to frame this issue.*

# YES

**Elaine A. Borawski et al.**

# Effectiveness of Abstinence-Only Intervention in Middle School Teens

National data has documented a decline in the rate of sexual activity among adolescents over the past 10 years, with the percentage of sexually experienced high school students dropping from 54.1% in 1991 to 45.6% in 2001.[1] However, for most, the age of sexual initiation still occurs during the teen years,[2] and the rates of early sexual initiation (ie, prior to age 13) remains high, particularly among minority youth.[2,3] In 2001, rates of early sexual initiation among African Americans were twice that of Hispanic youth and 3 times that of white youth (16.3%, 7.6%, 4.7%, respectively).[2]

The consequences of and risks related to early sexual initiation are well documented,[4–9] including increased likelihood of multiple partners and the increased risk of teen pregnancy and STDs, as well as the social and emotional consequences such as reduced likelihood of finishing high school, the increased likelihood of being a single parent, and the likelihood of regretting having been sexually active so early in life.[5,9,10]

For these reasons, health educators and public health officials continue to seek effective methods to reduce the incidence of early sexual initiation and the rates of high-risk sexual activity among young adolescents.[11] A common approach is the classroom-based curriculum, and over the past decade the content of these curricula have increasingly focused on abstinence.[12,13] This evolution has been influenced by the concerns listed, as well as a change in the federal welfare law in 1996 that has allocated at least $50 million per year since then to abstinence-only education.[14,15] The premise of this law is to encourage teens to abstain from, or at the very least postpone, sexual initiation, arguing that a delay in initiation would reduce the number of years of sexual activity and the potential number of partners, which in turn would reduce the exposure to disease and risk of pregnancy. A delay is also thought to be beneficial as it provides more time for adolescents to develop the cognitive and emotional maturity needed in a healthy sexual relationship.[14]

The eligibility criteria for funding through this federal mechanism is quite explicit, with the law outlining specific characteristics that programs must include, such as the physical, social, psychological, and emotional consequences of early sexual experimentation and the value of sexual abstinence.[15] In addition, it is assumed that because sex in a monogamous, married relationship is the expected standard of behavior, discussion of contraceptives (i.e., condoms) as protection against disease is not included in the list.

This has led to concerns by health educators that the absence of contraceptive information in abstinence-only programs will place adolescents at a higher risk for STDs once they engage in sexual intercourse because they will lack the information needed to protect themselves from pregnancy or disease.[13] In addition, some argue that due to the strong emphasis on virginity there is an inherent focus on the sexually uninitiated, potentially ignoring or alienating the sexually experienced.[16] However, few studies have assessed these concerns. In fact, there have been only a few published evaluations of abstinence-only programs,[13,17–19] as compared to the numerous evaluations of more comprehensive sex education curricula (see reviews[12,20–23]).

The purpose of this study was to examine the effectiveness of a school-based, Title V compliant, abstinence-until-marriage curriculum taught to middle school adolescents. Using a theoretical framework that draws primarily from social cognitive theory,[24,25] we hypothesized that the intervention would affect sexual behavior both directly and indirectly through cognitive mediators (eg, knowledge, beliefs, efficacy, intentions) that are considered to be antecedent to sexual behavior in adolescents[13] and that these effects could be modified by the adolescent's gender and prior sexual experience.

We hypothesized that students exposed to the intervention would report an increase in knowledge regarding HIV/AIDS, stronger beliefs in abstinence, greater confidence in resisting sexual advances, and greater intentions to abstain from sex in the future when compared to a control group of their peers. Due to the lack of contraceptive information, we hypothesized that there would be no group differences in condom-use efficacy or in the intention to use a condom in the future. Moreover, due to the emphasis on abstinence and the emotion-focused nature of the message, we hypothesized that the intervention would be strongest among the sexually inexperienced and female students. With regard to behavior, we hypothesized that the inexperienced students exposed to the intervention would be less likely to initiate, but that there would be no group differences in sexual activity (frequency, number of partners, condom use) among the sexually experienced.

## Methods

### Participants

The study population comprised 3017 adolescents in seventh and eighth grades enrolled in 5 urban and 2 suburban middle schools in the Midwest during the 2001–2002 school year. . . . Data for the current study were derived from the 7 schools that were assigned by the school districts to receive the abstinence-until-marriage (For Keeps) curriculum. The authors served as the independent evaluators of the countywide program (ie, funded through the local Children and Family First Council) and were granted usage of the data for research purposes. The authors have no affiliation or conflicts of interest (financial or otherwise) with the evaluated program. . . .

### Curriculum

For Keeps is a 5-day (40-minute sessions) classroom-based curriculum that stresses abstinence until marriage and focuses on the benefits of abstinence and the physical, emotional, psychological, and economic consequences of early sexual activity. The curriculum emphasizes character development, and future orientation, and presents virginity as a "gift" that is shared in marriage at a time when individuals are more prepared for sexual relationships. It also emphasizes how teen pregnancy and disease can interfere with life goals, the need for and development of resistance skills, and the links between alcohol, drugs, and vulnerability to sexual advances/desires, all deemed important elements of successful prevention programs involving teens.[14] The curriculum does emphasis that condoms are not 100% effective in preventing pregnancy and disease, but more emphasis is placed on how condoms and other contraceptives do not protect adolescents from the emotional consequences of sexual activity (eg, broken hearts). Finally, the curriculum is designed to address both

the sexually experienced and inexperienced by emphasizing the value of renewed abstinence among the sexually experienced. In this project, the curriculum was taught by outside facilitators, recruited and trained by the locally funded agency.

### Data Collection

All students were assessed at baseline via self-administered paper-based surveys (72 questions), 1 to 5 days prior to the intervention. Classrooms within each school were then assigned, based on class scheduling, to either the intervention or control arm of the study, with the intervention classrooms receiving the abstinence-until-marriage curriculum in the fall semester. (Authors of study were contracted evaluators of this community-based program and unable to dictate randomization of classrooms to intervention and control arms). A post intervention survey (70 questions) was completed by all students after a period of time ranging from 16 to 25 weeks after the end of the curriculum (mean=149 days or approximately 21 weeks). Students in classrooms assigned to the control arm then received the curriculum during spring semester, following the posttest survey.

In order to match pre- and posttest data of individual students, unique identifiers were asked (initials, classroom, date of birth, student ID, gender, race, and last 4 digits of the home phone number). . . .

### Measures

#### Demographics
Baseline demographic measures included age (in years), gender (F=1, M=0), living arrangements (dual parents=0, other=1), self-identified ethnicity (assessed with 3 index variables for African American, Hispanic, and Other, respectively, with white students serving as the reference category), and whether students attended an urban (1) or suburban (0) school.

#### Knowledge
HIV/STD knowledge was assessed using a 7-item index with a true/false/not sure format, scoring the number of correct responses (range=0–7). Item examples include: "AIDS can be cured" and "a pregnant woman who has a STD can give it to her baby."

#### Abstinence Values
Beliefs in abstinence were assessed with 2 composites of 2 items each, one assessing the belief in abstinence until "older" and the other in abstinence until "marriage." Examples from domains include "I believe people my age

should wait until they are older before they have sex" and "It is important to me that I get married before having sexual intercourse." Responses to these items range from (1) definitely no to (4) definitely yes.

### Self-efficacy

Self-efficacy was assessed with 2 composites of 2 items each: *impulse control efficacy*, assessing the adolescent's confidence in his or her ability to resist sexual advances; and *condom use efficacy*, assessing the confidence in his or her ability to (a) obtain and (b) correctly use a condom (or explain use to a partner). Responses for both efficacy composites ranged from 1 to 4, based on the original response categories of (1) totally unsure to (4) totally sure; thus, the higher the score, the greater the efficacy.

### Behavioral Intentions

Behavioral intentions included intentions to have sex and to use a condom in the future. Intention to have sex was assessed with 2 single-item questions: intention to have sex in the next 3 months and in the next year, with responses ranging from (1) not at all likely to (4) definitely likely. Intention to use a condom was assessed with a single item, asking the likelihood of using a condom in the future, with similar response categories.

### Behavioral Outcomes

With the exception of frequency of sexual intercourse and condom use, binary measures of sexual activity served as our primary outcomes. Prior sexual experience was assessed at baseline ("ever had sexual intercourse?" no=0; yes=1). At follow up, sexual activity was assessed as reports of sexual intercourse during the evaluation period (no=0; yes=1). Specific to these episodes of recent sexual intercourse, students were asked the frequency of intercourse, which was included in the analyses as both a continuous variable and dichotomized at the 75/25 split as (5 times or fewer=0 and 6 or more=1). The number of sexual partners during the evaluation period was dichotomized into 1 partner (0) and 2 or more (1) to reflect multiple partnerships. Condom-use frequency was assessed by a question asking how often a condom was used during sexual intercourse during the evaluation period, with responses ranging from never (0) to every time (4). We utilized the measure as a continuous variable and as a dichotomous variable reflecting consistent condom use with those reporting use every time (1) being compared to all other responses (0).

Although we acknowledge the limitation of grouping adolescents based on very different circumstances or experiences, for descriptive brevity, we refer to adolescents who report ever having sexual intercourse are referred to as "sexually experienced" and adolescents who report sexual intercourse during the evaluation period are referred to as "sexually active."

## Analyses

To test the impact of the curriculum on the change in cognitive mediators, general linear model (GLM) analyses were used, with group membership (Intervention=1; Controls=0) as the fixed effect and covariates (age, gender, ethnicity, urban vs suburban school, sexual experience at baseline, time from pretest to posttest, and baseline measure of the outcome variable) included, producing adjusted group means for comparison. Intervention effects, when found, indicate that the change in the variable (eg, knowledge) is significantly different (larger) in the intervention group than the control group. To test whether intervention effects were conditional upon gender or sexual experience at baseline, all significant direct effects analyses were repeated, adding 2 cross-product terms (group * sexually experience and group * gender) after the main effects. These results are discussed separately within each results section.

Sexual behavior at follow-up was assessed using logistic regression (for binary outcomes) and linear regression (for continuous variables), including the same set of covariates and interaction effects as discussed above.

. . .

## Results

3017 students from the 7 middle schools were assessed at baseline. Of these, 2069 (69%) students completed a follow-up survey that could be successfully linked to their pretest survey through the demographic identifiers. . . .

On average, the students in the sample were 13 years of age; a little over half were female and a similar proportion (52%) lived with 2 parents and attended an urban (53%) school. The sample was predominantly African American (73%), followed by white (19%) and Hispanic/Latino (6%) students, and students of other racial/ethnic groups (2%). Less than a quarter (23%) of students were sexually experienced at baseline; however, among these students, nearly half (46%) reported having sex during the past 3 months.

The intervention and control groups differed on 2 variables at baseline: more suburban schools included intervention classrooms than did urban schools, and the length of time between the pretest and posttest differed between with intervention and controls, with the follow-up period being approximately 5 days longer for intervention students than controls. Otherwise, the intervention and control students were nearly identical with regard to sociodemographic characteristics and baseline sex-related attitudes, perceptions, and behaviors.

## Cognitive Mediators

### HIV/STD Knowledge
Students exposed to the intervention demonstrated and maintained a significant increase in HIV/ STD knowledge at follow-up when compared to controls (P<.001; partial $\eta^2$=.012). These results did not differ by gender or sexual experience at baseline.

### Belief in Abstinence
Students exposed to the intervention reported a significant increase in their beliefs in being abstinent until older (P<.01; partial $\eta^2$=.005) and abstinent until marriage (P<.001; partial $\eta^2$=.010) at follow-up than did controls. A significant interaction was found in the model predicting abstinence-until-older beliefs, with the intervention effect being found only among female students and sexually inexperienced at baseline (P<.02).

### Efficacy—Impulse Control and Condom Use
No intervention effects were found with regard to students' perception of confidence in resisting sexual advances or in their confidence to obtain and use a condom.

### Intentions—Sex and Condom Use
Students exposed to the intervention reported a *decline* in their intention to have sex in the next 3 months (P<.05; cluster adjusted P value <.09), and in the next year (P<.03; partial $\eta^2$=.004), as well as a decline in their intentions to use a condom in the future (P<.01; partial $\eta^2$=.006) when compared to controls. That is, although they reported lower intentions to have sex in the future, they also reported lower intentions to use a condom if they had sex. The intervention effects on intentions to have sex did not differ by gender or sexual experience at baseline (ie, significant for all groups); however, the impact on condom-use intentions was found only among the sexually inexperienced (irrespective of gender; P<.05).

### Behavioral Outcomes
Table 1 provides the results of the multivariate analyses examining the intervention effects on behavioral outcomes. Although some of the results were conditional on sexual experience at baseline, there were no gender*group interactions found in any of the behavioral analyses.

The unadjusted rate of sexual intercourse among the sexually inexperienced was 5.6% (n=75/1329; 5.2% for intervention group; 6.1% for controls), and the rate of continued sexual activity among the sexually experienced was 52.2% (n=211/404; 51.2% for intervention group; 53.4% for controls). When examined within the multivariate model (Table 4), controlling for covariates, students exposed to the intervention were not statistically different from controls in their reporting of sexual activity during the 5-month period. Moreover, these results were similar for both the sexually inexperienced and experienced at baseline.

The final analyses tested the intervention effects on frequency of sexual intercourse, number of partners, and condom use among students who said that they had sexual intercourse at least once during the 5-month period. Results revealed that students exposed to the intervention reported fewer episodes of sexual intercourse (P<.05) and fewer partners (P<.01) during the 5-month period than did controls. Although the effects were most pronounced among the sexually experienced at baseline when compared to those who initiated during the evaluation, the differences were not statistically significant. Lastly, there were no group differences observed with regard to condom use, when examined as a continuous measure or as a binary measure reflecting consistent condom use, nor did the relationships vary by sexual experience at baseline.

## Discussion

This study examined the effectiveness of an abstinence-until-marriage sex education intervention intended to increase abstinence beliefs and intention, increase efficacy in situational resistance, reduce early sexual experimentation among the sexual inexperienced, and encourage renewed abstinence among the sexually experienced. We found that compared to controls, intervention students reported significant increases in their HIV/STD knowledge, their personal beliefs about the importance of abstinence, and their intentions to remain abstinent in the near future when queried 5 months after the completion of the school-based program. The program did not have an effect on students' confidence to avoid a risky sexual situation, and intervention students who were sexually inexperienced at baseline reported a decrease in their intention to use a condom in the future.

With regard to the impact on sexual intercourse, intervention results (i.e., odds ratio) went in the hypothesized (ie, protective) direction; however, the group differences were not statistically significant. That is, the program did not

*Table 1*

**Multivariate Results:[a] Impact of Abstinence-Until-Marriage Intervention on Sexual Behavior Among Middle School Adolescents**

| | OR(95%CI) |
|---|---|
| **Among all students (n=2069)** | |
| Recent Sex[b,c] | 0.85(0.62,1.15) |
| **Among sexually inexperienced students at baseline (n=1462)** | |
| Recent Sex[b,c] | 0.83(0.52, 1.33) |
| **Among sexually experienced students at baseline (n=439)** | |
| Recent Sex[b,c] | 0.87(0.58,1.31) |
| **Among all students who reported sexual intercourse during evaluation period (n=311)** | |
| Frequency of sexual intercourse[d] | $\beta = -1.74$ s.e.$=0.83$ $\beta=-.127$*[e] |
| Multiple episodes of sexual intercourse (6 or more vs 5 or less) | 0.47 (0.26, 0.84)* |
| Two or more sexual partners | 0.50(0.30,0.83)** |
| Consistent condom use[f] | 1.19(0.71,1.99) |

*Note*

* $P < .05$; ** $P < .01$; *** $P < .001$

a  All models adjusted for gender, age, race, sexual experience at baseline, and time between pretest and posttest.
b  Defined as sexual activity during the time between pretest and posttest.
c  Results from binary logistic regression: odds ratio and 95% confidence intervals associated with group membership (intervention vs control).
d  Results from linear regression: unstandardized coefficient ($\beta$), standard error, and standardized coefficient b(beta) associated with group membership (intervention vs control).
e  Results from linear regression: unstandardized coefficient ($\beta$), standard error, and standardized coefficient b(beta)
f  Defined as using a condom during every sexual encounter during the evaluation period.

significantly reduce the likelihood of sexual initiation among the sexually inexperienced, nor did it reduce the likelihood of sexual intercourse among the sexual experienced.

In contrast, and somewhat surprising, our study revealed that although sexually experienced students were not more likely to abstain from sex during the follow-up period, those who did engage in intercourse reported fewer episodes and fewer sexual partners than did their sexually active peers who did not receive the intervention. That is, although the incidence of abstinence did not increase in this group, students who engaged in sexual intercourse during the evaluation period appeared to reduce the amount of casual sex, as evidenced by fewer episodes of sex and fewer sexual partners reported in the 5-month period.

Some of the study results seem counterintuitive in nature, particularly the impact of the intervention among the already sexually experienced. Some have argued that the abstinence-until-marriage message will not appeal to students who have already had sex.[16] Yet, sexually experienced intervention students were just as likely to report increases in their abstinence-until-marriage beliefs and intentions to remain abstinent in the future as their inexperienced peers. It is possible that it is because of their prior sexual experience that the abstinence message is appealing. Researchers have shown that young adolescents are highly

motivated by affective cues,[26] and sexual intercourse certainly has strong affective appeal. Although certainly not all adolescents, some may have found that the experience of sexual intercourse was far less romantic, exciting, or pleasurable than they had expected,[5] and perhaps for some, the initial act of sex may have been forced, unwanted, or unintended.[4-5] Thus, the appeal of sex may have been lessened by reality, giving more consideration to the alternative, a similarly affective, emotion-focused message.

. . .

Due to the paucity of rigorously evaluated abstinence-only programs,[13] it is unclear whether our results are generalizable to other abstinence-only programs or only the specific program evaluated in this study (ie, Operation Keepsake). Kirby concluded in his most recent review of teen pregnancy prevention programs[13] that there have been only 3 studies of abstinence-only programs and none of these offered evidence that they delay initiation or reduce the frequency of sexual intercourse.

Postponing Sexual Involvement (PSI) is one of the most highly cited "successful" abstinence programs[12,14,23,27,28] based on an initial study that found significant reduction in sexual initiation among adolescents exposed to the intervention.[17] The success was limited to the sexually inexperienced, with the program having little to no impact on sexual behavior of students sexually experienced at baseline or those who engaged in sexual intercourse after the program. However, the measures assessing sexual behavior (eg, frequency, partners, etc) were severely limited. Kirby and colleagues evaluated the impact of PSI among more than 10,000 adolescents in California and found no intervention effects on sexual initiation or on frequency of intercourse of number of partners among the sexually active.[29]

In their randomized trial involving a comparison of a safer-sex curriculum to an abstinence-based curriculum,[30] Jemmott and colleagues reported that the abstinence-based curriculum had a short-term protective effect on sexual initiation, but these effects washed out by 6 months. However, the abstinence-based program was not found to impact frequency of sex, frequency of unprotected sex, or condom use, with the exception of a protective effect on condom use at 12 months. Thus, our results do seem to be unique in that the program did appear to have an effect on sexual behavior of the sexually experienced. However, we do not know whether these effects are sustainable beyond the 5-month follow-up.

. . .

In conclusion, this study provides some evidence that an abstinence-until-marriage program can affect short-term sexual behavior among adolescents. Although the program did not impact sexual initiation among the sexually inexperienced, it had a significant, unexpected effect on sexually active students, with a possible reduction in casual sex as evidenced by the reduction in multiple partners and frequency of sexual intercourse. The reduction in condom use intentions among the sexually inexperienced merits further study to determine the long-term implications; however, in this study, the reduction did not equate to less consistent condom use.

## References

1. Trends in the Prevalence of Sexual Behaviors (1991–2001). *Centers for Disease Control and Prevention* [Internet site]. January 12, 2004. Available at: http://www.cdc.gov/nccdphp/dash/yrbs/pdf-factsheets/sex.pdf. Accessed March 8, 2004.

2. Youth Risk Behavior Surveillance-United States, 2001. *MMWR*. June 28, 2002 2002;51(SS-4).

3. Miller KS, Boyer CB, Cotton G. The STD and HIV epidemics in African American youth:
Reconceptualizing approaches to risk reduction. *Journal of Black Psychology*. 2004;30(l):124–137.

4. O'Donnell BL, O'Donnell CR, Stueve A. Early sexual initiation and subsequent sex-related risks among urban minority youth: The reach for health study. *Fam Plan Perspect*. 2001;33(6):268–275.

5. Dickson N, Paul C, Herbison P, et al. First sexual intercourse: Age, coercion, and later regrets reported by a birth cohort. *Br Med J*. 1998;316(7124):29–33.

6. Aten MJ, Siegel DM, Enaharo M, et al. Keeping middle school students abstinent: Outcomes of a primary prevention intervention. *J Adolesc Health*. 2002;31(l):70–78.

7. Paul C, Fitzjohn J, Herbison P, et al. The determinants of sexual intercourse before age 16. *J Adolesc Health*. 2000;27(2): 136–147.

8. Harvey SM, Spigner C. Factors associated with sexual behavior among adolescents: A multivariate analysis. *Adolescence*. 1995;30(118): 253–264.

9. Besharov DJ, Gardiner KN. Sex education and abstinence: Programs and evaluation. *Children & Youth Services Review*. 1997;19(5/6):327–339.

10. Wight D, Henderson M, Raab G, et al. Extent of regretted sexual intercourse among young teenagers in Scotland: A cross sectional survey. *Br Med J*. 2000;320(7244): 1243–1244.

11. Kirby D. Reflections on two decades of research on teen sexual behavior and pregnancy. *J Sch Health*. 1999;69(3):89–94.

12. Kirby D, Short L, Collins J, et al. School-based programs to reduce sexual risk behaviors: A review of effectiveness. *Public Health Rep (Washington DC :1974)*. 1994;109(3):339–360.

13. Kirby D. Emerging Answers: Research Findings on Programs to Reduce Teen Pregnancy: The National Campaign to Prevent Teen Pregnancy, 2001:1–186.

14. Thomas MH. Abstinence-based programs for prevention of adolescent pregnancies. A review. *J Adolesc Health*. 2000;26(l):5–17.

15. U.S. Social Security Act 510(b)(l). Available at: http://www.ssa.gov/OP_Home/ssact/title05/0510.htm. Accessed December 14, 2004.

16. Lamstein E, Haffner DW. Abstinence-only guidelines restrict postponing sexual involvement adaptation. *SIECUS Report*. 1998;26(3):23.

17. Howard M, McCabe JB. Helping teenagers postpone sexual involvement. *Fam Plan Perspect.* 1990; 22(l):21–26.

18. Christopher F, Roosa M. An evaluation of an adolescent pregnancy prevention program. Is "Just say no enough?" *Family Relations.* 1990;42;401–406.

19. Jorgensen S, Potts V, Camp B. Project Taking Charge: six months of follow up of a pregnancy prevention program for early adolescents. *Family Relations.* 1993;42:401–406.

20. Kim N, Stanton B, Li X, et al. Effectiveness of the 40 adolescent AIDS-risk reduction interventions: A quantitative review. *J Adolesc Health.* 1997; 20(3):204–215.

21. Rotheram-Borus MJ, O'Keefe Z, Kracker R, et al. Prevention of HIV among adolescents. *Prev Sci.* 2000;l(l): 15–30.

22. Ogletree RJ, Rienzo BA, Drolet JC, et al. An assessment of 23 selected school-based sexuality education curricula. *J Sch Health.* 1995;65(5):186–191.

23. Frost JJ, Forrest JD. Understanding the impact of effective teenage pregnancy prevention programs. *Family Plan Perspect.* 1995;27(5):188–195.

24. Bandura A. Self-efficacy: Toward a unifying theory of behavioral change. *Psychol Rev.* 1977;84(2):191–215.

25. Bandura A, Adams NE, Beyer J. Cognitive processes mediating behavioral change. *J Pers Soc Psychol.* 1977;35(3):125–139.

26. Nelson C, Bloom F, Cameron J, et al. An integrative, multidisciplinary approach to the study of brain-behavior relations in the context of typical and a typical development. *Dev Psychopathol.* 2002; 14:499–520.

27. Aarons SJ, Jenkins RR, Raine TR, et al. Postponing sexual intercourse among urban junior high school students—A randomized controlled evaluation. *J Adolesc Health.* 2000;27(4):236–247.

28. Card JJ. Teen pregnancy prevention: Do any programs work? *Annu Rev Public Health.* 1999;20:257–285.

29. Kirby D, Korpi M, Barth RP, et al. The impact of the Postponing Sexual Involvement curriculum among youths in California. *Fam Plan Perspect.* 1997;29(3):100–108.

30. Jemmott JB, Jemmott LS, Fong GT. Abstinence and safer sex HIV risk-reduction interventions for African American adolescents: A randomized controlled trial. *JAMA.* 1998;279(19):1529–1536.

**ELAINE A. BORAWSKI** is professor in the Department of Epidemiology and Biostatistics and the Angela Bowen Williamson Professor in Community Nutrition at Case Western Reserve University. She has been elected as president of the American Academy of Health Behavior.

*Appendix*

Section 510 off Title V of the Social Security Act specifies 8 specific characteristics that abstinence education programs must possess to receive federal funding:

(a) has as its exclusive purpose, teaching the social, psychological, and health gains to be realized by abstaining from sexual activity;
(b) teaches abstinence from sexual activity outside marriage as the expected standard for all school age children;
(c) teaches that abstinence from sexual activity is the only certain way to avoid out-of-wedlock pregnancy, sexually transmitted diseases, and other associated health problems;
(d) teaches that a mutually faithful monogamous relationship in context of marriage is the expected standard of human sexual activity;
(e) teaches that sexual activity outside of the context of marriage is likely to have harmful psychological and physical effects;
(f) teaches that bearing children out-of-wedlock is likely to have harmful consequences for the child, the child's parents, and society;
(g) teaches young people how to reject sexual advances and how alcohol and drug use increases vulnerability to sexual advances; and
(h) teaches the importance of attaining self-sufficiency before engaging in sexual activity.

**Kathrin F. Stanger-Hall and David W. Hall**

 **NO**

# Abstinence-Only Education and Teen Pregnancy Rates: Why We Need Comprehensive Sex Education in the U.S.

## Introduction

The appropriate type of sex education that should be taught in U.S. public schools continues to be a major topic of debate, which is motivated by the high teen pregnancy and birth rates in the U.S., compared to other developed countries [1–4] (Table 1). Much of this debate has centered on whether abstinence-only versus comprehensive sex education should be taught in public schools. Some argue that sex education that covers safe sexual practices, such as condom use, sends a mixed message to students and promotes sexual activity. This view has been supported by the US government, which promotes abstinence-only initiatives through the Adolescent Family Life Act (AFLA), Community-Based Abstinence Education (CBAE) and Title V, Section 510 of the Personal Responsibility and Work Opportunity Reconciliation Act of 1996 (welfare reform), among others [5]. Funding for abstinence-only programs in 2006 and 2007 was $176 million annually (before matching state funds) [5,6]. The central message of these programs is to delay sexual activity until marriage, and under the federal funding regulations most of these programs cannot include information about contraception or safer-sex practices[5,7].

The federal funding for abstinence-only education expired on June 30, 2009, and no funds were allocated for the FY 2010 budget. Instead, a "Labor-Health and Human Services, Education and Other Agencies" appropriations bill including a total of $114 million for a new evidence-based Teen Pregnancy Prevention Initiative for FY 2010 was signed into law in December 2009. This constitutes the first large-scale federal investment dedicated to preventing teen pregnancy through research- and evidence-based efforts. However, despite accumulating evidence that abstinence-only programs are ineffective [6,8], abstinence-only funding (including Title V funding) was restored on September 29, 2009 [8] for 2010 and beyond

by including $250 million of mandatory abstinence-only funding over 5 years as part of an amendment to the Senate Finance Committee's health-reform legislation (HR 3590, Amendment #2786, section 2954). This was authorized by the legislature on March 23, 2010 [9].

With two types of federal funding programs available, legislators of individual states now have the opportunity to decide which type of sex education (and which funding option) to choose for their state, while pursuing the ultimate goal of reducing teen pregnancy rates. This large-scale analysis aims to provide scientific evidence for this decision by evaluating the most recent data on the effectiveness of different sex education programs with regard to preventing teen pregnancy for the U.S. as a whole. We used the most recent teenage pregnancy, abortion and birth data from all U.S. states along with information on each state's prescribed sex education approach to ask "what is the quantitative evidence that abstinence-only education is effective in reducing U.S. teen pregnancy rates?" If abstinence education results in teenagers being abstinent, teenage pregnancy and birth rates should be lower in those states that emphasize abstinence more. Other factors may also influence teenage pregnancy and birth rates, including socio-economic status, education, cultural influences [10–12], and access to contraception through Medicaid waivers [13–15] and such effects must be parsed out statistically to examine the relationship between sex education and teen pregnancy and birth rates. It was the goal of this study to evaluate the current sex-education approach in the U.S., and to identify the most effective educational approach to reduce the high U.S. teen pregnancy rates. Based on a national analysis of all available state data, our results clearly show that abstinence-only education does not reduce and likely increases teen pregnancy rates. Comprehensive sex and/or STD education that includes abstinence as a desired behavior was correlated with the lowest teen pregnancy rates across states. In alignment

Stanger-Hall KF, Hall DW (2011). Abstinence-Only Education and Teen Pregnancy Rates: Why We Need Comprehensive Sex Education in the U.S., *PLoS ONE*, vol. 6, no. 10, p. e24658. doi:10.1371/journal.pone.0024658

*Table 1*

| U.S. teenage pregnancy and birth rates are high compared to other developed countries | | | | | | |
|---|---|---|---|---|---|---|
| International Data | U.S. | France | Germany | Netherlands | Canada | UK |
| Pregnancy rate (2002–5) | 72.2 | 25.7 | 18.8 | 11.8 | 29.2 | 41.3^ |
| Birth rate (2006) | 41.9 | 7.8 | 10.1 | 3.8 | 13.3 | 26.7 |

Rates are listed as numbers per 1000 girls 15–19 years old,
^15–18 years old [1–4].
doi:10.1371/journal.pone.0024658.t001

with the *Precaution Adoption Process Model* advocated by the National Institutes of Health we suggest that comprehensive sex and HIV/STD education should be taught as part of the biology curriculum in middle and high school science classes, along with a social studies curriculum that addresses risk-aversion behaviors and planning for the future.

## Materials and Methods

### Level of Emphasis on Abstinence in State Laws

Data on abstinence education were retrieved from the Education Commission of the States [16]. Of the 50 U.S. states, only 38 states had sex education laws (as of 2007). Thirty of the 38 state laws contained abstinence education provisions, 8 states did not. Following the analysis of the Editorial Projects in Education Research Center [17], which categorizes the data on abstinence education into four levels (from least to most emphasis on abstinence: no provision, abstinence covered, abstinence promoted, abstinence stressed), we assigned ordinal values from 0 through 3 to each of these four categories respectively. A higher category value indicates more emphasis on abstinence with level 3 stressing abstinence only until marriage as the fundamental teaching standard (similar to the federal definition of abstinence-only education), if sex or HIV/STD education is taught (sex education is not required in most states) [16–18]. The primary emphasis of a level 2 provision is to promote abstinence in school-aged teens if sex education or HIV/STD education is taught, but discussion of contraception is not prohibited. Level 1 covers abstinence for school-aged teens as part of a comprehensive sex or HIV/STD education curriculum, which should include medically accurate information on contraception and protection from HIV/STDs [16–18]. Level 0 laws on sex education and/or HIV education do not specifically mention abstinence.

### Level of Emphasis on Abstinence in State Laws & Policies

States without sex education laws may nevertheless have policies regarding sex and/or HIV/STD education. These policies may be published as Health Education standards or Public Education codes [19]. These policies can also provide information on how existing sex education laws may be interpreted by local school boards. Information on the sex education laws and policies for all 50 US states was retrieved from the website of the Sexuality Information and Education Council of the US (SIECUS). We analyzed the 2005 state profiles on sex education laws and policy data for all 50 states [19] following the criteria of the Editorial Projects in Education Research Center [17] to identify the level of abstinence education. The coding for the state laws (N=38) and the coding for both laws and policies (N=48) was more or less the same for the states represented in both data sets with 6 exceptions. . . . Only two states had neither a state law nor a policy regarding sex or STD/HIV education (as of 2005): North Dakota and Wyoming. Analyses of the two data sets gave essentially identical results. In this paper we present the analyses of the more extensive (48 states) law and policy data set.

### Teen Pregnancy, Abortion and Birth Data

Data on teen pregnancy, birth and abortion rates were retrieved for the 48 states from the most recent national reports, which cover data through 2005 [11,12]. The data are reported as number of teen pregnancies, teen births or teen abortions per one thousand female teens between 15 and 19 years of age. In general, teen pregnancy rates are calculated based on reported teen birth and abortion rates, along with an estimated miscarriage rate [12]. We used these data to determine whether there is a significant correlation between level of prescribed abstinence education and teen pregnancy and birth rates across states. The expectation is that higher levels of abstinence education will be correlated with higher levels of abstinence behavior and thus lower levels of teen pregnancy.

## Other Factors

Data on four possibly confounding factors were included in our analyses.

### Socio-Economics

To account for cost-of-living differences across the US, we used the adjusted median household income for 2006 for each state from the Council for Community and Economic Research: C2ER [20]. These data are based on median household income from the *Current Population Survey for 2006* from the U.S. Census Bureau [21] and the 2006 cost of living index (COLI).

### Educational Attainment

As an estimate of statewide education levels among teens, we used the percentage of high school graduates that took the SAT in 2005/2006 in each state [22].

### Ethnic Composition

We determined the proportion of the three major ethnic groups (white, black, Hispanic) in the teen population (15–19 years old) for each state [12], and assessed whether the teen pregnancy, abortion and birth rates across states were correlated with the ethnic composition of the teen population. To account for the ethnic diversity among the teen populations in the different states in a multivariate analysis of teen pregnancy and birth rates, we included only the proportion of white and black teens in the state populations as covariates, because the Hispanic teen population numbers were not normally distributed (see below).

### Medicaid Waivers for Family Planning

Medicaid-funded access to contraceptives and family planning services has been shown to decrease the incidence of unplanned pregnancies, especially among low-income women and teens [13]. According to the Guttmacher Institute, the national family planning program prevents 1.94 million unintended pregnancies, including almost 400,000 teen pregnancies each year by providing millions of young and low-income women access to voluntary contraceptive services [13], Medicaid covered 71% of expenditures for these programs in 2006, and it is estimated that states saved $4 (associated with unintended births) for each $1 spend on contraceptive services [13]. . . .

## Statistical Analyses

. . .

### Multivariate Analyses

Only the two normally distributed dependent variables were included in the multivariate analysis (MANOVA and MANCOVA [23]): teen pregnancy and teen birth rates. We tested for homogeneity of error variances (Levene's Test) and for equality of covariance matrices (Box test) between groups. . . .

## Results

Among the 48 states in this analysis (all U.S. states except North Dakota and Wyoming), 21 states stressed abstinence-only education in their 2005 state laws and/or policies (level 3), 7 states emphasized abstinence education (level 2), 11 states covered abstinence in the context of comprehensive sex education (level 1), and 9 states did not mention abstinence (level 0) in their state laws or policies (Figure 1). In 2005, level 0 states had an average (± standard error) teen pregnancy rate of 58.78 (±4.96), level 1 states averaged 56.36 (±3.94), level 2 states averaged 61.86 (±3.93), and level 3 states averaged 73.24 (±2.58) teen pregnancies per 1000 girls aged 14–19 (Table 2). The level of abstinence education (no provision, covered, promoted, stressed) was positively correlated with both teen pregnancy (Spearman's $rho = 0.510$, $p = 0.001$) and teen birth ($rho = 0.605$, $p < 0.001$) rates (Table 3), indicating that abstinence education in the U.S. does not cause abstinence behavior. To the contrary, teens in states that prescribe more abstinence education are actually more likely to become pregnant. Abortion rates were not correlated with abstinence education level ($rho = -0.136$, $p = 0.415$). A multivariate analysis of teen pregnancy and birth rates identified the level of abstinence education as a significant influence on teen pregnancy and birth rates across states (pregnancies $F = 5.620$, $p = 0.002$; births $F = 11.814$, $p < 0.001$). The significant pregnancy effect was caused by significantly lower pregnancy rates in level 0 (no abstinence provision) states compared to level 3 (abstinence stressed) states ($p = 0.036$), and level 1 (abstinence covered) states compared to level 3 states ($p = 0.005$); the significant birth effect was caused by significantly lower teen birth rates in level 0 states compared to level 3 ($p = 0.006$) states, and significantly lower teen birth rates in level 1 states compared to level 3 states ($p < 0.001$).

Socio-economic status, educational attainment, and ethnic differences across states exhibited significant

*Figure 1*

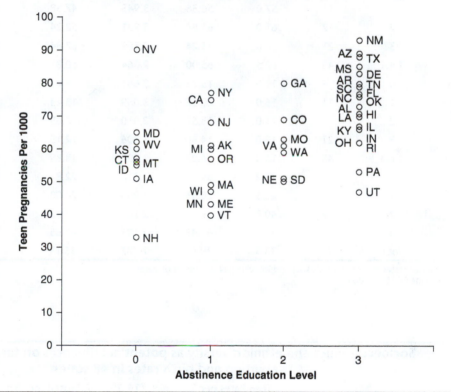

Abstinence education level prescribed in 2005 state laws or policies.
All 48 states with state laws or policies on sex and/or HIV education are shown (North Dakota and Wyoming are not represented).
doi:10.1371/journal.pone.0024658.g001

correlations with some variables in our model (Table 3). We examined the influence of each possible confounding factor on our analysis by including them as covariates in several multivariate analyses. However, after accounting for the effects of these covariates, the effect of abstinence education on teenage pregnancy and birth rates remained significant (Figure 2).

## Socio-Economic Status

There was a significant negative correlation between median household income (adjusted for cost of living) and level of abstinence education ($rho=-0.349$, $p=0.015$; Table 3), indicating a socio-economic bias at the state level on state laws and regulations with regard to sex education. The adjusted median household income was negatively correlated with teen pregnancy ($rho=-0.383$, $p=0.007$) and birth ($rho=-0.296$, $p=0.041$) rates across states: pregnancy and birth rates tended to be higher in lower-income states.

There was no correlation between household income and abortion rates ($rho = -0.116$, $p = 0.432$). When including the adjusted median household income as a covariate in a multivariate analysis (evaluated at $45,892), income significantly influenced teen pregnancy ($F = 5.427$, $p = 0.025$) but not birth ($F = 2.216$, $p = 0.144$) rates. After accounting for socioeconomic status, the level of abstinence education still had a significant effect on teen pregnancy ($F = 4.103$, $p = 0.012$) and birth rates ($F = 10.480$, $p < 0.001$).

## Educational Attainment

There was no significant correlation between statewide teen education (percentage of high school graduates that took the SAT in 2005/2006) and level of abstinence education ($rho=-0.156$, $p=0.291$). Education was not correlated with teen pregnancy rates ($rho=-0.014$, $p=0.925$), but it was positively correlated with teen abortion rates ($rho=0.662$, $p < 0.001$), and as a consequence, negatively

*Table 2*

## Teen pregnancy, abortion and birth rates (per 1000 girls aged 14–19) by level of abstinence education

| Descriptive Statistics by Abstinence Education Level | | | | | 95% Confidence Interval | | | |
|---|---|---|---|---|---|---|---|---|
| Outcomes | Level | N | Median | Mean | Std. Error | Lower Bound | Upper Bound | Minimum | Maximum |
| Teen Pregnancies | 0 | 9 | 57.0 | 58.78 | 4.966 | 47.43 | 70.23 | 33 | 90 |
| | 1 | 11 | 57.0 | 56.36 | 3.943 | 47.58 | 65.15 | 40 | 77 |
| | 2 | 7 | 61.0 | 61.86 | 3.931 | 52.24 | 71.47 | 50 | 80 |
| | 3 | 21 | 76.0 | 73.24 | 2.589 | 67.84 | 78.64 | 47 | 93 |
| | Total | 48 | 62.5 | 65.00 | 2.064 | 60.85 | 69.15 | 33 | 93 |
| Teen Abortions | 0 | 9 | 11.0 | 15.78 | 2.681 | 9.6 | 21.96 | 9 | 28 |
| | 1 | 11 | 16.0 | 20.27 | 3.069 | 13.43 | 27.11 | 10 | 41 |
| | 2 | 7 | 15.0 | 13.57 | 2.010 | 8.65 | 18.49 | 6 | 20 |
| | 3 | 21 | 12.0 | 14.86 | 1.306 | 12.13 | 17.58 | 6 | 27 |
| | Total | 48 | 15.00 | 16.08 | 1.096 | 13.88 | 18.29 | 6 | 41 |
| Teen Births | 0 | 9 | 35.2 | 34.82 | 3.316 | 22.8 | 41.5 | 18 | 50 |
| | 1 | 11 | 26.5 | 28.43 | 1.950 | 24.08 | 32.77 | 19 | 39 |
| | 2 | 7 | 40.0 | 39.29 | 2.765 | 32.52 | 46.05 | 31 | 53 |
| | 3 | 21 | 49.1 | 47.43 | 2.197 | 42.85 | 52.01 | 30 | 62 |
| | Total | 48 | 38.5 | 39.52 | 1.687 | 36.13 | 42.92 | 18 | 62 |

Based on 2005 data for all states except North Dakota and Wyoming, N = number of states.
doi:10.1371/journal.pone.0024658.t003

*Table 3*

## Socioeconomics and ethnic diversity as potential influences on teen pregnancy, abortion and birth rates in 48 states

| Correlation Coefficients | | Teen Rates per 1000 girls (14–19) | | | Adjusted median household income | % Teens in population[1] | | |
|---|---|---|---|---|---|---|---|---|
| | | Pregnancies | Abortions | Births | | White | Black | Hispanic |
| Abstinence Education level | Spearman's rho | 0.507** | −0.083 | 0.562** | −0.349* | −0.382** | 0.419** | 0.030 |
| | p (2-tailed) | <0.001 | 0.577 | <0.001 | 0.015 | 0.007 | 0.003 | 0.839 |
| Teen Pregnancies per 1000 girls | Spearman's rho | | 0.329* | 0.806** | −0.383* | −0.807** | 0.597** | 0.341* |
| | p (2-tailed) | | 0.022 | <0.001 | 0.007 | <0.001 | <0.001 | 0.018 |
| Teen Abortions per 1000 girls | Spearman's rho | | | −0.221 | −0.116 | −0.564** | 0.263 | 0.557** |
| | p (2-tailed) | | | 0.131 | 0.432 | <0.001 | 0.071 | <0.001 |
| Teen Births per 1000 girls | Spearman's rho | | | | −0.296* | −0.482** | 0.393** | 0.036 |
| | p (2-tailed) | | | | 0.041 | 0.001 | 0.006 | 0.806 |
| Adjusted median income | Spearman's rho | | | | | 0.298* | −0.238 | 0.089 |
| | p (2-tailed) | | | | | 0.040 | 0.103 | 0.547 |
| % white teens in population | Spearman's rho | | | | | | −0.566** | −0.532** |
| | p (2-tailed) | | | | | | <0.001 | <0.001 |
| % black teens in population | Spearman's rho | | | | | | | −0.014 |
| | p (2-tailed) | | | | | | | 0.925 |

Significant correlations are marked in bold type (* significant at p<0.05, ** significant at p<0.01).
[1]The % teen population variables are measures of the ethnic diversity of the states. Please note the teen pregnancy, abortion and birth data (per 1000) reflect the behavior of all teens in each state: they are not limited to the behavior within that particular ethnic teen population (see Table 4).
doi:10.1371/journal.pone.0024658.t004

*Figure 2*

Trends in teen pregnancy and birth rates after accounting for socioeconomics, education and ethnic diversity.
(A) The adjusted median household income significantly influenced teen pregnancy and birth rates, but the level
of abstinence education still had a significant influence on teen pregnancy and birth rates after accounting for
socioeconomic status. (B) Education had a significant influence on teen birth, but not on teen pregnancy rates.
After accounting for the influence of teen education, the level of abstinence education still had a significant
influence on both teen pregnancy and teen birth rates. (C) The proportion of white teens (but not black teens)
in the population had a significant influence on teen pregnancy and teen birth rates. After accounting for
this influence, the level of abstinence education still had a significant influence on teen pregnancy and birth rates.
doi:10.1371/journal.pone.0024658.g003

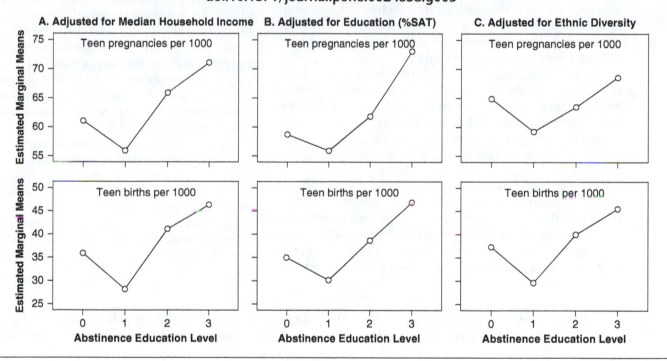

correlated with teen birth rates ($rho=-0.412$, p=0.004).
There was no correlation between socio-economic
status and teen educational attainment across states
($rho=-0.048$, p=0.748), suggesting that these trends
apply to both rich and poor states. When including education (% graduates taking the SAT) as a covariate in a multivariate analysis, education had a significant influence on
teen birth (F=8.308, p=0.006), but not on teen pregnancy
(F=0.161, p=0.690) rates, and after accounting for the
influence of teen education (evaluated at 39.7% of graduates taking the SAT), the level of abstinence education still
had a significant effect on both teen pregnancy (F=5.527,
p=0.003) and teen birth rates (F=10.772, p<0.001).

. . .

## Medicaid Waivers

If Medicaid waivers contribute to the positive correlation
between abstinence education and teen pregnancy at the
state level, then states with waivers should have different
teen pregnancy and birth rates than states without waivers.
This was not the case. States with waivers (N=17) were represented across all four abstinence education levels and did
not differ significantly in teen pregnancy rates from states
without waivers (N=21, Mann Whitney U=237, p=0.086),
suggesting no significant effect of waivers (at the state level)
on the correlation between abstinence levels and teen pregnancy rates. A recent study [14] found the same level of
(non-)significance (0.05<p<0.1) for the effect of waivers
on teen birth rates, but reported it as significant.

# Discussion

This study used a correlational approach to assess whether abstinence-only education is effective in reducing U.S. teen pregnancy rates. Correlation can be due to causation, but it can also be due to other underlying factors, which need to be examined. Several factors besides abstinence education are correlated with teen pregnancy rates. In agreement with previous studies, our analysis showed that adjusted median household income and proportion of white teens in the teen population both had a significant influence on teen pregnancy rates. Richer states tend to have a higher proportion of white teens in their teen populations, tend to emphasize abstinence less, and tend to have lower teen pregnancy and birth rates than poorer states. A recent study [24] found that higher teen birth rates in poorer states were also correlated with a higher degree of religiosity (and a lower abortion rate) at the state level. Medicaid waivers have previously been shown to reduce teen pregnancy rates [13], but our analysis shows that they do not explain our main result, the positive correlation between abstinence education level and teen pregnancy rates.

After accounting for other factors, the national data show that the incidence of teenage pregnancies and births remain positively correlated with the degree of abstinence education across states: The more strongly abstinence is emphasized in state laws and policies, the higher the average teenage pregnancy and birth rate. States that taught comprehensive sex and/or HIV education and covered abstinence along with contraception and condom use (level 1 sex education; also referred to as "abstinence-plus" [25], tended to have the lowest teen pregnancy rates, while states with abstinence-only sex education laws that stress abstinence until marriage (level 3) were significantly less successful in preventing teen pregnancies. Level 0 states present an interesting sample with a wide range of education policies and variable teen pregnancy and birth data [17–19]. For example, several of the level 0 states (as of 2007) did not mandate sex education, but required HIV education only (e.g. CT, WV) [19]. Only three of the level 0 states (IA, NH and NV) mandated both sex education and HIV education, but one of them (NV) did not require that teens learn about condoms and contraception. This state (NV) has the highest teen pregnancy and birth rates in that group (Figure 1). Nevada is also one of only five states (with MD in level 0, CO in level 2, and AZ and UT in level 3) that required parental consent for sex education in public schools instead of an opt-out requirement that is present in all the other states [16,19].

The effectiveness of Level 1 (comprehensive) sex education in our nation-wide analysis is supported by Kirby's meta-analysis of individual sex education programs [8], Underwood et al.'s analysis of HIV prevention programs [26], and a recent review by the CDC taskforce on community

*Table 4*

**Ethnic breakdown of teen pregnancy, birth, and abortion rates and their relationship with abstinence education, educational attainment (SAT), adjusted income and teen diversity in the states.**

| Correlation Coefficients for ethnic diversity in states | | Pregnancy rates (per 1000 girls) | | | Abortion rates (per 1000 girls) | | | Birth rates (per 1000 girls) | | |
|---|---|---|---|---|---|---|---|---|---|---|
| | | White | Black | Hispanic | White | Black | Hispanic | White | Black | Hispanic |
| Abstinence Education level | Spearman's rho | 0.360 | 0.029 | **0.489*** | 0.024 | −0.166 | 0.005 | **0.463**** | **0.332*** | **0.437**** |
| | p (2-tailed) | 0.071 | 0.890 | **0.011** | 0.909 | 0.417 | 0.980 | **0.002** | **0.030** | **0.003** |
| Percent of graduates taking SAT | Spearman's rho | −0.134 | 0.053 | 0.104 | **0.723**** | **0.461*** | **0.613**** | **−0.450**** | **−0.504**** | −0.258 |
| | p (2-tailed) | 0.514 | 0.796 | 0.614 | **<0.001** | **0.018** | **0.001** | **0.002** | **0.001** | 0.094 |
| Adjusted median household income | Spearman's rho | −0.033 | 0.143 | 0.103 | −0.348 | −0.171 | −0.240 | **−0.335*** | 0.106 | 0.099 |
| | p (2-tailed) | 0.873 | 0.486 | 0.617 | 0.081 | −0.404 | 0.238 | **0.028** | 0.500 | 0.529 |
| Proportion of white teens in population | Spearman's rho | −0.307 | 0.054 | −0.318 | −0.376 | −0.015 | −0.256 | −0.017 | 0.162 | 0.064 |
| | p (2-tailed) | 0.127 | 0.794 | 0.114 | 0.058 | 0.944 | 0.206 | 0.916 | 0.298 | 0.685 |
| Proportion of black teens in population | Spearman's rho | **0.550**** | **0.539**** | **0.393*** | 0.113 | 0.086 | 0.031 | 0.282 | **0.420**** | 0.215 |
| | p (2-tailed) | **0.004** | **0.004** | **0.047** | 0.584 | 0.675 | 0.880 | 0.067 | **0.005** | 0.166 |
| Proportion of hispanic teens in population | Spearman's rho | −0.366 | −0.226 | 0.071 | 0.093 | 0.108 | 0.262 | **−0.434**** | **−0.347*** | −0.140 |
| | p (2-tailed) | 0.066 | 0.267 | 0.730 | 0.652 | 0.600 | 0.196 | **0.004** | **0.023** | 0.370 |

Sample sizes for the analysis of ethnic breakdown (for all three ethnic groups) of teen pregnancy and abortion (N = 26 states) and birth rates (N = 43 states) are limited. Significant correlations are marked in bold type (* significant at $p<0.05$, ** significant at $p<0.01$).
doi:10.1371/journal.pone.0024658.t005

preventive services [27]. All these studies suggest that comprehensive sex or HIV education that includes the discussion of abstinence as a recommended behavior, and also discusses contraception and protection methods, works best in reducing teen pregnancy and sexually transmitted diseases.

## Individual Research Studies

Despite large differences between individual research studies that evaluate specific sex education programs (e.g. sample size, approaches to sex education studied, selection of participants, choice of control groups, types of data, control for cross-talk between students outside of class, etc.), several case studies show that abstinence-only education rarely has a positive effect on teen sexual behavior [6,8,28]. One of the few exceptions is the recent study by Jemmott et al. [29] on black middle school students in low-income urban schools: after receiving 8 hours of abstinence education as 12 year olds, significantly more students (64/95) reported to be abstinent after 24 months when compared to (control) students who received 8 hours of health education (without any form of sex education: 47/88; Fishers exact test, p=0.037), or students who received 8 hours of safe-sex education (without an abstinence component: 41/85, Fishers exact test, p=0.007). However, there was no significant difference in abstinence behavior between students who had received abstinence education (64/95) and students who received 8 hours of comprehensive sex education (combining sex education with abstinence education: 57/97; Fishers exact test, p=0.138). These two groups also did not differ in rates of reported unprotected sex (8/122 versus 8/115) or use of condoms (25/33 versus 29/37) in the previous 3 months. The abstinence-only intervention in that study was unique in that it increased knowledge about HIV/STD, emphasized the delay of sexual activity, but not necessarily until marriage, did not put sex into a negative light or use a moralistic tone, included no inaccurate information, corrected incorrect views, and did not disparage the use of condoms [29]. As a result, as pointed out by the authors, this successful version of abstinence education would not have met the criteria for federal abstinence-only funding [29]. While promoting an alternative and more effective form of abstinence education, these results also support Kirby's findings [8] and the data in the present study that comprehensive sex education that includes an abstinence (delay) component (level 1), is the most effective form of sex education, especially when using teen pregnancy rates as a measurable outcome.

Individual research studies also show that teaching about contraception is generally not associated with increased risk of adolescent sexual activity or sexually transmitted diseases (STDs) [8] as suggested by abstinence-only advocates, and adolescents who received comprehensive sex or HIV education had a lower risk of pregnancy and HIV/STD infection than adolescents who received strict abstinence-only or no sex education at all in the U.S. and in other high-income countries [26, 30].

## Abstinence-Only Education: Public Opinion and Associated Costs

Despite the data showing that abstinence-only education is ineffective, it may be argued that the prescribed form of sex education represents the underlying social values of families and communities in each state, and changing to a more comprehensive sex education curriculum will meet with strong opposition. However, there is strong public support for comprehensive sex education [31]. Approximately 82% of a randomly selected nationally representative sample of U.S. adults aged 18 to 83 years (N=1096) supported comprehensive programs that teach students about both abstinence and other methods of preventing pregnancy and sexually transmitted diseases. In contrast, abstinence-only education programs, received the lowest levels of support (36%) and the highest level of opposition (about 50%).

In addition to the federal and state funds spent on abstinence-only (level 3) education, there are other costs associated with the outcomes of failed sex education and family planning. When deciding state policies on sex education, State legislators should consider these additional costs. For example, based on estimates by the *National Campaign To Prevent Teen and Unplanned Pregnancy* [32], teen child bearing (compared to first birth at 20 years or older) in the U.S. cost taxpayers (in direct and indirect costs) more than $9.1 billion in 2004.

· · ·

As pointed out by the Society for Adolescent Medicine, the abstinence-only approach (as stressed by level 3 state laws and policies and funded by the federal abstinence-only programs) is characterized by the withholding of information and is ethically flawed [7]. Abstinence-only programs tend to promote abstinence behavior through emotion, such as romantic notions of marriage, moralizing, fear of STDs, and by spreading scientifically incorrect information [7,20,33]. For example a Congressional committee report found evidence of major errors and distortions of public health information in common abstinence-only curricula [34]. As a result, these programs may actually be promoting irresponsible, high-risk teenage behavior by keeping teens uneducated with regard to reproductive knowledge and sound decision-making instead of giving them the tools to make educated decisions regarding their reproductive health [35]. The effect of presenting inadequate or incorrect information to teenagers regarding sex and pregnancy and STD protection is long-lasting as uneducated teens grow into uneducated adults: almost half of all pregnancies in the U.S. were unplanned in 2001 [36]. Of these three million unplanned pregnancies, ~1.4 million resulted in live births, ~1.3 million ended in abortion, and over 400,000 ended in a miscarriage [34,35] at a financial cost (direct medical costs only) of ~$5 billion in 2002 [37].

The U.S. teen pregnancy rate is substantially higher than seen in other developed countries (Table 1) despite similar cultural and socioeconomic patterns in teen pregnancy rates [38]. The difference is not due to the onset of sexual activity [1]. Instead, the main factor seems to be sex education, especially with regard to contraception and prevention of STDs [39]. Sex education in Europe is based on the WHO definition of sexuality as a lifelong process, aiming to create self-determined and responsible attitudes and behavior with regard to sexuality, contraception, relationships and life strategies and planning [40]. In general, there is greater and easier access to sexual health information and services for all people (including teens) in Europe, which is facilitated by a societal openness and comfort in dealing with sexuality [38], by pragmatic governmental policies [41,42] and less influence by special interest groups.

. . .

As parents, educators or policy makers it should be our goals that (1) teens can make educated reproductive and sexual health decisions, that (2) teen pregnancy and STD rates are reduced to the rates of other developed nations, and that (3) these trends are maintained through the teenage years into adulthood. One possibility for achieving these goals is a close alignment and integration of sex education with the National Science Standards for U.S. middle and high schools [43]. In addition, the *Precaution Adoption Process Model* advocated by the National Institutes of Health [44] offers a good basis for communication and discussions between scientists, educators, and sex education researchers, and could serve as a reference for measuring progress in sex education (in alignment with the new evidence-based Teen Pregnancy Prevention Initiative). In addition, it could be used as a communication tool between sex education teachers and their students. It should be our specific goal to move American teens from Stages 1 or 2 (unaware or unengaged in the issues of pregnancy and STD prevention) to Stages 3–7 (informed decision-making) by providing them with knowledge, understanding, and sound decision-making skills. For example, a recent study [45] attributes 52% of all unintended pregnancies (teenagers and adults) in the U.S. to non-use of contraception, 43% to inconsistent or incorrect use, and only 5% to method failure.

Our analysis adds to the overwhelming evidence indicating that abstinence-only education does not reduce teen pregnancy rates. Advocates for continued abstinence-only education need to ask themselves: If teens don't learn about human reproduction, including safe sexual health practices to prevent unintended pregnancies and STDs, and how to plan their reproductive adult life in school, then when should they learn it, and from whom?

## References

1 Darroch JE, Singh S, Frost JJ (2001) Differences in Teenage Pregnancy Rates Among Five Developed Countries: The Roles of Sexual Activity and Contraceptive Use. *Family Planning Perspectives* 33(5): 244–250. Available: http://www.guttmacher.org/pubs/journals/3324401.html. Accessed 2011, Jan 10.

2 The National Campaign to prevent teen and unplanned pregnancy. Teen birth rates: International Comparison 2006. Available: www.thenationalcampaign.org/.../TBR_InternationalComparison2006.pdf. Accessed 2011, Jan 10.

3 Canada: Statistics Canada (2005) Pregnancy outcomes by age group. Available: http://www40.statcan.gc.ca/l01/cst01/hlth65a-eng.htm. Accessed 2010, Nov 20.

4 UK Department of Education 2011 Under 18 and under 16 conception statistics (2011) Available: http://www.education.gov.uk/childrenandyoungpeople/healthandwellbeing/teenagepregnancy/a0064898/under-18-and-under-16-conception-statistics. Accessed 2011, Aug 3.

5 Advocates for Youth (2007) The History of Federal Abstinence-Only Funding. Available: http://www.advocatesforyouth.org/publications/429?task=view. Accessed 2011, Jun 19.

6 Trenholm C, Devaney B, Fortson K, Quay L, Wheeler J, et al. (2007) "Impacts of four Title V, Section 510 abstinence education programs" (Mathematica Policy Research). Available: http://aspe.hhs.gov/hsp/abstinence07/. Accessed 2010, May 8.

7 Santelli JS, Ott MA, Lyon M, Rogers J, Summers D (2006) bstinence-only education policies and

programs: A position paper of the Society for Adolescent Medicine. *Journal of Adolescent Health* 38: 83–87.

8   Kirby D (2007) Emerging Answers, Research Findings on Programs to Reduce Teen Pregnancy and Sexually Transmitted Diseases (National Campaign to Prevent Teen and Unplanned Pregnancy, Washington, DC).www.thenationalcampaign.org/EA2007/EA2007_full.pdf. Accessed 2010, Jun 18.

9   SIECUS: Senate Finance Committee Votes to Fund Comprehensive Sex Education; Restore Failed Title V Abstinence-Only-Until-Marriage Funding. Available: http://www.siecus.org/index.cfm?fuseaction=Feature.showFeature&featureid=1816&pageid=525&parentid=523. Accessed 2011, Jan 10.

10  Horn B (1983) Cultural beliefs and teenage pregnancy. *Nurse Practitioner* 8: 35–39.

11  Martin JA, Hamilton BE, Sutton PD, Ventura SJ, Menacker F, et al. (2007) Births: Final data for 2005. National Vital Statistics Reports 56 #6: Available: http://www.cdc.gov/nchs/data/nvsr/nvsr56/nvsr56_06.pdf. Accessed 2010, May 8.

12  Kost K, Henshaw S, Carlin L (2010) U.S. Teenage Pregnancies, Births and Abortions: National and State Trends and Trends by Race and Ethnicity (Guttmacher Institute). Available: http://www.guttmacher.org/pubs/USTPtrends.pdf. Accessed 2010, Jan 30.

13  Benson Gold R, Sonfield A, Richards CL, Frost JJ (2009) Next Steps for America's Family Planning Program: Leveraging the Potential of Medicaid and Title X in an Evolving Health Care System, New York: Guttmacher Institute. Available: www.guttmacher.org/pubs/NextSteps.pdf. Accessed 2011, Jan 10.

14  Yang Z, Gaydos LM (2010) Reasons for and Challenges of Recent Increases in Teen Birth Rates: A Study of Family Planning Service Policies and Demographic Changes at the State Level. *Journal of Adolescent Health* 46(6): 517–524.

15  Benson Gold R, Richards CL, Ranji UR, Salganicoff A (2005) Medicaid: A critical source of support for family planning in the United States. Kaiser Family Foundation and Guttmacher Institute. Available: http://www.kff.org/womenshealth/7064.cfm. Accessed 2011, Jan 10.

16  Zinth K (2007) Sex education laws in the states. State Note (Education Commission of the States, Denver CO). Available:http://www.ecs.org/html/educationIssues/ECSStateNotes_2007.asp. Accessed 2011, Aug 1.

17  Callahan J (2007) Abstinence education in state laws. Editorial Projects in Education Research Center.

Available: http://www.edweek.org/rc/articles/2007/06/08/sow0608.h26.html. Accessed 2009, Jan 10.

18  Advocates for Youth. Sex Education Resource Center. State profiles. Washington, D.C.: Advocates for Youth, Available: http://www.advocatesforyouth.org/index.php?option=com_content&task=view&id=766&Itemid=123). Accessed 2010, Sep 20.

19  SIECUS State Profiles Fiscal Year 2005. Available: http://www.siecus.org/index.cfm?fuseaction=page.viewPage&pageID=1061&nodeID=1. Accessed 2011, Feb 10.

20  The Council for Community and Economic Research. ACCRA Cost of living index (COLI). The Council for Community and Economic Research, C2ER. Available:http://www.coli.org/COLIAdjustedMHI.asp. Accessed 2010, May 10.

21  Census Bureau US (2006) R1901: Median Household Income for 2006. http://factfinder.census.gov/servlet/GRTTable?_bm=y&-geo_id=01000US&-_box_head_nbr=R1901&-ds_name=ACS_2006_EST_G00_&-redoLog=false&-format=US-30&-mt_name=ACS_2007_1YR_G00_R1901_US30&-CONTEXT=grt. Accessed 2010, May 10.

22  National Center of Education Statistics (2007) SAT data. Tables and Figures: Table 137. US Department of Education. Available: http://nces.ed.gov/programs/digest/d07/tables/dt07_137.asp. Accessed 2010, Jun 10.

23  SPSS for MacInstosh, version 17.0. Chicago, , IL: SPSS Inc).

24  Strayhorn JM, Strayhorn JC (2009) Religiosity and teen birth rate in the United States. Reproductive Health 6: 14. doi:10.1186/1742-4755-6-14.

25  Collins C, Alagiri P, Summers T (2002) "Abstinence Only versus Comprehensive Sex education. What are the arguments? What is the Evidence?" Policy Monograph Series. San Francisco, CA: AIDS Policy Research Center & Center for AIDS Prevention Studies, AIDS Research Institute, UC San Francisco.

26  Underhill K, Operario D, Montgomery P (2007) Systematic Review of Abstinence-Plus HIV Prevention Programs in High-Income Countries. *PLoS Medicine* 4: e275.

27  CDC Taskforce on Community Preventive Services (2009) Guide to Community Preventive Services. Prevention of HIV/AIDS, other STIs and Pregnancy: Group-based comprehensive risk reduction interventions for adolescents. Available: www.thecommunityguide.org/hiv/riskreduction.html. Accessed 2011, Jun 20.

28  Goodson P, Pruitt BE, Buhi E, Wilson KL, Rasberry CN, et al. (2004) "Abstinence education evaluation phase 5 technical report." College Station, TX: Texas A&M University, Department of Health and Kinesiology.

29  Jemmott JB, Jemmott LS, Fong GT (2010) Efficacy of a Theory-Based Abstinence-Only Intervention Over 24 Months. A Randomized Controlled Trial With Young Adolescents. *Arch Pediatr Adolesc Med* 164(2): 152–159.

30  Kohler PK, Manhart LE, Lafferty WE (2008) Abstinence-Only and Comprehensive Sex Education and the Initiation of Sexual Activity and Teen Pregnancy. *Journal of Adolescent Health* 42(2): 344–351.

31  Bleakley A, Hennessy M, Fishbein M (2006) Public opinion on sex education in U.S. schools. *Archives of Pediatrics and Adolescent Medicine* 160(11): 1151–1156.

32  Hoffmann SD (2006) By the Numbers—The Public Costs of Teen Childbearing. Washington, DC: National Campaign to Prevent Teen and Unplanned Pregnancy, Available: www.thenationalcampaign.org/resources/pdf/pubs/btn_full.pdf. Accessed 2010, May 10.

33  Kreinin T, Waggoner J (2001) Towards a sexually healthy America. Washington, D.C.: Advocates for Youth, Sexuality Information and Education Council of the United States. (SIECUS. Available: www.naccho.org/topics/HPDP/infectious/hiv/.../abstinenceonly.pdf. Accessed 2010, Jan 10.

34  US House of Representatives Committee on Government Reform—Minority Staff Special Investigations Division. The Content of Federally Funded Abstinence-Only Education Programs. Available: http://oversight.house.gov/index.php?option=com_content&view=article&id=2487&catid=44:legislation. Accessed 2010, Nov 1.

35  Kaye K, Suellentrop K, Sloup C (2009) The Fog Zone: How Misperceptions, Magical Thinking, and Ambivalence Put Young Adults at Risk for Unplanned Pregnancy, Washington, DC: The National Campaign to Prevent Teen and Unplanned Pregnancy, Available: www.thenationalcampaign.org/fogzone/pdf/fogzone.pdf. Accessed 2010, Jun 10.

36  Finer LB, Henshaw SK (2006) Disparities in Rates of Unintended Pregnancy in the United States, 1994 and 2001. *Perspectives on Sexual and Reproductive Health* 38(2): 90–96.

37  Trussel J (2007) The cost of unintended pregnancy in the United States. *Contraception* 75(3): 168–170.

38  Singh S, Darroch JE, Frost JJ (2001) Socioeconomic disadvantage and adolescent women's sexual and reproductive behavior: The case of five developed countries. *Fam Plann Perspect* 33: 251–258.

39  Schalet A (2004) Must we fear adolescent sexuality? *Med Gen Med* 6(4): 44. Available: http://www.ncbi.nlm.nih.gov/pmc/articles/PMC1480590/. Accessed 2010, Oct 1.

40  Advocates for Youth (2009) Adolescent Sexual Health in Europe and the U.S.— Why the Difference? 3rd edition: Sue Alford and Debra Hauser. Available: www.advocatesforyouth.org/storage/advfy/documents/fsest.pdf. Accessed 2011, Jan 30.

41  Bundeszentrale fuer gesundheitliche Aufklaerung (BZgA) (2006) BZgA/WHO Conference on Youth Sex Education in a Multicultural Europe, Cologne, Germany, 2006. Available: http://www.sexualaufklaerung.de/index.php?docid=1111. Accessed 2010, Jun 10.

42  Bundeszentrale fuer gesundheitliche Aufklaerung (BZgA) (2006) Country papers on youth sex education in Europe. BZgA/WHO Conference, Cologne, Germany, 2006. Available: http://www.sexualaufklaerung.de/index.php?docid=1039. Accessed 2010, Jun 10.

43  National Research Council (1996) "National Science Education Standards" (National Academy Press, Washington, DC). Available: http://www.nap.edu/openbook.php?record_id=4962. Accessed 2010, Oct 8.

44  National Institutes of Health (2005) Theory at a Glance, Application to Health Promotion and Health Behavior (Second Edition). U.S. Department of Health and Human Services, National Institutes of Health. Available: Available: http://www.cancer.gov/PDF/481f5d53-63df-41bc-bfaf-5aa48ee1da4d/TAAG3.pdf. Accessed 2009, Jan 10.

45  Frost JJ, Darroch E, Remez L (2008) Improving contraceptive use in the United States New York: Guttmacher Institute, No. 1. Available: www.guttmacher.org/pubs/2008/05/.../ImprovingContraceptiveUse.pdf. Accessed 2010, Oct 1.

**KATHRIN F. STANGER-HALL** is Associate Professor of Plant Biology at the University of Georgia.

**DAVID W. HALL** is Associate Professor of Genetics at the University of Georgia.

# EXPLORING THE ISSUE

## Is There Anything Good about Abstinence-Only Sex Education?

## Critical Thinking and Reflection

1. Do you think region of the country, culture, and religion should be factors in deciding what type of sex education should be taught in schools? Why or why not?
2. Do you think abstinence-only programs will help decrease or impede the teen pregnancy and sexually transmitted disease problem?
3. If you were the parent of an adolescent, what type of sex education program would you feel most comfortable with your child being exposed to, abstinence-only education or comprehensive? Why?

## Is There Common Ground?

Common ground in this debate is easily attained. We can accept the findings of both studies as they are not contradictory to each other. The Borawski et al. (2005) study simply showed that doing something, i.e., abstinence only, can be beneficial, particularly compared to doing nothing. The study had its limitations, namely in its nonrandom assignment to groups, but its strength is in the matched control comparison. However, these positive outcomes are not typical according to a review conducted by Kirby (2008), who found that abstinence-only programs did not delay initiation and only a handful of studies, of which this study was part of, registered positive effects.

Even though abstinence-only programs may not be the preferred curriculum if evidence-based results are valued, it provides a sex education. A study by Jeffries, Dodge, Bandiera, & Reece (2010) reported that based on a survey of teachers who taught abstinence-only and comprehensive courses, the odds of teaching comprehensive sex education topics increased as teachers taught more of the federal government's abstinence guidelines.

Finally, the Stanger-Hall and Hall (2011) study shows that there is a highly significant correlation that does not favor abstinence-only state policies, even after controlling for a host of other factors related to teen pregnancy and birth rates. The authors point out that an abstinence-only curriculum withholds information and can spread scientifically incorrect information. Thus, while abstinence-only is better than no formal sex education, there is a great deal of consensus formed that comprehensive sex education is the ideal way to educate American youth in the schools.

## References

W. L. Jeffries, B. Dodge, F. C. Bandiera, and M. Reece, "Beyond abstinence-only: Relationships between abstinence education and comprehensive topic instruction," *Sex Education* (vol. 10, 2010).

D. B. Kirby, "The impact of abstinence and comprehensive sex and STD/HIV education programs on adolescent sexual behavior," *Sexuality Research & Social Policy* (vol. 5, 2008).

T. E. Mueller, L. E. Gavin, and A. Kulkarni, "The association between sex education and youth's engagement in sexual intercourse, age at first intercourse, and birth control use at first sex," *Journal of Adolescent Health* (vol. 42, 2008).

## Additional Resources

S. Arsneault, "Values and virtue: The politics of abstinence-only sex education," *American Review of Public Administration* (vol. 31, 2001).

P. K. Kohler, L. E. Manhart, and W. E. Lafferty, "Abstinence-only and comprehensive sex education and the initiation of sexual activity and teen pregnancy," *Journal of Adolescent Health* (vol. 42, 2007).

# *Internet References . . .*

**CDC: Sexual Risk Behaviors: HIV, STD, & Teen Pregnancy Prevention**

www.cdc.gov/healthyyouth/sexualbehaviors

**Planned Parenthood on Abstinence-Only Programs**

www.plannedparenthoodaction.org/issues/sex -education/abstinence-only-programs

**SIECUS: Abstinence-Only-Until-Marriage Programs**

www.siecus.org/index.cfm?fuseaction=Page.view Page&pageId=523&parentID=477

**Selected, Edited, and with Issue Framing Material by:**
Esther S. Chang, *Soka University of America*

# ISSUE

# Does Reducing Class Size Improve Student Achievement?

**YES:** Jeremy D. Finn, Susan B. Gerber, and Jayne Boyd-Zaharias, from "Small Classes in the Early Grades, Academic Achievement, and Graduating from High School," *Journal of Educational Psychology* (2005)

**NO:** Eric A. Hanushek, from "The Tennessee Class Size Experiment (Project STAR)," Economic Policy Institute (2002)

---

## Learning Outcomes

**After reading this issue, you will be able to:**

- Design a field experiment that would successfully determine that small class sizes are promotive of student achievement.
- Draw out Project STAR's actual study design.
- Identify weaknesses in Project STAR's methods.
- Explain how class size has been defined in field experiments.

---

## ISSUE SUMMARY

**YES:** Jeremy Finn and colleagues analyzed longitudinal data based on a subsample of children who were tracked from kindergarten to high school because they participated in Project STAR. They found that 4 years of small classes in K-3 during Project STAR was associated with a significant increase in the likelihood of graduating from high school.

**NO:** Eric Hanushek contends that there is little evidence that supports any beneficial effects of classroom reduction, nor does it indicate what effects could be expected from reductions.

Among the most common visual metaphors for public education in the United States is the one-room schoolhouse. Children of all ages and abilities were taught as a single class in one room under one roof. In a largely agrarian society, the arrangement was one of necessity. Following the arrival of the Industrial Revolution, rapid urbanization, and population growth compulsory education emerged, in part, to supply an educated labor force. School enrollments increased and children were stratified into graded classrooms by chronological age. But was this out of necessity? As can be seen throughout history, the structure of schools and classrooms have changed in response to the changing needs of societies and their usefulness to the economy. Yet, in educational psychology, the questions tend to focus on the extent to which the structure of classrooms influences teaching quality and student achievement.

Concerns about class size in relation to student outcomes appear by as early as the 1920s, and for the next four decades informal and opinion-based reviews seemed to support the generally held view that class size was unrelated to academic outcomes. Then, a series of research method innovations led to quantitative reviews of the available research literature suggesting the opposite; student outcome and class size appeared to be positively related. At the same time, dramatic sociopolitical changes were occurring with respect to civil rights and equal access to education opportunities. Schools changed again with further diversity and increasing enrollment. Open education became a prominent perspective, with issues related to student grouping and classroom arrangement practices receiving further scrutiny.

The argument concerning class size continues unresolved in contemporary education but it is politically popular to reduce them, and states have experimented with making small classes policy with mixed results. As in many issues in education, there are many stakeholders with conflicting points of view that involve rhetoric as much as research, and values as much as facts. In general, proponents maintain on logical and empirical grounds that smaller class size makes sense because of increased opportunities for student–teacher interaction and therefore learning, reduced problem behavior because of a smaller student–teacher ratio, and overall improved classroom climate. Teachers may also be effective in smaller classes because they can assign more writing assignments and provide more feedback and help to students. In any case, teachers like having small classes because they think that it improves their teaching. According to Hattie (2005), teachers believed that there are fewer disciplinary problems in small classes and report that they cover more content in depth. Parents also tend to prefer their children to be in small classes.

Opponents, however, contend that the evidence supporting these claims are not straightforward and much more complex, that reducing class size is a costly venture, and that student outcomes are better served by increasing the quality, not the quantity of teachers. Among the many problems associated with reduced class size policies has been the lack of teacher supply and building space for more classes. The issue is never far from a political platform and in the late 1990s through the early part of the twenty-first century class size reduction moved through the legislative process and became a provision of the Elementary and Secondary Education Act (ESEA).

The debate between class size and student achievement is illustrated in the following selections. For the "Yes" side, Jeremy Finn and colleagues report on the enduring and positive impact of Project STAR in Tennessee. In 1985, Tennessee State Department of Education undertook a $12 million project to evaluate the effectiveness of class size on student achievement. It was the largest, randomized, controlled field test at the time and has been widely cited as empirical evidence for the positive achievement outcomes the researchers found. Finn and colleagues in the "Yes" side article review the key findings and test for any benefits of small class size on long-term outcomes since the 1985 cohort of kindergarteners have long graduated from high school. Readers interested in examining the study measures, such as the definition of class size, and the powers and pitfalls of its study design are recommended to refer to Ehrenberg, Brewer, Gamoran, and Willms (2001). Critics of Project STAR's findings also provide details on the methodological flaws, such as the "No" position's article by Hanushek (2002).

Critics of class size reduction contend that there should be tangible evidence of large benefits associated with reduced numbers. The standard should be high, the argument goes, because the financial costs underlying reducing class size are high. Limitations of Project STAR's study design have thus fueled a publication surge. The selection of project participants were found to be different than the average Tennessee student, random assignment was tainted as parents may have pressured school staff to allow their child to be in the "treatment," and high attrition rates have been voiced as major concerns. Even if there is some evidence that some students benefit, the majority of the evidence is mixed and policymakers should be reluctant to take up such measures in the absence of clear and compelling data. Hanushek summarizes these arguments in the "No" selection. (Introduction by L. Abbeduto and F. Symons.)

# YES

Jeremy D. Finn et al.

# Small Classes in the Early Grades, Academic Achievement, and Graduating from High School

The purpose of this investigation was to address three questions about the long-term effects of early school experiences: (a) Is participation in small classes in the early grades (K–3) related to the likelihood that a student will graduate from high school? (b) Is academic achievement in the early grades related to high school graduation? (c) If class size in K–3 is related to high school graduation, is the relationship attributable to the effect of small classes on students' academic achievement and the subsequent effect of achievement on graduation?

This study is unique in several ways. Although the relationship of class size with achievement and behavior has been documented elsewhere, no formal examination of early class sizes and graduating or dropping out 6 to 9 years later has been published previously. Also, the study was based on an extraordinary database—a large sample of students followed for 13 years,[1] with norm-referenced and criterion-referenced achievement tests administered annually and graduation/dropout information collected from official school and state records.

## Early Academic Achievement and Dropping Out

There is long-standing evidence that students' academic achievement in the early grades sets the stage for much that happens in the ensuing years (see Bloom, 1964). It is also clear that academic achievement throughout the school years is related to students' leaving school without graduating. In an overview of research, the National Research Council (2001) identified a history of poor academic performance as one of three leading schoolrelated characteristics associated with dropping out.[2]

Research on students in the middle grades (5–9) has found that when several antecedents are studied together, academic achievement makes a consistent, independent contribution to graduating from or dropping out of school (Battin-Pearson et al., 2000; Kaplan, Peck, & Kaplan, 1997). Other studies have traced the origins of dropping out to academic performance in the early grades. Barrington and Hendricks (1989) examined retrospectively the permanent records of students entering two high schools in 1981 and then followed the students through high school. Dropouts had been distinct in academic achievement and attendance from as early as third grade but did not differ on home-related characteristics. Significant differences between graduates and dropouts at the .01 level were found in third-grade scores on the Iowa Achievement Tests and, later on, the number of courses failed in Grades 7 to 12. Garnier, Stein, and Jacobs (1997) followed children in 194 families from birth through age 19. Their study used structural equation modeling to describe the relationships of family, individual, and school factors to school noncompletion. A composite of mathematics and reading grades and teacher ratings in Grade 1 had a significant influence on performance in Grade 6 ($r = -0.24$), which, in turn, had a direct impact on dropping out ($r = -0.30$).

Two prospective studies followed urban Grade 1 children through their high school years, examining a range of parent and student behaviors. Ensminger and Slusarcick (1992) studied a sample of 1,242 African American students in Chicago, Illinois, about one half of whom did not graduate from high school. Among the significant predictors of dropping out were poverty, sex (female students were more likely to graduate than were male students), family structure interactively with sex, aggressive behavior in first grade, and school performance from first grade onward. The odds of graduating for male students who received As or Bs in first grade were more than twice as high as the odds for male students who received Cs or Ds;

Finn, Jeremy D.; Gerber, Susan B.; Boyd-Zaharias, Jayne, "Small Classes in the Early Grades, Academic Achievement, and Graduating from High School," *Journal of Educational Psychology*, vol 92, no. 2, May 2005, pp. 214–223. No further reproduction or distribution is permitted without written permission from the American Psychological Association.

for female students, the odds for those who received As or Bs were more than 1.5 times as great. The authors noted, "Although later educational expectations and assessments of educational performance also mattered, they did not diminish the impact of earlier performance. Children's early school performance and adaptation may help establish patterns that remain relatively stable" (Ensminger & Slusarcick, 1992, p. 110).

As part of the Beginning School Study, Alexander et al. (1997) followed a sample of 790 African American and White students from the time they entered first grade in 1982 through spring of 1996. The study included an extensive set of measures including family stressors, parents' attitudes and practices, children's attitudes and school engagement, and school experiences—data gathered from school records, interviews, and parent and teacher questionnaires. A number of significant antecedents of dropping out were identified, including first-grade marks and first-grade test scores; zero-order correlations with dropping out were in the range from 0.30 to 0.38. This study also found measures of student engagement to be important to graduation, including absences from school and teachers' ratings of engagement in the classroom.

Several theoretical perspectives explain dropping out as the culmination of experiences that may begin in the early grades; the models and the data that support them have been given in Finn (1989); Newmann, Wehlage, and Lamborn (1992); Rumberger (2001); and Wehlage, Rutter, Smith, Lesko, and Fernandez (1989). All give a central role to student engagement (or disengagement) and depict dropping out as the final step in a gradual process of disengagement from school. Student behavior and academic achievement in the early grades are portrayed as important antecedents of engagement (or disengagement) in later years; studies are reviewed that have supported this premise. Student engagement (and disengagement) can also be impacted by school characteristics and practices. For example, the practice of retaining students in one or more grades—as early as first grade—is significantly related to the likelihood of leaving school without graduating (Goldschmidt & Wang, 1999; National Research Council, 2001; Randolph, Fraser, & Orthner, 2004).

The main theme of this research and theory is that dropping out of high school is not a spontaneous event but is often the culmination of a history of school experiences. These experiences may date back to the earliest grades in school or before. The present study examined the relationship of early academic achievement and early class sizes[3] with dropping out in a sample of students followed from kindergarten through high school.

# Small Classes in the Early Grades

It is now established that classes of fewer than 20 pupils in Grades K–3 have a positive effect on student achievement. Three phases of research, taken together, have confirmed this relationship. Prior to the 1980s, several hundred studies appeared on the topic; this work was summarized in a meta-analysis by Glass and Smith (1978) and a review by Robinson (1990). The studies showed that classes with fewer than 20 pupils were likely to benefit students' achievement in mathematics and reading. Furthermore, the benefits seemed to be greatest in the early grades and for students from low-income homes. Many of the studies were of poor quality, however, and none was a randomized experiment.

In 1985, the Tennessee State Department of Education undertook a large randomized experiment, Project STAR, to provide more definitive answers to the class-size question. In Project STAR, students entering kindergarten were assigned at random to a small class (13–17 students), a full-size class (22–26 students), or a full-size class with a full-time teacher aide within each participating school. The class size was maintained throughout the day, all year long. Students were kept in the same class arrangement for up to 4 years (Grade 3), with a new teacher assigned at random to the class each year. Norm-referenced and criterion-referenced achievement tests were administered in the spring of each school year. In all, almost 12,000 students participated in the STAR experiment in more than 300 classrooms in schools across the state. All students returned to full-size classes in Grade 4 when the experiment ended.[4]

Project STAR results have been published elsewhere (e.g., Achilles, 1999; Finn & Achilles, 1990; Finn, Gerber, Achilles, & Boyd-Zaharias, 2001; Word et al., 1990). Secondary analysts have confirmed the basic findings using a variety of statistical approaches (Goldstein & Blatchford, 1998; Hedges, Nye, & Konstantopoulos, 2000; Krueger, 1999). Four findings are central: First, small classes were associated with significantly higher academic performance in every school subject in every grade during the experiment (K–3) and in every subsequent grade studied (4–8). Second, many of the academic benefits of small classes were greater for students at risk, that is, minority students, students attending inner-city schools, or students from low-income homes. Krueger and Whitmore (2001) used the STAR data to estimate that the White–minority achievement gap would be reduced by 38.0% if all students attended small classes in K–3. Third, students in small classes were more engaged in learning than were students in larger classes (Evertson & Folger, 1989; Finn,

Fulton, Zaharias, & Nye, 1989; Finn, Pannozzo, & Achilles, 2004); this provides a partial explanation of the process by which small classes are academically beneficial. Fourth, no significant differences were found between full-size classes with teacher aides and classes without teacher aides on any test in any grade.

The third phase of research consisted of the district- and statelevel class-size-reduction (CSR) initiatives that followed Project STAR. Several initiatives have been accompanied by high-quality evaluations, for example, Tennessee's Project Challenge (Achilles, Nye, & Zaharias, 1995); Wisconsin's Student Achievement Guarantee in Education (SAGE) program (Molnar, Smith, & Zahorik, 1999; Molnar et al., 2000); the CSR initiative in Burke County, North Carolina (Achilles, Harman, & Egelson, 1995; Egelson, Harman, & Achilles, 1996); and the statewide program in California (CSR Research Consortium, 2000). The outcomes of these efforts were highly consistent with STAR findings. For example, SAGE demonstrated greater effects for students at risk, with effect sizes similar to those reported for STAR (Finn et al., 2001). The weak results found in California were also consistent: The California evaluation focused on Grade 3 students, and the (significant) effect sizes were similar to those obtained in STAR for Grade 3 students who spent just 1 or 2 years in small classes (Finn et al., 2001).

## Enduring Effects

The primary question of the present study is one of enduring impact: Does attending small classes in the early grades affect the likelihood of graduating from or dropping out of high school? Both empirical findings from Project STAR and theory about interventions that have lasting effects lead to the hypothesis that the answer is yes.

Although the class-size experiment ended in Grade 3,[5] researchers continued to collect achievement test data on the STAR participants through Grade 8. Attending small classes in K–3 was significantly related to academic achievement in all grades (4–8) in all subject areas (Finn et al., 2001; Hedges, Nye, & Konstantopoulos, 1999). The analysis by Finn et al. (2001) took advantage of the fact that some STAR participants attended small classes for 1, 2, or 3 years, as well as the full 4 years, and controlled for student race, socioeconomic status (SES), urbanicity, and movement into or out of STAR. Results showed that the carryover to Grades 4, 6, and 8 was strongest for students who entered small classes in kindergarten or Grade 1 and who remained in small classes for 3 or more years. Krueger and Whitmore (2001) also found that STAR students' likelihood of taking college admissions tests (ACTs/SATs)

in high school was increased by participation in small classes in K–3. The increase was especially large for African American students.

To be sure, not all early interventions have long-term effects. With some programs, short-term academic benefits decrease over time even if nonachievement outcomes persist (Barnett, 1992, 1995; Lazar & Darlington, 1982; White, 1986). Both the Perry Preschool Project and most Head Start programs have exhibited this pattern (Haskins, 1989; McKey et al., 1985). Evaluators have found that achievement benefits disappeared 3 years after students left those programs, but students continued to be less likely to be placed in special education, less likely to be retained in grade, and more likely to graduate than were their nonprogram counterparts (Berrueta-Clement, Barnett, Epstein, & Weikart, 1984; McKey et al., 1985).

In contrast, the Chicago Parent–Child Centers (CPC) program has documented continuing academic benefits (Reynolds, 1997; Reynolds, Temple, Robertson, & Mann, 2001). CPC was designed to aid low-income students, especially those not served by Head Start. The program has components for preschool through Grade 3, including high-quality educational, family, and health services. Individual children participate for up to 6 years. In an evaluation of continuing effects, CPC students outperformed nonprogram students in reading and mathematics in Grades 3 and 5 and in mathematics in Grade 8 (Reynolds, 1997). CPC students were also less likely to be retained in grade, were likely to complete more years of education, and were less likely to drop out compared with nonprogram students (Reynolds et al., 2001).

What features of educational programs are likely to produce long-term benefits? Barnett (1995) summarized the evaluations of 36 early childhood programs and concluded that to have any long-term effects at all, school-age services "must actually change the learning environment in some significant ways" (p. 43). Ramey and Ramey (1998) identified six principles of program efficacy for early interventions. The most important principles are (a) developmental timing, that is, start early and continue; (b) program intensity, that is, the importance of many hours per day, days per week, and weeks per year of the intervention; and (c) direct provision of learning experiences rather than relying on intermediary sources—parent training alone, for example, is not likely to have an enduring impact on school performance.

The Perry Preschool Project and most Head Start programs in the evaluation were of limited intensity (see Zigler & Styfco, 1994). Although beginning at an early age (3 or 4 years), the Perry program lasted for 2 years, and most Head Start programs lasted for 1 or, at most,

2 years. Neither program engaged pupils for the full day; the Perry intervention involved about 2.5 hours of school time daily, and typical Head Start programs involve about 3.5 hours of class time, 4 or 5 days per week. When students leave programs such as Perry, CPC, or Head Start, they often enter half-day kindergartens targeted to non-accelerated children. It comes as little surprise that early advantages are lost after several years in these settings.

Tennessee's Project STAR started early, beginning with full-day kindergartens. By Ramey and Ramey's (1998) definition, STAR was a high-intensity intervention. Children attended small classes for the entire school day every day of the school year, for up to 4 consecutive years. STAR impacted the learning setting directly and influenced all student–teacher interactions taking place in that setting. The present study asked if all-day, multiple-year participation in small classes in K–3 affected the likelihood of dropping out and if the effect on graduation rates was greater for lower than for higher SES students.

## Method

### The STAR Sample

The sample for this investigation consisted of a subset of students who participated in Tennessee's Project STAR. Although STAR ended when students reached Grade 4, researchers continued to follow as many students as possible through high school. The investigators for this study collected high school transcripts for 5,335 STAR students in 165 schools, 4,948 of whom could be classified clearly as graduating or dropping out and who had achievement data from K–3.[6] When the high school information was unclear, the individual's status was confirmed through Tennessee State Education Department records.

A comparison of the entire STAR sample with the sample for this investigation is shown in Table 1. In general, the two samples had similar compositions. The sample for the present investigation had a somewhat lower percentage of minority students, but the percentage of students receiving free lunch was close to that of the full STAR sample. All demographic characteristics in Table 1 were included in the statistical analysis.

### Measures

#### Student Data

In addition to demographic information and the number of years of participation in small or full-sized classes, we computed two achievement composites for each student,

*Table 1*

**Characteristics of Project STAR Samples**

| Characteristic | Full Project STAR sample | Transcript sample |
|---|---|---|
| Number of students | 11,601 | 4,948 |
| Percentage graduating | — | 77.5 |
| Percentage male | 52.9 | 49.8 |
| Percentage minority[a] | 36.9 | 31.6 |
| Percentage free lunch | 55.3 | 55.8 |
| Percentage in small classes[b] | 31.7 | 33.8 |

[a] Minority students were 98.7% African American. Nonminorities included White students and 0.4% Asian students.

[b] For 1 or more years.

one in mathematics and one in reading. Each composite was a principal component obtained from normreferenced and criterion-referenced achievement tests administered in K–3. The Stanford Achievement Tests (StATs; Psychological Corporation, 1983) were administered to all STAR participants in the spring of each year. In addition, beginning in Grade 1, the Basic Skills First (BSF) tests, a set of curriculum-referenced tests developed by the Tennessee State Education Department, were also administered to each student. These were constructed from well-specified lists of objectives in reading and mathematics at each grade level. The number of objectives covered by a test ranged from 8 to 12 depending on the subject and grade level; a student was considered to have mastered an objective if she or he answered 75.0% of the items correctly. Our analyses used the number of objectives passed on each year's reading and mathematics tests.

For the present study, the reading composite score was the first principal component of four StAT Total Reading scores (Grades K, 1, 2, and 3) and three BSF Reading scores (Grades 1, 2, and 3). Similarly, the mathematics composite was the first principal component of four StAT Total Mathematics scores and three BSF Mathematics scores.[7] These composites accounted for 72.7% of variation in the seven reading tests and 71.0% of variation in the mathematics tests. Each composite had high positive correlations with the seven respective tests, all in the range from 0.73 to 0.92. The second component of each set accounted for less than 10.0% of the variance in the seven tests and had correspondingly low eigenvalues; thus, they were not used in our analyses.[8]

Students who did not participate in STAR for all 4 years were missing 1 or more years of test scores. Scores were imputed for those individuals prior to the principal component analysis using the expectation maximization

(EM) method (Schafer, 1997) as implemented in the SPSS Missing Values program (Hill, 1997); this is superior to techniques such as listwise or pairwise deletion or mean substitution (Little & Rubin, 1990). The EM algorithm approach is especially useful in individual studies and for data sets for which the assumptions of data that are missing at random are not strictly met (Little & Schenker, 1995).

In the STAR data, as many as one third of the values were missing on some achievement variables (e.g., in kindergarten). However, we viewed the imputations as adequate for several reasons. For one, the correlations among the 14 reading and mathematics tests were consistently high, thus providing good information for estimating missing test scores, and the squared multiple correlations of each individual test with all others were uniformly strong.[9] Furthermore, a good set of covariates was added to the imputation process on which no values were missing, namely, school urbanicity and student sex, race/ethnicity, free-lunch participation, years in a small class, and years in Project STAR. These helped to adjust for the possibility that missing values were related to SES and student mobility.

After the imputation process, we conducted thorough checks on the reasonableness of the results; 45 students were eliminated who had test scores for just 1 year and imputed values well outside the distribution of observed scores on one or more tests.[10] Also, for each subject area, we correlated the first principal component computed using the original test scores (before the missing values analysis) with the first principal component computed using test scores after the missing values analysis. For both reading and mathematics, the correlation was above 0.99.

### School Data

Two characteristics of the high schools attended by participants in the study were also examined, total enrollment and school urbanicity. Schools were identified as suburban, rural, or inner city; we created two dummy variables to compare suburban schools with inner-city schools and rural schools with inner-city schools, respectively.

## Analyses

The basic model used in the analysis was a logistic regression model for multilevel data, using the HLM5 program (Raudenbush, Bryk, Cheong, & Congdon, 2000). The first level of data comprised students, nested within high schools (the second level). The dependent variable for all analyses was the dichotomous indicator of whether or not the student had graduated from high school.

The analyses involved a set of computer runs addressing each of the three research questions. The first set addressed the effect of small-class participation on the likelihood of graduation (Question 1), the second set examined the relationship between academic achievement and likelihood of graduation (Question 2), and the third set included both small-class participation and early academic achievement (Question 3). Each set consisted of three computer runs to (a) test main effects alone, (b) test interactions above and beyond main effects, and (c) estimate strength-of-effect measures from a reduced model containing those effects found to be important and significant.

The variables in each analysis are listed in the Appendix. For analyses of class size (Questions 1 and 3), each student was coded as having attended small classes for 0, 1, 2, 3, or 4 years during Grades K–3. Four contrasts were tested to compare students who attended small classes for 1, 2, 3, or 4 years, respectively, with students who attended full-size classes for all 4 years.

All analyses also included student sex, student race/ethnicity, student participation in the free-lunch program, school enrollment, and two school-urbanicity contrasts. Race/ethnicity, free-lunch participation, and school urbanicity provided some control for SES and student mobility into and out of STAR schools or between one STAR school and another. Interactions between small-class participation and eligibility for free lunch and between small-class participation and race/ethnicity were tested in the interaction model (Step b).

For the analysis of academic achievement (Question 2), the reading and mathematics composite scores were used in place of the class-size variable, and the interactions of mathematics and reading with free-lunch and race/ethnicity replaced the interactions of class size with free-lunch and race/ethnicity. All other effects were the same. A combined model with class-type contrasts and achievement test scores was tested to address Question 3. This model included the interactions of race and free-lunch participation with class type and with the achievement tests.

All terms in the hierarchical linear modeling (HLM) models were treated as fixed effects except for the intercepts at the student and school level, which were treated as random. All student-level characteristics were centered around the school means. Although the sample sizes were large, an alpha level of .05 was used for tests of significance. The outcomes, if they occurred, would take place 7 to 9 years after Grade 3 and may have been difficult to detect.

Strength-of-effect measures were obtained from final regression models after eliminating nonsignificant main effects and interactions; they were computed holding constant all predictor variables that remained in the model. Because the outcome measure was dichotomous (graduate or drop out), the strength-of-effect measures were odds ratios. This is the common strength-of-effect measure for logistic regression and has a direct relationship to the logistic regression coefficients (odds ratio = $e^\beta$ where $\beta$ is a specific regression weight; see Hosmer & Lemeshow, 2000).[11] The odds that a member of one group (e.g., White students) would graduate are the estimated percentage of Whites who graduate divided by the percentage who drop out. The odds for the second group (e.g., minority students) are the estimated percentage of minorities who graduate divided by the percentage who drop out. The odds ratio is the ratio of the two (White odds/minority odds). When the independent variable is numerical rather than categorical (e.g., mathematics achievement or reading achievement), the odds ratio is the change in odds associated with a one-standard-deviation change in the respective achievement scale.

## Results

The percentage of all students who graduated from high school was 77.5% in the transcript sample. Graduation rates were higher for female students (81.8%) than for male students (73.1%), higher for White students (81.8%) than for minority students (67.9%), and higher for students who did not receive free lunches (83.4%) than for students who received free lunches (72.8%).

Table 2 shows the graduation rates for students who attended full-size classes or small classes for 1 or more years. Graduation rates (and academic achievement) increased monotonically with additional years in a small class. Furthermore, the benefit of 3 or 4 years in a small class was greater for free-lunch students than for non-free-lunch students. Indeed, after 4 years in a small class, the graduation rate for free-lunch students was as great as or greater than that for non-free-lunch students. These effects were tested for significance in the regression analyses.

Table 2 also shows that the graduation rates of students in full-size classes were higher than those of students who spent 1 year in a small class. This may be due to the fact that students who attended small classes for 1 year were more transient than others; their families most likely moved into or out of the school's catchment area during the STAR years. In contrast, the full-size class group included the whole range of transience, including none. On average, the full-size group was less transient than groups who had 1 (or 2) years in small classes, and the lower graduation rate for 1 year in a small class may reflect transience as well as class size.[12]

The results for background demographic characteristics of schools and students (sex, race/ethnicity, free lunch) were consistent across the three sets of analyses, whether class size was the main independent variable (Question 1), academic achievement was the main independent variable (Question 2), or both (Question 3). (See Table 3.)

With respect to school characteristics, graduation rates were significantly higher in suburban and rural schools than they were in inner-city schools and were positively related to school size. With respect to student characteristics, female students had a significantly higher graduation rate than did male students (odds ratio = 1.67); in the sample, the difference was 8.7%. The difference between White and minority students was not statistically significant.[13] Free-lunch status was significantly related to likelihood of graduation. In the sample, the graduation rate for nonfree-lunch students was 10.6% higher than for free-lunch students; the odds ratio was 1.89.

*Table 2*

### Graduation Rates and Academic Achievement by Small-Class Participation

| | Percentage graduating | | | Mean achievement score[a] | |
|---|---|---|---|---|---|
| Years in a small class | Free lunch | No free lunch | All | Reading | Mathematics |
| 0 (full-size classes) | 70.2 | 83.7 | 76.3 | 49.58 | 49.59 |
| 1 | 68.1 | 78.3 | 72.8 | 49.33 | 49.32 |
| 2 | 70.1 | 85.2 | 76.8 | 50.00 | 50.01 |
| 3 | 79.6 | 82.8 | 81.1 | 50.75 | 50.72 |
| 4 | 88.2 | 87.0 | 87.8 | 52.83 | 52.81 |

[a] Principal component scores plus constant (50). Standard deviations are 5.19 (Reading) and 5.18 (Mathematics).

*Table 3*

## Logistic HLM Results

| Independent variable | Class-size analysis | Achievement analysis | Class size and achievement |
|---|---|---|---|
| School level | | | |
| Urbanicity | | | |
| Suburban–inner city | 0.54* | 0.56* | 0.56* |
| Rural–inner city | 0.60** | 0.73** | 0.73** |
| Enrollment | 0.001* | 0.001* | 0.001* |
| Student level | | | |
| Sex (M–F) | −0.58*** | −0.52*** | −0.51*** |
| Race (White–minority) | 0.05 | −0.24 | −0.22 |
| Free-lunch status (nonfree–free) | 0.66*** | 0.64*** | 0.65*** |
| Years in small class | | | |
| 1–none | −0.18 | | −0.21 |
| 2–none | 0.05 | | 0.00 |
| 3–none | 0.22 | | 0.07 |
| 4–none | 0.68*** | | 0.36* |
| Mathematics | | 0.06*** | 0.06*** |
| Reading | | 0.06*** | 0.05*** |
| Free-Lunch Status × Years in Small Class | | | |
| 1–none | −0.18 | | −0.20 |
| 2–none | 0.33 | | 0.22 |
| 3–none | −0.73* | | −0.83* |
| 4–none | −0.74* | | −0.87** |
| Free-Lunch Status × Mathematics | | 0.05 | 0.06* |
| Free-Lunch Status × Reading | | −0.03 | −0.02 |
| Race × Years in Small Class | | | |
| 1–none | −0.42 | | −0.25 |
| 2–none | 0.12 | | 0.22 |
| 3–none | 0.05 | | 0.06 |
| 4–none | 0.10 | | 0.13 |
| Race × Mathematics | | −0.04 | |
| Race × Reading | | 0.05 | |

*Note.* All results are regression coefficients. Main-effects results from main-effect analyses (Step a). Interaction results from analysis (Step b). HLM = hierarchical linear modeling; M = male; F = female. *$p < .05$. **$p < .01$. ***$p < .001$.

## Class Size

In the class-size analysis (Question 1), neither 1, 2, nor 3 years in a small class was significantly different from full-size classes. However, 4 years in a small class was associated with a significantly higher graduation rate than attending full-size classes. Table 4 displays odds ratios for this effect, obtained from the final reduced model. The overall odds ratios were greater than 1.00 for 2, 3, and 4 years in a small class, ranging from 1.08 to 1.21 to 1.80. These figures show that more years in small classes had an increasing effect on the odds of completing high school.

*Table 4*

**Odds Ratios for Small Class × Free-Lunch Participation**

| Years in small class | Free lunch | No free lunch | All |
|---|---|---|---|
| 1 | 0.89 | 0.75 | 0.83 |
| 2 | 0.94 | 1.27 | 1.08 |
| 3 | 1.67 | 0.80 | 1.21 |
| 4 | 2.49 | 1.19 | 1.80 |

*Note.* Odds ratios computed from final reduced models; each odds ratio is the comparison of small-class participation to full-size classes.

None of the interactions of class size with race/ethnicity were statistically significant; the effect of small classes on graduation rates did not impact White and minority students differently. In contrast, several of the interactions of class size with free lunch were statistically significant, specifically those for 3 and 4 years in a small class. To examine this interaction further, we conducted tests of significance separately for free-lunch and non-free-lunch groups (simple main effects). Overall, there was a significant effect for participation in small classes for students eligible for free lunches, $\chi^2(4) = 30.34$, $p < .001$, but not for students who were not eligible, $\chi^2(4) = 4.08$, $p > .05$.[14]

Odds ratios for small-class participation were also computed separately by free-lunch status (Table 4). The odds ratios for students not receiving free lunch do not differ significantly from 1.0. That is, for non-free-lunch students there were no significant differences in graduation rates based on participation in small classes. Among free-lunch students, however, the odds ratio for 3 years in a small class was large and significant, $t(2737) = 2.50$, $p < .02$, odds ratio = 1.67, and was larger still for 4 years, $t(2737) = 5.10$, $p < .001$, odds ratio = 2.49. The odds of graduating were 67.0% greater for students attending small classes for 3 years and almost 2.5 times greater for students attending small classes for 4 years. Table 2 shows that the difference between 3 years in a small class and attending full-size classes was associated with a 9.4% difference in graduation rates; for 4 years, it was 18.0%.

*Achievement Tests*

The analysis of achievement scores showed that both reading achievement and mathematics achievement in K–3 were significantly, positively related to the likelihood of graduating from high school. Odds ratios were computed for a 5-point interval on the achievement measures; this is approximately equal to one standard deviation on the achievement composites (5.09 and 5.03, respectively).[15]

The odds ratios were 1.32 for reading and 1.35 for mathematics. A one-standard-deviation increase in achievement in either area increased the odds of graduating from high school by about one third. The origins of high school graduation or dropping out can be seen clearly in academic achievement in the early grades.

When both class size and academic achievement were entered in a single HLM model (Question 3), the pattern of significant results was largely unchanged: Four years of small-class participation remained significantly superior to attending full-size classes, although at a lower level of significance, and the interaction of class size with free-lunch participation remained significant for the 3-year and 4-year contrasts. That is, after controlling for academic achievement in K–3, consistent small-class participation still increased the likelihood of graduating from high school. Stated another way, attending small classes for 3 or 4 years in the early grades had a positive effect on high school graduation above and beyond the effect on early academic performance.

## Conclusions

This investigation addressed three questions about the relationships of early school experiences with graduating from or dropping out of school. One was a basic question about students' academic achievement in the primary grades. On the basis of a large sample of White and minority students followed from kindergarten through Grade 12, the analysis revealed a strong relationship between mathematics and reading achievement in K–3 and graduation from high school. The nonsignificant interactions indicated that these relationships held for White and minority students and for higher and lower SES students alike. The results are consistent with the findings of other research (Alexander et al., 1997; Barrington & Hendricks, 1989; Ensminger & Slusarcick, 1992; Garnier et al., 1997) and support theories that explain dropping out or withdrawing from school as a process that may begin in the early grades. The findings point once again to the need to identify and address learning and behavior problems at the earliest time feasible.

The other questions concerned the impact of small classes in the early grades on the likelihood of graduating from high school. The hypothesis of a positive long-term impact was predicated on research showing long-term effects of small classes on other outcomes and theory about the types of programs likely to have lasting benefits (e.g., Barnett, 1995; Ramey & Ramey, 1998).

The results support this hypothesis. For all students combined, 4 years in a small class in K–3 were associated with a significant increase in the likelihood of graduating from high school; the odds of graduating after having attended small classes for 4 years were increased by about 80.0%. Furthermore, the impact of attending a small class was especially noteworthy for students from low-income homes. Three years or more of small classes affected the graduation rates of low-SES students, increasing the odds of graduating by about 67.0% for 3 years and more than doubling the odds for 4 years. These findings are consistent with research showing that the immediate academic impact of small classes is greater for minority students and low-SES students (Finn & Achilles, 1990; Krueger & Whitmore, 2001) and that the percentage of minority students taking college entrance exams is increased by small-class participation (Krueger & Whitmore, 2001).

It is possible that the small-class effect on graduation rates is more far reaching than found in this investigation. Student mobility in the study may have played a role: Students who spent 1 or 2 years in small classes probably had higher mobility, on average, than students with 4 years of full-size classes. Thus, mobility may have decreased the graduation rates of 1- and 2-year groups relative to the comparison group, contributing to nonsignificant findings. Viewed in isolation, graduation rates did increase monotonically with additional years in a small class for all students combined and for each subgroup.

Finally, the long-term effects of small classes on dropout rates were not explained entirely by improvements in academic performance, even if the improvements carried through later grades. Other dynamics must have been occurring as well, for example, effects on students' attitudes and motivation, students' pro- or antisocial behavior, or students' learning behavior. The latter two have been termed social and academic engagement in school and have been posed as possible explanations in a recent review article (Finn et al., 2004). Further research is needed to understand the processes that connect early school experiences with long-term benefits. Even studies that have demonstrated connections between them have not given adequate consideration to the processes that lead from one to the other.

This study contradicts the argument that 1 year in a small class is sufficient to realize all the noteworthy benefits (Hanushek, 1999). Three or 4 years of small classes are needed to affect graduation rates, and 3 or 4 years have been found necessary to sustain long-term achievement gains (Finn et al., 2001). Our findings also raise a question about attempts to analyze the costs of small classes (e.g., Brewer, Krop, Gill, & Reichardt, 1999). To our knowledge, no cost analysis has weighed the benefits of small-class participation, which include increased high school

graduation rates and increased aspirations to attend postsecondary school (Krueger & Whitmore, 2001).

This study did not ask whether the findings would be the same in locales with different populations or with particular programs to increase graduation rates. The results are in agreement with other research on academic achievement and dropping out, and the short-term impact of small classes on academic achievement has been found in other large-scale programs. However, the connections between early educational interventions—small classes among them—and long-range outcomes remain to be examined in other settings.

Furthermore, the theory about long-term impact and these findings raise the question, How can the magnitude of the effect be increased still further, perhaps by continuing small classes into later grades or by combining small classes with other educational interventions? Little if any research has examined the joint impact of reduced-size classes with programs such as an intensive reading curriculum in kindergarten (see Hanson & Farrell, 1995), full-day kindergartens, intensive preschool programs, or others. It seems that the potential for improved educational outcomes, especially among low-SES students, is considerable.

# References

Achilles, C. M. (1999). *Let's put kids first, finally: Getting class size right*. Thousand Oaks, CA: Corwin Press.

Achilles, C. M., Harman, P., & Egelson, P. (1995). Using research results on class size to improve pupil achievement outcomes. *Research in the Schools, 2*(2), 2–30.

Achilles, C. M., Nye, B. A., & Zaharias, J. B. (1995, April). *Policy use of research results: Tennessee's Project Challenge*. Paper presented at the annual meeting of the American Educational Research Association, San Francisco, CA.

Alexander, K. A., Entwisle, D. R., & Horsey, C. S. (1997, April). From first grade forward: Early foundations of high school dropout. *Sociology of Education, 70*(2), 87–107.

Barnett, W. S. (1992). Benefits of compensatory preschool education. *Journal of Human Resources, 27*, 279–312.

Barnett, W. S. (1995, Winter). Long-term effects of early childhood programs on cognitive and school outcomes. *Future of Children, 5*(3), 25–50.

Barrington, B. L., & Hendricks, B. (1989). Differentiating characteristics of high school graduates, dropouts, and nongraduates. *Journal of Educational Research, 82*, 309–319.

Battin-Pearson, S., Newcomb, M. D., Abbott, R. D., Hill, K. G., Catalano, R. F., & Hawkins, J. D. (2000). Predictors of early high school dropout: A test of five theories. *Journal of Educational Psychology, 92*, 568–582.

Berrueta-Clement, J. R., Barnett, W. S., Epstein, A. S., & Weikart, D. P. (1984). *Changed lives: The effects of the Perry Preschool Program on youths through age 19.* Ypsilanti, MI: High Scope Press.

Bloom, B. S. (1964). *Stability and change in human characteristics.* New York: Wiley.

Brewer, D., Krop, C., Gill, B. P., & Reichardt, R. (1999). Estimating the cost of national class size reductions under different policy alternatives. *Educational Evaluation and Policy Analysis, 21*, 179–192.

CSR Research Consortium. (2000). *Class size reduction in California: The 1998–99 evaluation findings.* Sacramento, CA: California Department of Education.

Egelson, P., Harman, P., & Achilles, C. M. (1996). *Does class size make a difference? Recent findings from state and district initiatives.* Greensboro, NC: Southeast Regional Vision for Education (SERVE).

Ensminger, M. E., & Slusarcick, A. L. (1992, April). Paths to high school graduation or dropout: A longitudinal study of a first-grade cohort. *Sociology of Education, 65*(2), 95–113.

Evertson, C. M., & Folger, J. K., (1989, March). *Small class, large class: What do teachers do differently?* Paper presented at the annual meeting of the American Educational Research Association, San Francisco, CA.

Finn, J. D. (1989). Withdrawing from school. *Review of Educational Research, 59*, 117–142.

Finn, J. D., & Achilles, C. M. (1990). Answers and questions about class size: A statewide experiment. *American Educational Research Journal, 27*, 557–577.

Finn, J., D., Fulton, B. D., Zaharias, J., & Nye, B. A. (1989). Carry-over effects of small classes. *Peabody Journal of Education, 67*, 75–84.

Finn, J. D., Gerber, S. B., Achilles, C. M., & Boyd-Zaharias, J. (2001). The enduring effects of small classes. *Teachers College Record, 103*, 45–83.

Finn, J. D., Pannozzo, G. M., & Achilles, C. M. (2004). The "why's" of class size: Student behavior in small classes. *Review of Educational Research, 73*, 321–368.

Garnier, H. E., Stein, J. A., & Jacobs, J. K. (1997). The process of dropping out of high school: A 19-year perspective. *American Educational Research Journal, 34*, 395–419.

Glass, G. V., & Smith, M. L. (1978). *Meta-analysis of research of the relationship of class size and achievement.* San Francisco: Far West Laboratory for Educational Research and Development.

Goldschmidt, P., & Wang, J. (1999). When can schools affect dropout behavior? A longitudinal multilevel analysis. *American Educational Research Journal, 36*, 715–738.

Goldstein, H., & Blatchford, P. (1998). Class size and educational achievement: A review of methodology with particular reference to study design. *British Educational Research Journal, 24*, 255–268.

Hanson, R. A., & Farrell, D. (1995). The long-term effects on high school seniors of learning to read in kindergarten. *Reading Research Quarterly, 30*, 908–933.

Hanushek, E. A. (1998). *The evidence on class size.* Rochester, NY: University of Rochester, W. Allen Wallis Institute of Political Economy.

Hanushek, E. A. (1999). Some findings from an independent investigation of the Tennessee STAR experiment and from other investigations of class size effects. *Educational Evaluation and Policy Analysis, 21*, 143–164.

Haskins, R. (1989). Beyond metaphor: The efficacy of early childhood education. *American Psychologist, 44*, 274–282.

Hedges, L. V., Nye, B., & Konstantopoulos, S. (1999). The long-term effects of small classes: A five-year follow-up of the Tennessee class size experiment. *Educational Evaluation and Policy Analysis, 21*, 127–142.

Hedges, L. V., Nye, B., & Konstantopoulos, S. (2000). The effects of small classes on academic achievement: The results of the Tennessee class size experiment. *American Educational Research Journal, 37*, 123–151.

Hill, M. (1997). *SPSS missing value analysis 7.5.* Chicago: SPSS.

Hosmer, D. W., & Lemeshow, S. (2000). *Applied logistic regression*. New York: Wiley.

Kaplan, D. S., Peck, B. M., & Kaplan, H. B. (1997). Decomposing the academic failure– dropout relationship: A longitudinal analysis. *Journal of Educational Research, 90*, 331–343.

Krueger, A. B. (1999). Experimental estimates of education production functions. *Quarterly Journal of Economics, 114*, 497–532.

Krueger, A. B., & Whitmore, D. (2001, March). *Would smaller classes help close the Black–White achievement gap?* (Princeton University Industrial Relations Section Working Paper No. 451). Retrieved January 18, 2005, from www.irs.princeton.edu/pubs/frame.html

Lazar, I., & Darlington, R. (1982). *Lasting effects of early education: A report from the Consortium for Longitudinal Studies*. Chicago: University of Chicago Press.

Lewit, E. M., & Baker, L. S. (1997, Summer/Fall). Class size. *Future of Children, 7*(2), 112–121.

Little, R. J. A., & Rubin, D. B. (1990). The analysis of social science data with missing values. In J. Fox & J. S. Long (Eds.), *Modern methods of data analysis* (pp. 374–409). Newbury Park, CA: Sage.

Little, R. J. A., & Schenker, N. (1995). Missing data. In G. Arminger, C. C. Clogg, & M. E. Sobel (Eds.), *Handbook of statistical modeling for the social and behavioral sciences* (pp. 39–75). New York: Plenum Press.

McKey, R. H., Condelli, L., Granson, H., Barnett, B., McConkey, C., & Plantz, M. (1985) *The impact of Head Start on children, families, and communities*. Washington, DC: Head Start Bureau, U. S. Department of Health and Human Services.

Miles, K. H. (1995). Freeing resources for improving schools: A case of teacher allocation in Boston public schools. *Educational Evaluation and Policy Analysis, 17*, 476–493.

Molnar, A., Smith, O., & Zahorik, J. (1999). *1998–99 evaluation results of the Student Achievement Guarantee in Education (SAGE) program*. Milwaukee: University of Wisconsin School of Education.

Molnar, A., Smith, O., Zahorik, J., Ehrle, K., Halbach, A., & Kuehl, B. (2000). *1999–2000 evaluation of the Student Achievement Guarantee in Education (SAGE) program*. Milwaukee: University of Wisconsin School of Education.

National Research Council. (2001). *Understanding dropouts: Statistics, strategies, and high-stakes testing*. Washington, DC: National Academy Press.

Newmann, F. M., Wehlage, G. G., & Lamborn, S. D. (1992). The significance and sources of student engagement. In F. M. Newmann (Ed.), *Student engagement and achievement in American secondary schools* (pp. 11–39). New York: Teachers College Press.

Psychological Corporation. (1983). *Stanford Achievement Tests* (7th ed.). San Diego, CA: Author.

Ramey, C. T., & Ramey, S. (1998). Early intervention and early experience. *American Psychologist, 53*, 109–120.

Randolph, K. A., Fraser, M. W., & Orthner, D. K. (2004). Educational resilience among youth at risk. *Substance Use and Misuse, 39*, 747–767.

Raudenbush, S. W., Bryk, A. S., Cheong, Y. F., & Congdon, R. T. (2000). *HLM5: Hierarchical linear and nonlinear modeling*. Lincolnwood, IL: Scientific Software International.

Reynolds, A. J. (1997). *The Chicago child–parent centers: A longitudinal study of extended early childhood intervention* (Discussion Paper No. 1126–97). Madison, WI: Institute for Research on Poverty.

Reynolds, A. J., Temple, J. A., Robertson, D. L., & Mann, E. A. (2001). Long-term effects of an early childhood intervention on educational achievement and juvenile arrest. *JAMA, 285*, 2339–2346.

Robinson, G. E. (1990). Synthesis of research on effects of class size. *Educational Leadership, 47*(7), 80–90.

Rumberger, R. W. (2001, January). *Why students drop out of school and what can be done*. Paper presented at the "Dropouts in America: How Severe Is the Problem? What Do We Know About Intervention and Prevention?" conference, Cambridge, MA.

Schafer, J. L. (1997). *Analysis of incomplete multivariate data*. London: Chapman & Hall.

Wehlage, G. G., Rutter, R. A., Smith, G. A., Lesko, N., & Fernandez, R. R. (1989). *Reducing the risk: Schools as communities of support*. London: Falmer Press.

White, K. R. (1986). Efficacy of early intervention. *Journal of Special Education, 19*, 400–416.

Word, E., Johnson, J., Bain, H. P., Fulton, D. B., Boyd-Zaharias, J., Lintz, M. N., et al. (1990). *Student/teacher achievement ratio (STAR): Tennessee's K–3 class-size study.* Nashville, TN: Tennessee State Department of Education.

Zigler, E., & Styfco, S. J. (1994). Is the Perry Preschool better than Head Start? Yes and no. *Early Childhood Research Quarterly, 9,* 269–287.

## Notes

1 Two other studies of early academic achievement and dropping out are cited in the introductory section of this article, one conducted in Chicago, Illinois (Ensminger & Slusarcick, 1992), and one in Baltimore, Maryland (Alexander, Entwisle, & Horsey, 1997). The sample in the present study was a larger and more diverse sample than in either of those studies.

2 The other pervasive correlates of high school graduation/dropping out named were educational engagement and academic delay.

3 Class size is the number of students who are regularly in a classroom with a teacher and for whom that teacher is responsible. Other writing about pupil–teacher ratios for schools, districts, or states (e.g., Hanushek, 1998) does not pertain to the educational effects of small or large classes. Actual class sizes may vary dramatically within a school or district. At times, even in districts with low pupil–teacher ratios, students may spend most of their school time in large classes (Lewit & Baker, 1997; Miles, 1995).

4 Achievement scores, behavior ratings, and other data continued to be collected through high school.

5 All students returned to full-size classes in Grade 4.

6 Graduation information was available for 4,993 students, but 45 were eliminated from the analysis due to inadequate K–3 achievement data. Of the 342 students who could not be classified definitively as graduates or dropouts, 7 were listed as deceased.

7 Components were obtained from the correlation matrices.

8 We also considered using Grade 3 tests alone, considering them to be a composite that reflected 4 years of learning. The correlations between Grade 3 achievement and the principal component scores were 0.91 in both subjects.

9 In reading, the correlations ranged from 0.65 to 0.85 for StAT tests and from 0.46 to 0.55 for BSF tests. In mathematics, the correlations ranged from 0.80 to 0.86 for StAT tests and from 0.44 to 0.57 for BSF tests.

10 Because these students never entered any subsequent analyses, they are not included in the subsample described in Table 1.

11 This is analogous to the way that effect-size measures are directly related to regression coefficients in ordinary least squares by dividing $\beta$ by the standard deviation of the outcome variable.

12 A rough approximation to transience rates was used to confirm this. School identifiers were not available for students when they were not attending a STAR school. However, we computed the number of years each student participated in Project STAR out of 4 possible (or 3 possible if the student began in Grade 1). A transience indicator was defined as 0 if the student participated in STAR for all 4 years (or 3 years if the student began in Grade 1) and 1 otherwise. Of students in full-size classes, 52.0% had made one or more school moves according to this indicator. Of 537 students in small classes for 1 year, 74.9% had made one or more school moves—clearly more than students in full-size classes. For students in small classes for 2, 3, and 4 years, the transience percentages were 70.5%, 20.7%, and 0.0%, respectively. Also, the actual differences in dropout rates were tested for significance in the regressions, both in the total sample and in each free-lunch group (see the *Analyses* section). None of the differences between 0 years in a small class and 1 or 2 years in a small class were statistically significant.

13 As follow-up, we tested the significance of racial/ethnic differences in a model that did not include free-lunch status. The relationship was still nonsignificant.

14 Tests were conducted using a Wald test of overall differences among the percentages.

15 Also, if thirds of the scores distributions are viewed as achievement levels, the 5-point interval is the number of points required to move from the middle of one achievement level to the bottom of the next higher level.

**JEREMY D. FINN** is Distinguished Professor and Chair of the Department of Counseling, School, and Educational Psychology at the State University of New York, Buffalo. Susan B. Gerber was adjunct assistant professor in the Graduate School of Education at State University of New York, Buffalo. Jayne Boyd-Zaharias was executive director of HEROS, Inc. at the time of publication.

Eric A. Hanushek

# The Tennessee Class Size Experiment
# (Project STAR)

A different form of evidence—that from random assignment experiments—has recently been widely circulated in the debates about class size reduction. Following the example of medicine, one large-scale experimental investigation in Tennessee in the mid-1980s (Project STAR) pursued the effectiveness of class size reductions. Random-assignment experiments in principle have considerable appeal. The underlying idea is that we can obtain valid evidence about the impact of a given well-defined treatment by randomly assigning subjects to treatment and control groups. This random assignment eliminates the possible contaminating effects of other factors and permits conceptually cleaner analysis of the outcomes of interest across these groups. The validity of any particular experiment nonetheless depends crucially on the implementation of the experiment. On this score, considerable uncertainty about the STAR results is introduced. But, ignoring any issues of uncertainty, the estimated impacts of large class size reductions are small and have limited application to the current policy proposals.

Project STAR was designed to begin with kindergarten students and to follow them for four years. Three treatments were initially included: small classes (13–17 students); regular classes (22–25 students); and regular classes (22–25 students) with a teacher's aide. Schools were solicited for participation, with the stipulation that any school participating must be large enough to have at least one class in each treatment group. The initial sample included 6,324 kindergarten students. These were split between 1,900 in small classes and 4,424 in regular classes. (After the first year, the two separate regular class treatments were effectively combined, because there were no perceived differences in student performance). The initial sample included 79 schools, although this subsequently fell to 75. The initial 326 teachers grew slightly to reflect the increased sample size in subsequent grades, although of course most teachers are new to the experiment at each new grade.

The results of the Project STAR experiment have been widely publicized. The simplest summary is that students in small classes performed significantly better than those in regular classes or regular classes with aides in kindergarten and that the achievement advantage of small classes remained constant through the third grade.

This summary reflects the typical reporting, focusing on the differences in performance at each grade and concluding that small classes are better than large. But it ignores the fact that one would expect the differences in performance to become wider through the grades because they continue to get more resources (smaller classes) and these resources should, according to the hypothesis, keep producing a growing advantage. Figure 1 shows the difference in reading performance in small classes that was observed across grades in Project STAR. (The results for math performance are virtually identical in size and pattern). It also shows how the observed outcomes diverge from what would be expected if the impact in kindergarten were also obtained in later grades. As Krueger (1999) demonstrates, the small class advantage is almost exclusively obtained in the first year of being in a small class—suggesting that the advantages of small classes are not general across all grades.

The gains in performance from the experimental reduction in class size were relatively small (less than 0.2 standard deviations of test performance), especially in the context of the magnitude of the class size reduction (around eight students per class). Thus, even if Project STAR is taken at face value, it has relatively limited policy implications.

While the experimental approach has great appeal, the actual implementation in the case of Project STAR introduces uncertainty into these estimates. The uncertainty arises fundamentally from questions about the quality of the randomization in the experiment. In each year of the experiment, there was sizable attrition from the prior year's treatment groups, and these students

*Figure 1*

**Expected vs. Actual STAR Results, Stanford Achievement Test, Reading**

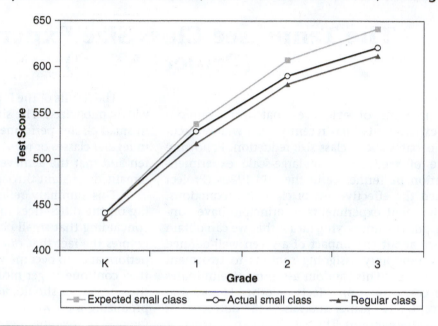

were replaced with new students. Of the initial experimental group starting in kindergarten, 48% remained in the experiment for the entire four years. No information, such as pretest scores, is available to assess the quality of student randomization for the initial experimental sample or for the subsequent additions to it. (The data in Figure 1 are equally consistent with either a true small class advantage or an initial assignment of somewhat better students to small kindergartens). It is also impossible to assess adequately the impact of differential attrition of experimental subjects, particularly of those in larger classes disappointed over their placement. Substantial, non-random test taking occurs over the years of the experiment.

But, most important, the STAR results depend fundamentally on the choice of teachers. One measure of the importance of teachers relative to class size effects is that the average kindergarten achievement in small classes exceeds that in regular classes and regular-with-aide classes in only 40 of the 79 schools. While the teachers were to be randomly assigned to treatment groups, there is little description of how this was done. Nor is it easy to provide any reliable analysis of the teacher assignment, because only a few descriptors of teachers are found in the data and because there is little reason to believe that

they adequately measure differences in teacher quality. The teacher data include race, gender, teaching experience, highest degree, and position on the Tennessee career ladder. While there is no information about the effect of career ladder position on student performance, none of the other measures has been found to be a reliable indicator of quality. Moreover, teachers all knew they were participating in an experiment that could potentially affect the future resources available from the state. The schools themselves were self-selected and are clearly not random. Small schools were excluded from the experiment, and all participating schools were willing to provide their own partial funding to cover the full costs. (This school selection issue is important, because the STAR experiment heavily oversampled urban and minority schools where the achievement response to the program is thought to be largest). The net result of each of these effects is difficult to ascertain, but there is prima facie evidence that the total impact is to overstate the impact of reduced class size.

The STAR experiment is very important from a methodological perspective. . . . More random-assignment experimentation is desperately needed in schools. But the evidence from this specific experiment should be interpreted with caution. Mosteller (1995) makes a clear distinction between supporting the methodology of random assignment experimentation and ratifying the results from the single major experiment that currently exists.

Moreover, the evidence as it stands speaks just to the possible small effects of major and costly reductions in class size at kindergarten or first grade. It provides no evidence about beneficial effects at later grades. Nor does it indicate what effects could be expected from reductions

of a smaller magnitude than the one-third reductions in Project STAR.

---

ERIC A. HANUSHEK is the Paul and Jean Hanna Senior Fellow at the Hoover Institution at Stanford University. He has authored numerous, highly cited studies on the effects of class size reduction, high stakes accountability, the assessment of teacher quality, and other education related topics.

# EXPLORING THE ISSUE

## Does Reducing Class Size Improve Student Achievement?

### Critical Thinking and Reflection

1. Are there any disadvantages to small class size?
2. Can there ever be a perfect field study in education?
3. In addition to the factors mentioned in the articles, could there be cultural factors that make small class sizes more conducive to student achievement in the United States?

### Is There Common Ground?

In the first selection Finn and colleagues demonstrated the positive and enduring effects of class size reduction based on a well-conceived and controlled longitudinal study with multiple levels modeled simultaneously. These results provide an increasingly strong platform from which to make several conclusions with respect to class size and educational outcomes. Most notably, they underscore that early grade experience matters with greater gains associated with longer exposure to smaller classes. And, although all types of students can benefit from smaller class sizes, the greatest gains were reported for historically disadvantaged groups of schoolchildren. In the second selection, Erik Hanushek argues that the evidence is less than compelling that small class size is essential for positive academic outcomes and further, that the cost associated with reducing class size may be too high a price pay given any gains. He pointed out that one would expect smaller classrooms to produce bigger effects throughout the experiment because they get more resources throughout the study, but the magnitude of effects was very small compared to normal class sizes and much smaller than expected (see Figure 1). Hanushek's article was written prior to Finn et al.'s study of enduring effects, which estimated that the odds of graduating after small classes for 4 years were increased by 80 percent, but it is doubtful that he would be convinced to change his position on the issue. The reason may be that there is high attrition and the longitudinal samples tracked throughout high school were very different despite Finn et al.'s demonstration that the sample did not differ that

much (see their Table 1). In particular, participants may have exhibited the Hawthorne effect because they were being tracked by researchers.

One point that must be made in order to seek common ground is that there will always be a problem with any field study, no matter how large and no matter how generously funded. Human behavior can't be observed the way that we used to observe animals in cages for research after doing something to them. Given what we have, however, proponents note that research studies addressing the issue of class size and student achievement may be among the most abundant in all of educational research (see references to such research in Finn et al.) and yet there remain no coordinated policies based on consensual agreement. They summarize several likely causes for this, including different perspectives of what is at issue, confusion concerning research results and their interpretation, poorly disseminated findings, political agendas, and practical realities confronting local decision making to name a few. Perhaps the research agenda needs to continue forward with an even more refined eye toward exploring in greater detail the circumstances under which class size reduction is and is not beneficial and for which students. The problem may be that the cost of conducting a better class size reduction experiment in education will most likely prevent a future one given the growing consensus in educational psychology that class size is a positive intervention despite the expected methodological problems in conducting experiments in the real world with real people in real time. Perhaps it's time that the "No" side has to ask themselves a different question: is reducing the achievement gap through class size reduction worth it?

## Reference

R. G. Ehrenberg, D. J. Brewer, A. Gamoran, and J. D. Willms, "Class size and student achievement," *Psychological Science in the Public Interest* (2001).

## Additional Resources

J. D. Finn, G. M. Pannozzo, and C. M. Achilles, "The 'why's' of class size: Student behavior in small classes," *Review of Educational Research* (vol. 73, no. 3, 2003).

A. B. Krueger, "Understanding the magnitude and effect of class size on student achievement," *The Class Size Debate* (2002).

W. L. Sanders, S. P. Wright, and S. P. Horn, "Teacher and classroom context effects on student achievement: Implications for teacher evaluation," *Journal of Personnel Evaluation in Education* (vol. 11, no. 1, 1997).

R. E. Slavin, "Class size and student achievement: Small effects of small classes," *Educational Psychologist* (vol. 24, no. 1, 1989).

# *Internet References . . .*

**Center for Public Education: Class Size and Student Achievement**

www.centerforpubliceducation.org/Main-Menu /Organizing-a-school/Class-size-and-student -achievement-At-a-glance

**Class Size Reduction Research**

www.classsizematters.org/research-and-links

**Class Size: What Research Says and What It Means for State Policy**

www.brookings.edu/research/papers/2011/05 /11-class-size-whitehurst-chingos

Selected, Edited, and with Issue Framing Material by:
Esther S. Chang *Soka University of America*

# ISSUE

# Are School-Wide Anti-Bullying Programs Effective?

**YES: Antti Kärnä, et al.,** from "Going to Scale: A Nonrandomized Nationwide Trial of the KiVa Antibullying Program for Grades 1–9," *Journal of Consulting and Clinical Psychology* (2011)

**NO: Sabina Low and Mark Van Ryzin,** from "The Moderating Effects of School Climate on Bullying Prevention Efforts," *School Psychology Quarterly* (2014)

---

| Learning Outcomes |
| --- |
| After reading this issue, you will be able to: |

- Define bullying and victimization.
- Identify all the potential "actors" involved in instance of bullying.
- Discuss the strategies of anti-bullying prevention programs like KiVA (Finland).
- Discuss the strategies of Steps to Respect (STR; USA).

## ISSUE SUMMARY

**YES:** Antti Kärnä, with support from a team of experts and colleagues, reported upon the positive effects of a nationwide school-based anti-bullying program in Finland.

**NO:** Sabina Low and Mark Van Ryzin propose and provide evidence that a positive psychosocial school climate plays a foundational role in the effective prevention of bullying.

Eric Harris, one of the shooters in the 1999 Columbine High School shootings, was known to have written the following in his journal:

> "Everyone is always making fun of me because of how I look, how fucking weak I am and shit, well I will get you all back: ultimate fucking revenge here. You people could have shown more respect, treated me better, asked for my knowledge or guidance more, treated me more like senior, and maybe I wouldn't have been as ready to tear your fucking heads off" and "Whatever I do people make fun of me, and sometimes directly to my face. I'll get revenge soon enough. fuckers shouldn't have ripped on me so much huh!"

Eric Harris was most likely suffering from a severe mental illness and personality disorder but the fact that he came to school and killed students forced schools to think more seriously about security on campus as well as its responsibility in creating a positive social and emotional climate on campus. Despite school's focus on academic achievement, this type of event reminds us all that schools harbor some responsibility for the social and emotional environment of its students simply because they host massive amounts of similarly aged children and youth for much of the day.

More recently, in 2013, when 12-year-old Rebecca Sedwick committed suicide by jumping to her death, the messages on social media she received from two other girls of similar age were the focus of much media attention and personally shocked many. The content and quality of the messages that Rebecca Sedwick received from the other girls was overtly aggressive (e.g., media outlets quoted one message: "drink bleach and die") and the social context within which this high level of aggression was permitted to flourish, even after Rebecca's death, was concerning for us all. One of the girls who allegedly tormented Rebecca Sedwick posted "Yes, I bullied Rebecca and she killed herself but I don't give a . . . and you can add the last word yourself,' to her Facebook account. It can be easily argued that many factors led to Rebecca's choice to kill herself (i.e., she was depressed, had high levels of parent–child conflict, experienced a failed romantic relationship, etc.) and the school reportedly attempted to help her manage peer rejection and exclusion. However, what social context is being created on Facebook among "friends" to allow such messages after a horrible death? What can schools do to help its youth create a more honorable community?

In much psychological research, bullying has been defined as the repeated and proactive aggression in which one or more persons intend to harm or disturb another person physically and/or psychologically. Bullying can take on physical, verbal, and indirect forms and often takes place within interpersonal relationships that have some type of power imbalance whereby the "weaker" is the target. Bullying is often without provocation, which may explain why perceptions of bullying differs across different types of people reporting on it. Most of psychological research however has relied on self-reported bullying and victimization to report upon the prevalence of bullying with the limitations of self-reports acknowledged.

When researchers provide children with a brief definition of what bullying is and then ask them if they have ever bullied someone, prevalence rates have varied significantly between studies, but in general the prevalence of bullying in elementary and secondary school is estimated to be between 15 and 25 percent with rising prevalence in the United States (e.g., Glew et al., 2005; Nansel et al., 2001). An interesting study of kindergarten school children indicated that when combining teacher and peer ratings, 28 percent of girls and 45 percent of boys were involved in bullying and/or victimization incidents (Perren & Alasker, 2006). Thus, it appears that all school-aged children can benefit from effective anti-bullying prevention efforts.

Parents and educators at all levels have been more concerned with bullying not only because of its high prevalence but also because of the potential problems that experiences with bullying and victimization have had with mental health and academic development. Much developmental research has reported that bullies tend to be aggressive, impulsive, hostile, antisocial, and uncooperative. Interestingly, they make friends easily (based on their own self report) but they are usually lower in achievement and psychological well-being compared to children who are uninvolved in bullying. Victims tend to be characterized as withdrawn, depressed, anxious, quiet, and insecure. Many victims report that they don't fit in and are lonely and less happy at school. In addition to bullies and victims, there are bully-victims who report both being a bully and a victim. Research has observed that half of bullies are bully-victims (Veenstra et al., 2005). Bully-victims have been found to be a high-risk group. They tend to be very aggressive and very depressed, are involved in problem behaviors, and are the most disliked at school.

Although less research attention has discussed the impact of bystanders on bullying and victimization, bystanders are thought to be key in prevention efforts in Finland. As described in the "Yes" side article, first authored by Antti Kärnä, the authors point out that bystanders can stop or maintain bullying by whether or not the bullying is rewarded. When bystanders defend the victim, bullying becomes an unsuccessful strategy to gain status in the group. Thus, their anti-bullying prevention program (KiVa) emphasizes student lessons teaching bystanders to act in support of the victim. In addition to prevention efforts, they provide intervention discussions for bullies and victims. Kärnä and colleagues provide evidence in their study from a nationwide trial of the KiVa program in Finland for grades 1 to 9.

Sabina Low and Mark V. Ryzin argue on the "No" side that while prevention programs are desirable in theory and it appears that they work in Europe, there is less convincing evidence that anti-bullying efforts are effective in the United States. Low and Ryzin measure the perceived school climate as a prevention program is implemented (STR). They test the idea that a stand-alone program cannot be successful without a positive school climate to support it in the United States. They argue that school climate, as reported by either students or teachers, has long been associated with lower bullying incidents, and focusing efforts in creating and maintaining a positive and trusting school climate can function as a form of prevention.

# YES ←

**Antti Kärnä, Marinus Voeten, Todd D. Little, Elisa Poskiparta, Erkki Alanen, and Christina Salmivalli**

# Going to Scale: A Nonrandomized Nationwide Trial of the KiVa Antibullying Program for Grades 1–9

Bullying in schools is a pervasive problem threatening the psychosocial development of children and youths all over the world. Being victimized is related to a multitude of problems from school avoidance, depression, anxiety, and lowered academic functioning (e.g., Card & Hodges, 2008; Kochenderfer & Ladd, 1996; Nakamoto & Schwartz, 2010) to tragedies such as suicides (Olweus, 1993) and even school shootings (Leary, Kowalski, Smith, & Phillips, 2003). There is a pressing need for effective interventions—a call that has resulted in numerous school-based antibullying programs and studies on their effects (Smith, Pepler, & Rigby, 2004). The most comprehensive meta-analysis conducted so far (Farrington & Ttofi, 2009) concluded that antibullying programs *are* effective. On the basis of 44 evaluation studies, it reported average reductions of 20%–23% and 17%–20% for bullying and victimization, respectively (Farrington & Ttofi, 2009). These effects are not very large as such, but the reductions would be practically significant if they could be replicated in a well-conducted, large-scale evaluation. Farrington and Ttofi (2009) stated that the generalizability of results from an antibullying program (i.e., their external validity) "can best be established in a systematic review" (p. 13). This method is compromised, however, if the studies included have similar kinds of selection biases (e.g., with more problematic students dropping out). Furthermore, most often we are interested in the generalizability of the effects of a *particular* program when it is implemented to a sample from *its target population*.

The aim of the present study was to examine the effectiveness of the recently developed KiVa antibullying program (Salmivalli, Kärnä, & Poskiparta, 2010a, Salmivalli, Kärnä, & Poskiparta, 2010b) in the beginning of its nationwide dissemination. We tested the generalizability of the previous evaluation results

(Kärnä, Voeten, Little, Alanen, et al., 2011; Kärnä, Voeten, Little, Poskiparta, et al., 2011) to the population of Finnish comprehensive schools and across Grades 1–9 with a sample of 888 schools (28% of the school population) and about 150,000 students (30% of the student population) during the first 9 months (i.e., 1 school year) of implementation.

## KiVa Antibullying Program

In 2006, the Finnish Ministry of Education and Culture made a contract with the University of Turku concerning the development and initial evaluation of an antibullying program for comprehensive schools (Grades 1–9 in the Finnish school system). From the very beginning, the vision was to develop a program that would be suitable for nationwide distribution in Finland. The program, KiVa, was a collaborative development between the Department of Psychology and the Centre for Learning Research at the University of Turku.

The KiVa program has its theoretical background in recent research on bullying and on the social status of aggressive children in general (see also Salmivalli et al., 2010a, Salmivalli et al., 2010b). More specifically, it is assumed that bullies demonstrate their high status by harassing their low-status victims and that bullying is actually a strategy for gaining a powerful position in the peer group (e.g., Juvonen & Galván, 2008; Salmivalli & Peets, 2008). Furthermore, in the KiVa program, bullying is viewed as a group phenomenon, in which bystanders' behaviors have an effect on the maintenance of bullying (Salmivalli, 2010; Salmivalli, Lagerspetz, Björkqvist, Österman, & Kaukiainen, 1996). According to this view, supported by empirical findings (Salmivalli, Voeten, & Poskiparta, 2011), bystanders maintain the bullying behavior in part by assisting and reinforcing the bully, because such behaviors

Kärnä, Antti; Voeten, Marinus; Little, Todd D.; Poskiparta, Elisa; Alanen, Erkki; Salmivalli, Christina, "Going to Scale: A Nonrandomized Nationwide Trial of the KiVa Antibullying Program for Grades 1–9," *Journal of Consulting and Clinical Psychology*, vol 79, no. 6, December 2011, pp. 796–805. No further reproduction or distribution is permitted without written permission from the American Psychological Association.

provide the bullies the position of power they seek after. On the other hand, if bystanders defend the victim, this turns bullying into an unsuccessful strategy for attaining and demonstrating high status. These views imply that a positive change in the bystanders' behaviors will reduce the rewards gained by bullies and consequently their motivation to bully in the first place. KiVa is designed to bring about change in the bystanders' behaviors by increasing their empathy, self-efficacy, and antibullying attitudes, because these characteristics have been found to predict defending and supporting the victimized peers (Caravita, DiBlasio, & Salmivalli, 2009; Pöyhönen, Juvonen, & Salmivalli, 2010; Salmivalli & Voeten, 2004). A central goal of the KiVa program is therefore to make bystanders, instead of encouraging the bully, show that they are against bullying and to make them support the victim. However, as an equally important intervention strategy, the KiVa program includes also procedures for handling the acute bullying cases that come to the attention of the school personnel. Thus, both universal (targeted at all students) and indicated (targeted at students involved in bullying) actions are involved in the program. The KiVa program is assumed to produce its effects by (a) encouraging all students to support the victimized peers instead of providing social rewards to the bullies, (b) communicating to children involved in bullying that such behavior cannot be tolerated, and (c) providing adults (parents as well as school personnel) information about bullying and efficacy to prevent it and to intervene in it.

Overall, the KiVa program includes several elements that Farrington and Ttofi (2009) found to be associated with reductions in bullying, victimization, or both. These include disciplinary methods, improved playground supervision, teacher training, classroom rules, whole-school antibullying policy, school conferences, information for parents, videos, and cooperative group work. In addition, the KiVa program consists of several elements and is quite intensive and long lasting (the program implementation takes 1 whole school year). These are characteristics that have been found to describe effective antibullying programs (Farrington & Ttofi, 2009).

The KiVa program was first evaluated in a randomized controlled trial (RCT) involving 234 schools. The findings from the evaluation studies were promising: The odds of being a victim or being a bully were about 1.3 times higher for a control-school student than for a KiVa-school student (for victimization, odds ratio [OR] = 1.28, 95% CI [1.17, 1.40]; for bullying, OR = 1.30, 95% CI [1.15, 1.48]; Kärnä, Voeten, Little, Alanen, et al., 2011). In Grades 4–6, KiVa brought about positive changes also in other outcomes as well: Students in KiVa schools assisted

and reinforced the bully less, had an increased self-efficacy to defend the victims, and enhanced well-being at school (Kärnä, Voeten, Little, Poskiparta, et al., 2011; Salmivalli, Garandeau, & Veenstra, in press). The results nevertheless indicated that the effectiveness of the program varied across grade levels, with the largest effects in elementary school (Grades 1–6: ORs around 1.3–1.5) and the smallest (and mostly statistically nonsignificant) effects in the lower secondary grade levels (Grades 7–9: ORs around 1.1–1.2; Kärnä, Voeten, Little, Alanen, et al., 2011; Kärnä, Voeten, Little, Poskiparta, et al., 2011).

The main components of KiVa (i.e., student lessons and discussions with bullies and victims) were implemented during both the RCT and the broad dissemination. However, there were several differences between these two phases. The procedures differed in the support provided to schools, in the recommended delivery of student lessons, and in the freedom of schools to choose between two possible approaches to be utilized in discussions with the bullies. First, school networks were created during the RCT to enhance the implementation of the KiVa program. Three teachers or other personnel formed a KiVa team for each school, and the KiVa teams of three schools in a same geographical area formed a school network. This network met, together with a key person representing the program providers, three times during the school year. The aims of the meetings were to exchange ideas and experiences, to get support in implementation, and to enhance the motivation to implement the program with fidelity. During the broad dissemination period, there was no regular face-to-face contact between the schools and program developers besides the initial 2 days of preimplementation training—this was due to the large number of schools (nearly 1,500) implementing the KiVa program. Second, during the RCT, the student lessons were delivered in all grade levels in the intervention schools, whereas during the broad rollout of the intervention, we recommended to utilize the lessons in Grades 1, 4, and 7. This recommendation was based on the fact that there are three versions of the KiVa program, and in this schedule, each series of the lessons is implemented only once (i.e., the same lessons are not repeated several times during consecutive years). Third, during the RCT, the schools were randomly assigned to groups utilizing two different approaches to discussions with the bullies: the No Blame Approach and the Confronting Approach. During the large-scale implementation, the school teams could freely choose between the two.

In the present study, the main questions were (a) whether the effects obtained during the RCT (Kärnä, Voeten, Little, Alanen, et al., 2011; Kärnä, Voeten, Little, Poskiparta, et al., 2011) also appear during a broad implementation, and (b) whether the effects vary across grade levels. Because of the differences with the RCT, we expected to find somewhat smaller effects during the nationwide implementation compared with the initial evaluation. We also expected to find the largest effects in Grades 1, 4, and 7, where the student lessons were delivered during broad diffusion. Contrary to findings of Farrington and Ttofi (2009) and in accordance with our previous results (Kärnä, Voeten, Little, Alanen, et al., 2011), we hypothesized that the effects would be stronger in elementary than in lower secondary grades. Such a difference could be due to developmental changes in adolescence (e.g., in attitude to adults) and to the more complex organization of lower secondary schools, which may complicate the intervention implementation (Smith, 2010).

## Method

### Design

Because the program was disseminated throughout the country and all the participating schools were implementing KiVa, it was not possible to use a traditional experimental design. We therefore used a particular form of a quasi-experimental design, a cohort-longitudinal design with adjacent cohorts (Olweus & Alsaker, 1991), to evaluate the program effects. This design has been used previously in some evaluation studies of antibullying programs (Olweus & Alsaker, 1991; Salmivalli, Kaukiainen, & Voeten, 2005), and it has been recommended as a useful approach in situations such as the present one (Olweus, 2005). In this design, posttest data from students in each grade cohort are compared with pretest data from same-age students from the same schools (i.e., the previous cohort) who have not yet been exposed to the intervention. For instance, data from first-graders in May 2010 (when they have been exposed to the KiVa program for 1 year) were compared with data from students who were in Grade 1 in May 2009 and who were not yet exposed to the intervention program. By doing these kinds of comparisons, we were able to rule out maturation effects as an alternative explanation. This is important, because bullying and victimization change with age (see, e.g., the Control % columns in Tables 1 and 2). As noted by Olweus (2005), it is plausible to assume with this design that a cohort differs in only nonsignificant ways from its contiguous cohort(s). This is because, in the usual case, the majority of the members in the grade cohorts stem from the same, relatively stable population, and the students have been in the same schools for many years.

### Sample

As soon as the first results from the evaluation of the KiVa program for Grades 4–6 were available in 2008 (Kärnä, Voeten, Little, Poskiparta, et al., 2011), the Finnish Ministry of Education and Culture made a decision to support the diffusion of the program across the entire country. All Finnish comprehensive schools were provided with the opportunity to get the material and the training for free during the next 2 school years. All schools that started implementing KiVa in Fall 2009 or Fall 2010 got this benefit.

In recruiting the schools (October 2008), letters were sent to all schools providing comprehensive education (compulsory schooling in Grades 1–9) in mainland Finland. Along with basic information about the program, the letters explained what it means to be a KiVa school, that is, what kind of efforts they should be ready to invest in the implementation. The schools were given guidelines for registering as KiVa schools in the web-based system. Of the 3,218 schools contacted, 1,827 were willing to adopt the program. We were able to include the first 1,450 schools into the first round of teacher training and program implementation, whereas the rest of the schools remained on the waiting list because of limited resources. One year later, the new call for registration resulted in a total number of 2,260 schools that started the implementation during the first 2 years of national diffusion. The target sample of the present study was composed of the schools that registered in the first round ($N = 1,450$) and started the implementation in the beginning of the school year 2009 (August). At the time of the registration, the schools received passwords for the web-based student questionnaire by which they could get feedback about their own current situation and could compare themselves with the other schools starting to implement KiVa.

Of the 1,450 schools, 1,189 organized the web-based survey in May 2009, and 888 (74.7%) of them also responded in May 2010. To be able to compare the situation at pretest and posttest in the same schools, only those who participated in both measurements were included into the final sample. These schools had on average 226 students and 13 classrooms, with 18 students in a classroom. The sample schools were therefore somewhat larger than Finnish comprehensive schools in general ($M = 181$ students per school), but the mean classroom size corresponded well to the national average (17–20 students depending on the grade level). The respondents consisted of an equal number of boys (51%) and girls (49%). Data on socioeconomic status or ethnic

*Table 1*

## Odds Ratios Indicating the Intervention Effects on Self-Reported Victimization

| Grade | N | Sample size | | | | | Control | | | KiVa | | | | | |
| | | KiVa | Control | Schools | ICC | DEFF | Nonvictim | Victim | % | Nonvictim | Victim | % | OR | 95% CI | p |
|---|---|---|---|---|---|---|---|---|---|---|---|---|---|---|---|
| 1 | 34,241 | 16,370 | 17,871 | 675 | 0.07 | 1.61 | 13,242 | 4,629 | 25.9 | 12,598 | 3,772 | 23.0 | 1.17 | [1.08,1.26] | <.001 |
| 2 | 34,442 | 16,612 | 17,830 | 664 | 0.07 | 1.67 | 13,641 | 4,189 | 23.5 | 13,286 | 3,326 | 20.0 | 1.23 | [1.13,1.34] | <.001 |
| 3 | 35,164 | 16,903 | 18,261 | 668 | 0.06 | 1.61 | 14,773 | 3,488 | 19.1 | 14,187 | 2,716 | 16.1 | 1.23 | [1.13,1.35] | <.001 |
| 4 | 35,696 | 17,154 | 18,542 | 694 | 0.07 | 1.63 | 15,534 | 3,008 | 16.2 | 14,968 | 2,186 | 12.7 | 1.33 | [1.20,1.46] | <.001 |
| 5 | 34,231 | 16,297 | 17,934 | 651 | 0.05 | 1.54 | 15,509 | 2,425 | 13.5 | 14,552 | 1,745 | 10.7 | 1.30 | [1.18,1.44] | <.001 |
| 6 | 31,342 | 14,768 | 16,574 | 602 | 0.06 | 1.57 | 14,624 | 1,950 | 11.8 | 13,317 | 1,451 | 9.8 | 1.22 | [1.09,1.37] | <.001 |
| 7 | 28,169 | 13,411 | 14,758 | 231 | 0.03 | 1.71 | 13,044 | 1,714 | 11.6 | 11,986 | 1,425 | 10.6 | 1.11 | [0.97,1.26] | .123 |
| 8 | 26,548 | 12,489 | 14,059 | 221 | 0.03 | 1.67 | 12,653 | 1,406 | 10.0 | 11,389 | 1,100 | 8.8 | 1.15 | [1.00,1.32] | .047 |
| 9 | 21,177 | 10,486 | 10,691 | 195 | 0.03 | 1.53 | 9,697 | 994 | 9.3 | 9,614 | 872 | 8.3 | 1.13 | [0.98,1.31] | .100 |
| 1–9 | 297,737 | 141,103 | 156,634 | 888 | 0.05 | 3.05 | 131,107 | 25,527 | 16.3 | 121,578 | 19,525 | 13.8 | 1.21[a] | [1.14,1.29] | <.001 |

*Note.* ICC = school-level intraclass correlation for the dichotomous victimization variable (estimated with Mplus 6.1). ICC = $\tau_0^2/(\tau_0^2 + \pi^2/3)$, where $\tau_0^2$ = intercept variance and $\pi^2/3 \approx 3.29$ (Snijders & Bosker, 1999). DEFF = design effect; % = prevalence of victimization in percentages; OR = odds ratio; CI = confidence interval.
[a]The corresponding average weighted odds ratio across Grades 1–9 was 1.22, 95% CI [1.19, 1.24].

*Table 2*

## Odds Ratios Indicating the Intervention Effects on Self-Reported Bullying

| Grade | N | Sample size | | | | | Control | | | KiVa | | | | | |
| | | Control | KiVa | Schools | ICC | DEFF | Nonbully | Bully | % | Nonbully | Bully | % | OR | 95% CI | p |
|---|---|---|---|---|---|---|---|---|---|---|---|---|---|---|---|
| 1 | 34,238 | 16,369 | 17,869 | 675 | 0.07 | 1.65 | 15,445 | 2,424 | 13.6 | 14,410 | 1,959 | 12.0 | 1.15 | [1.04,1.28] | .007 |
| 2 | 34,440 | 16,611 | 17,829 | 664 | 0.09 | 1.77 | 15,600 | 2,229 | 12.5 | 14,970 | 1,641 | 9.9 | 1.30 | [1.16,1.47] | <.001 |
| 3 | 35,164 | 16,903 | 18,261 | 668 | 0.08 | 1.77 | 16,501 | 1,760 | 9.6 | 15,602 | 1,301 | 7.7 | 1.28 | [1.12,1.46] | <.001 |
| 4 | 35,696 | 17,154 | 18,542 | 694 | 0.12 | 1.99 | 16,800 | 1,742 | 9.4 | 15,919 | 1,235 | 7.2 | 1.34 | [1.15,1.55] | <.001 |
| 5 | 34,230 | 16,297 | 17,933 | 651 | 0.09 | 1.84 | 16,378 | 1,555 | 8.7 | 15,127 | 1,170 | 7.2 | 1.23 | [1.06,1.42] | .006 |
| 6 | 31,342 | 14,768 | 16,574 | 602 | 0.11 | 1.91 | 14,920 | 1,654 | 10.0 | 13,509 | 1,259 | 8.5 | 1.19 | [1.03,1.38] | .021 |
| 7 | 28,168 | 13,410 | 14,758 | 231 | 0.05 | 2.06 | 13,084 | 1,674 | 11.3 | 11,958 | 1,452 | 10.8 | 1.05 | [0.90,1.23] | .505 |
| 8 | 26,547 | 12,488 | 14,059 | 221 | 0.05 | 1.96 | 12,385 | 1,674 | 11.9 | 11,058 | 1,430 | 11.5 | 1.05 | [0.90,1.21] | .557 |
| 9 | 21,177 | 10,486 | 10,691 | 195 | 0.03 | 1.69 | 9,276 | 1,415 | 13.2 | 9,178 | 1,308 | 12.5 | 1.07 | [0.93,1.23] | .328 |
| 1–9 | 297,728 | 141,099 | 156,629 | 888 | 0.05 | 3.11 | 139,266 | 17,363 | 11.1 | 127,569 | 13,530 | 9.6 | 1.18[a] | [1.09,1.27] | <.001 |

*Note.* ICC = school-level intraclass correlation for the dichotomous bullying variable (estimated with Mplus 6.1). ICC = $\tau_0^2/(\tau_0^2 + \pi^2/3)$, where $\tau_0^2$ = intercept variance and $\pi^2/3 \approx 3.29$ (Snijders & Bosker, 1999). DEFF = design effect; % = prevalence of bullying in percentages; OR = odds ratio; CI = confidence interval.
[a]The corresponding average weighted odds ratio across Grades 1–9 was 1.18, 95% CI [1.15, 1.21].

background of the students were not collected; however, in the Finnish population, about 3% of the students are immigrants, whereas the vast majority of Finns are Caucasian. The participating schools had elementary (70.8%), lower secondary (13.3%), and both elementary and lower secondary (15.9%) grades. These percentages follow quite closely the population figures (76%, 13.4%, and 10.5% for elementary, lower secondary, and combined schools, respectively). There are fewer schools for the lower secondary grade levels (Grades 7–9), because they are usually much larger organizational units than elementary schools (Grades 1–6). In 8.9% of schools, instruction was given in the Swedish language, which corresponds well to the percentage of these schools in the population (8.6%). Overall, on the basis of several characteristics described above, our sample may be considered fairly representative of Finnish schools in general.

There was a small number of schools ($N = 26$) with a prior involvement in the RCT of the KiVa program. In these schools, the prevalence of victimization was slightly lower ($-1.5\%$), whereas the prevalence of bullying was equal to the rest of the sample ($+0.03\%$). It was therefore improbable that the inclusion of these schools would bias the results, but we nevertheless tested for differences in the intervention effectiveness for these schools and the rest of the sample.

Of the 1,189 schools participating at Wave 1,301 schools responded only once and were therefore excluded from the study. In these schools, victimization and bullying behaviors were slightly more prevalent (victimization = $+1.4\%$, and bullying = $+1.1\%$) than in the sample studied. Furthermore, a group of students were excluded from analyses because of obviously contradictory responding (in total, 403 respondents at Waves 1 and 2). This left us with control and intervention samples of 156,634 and 141,103 for victimization and 156,629 and 141,099 for bullying. There were approximately 200,000 students in these 888 schools included in the present study,[1] which resulted in response rates of 78% and 70% at Waves 1 and 2, respectively. Sensitivity analyses were conducted to account for potential differential attrition.

### Intervention

The KiVa program consists of both universal and indicated actions, as mentioned above (for the program manuals, see Salmivalli, Poskiparta, Tikka, & Pöyhönen, 2009; Salmivalli, Pöyhönen, & Kaukiainen, 2009; Sainio et al., 2009). The core of the universal components consists of student lessons and virtual learning environments. Both elementary

school versions (for Grades 1 and 4) include 10 double lessons ($2 \times 45$ min) that classroom teachers implement according to the teacher's manual during the school year (one per month from August until May). The general aims of these lessons are (a) to raise awareness of the role that the group plays in maintaining bullying, (b) to increase empathy toward victims, (c) to promote children's strategies of supporting the victim and their self-efficacy to do so, and (d) to increase children's coping skills when victimized. In the lower secondary school version (for Grade 7), four themes are described in the teachers' manual that can be introduced to students as a series of lessons, whole theme days, or otherwise. The themes are (a) "group interaction," (b) "me and the others," (c) "forms of bullying," and (d) "the consequences and counterforces of bullying." The recommended time to be dedicated for the kick-off session, the four themes, and the concluding session is 13–23 hr in total.

In addition to student lessons, the KiVa program utilizes virtual learning environments: an antibullying computer game for elementary school students and an Internet forum "KiVa Street" for lower secondary school students. The virtual learning environments are closely connected to the topics of the lessons and themes, enhancing the learning process and motivating students to apply the learned skills in everyday interactions with peers. Furthermore, the universal actions include a parents' guide as well as symbols (posters, highly visible vests for teachers supervising recess time), reminding both students and school personnel about KiVa.

The indicated actions involve discussions with victims and bullies, and with selected prosocial classmates as well, who are invited to support the victimized classmate. The discussions with the bullies and victims are conducted by a team of three teachers or other school personnel, called a KiVa team, whereas the classroom teacher organizes separate meetings with potential supporters of the victim (for a more detailed description of program contents, see Salmivalli et al., 2010a, Salmivalli et al., 2010b).

### Preimplementation Training

The schools in the target sample were provided 2 days of preimplementation training in 2009. Due to the large number of schools, there were several teacher training days in all provinces of Finland, and the number of participating personnel from each school was limited to four, except for schools including both elementary (Grades 1–6) and lower secondary (Grades 7–9) grades, from which a maximum of six persons could participate.

The participants included principals and teachers but also school social workers and school psychologists. They were provided with presentation graphics to educate other staff members in their schools about KiVa.

## Data Collection

In May 2009, the students from all participating schools were invited to complete a short, anonymous web-based questionnaire about bullying others, being bullied, telling about bullying, attitudes related to bullying, and classroom and school atmosphere. The survey took place before the summer break, and the school year started again in August. One year later, in May 2010, the schools were asked to organize the web-based survey again. The second assessment took place in the same time of the following school year to avoid any season effects and to have same-age students in the grade-wise comparisons. At that time, the KiVa program had been implemented in the participating schools for 9 months (i.e., 1 entire school year).

Students filled in the questionnaires in the schools' computer laboratories during regular school hours while the teachers administered the process. The teachers had been provided with detailed instructions about the procedure well in advance, including guidelines on how to protect the confidentiality of the responses. No consent forms were collected from the students, because the anonymous KiVa questionnaires were now a part of normal educational practices (American Psychological Association, 2010, p. 233). Only data concerning school, gender, grade, and bullying others and being bullied by others were utilized in the present study.

## Measures

The participants logged into the questionnaire with their school-specific passwords, so each student's school identification was automatically saved into the data set. The participants were asked to choose their gender and grade level from the options appearing on the computer screen. They were then provided with the standard definition of bullying (Olweus, 1996), followed by questions about bullying others and being bullied by others. These questions were the global items from the Revised Olweus Bully/Victim Questionnaire (Olweus, 1996): "How often have you been bullied at school in the last couple of months?" and "How often have you bullied others at school in the last couple of months?" Students chose their answer from five frequency categories (0 = *not at all*, 1 = *only once or twice*, 2 = *two or three times a month*, 3 = *about once a week*, 4 = *several times a week*).

Students who were systematically being bullied by their peers at school or bullied their peers at school were identified by the criterion suggested by Solberg and Olweus (2003). More specifically, students who reported they had been bullied 2–3 times a month, every week, or several times a week (response alternatives 2–4) during the past couple of months were categorized as victims, whereas those reporting they had bullied others at the same frequency were categorized as bullies. Solberg and Olweus found in their study that with this cutoff point, victims and bullies differed markedly from noninvolved students in conceptually related variables. Furthermore, Farrington and Ttofi (2009) used this criterion (i.e., more than once or twice) in their meta-analysis, and adopting this cutoff point also facilitates comparisons between the present study and the previous studies reviewed by them.

We investigated the validity of the dichotomized versions of these global bullying and victimization questions in a Finnish sample consisting of the students in Grades 1–9 ($N = 25,833$) that took part in the RCT of the KiVa program (Kärnä, Voeten, Little, Alanen, et al., 2011; Kärnä, Voeten, Little, Poskiparta, et al., 2011). More specifically, we calculated school-level correlations (cf. Solberg & Olweus, 2003) between the (a) dichotomized global bullying and victimization items (used in the present study) and (b) averages for the dichotomized self-reported forms of bullying and victimization (e.g., name calling) and (c) peer reports of bullying and victimization. The peer reports were formed by calculating averages of proportion scores (number of nominations divided by the number of classmates nominating) on three items for both bullying (e.g., "Starts bullying") and victimization (e.g., "He/she is being pushed around and hit"). The results indicated that correlations between the global questions and the questions concerning the respective forms of bullying or victimization were substantial at Grades 1–9 ($rs = .65–.87$, $p < .001$). The correlations between the global bullying and victimization items were of similar magnitude across all grades ($rs = .59–.65$, $p < .001$). For the RCT concerning Grades 1–3, we did not have data on peer-reports; however, for Grades 4–9, the global self-report items and peer-reported bullying and victimization correlated significantly as well ($rs = .46–.75$, $p < .001$). The results are consistent with the findings of Solberg and Olweus (2003), who reported correlations of .79 (victimization) and .77 (bullying) between the global questions and the questions concerning the respective forms. Overall, these results indicate that the measures used in the present study have construct validity in the Finnish student population as well.

# Results

## Implementation Dosage

In May 2010, schools reported the amount of implementation of the KiVa program. For the elementary grades, respondents included the homeroom teachers of 749 classrooms in 425 schools (55.2% of the 770 schools with Grades 1–6). These teachers indicated that they had implemented at least partially eight out of the 10 prescribed lessons ($M = 7.90$, $SD = 2.48$), whereas the number of fully implemented lessons (2 × 45 min) was lower ($M = 4.50$, $SD = 3.57$). The KiVa computer game had been played in 69.6% of these classrooms.

In the lower secondary grades, the respondents included 113 schools (43.6% of the 259 schools with Grades 7–9). In case there were several respondents per school, their answers were averaged to get a single estimate of the time devoted to the KiVa program. Schools reported having used on average 9 hr for implementing the themes ($M = 8.68$, $SD = 5.19$). The Internet forum KiVa Street had been utilized in 62.1% of these schools.

The schools reported also the number of bullying cases that had been handled with the discussion methods during the school year. We received valid answers from 372 schools (41.9% of the sample), and they indicated that the school teams had processed on average six bullying cases ($M = 5.69$, $SD = 5.70$).

In addition, we received some implementation data also from schools that did not respond twice to the student questionnaire. Compared with the study sample, there were slightly higher or lower levels of implementation of different components in these schools: Student lessons were implemented a little less ($M = 7.39$, $SD = 2.83$, and $M = 4.08$, $SD = 3.52$, for partially and fully implemented lessons, respectively), and the game was played in fewer classrooms (58.4%) in Grades 1–6 (school $N = 100$, and classroom $N = 173$). On the other hand, a bit more time was devoted in these schools to implementing the themes in Grades 7–9 ($M = 9.40$, $SD = 4.47$), and the Internet forum had been used more frequently (in 74.5% of the 34 schools responding). A slightly larger number of bullying cases had been handled in the 103 schools that reported about the activity of the KiVa teams ($M = 7.47$, $SD = 9.73$). The data did not therefore reveal any systematic difference between the dropouts and the study sample with regard to program implementation.

Considered as a whole, the results indicate that the schools had implemented the KiVa program to some extent, but there was notable variation between teachers and schools. Compared to the recommendations, teachers had used clearly less time for implementing the lessons and themes. This may suggest that teachers adapted the program by selecting the components that they viewed as the most suitable for their students.

## Program Effects

The percentages of students who reported being bullied or bullying others in the first student questionnaire (May 2009) are reported in Tables 1 and 2 (under Control %) for the entire sample and separately for each grade level. The overall prevalence rates for victimization and bullying were 16.3% and 11.1%, respectively. Victimization decreased with age from Grade 1 (25.9%) to Grade 9 (9.3%), the decrease being largest during Grades 1–6. Bullying decreased from Grade 1 (13.6%) to Grade 5 (8.7%), after which there was some increase until Grade 9 (13.2%). After the intervention, the prevalence rates of bullying and victimization were lower in each grade level (see the KiVa % columns in Tables 1 and 2). The age-related trends were parallel to those described above, except for Grade 7, where the level of victimization was slightly higher compared with adjacent grades.

To estimate the effect sizes, we calculated ORs with 95% confidence intervals for victimization and bullying while correcting the standard errors for clustering at the school level. The ORs represented the odds of victimization (bullying) in the control group compared with the odds of victimization (bullying) in the intervention group. The standard errors were multiplied by the design effect calculated on the basis of the cluster sizes (harmonic averages) and intraclass correlations in our sample (for the formulas, see Farrington & Ttofi, 2009; Kline, 2010, p. 344; Snijders & Bosker, 1999, p. 224). The results are presented in Tables 1 and 2. Based on the entire sample, the average weighted ORs were 1.22 for victimization and 1.18 for bullying. These results mean that the odds of being a victim or a bully were about 1.2 times higher in the comparison group, compared with the intervention group. The ORs obtained correspond to reductions of 15% and 14% in the prevalence rates of victimization and bullying, respectively. The intervention effects increased from Grade 1 until Grade 4, where the effects on victimization ($OR = 1.33$) and bullying ($OR = 1.34$) were largest. After Grade 4, the effects decreased and became statistically nonsignificant in the lower secondary school, except for victimization in Grade 8. The KiVa program effects on victimization were not far from statistical significance in Grades 7 and 9 either. There was a larger drop in the program effectiveness for bullying than for victimization. Doing the calculations separately for boys and girls and testing the differences in ORs did not reveal any gender differences in the overall effectiveness of the intervention or across the grade levels. In addition, analyses did not reveal any statistically significant differences in program effectiveness between (a) mainstream schools and special education schools, (b) Finnish-and Swedish-language schools, and (c) schools with and without prior involvement in the evaluation study.

We conducted some simple sensitivity analyses to investigate the robustness of our results with respect to differential attrition. It may be the case that bullies and/or victims drop out of the study more easily than noninvolved children, which would inflate the intervention effects. To examine this issue, we assumed (a) equal sample sizes at both waves (no drop-out) and (b) prevalence rates of 29% for victimization and 16% for bullying among the students whose responses can be considered missing at Wave 2. These assumptions mean that among the students with missing values, the risk for victimization would be 1.8 times higher, and the risk for bullying would be 1.5 times higher than in the sample in general, in spite of the intervention. Furthermore, the assumed prevalence rates were 1.6 times higher for victimization and 1.3 times higher for bullying than those observed in the 301 schools that dropped out of the study. Even in this unlikely situation, the effects of the KiVa program would be statistically significant with $ORs$ of 1.07 (95% CI [1.01, 1.14]) for victimization and 1.09 (95% CI [1.01, 1.17]) for bullying. Therefore, even with the strong selective attrition assumed above, we obtain qualitatively the same conclusions as with our main analysis.

To investigate the internal validity of the findings, we calculated school-level correlations between reductions in victimization and bullying and the intervention dosage. The dosage was defined here as (a) the hours spent in implementing the universal program components and (b) the number of bullying cases processed by the school team. The reduction was calculated by subtracting the posttest prevalence of victimization and bullying from the pretest prevalence in the particular schools. The teacher reports of hours devoted to the program were averaged within schools, and the number of bullying cases handled with discussions was divided by the number of students in the school. This was done because in large schools, there tend to be more bullying cases and more indicated actions as well.

At the school level, the average reduction for victimization was 2.7% ($SD = 6.4\%$), and for bullying it was 1.9% ($SD = 5.4\%$). A statistically significant positive correlation was obtained between the time devoted to universal actions and the reduction in both victimization ($r = .11$, 95% CI [.03, .20], $p = .011$, $N = 498$) and bullying ($r = .11$,

95% CI [.02, .20], $p = .015$, $N = 498$). In addition, the analyses revealed a positive correlation of the dosage of indicated actions with the reduction in bullying ($r = .16$, 95% CI [.06, .26], $p = .002$, $N = 372$) but not with the reduction in victimization ($r = .04$, 95% CI [−.06, .15], $p = .412$, $N = 372$). A reduction in bullying was associated with a corresponding decrease in victimization ($r = .41$, 95% CI [.35, .47], $p < .001$, $N = 888$). The change in bullying and victimization was approximately equal in schools that reported on implementation and in those schools that did not provide that information. It can therefore be concluded that those schools that implemented a higher dosage of the intervention obtained somewhat larger reductions in bullying and victimization, and a decrease in bullying was associated with a corresponding decrease in victimization. Both these findings suggest that the obtained results represent actual intervention effects.

Finally, to make the obtained results more concrete, we calculated corresponding reductions in absolute number of victims and bullies. Assuming random missingness, we estimated that during the first year of broad implementation, the KiVa program reduced the number of victims by 3,900 and reduced the number of bullies by about 2,300.[2]

## Discussion

The purpose of the present study was to test the effectiveness of the KiVa antibullying program when it is widely implemented in Finnish elementary and lower secondary schools (Grades 1–9). It was found that during the first 9 months of implementation, there was a decrease in the prevalence rates for both victimization and bullying. The effects were generally somewhat weaker than those obtained in the RCT (Kärnä, Voeten, Little, Alanen, et al., 2011; Kärnä, Voeten, Little, Poskiparta, et al., 2011). It may be concluded, however, that the KiVa program can effectively reduce bullying among peers at schools, even when implemented widely at the national level.

The smaller program effects during the broad dissemination ($OR = 1.2$) compared with the RCT ($OR = 1.3$; Kärnä, Voeten, Little, Alanen, et al., 2011) may result from the fact that some of the most motivated schools joined in already during the RCT, and the schools participating in the nationwide rollout were probably a more heterogeneous group. The heterogeneity may have resulted in lower quality of implementation during broad rollout, also because schools got less support for the implementation. This reduced support may have led to fewer actions taken and to local adaptations of the program.

The results concerning program implementation and its association to outcomes provide some evidence for this explanation.

The effects were statistically significant in elementary school (Grades 1–6); however, in lower secondary school, the effects reached statistical significance only for victimization in Grade 8. Overall, the effect sizes were largest in Grade 4 and smallest in lower secondary grades. These results confirm the findings of our previous evaluation studies, where we found that the KiVa program is more effective in Grades 1–6 than in Grades 7–9 (Kärnä, Voeten, Little, Alanen, et al., 2011; Kärnä, Voeten, Little, Poskiparta, et al., 2011). Farrington and Ttofi (2009) argued in their meta-analysis that the effects of antibullying programs increase steadily as a function of age, and they recommended that antibullying programs should be targeted at children 11 years of age or older. This recommendation is in stark contrast with our results, in which program effects increase until 11 years of age (at the end of Grade 4) and diminish thereafter. Furthermore, Farrington and Ttofi found in their meta-analysis that the average $OR$ for antibullying intervention programs (excluding the KiVa program) was 1.29 (95% CI [1.17, 1.41]) for victimization and 1.36 (95% CI [1.26, 1.47]) for bullying (D. Farrington, personal communication, March 8, 2010). In comparison to those results, the $OR$s from the current study (1.21 for victimization and 1.17 for bullying) are somewhat smaller. However, none of the studies included in that meta-analysis reported as broad a nationwide rollout of an antibullying program as the present study. Furthermore, it can be noted that the effect on victimization is slightly larger than the effect on bullying. Perhaps some students can be protected relatively easily from victimization compared with the effort required to completely stop the bullying behaviors of the perpetrators.

In our view, the effects reported here can be considered important and practically significant. As estimated above, the first-year implementation of the KiVa program may have resulted in reduction of about 3,900 victims and 2,300 bullies, and this result alone shows that the program has positively influenced the lives of a large number of children and youths. Additionally, we can estimate how much KiVa would have reduced bullying and victimization had all Finnish comprehensive schools implemented KiVa with the effects reported above. In this population consisting of around 500,000 students in Grades 1–9, the reductions would have amounted to about 7,500 bullies and 12,500 victims during the first year of implementation.

In the present study, we could not use a randomized design because all participating schools were implementing the KiVa program. It is therefore important to rule out plausible alternative interpretations for the results (Shadish, Cook, & Campbell, 2002). The pattern of results obtained with the cohort-longitudinal design was similar to the pattern of results obtained with the RCT (Kärnä, Voeten, Little, Alanen, et al., 2011; Kärnä, Voeten, Little, Poskiparta, et al., 2011). This contributes to confidence in the internal validity of the present findings. Furthermore, the statistically significant positive correlations between the program dosage and reduction in bullying and victimization suggest that the intervention has indeed decreased these problems. According to Cohen (1988), effect sizes of this magnitude ($r$s = .11 and .16) can be considered small. However, effects of this size are common in behavioral sciences, where measurements often have less than perfect reliability, which in turn leads to attenuation of the correlation coefficients (Cohen, 1988). The small magnitude of the correlations is probably partly due to difficulty in measuring precisely the quantity of program implementation. Furthermore, skewed distributions may lower correlations (Kendall & Stuart, 1958), and the frequency distribution of the rate of indicated actions was quite skewed.

Next, we discuss the specific confounding factors for the cohort-longitudinal design (Olweus, 2004). The comparability of the cohorts is an important assumption in the present study. As explained in the Method and Results sections, age-related changes, seasonal variations, and differential attrition are implausible as alternative explanations. Selection bias in the cohort-longitudinal design would mean that the cohorts included in the study inadvertently represent different populations with differing characteristics. This threat to validity is not likely either, because the cohorts were sampled from the same schools, and they were separated by only 1 year in age. The selection-bias interpretation is also contradicted by the fact that the results consistently favored KiVa schools in all the grade levels. Having cohort(s) with unusually high or low prevalence rates for bullying and victimization would have created some inconsistency in the results, because the cohorts serve as both baseline and intervention groups (except for Cohorts 1 and 10; see Figure 1). Another possible threat is that answering is influenced by repeated measurements. In this study, however, the questionnaires used were rather brief, and the measurement occasions were separated by an entire year, which makes a carryover from the first measurement to the second unlikely. Finally, there are no grounds for assuming a history effect either: We are not aware of any event concurrent to the intervention program that might have significantly influenced the study results.

## Strengths and Limitations

The present study is unique with respect to the number of schools and students involved. Whereas the typical number of schools involved in the evaluations of anti-bullying programs has varied from 1 to 78 (Farrington & Ttofi, 2009), our study included 888 schools and about 150,000 students. Furthermore, the sample involved the entire range of grade levels (Grades 1–9; 8–16 years of age during the measurements) in the Finnish compulsory school system, with thousands of participants in each grade level.

Our outcome variables were limited to self-reported bullying and victimization. In the previous evaluation studies (Kärnä, Voeten, Little, Alanen, et al., 2011; Kärnä, Voeten, Little, Poskiparta, et al., 2011), however, we have reported findings for many more outcomes, including peer-reports. In the study by Kärnä, Voeten, Little, Poskiparta, et al. (2011), the effect sizes for peer-reported victimization and bullying were converted into $ORs$, and the effects were at least of equal magnitude compared with self-reports. One further limitation is that the missing data create some uncertainty about the exact magnitude of the effects. If a large number of problematic students or classrooms did drop out during the study, this may have created some bias to the results. However, as argued above in the Results section, the conclusions tolerate quite a strong selective attrition. Note that to demonstrate this, we assumed a selection bias that was much larger than the actual observed difference between the study sample and the dropout schools.

## Future Research

It will be an interesting task to follow the KiVa effects during the next years. Ryan and Smith (2009) recommended the use of a 3-year follow-up period to properly investigate the effects of an intervention program. Enough time is needed so that teachers can solve the initial implementation problems and the program effects can fully unfold. It may even happen that some program effects become stronger over time (Olweus & Alsaker, 1991). The attempts to maintain the motivation and fidelity of implementation in Finnish schools include biannual KiVa conference days, regular newsletters to schools, and an online discussion forum for school personnel. The assessment of both implementation quantity and student outcomes in schools implementing the KiVa program will enable future studies on the long-term effects of the program as well as the implementation process itself.

## References

American Psychological Association. (2010). *Publication manual of the American Psychological Association* (6th ed.). Washington, DC: Author.

Caravita, S., DiBlasio, P., & Salmivalli, C. (2009). Unique and interactive effects of empathy and social status on involvement in bullying. *Social Development, 18,* 140–163. doi:10.1111/j.1467-9507.2008.00465.x

Card, N. A., & Hodges, E. V. E. (2008). Peer victimization among schoolchildren: Causes, consequences, and considerations in assessment and intervention. *School Psychology Quarterly, 23,* 451–461. doi: 10.1037/a0012769

Cohen, J. (1988). *Statistical power analysis for the behavioral sciences* (2nd ed.). Hillsdale, NJ: Erlbaum.

Farrington, D. P., & Ttofi, M. M. (2009). School-based programs to reduce bullying and victimization. *Campbell Systematic Reviews,* 2009:6. Retrieved from http://www.d300.org/files/School-based%20Anti-Bullying%20Programs%20v2_R.pdf

Juvonen, J., & Galván, A. (2008). Peer influence in involuntary social groups: Lessons from research on bullying. In M. J. Prinstein & K. A. Dodge (Eds.), *Understanding peer influence in children and adolescents* (pp. 225–244). New York, NY: Guilford Press.

Kärnä, A., Voeten, M., Little, T. D., Alanen, E., Poskiparta, E., & Salmivalli, C. (2011). *Effectiveness of the KiVa antibullying program: Grades 1–3 and 7–9.* Manuscript submitted for publication.

Kärnä, A., Voeten, M., Little, T., Poskiparta, E., Kaljonen, A., & Salmivalli, C. (2011). A large-scale evaluation of the KiVa antibullying program. *Child Development, 82,* 311–330. doi:10.1111/j.14678624.2010.01557.x

Kendall, M. G., & Stuart, A. (1958). *The advanced theory of statistics.* New York, NY: Hafner.

Kline, R. (2010). *Principles and practice of structural equation modeling* (3rd ed.). New York, NY: Guilford Press.

Kochenderfer, B. J., & Ladd, G. W. (1996). Peer victimization: Cause or consequence of school maladjustment? *Child Development, 67,* 1305–1317. doi:10.2307/1131701

Leary, M. R., Kowalski, R. M., Smith, L., & Phillips, S. (2003). Teasing, rejection, and violence: Case studies of the school shootings. *Aggressive Behavior, 29,* 202–214. doi:10.1002/ab.10061

Nakamoto, J., & Schwartz, D. (2010). Is peer victimization associated with academic achievement? A meta-analytic review. *Social Development, 19,* 221–242. doi:10.1111/j.1467-9507.2009.00539.x

Olweus, D. (1993). Victimization by peers: Antecedents and long-term outcomes. In K. H. Rubin & J. B. Asendorf (Eds.), *Social withdrawal, inhibition, and shyness* (pp. 315–341). Hillsdale, NJ: Erlbaum.

Olweus, D. (1996). *The Revised Olweus Bully/Victim Questionnaire.* Bergen, Norway: University of Bergen, Research Center for Health Promotion (HEMIL Center).

Olweus, D. (2004). The Olweus Bullying Prevention Programme: Design and implementation issues and a new national initiative in Norway. In P. K. Smith, D. Pepler, & K. Rigby (Eds.), *Bullying in schools: How successful can interventions be?* (pp. 13–36). New York, NY: Cambridge University Press. doi:10.1017/CBO9780511584466.003

Olweus, D. (2005). A useful evaluation design, and effects of the Olweus Bullying Prevention Program. *Psychology, Crime & Law, 11,* 389–402. doi:10.1080/10683160500255471

Olweus, D., & Alsaker, F. (1991). Assessing change in a cohort-longitudinal study with hierarchical data. In D. Magnusson, L. Bergman, G. Rudinger, & B. Törestad (Eds.), *Problems and methods in longitudinal research: Stability and change* (pp. 107–132). New York, NY: Cambridge University Press. doi:10.1017/CBO9780511663260.008

Pöyhönen, V., Juvonen, J., & Salmivalli, C. (2010). What does it take to stand up for the victim of bullying? The interplay between personal and social factors. *Merrill-Palmer Quarterly, 56,* 143–163. doi:10.1353/ mpq.0.0046

Ryan, W., & Smith, J. D. (2009). Antibullying programs in schools: How effective are evaluation practices? *Prevention Science, 10,* 248–259. doi:10.1007/s11121-009-0128-y

Sainio, M., Kaukiainen, A., Willför-Nyman, U., Annevirta, T., Pöyhönen, V., & Salmivalli, C. (2009). *KiVa: Teacher's guide, unit 3* (Research Into Practice Publication Series, No. 4). Turku, Finland: University of Turku, Psychology Department.

Salmivalli, C. (2010). Bullying and the peer group: A review. *Aggression and Violent Behavior, 15,* 112–120. doi:10.1016/j.avb.2009.08.007

Salmivalli, C., Garandeau, C., & Veenstra, R. (in press). KiVa antibullying program: Implications for school adjustment. In G. Ladd & A. Ryan (Eds.), *Peer relationships and adjustment at school.* Charlotte, NC: Information Age Publishing.

Salmivalli, C., Kärnä, A., & Poskiparta, E. (2010a). Development, evaluation, and diffusion of a national anti-bullying program, KiVa. In B. Doll, W. Pfohl, & J. Yoon (Eds.), *Handbook of youth prevention science* (pp. 238–252). New York, NY: Routledge.

Salmivalli, C., Kärnä, A., & Poskiparta, E. (2010b). From peer putdowns to peer support: A theoretical model and how it translated into a national anti-bullying program. In S. Jimerson, S. Swearer, & D. Espelage (Eds.), *Handbook of bullying in schools: An international perspective* (pp. 441–454). New York, NY: Routledge.

Salmivalli, C., Kaukiainen, A., & Voeten, M. (2005). Anti-bullying intervention: Implementation and outcome. *British Journal of Educational Psychology, 75,* 465–487. doi:10.1348/000709905X26011

Salmivalli, C., Lagerspetz, K., Björkqvist, K., Österman, K., & Kaukiainen, A. (1996). Bullying as a group process: Participant roles and their relations to social status within the group. *Aggressive Behavior, 22,* 1–15. doi:10.1002/(SICI)1098-2337 (1996)22:1<1::AID-AB1>3.0 .CO;2-T

Salmivalli, C., & Peets, K. (2008). Bullies, victims, and bully–victim relationships. In K. Rubin, W. Bukowski, & B. Laursen (Eds.), *Handbook of peer interactions, relationships, and groups* (pp. 322–340). New York, NY: Guilford Press.

Salmivalli, C., Poskiparta, E., Tikka, A., & Pöyhönen, V. (2009). *KiVa: Teacher's guide, unit 1* (Research Into Practice Publication Series, No. 2). Turku, Finland: University of Turku, Psychology Department.

Salmivalli, C., Pöyhönen, V., & Kaukiainen, A. (2009). *KiVa: Teacher's guide, unit 2* (Research Into Practice Publication Series, No. 3). Turku, Finland: University of Turku, Psychology Department.

Salmivalli, C., & Voeten, M. (2004). Connections between attitudes, group norms, and behaviors associated with bullying in schools. *International Journal of Behavioral Development, 28,* 246–258. doi:10.1080/01650250344000488

Salmivalli, C., Voeten, M., & Poskiparta, E. (2011). Bystanders matter: Associations between reinforcing, defending, and the frequency of bullying in classrooms. *Journal of Clinical Child and Adolescent Psychology, 40,* 1–9.

Shadish, W., Cook, T., & Campbell, D. (2002). *Experimental and quasi-experimental designs for generalized causal inference.* Boston, MA: Houghton Mifflin.

Smith, P. K. (2010). Bullying in primary and secondary schools: Psychological and organizational comparisons. In S. Jimerson, S. Swearer, & D. Espelage (Eds.), *Handbook of bullying in schools: An international perspective* (pp. 137–150). New York, NY: Guilford Press.

Smith, P. K., Pepler, D., & Rigby, K. (Eds.). (2004). *Bullying in schools: How successful can interventions be?* New York, NY: Cambridge University Press. doi:10.1017/CBO9780511584466

Snijders, T., & Bosker, R. (1999). *Multilevel analysis: An introduction to basic and advanced multilevel modeling.* London, England: Sage.

Solberg, M. E., & Olweus, D. (2003). Prevalence estimation of school bullying with the Olweus Bully/Victim Questionnaire. *Aggressive Behavior, 29,* 239–268. doi:10.1002/ab.10047

## Notes

1. When these 888 schools registered as KiVa schools, they reported having 200,482 students.
2. Assuming an equal number of respondents in the intervention and control groups, the number of victims would have been 156,634 $\times$ 13.8% = 21,615. This corresponds to a reduction of 25,527 − 21,615 = 3,912 students. The number of bullies would have been 156,629 $\times$ 9.6% = 15,036, which corresponds to a reduction of 17,363 − 15,036 = 2,327 students.

**ANTTI KÄRNÄ** is postdoctoral research fellow in the Department of Psychology at University of Turku. Marinus Voeten is educational and psychological researcher in Nijmegen, Netherlands. Todd D. Little, PhD, is professor of educational psychology at Texas Tech University. Elisa Poskiparta and Christina Salmivalli are research staffers in the Department of Psychology at University of Turku. Erkki Alanen is retired and was a research staffer in the Department of Psychology at University of Turku.

**Sabina Low and Mark Van Ryzin**

# The Moderating Effects of School Climate on Bullying Prevention Efforts

**D**ue to the high prevalence of bullying in schools and its strong relationship to adverse mental health and academic outcomes, there has been considerable growth in the number and dissemination of school-based bullying prevention programs over the past 20 years (Espelage & Swearer, 2003). Part of this growth is spurred by states requiring schools to adopt policies and practices to assess and address bullying and harassment among students. However, policies alone or in combination with bullying prevention curricula do not automatically translate to behavioral change and, ultimately, strong public health impact. Indeed, several recent meta-analyses reveal that over the last decade, school-wide bullying prevention evaluations have demonstrated negligible to nonsignificant results (Merrel, Gueldner, Ross, & Isava, 2008; Smith, Schneider, Smith, & Ananiadou, 2004), with the more promising studies being based in Europe (Farrington & Ttofi, 2009).

Studies on the effectiveness of bullying prevention programs have tended to focus on features and delivery of the programs as important determinants of their success (see Durlak & DuPre, 2008) with particular attention to implementation (Hirschstein, VanSchoiack, Frey, Snell, & MacKenzie, 2007; Low, Van Ryzin, Brown, Smith, & Haggerty, 2014; Olweus, 1991; Smith et al., 2004). Yet, as Orpinas (2009) articulated, such programs do not operate in a vacuum, and we may be limiting our knowledge of bullying prevention efforts (and how to optimize these efforts) if we ignore the broader context in which these programs are delivered. Orpinas (2009) argued that having a positive school climate is pivotal to reducing aggression, and a necessary foundation for any stand-alone bullying prevention efforts. Yet, few (if any) scholars have formally tested the moderating role of school climate on the effects of an adopted bullying prevention program, masking important information on whether and to what extent the larger environment shapes bullying prevention impacts. The current study aims to address this gap by examining the moderating effects of school climate on the effectiveness of Steps to Respect (STR; Committee for Children, 2005), a bullying prevention program with demonstrated efficacy in reducing bullying behavior (Brown et al., 2011).

## School Climate and Bullying

School climate refers to the culture, milieu, or character of a school, capturing its sense of community and overall organizational health (Cohen, McCabe, Michelli, & Pickeral, 2009; Hoy, Smith, & Sweetland, 2002). Climate is foundational to students' values, behaviors, and peer group norms, and there is a robust literature suggesting relations between school climate and students' academic achievement, commitment to school, and conduct problems (McEvoy & Welker, 2000; Mehta, Cornell, Fan, & Gregory, 2013). Climate has long been considered a critical component to targeting peer violence and aggression, and particularly bullying, given that a systems framework is necessary to assess and respond to the complex origins, manifestations, and underlying maintenance factors of bullying. Indeed, several studies have documented relations between positive school climate and reduced bullying and victimization (Guerra, Williams, & Sadek, 2011; Meyer-Adams & Connor, 2008; Plank, Bradshaw, & Young, 2009), more prosocial responses to bullying behavior (Lindstrom Johnson, Waasdorp, Debnam, & Bradshaw, 2013), greater willingness to intervene (Syvertsen, Flanagan, & Stout, 2009), and greater willingness to seek help for bullying or threats of violence (Eliot, Cornell, Gregory, & Fan, 2010). In particular, the relational aspects of the community (e.g., connectedness, having trusting relationships with teachers, availability of caring adults) has been associated with lower rates of aggression and victimization in schools (Corrigan, Klein, & Isaacs, 2010; Gregory et al., 2010) and

Low, Sabina; Van Ryzin, Mark, "The Moderating Effects of School Climate on Bullying Prevention Efforts," *School Psychology Quarterly*, vol. 29, no. 3, September 2014, pp. 306–319. No further reproduction or distribution is permitted without written permission from the American Psychological Association.

greater likelihood of help-seeking behaviors (Gregory, Cornell & Fan, 2011).

## School Climate Can Facilitate Program Effectiveness

Based on the aforementioned studies, there is accumulating evidence that creating and maintaining a positive, trusting school climate can function as a form of bullying prevention. After all, climate affects norms and social interactions at the level of the school (e.g., commitment to academics, relations with parents), classroom (trusting relations with peers and teachers), and individual (enhanced willingness to report or intervene) that should theoretically combat the origins and maintenance of bullying (Eliot et al., 2010; Orpinas, 2009; Unnever & Cornell, 2004). However, climate may also function at different ecological levels to enhance the adoption, commitment to, and implementation of prevention programs as well as the deployment of skills taught in bullying prevention programs. For example, Eliot, Cornell, Gregory, and Fan (2010) examined the role of climate among students participating in the Virginia High School Safety Study and found that positive school climate engendered more positive bystander behavior. The authors concluded that fostering more positive and supportive relations may be valuable to engaging students in bullying prevention efforts. Similarly, Unnever and Cornell (2004) found that a positive psycho–social climate encourages help-seeking in schools in response to bullying or peer violence, which is a critical cornerstone to the success of stand-alone violence prevention programs. Bradshaw, Koth, Thornton, and Leaf (2009) found that schools with higher levels of organizational health (indicated by leadership, academic emphasis, and staff climate) at baseline saw better implementation and greater improvement in organizational health over a 5-year trial of Positive behavioral Interventions and Supports (PBIS). Lastly, in a trial of Expect Respect, a bullying prevention program, the authors found that school climate served as a key mechanism (i.e., mediator) for behavior change (Meraviglia, Becker, Rosenbluth, Sanchez, & Roberston, 2003).

## Summary and Aims

Taken together, prior research would suggest that the effects of bullying prevention programs shape, are shaped by, the school climate. However, few if any studies have examined the relationship between climate and bullying prevention programming impact. Thus, the overarching aim of the current article is to explore this relationship so as to better understand the independent and or synergistic effects of the environment in which bullying programs (or violence prevention programs more generally) are delivered. Specifically, we sought to answer two questions: (a) After controlling for intervention status (STR), does school climate (operationalized below) relate to decreases in bullying behaviors and attitudes over time? and (b) Does school climate magnify the effects of a bullying intervention on bullying behaviors and attitudes?

In addition to exploring these questions, the current study advances the field in three novel and important ways. First, we utilize both teacher/staff perceptions of climate as well as student, to capture a broader and more diverse sampling of perspectives of school environment. Second, we recognize that climate is multidimensional, and contrast two related but potentially distinct dimensions of climate, relational (or psychosocial) and organizational (see Roeser, Eccles, & Sameroff, 2000). For this study, "staff psychosocial school climate" is operationalized as perceived relations with teachers, parents, and students, whereas the "organizational climate" component is captured by teacher/staff perceptions of policies and administrative commitment to bullying prevention. In contrast, "student psychosocial climate" measures students' relationships with peers and teachers, and perceived connectedness to school. Third, use of multilevel modeling allowed for us to examine the relations between climate and bullying outcomes as contextualized (i.e., nested) within school demographic characteristics and intervention status. Moreover, multilevel modeling allowed for us to examine staff reports of climate as a settinglevel (Level 2) variable (Marsh et al., 2012), in contrast with student climate (which was assessed at the individual level).

The current study draws upon data from a 1-year elementary school bullying prevention trial of STR. The STR program is based on a social-ecological model of bullying which views youth behavior as shaped by multiple factors within nested contextual systems at the school, peer, and individual levels (Swearer, Espelage, Vaillancourt, & Hymel, 2010). School-wide components are intended to foster a positive school climate and positive norms through a one-time teacher and staff training focused on improved monitoring of students and instruction on how to effectively intervene with students involved in bullying situations (i.e., coaching). Classroom curricula are intended for the upper three elementary grades and seek to promote socially responsible norms and behavior and increase social–emotional skills. Lessons help students recognize bullying, increase empathy for students that are bullied, build friendship skills to increase protective social connections, improve assertiveness and communication skills to help students deter and report bullying, and teach appropriate bystander responses to bullying. A randomized controlled trial of STR (Brown, Low, Smith, & Haggerty, 2011) indicated positive main effects on student attitudes, bullying related behavior (e.g., social competence, physical bullying perpetration, positive bystander behavior), and school climate. In addition, when examining implementation as a moderator of program impact, Low, Van Ryzin, Brown, Smith, and Haggerty (2014) found that high levels of engagement (but not adherence to program components) was related to lower levels of school bullying problems, enhanced school climate and attitudes less supportive of bullying. Notably, psychosocial climate was predictive of student engagement, though organizational climate was not.

Drawing upon the previous findings from the STR study and the extant literature previously discussed, we hypothesized both main and moderation effects for school climate. First, we expected climate to contribute to improved outcomes regardless of intervention status. Second, we expected that intervention schools with more positive school climate would see greater program impact when compared with intervention schools with less positive climate. Finally, we did not anticipate that climate as measured in terms of policies/administrative commitment (i.e., organizational climate) would have a significant impact, either as a main effect or when interacted with intervention status. Finally, staff and students perceptions of climate have functioned similarly in prior STR analyses (i.e., showed high correspondence in relations to outcomes; see Brown et al., 2011; Low et al., 2014), and thus, we anticipated similar patterns of relations across reporters here.

# Method

## Participants

### Schools

The data for this study were derived from a 1-year (pre to post) STR efficacy trial that was conducted in 33 elementary schools in north-central California. Based on power analyses using parameter estimates from Frey et al. (2005) and Jenson and Dietrich (2007) we targeted 34 schools for the trial. The 34 schools were matched into pairs within each geographic area using NCES data (http://www.ed-data.k12.ca.us) on the characteristics of the school environment (e.g., total student enrollment, change in student enrollment from 2006 to 2007, number of teachers), and characteristics of the student population (e.g., percentage eligible for the free or reduced-price lunch program, ethnic/racial percentages, and percentage of students for whom English was not their primary language). Schools within each matched pair were assigned randomly to either the intervention or wait-listed control condition using a random number table. Between random assignment and program implementation, two schools withdrew from the study (one because of turnover in leadership, and one because of building remodeling). One school was immediately replaced by another eligible school, which was an adequate match on all criteria. A replacement was not found, however, for the second school, leaving us with 33 schools for the trial; the matching school was not removed to preserve statistical power. Overall, the schools had an average enrollment (school size) of 480 ($SD = 170$, range = 77–748) and an average free or reduced-lunch percentage of 43.45 ($SD = 30.72$, range = 0.00–99.00); intervention and control schools were not significantly different on these measures, $F(1, 31) = 2.09$, $ns$, and $F(1, 31) = .19$, $ns$, respectively. Twenty-five percent of the schools were from rural areas, 10% were from small towns, 50% were from suburban areas, and 15% were located in midsized cities. On average, 40% of students received free or reduced-price lunch ($SD = 29\%$). The mean number of students per school was 479 ($SD = 177$, range = 77–749 students) and the mean number of teachers per school was 24.

### School Staff

We asked all school staff from each of the 33 participating schools to voluntarily complete pretest and posttest versions of the School Environment Survey. School staff participants included all paid and volunteer staff including: administrators, teachers, paraprofessionals, support staff, custodial and cafeteria personnel, and so forth. At pretest, 1,307 individuals completed a survey (77% of the total population of school staff). At posttest, 1,296 individuals (76%) completed a survey. Respondents represented school administrators (2.8%), teachers (58%), paraprofessionals (10%), cafeteria staff (3.3%), school counselors/psychologists (1.4%), custodial staff (1.4%), bus drivers (0.7%), volunteers (0.1%), and other positions (7.6%). School staff participants were 90% female, 12% Hispanic, and 88% White. School staff averaged 46 years of age and worked at their schools a median of 3 to 5 years.

### Students

All students in each of the selected classrooms were included in the target sample of 3,119 students for completion of the student survey; 2,940 (94%) provided data at both time points, which comprised the analytic sample for this study. Approximately half (50. 4%) of the analytic sample was male, 52.5% were White, and 6.6% were African American; 41.7% of students identified as of Hispanic origin via self-report. Students ranged in age from 7 to 11 years, with 2.3% being age 7, 27.7% being age 8, 48.1% being age 9, 19.1% being age 10, and 2.8% being age 11 ($M = 8.92$, $SD = .92$). Surveys were conducted in class (proctored by research staff), and took approximately one class period to complete. Students received a small gift worth about $5 for each interview they completed in the fall (pretest) and spring (posttest).

## Steps to Respect

The program included 11 semiscripted skills lessons focusing on social–emotional skills for positive peer relations, emotion management, and recognizing, refusing, and reporting of bullying behavior were delivered by teachers. Lesson topics included joining groups, distinguishing reporting from tattling, and being a responsible bystander. Instructional strategies included direct instruction, large- and small-group discussions, skills practice, and games. Weekly lessons, totaling about 1 hr, were taught over 2 to 3 days. Overall, fidelity to the program was high. Third through sixth grade teachers' ratings of school-wide implementation on a four-item scale (1 = *poor*, 4 = *excellent*) indicated that, by the end of the school year, program policies and procedures were well implemented ($M = 3.25$, $SD = 0.44$). Teachers reported teaching 99.2% of

all classroom skill lessons. Approximately 75% of students were exposed to at least 95% of all lessons and an additional 22% of students were exposed to between 75% and 94% of the lessons. Overall, program engagement (e.g., asking questions, volunteering) was high ($M = 3.67$, $SD = .54$). Across all lessons, 18% of teachers reported omitting one or more elements from a lesson. Despite this, a high percentage of teachers (92%) reported completing all objectives.

## Measures

### Student survey

Student pre- and posttest survey data (October and April, approximately) were collected using a revised version of the Colorado Trust's Bullying Prevention Initiative Student Survey (Csuti, 2008a). The outcome scales used in this study, the number of items per scale, scale coefficient alphas, intraclass correlations, and sample items for the posttest administrations of the survey are presented in Table 1. Scale scores for student survey measures were constructed as the mean of all nonmissing items. The school psychosocial climate construct is composed of three subscales for student climate, connectedness, and support.

### School environment survey

Pretest and posttest data were collected from school staff during school staff training sessions (in intervention schools only) or during in-service meetings using the

*Table 1*

**Student Survey Measures**

| Variable | Number of items | Coefficient alpha | ICC | Sample item/response options |
|---|---|---|---|---|
| School climate (pre) | 15 | .87 | — | This is a close-knit school where everyone looks out for each other; students in my school are willing to help each other. (1 = *Strongly disagree* to 4 = *Strongly agree*) |
| Bullying perpetration (post) | 7 | .87 | .07 | I teased or said mean things to certain students. (1 = *Never* to 5 = *A lot*) |
| Bullying victimization (post) | 4 | .75 | .04 | A particular student or group of students pushed, shoved, tripped, or picked a fight with me. (1 = *Never* to 5 = *A lot*) |
| Positive bystander behavior (post) | 5 | .71 | .05 | I ignored rumors or lies that I heard about other students. (1 = *Never* to 5 = *A lot*) |
| Student attitudes against bullying (post) | 7 | .87 | .04 | How okay is it when students tease weaker students in front of others? (1 = *Extremely wrong* to 5 = *Very okay*) |
| Student attitudes toward intervention in bullying incidents (post) | 4 | .79 | .08 | How okay is it when students defend others who are being shoved around by strong students? (1 = *Extremely wrong* to 5 = *Very okay*) |

*Note.* ICC = intraclass correlation.

School Environment Survey (SES). The SES is a brief (10-min), anonymous, paper-and-pencil survey, which was adapted for the current study from the Colorado Trust's 3-year statewide Bullying Prevention Initiative (Csuti, 2008b). The SES was designed to parallel several of the measures collected from the student surveys to provide an alternative source of information on the social–ecological context of the school environment. School staffs were asked about their perceptions of their school's climate, their school's antibullying policies and strategies, and background demographic information (age, gender, race/ethnicity, how many years they worked at the school, and their position at the school). Scale scores for outcome measures were created as the mean of all non-missing items on the scale, and teacher reports were averaged across school. The two SES measures used in this study were as follows:

*Organizational climate* was measured by eight items from the School Antibullying Policies and Strategies scale that asked school staff about how much their school was doing with regard to policies and strategies to prevent bullying (e.g., *Demonstrating administrator commitment and leadership to address bullies, bullied, and bystanders*). Responses were recorded on a 4-point Likert-type scale ranging from (1 = *Not at all* to 4 = *A lot*, *M = 2.83, SD = .76*). Coefficient alpha for this measure was .93.

*Psychosocial school climate* was measured by seven items that asked school staff how much they were connected or bonded, or shared the same values with each other, with students, and with parents (e.g. *Staff in this school can be trusted.*). Responses were recorded on a 4-point Likert-type scale ranging from 1 = *Strongly disagree* to 4 = *Strongly agree (M = 3.46, SD = .47)*. Coefficient alpha for this measure was .91.

### School characteristics

Data on school size and the demographic characteristics of students were obtained from the National Center for Educational Statistics (NCES; http://www.ed-data.k12.ca.us). The following variables were used as school-level predictors of bullying outcomes: total student enrollment (*M = 479, SD = 180*); percentage eligible for the free or reduced-price lunch program (*M = 40, SD = 29*); and percentage White (*M = 50, SD = 30*).

## Statistical Analyses

In order to assess the unique effects of climate (after controlling for intervention status), as well as the moderating effects of climate on intervention status, hierarchical

linear models (HLM 7.0; Raudenbush & Bryk, 2002), were conducted wherein the student outcome measures were regressed on pretest staff (Level 2) and student-report climate (at Level 1), with school intervention status and characteristics at Level 2.

The impacts of student-reported and staff-reported climate were examined in separate models, and each outcome was examined separately according to standard HLM practice. Variables were grand-mean centered and random effects were included in all model equations to account for variability across schools. Robust standard errors were used to address any issues with non-normality. School size was divided by 100 before being entered into the analyses. Models were estimated using Restricted Maximum Likelihood analysis, which can provide unbiased estimates in the presence of missing data. The tenability of regression assumptions was evaluated with each model, but no significant violations were found (not presented).

To examine moderation, staff-report climate and policy variables were multiplied with intervention condition at Level 2, or in the case of student-report climate, we calculated a cross-level interaction. If interaction effects between climate and intervention condition were not significant, models were rerun without the interaction effects in order to examine main effects of climate and the intervention independently (to maximize power). For example, students' self-reported level of bullying at posttest was regressed upon (a) pretest levels of bullying, (b) levels of Staff Psychosocial Climate (PCLM) measured at pretest, and (c) school size (SZE), school-level percentage of White students (WHT) and eligible for free or reduced-price lunch (FRL), intervention condition (STR), and the interaction term (INT); this is illustrated in the following model:

### Model 1: Level 1 (Student)

$$POST - BULLYING = \beta_{0j}$$
$$+\beta_{1j}(PRE - BULLYING) + e$$

### Level 2 (School)

$$\beta_{0j} = \gamma_{00} + \gamma_{01}(SZE) + \gamma_{02}(WHT) + \gamma_{03}(FRL)$$
$$+\gamma_{04}(STR) + \gamma_{05}(PCLM) + \gamma_{06}(INT) + u_{0j}$$
$$\beta_{1j} = \gamma_{10} + \gamma_{11}(SZE) \gamma_{12}(WHT) + \gamma_{13}(FRL)$$
$$+\gamma_{14}(STR) + \gamma_{15}(PCLM) + \gamma_{16}(INT) + u_{1j}$$

To examine moderation by student-report climate, students' self-reported level of bullying at posttest was regressed upon (a) pretest levels of bullying; (b) levels of

Student-Perceived Psychosocial Climate (PCLM) measured at pretest; and (c) school size (SZE), school-level percentage of White students (WHT) and eligible for free or reduced-price lunch (FRL), and intervention condition (STR); this is illustrated in the following model:

## Model 2: Level 1 (Student)

$$POST - BULLYING = \beta_{0j}$$
$$+ \beta_{1j}(PRE - BULLYING)$$
$$+ \beta_{2j}(PCLM) + e$$

## Level 2 (School)

$$\beta_{0j} = \gamma_{00} + \gamma_{01}(SZE) + \gamma_{02}(WHT)$$
$$+ \gamma_{03}(FRL) + \gamma_{04}(STR) \, u_{0j}$$
$$\beta_{1j} = \gamma_{10} + \gamma_{11}(SZE) + \gamma_{12}(WHT)$$
$$+ \gamma_{13}(FRL) + \gamma_{14}(STR) + u_{1j}$$
$$\beta_{2j} = \gamma_{20} + \gamma_{21}(SZE) + \gamma_{22}(WHT)$$
$$+ \gamma_{23}(FRL) + \gamma_{24}(STR) + u_{2j}$$

In this model, the interaction between student report climate and intervention condition does not require the insertion of an interaction effect; rather, this effect is captured by $\gamma_{24}$, a fixed effect representing a cross-level interaction.

## Missing Data

For the SES and student survey instruments, 39.3% and 11.5% of school staff and students, respectively, were missing 67% or more of items on at least one of each survey's scales. A statistical comparison of participants that had missing scale data versus those who did not have missing scale data indicated that rates of missingness did not differ by participants' gender, race/ethnic group, age, grade, or intervention status (all $ps > .05$). Rates of missing scale data, however, were significantly different by geographic area, with one area demonstrating lower rates of missing data than the other two geographic areas, $\chi^2(1, N = 3,048) = 4.81, p < .05$.

To account for the missing data at the scale level, we conducted multiple imputation analyses (Graham, 2009) using NORM version 2.03 (Schafer, 1999), separately for each of the three surveys. To preserve the unique variance-covariance structures of the data by intervention status, we conducted separate imputation analyses for experimental and control schools. Imputation

analyses included all respective outcome measures, participants' background demographic information, and dummy-coded indicator variables representing the matching of schools into pairs. Forty imputed data sets were created for each survey by intervention status group. Imputed data sets were combined subsequently to include both intervention and control groups for analysis of outcome measures.

## Results

Correlations and sample descriptive data for all variables at Level 1 are provided in Table 2. The bullying measures demonstrated significant stability across time (i.e., from pretest to posttest). Descriptive data for the schools (i.e., size, free or reduced-price lunch) is presented in the Method section. Descriptive data for staff-report climate is as follows: psychosocial climate ($M = 3.33$, $SD = .20$, range = 2.86 to 3.74); organizational climate ($M = 2.85$, $SD = .33$, range = 2.27 to 3.47). The two staff measures of climate were significantly correlated, $r = .59, p < .001$, but were not correlated with size, ethnicity, or free or reduced-price lunch, with the following exceptions: psychosocial climate was correlated free or reduced-price lunch, $r = -.56, p < .001$, and with percentage White, $r = .63, p < .001$.

## Staff Psychosocial Climate

To evaluate the effects of staff-report psychosocial climate, we initially fit a model evaluating whether staff-report climate moderated the effect of the intervention on student-report outcomes (as in Model 1); the results are presented in Table 3. Victimization was the only outcome that demonstrated a significant interaction effect (effect size, $R^2 = .24$); the negative coefficient for this effect indicated that a more positive psychosocial school climate, as reported by the teachers and staff, was associated with a larger drop in student-reported victimization at posttest.

Because the interaction term was significant for only one outcome, we removed it and reran the models (excluding the model for victimization) in order to obtain an estimate of the main effect of staff-report psychosocial climate; the results are presented in Table 4. Staff-report psychosocial climate was linked with a variety of improvements in student outcomes by posttest, including lower levels of bullying perpetration and higher levels of positive bystander behavior (the effect for attitudes against bullying was marginal). Effects sizes ranged were in the medium range ($R^2 = .24–.25$).

*Table 2*

### Correlations and Sample Descriptives for Level 1 Variables from Student Survey

| Variable | 1 | 2 | 3 | 4 | 5 | 6 | 7 | 8 | 9 | 10 | 11 |
|---|---|---|---|---|---|---|---|---|---|---|---|
| 1. School climate (pre) | — | | | | | | | | | | |
| 2. Bullying perpetration (pre) | −.30*** | — | | | | | | | | | |
| 3. Bullying victim (pre) | −.22*** | .33*** | — | | | | | | | | |
| 4. Positive bystander behavior (pre) | −.02 | −.02 | −.20*** | — | | | | | | | |
| 5. Student attitude against (pre) | .20*** | −.16*** | −.05* | −.19*** | — | | | | | | |
| 6. Student attitude intervention (pre) | .15*** | −.14*** | −.12*** | −.27*** | .44*** | — | | | | | |
| 7. Bullying perpetration (post) | −.19*** | .42*** | .18*** | .04* | −.18*** | −.10*** | — | | | | |
| 8. Bullying victim (post) | −.16*** | .16*** | .47*** | −.08*** | −.06** | −.07*** | .27*** | — | | | |
| 9. Positive bystander behavior (post) | .10*** | .13*** | −.11*** | .33*** | −.09*** | −.16*** | .02 | −.19*** | — | | |
| 10. Student attitude against (post) | .17*** | −.19*** | −.07*** | −.07*** | .16*** | .09*** | −.08*** | −.05* | .32*** | — | |
| 11. Student attitude intervention (post) | .12*** | −.19*** | −.09*** | −.15*** | .15*** | .23*** | −.03 | −.09*** | .37*** | .58*** | — |
| *M* | 2.99 | 1.27 | 2.11 | 2.36 | 3.70 | 2.30 | 1.61 | 2.16 | 2.64 | 3.53 | 3.02 |
| *SD* | .46 | 1.78 | 1.04 | .90 | .50 | .98 | 1.87 | 1.04 | 1.11 | .52 | 1.41 |

$*p < .05.$    $**p < .01.$    $***p < .001.$

*Table 3*

### Multilevel Models of Staff-Report Psychosocial Climate (with Interaction Terms)

| | Bullying perpetration | Victimization | Positive bystander behavior | Attitudes against bullying | Attitudes toward intervention |
|---|---|---|---|---|---|
| **Predictors (all assessed at pretest)** | | | | | |
| Baseline measure | .44 (.03)*** | .46 (.02)*** | .38 (.02)*** | .19 (.03)*** | .26 (.03)*** |
| **School level** | | | | | |
| School size (enrollment) | .00 (.03) | .00 (.04) | .01 (.02) | .09 (.04)* | .07 (.03)* |
| Ethnicity (% White) | −.009 (.002)*** | .001 (.002) | .003 (.001)* | .004 (.003) | .002 (.002) |
| SES (% FRL) | −.005 (.002)** | .001 (.002) | .001 (.001) | −.001 (.003) | −.004 (.002)† |
| Intervention condition | 1.27 (1.24) | 2.58 (.92)** | 1.33 (.81) | 2.85 (2.10) | 1.72 (1.58) |
| Psychosocial climate (staff) | −.43 (.34) | .34 (.18)† | .65 (.17)*** | 1.17 (.53)* | .77 (.40)† |
| Intervention × Climate | −.43 (.37) | −.80 (.28)** | −.42 (.24) | −.84 (.63) | −.50 (.47) |
| Effect size (interaction) | .04 | .24 | .04 | .07 | .00 |

*Note.* SES = School Environment Survey; FRL = free or reduced-price lunch.

$†p < .10.$    $*p < .05.$    $**p < .01.$    $***p < .001.$

*Table 4*

## Multilevel Models for Staff-Report Psychosocial Climate (without Interactions)

| | Bullying perpetration | Victimization | Positive bystander behavior | Attitudes against bullying | Attitudes toward intervention |
|---|---|---|---|---|---|
| Predictors (all assessed at pretest) | | | | | |
| Baseline measure | .44 (.03)*** | — | .38 (.02)*** | .19 (.03)*** | .26 (.03)*** |
| School level | | | | | |
| School size (enrollment) | .00 (.03) | — | .01 (.02) | .08 (.04)* | .07 (.03)* |
| Ethnicity (% White) | −.009 (.002)*** | — | .003 (.001)† | .003 (.003) | .002 (.002) |
| SES (% FRL) | −.005 (.002)** | — | .001 (.001) | −.001 (.003) | −.004 (.002)† |
| Intervention condition | −.15 (.08)† | — | −.06 (.06) | .05 (.13) | .05 (.10) |
| Psychosocial climate (staff) | −.64 (.26)* | — | .43 (.19)* | .74 (.42)† | .50 (.31) |
| Effect size (climate) | .24 | — | .25 | .08 | .06 |

*Note.* SES = School Environment Survey; FRL = free or reduced-price lunch. Because the Victimization model had a significant interaction term, it was not rerun to examine main effects.

†$p < .10$.    *$p < .05$.    **$p < .01$.    ***$p < .001$.

## Staff Organizational Climate

We then ran similar models for teacher reports of school organizational climate; these models were similar to Model 1 but made use of organizational climate rather than psychosocial climate. We initially fit a model evaluating whether staff-report organizational climate moderated the effect of the intervention on student-report outcomes; the results indicated no significant interactions. Thus, we removed the interaction terms and reran the models in order to obtain estimates of the main effect of organizational climate; the results are presented in Table 5. Staff-report organizational climate was linked with a decrease in bullying perpetration at posttest ($R^2 = .43$).

## Student-Report Psychosocial Climate

Finally, to evaluate the effects of student-report climate on intervention outcomes, we ran a model with student reports of climate at Level 1 (while including the intervention condition at Level 2) and a cross-level (Climate X Intervention Status) interaction. The results are presented in a single table (see Table 6) because there were no significant cross-level interactions. Although no cross-level interactions with intervention condition were significant, student-report psychosocial climate was linked with a variety of improvements in student outcomes by posttest, including lower levels of bullying perpetration and victimization and higher levels of positive bystander behavior, attitudes against bullying and attitudes toward bullying intervention. As shown in the table, effect sizes for climate effects ranged from small to medium (.08–.21). There was one significant intervention effect on bullying perpetration.

## Discussion

Social–ecological theory is a guiding tenet of bullying prevention, insofar as bullying is a school-wide problem (see Mehta et al., 2013; Unnever & Cornell, 2004). Just as much as bullying creates a climate of fear, mistrust and intimidation, several studies suggest that a supportive, fair and respectful school climate provides a host environment that engenders the norms, behaviors, and attitudes/values that are incompatible with aggressive behavior (Bryk & Driscoll, 1988; Gottfredson et al., 2005; Zaykowski & Gunter, 2012), including bullying as a specific subclass (Guerra et al., 2011; Meyer-Adams &

*Table 5*

## Multilevel Model for Staff-Report Organizational Climate

| | Bullying perpetration | Victimization | Positive bystander behavior | Attitudes against bullying | Attitudes toward intervention |
|---|---|---|---|---|---|
| **Predictors (all assessed at pretest)** | | | | | |
| Baseline measure | .44 (.03)*** | .46 (.02)*** | .39 (.02)*** | .18 (.03)*** | .26 (.03)*** |
| **School level** | | | | | |
| School size (enrollment) | .01 (.02) | −.01 (.02) | .01 (.02) | .08 (.04)† | .06 (.04)† |
| Ethnicity (% White) | −.001 (.002) | .001 (.002) | .004 (.001)** | .005 (.003) | .003 (.003) |
| SES (% FRL) | −.003 (.002)† | .001 (.002) | .000 (.001) | −.002 (.003) | −.005 (.003) |
| Intervention condition | −.15 (.08)† | −.08 (.06) | −.06 (.06) | .05 (.13) | .05 (.08) |
| Organizational climate (staff) | −.38 (.10)*** | .01 (.09) | .10 (.09) | .20 (.22) | .14 (.18) |
| Effect size (climate) | .43 | .00 | .00 | .00 | .00 |

*Note.* SES = School Environment Survey; FRL = free or reduced-price lunch. The interaction term between Organizational Climate and Intervention Condition was not significant in any model.

†$p < .10$.    *$p < .05$.    **$p < .01$.    ***$p < .001$.

*Table 6*

## Multilevel Model for Student-Report Psychosocial Climate

| | Bullying perpetration | Victimization | Positive bystander behavior | Attitudes against bullying | Attitudes toward intervention |
|---|---|---|---|---|---|
| **Predictors (all assessed at pretest)** | | | | | |
| Baseline measure | .44 (.03)*** | .45 (.02)*** | .40 (.02)*** | .29 (.03)*** | .31 (.03)*** |
| Psychosocial climate (students) | −.21 (.06)*** | −.13 (.04)** | .20 (.05)*** | .59 (.07)*** | .20 (.06)** |
| Effect size (climate) | .21 | .14 | .10 | .14 | .08 |
| **School level** | | | | | |
| School size (enrollment) | −.01 (.02) | −.01 (.02) | .01 (.02) | .08 (.03)* | .05 (.03) |
| Ethnicity (% White) | −.010 (.002)*** | .001 (.002) | .004 (.001)* | .004 (.003) | .003 (.003) |
| SES (% FRL) | −.004 (.002)† | .001 (.002) | .000 (.001) | −.001 (.002) | −.005 (.003) |
| Intervention condition | −.16 (.08)* | −.09 (.05) | −.07 (.07) | .03 (.12) | .03 (.08) |

*Note.* SES = School Environment Survey; FRL = free or reduced-price lunch. The cross-level interaction between Intervention Condition and Student-Report Climate was not significant for any outcome.

†$p < .10$.    *$p < .05$.    **$p < .01$.    ***$p < .001$.

Connor, 2008; Nansel et al., 2001). Additionally, a handful of studies suggest that a positive psychosocial climate is pivotal to the success of violence prevention programs (Bradshaw et al., 2009; Eliot et al., 2010; Meraviglia et al., 2003). Yet, few of these studies have been specific to bullying prevention (where context is particularly critical), and most have utilized single reporters, have a limited sampling of bullying (and related) outcomes, and have not utilized multilevel modeling. In addition to addressing these methodological limitations, there remains a paucity of studies that disentangle the relation between context (i.e., climate) and bullying prevention programming, as if these were orthogonal to each other. Doing so will provide valuable information for theory building and prevention.

The current article is predicated on the belief that in order to understand how bullying prevention programs work (or fail to work), we must understand the broader context and elucidate the role of the host environment, or school climate. Scholars can agree that context matters with bullying prevention, but the novel contribution of the current study is examining how bullying prevention programs (in this case, STR) work in conjunction with existing school climate. The goals of the current study were to examine the main effects of climate (i.e., psychosocial and organizational dimensions) and STR, as well as the moderating role of school climate on the impact of STR. Specifically, we examined whether the effects of STR were strengthened by positive school climate (i.e., a synergistic or interactive effect), or whether the relation between STR and outcomes was largely nonconditional upon climate. Findings from the current article yield a consistent pattern, across both student and staff reports, wherein the psychosocial dimension of climate is predictive of positive changes in bullying attitudes and behavior, but does not appear to enhance STR intervention effects. For example, students who reported more positive psychosocial climate, regardless of intervention group, also endorsed stronger attitudes toward intervention and attitudes against aggression, as well as improved bystander behavior; students' perceived psychosocial climate also predicted lower levels of victimization and perpetration. In the case of staff perceptions, more positive psychosocial climate was related to lower levels of perpetration and improved bystander behavior. In only one instance, climate demonstrated a synergistic effect with STR: staff-report psychosocial climate appeared to strengthen the effects of STR on student-report victimization. Interestingly, when the effects of STR and climate are considered simultaneously (e.g., Table 4), most of the main effects of intervention condition are nonsignificant,

even though they were found to be significant previously (Brown et al., 2011); a reminder of the potent role of environment. In sum, our results also suggest that bullying programs such as STR may have a smaller impact on bullying behaviors and attitudes in schools that already possess positive psychosocial climates.

At the same time, it is important to not diminish the synergistic effect between staff-report psychosocial climate and reduced victimization among STR intervention schools. This finding suggests that intervention schools with more supportive psychosocial communities will see greater program impacts on student-report victimization. Positive psychosocial environments may not only model and reinforce more pro-social behavior, but there is literature suggesting that supportive school climates correspond with greater levels of critical coping skills among students, such as seeking help from adults, because youth feel safer (Williams & Cornell, 2006; Wilson & Deanne, 2001). Thus, positive school climates may serve as an importance bridge between skill acquisition and skill deployment, to the extent that these skills are contingent upon on having trusting, caring relationships with adults.

Because STR can significantly and positively impact school climate (both staff and student report; Brown et al., 2011), it may be that the effects of STR (and, by extension, other bullying prevention programs) are *mediated* by school climate. In other words, the effects of STR on bullying behavior and attitudes may come about due to an STR-generated improvement in psychosocial climate. With only two waves of data, we were not able to adequately evaluate this hypothesis, but it presents an intriguing topic for future research. Furthermore, these data do not preclude what is likely a recursive relationship between bullying and psychosocial climate, in which climate leads to reductions in bullying behavior, which in turn improves the psychosocial climate. Thus, transactional models (with ample time points) would be a significant contribution to the field of bullying prevention.

In contrast to the relationship aspects of climate, the organizational component (i.e., school policies/administrative commitment) was not as strongly related to attitudes and bystander behavior or victimization, but did predict less bully perpetration over a 1-year period. This was the case for all schools, regardless of intervention condition. Administrative leadership and commitment may help create norms wherein violence is less normative; or it may be that this construct is a proxy for the disciplinary climate of the school, implying that bullying behavior receives stronger corrective action from staff. It is important to note that we did not gather more detailed information about other programs/practices adopted by administration, and policies were not evaluated for merit; thus, it is difficult to disentangle staff commitment from genuine evidence-based or "gold standard" practices. In other words, because many schools have antibullying policies in place, higher levels of staff-report organizational climate may represent something as simple as staff "buy-in" to school policy.

The marked contrast between main effects of climate versus intervention status suggests that bullying prevention is not a simple or quick fix. Rather, the current data validate a social–ecological or comprehensive approach to violence prevention (Espelage & Swearer, 2003) and suggest that establishing a positive school climate is foundational to reducing violence and aggressive behavior. A positive psychosocial climate appears to not only elevate the skill levels among students, but in some cases, may enhance (or facilitate) behavioral changes from stand-alone prevention programs such as STR. Because improvement in skills doesn't automatically translate to behavioral change, our results suggest that one way in which psychosocial climate may facilitate bullying curriculum is via relationships, insofar as supportive, trusting relationships provide a context (characterized by more connectedness and a greater sense of safety) wherein students are more likely to utilize or apply their acquired skills. In addition, facilitation of behavioral changes may happen at the programmatic level (see Orpinas, 2009). That is, staff/teachers who feel they are part of a positive, close school community may show greater adoption of programs and more efforts at engaging students in the curriculum. Of course, both of these are hypothetical mediational mechanisms that warrant further analysis but were not addressed in the current study.

Consistent with our hypothesis, it is noteworthy that there was generally strong overlap across reporters in the observed pattern of relations. This was the case, despite slightly different constructs and different methodological approaches (i.e., aggregated at school level for staff, vs. individual level for students). In this study, the psychosocial climate scales across reporters were not identical, but both were meaningfully related to bullying behavior and attitudes, suggesting that they both tapped the same core construct. It is also important to highlight that we assessed climate in multilevel models, wherein we controlled for several school-level demographic factors that correlated significantly with psychosocial climate (i.e., ethnicity and socioeconomic

status), so our measurement approach departs from what scholars have done previously. Despite strong similarities in relations between climate and bullying behavior across reporters/perspectives, the only moderating effect was specific to staff-report perceptions of psychosocial climate. One could argue that staff climate captured a more diverse set of relations, that is, between staff, parents, and students. Thus, perhaps staff perceptions reflect a broader, more comprehensive view of the social environment, although other scholars have found the opposite (i.e., that staff perceived climate is driven more by classroom characteristics; Mitchell et al., 2010). Or, perhaps the social culture among teachers, and between teachers and parents, is particularly salient for understanding and unpacking the effects of stand-alone bullying prevention programs. Further studies on the specific aspects of climate that are driving behavioral change are needed, and will help in more precise targeting of prevention strategies.

It remains an important public health priority to understand the nature and timing of shifts in peer violence and aggression in schools and how stand-alone programs operate dynamically in response to their host environments. The field could also benefit from a deeper understanding of the mutuality between the different dimensions of climate and bullying behavior within schools, given the translational value of such knowledge. Indeed, there remains a gap between research validating a social–ecological approach to bullying prevention and the number of "multitiered," "whole school," or "comprehensive," programs that target and promote positive social-interactions across different microcontexts. Current limitations of our study notwithstanding, our findings cannot only spark dialogue about how bullying prevention programs operate (or are optimized) within a given ecology, but also have important implications for school decision makers around factors of adoption, efficiency, and resource allocation.

# References

Bradshaw, C. P., Koth, C. W., Thornton, L. A., & Leaf, P. J. (2009). Altering school climate through school-wide positive behavioral interventions and supports: Findings from a group-randomized effectiveness trial. *Prevention Science, 10*, 100–115. doi:10.1007/s11121-008-0114-9

Brown, E. C., Low, S., Smith, B. H., & Haggerty, K. P. (2011). Outcomes from a school-randomized controlled trial of Steps to Respect: A Bullying Prevention Program. *School Psychology Review, 40,* 423–443.

Bryk, A. S., & Driscoll, M. E. (1988). *The high school as community: Contextual influences and consequences for students and teachers.* Madison, WI: National Center on Effective Secondary Schools, University of Wisconsin.

Cohen, J., McCabe, L., Michelli, N. M., & Pickeral, T. (2009). School climate: Research, policy, practice, and teacher education. *The Teachers College Record, 111,* 180–213.

Committee for Children. (2005). *Steps to respect: A bullying prevention program.* Seattle, WA: Committee for Children.

Corrigan, M. W., Klein, T. J., & Isaacs, T. (2010). Trust us: Documenting the relationship of students' trust in teachers to cognition, character, and climate. *Journal of Research in Character Education, 8*(2), 61–73.

Csuti, N. (2008a). *The Colorado trust bullying prevention initiative student survey.* Retrieved from http://www.coloradotrust.org/attachments/0001/4051/BPI_Student_Survey.pdf

Csuti, N. (2008b). *The Colorado trust bullying prevention initiative student survey.* Retrieved from http://www.coloradotrust.org/attachments/0001/4051/BPI_Student_Survey.pdf

Durlak, J. A., & DuPre, E. P. (2008). Implementation matters: A review of research on the influence of implementation on program outcomes and the factors affecting implementation. *American Journal of Community Psychology, 41,* 327–350. doi:10.1007/s10464-008-9165-0

Eliot, M., Cornell, D., Gregory, A., & Fan, X. (2010). Supportive school climate and student willingness to seek help for bullying and threats of violence, *Journal of School Psychology, 48,* 533–553. doi:10.1016/j.jsp.2010.07.001

Espelage, D. L., & Swearer, S. M. (2003). Research on school bullying and victimization: What have we learned and where do we go from here? *School Psychology Review, 32,* 365–383. Retrieved from http://www.nasponline.org/publications/spr/index.aspx?vol=32&issue=3

Farrington, D. P., & Ttofi, M. M. (2009). *Campbell systematic reviews: School-based programs to reduce bullying and victimization.* Retrieved May 18, 2010, from www.campbellcollaboration.org/lib/download/718/

Frey, K. S., Hirschstein, M. K., Snell, J. L., Edstrom, L. V. S., MacKenzie, E. P., & Broderick, C. J. (2005). Reducing playground bullying and supporting beliefs: An experimental trial of the Steps to Respect program. *Developmental Psychology, 41,* 479–491.

Gottfredson, G. D., Gottfredson, D. C., Payne, A., & Gottfredson, N. C. (2005). School climate predictors of school disorder: Results from national delinquency prevention in school. *Journal of Research in Crime and Delinquency, 42,* 412–444. doi:10.1177/0022427804271931

Graham, J. W. (2009). Missing data analysis: Making it work in the real world. *Annual Review of Psychology, 60,* 549–576.

Gregory, A., Cornell, D., & Fan, X. (2011). The relationship of school structure and support to suspension rates for Black and White high school students. *American Educational Research Journal, 48,* 904–934. doi:10.3102/0002831211398531

Gregory, A., Cornell, D., Fan, X., Sheras, P., Shih, T., & Huang, F. (2010). Authoritative school discipline: High school practices associated with lower student bullying and victimization. *Journal of Educational Psychology, 102,* 483–496. doi: 10.1037/a0018562

Guerra, N. G., Williams, K. R., & Sadek, S. (2011). Understanding bullying and victimization during childhood and adolescence: A mixed methods study. *Child Development, 82,* 295–310. doi:10.1111/j.1467-8624.2010.01556.x

Hirschstein, M. K., Van Schoiack Edstrom, L., Frey, K. S., Snell, J. L., & MacKenzie, E. P. (2007). Walking the talk in bullying prevention: Teacher implementation variables related to initial impact of the steps to respect program. *School Psychology Review, 36,* 3–21.

Hoy, W. K., Smith, P. A., & Sweetland, S. R. (2002). The development of the organizational climate index for high schools: Its measure and relationship to faculty trust. *The High School Journal, 86,* 38–49. doi:10.1353/hsj.2002.0023

Jenson, J. M., & Dieterich, W. A. (2007). Effects of a skills-based prevention program on bullying and bully victimization among elementary school children. *Prevention Science, 8,* 285–296.

Lindstrom Johnson, S., Waasdrop, T. E., Debnam, K., & Bradshaw, C. P. (2013). The role of bystander perceptions and school climate in influencing victims' responses to bullying: To retaliate or seek support? *Journal of Criminology, 2013.* doi: 10.1155/2013/780460

Low, S., Van Ryzin, M. J., Brown, E. C., Smith, B. H., & Haggerty, K. P. (2014). Engagement matters: Lessons from assessing classroom implementation of Steps to Respect: A bullying prevention program over a one-year period. *Prevention Science, 15,* 165–176.

Marsh, H. W., Lüdtke, O., Nagengast, B., Trautwein, U., Morin, A. J., Abduljabbar, A. S., & Köller, O. (2012). Classroom climate and contextual effects: Conceptual and methodological issues in the evaluation of group-level effects. *Educational Psychologist, 47,* 106–124. doi:10.1080/00461520 .2012.670488

McEvoy, A., & Welker, R. (2000). Antisocial behavior, academic failure, and school climate: A critical review. *Journal of Emotional and Behavioral Disorders, 8,* 130–140. doi:10.1177/106342660000800301

Mehta, S. B., Cornell, D., Fan, X., & Gregory, A. (2013). Bullying climate and school engagement in ninth grade students. *Journal of School Health, 83,* 45–52. doi:10.1111/j.1746-1561.2012.00746.x

Meraviglia, M. G., Becker, H., Rosenbluth, B., Sanchez, E., & Robertson, T. (2003). The Expect Respect Project. Creating a positive elementary school climate. *Journal of Interpersonal Violence, 18,* 1347–1360. doi:10.1177/0886260503257457

Merrell, K. W., Gueldner, B. A., Ross, S. W., & Isava, D. M. (2008). How effective are school bullying intervention programs? A meta-analysis of intervention research. *School Psychology Quarterly, 23,* 26–42. doi:10.1037/1045-3830.23.1.26

Meyer-Adams, N., & Connor, B. T. (2008). School violence: Bullying behaviors and psychosocial school environment in middle schools. *Children & Schools, 30,* 211–221. doi:10.1093/cs/30.4.211

Mitchell, M. M., Bradshaw, C. P., & Leaf, P. J. (2010). Student and teacher perceptions of school climate: A multilevel exploration of patterns of discrepancy. *Journal of School Health, 80,* 271–279. doi:10.1111/j.1746-1561.2010.00501.x

Nansel, T. R., Overpeck, M., Pilla, R. S., Ruan, W. J., Simons-Morton, B., & Scheidt, P. (2001). Bullying behaviors among U.S. youth. *Journal of the American Medical Association: The journal of the American Medical Association, 285,* 2094–2100. doi:10.1001/jama.285.16.2094

Olweus, D. (1991). Bully/victim problems among schoolchildren: Basic facts and effects of a school based intervention program. In D. Pepler & K. Rubin (Eds.), *The development and treatment of childhood aggression* (pp. 411–448). Hillsdale, NJ: Erlbaum.

Orpinas, P. (2009). *Manual measurement-aggression, victimization, & social skills scales.* Athens, GA: The University of Georgia.

Plank, S. B., Bradshaw, C. P., & Young, H. (2009). An application of "broken windows" and related theories to the study of disorder, fear, and collective efficacy in schools. *American Journal of Education, 115,* 227–247. doi:10.1086/595669

Raudenbush, S. W., & Bryk, A. S. (2002). *Hierarchical linear models* (2nd ed.). Thousand Oaks, CA: Sage.

Roeser, R. W., Eccles, J. S., & Sameroff, A. J. (2000). School as a context of early adolescents' academic and social-emotional development: A summary of research findings. *The Elementary School Journal, 100,* 443–471. doi:10.1086/499650

Schafer, J. L. (1999). Multiple imputation: a primer. *Statistical methods in medical research, 8,* 3–15.

Smith, J. D., Schneider, B. H., Smith, P. K., & Ananiadou, K. (2004). The effectiveness of wholeschool antibullying programs: A Synthesis of evaluation research. *School Psychology Review, 33,* 548–561.

Swearer, S. M., Espelage, D. L., Vaillancourt, T., & Hymel, S. (2010). What can be done about school bullying? Linking research to educational practice. *Educational Researcher, 39,* 38–47. doi:10.3102/0013189X09357622

Syvertsen, A. K., Flanagan, C. A., & Stout, M. D. (2009). Code of silence: Students' perceptions of school climate and willingness to intervene in a peer's dangerous plan. *Journal of Educational Psychology, 101,* 219–232. doi:10.1037/a0013246

Unnever, J. D., & Cornell, D. G. (2004). Middle school victims of bullying: Who reports being bullied? *Aggressive Behavior, 30,* 373–388. doi: 10.1002/ab.20030

Williams, F., & Cornell, D. (2006). Student willingness to seek help for threats of violence. *Journal of School Violence, 5,* 35–49. doi: 10.1300/J202v05n04_04

Wilson, C. J., & Deanne, F. P. (2001). Adolescent opinions about help seeking barriers and increasing appropriate help engagement. *Journal of Educational and psychological Consultation, 12,* 345–364. doi:10.1207/S1532768XJEPC1204_03

Zaykowski, H., & Gunter, W. D. (2012). Youth victimization: School climate or deviant lifestyles? *Journal of Interpersonal Violence, 27,* 431–452. doi:10.1177/0886260511421678

**SABINA LOW** is assistant research professor in the T. Denny Sanford School of Social and Family Dynamics at Arizona State University. Mark Van Ryzin is a lecturer in the Department of Educational Methodology, Policy, and Leadership at University of Oregon.

# EXPLORING THE ISSUE

## Are School-Wide Anti-Bullying Programs Effective?

## Critical Thinking and Reflection

1. Would you make any changes to the KiVA program if it were implemented in U.S. schools?
2. How is the STR program similar to or distinct from KiVa? Identify the biggest similarity and the biggest difference.
3. Given Low and Ryzin's findings, how would you alter STR?

## Is There Common Ground?

In order to find common ground, the two school-based violence prevention programs must be compared since one found a general positive effect (KiVa), whereas the other generally did not (STR). KiVa in Finland was distinguished by actively targeting student bystanders (all students), whereas STR mainly focused on training teacher and staff on improved monitoring of students and on intervening in bullying situations. Thus, the two interventions differed fundamentally and could explain the difference in outcome. A comparison of the KiVa program and Low and Ryzin's measure of positive school climate are strikingly similar. School psychosocial climate was assessed by the following items by asking students to agree to statements such as: "This is a close-knit school where everyone looks out for each other"; "Students in my school are willing to help each other." Teachers were asked to respond to two types of climate: psychosocial ("staff at this school can be trusted") and organizational (administrated is committed to address bullies). Unfortunately, both studies did not measure school climate, but it can be argued that violence prevention programs at schools work through (e.g., mediated) its effects on school climate or in changing the school climate.

Finally, it is important to note that simply going through a school-based anti-bullying prevention program can be beneficial to the school community for other important outcomes beyond bullying and victimization. Adults can learn as much as the children. When an intervention is active, the whole school community becomes aware of the values that the larger community prioritizes. It has often been assumed that parents, staff, and teachers are socially competent and know how to teach socially competent interpersonal behaviors. Anti-bullying interventions that target a culture of trust are most likely beneficial in many more respects than just preventing bullying and victimization.

## References

G. M. Glew, M. Fan, W. Katon, F. P. Rivara, and M. A. Kernic, "Bullying, psychosocial adjustment, and academic performance in elementary school," *Archives of Pediatrics and Adolescent Medicine* (vol. 159, 2005).

T. R. Nansel, M. Overpeck, R. S. Pilla, W. J. Ruan, B. Simons-Morton, and P. Scheidt, "Bullying behaviors among US youth: Prevalence and association with psychosocial adjustment," *Journal of the American Medical Association* (vol. 285, 2001).

S. Perren, and F. D. Alsaker, "Social behavior and peer relationships of victims, bully-victims, and bullies in kindergarten," *Journal of Child Psychology and Psychiatry* (vol. 47, 2006).

R. Veenstra, S. Lindenberg, A. J. Oldehinkel, A. F. De Winter, et al. "Bullying and victimization in elementary schools: A comparison of bullies, victims, bully/victims, and uninvolved preadolescents," *Developmental Psychology* (vol. 41, 2005).

## Additional Resources

K. W. Merrell, B. A. Gueldner, S. W. Ross, and D. M. Isava, "How effective are school bullying intervention programs? A meta-analysis of intervention research," *School Psychology Quarterly* (vol. 23, 2008). doi:10.1037/1045-3830.23.1.26

K. Rigby, *Children and Bullying: How Parents and Educators Can Reduce Bullying at School* (Blackwell Publishing, 2008).

P. K. Smith, and K. Ananiadou, "The nature of school bullying and the effectiveness of school-based interventions," *Journal of Applied Psychoanalytic Studies* (vol. 5, 2003). doi:10.1023/A:1022991804210

S. M. Swearer, D. L. Espelage, T. Vaillancourt, and S. Hymel, "What can be done about school bullying? Linking research to educational practice," *Educational Researcher* (vol. 39, 2010). doi:10.3102/0013189X09357622

# *Internet References . . .*

**An All-Out Anti-Bullying Focus**

www.apa.org/monitor/2014/03/anti-bullying.aspx

**Bully Prevention**

www.pbis.org/school/bully-prevention

**KiVa School: Let's Make It Together**

www.kivaprogram.net

**Reducing Bullying: Meeting the Challenge**

www.teachsafeschools.org/bullying -prevention.html

**Steps to Respect: Bullying Prevention for Elementary School**

www.cfchildren.org/steps-to-respect

Selected, Edited, and with Issue Framing Material by:
Esther S. Chang, *Soka University of America*

# ISSUE

# Are Charter Schools Advancing Educational Reforms?

**YES: RAND Education**, from "Are Charter Schools Making a Difference? A Study of Student Outcomes in Eight States (Research Brief)," RAND Corporation (2009)

**NO: Martin Carnoy, et al.**, from "Worth the Price? Weighing the Evidence on Charter School Achievement," *Education Finance and Policy* (2006)

---

## Learning Outcomes

**After reading this issue, you will be able to:**

- Define charter school and why they are considered an educational reform.
- Define what unions are and why teachers have unions in schools.
- Describe the advantages and disadvantages of using charter schools as an educational reform strategy.

---

## ISSUE SUMMARY

**YES:** Based on the results from data gathered across eight states, RAND researchers found that charter schools can make a difference with regard to long-term student attainment despite their lack of progress on achievement-related indicators compared to traditional public schools.

**NO:** Martin Carnoy and colleagues question whether any gains observed by charter schools is worth the price of closing down traditional public schools. They point out that charters have not made any progress related to achievement when compared to traditional public schools and recreate many of the same problems associated with public schools rather than take advantage of the autonomy to create educational innovations.

*"The overall vision is that every child has access and every family has access to a high-quality education, we have to find a way to give better options to families, and we have to do that as soon as we can."*

—Executive Director Gregory McGinity
from Broad Foundation
(*LA Times*, November 12, 2015)

*"This is not a conversation about choice [or competition or innovation]. It draws us to a very honest and open place about the future of the Los Angeles Unified School District. . . . This is about: Is there a future for L.A. Unified?"*

—LAUSD School Board President Steve
Zimmer (*LA Times*, November 12, 2015)

Charter schools receive funding from the public school system but operate with a great deal of relative autonomy regarding staffing, curriculum, and spending. The first school charter was given in Minnesota in 1991 through legislative action prompted by grassroots advocates. In return for their relative autonomy and public funding, charter schools must meet accountability standards and are reviewed periodically. Since 1991, the percentage of all public schools that were public charter schools has increased ever since and each school's enrollment size has generally increased over time (U.S. Department of Education, 2015). Some states have been more receptive than others. Among the states that have been receptive are those that have struggled with bureaucratic problems and serve the largest proportion of disadvantaged children. For example, among all states in school year 2012–13, California enrolled the largest number of students in charter schools (8 percent of total public school students), and the District of Columbia enrolled the highest percentage of public school students in charter schools (42 percent) (U.S. Department of Education, 2015).

The growth of the charter school movement in recent years and their expansion plans suggest that it is the most popular solution to what was the most widely cited problem in American education: the school monopoly. It has long been argued that schools act like monopolies when parents don't have a choice in sending their children to a different school than the one operating in their neighborhood. Monopolies are bad because they foreclose educational opportunities for children and families. Without a choice in schools, the main problem is that schools are not effectively motivated to improve because parents have to send their children to the school that one's home is zoned for—or pay for a private education. The result is often an inefficient and growing school bureaucracy (e.g., district offices) that is not designed to respond to the changing demands of parents and communities.

Complicating matters in the charter school debate is the role of teacher unions, their historical development, and their power throughout the educational reform movement. In short, unions are workplace organizations that serve to protect the interest of the workers. In all workplaces, it is an attempt to level the authority of "the boss" with a unified voice among the workers. The underlying power of unions is directly proportional to the amount of unity found among its workers because they can stop work if their demands are not met. Unions function somewhat independently at each workplace but are usually affiliated with local and national unions within their industry. This is because workers are more powerful when their colleagues at similar other workplaces are coordinated. As it relates to education, unions operate in schools to protect the interest of teachers (it should be noted that they do not protect the interests of parents or the children they teach). They developed as a direct result of low salaries and economic insecurity among teachers at the turn of the twentieth century. Women teachers in the early 1900s were also faced with policies that discriminated against them, such as rules that governed their dress (e.g., "keep their galoshes buckled") and personal life (e.g., "not receive gentleman callers more than 3/week"). Union contracts helped to solve these "bread and butter" issues and have grown in number and power over the years.

Two of the top three largest unions in the United States today are teachers' unions, the American Federation of Teachers (AFT), and the nation's largest union, the National Education Association of the United States (NEA). As a result of their numbers, the teacher unions are considered among the most powerful voices in educational policy making. Although charters typically begin as a non-union workplace, many have organized unions at charters much to the dismay of those who formed and lead the charters. Union contracts are extremely difficult to work around because all teachers are evaluated similarly (by their contract guidelines) and salaries and raises are predetermined and apply to all. Many assume that unions add more barriers to implementing creative solutions to teaching and student learning. Among the most prominent images of this idea are embodied by the negative interactions between Michelle Rhee, former Chancellor of DC Public Schools, and DC's unionized teachers in a *Frontline* special entitled, "The Education of Michelle Rhee" (PBS, 2013). The documentary "Waiting for 'Superman'" also emphasized the images of what they labeled as teacher jails in NYC. Teachers accused of abuse are removed from their classrooms and asked to report to an office to wait until an investigation produces an outcome of their innocence or guilt. Some cases can take years to resolve as the accused teacher gets paid a union salary "doing nothing" in teacher jail (Takepart, 2010). The role of unions has not been very prominent in the public mind when discussing the issue of charter schools, but will inevitably be as charters gain ground. Schools are workplaces with power dynamics and struggles of competing interests. It is obvious that classrooms are not industrial factory work floors, but the issues pertaining to who has the power to implement rules at school are similar to traditional factory floors.

The charter school movement has certainly brought variety to the school system menu and has expanded parental choice. Community groups, activists, and entrepreneurs seem to be clamoring for available charters for KIPP schools, Oxford Academies, Core Knowledge schools, Paideia schools, fine arts academies, Afrocentric schools, schools for at-risk students and dropouts, technology schools, character education-based schools, job-training academies, and so on. The National Commission on Governing America's Schools has recommended that every school become a charter school, which would bring an end to the era of centralized bureaucratic control of public school districts and release from union contracts with teachers. For example, the Sarasota County School District in Florida has already embarked on a decentralized organizational model offering a "100% School Choice Program" through newly conceived "conversion, deregulated, and commissioned schools." In Los Angeles, the Broad Foundation announced a $490 million plan that would target half of Los Angeles Unified School District's (LASUD) students to be enrolled in charters in the next 8 years. Currently, 16 percent of LAUSD students are in charters and has the most charters and charter students of any district in the country (as cited in Blume, 2015).

There are obstacles to charter school success, however, and indeed many have closed since 1991. Among the notable concerns related to charter schools has been a pattern of self-segregation, or Balkanization among schools that appeared to counter school integration efforts since the ruling of *Brown v. Board of Education* in 1954. Charters were also criticized for selecting for the most intelligent among the public school population and at the same time arguing that they serve the most disadvantaged. Charter schools have also been in the news for operating while being found guilty of financial mismanagement (e.g., Watanabe, 2014), thus re-creating the original problem cited of public schools. Still others accuse the charter school movement as being a privatization movement that attracts private companies (e.g., Microsoft) and businessmen (such as Eli Broad and Bill Gates) to develop private alternatives designed with private interests in mind.

Research on charter schools has been interdisciplinary in nature and is usually published in educational journals rather than in journals devoted to psychology. The main empirical questions that have been examined have focused on whether students in charter schools are performing better on standardized tests than students in traditional public schools. The "Yes" selection is a research brief prepared by RAND (Jennifer Li) that summarizes the findings of a systematic study of eight states and explores several indicators of school efficiency, including long-term outcomes, and tests the assumptions made by charter school critics (Zimmer, Gill, Booker, Lavertu, Sass, & Witte, 2009). The "No" selection by Carnoy and colleagues weighs the available evidence of charter school achievement and examines whether charter schools are taking advantage of their relative freedom to be creative and innovative.

# YES

**RAND Education**

## Are Charter Schools Making a Difference?
## A Study of Student Outcomes in Eight States
## (Research Brief)

Charter schools are publicly funded schools that operate outside the direct control of local school districts, under a publicly issued charter that gives them greater autonomy than other public schools have over curriculum, instruction, and operations. Their students, or the students' parents, choose the school rather than being assigned based on residential location. The first U.S. charter school opened in 1992. Since then, the number of charter schools has grown to more than 4,000 in 40 states, and the schools serve more than 1.2 million students.

While both President Barack Obama and Secretary of Education Arne Duncan support charter schools, there continues to be a contentious debate over such schools. Proponents contend that charter schools expand educational choices for students, increase innovation, improve student achievement, and promote healthy competition with traditional public schools. Opponents argue that charter schools lead to increased racial or ethnic stratification of students, skim the best students from traditional public schools, reduce resources for such schools, and provide no real improvement in student outcomes.

Although the body of research on these issues is growing, many key outcomes have not been adequately examined, or they have been studied only in individual cities and states. RAND researchers therefore set out to shed more light on charter-school effects, examining data on achievement trajectories of individual students in communities and states with varying charter policies, and exploring—for the first time—how charter schools affect long-term student outcomes. The research team analyzed longitudinal, student-level data from Chicago, San Diego, Philadelphia, Denver, Milwaukee, and the states of Ohio, Texas, and Florida. Consistent with other studies, they found that some of the concerns about charter schools can be put to rest and that some of the anticipated benefits of

## Key findings:

- Charter schools do not generally draw the top students away from traditional public schools.
- Charter middle and high schools produce test-score achievement gains that are, on average, similar to those of traditional public schools.
- The RAND team found no evidence that charter schools substantially affect achievement in nearby traditional public schools.
- However, in this first study to examine how charter schools affect long-term student attainment, the authors found that charter–high school students had a higher probability of graduating and attending college.

charter schools have not become a reality. The most striking finding was that charter–high school attendance may positively affect the chance that a student will graduate and go on to college—two critical outcomes that have not been examined in previous research—suggesting the need to look beyond achievement-test scores when measuring the effectiveness of charter schools. This brief describes the key research findings and their implications for policy and future investigation.

*Charter schools are not skimming the highest-achieving students from traditional public schools, nor are they creating racial stratification.* When researchers examined the prior achievement-test scores of students transferring to charter schools, they found that those scores were near or below the local district or state average. This suggests that charter schools are not drawing the best students away from traditional public schools, as some opponents predicted that they would. Similarly, when the researchers looked at whether transfers to charter schools affected the

Zimmer, Ron, Brian Gill, Kevin Booker, Stephane Lavertu, Tim R. Sass and John Witte, "Are Charter Schools Making a Difference? A Study of Student Outcomes in Eight States," Santa Monica, Calif.: RAND Corporation, RB-9433-BMG/JOY/WPF, 2009. As of August 18, 2015: http://www.rand.org/pubs/research_briefs/RB9433. Used with permission.

distribution of students by race or ethnicity, they found that, in most sites, the racial composition of the charter school entered by a transferring student was similar to that of the traditional public school that he or she had left.

***On average, across varying communities and policy environments, charter middle and high schools produce achievement gains that are about the same as those in traditional public schools.*** However, the achievement gains for charter elementary schools are challenging to estimate and remain unclear because elementary students typically have no baseline test scores at the time they enter kindergarten. For middle- and high-school levels, the research team found that achievement gains in charter schools and traditional public schools were about the same, with two exceptions. First, charter schools generally do not perform well in the first year of operation, when their students tend to fall behind. Gains generally occur thereafter. Second, there is reason for concern about the performance of virtual charter schools, which serve their students remotely in the students' homes rather than in a school building. In the one location with a substantial number of virtual charter schools (Ohio), their students showed achievement gains that fell significantly short of those in traditional public schools and classroom-based charter schools.

***Charter schools do not appear to help or harm student achievement in nearby traditional public schools.*** Some proponents have predicted that the presence of charter schools would have a positive effect on nearby traditional public schools by exerting positive competitive pressure; some opponents have worried that charter schools would harm students in nearby traditional public schools by draining resources. Neither theory was borne out by the study. The researchers examined student achievement in traditional public schools that had charter schools nearby, and they found that the presence of the charter schools did not appear to help or harm student achievement in the traditional public schools.

***Students who attended charter high schools were more likely to graduate and go on to college.*** For the locations for which charter–high school graduation and college attendance rates were available—Chicago and Florida—the researchers found that attending a charter high school appeared to boost a student's probability of graduating by 7 to 15 percentage points. Similarly, students who attended a charter high school appeared to benefit from an 8 to 10 percentage point increase in the likelihood that they would enroll in college. Although there are some limitations to these results, they provide reason for encouragement in terms of the long-term benefits of charter schools. They also suggest a need to look beyond test scores to fully assess charter school's performance.

## Policy Implications

The study holds several implications for policy and future research. First, the finding that charter schools are not drawing the highest-achieving students from traditional public schools can help alleviate some of the concerns held by policymakers. Second, the absence of effects on achievement in nearby traditional public schools suggests that the loss of students to charter schools is not having negative achievement effects on traditional public schools, but it also suggests that charter schools may not produce the hoped-for positive competitive effects in traditional public schools. Finally, this research makes clear the need to move beyond test scores and broaden the scope of measures used to evaluate success. This was the first study to extend the scope of outcome measures to include long-term outcomes, such as high-school graduation and college attendance, in addition to test scores, and the results are more encouraging than test scores alone would indicate. Future research on charter schools should seek to examine a broader and deeper range of student outcomes.

---

**RAND Education**, a division of the nonprofit institution RAND Corporation, focuses on using accurate data and objective research analysis to improve educational policy and decision making.

**Martin Carnoy, et al.**

 **NO**

# Worth The Price? Weighing the Evidence on Charter School Achievement

In the summer of 2004, the American Federation of Teachers (AFT) published data from the National Assessment of Educational Progress (NAEP) showing that average fourth-grade achievement is higher in regular public schools than in charter schools, both for students overall and for low-income students. For black students, a group that many charter schools are designed to serve, the analysis showed that average achievement is no better in charter schools than in regular public schools. These conclusions were reported in a front-page article in the *New York Times*. Their accuracy has not subsequently been challenged.[1]

Some charter school supporters claimed that the NAEP data provided only misleading information about the quality of charter schools because: (1) NAEP only assessed a single year (2003) of fourth-grade scores and so could not detect whether charter school scores were low because their students had even lower scores in earlier grades. If so, charter school students could have made more progress even if they still had not caught up to regular public school students by the fourth grade; (2) black and low-income students in charter schools are more disadvantaged than black and low-income students in regular public schools. To make valid comparisons of charter and regular public school test scores, more demographic information is required than simply whether students are minority or eligible for free or reduced-price lunches. Parental education, specific income levels, and home environment must also be controlled; and (3) charter school performance may be poor because so many charter schools are new, experiencing "growing pains" or "shakedown" problems; studies restricted to mature charter schools would show superior results.

While it is important to analyze these claims, it is curious that the average underperformance of charter schools came as such a surprise. The original intent of charter schools was to allow for experimentation; an

expected outcome of experimentation in any field is many failures before successes are identified. While the controversy that erupted in the wake of the *Times* article focused on whether students in charter schools, on average, outperform students in regular public schools, it missed a more important policy discussion regarding the costs of pursuing charter school policies—weighing whether the successes are worth the failures. The costs of chartering policies include high student mobility, increased corruption and mismanagement of some deregulated schools, and more inexperienced and underqualified teachers working in schools with fewer hiring restrictions. Only then will we be able to say whether the underperformance of some charter schools is a price worth paying for the successes realized by others.

In a *New York Times* advertisement published eight days later, and in several other op-ed articles and web postings, some charter school supporters' criticism of the use of NAEP data to support claims about charter school underperformance made a lot of sense. NAEP scores themselves are not a sufficient basis to conclude that charter school performance is lacking. Nonetheless, there is extensive corroboration of this finding.

From NAEP itself, we can reasonably conclude that charter schools do not, on average, serve students who are more disadvantaged than superficially similar students in regular schools. Although NAEP reveals that charter schools have a higher proportion of black students than regular schools, black students in charter schools are apparently less disadvantaged, not more so, than black students in regular public schools. As Table 1 shows, while 76 percent of black students in regular public schools are low-income, only 68 percent of black students in charter schools are low-income. In central cities especially, black students are more likely to be low-income in regular public schools (83 percent) than in charter schools (72 percent).

*Table 1*

**Percent of Lunch-Eligible Students, by Race and Location**

| | PERCENT LUNCH-ELIGIBLE | | |
|---|---|---|---|
| | Charter Schools | Regular Public Schools | Difference |
| **Total** | 47 | 46 | 1 |
| Central city | 65 | 65 | 0 |
| Urban fringe | 29 | 36 | −7 |
| Rural | 30 | 41 | −11 |
| **Black Students** | 68 | 76 | −8 |
| Central city | 72 | 83 | −11 |
| Urban fringe | 49 | 64 | −15 |
| Rural | 92 | 76 | 16 |

*Note:* Data are for students who took the NAEP Fourth Grade Math Assessment and who reported whether they were eligible for free or reduced-price lunch.

*Source:* NAEP 2005, supplemented by unpublished data furnished to the authors by the National Center for Education Statistics.

Only in rural schools are black students in charter schools more likely to be lunch-eligible than black students in regular public schools.

About 10 percent of charter school and 4 percent of regular public school students in the NAEP sample did not provide information about their lunch eligibility. Under the strongest assumptions about these nonresponders, the result holds that urban black students in charter schools are less likely to be lunch-eligible than their peers in regular public schools. If all nonresponders in the charter school sample are assumed to be lunch-eligible, and no nonresponders in the regular public school sample are assumed to be, then the low-income percentages for black students in charter and in regular public schools would be 71 and 74, respectively. For black students in central city charter and regular public schools, the low-income percentages would be 75 and 81, respectively.

Many studies have compared charter and regular public schools at the state level, and they usually confirm these NAEP data. We base this conclusion on an examination of every state-level study we could find that had been published or made available through April 2005.[2] In general, state studies show that charter schools have a higher proportion of black students but a lower proportion of lunch-eligible students than regular public schools. This probably means that black students in charter schools are less likely to be lunch-eligible than black students in regular public schools, because black students generally are more likely to be lunch-eligible than white students. This pattern—more black students but fewer lunch-eligible students—characterizes charter schools in California, Florida, Illinois, Massachusetts, Michigan, North Carolina, and Wisconsin. Other state studies cannot confirm this pattern because they did not collect adequate demographic data, but only one study, that of schools in the District of Columbia, suggests the opposite—black students are more likely to be lunch-eligible in charter than in regular schools.

In short, the notion that NAEP charter school scores are no better than those of regular public schools, among all students and particularly for black students, because charter school students are more disadvantaged is not supported by hard evidence.

Many anecdotal accounts, however, do suggest that charter school students are more disadvantaged than regular public school students who seem superficially similar. These anecdotes may be accurate, but the data we report here make sense because such schools are offset by at least as many unnoticed examples of charter schools where students are more advantaged than superficially similar students in regular schools.

And some anecdotes, however well-intentioned, are simply exaggerated. We examined, for example, Knowledge Is Power Program (KIPP) schools, a highly publicized network of grades 5–8 middle schools serving central city minority children. Charter school supporters (and KIPP leaders) often claim that KIPP serves the most disadvantaged students, but careful examination suggests otherwise. Where fourth-grade test scores are available for a KIPP school and for the neighborhood schools from which it draws, test scores of students who transfer to KIPP are consistently higher than neighborhood averages. Fourth-grade teachers in regular public schools who refer students to KIPP consistently report that they recommend their most able students, or those with the greatest parental support.

With access to cross-tabulated NAEP data by race, residence, and lunch eligibility that were not available in August 2004, we can now confirm that charter school test scores are not higher than those in regular public schools. As Table 2 shows, black students living in central cities and attending regular public schools are not only apparently less advantaged than black central city students in charter schools; they also do better academically, on average, in regular public than in charter schools. This is true in both math and reading and is statistically significant in math.

NAEP data also fail to confirm claims that charter school performance improves as schools gain experience. In both math and reading, charter schools that have been providing instruction for four years or more have lower scores than new charter schools.

These findings, too, are confirmed in state studies. Although a few find a charter school advantage in narrowly defined categories (for example, California studies find that charter schools that converted from regular school status perform relatively well, but start-up charter schools do not), most find that charter school students perform less well than regular public school students. States where such is apparently the case include Arizona, California, the District of Columbia, Illinois (with the exception of

Chicago), Michigan, North Carolina, and Texas (except for schools chartered by local districts). In other states, charter school students seem to do better in some grades but worse in others.

Seven studies (in Arizona, California, Florida, Michigan, North Carolina, and two separate studies in Texas) compare like students and estimate score gains for one or more cohorts as students progress from year to year. Three of these studies (the Florida and North Carolina studies published in this issue, and one study in Texas) make strong corrections for selection bias. Such studies meet or exceed the quality standard set by charter school supporters who signed the *New York Times* advertisement. Six of the seven studies (Arizona was the exception) estimate that gains were either the same in charter schools as they were in regular public schools or lower.

In sum, the results of state-level studies, including the most methodologically sophisticated ones, accord with the "no charter school achievement advantage" inferences drawn from the NAEP data, even though NAEP data were only for a single year and demographic controls were minimal. The state-level studies seem strongly to suggest that generally charter schools do not outperform regular public schools even when the charter schools have had time to mature and shake out early problems. In a North Carolina study, when the strictest controls were used to correct for selection bias by comparing the same student's performance when that student transferred back and forth between charter and regular public schools, the

*Table 2*

**Fourth-Grade Test Scores of Black Students in Charter and Other Public Schools by Eligibility for Free and Reduced-Price Lunch and Location, 2003**

| | MATHEMATICS | | | READING | | |
|---|---|---|---|---|---|---|
| | Charters | Other public | Difference (Charters less others) | Charters | Other public | Difference (Charters less others) |
| *Lunch-eligible* | 210 | 212 | −2 | 188 | 193 | −5 |
| Central city | 208 | 211 | −3 | 188 | 191 | −3 |
| Urban fringe | 218 | 214 | 4 | n/a | 196 | n/a |
| *Not lunch-eligible* | 220 | 227 | −6 | 208 | 211 | −3 |
| Central city | 217 | 225 | −8* | 208 | 207 | 0 |
| Urban fringe | 226 | 229 | −3 | 205 | 214 | −9 |
| *Info n.a.* | 219 | 219 | 0 | 198 | 199 | −1 |

*Notes:* Data on rural students not available.

*Statistically significant at the 5% level.

*Source:* NAEP 2005, and unpublished data provided to authors by the National Center for Education Statistics.

effect on students of being in charter schools tended to be negative.

. . .

The lack of a charter school achievement advantage suggests that if there are excellent charter schools that provide better educations than the regular schools from which students came, there are also many ineffective charter schools where education is worse. In average data, the better and worse may offset each other. NAEP strongly suggests, but does not prove, that most ineffective charter schools are not being closed, even after academic shortcomings become obvious.

Just as institutional inertia protects low-performing regular public schools from reform, it also protects low-performing charter schools from reform or closure. Charter schools often enjoy the support of organized political, parental, and community forces; it is much easier for state and district officials to ignore poor performance than to intervene and provoke unwelcome controversy. The insistence of some charter school supporters that NAEP data did not reveal real problems avoids addressing the failure to hold charter schools accountable, in view of the inevitable barriers to such accountability that exist in a democratic political environment.

Many charter school supporters have not resolved a theoretical ambivalence about whether market forces (parent choices) are sufficient regulatory mechanisms, or whether states should ensure that charter schools really do operate in ways that are likely to, and in fact do, raise student achievement. And this conflict, in turn, reflects (and in some ways distorts) a deeper ambivalence that runs through the charter school movement. Are charter schools intended to give parents the ability to choose their own goals, whatever those goals might be, or should the public insist that public money be spent and charters granted only to pursue the public's goal of higher student achievement? If charter schools' purpose is the former, then it really shouldn't matter whether NAEP scores, or any other measure, indicate that average charter school performance is low; if parents are comfortable in schools that produce low achievement, they should be permitted to enroll their children in them.

Charter school proponents with this view should not only be unworried about low NAEP scores but should also be hesitant about the No Child Left Behind law and its national requirements for minimal academic sufficiency. If parental choice were a sufficient guarantee of school quality, then any regular public school in a district where parents can choose to remain in a zoned school (or switch to a magnet or charter) should be exempt from further accountability.

The negligible achievement differences between disadvantaged students in charter and regular public schools also raises questions about early charter school theory, which assumed that regular public school student performance was inadequate, especially for disadvantaged students, because union contracts and school district bureaucratic procedures prevent dedicated, creative, and innovative school leaders from developing new and more effective ways of running schools. Early charter school advocates argued that, freed from constraints of bureaucratic rules and union contracts, schools would improve instruction.

If, however, charter schools are not raising disadvantaged children's achievement, the cause of low student performance may not be bureaucratic rules. When a treatment doesn't work, it is prudent to examine not only whether the treatment should be improved, but also whether the diagnosis might be flawed.

The flaw stems from a failure of charter school proponents to distinguish between exceptional or anecdotal experiences and the typical experiences of schools. It is doubtlessly true that creative and effective school leaders, freed from bureaucratic regulations and union contracts, can design excellent schools that do a better job of educating disadvantaged children than do typical regular public schools.

But bureaucratic regulations and union rules do not exist for the purpose of suppressing creative practices. They mostly aim at preventing corrupt, incompetent, and ineffective practices. Freed from regulations, the best educators can design excellent charter schools. But freed from the same rules, the worst educators can also design terrible schools.

Financial management is one area where this has become clear. Many school districts are notorious for their bureaucratic mazes, but almost every rule can be traced to earlier reforms to curb corruption. Because purchasing department employees were once caught in kickback schemes, districts now require multiple signatures and reviews of major purchases. School principals in regular public schools often complain that civil service rules prevent them from firing janitors whose work is mediocre, but it is also nearly impossible for them to hire cousins or in-laws for maintenance positions, a practice that was once routine in public employment.

Charter schools are designed to avoid these rules and thus to enable principals to hire the most qualified people and to purchase supplies quickly and at low cost. As a result, many charter schools can function more efficiently. Some charter schools spend funds in creative ways that would be prohibited in the public school bureaucracy: one of the most widely noticed strategies is to hire younger teachers to work longer hours than regular public school teachers. Charter schools can pay these teachers more than young teachers in regular schools but less than typical teachers in regular schools, at the same overall payroll cost. The strategy requires that many teachers leave as they mature, but if a charter school can continue to attract young enthusiastic teachers who are inspired by the challenge, the strategy can be cost-effective.

But many other charter schools, freed from bureaucratic rules that are designed to ensure a minimum level of competence, have developed approaches that are ineffective. Some charter schools, freed from bureaucratic rules, are tainted by corruption and mismanagement, cronyism and nepotism. While the CER's survey found that fewer than 1 percent of charter schools had been closed for academic shortcomings, over seven times that many had been closed for financial or other mismanagement. Freedom from bureaucratic rules permits some charter schools to be unusually creative and others to be corrupt or inefficient. Many charter school supporters repeat anecdotal accounts only of the creative schools, but the evidence suggests that these are not predominant.

Many charter school supporters have seized upon evidence that teachers are more effective if they attended more selective colleges themselves, had higher test scores, or had more college coursework in subjects they were teaching, especially high school science and math. If so, charter schools could outperform regular public schools if freed from state teacher certification requirements, hiring teachers without formal training in education but with high test scores and degrees from more selective colleges.

But while some charter schools will hire more qualified teachers if freed from certification requirements, other charter schools will hire less qualified teachers. They are unlikely to post high performance if their teachers have neither high test scores and selective baccalaureates nor the pedagogical training, background in child development, and supervised practice that traditionally certified young teachers possess.

Data from the federal government's 1999 Schools and Staffing Survey (SASS) show that, on average, charter schools have probably not hired more qualified teachers. Charter schools were slightly more likely to hire teachers who had graduated from the most selective colleges (14 percent of charter school teachers vs. 10 percent of regular public school teachers). But on other available measures, charter school teachers seem to be less qualified. For example, the SASS data show that in mathematics,

charter schools were less likely to hire teachers with extensive mathematics backgrounds. At the secondary level, where content knowledge is especially important, only 56 percent of charter school math teachers had extensive content knowledge in mathematics, compared to 70 percent of regular public school teachers.

For science, charter schools and regular public schools overall hired nearly the same percentage of teachers with a major or minor in science. But at the secondary level, where it most matters, only 67 percent of charter school teachers had college majors or minors in science, compared to 78 percent of regular public school teachers.

On average, teachers typically gain in effectiveness as they gain in experience, up to about five years, although a few studies find effects of experience that end earlier or later than five years. The SASS data show that charter schools have less effective teachers measured in this way. About twice the proportion of charter school teachers as regular public school teachers had five years' experience or less in 1999. This is a problem not only because of the inferior instruction that teachers who lack sufficient experience may deliver but also because the high concentration of inexperienced teachers in charter schools also deprives these teachers of opportunities for mentoring by more experienced teachers, one of the most effective ways in which teachers typically gain skill.

In sum, while freedom from certification rules undoubtedly permit charter schools to hire teachers who are more qualified than typical teachers in regular public schools, the data do not reveal evidence that charter schools consistently use their freedom to do so.

The more important question that policy makers should confront is not one that NAEP data stimulated—whether charter schools, on average, outperform regular public schools—but rather whether the underperformance of some charter schools is a price worth paying for the high performance of others. How much experimentation should we do on children, knowing that failures as well as successes may result? This is a much trickier public policy issue, and it has no easy answer.

# Notes

1. The National Center for Education Statistics (NCES) did subsequently reclassify twelve schools in its national sample from regular public to charter schools, but this reclassification did not affect the broad conclusions reached by the AFT in its earlier analysis.

2. More detailed descriptions of each of these state studies, including full bibliographic references, are provided in our book, *The Charter School Dust-Up* (Teachers College Press, 2005).

**MARTIN CARNOY** is Vida Jacks Professor of Education in Graduate School of Education at Stanford University. Rebecca Jacobsen is associate professor in the Department of Teacher Education at Michigan State University. Lawrence Mishel is president of the Economic Policy Institute, and Richard Rothstein is a research associate at the Economic Policy Institute.

# EXPLORING THE ISSUE

## Are Charter Schools Advancing Educational Reforms?

## Critical Thinking and Reflection

1. What do you think is a better indicator of charter school effectiveness: student test performance or college entry and graduation? Explain why.
2. How can unions help both sides seek common ground?
3. Who represents the interest of parents and students in traditional and charter schools?
4. Design a field experiment that would test the effectiveness of charter schools and identify the major reasons why psychological research is prevented in this area.

## Is There Common Ground?

At first, the question of charter schools revolved around their ability to revitalize schools and offer parents and the community a greater diversity of schooling experiences. As Carnoy and colleagues also point out in the "No" side article, charter schools were therefore intended to be a source of innovation, experimentation, and creative inspiration. Thus, the original question of charter schools was whether the introduction of competition would motivate traditional public schools to be better and more efficient. Among school district officials and teachers unions, there is growing consensus that the charter school movement threatens to destroy traditional public schools and the rules of shared governance developed between school administration and teachers over a century. Despite the original intentions of charter schools, the situation today is that they can't compete fairly with cash. Is this a good or bad thing for education? As LAUSD and other school districts face an insecure future, the empirical question becomes centered on whether charter schools are advancing educational reforms. In seeking common ground it is apparent that all stakeholders in education have been more enlightened by the charter school movement. Charters appear to be in motivating parents, who may not have been motivated in the past to become more involved in selecting or settling with schools as well as asked to personally evaluate the importance of test scores in assessing schools for their unique child. Traditional public schools have also been compelled to search for their true meaning and purpose, and to put aside their self-interest in the common interest of education for all.

Charter schools have definitely brought more choices to parents even though there can be a great deal of selection bias within any charter school population. Children are randomly selected at charter schools but they didn't enter the lottery randomly. Parents who are concerned about their child's education and intend for their child to pursue their studies are obviously more likely to look into alternatives. However, it is possible that the existence of a public charter has elicited more parental involvement in their child's education merely because there is an opportunity for school choice. In the past, this did not exist because a private school education is not affordable for all families. Even Carnoy and colleagues stated that "if parents are comfortable in schools that produce low achievement, they should be permitted to enroll their children in them." In order to be *comfortable*, parents need to know their child's needs and the opportunities for their education. Therefore, the question remains regarding whether parents know more about their child and their child's school. Educational psychologists can examine the extent to which parents have engaged more in their child's education as a result of school choice in order to inform this aspect of the debate in the future.

As for the work of schools, the results trickling in on studies comparing charters and traditional schools within and between states indicate that it is a "draw" when student test scores are being used as a criterion for success. Authors of the "Yes" and "No" sides provide evidence that there is either no difference in achievement or a lack of charter school achievement when compared to traditional public schools. This makes a great deal of sense given our cultural tendency to foster children's self-esteem and our responsivity to children's unique needs. RAND reports that positive long-term outcomes, such as college enrollment, have been found in some states and the authors push educators to use other indicators valued in education. Thus, the scale may be tipping in the favor of charters as they provide greater choices for parents to select environments for their child to succeed.

As for the apparent destruction of traditional public schools in some local areas, such as in Los Angeles, it seems that school staff at all levels of leadership and rank-and-file membership have been put on notice. The threat of charter school expansion, with the support of big businessmen and their vaults of cash, may be what it ultimately takes to ask the tough questions that Carnoy and colleagues pose in their "No" side article within the LAUSD bureaucracy. The challenge for school staff will be to form a unified vision of public school education that parents and community members can be happy and proud of, and with rules that involve the interest of all of our children (not just bread and butter trade union issues). Yes, schools are workplaces but they are educational institutions serving communities.

## References

H. Blume, "Charter school expansion could reshape L.A. Unified, officials say," *LA Times*, www.latimes.com (2015, November 12).

PBS (Producer), *The Education of Michelle Rhee* [DVD], www.pbs.org/frontline (2013).

Takepart (Producer), *Waiting for "Superman"* [DVD], www.takepart.com/waiting-for-superman (2010).

U.S. Department of Education, National Center for Education Statistics, *The Condition of Education 2015* (NCES 2015–144), https://nces.ed.gov/programs/coe/indicator_cgb.asp (2015).

T. Watanabe, "Judge tentatively allows 2 charter schools to keep operating," *LA Times*, www.latimes.com (2014, July 24).

R. Zimmer, B. Gill, K. Booker, S. Lavertu, T. R. Sass, and J. Witte, *Charter Schools in Eight States: Effects on Achievement, Attainment, Integration, and Competition* (RAND Education, 2009).

## Additional Resources

K. Bulkley, and J. Fisler, "A decade of charter schools: From theory to practice," *Educational Policy* (vol. 17, 2003).

C. E. Finn Jr, B. V. Manno, and G. Vanourek, *Charter Schools in Action: Renewing Public Education* (Princeton University Press, 2001).

C. Lubienski, "Innovation in education markets: Theory and evidence on the impact of competition and choice in charter schools," *American Educational Research Journal* (vol. 40, 2003).

P. Wohlstetter, R. Wenning, and K. L. Briggs, "Charter schools in the United States: The question of autonomy," *Educational Policy* (vol. 9, 1995).

# Internet References . . .

**American Federation of Teachers (AFT)**

www.aft.org

**National Alliance for Public Charter Schools**

www.publiccharters.org

**National Center for Education Statistics**

https://nces.ed.gov/fastfacts/display.asp?id=30

**National Education Association (NEA)**

www.nea.org

**Students First (Founded by Michelle Rhee)**

www.studentsfirst.org